Global Marketing

CONTEMPORARY THEORY, PRACTICE, AND CASES

ILAN ALON
Rollins College, USA

EUGENE JAFFE
Ruppin Academic Center, Israel

WITH DONATA VIANELLI
University of Trieste, Italy

GLOBAL MARKETING: CONTEMPORARY THEORY, PRACTICE, AND CASES

Published by McGraw-Hill, a business unit of The McGraw-Hill Companies, Inc., 1221 Avenue of the Americas, New York, NY 10020. Copyright © 2013 by The McGraw-Hill Companies, Inc. All rights reserved. Printed in the United States of America. No part of this publication may be reproduced or distributed in any form or by any means, or stored in a database or retrieval system, without the prior written consent of The McGraw-Hill Companies, Inc., including, but not limited to, in any network or other electronic storage or transmission, or broadcast for distance learning.

Some ancillaries, including electronic and print components, may not be available to customers outside the United States.

This book is printed on acid-free paper.

1 2 3 4 5 6 7 8 9 0 RJE/RJE 1 0 9 8 7 6 5 4 3 2

ISBN 978-0-07-802927-1
MHID 0-07-802927-9

Vice President & Editor-in-Chief: *Brent Gordon*
Vice President & Director Specialized Publishing: *Janice M. Roerig-Blong*
Sponsoring Editor: *Daryl C. Bruflodt*
Marketing Campaign Coordinator: *Colleen P. Havens*
Developmental Editor: *Robin A. Reed*
Project Manager: *Melissa M. Leick*
Design Coordinator: *Brenda A. Rolwes*
Cover Design: *Studio Montage, St. Louis, Missouri*
Cover Image Credit: *Pompidou Centre: © Getty Images RF; Asian Street at Night: © Corbis RF; Vehicles in London at Night: © Dynamic Graphics/Jupiter Images RF*
Buyer: *Susan K. Culbertson*
Media Project Manager: *Balaji Sundararaman*
Compositor: *Laserwords Private Limited*
Typeface: *10.5/12 Times New Roman PS*
Printer: *R. R. Donnelley*

All credits appearing on page or at the end of the book are considered to be an extension of the copyright page.

Library of Congress Cataloging-in-Publication Data
Alon, Ilan.
    Global marketing: contemporary theory, practice, and cases / Ilan Alon, Eugene Jaffe, with Donata Vianelli.
        p. cm.
    ISBN-13: 978-0-07-802927-1 (alk. paper)
    ISBN-10: 0-07-802927-9
  1. Export marketing. 2. Export marketing—Case studies. I. Jaffe, Eugene D. II. Vianelli, Donata. III. Title.

    HF1416.A47 2013
    658.8'4—dc23   2011042361

To my wife
—Ilan Alon

To Liora
—Eugene Jaffe

BRIEF CONTENTS

CONTENTS

PREFACE

OVERVIEW

Taking the marketing function global is no easy task. It requires managers to think globally and strategically about global markets and comparative marketing environments. International markets pose the challenge of differing political, social, economic, and technological environments. Regional and national differences may render some marketing strategies and tactics ineffectual in new environments.

Identifying opportunities in the global environment requires market research and analysis that spans national boundaries. Segmentation, targeting, and positioning strategies of multinational firm must look for the commonalities across markets as well as take into account the idiosyncrasies of individual markets. It is in this context that the 4Ps (product, price, place, and promotion) are implemented. This book examines the 4Ps and gives students tools for analyzing the pros and cons of related international marketing decisions. The individual decisions of the marketer have to be examined holistically. Coordination, design, and control of marketing across markets and functions are, thus, critical.

Recent years were accentuated by a rise of new technologies, such as social media, and new attention to social responsibility and ethics in corporate leadership. This book captures these new developments by adding a Technology in Focus boxed feature in many chapters, and by dedicating chapters to the subjects of social responsibility, ethics, and social media in global marketing.

THE APPROACH OF THIS TEXT

Our objective in writing *Global Marketing* was to publish a marketing textbook with a truly global orientation. This objective has been carried out by three authors who not only live in different areas of the world, the United States, Europe and Israel, but also have extensive international teaching and consulting experience (Austria, Australia, China, Croatia, Denmark, France, Germany, India, Israel, Italy, Slovenia, and United States of America among others). Taken together, the three authors have over 80 years of international business and marketing teaching experience. This global orientation is also exemplified by the cases found at the end of each chapter. They cover a large number of countries and were written by an international group of educators. Most of the cases were solicited specifically for this book. We have endeavored to include material about marketing from not only developed countries, but also emerging markets, including strategies for large multinational corporations and small/medium firms. Both long analytical cases, at the last section of the book (Part 5), and short discussion cases at the end of each chapter, add to the pedagogical milieu available for professors and a variety of learning materials for the students. The book attempts to strike a balance between theory and practice that will allow students to enrich their international marketing vocabulary, comprehend international marketing models, apply their learning in cases, and contend with problems facing the global marketing manager.

ORGANIZATION

This book is organized into five sections. Part 1 of the book sets the context by reviewing the global marketing environments. Particular attention is paid to market assessment and situation analysis tools, such as CAGE (cultural, administrative, geographic, and economic distances) and PEST (political, economic, social, and technological environments), in Chapters 1 and 2. Drilling more deeply on the cultural and political/legal environments, Chapter 3 reviews models of cross-cultural management and their implications to marketing strategies and Chapter 4 develops a political risk model that helps in risk assessment. Chapter 5 closes the first part of the section by examining global, regional and national market similarities and differences. The chapter also discusses the important trade blocs that facilitate international trade. Taken together, Part 1 deals with an analysis of the external, mostly uncontrollable, marketing environment.

Part 2 consists of four chapters relating to functional marketing strategies, including global marketing research, international market selection, global market entry strategies, and segmentation, targeting and positioning. Marketing research in the international environment is more complex and riddled with cultural and legal variations that make the collection and interpretation of results difficult to apply uniformly across countries. Marketing managers may make the mistake that if it works at home, it will also work abroad. Searching for opportunities around the world necessitates both market research and a deliberate, systematic analysis of varying conditions that drive demand. International market selection models are covered next. International marketing entry decisions often follow market selection decisions and involve a tradeoff between risk and control. Marketers willing to invest in markets must also realize financial returns to justify it. Non-equity modes of market entry are growing as a result of firms' increasing sophistication in managing at arm's length and the increase of international marketing activities in emerging markets, which embody more risks, such as those emanating from political risk, cultural distance, and economic under development.

STP (segmentation, targeting, and positioning) strategies can be applied both at the national and international level. A product targeted at middle-income consumers in North America may also attract a high-income consumer from Brazil. Lifestyles of young and urban consumers are converging as a result of international media, the activities of multinational advertisers, and increased connectivity via the Internet and social media. Marketers are increasingly able to target like-minded consumers across markets by using Web-based technologies to identify, reach out and sell to those segments.

Part 3 of the book covers the traditional 4Ps (product, price, place, and promotion). Much of the controllable environment for marketers involves 4P decisions. These decisions need to be coordinated, resulting in appeal to the targeted group. The book reviews in detail the elements of product and branding strategies, pricing strategies, global placement, and distribution strategies and, finally, global communication and advertising strategies. Taken together, these strategies form the foundation for international marketing planning and the basis for competitiveness in international markets.

Part 4 is among the most innovative in the book, focusing on emerging technologies in international marketing, such as the development of social media, the design and control of global marketing, as well as the ethical and socially responsible actions of the marketing manager. Social media is a disruptive technology that will especially shape marketing and advertising in future years. It is a medium of advertising, a method to connect to dispersed consumers, a market research tool for both consumers and markets, and an opportunity for consumers to shape the message of the company by sharing their thoughts about the brand with friends, peers and colleagues. The recession that has had a grip on global markets since 2008 has also spurred an introspection of the role of marketing in society and the responsibility of the company to its environment. Marketers are increasingly being asked to be accountable to more than just the "bottom line," but also to those aspects of society upon which they have an influence.

Long, analytical cases are provided in Part 5 of the book. These cases are mostly collated from the Ivey Case Clearing House and represent realistic situations and opportunities for students to engage in formal case analysis. They will need to analyze the situation, identify a problem and develop alternative solutions.

SPECIAL FEATURES

This book covers the foundations of global marketing, including a strong overview of international marketing environments, including external uncontrollable factors as well as tools and strategies available for the international manager to cope with them.

To our knowledge, this is the only global marketing text that has included separate chapters on business ethics and social marketing. The increase in ethical dilemmas faced by managers in multinational firms or those that have to do business in different cultures demand increased attention to this subject. This demand has guided our formulating a chapter on ethics and corporate social responsibility in the international marketplace. An additional chapter devoted to global social marketing was thought necessary owing to the growth and usage of social media in international markets. As the reader will learn, the use of social marketing strategies is not limited to developed countries in the Western world, but to emerging markets as well.

Another feature of the book is the use of box examples in every chapter that contain a mini-case or short story focused on countries, companies, people or technology. These mini-cases add to a particular chapter section by focusing on a recent global marketing event or person.

The book has both short cases at the end of each chapter as well as long Ivey-style cases in Part 5. Cases at the end of each chapter help highlight the application of chapter materials and are designed to provide in-class activities and discussions that help demonstrate how to apply models and theories from the chapter. The long cases are best used to integrate materials which require the students to analyze the marketing environment and industry, identify a problem and develop alternative solutions. The cases are carefully selected to provide a balance of small and medium to large companies, different areas of the world, and varying industries (including not-for-profit companies). The Ruth's Chris case, for example, is one of Ivey's best-selling cases for three years in a row.

The world of global marketing is continuously changing. To keep abreast of changes, students and teachers of international marketing are advised to go beyond the book's theories and cases to examine how they are applied in the real world. A variety of resources are available through McGraw-Hill to help both groups stay connected and updated with the materials.

SUPPLEMENTS

McGraw-Hill has a variety of tools online to help engage the student with the materials. Visit our Online Learning Center (OLC) at www.mhhe.com/alon1e for additional student and instructor resources. The following supplemental aids accompany *Global Marketing:*

For Students

A variety of exercises and internet links to current events are developed to enhance the learning outcomes. Students also have access to PowerPoint presentations for the book chapters to help them study the material.

For Instructors

The password-protected instructor portion of the OLC includes the Instructor's Manual, a comprehensive computerized test bank using the EZ Test test generator, and PowerPoint lecture slides. Teaching notes for both the long and short cases are also available on the book's Online Learning Center.

This text is available as an eBook at www.Course-eSmart.com. At CourseSmart your students can take advantage of significant savings off the cost of a print textbook, reduce their impact on the environment, and gain access to powerful Web tools for learning. CourseSmart eBooks can be viewed online or downloaded to a computer. The eBooks allow students to do full text searches, add highlighting and notes, and share notes with classmates. CourseSmart has the largest selection of eBooks available anywhere. Visit www.CourseSmart.com to learn more and to try a sample chapter.

Craft your teaching resources to match the way you teach! With McGraw-Hill Create™, www.mcgrawhillcreate.com, you can easily rearrange chapters, combine material from other content sources, and quickly upload content you have written like your course syllabus or teaching notes. Find the content you need in Create by searching through thousands of leading McGraw-Hill textbooks. Arrange your book to fit your teaching style. Create even allows you to personalize your book's appearance by selecting the cover and adding your name, school, and course information. Order a Create book and you'll receive a complimentary print review copy in 3–5 business days or a complimentary electronic review copy (eComp) via e-mail in minutes. Go to www.mcgrawhillcreate.com today and register to experience how McGraw-Hill Create™ empowers you to teach *your* students *your* way.

ACKNOWLEDGMENTS

The following reviewers provided valuable feedback to help shape our final product:

Susan Baxter, Farmingdale State College–SUNY

Catherine Campbell, University of Maryland University College

Scott R. Davidson, University at Albany

Eileen Fischer, New York University

John Hadjimarcou, The University of Texas at El Paso

Anna Helm, George Washington University

Lynn Kahle, University of Oregon

Joe Kim, Rider University

Maria Kniazeva, University of San Diego

Dennis Langhofer, Fresno Pacific University

Luis Larrea, DePaul University

Sangwon Lee, University of Central Florida

Behnam Nakhai, Millersville University of Pennsylvania

Pallab Paul, University of Denver

Rajani Ganesh Pillai, North Dakota State University

Brenda Ponsford, Clarion University

George Priovolos, Iona College

Brent Smith, Saint Joseph's University

Jill Solomon, University of South Florida

Ven Sriram, University of Baltimore

Verna Swanljung, North Seattle Community College

Alexia Vanides, Intrax International Business Institute, San Francisco

John Wood, West Virginia University

Also, we would like to thank the editorial staff, particularly Robin Reed of McGraw-Hill, for moving us through the process of publishing a textbook.

We would also like to acknowledge Professor Donata Vianelli, from the University of Trieste, Italy, for contributing Chapters 10, 11, and 12, and Nadia Ballard, a seasoned international marketing consultant, for helping in the researching, writing, and/or editing parts of Chapters 6, 9, 13, and 15.

ABOUT THE AUTHORS

Dr. Ilan Alon is George D. and Harriet W. Cornell Chair of International Business and Marketing and Director of *The China Center* at Rollins College, as well as a Visiting Scholar and Asia Fellow at Harvard University.

Alon has consulted for both multinational businesses and government organizations relating to marketing and international business issues. Alon is particularly an expert on global franchising, which accounts for much of the service economy and its globalization.

Alon's teaching and consulting work spans the globe, covering America, Europe, Asia, and the Middle East. He has taught in top business programs globally, including Shanghai JiaoTong University, Ben Gurion University, Washington University, Bilkent University, and University of New South Wales, among others.

He recently authored *Entrepreneurial and Business Elites of China* (Emerald, 2011), *Franchising Globally* (Palgrave, 2010), *Chinese Entrepreneurs* (Edward Elgar, 2009), *China Rules* (Palgrave, 2009), and *Service Franchising: A Global Perspective* (Springer, 2006) among others. He also published in numerous prestigious refereed journals, such as *Journal of International Marketing, Management International Review, Thunderbird International Business Review, Journal of Small Business Management, Business Horizons, Journal of Macromarketing* and others.

E-mail: ialon@rollins.edu

Eugene D. Jaffe is Professor at the School of Economics and Management and Head, MBA Programs, Ruppin Academic Center and Emeritus Professor, Graduate School of Business Administration, Bar-Ilan University, both in Israel. He holds B.S. (Econ.) and Ph.D (Econ.) degrees from the Wharton School, University of Pennsylvania and an MBA in International Business from the Graduate School of Business, New York University. He has been a Visiting Professor in the United States, Denmark and Mexico.

Jaffe has authored/edited six books; his latest publication (co-authored with Israel Nebenzahl) is *National Image & Competitive Advantage: The Theory and Practice of Place Branding*, 2/e, Copenhagen Business School Press, 2006, was translated into Italian and Korean.

He has 90 refereed publications and conference proceedings that have appeared in the *Journal of Marketing Research, Columbia Journal of World Business, Long-Range Planning, European Journal of Marketing, International Marketing Review, Journal of Global Marketing, Management International Review* (he is listed among the authors of the "Most Influential Articles Published in MIR 1993–2007"), *International Business Review, Journal of Business Ethics, Business Ethics: A European Review* and others.

He has been a member of the Academy of International Business, European International Business Academy (President, 1998), Association for Global Business, the Centre for National Competitiveness, Institute of Industrial Policy Studies (South Korea), Academy of Market Intelligence, and the Society for Business Ethics.

E-mail: eugenej@ruppin.ac.il

Donata Vianelli is Professor at the University of Trieste, Italy, where she teaches International Marketing and International Business and is the Head Coordinator of the Bachelor Degree in Management.

She also holds a position as Academic Coodinator of Marketing at MIB School of Management, one of the most accredited business schools in Italy and with an excellent positioning in the European market.

She holds a B.S. and a M.S. degree in Business from the University of Trieste and a Ph.D degree in Management from the University Ca' Foscari of Venice. During her 20 years of teaching experience, she collaborated with numerous universities and business schools in France, China, Austria, Slovenia, and the United States.

Vianelli has authored two books and 50 refereed publications that have appeared in national and international books and journals. Her research focus is on global distribution and cross-cultural consumer behavior, with a regional focus on Europe and Asia, where she has recently coordinated a large research program on distribution and sales of Italian products in the Chinese market, sponsored by the Italian Ministry of Education, Universities and Research.

E-mail: donata.vianelli@econ.units.it

PART 1

Global Marketing Environments

Understanding Global Markets and Marketing

Companies must learn to operate as if the world were one large market—ignoring superficial regional and national differences.

THEODORE LEVITT

LEARNING OBJECTIVES

After reading this chapter, you should be able to:

■ Understand how globalization impacts marketing strategy.

■ Define what is meant by "global marketing."

■ Use the CAGE model to understand the differences between countries.

■ Determine how a firm is organized according to the EPRG framework.

■ Identify three approaches to developing a global marketing strategy.

■ Know why a global vision is important in order to develop a global marketing strategy.

MARKETS ARE BECOMING GLOBAL

Traveling abroad, you encounter familiar brand names like Kentucky Fried Chicken, Coca-Cola, and McDonald's that you assumed are American owned (they are). Perhaps you thought that some of these products tasted a bit different from the ones sold in the United States, even though the products looked the same. If so, they were adapted by changing the formula to conform to local tastes. If you were lucky enough to ride in a Rolls-Royce, you probably assumed it was British (*very* British, but German-owned). Maybe you drove a Land Rover, a British landmark; or a Volvo automobile, Swedish-made; they were sold to Ford Motor Co. The fact that American products can compete in local markets throughout the world and that European and Asian manufacturers can compete in America (who would have thought that Chinese and Indian-made cars would sell in the United States?) is a consequence of the globalization of markets and marketing.

Consider this. In Copenhagen, 18-year-old Hanna logs on to a Canadian website, orders the latest CD recorded by Madonna, and pays for it in Kroner, using a Danish credit card issued by her local bank. Her cousin Jacques, visiting from France, logs on to a consumer electronics site, where he notices an advertisement for a new recording gadget developed in Japan but not available in European stores. Jacques enters a

BOX 1-1   COUNTRY IN FOCUS: INDIA

Your office phone rings. On the other end is an unfamiliar voice speaking in accented but very good English: "Good morning, sir, my name is accountant Bawa Singh and I would like to do your personal income tax return." While you probably will not receive such a phone call—and anyway you have a local accountant doing your tax returns—nevertheless, it is very possible that your returns are actually filled out by someone like Bawa Singh. While you have never heard of him, he is one of thousands of Indians employed in a string of offshore accounting firms located in Bangladore and

Delhi. Mr. Singh explains: "We have agreements with a number of American CPA firms. We are linked to their databases, to which we have instant access. Using these databases, our accountants do the tax returns. The American firms can then concentrate on account servicing, customer relations, and the more complicated returns, while we do the basics at a fraction of the cost."

In a similar fashion, Indian offshore companies do account billing for retail chains and banks and specialize in building websites and software development.

search engine and finds that the gadget is available for sale in Macau. He orders the gadget from a Macau dealer, has it sent to his home address in Paris, pays for it in euros, and receives a receipt for payment sent to his e-mail address. These transactions represent global marketing that permits buyers and sellers the world over to meet and do business online in virtually any language and currency, with ease, precision, security, and reliability.

Another phenomenon of global markets is the growth of **social networking** websites such as Facebook and Twitter. For example, Facebook's international audience totaled 34 million people at the beginning of 2008, and at the beginning of 2009 that number had increased to 95 million. Many of Facebook's markets are growing by double digits every month. Are you connected? These websites have information about their subscribers' interests, hobbies and in some cases, consumption habits. In a sense, Facebook's analysts may know a lot about people and their friends in terms of what they may be interested in! This information is very valuable to global advertisers who choose to communicate via these websites.

All of these examples have occurred mainly as a result of globalization (see Box 1-1). **Globalization,** a process of interaction and integration among people, companies, and governments of many nations, is driven by international trade and investment and has resulted in what some call a global economy.

GLOBALIZATION: THE WORLD IS BECOMING SMALLER

Businesses in every corner of the world, both large and small, must be aware of the impact that the global economy is having on their performance. The Internet, e-commerce, digital communication, and information transparency have led to an increasingly mobile workforce, more informative customers, and rapidly changing technologies and business models. As a result, many business organizations must choose a global marketing strategy to enable them to win market share and capture

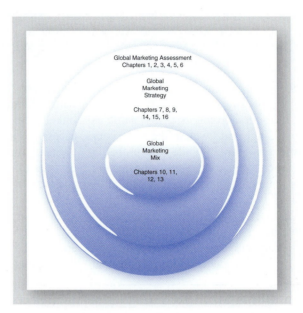

Figure 1-1 Global Marketing Book Organization

and retain current and prospective customers. Marketing is becoming more important as organizations around the world strive to develop products and services that appeal to their customers and aim to differentiate their offering in the increasingly crowded global marketplace.

We believe that marketing strategy is the key to attaining competitive advantage in the global marketplace. Therefore, the objective of this book is show how a successful global marketing strategy can be developed and sustained.

The book is organized around three global marketing activities: assessment, strategy, and the marketing mix. These three steps are shown in Figure 1-1. Before entering global markets, an assessment must be made of their economic, political, and cultural environments. After making the assessment, the next step in the determination of global marketing strategy concerns selecting markets and market entry strategies. Finally, a marketing mix and product, promotion, distribution, and pricing strategies are determined for each market. Figure 1-1 shows the sequence of chapters for each of the three activities.

GLOBALIZATION AND GLOBAL MARKETING

Globalization is changing the competitive environment in which companies must determine marketing strategy. The growing use of e-commerce, the spread of technological drivers such as the Internet and mobile phones, improved transportation facilities, and the removal of political and economic borders in many regions of the world allows companies to focus not only on domestic markets but on diverse global markets as well. As global markets become more interconnected and dynamic over time, effective monitoring of the external environment and maximum use of company-specific resources will be imperative in order to gain competitive advantage.

The global firm deals constantly with a paradox. On the one hand, global reach implies general objectives and skills that transcend any particular country. Indeed, a firm may enter a country because its vision and advanced skill set can make more of that country's productive resources than local firms. On the other hand, global firms are challenged by their comparative disadvantage in navigating many features of local markets. Success means adapting general knowledge to the particular circumstances of each country. The strategic challenge of the global firm entering a new country is determining which business tactics and practices to import, which to evolve onsite, and how to combine them within a working global enterprise.[1]

The technological advances spurred by globalization have enabled a significant growth of worldwide outsourcing, as illustrated by the example in Box 1-1. An example of how globalization affects international corporate culture and strategy is the emergence of diversified global conglomerates (based in two or more countries). An example of a conglomerate/merger is Daimler-Benz's (now Daimler) takeover of Chrysler, intended to shore up both Daimler and Chrysler in their respective markets.[2]

The DaimlerChrysler merger resulted in a large car manufacturing company, ranked third in the world in terms of revenue, market capitalization, and earnings and fifth in passenger cars and commercial vehicles sold. However, the merger actually strengthened their Japanese rival, Toyota. The combined stock market value of both companies in 2003 was half the sum of their separate valuations before they merged in 1998.[3]

Why did the merger fail to reach its objectives? A major reason was the difference in organizational cultures of the two companies. Because American and German managerial styles differed widely, a culture clash soon occurred that could not be resolved even with the use of sensitivity workshops. Another problem was that the Americans earned significantly higher salaries than their German counterparts, especially at managerial levels. The disparity in salary levels had made German employees envious of the Americans—not a good contributing factor to cooperation between the two sides.

Marketing considerations also played a part. The brand images of both Chrysler and Daimler-Benz automobiles were quite different. Chrysler's "image was one of American excess . . . its brand value lay in its assertiveness and risk-taking cowboy aura . . . [While] Mercedes-Benz . . . exuded disciplined German engineering coupled with uncompromising quality."[4] In 2007, Daimler sold an 80 percent stake in its Chrysler brand to Cerberus Capital Management, a private equity investment firm. However, the financial crisis took its toll when, in 2009, Chrysler filed for bankruptcy. The bankruptcy allowed Chrysler to conclude an alliance with Italy's Fiat, which took a 20 percent stake in the company. The alliance could help Chrysler to survive with a partner that makes small and midsize passenger cars.

The difficulty with such transatlantic mergers is that they not only transcend country and cultural boundaries but also necessitate new legal, financial, and managerial considerations.[5] Therefore, in designing strategies for firms operating in the global age, not only are technological competencies required, but also geographical scope and expertise for managing and marketing in foreign environments.

1. Calomiris, C. (30 August 2004). *What does it mean to have a global vision?* Columbia Business School.

2. DaimlerChrysler was ejected from membership in the American Automobile Manufacturers association because Chrysler was no longer considered to be an "American" producer.

3. The New European order [Special report]. (2 September 2004). *The Economist.* Retrieved from www.economist.com/node/3127264.

4. Finkelstein, S. (2002). *The DaimlerChrysler merger.* Tuck School of Business.

5. Lazer, W., & Shaw, E. (2000). Global marketing management: at the dawn of the new millennium. *Journal of International Marketing, 8*(1), 65–77; Meyer, K. (2006). Global focusing: from domestic conglomerates to global specialists. *Journal of Management Studies, 43*(5), 1109–1144.

Globalization: Opportunity or Threat?

Globalization—the trend toward a single integrated and interdependent world—is driven by international trade and made possible largely by information technology. Globalization may be understood by different perspectives. To the economist, globalization refers to the emergence of global markets. On the other hand, sociologists see globalization as the convergence of lifestyles and social values. To the political scientist, globalization reduces national sovereignty. While aspects of globalization have been around for more than a hundred years, one of the first to recognize it as such was Marshall McLuhan. He coined the term "global village," wherein people who are physically separated by time and space are interconnected by electronic media. This linkage, while having positive benefits, also carries responsibilities on a global level.[6]

The world turns into a "global village" as national borders disappear and time and space distances contract. This contraction has come about because air, sea, and communication costs have declined significantly during the twentieth century. Average ocean freight and port charges per ton fell from $95 in 1920 to $60 in 1930 and fell again to $29 by 1990. Freight costs declined owing mainly to containerization of cargo, which increased from about 20 percent of total cargo in 1980 to about 65 percent in 2000.

Communication costs declined owing to improvements in information technology. For example, a three-minute phone call from New York to London cost $245 in 1930; the same call cost only $3 in 1990. Making a bank transaction by telephone costs about $0.55; making the same transaction in an ATM machine reduces the cost to $0.45, and by the Internet to less than $0.10.

What are the opportunities driven by globalization? Trade liberalization means that the demand for a country's products is not limited to the home market, while investment, technology, and know-how move more freely across borders to both developed and developing countries. Nevertheless, globalization has its detractors, as evidenced by the some 40,000 protestors who interrupted the Third Ministerial Conference of the World Trade Organization held in Seattle in late 1999. Much of the discontent concerns the fact that the benefits of globalization have not been spread equally among peoples and countries.

Yet most people around the world have positive attitudes toward globalization. The majority of 38,000 people in 35 out of 44 developed and developing countries surveyed by the Pew Global Attitudes Project[7] believed that the growth in trade was very good or somewhat good for their country. While it is not surprising that Americans and Europeans hold positive attitudes toward globalization, it is surprising to find that African and Asian respondents had equally if not stronger support for globalization as compared to people in more developed countries.

The Global Marketing Approach

How to take advantage of the opportunities offered by technological breakthroughs and the growth of both developed and emerging markets have become a critical task for management, requiring a global approach to marketing strategy development and implementation. A global approach requires the firm to focus its efforts worldwide, rather than developing marketing strategies on a country-by-country basis. It also requires the coordination and integration of production, marketing, and other functional activities across countries. For many firms, a global marketing

6. McLuhan, M. (1964). *Understanding media.* New York: Mentor.

7. The Pew Global Attitudes Project. (2003). *Views of a changing world.* The Pew Research Center, Washington, D. C.

strategy requires a centralized operation to leverage scale advantages and optimize resources and reduce costs.

Specifically, the objective of **global marketing** is to attain worldwide coordination, rationalization, and integration of all marketing activities including target market selection, marketing-mix decisions, and organizational design and control mechanisms.[8] The world-wide integration of marketing activities includes the development of global products and brands and global communication and distribution strategies.

GLOBAL MARKETING AND GLOBAL MARKETS

Some proponents of global marketing contend that as markets are becoming homogeneous, country differences are less important to international marketing decisions.[9] Others take an opposite view and claim that *global markets* are few, so that customizing marketing strategies to the needs of local markets is still necessary.[10] While the formation of regional, integrated markets such as the European Union, the North American Free Trade Agreement (NAFTA), and Mercosur (Southern Common Market)[11] have indeed brought us further toward a "borderless world," there are still significant differences in consumer motivations and preferences across markets. Therefore, there is a fundamental difference between *global marketing*, the integration and control of marketing activities on a global basis, and *global markets*, the idea that regional and/or world markets are converging, allowing for a standardized marketing strategy. Implementing a global strategy depends on the distance (or closeness) between regions and countries. A framework for measuring distances is discussed below.

THE CAGE DISTANCE FRAMEWORK

According to the **CAGE framework,** distance between two or more countries can be measured along four dimensions: **C**ultural, **A**dministrative, **G**eographic, and **E**conomic.[12] Cultural differences include language, ethnicities, religion, values, and norms. Administrative distance measures differences in laws, political risk, and government structure. Geographic distance includes country size, infrastructure, climate, and remoteness from neighboring countries. Economic distance refers to differences in national income, costs of doing business, prices, and availability of human and natural resources. These factors affect not only differences between countries but also between industries.

Which of these factors is most important to international marketing decisions? It depends. For example, two countries might be close to each other geographically, but administrative distance might be large because of political hostility. In other cases, cultural distance might be the dominant factor in creating distance between two countries, for example, in the case of food products. In other cases, economic distance may be too great to overcome, such as low consumer income, unless products can be tailored down and priced accordingly. The relevance of these differences will be

8. Douglas, S., & Craig, C. S. (1989, Fall). Evolution of global marketing strategy: scale, scope and synergy. *Columbia Journal of World Business*, 47–59.

9. Sheth, J., & Parvatiyar, A. (2001). The antecedents and consequences of integrated global marketing. *International Marketing Review*, *18*(1), 16–34.

10. Quelch, J. A., & Hoff, E. J. (1986, May–June). Customizing global marketing. *Harvard Business Review*, *64*, 59–68; Douglas, S. P., & Wind, Y. (1987, Winter). The myth of globalization. *Columbia Journal of World Business*, 19–29.

11. NAFTA members include the United States, Canada, and Mexico; Mercosur members are Brazil, Argentina, Uruguay, Paraguay, and Venezuela. See Chapter 5 for a detailed discussion of these and other trade agreements.

12. Ghemawat, P. (2001, September). Distance still matters: the hard reality of global expansion. *Harvard Business Review*, 137–147.

TABLE 1-1 CAGE Distance Dimensions		
Dimension	**Source**	**Number of Countries Available**

1. Cultural
   Power distance
   Uncertainty avoidance
   Individualism
   Masculinity
	Hofstede (2001)
	World Values Survey
	   (WVS; Inglehart, 2004)[13]
		
		68
		66
		69
		69

2. Administrative
   Colonizer-colonized link
   Common language
   Legal system
	CIA Factbook
	La Porta et al. 1998[14]
		
		198

3. Geographic Great circle distance	CIA Factbook	196

4. Economic
   Income
   Inflation
   Exports
   Imports
	World Development Indicators
	(World Bank)
		
		179
		157
		165
		165

Source: Adapted from: Berry, H., Guillén, M. F., & Zhou, N. (2010). An institutional approach to cross-national distance. *Journal of International Business Studies, 41*(9), 1460–1480.

discussed below and elsewhere in this book. Suggested measures of CAGE distances may be found in Table 1-1.

DOMESTIC AND GLOBAL MARKETING COMPARED

What distinguishes domestic from global marketing? There are three major differences between the two. Global marketing is characterized by:

1. Greater uncertainty in markets and environments.

Many global strategies do not succeed—either because they are never implemented or because the business environment changes before the strategy can deliver its full effect. In a symposium sponsored by the Wharton School, speakers identified two major factors that determine the future economic environment. The first is "whether external events that have the potential to affect economics are known and understood or unknown and surprising" and the second is "whether corporations have the culture, history and ability to be opportunistic in the face of rapidly changing conditions."[15] Moreover, successful firms understand the difference between taking active risks and sitting by passively at risk.[16]

2. Global markets are more diverse and dynamic than domestic, internal markets.

On the downside, economic, legal, social, and cultural differences in global markets make the task of the international marketing manager much more difficult than in a domestic market. While there are similarities across markets, the differences may be

13. Inglehart, R. (2004). *Human Beliefs and Values.* Madrid: Siglo XXI.

14. La Porta, R., Lopez-de-Silanes, F., Shleifer, A., & Vishny, R. W. (1998). Law and finance. *Journal of Political Economy, 106*(6), 1113–1155.

15. Knowledge@Wharton. (5 December 2001). Retrieved from http://knowledge.wharton.upenn.edu/article.cfm?>articleid=470.

16. Laudicina, P. (2005, March/April). Managing global risk to seize competitive advantage. *Ivey Business Journal*, 1–7.

greater. On the upside, the diversity of global markets exposes multinational companies to multiple experiences that can be used to gain competitive advantage over rivals that have not been exposed to the same learning experience. The transfer and use of such knowledge throughout subsidiaries of a multinational company enables the multinational firm to be a step ahead of rivals. Best practices, for example, can be transferred and shared throughout the organization.

Emerging markets provide new opportunities for investment and marketing. For example, the industrialization of China has been unparalleled in the twentieth and twenty-first centuries. China has steadily increased its share of global industrial output, including a gradual shift in the production of cheap and simple products to higher quality ones. Other emerging markets have also shown significant growth. India had become the world's leading provider of IT and telecommunication services by the end of the twentieth century. Emerging countries such as China, India, and Poland not only provide opportunities, but also a double challenge for global firms; first, the question of how to penetrate their home markets, and second, how to compete with emerging market firms in global markets.

Demographic changes have also been significant. A decline in births and an increase in aging populations has been the case in Europe and Japan. For example, birthrates in the UK, Japan, and the United States have fallen over the last decade resulting in zero population growth. Some see this as a positive development. Dr. John Guillebrand, a retired professor of family planning in the UK, said that lower population growth will result in less pressure on the planet's resources and increase the output of greenhouse gases. Overall population growth is increasing at a slightly declining rate (see Figure 1-2), but is expected to increase to nine billion people by 2050. Yet low birthrates means an aging population, increased pension payments, changes in work patterns, and increased healthcare costs. These changes will pose a major challenge to consumption-related sectors of the economy and, of course, the demand for specific products and services aimed at an aging population.

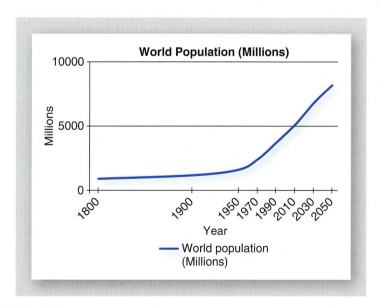

Figure 1-2 World Population Growth

Source: Data from *Internet Geography.* Retrieved from www.geography.learnontheinternet.co.uk.

BOX 1-2   TECHNOLOGY IN FOCUS: HOME SHOPPING

Technology and Retail Jobs

"Is home shopping the beginning of an irreversible trend, with specific TV channels devoted to selling every type of merchandise or service?

While the current channels, with their zircons, skin creams, and hair-replacement products, may not look attractive to many consumers, technology and marketing support should eventually make home shopping a sophisticated, viable alternative to traditional retailing. Interactive high-definition televisions will allow you to manipulate a product onscreen, looking at it from different perspectives or zooming in to examine a detail.

Most of us will still buy many items at the store, but the new approach to shopping could save consumers money because it will cut out the wholesalers, distributors, and retailers. As a result, many people in retail sales could find themselves out of a job. The number of people in delivery jobs who can provide speedy service, on the other hand, should increase."

Source: Campbell, C. (1994). *Where the jobs are: Career survival for Canadians in the new global economy.* Toronto: Macfarlane, Walter & Ross, 6–8.

Another dynamic aspect of global markets is the problem of global overcapacity in so-called traditional industrial nations such as the United States, Japan, and Western Europe as production increases in the emerging economies of Eastern Europe, China, and India. Overproduction increases price competition and lowers profits.

3. Global markets are separated by greater geographical and psychological distances.

Geographic or Spatial Distance

Spatial distances between domestic and global marketing have been reduced by the substitution of IT media for face-to-face contact between buyers and sellers. Consumers in one area of the world can be in instantaneous communication with sellers in another part of the world through the Internet and videoconferencing. Transactions that once took a long time to consummate can now be accomplished immediately over the internet. Business meetings that require the presence of people scattered across regions can now be held through videoconferencing, obviating the need for frequent travel by managers. The billions of mobile and online Internet users worldwide are creating huge opportunities for the development of electronic commerce and mobile commerce.

E-commerce revolutionizes the way consumers acquire information about products and services offered globally. The Internet allows manufacturers the alternative to shift from standardization to mass customization of products, as in the case of Dell Computer Corporation, which can offer computers to order. Moreover, the Internet overcomes global time and space barriers[17] and removes many barriers to communication with customers and employees by eliminating the obstacles created by geography, time zones, and location, thereby creating a "frictionless" business environment.[18]

17. Lazar, I. (16 October 2006). Counterpoint: demand for video conferencing seems weak. *BCR Magazine.* Retrieved from www.collaborationloop.com/blogs/video-conferencing-market-demand-2.htm.

18. Colony, G., Deutsch, H., & Rhinelander, T. (1995, May). Network strategy service: CIO meets the Internet. *The Forrester Report*, 12.

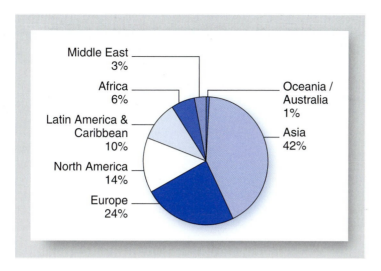

Figure 1-3   World Internet Users by Region

Source: Adapted from: Internet World Stats (www.internetworldstats.com/stats.htm). Basis: 1,966,514,816 Internet users on June 30, 2010. Miniwatts Marketing Group.

Internet usage is pronounced in Asia, North America, and Europe, as shown in Figure 1-3. Among developed countries, Iceland, Greenland, Norway, and Sweden had penetration rates (usage as a percent of population) of over 90 percent of the population by 2010. Note that these countries have sparse populations separated by land mass or water, and therefore the use of the Internet and its communication facilities is very important for human contact. Additional countries with high penetration rates include Germany (79 percent of the population), Japan (78 percent) and the United States (77 percent). Considering total Internet users (not as a percent of the population), China has more total Internet users than the United States. The world total penetration rate was 28.7 percent in 2010.[19]

There are constraining factors that may limit the use of telecommunication as a substitute for travel. An earlier study of the use of telecommunications[20] found that recall was better without face-to-face contact, but that persuasion levels were higher in face-to-face communication. The fact that the study took place in London may have influenced the results, as a "lingering Puritan ethic still keeps many people from accepting the idea that work can be successfully accomplished in a comfortable setting." A more recent study[21] found that videoconferencing growth may be stalled because people "don't want to be seen." Lazar (2006) comments that while videoconferencing makes meetings more effective by forcing individuals to pay attention rather than check e-mail or surf the web, its growth is constrained by a strong preference for being heard rather than seen.

One of the most dramatic developments of the start of the new millennium was a shift of advertising expenditure on traditional media to the Internet (see Table 1-2). Advertising on television, radio, and print media is growing slowly, while that on the Internet is increasing at higher rates. For example, the Internet's share of advertising expenditure was 19.2 percent of total UK advertising expenditure in 2009, an increase

19. Miniwatts Marketing Group. (2010).

20. Albertson, L. (1977). Telecommunications as a travel substitute—some psychological, organizational, and social aspects. *Journal of Communication*, 27(2), 32–45.

21. Lazar, I. (16 October 2006). Counterpoint: demand for video conferencing seems weak. *BCR Magazine*. Retrieved from www.collaborationloop.com/blogs/video-conferencing-market-demand-2.htm.

TABLE 1-2 Online Advertising Spending in the United States (2001–2011)	
2001	$7.1 (billion)
2002	$6
2003	$7.3
2004	$9.6
2005	$12.5
2006	$16.9
2007	$21.4
2008	$27.5
2009	$32.5
2010	$37.5
2011	$42

Source: Data from eMarketer. (2007, October). Retrieved from www.eMarketer.com.

of 3.7 percent over 2007 (15.5 percent). In 2002, the UK Internet share of mind (a limited list of products or services that a consumer considers purchasing) was only 1.4 percent. Growth of Internet advertising in the United States during the same period was also significant, although less than that of England. In 2002, the United States Internet share of mind was 2.5 percent, in 2006, 5.6 percent and in 2008, 12.9 percent.

Internet advertising reached double-digit figures in eight countries by the year 2008. In the United States, Internet advertising increased from $7.1 billion in 2001 to $37.5 billion in 2010 (see Table 1-2). In addition to the UK and the United States, additional countries include Sweden, Australia, Israel, Japan, Norway, South Korea, and Taiwan.

Psychic/Cultural Distance

The internationalization of the firm often means venturing into the unknown. Part of this "unknown" relates to the culture of the host nation. When operating in foreign environments, management must decide whether to adapt to the host culture, with its language, lifestyle, behavioral standards (ethics, for example), and consumer preferences, or operate under the rules and assumptions of the home culture. Both the adherence to host or home managerial styles has been used and can be explained by the EPRG framework discussed below. Before looking at the EPRG framework, however, a definition of psychic and cultural distances is necessary.

Cultural distance may be defined as *some measure of the extent to which cultures are similar or different.* A number of frameworks for this purpose have been suggested and will be discussed in Chapter 3. What is important to understand at this point is that cultural distance is measured on the country level. It is a given and cannot be controlled by management. **Psychic distance,** on the other hand, exists in the mind of the individual;[22] it is the perceptual distance between the home country culture and the host country culture. Psychic distance occurs when management believes there are significant differences between home and host cultures. Therefore, it is measured on the individual level and not the country level, as is the case with cultural distance.

Both cultural and psychic distances affect how management formulates global marketing strategy. Cultural differences influence consumer behavior and preferences for various products. Culture-bound products such as food and home furnishings may therefore have to be adapted to meet differences in consumer needs. Likewise, psychic

22. Sousa, C., & Bradley, F. (2006). Cultural distance and psychic distance: two peas in a pod? *Journal of International Marketing, 14*(1), 49–70.

distance may color managerial beliefs that the greater the distance between two or more countries, the greater the differences in consumer preferences. While psychic distance is perceptual, and may not accurately reflect actual differences, or lack of them, it nevertheless influences managerial decision making. Psychic distance may also affect a multinational firm's organization during its internationalization process, especially entry mode choices and the way it governs its operations abroad. This may be explained by referring to the EPRG typology developed by Perlmutter (1969).[23]

The EPRG Framework

The **EPRG framework** is based on management's worldview of the firm, which determines the way in which its foreign market activities are organized. According to the framework, there are four approaches or orientations by which a firm is managed in foreign markets. These approaches or orientations also reflect different stages in the internationalization of the firm, from solely a domestic player to a world competitor.

1. **Ethnocentric orientation:** In this stage, the focus is on the home market. Firms holding this view believe that domestic strategies are superior to foreign ones, and therefore are applied in overseas operations as well. Overseas operations are considered secondary to domestic operations. No systematic marketing screening is made to search for foreign markets. An example of this approach was the initial expansion of the American pharmaceutical company Eli Lilly into overseas markets. It established offices in key markets, hired local nationals to staff them, and maintained tight control by measuring each country on bottom-line profitability. Operations of foreign subsidiaries were limited to downstream activities required to support local sales, while marketing programs were developed at headquarters.[24]

2. **Polycentric orientation:** Unlike ethnocentric firms, those following this approach use decentralized management, allowing affiliates to develop their own marketing strategy. However, the mindset of management is focused on the host country in the belief that because country markets are dissimilar, marketing strategies must be adapted to the specific needs of each. There is little room in this orientation for standardized marketing. Overseas markets are screened individually. Each market operation functions independently without any meaningful coordination or integration between them. Marketing activities are organized and carried out country by country, modifying the marketing mix as necessary to meet the requirements of each market. An example of this orientation was Ford's marketing of the Escort. The UK version was differentiated from the American model, not only because the steering apparatus had to be shifted from the right to the left side, but also because the engine displacement was greater in the United States, and styling was also different.

3. **Regiocentric orientation:** A particular region is viewed as comprising a single market. Thus, regional trade areas such as the European Union and Mercosur may be the focus of marketing activities. An attempt is made to develop and implement marketing strategy for all countries comprising an entire region. However, unlike the polycentric approach, emphasis is on coordination of marketing in the region and standardization whenever possible.

23. Perlmutter, H. (1969, January/February). The tortuous evolution of the multinational corporation. *Columbia Journal of World Business, 4,* 9–18.

24. Malnight, T. (1995). Globalization of an ethnocentric firm: an evolutionary perspective. *Strategic Management Journal, 16,* 119–141.

An example of a company organized along regiocentric lines is Toyota. About 45 percent of its sales revenues are generated in Japan, with another 39 percent originating in North America. Toyota's success in North America stems from its customer-driven new product development, aimed at this regional market.

4. **Geocentric orientation:** Firms adopting this approach view the world as a potential market. In these markets, an attempt is made to implement global marketing by integrating worldwide operations. Global products and brands are produced in large volumes in order to achieve scale economies. A standardized product, brand, image, and positioning (as well as standardized advertising whenever possible) with minimal adaptations are offered in all markets. In both regiocentric and geocentric orientations, the ability to acquire and share knowledge (such as best practices) among the various components of the global, corporate network is maximized in order to attain and sustain competitive advantage. For example, the Tide brand of laundry detergent marketed in the United States by Procter & Gamble was first developed by its German subsidiary and then introduced in Germany (under the brand name Vizer) and later produced and marketed in several other European countries. The European and later Latin American introduction of Vizer/Tide was made possible by the experience and knowledge gained by German management that was shared with other subsidiaries of P&G. Table 1-3 summarizes product strategy of a multinational firm under each of the above conditions.

Developing Global Marketing Strategies

In order for firms to successfully compete globally, they must achieve significant competitive advantage over their rivals. To do so, a firm must develop a global marketing strategy. There are three approaches to global marketing strategy: Standardization, Configuration/Coordination and Integration of the Firm's Value Chain.

The Standardization versus Localization–Adaptation School

If we could put together a seminar attended by marketing managers of multinational corporations, one of the main topics for discussion would be whether a standardized marketing approach to markets is preferable to a localized (differentiated) approach. A truly globalized marketing strategy would aim to standardize elements of the marketing mix in all markets served by the company. In reality, it is rare to find a completely standardized marketing mix. Some companies may be able to standardize products but have to localize advertising campaigns. Others may have to localize product strategy but are able to standardize advertising. The Dell Computer Company, for example, standardizes its direct sales strategy in all its markets but localizes advertising strategy.

TABLE 1-3 EPRG and Global Product Strategy

Orientation	Product Strategy
Ethnocentric	Product development determined by needs of home country customers.
Polycentric	Local product development based on local needs.
Regiocentric	Standardized within region, but not across regions.
Geocentric	Global product with local variations.

Source: Thomson, A. Jr. & Strickland, A. *Strategic Management,* 13e © 2003 The McGraw-Hill Companies, Inc.

Figure 1-4 The Need for Localization Varies by Business Function

Source: Adapted from: ITSMA *Viewpoint,* June 2005, p. 3.

On the other hand, Nestlé localizes some of its products but attempts to standardize advertising campaigns as much as possible.

Figure 1-4 illustrates that the degree of localization needed depends on the business function performed. Most marketing functions need some sort of adaptation across markets, whereas such functions as finance need very little adjustment. Brand identity is a function that most companies want to standardize, in order to maintain a uniform image worldwide.

When is a standardized strategy preferable? There are several reasons why manufacturers and service providers prefer standardized marketing strategies on a global basis. These include gaining economies of scale in production and marketing, lowering costs—especially high R&D and development costs —and easing pressures exerted by global customers for the supply of uniform products. In industries that have high development and set-up costs and rapid technological obsolescence, it is to their advantage to develop standardized products that can be rapidly introduced in a large number of markets in order to recoup investment. Likewise, in industries where learning curve advantages are important, **standardization** can lower costs. Global customers can also pressure their suppliers to offer uniform products to their various manufacturing facilities that are located in a number of countries. For example, global suppliers of paint products to global car manufacturers must provide a standardized product from their different plant locations to ensure that all cars will have the same exterior finish. Table 1-4

TABLE 1-4 Companies Using Standardized Marketing Strategies	
Strategy	**Company**
Product Design	Ford (Escort), Nokia Mobile Phones, Gillette (razors), Kodak (cameras)
Brand Name	Heineken, Coca-Cola, Reebok, Nivea, Ikea
Product Positioning	Colgate (toothpaste)
Packaging	Gillette (razors)
Advertising	McDonald's, Kodak (cameras)
Sales Promotion	Thane International (exercise equipment)
Distribution	Mary Kay (cosmetics), Ikea

shows selected companies that use standardized marketing strategies. Some may design products globally but localize distribution (e.g., Gillette razors). Others may have two or more of the listed standardized strategies (e.g., Kodak).

On the other hand, there are factors working against the ability of firms to standardize marketing strategies: different tastes and customer preferences and performance requirements and standards across countries inhibit the ability to standardize. When Nestlé introduced its coffee products into China, it created a blend adapted to the particular tastes of Chinese consumers. Nestlé's wafer bar brand Kit Kat generates roughly $1 billion in sales worldwide. This product is adapted in many markets. For example, in Russia, its size is smaller than in Western countries and the chocolate is coarser, while in Japan the flavor is strawberry. Kenichi Ohmae[25] writes that "When it comes to product strategy, managing in a borderless economy doesn't mean managing by averages. It doesn't mean that all tastes run together into one amorphous mass of universal appeal. And it doesn't mean that the appeal of operating globally removes the obligation to mobilize products. The lure of a universal product is a false allure." However, in a revised edition,[26] Ohmae observes that "young people of the advanced countries are becoming increasingly nationality-less and more like 'Californians' all over the Triad countries—the United States, Europe, and Japan. . . ." The inference here is that this particular market segment of young people in developed countries may be targets for standardized products. We can think of some: Levi's jeans, iPods, and Timberland shoes. These are some examples of products that are standardized across borders.

Even when products are standardized, it may not be possible to standardize other elements of the marketing mix. A case in point was a Nescafé commercial aired in Chile. The commercial showed a house by a lake. Inside, the father tries to wake his son to go fishing, but the son prefers to stay in bed. Soon, the son wakes up and prepares a cup of coffee. Reinvigorated, he brings a cup of coffee to his father who is sitting by the lake, disappointed by his son's decision not to join him. However, father and son are reunited over a cup of coffee. The message is that coffee helped the relationship of both. However, the same commercial aired, for example, in Paris, might simply be viewed as an environmental statement. While coffee tastes may conceivably be the same in both countries, perception of the same advertising appeal might be quite different.

Another example of different perceptions of the same advertising message occurred when a television commercial produced for North American audiences was aired in several Latin America countries. The idea behind the message was to encourage the sale of additional telephone sets in two-story homes. A phone call for the husband was received by his wife who was working in the kitchen. The husband was on the second floor, without a telephone installation. The housewife shouted to her husband to come down right away and answer the phone. The ad was perceived negatively because the wife gave an order to her husband in a very masculine country, and she seemed to be impatient in a society where orientation to time and urgency were much different than in North America.

Levitt and the Globalization of Marketing

The late Theodore Levitt (1925–2006), longtime professor at the Harvard Business School, was one of the first marketers to envisage the possibility of a global marketing strategy. His vision contemplated the convergence (the tendency for everything to

25. Ohmae, K. (1990). *The borderless world*. New York: HarperCollins Publishers, Inc.

26. _____ (1999). *The borderless world* (Rev. ed.). New York: HarperCollins Publishers, Inc.

become more like everything else) of consumer demand worldwide.[27] Levitt believed that accustomed differences in national or regional preferences were a thing of the past. If marketers could provide high-quality products at reasonable, low prices, they would appeal to consumers in different countries. The ability of manufacturers to do so, however, depends on three factors: (1) substantial economies of scale, (2) consumer sensitivity to price and quality above all other considerations, and (3) homogenization of consumer desires and tastes across national boundaries. Levitt's assumptions have been questioned, especially the second and third above. There are significant differences between national markets that require adaptation and customization in, if not all of marketing programs, then at least in some parts, such as product and promotional strategies. Whether consumers everywhere will prefer less expensive, standardized products over differentiated ones (remember Ford's Model T—"You can choose any color as long as it's black"?) has been largely discounted. Levitt himself toned down his vision and realized that companies had to balance persistent national cultural patterns with the general trend toward the embrace of global brands. Thus, he acknowledged tactics like McDonald's supplementing its standard menus with local fare like vegan meals in India, Coca-Cola varying the sugar content of its soft drinks, and Nestlé developing products to meet local tastes if a global brand is not acceptable.

Standardization versus Mass Customization

Pine's (1993) theory[28] of "mass customization" challenges the globalization (standardization) of marketing approach. **Mass customization** has been defined as "a strategy that creates value by some form of company-customer interaction at the fabrication/assembly stage of the operations level to create customized products with production cost and monetary price similar to those of mass-produced products."[29] Pine asserts that many consumers are unwilling to purchase standardized products even though they are sold for lower prices. On the contrary, many people are willing to pay more for customized products that meet specific desires. In effect, the concept of customization views each consumer as a segment. Proponents of such an approach maintain that it is possible owing to the achievement of economies of scale through computer aided manufacturing (CAM).

Some examples of successful customization of consumer goods and services include:

- Dell's famous "build-to-order" model facilitated its rise to dominance in the PC direct-purchase industry.
- The Architectural Skylight Company is a firm in Maine that uses CAD to automate the production of windows to architects' specifications.
- Companies throughout the tourism industry have been offering package holiday alternatives through mass customization.

Additional examples of mass customization are operational today, such as software-based products that make it possible to add and/or change functionalities of a core product or to build fully custom enclosures from scratch. This degree of mass customization has only seen limited adoption, however. If an enterprise's marketing department offers individual products (atomic market fragmentation) it doesn't often mean that a product is produced individually, but rather that similar variants of the same mass produced item are available.

27. Levitt, T. (1983, May/June). The globalization of markets. *Harvard Business Review, 61,* 92–102.

28. Pine, B. J. (1993). *Mass customization: the new frontier in business competition.* Boston, MA: Harvard Business School.

29. Kaplan, A., & Haenlein, M. (2006). Toward a parsimonious definition of traditional and electronic mass customization. *Journal of Product Innovation Management, 23*(2), 168–182.

While theoretically feasible, the customization approach has not received much support in the marketing literature. Some of its drawbacks include longer waiting times for customized products, longer searching times for retail outlets, and of course higher prices. Many industries have found that lengthy supply chains and the economics of configurability do not allow them to economically offer mass customization. Some of the early businesses attempting mass customization (e.g., in bicycle production) went out of business. Supporters of the mass customization trend gave Cannondale as the exemplar of the new model. For instance, Wind and Rangaswany[30] (2000) cited the Cannondale bicycle company's ability to mass customize. Although the company's subsequent bankruptcy in 2003 was blamed on other causes (including a failed attempt to enter the motor sports market), the mass customization "revolution" certainly failed to save it, and it was dropped as a role model by business gurus. The company later became part of Dorel industries, a multinational leisure and recreational products (Schwinn and Cannondale bicycles) manufacturer headquartered in Canada (www.dorel.com).

In spite of these failures, the "customized consumer" does exist as a separate, niche segment alongside those willing to accept standardized products.[31]

Managing the Firm's Value Chain

A key tool for developing and sustaining competitive advantage is configuring and coordinating the firm's value chain. Briefly, a **value chain** is the sequence of activities required to make a product or provide a service.[32] A firm's survival depends upon its ability to create value which is demanded by customers. An example of a firm's value chain is shown in Table 1-5.

The value chain concept developed by Michael Porter[33] is based on the premise that organizations consist of activities that when linked together provide value to both the firm and to the final consumer. These activities are categorized as primary, such as production and marketing, and support activities that provide the facilities that contribute to the effectiveness and efficiency of the firm, such as research and development and human resource management. Primary value chain activities are:

- Inbound Logistics: receiving and warehousing of raw materials and distribution to manufacturing
- Operations: transforming inputs into finished products and services
- Marketing and Sales: identification and satisfaction of customer needs
- Service: after sales support

Secondary value chain activities support the primary activities. These include:

- Firm Infrastructure: organization and control mechanisms, company culture
- Human Resource Management: recruiting, hiring, training, development, and compensation of employees
- Technology: development of technology to support value-creating activities
- Procurement: purchasing material, supplies, and equipment inputs

30. Wind, J., & Rangaswamy, A. (2000). Customerization: the next revolution in mass customization. *eBusiness Research Center Working Paper 06-1999*. Penn State School of Information Sciences and Technology.

31. Bardacki, A., & Whitelock, J. (2004). How "ready" are customers for mass customization? An exploratory investigation. *European Journal of Marketing, 38*(11/12), 1396–1416.

32. Schmitz, H. (2005). *Value chain analysis for policy-makers and practitioners*. Geneva: International Labour Office.

33. Porter, M. (1985). *Competitive advantage: creating and sustaining superior performance*. New York: The Free Press.

TABLE 1-5 Value Chain Framework	
Primary Activities	**Support Activities**
Inbound Logistics	Infrastructure
Operations	Human Resource Management
Marketing and Sales	Technology Development
Service	Procurement

Source: Adapted from: Porter, M. (1985). *Competitive advantage: creating and sustaining superior performance.* New York: The Free Press.

Each link in the chain provides value, with some providing more value than others. The end result is "margin," or the difference between the total value (the price the consumer is willing to pay) and the cost of performing all the activities in the chain. Margin can be improved by either reducing activity costs or by increasing their value. It should be emphasized that not all firms perform all activities in a value chain; some are farmed out, or outsourced to other firms that can provide them more effectively and/or more efficiently; e.g., at lower cost. This is what Porter[34] termed a "value system," a set of inter-linked firms that perform all the functions in a given value chain, say for the production of computers. An example of such a chain-value system is the design of notebook computers in Taiwan and their assembly in China for most of the well-known brands sold today. Marketing strategy is planned at company headquarters. In this example, the design, production, and marketing of the computers is executed in at least three countries. As a result, the coordination of these value activities has to be controlled by a strong governance structure because of the risk of supplier failure to maintain quality and to deliver on schedule. In these cases, there is usually a "lead firm" that takes control, often the owner of the brand, such as Dell or Hewlett Packard (HP). Control and coordination are exercised by the lead firm in defining the products to be produced by suppliers and by providing key resources needed in the chain. In most cases value chains are producer-driven, as in the case of notebook computer manufacturers. However, there are buyer-driven chains, which include industries where large retailers and trading companies are lead firms, such as the British-headquartered chain Marks & Spencer.

Global Value Chain Configuration

In a global marketing system, there is a growing spatial dispersion of activities that comprise a value chain. This is one of the major distinctions between a domestic and international chain. According to Michael Porter, these distinctions revolve around two dimensions: configuration and coordination of the activities in the chain. **Configuration** refers to where and how the activities will be located, either concentrated in one country or dispersed in many countries. **Coordination** refers to the governance of the activities, how they are linked together throughout a chain which is dispersed geographically in different countries. Therefore, configuration and coordination are the major tools by which a value chain is managed.

Table 1-6 shows two primary activities and one support activity that are configured and coordinated globally by a multinational manufacturer of high-quality shoes with corporate headquarters located in Denmark.[35] Shoe components (uppers, soles, etc.)

34. Porter, M. (1990). *The competitive advantage of nations.* New York: The Free Press.

35. Er, M., & MacCarthy, B. (n.d.). *Configuration of international supply networks and their operational implications: Evidences from manufacturing companies in Indonesia.* University of Nottingham.

TABLE 1-6 Global Value Chain Configuration	
Primary Activities	**Support Activities**
Inbound Logistics **Production in Indonesia, Denmark, Portugal, Slovakia, and Thailand**	Infrastructure
Operations	Human Resource Management
Marketing and Sales **Marketing plans developed in Denmark**	Technology Development **Product development in Denmark & Indonesia**
Service	Procurement

Source: Adapted from: Porter, M. (1985). *Competitive advantage: creating and sustaining superior performance.* New York: The Free Press.

are manufactured in five locations: Indonesia, Denmark, Portugal, Slovakia, and Thailand. However, nearly 50 percent of the upper shoe is produced in Indonesia, and these parts are then shipped to other facilities where soles are added. Product development and marketing strategy, including sales forecasting and production quotas for the company's subsidiaries and licensees, is determined by headquarters management in Denmark. Of course, there are many other activities, such as procurement, distribution, and services that are configured globally as well, which illustrates the complexity of a global value chain. Indeed, the competitive advantage of a firm may well depend on its effectiveness in managing the set of value-adding activities across borders.

Integrating the Firm's Competitive Strategy

Other marketing scholars argue that the key to competitive advantage and global marketing success is participation in major world markets and integration of competitive strategies across these markets. Central to this line of reasoning are two tactics: cross-subsidization of operations in one market by shifting resources (capital, managerial talent) to other markets and responding to competitive pressures in one market (e.g., a firm's home market) by counterattacking competitors in their home market or in other key markets. By entering a rival's home market, a global competitor may motivate the rival to deploy resources in order to defend its home. By allocating resources in defense of the home market, the rival will have fewer resources to compete in other markets.

Global Competition

Global players can choose where to compete and invest the most resources against rivals—in their home market, in the competitor's home market, or in third markets where both compete. For example, in 1998, Michelin, the French tire manufacturer, was planning to enter the United States, the home market of Goodyear Tire. At the time, Michelin had an 18 percent world share of tire sales, compared to 17 percent for Goodyear. In order to strengthen its European position and compete against Michelin, Goodyear negotiated a joint venture (JV) with Somitomo, a Japanese manufacturer that had a 5.5 percent world market share. The JV gave Goodyear control over Somitomo's European operations, including more distribution channels. The result for Goodyear was increased market share in Europe that stalled, for a time, Michelin's challenge to its home market in the United States. Michelin had to concentrate resources in Europe in order to thwart Goodyear's challenge to its home market.

Another case of global competition is called cross-subsidization. Cross-subsidization is applicable when firms can benefit from sharing costs and/or revenues.[36] A global firm can shift resources from more profitable subsidiaries to less profitable ones. Cost sharing among subsidiaries to support R&D for product development is another possibility. Knowledge sharing among subsidiaries or affiliates is another area that can create synergy for firms operating in global industries. A lack of knowledge sharing resulted in huge losses for Caterpillar—the world's largest tractor manufacturer since the 1960s—during 1982–1984 and 1991–1992, when its Japanese rival Komatsu gained market share in both European and North American markets. However, by 1999, Caterpillar was profitable again, owing mainly to a strengthened global marketing and sales network and strict financial controls.

A GLOBAL MARKETING MANAGEMENT FRAMEWORK

A number of researchers[37] argue that global marketing strategy influences a firm's global marketing performance. Global marketing strategy, in turn, is mediated by external market drivers and internal drivers, which are in effect internal characteristics of the firm. Studies in industrial economics have shown that a firm's external environment influences its strategy and hence its performance.[38] Those firms that are able to "read" and understand these drivers are more likely to perform well. It is imperative for firms operating globally to respond quickly and effectively to changes in the economy, competition, consumer requirements, and technology. The boycott of French wine in the United States briefly during 2003, owing to France's opposition to the invasion of American forces in Iraq, and the boycott against Danish products in Middle Eastern countries stemming from the Danish Mohammed cartoon crisis in 2005, demonstrate the importance of keeping an ear open to such changes. Likewise, a firm's success will depend upon the extent to which it develops internal capabilities and resources to implement its strategy. Needed are managers who both recognize the importance of internationalizing the firm and who succeed in implementing a global marketing strategy.

As outlined at the beginning of this chapter, a global strategy is an organization-wide plan designed to enable the firm to develop a strong global presence, especially in terms of marketing and production. The elements of a global marketing strategy and its internal and external drivers are shown in Figure 1-5. Internal drivers are those that emanate from within the firm, and are thus controllable by management, such as a global vision and firm capabilities and the financing and international experience of executives. External drivers, on the other hand, are not controllable by the firm, but impact its ability to determine and execute a global strategy. Among these drivers are the global economy, culture, political-legal systems, and technology. All of these drivers will be discussed in the chapters that follow. We begin a discussion of the Global Marketing framework with attention to the dependent variable: Global Marketing Performance.

36. Ghoshal, S. (1987). Global strategy: an organizing framework, *Strategic Management Journal, 8,* 425–440.

37. Porter, M. (1986, Winter). Changing patterns of international competition. *California Management Review, 28,* 9–40; Ohmae, K. (1989, May/June). Managing in a borderless world. *Harvard Business Review, 67,* 152–161; Yip, G. (1995). *Total global strategy: managing for worldwide competitive advantage.* Englewood Cliffs, NJ: Prentice-Hall; Zou, S., & Cavusgil, T. (2002, October). The GMS: a broad conceptualization of global marketing strategy and its effect on firm performance. *Journal of Marketing, 66,* 40–56; Townsend, J., Yeniyurt, S., Deligonul, S., & Cavusgil, S. (2004, March). Exploring the marketing program antecedents of performance in the global company. Unpublished working paper.

38. Porter, M. (1980). *Competitive strategy.* New York: The Free Press.

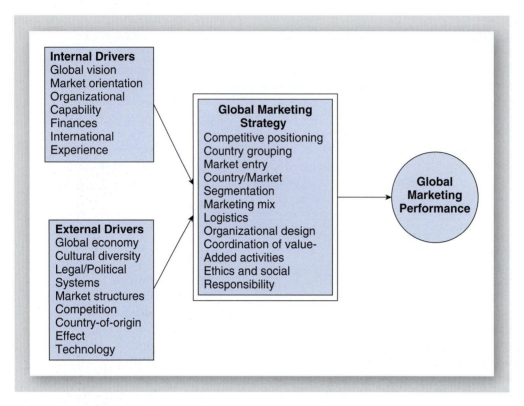

Figure 1-5 A Framework for Global Marketing Strategy

Global Marketing Performance

Ambler and Xiucun[39] (2003) suggest that marketing effectiveness or performance can be measured within four dimensions of business activity, as shown in Table 1-7. While financial outcomes measure overall firm performance, market and consumer-oriented metrics are better indicators of marketing success. If global marketing strategy takes into consideration external globalizing drivers, there should be a significant impact on the firm's global performance.[40] Moreover, there is evidence of a positive relationship between the development of customer knowledge, new product advantage, and market performance.[41]

As shown in Table 1-7, innovativeness also impacts marketing performance. Booz Allen Hamilton consulting found that firms having the highest rates of R&D spending as a percentage of sales are more likely than other companies in their industries to achieve superior gross margins.[42] Higher gross margins allow more to be spent on marketing programs, including research and development. Among the world's top R&D spenders (R&D/sales) are firms in the health and electronic industries. These include

39. Ambler, T., & Xiucun, W. (2003). Measures of marketing success: a comparison between China and the United Kingdom. *Asia Pacific Journal of Management, 20,* 267–281.

40. Zou, S., & Cavusgil, T. (2002, October). The GMS: a broad conceptualization of global marketing strategy and its effect on firm performance. *Journal of Marketing, 66,* 40–56.

41. Li, T., & Cavusgil, S. (2000). Decomposing the effects of market knowledge competence in new product export: a dimensionality analysis. *European Journal of Marketing, 34*(1/2), 57–79.

42. Jaruzelski, B., Dehoff, K., & Bordia, R. (2006). Smart spenders: the global innovation. *Special Report.* Booz Allen Hamilton.

TABLE 1-7 Measures of Marketing Performance	
Dimension	**Measure**
Market	Market share
	Advertising share of mind
	Promotional share of mind
Consumer	Customer penetration
	Customer loyalty
	New customers gained
	Brand recognition
	Brand equity
	Satisfaction
	Purchase intention
Innovativeness	New products launched
	Revenue from new products/total turnover
Financial	Turnover
	Contribution margin
	Profits

Source: Adapted from: Ambler, T., & Xiucun, W. (2003). Measures of marketing success: a comparison between China and the United Kingdom. *Asia Pacific Journal of Management, 20,* 267–281.

Roche Holdings (16 percent ratio of R&D/sales), Microsoft (16 percent), Novartis and Pfizer (15 percent), GlaxoSmithKline (14 percent) and Nokia (14 percent). All of these firms are large global competitors. Smaller firms must spend a higher proportion of their sales on R&D to compete with them. One way to do this is to outsource research and development to lower cost regions of the world. A study by Booz Allen Hamilton and INSEAD[43] found that 75 percent of new R&D centers that were planned were to be located in China and India.

Global Vision—The World Is My Oyster

One of the first perquisites to formulating a global marketing strategy is determining a global vision. A strategic vision states where a company wants to go, how it will get there, and why it should be successful in doing so. **Global vision** is the ability to look into the future or the capacity to visualize the image that the company is seeking to create on a worldwide basis. Entrepreneurs need a clear global vision to know where to go and how to achieve their objectives.

Every year, aspiring entrepreneurs create startups with the hope that they will go global almost instantly, but few of them survive. In some situations, starting a business is not so difficult because entrepreneurs already have sufficient resources, which include venture capital, a willingness to take risks and to recognize and exploit business opportunities in the international economy. But few of them can lead their new businesses to growth and global expansion owing to the lack of a clear vision and an appropriate strategy. Without a clear vision, they cannot plan for the future, and thus they are not prepared for growth, competition, and threats from changes in international markets.

A global mission statement is also necessary for well-established firms in order to plan for the long run. The following example is taken from Matsushita Electric Industrial Company's report to its stakeholders:

43. Duhoff, K., & Sehgal, V. (2006, Autumn). *Innovators without borders.* Retrieved from www.strategy-business.com/press/article/06305.

BOX 1-3   COMPANY IN FOCUS: MATSUSHITA

The current business environment remains uncertain, with volatile conditions expected to continue in the consumer electronics industry. Guided by its new management, Matsushita will bolster proprietary technologies as the basis for developing competitive products, focus management resources into strategic businesses, consistently strengthen management structures, and further promote global business expansion to achieve the targets of the Leap Ahead 21 plan. Such targets include an operating profit to sales ratio of 5 percent or more. . . . Furthermore, to achieve global excellence in 2010, Matsushita will continue efforts to realize its corporate twin vision of realizing a ubiquitous networking society and coexistence with the global environment. Moreover, we place a high priority on accountability for the benefit of our shareholders, investors, customers, and all other stakeholders, and will continue efforts to further increase corporate value.

Source: Matsushita Electric Industrial Co., Ltd., Annual Report, 2007.

SUMMARY

- This chapter has explored what is meant by global marketing and global marketing strategy and how they may be implemented.

- Global firms must plan globally while acting locally and determine the extent to which marketing activities can be standardized across national borders.

- Globalization, a process of interaction and integration among people, companies, and governments of many nations, is driven by international trade and investment.

- How similar or dissimilar are country markets to each other? The CAGE model is a good start to determine distances between countries. Absolute distances between countries are easily measured. However, there are also subjective distances that may impact on market entry. Psychic and cultural distances are additional measures that should be taken into consideration.

- How well has a firm performed internationally? We have suggested a number of measures to determine performance based on the consumer, product development, and financial returns.

- We have suggested a framework for global marketing strategy that will serve as the agenda for topics discussed in the chapters that follow.

DISCUSSION QUESTIONS

1. Give four reasons and explain why a domestic firm would choose to "go global."

2. As the manager of an SME (small–medium enterprise), which EPRG orientation would you implement in going global?

3. Which drivers of global marketing do you think are the most important in shaping marketing strategy: internal or external? Explain the reasons for your answer.

EXPERIENTIAL EXERCISES

1. Do research on the Internet and use the CAGE framework to discuss the distances between Japanese and United States automotive manufacturers.

2. Construct a global value chain for the production of a Toyota Corolla.

KEY TERMS

CAGE framework, p. 7

Configuration, p. 19

Coordination, p. 19

Cultural distance, p. 12

Emerging markets, p. 9

EPRG framework, p. 13

Ethnocentric orientation, p. 13

Geocentric orientation, p. 14

Global marketing, p. 7

Global markets, p. 7

Global vision, p. 23

Globalization, p. 3

Integration, p. 20

Mass customization, p. 17

Polycentric orientation, p. 13

Psychic distance, p. 12

Regiocentric orientation, p. 13

Social networking, p. 3

Standardization, p. 15

Value chain, p. 18

CASE 1-1

A Tortuous Road Ahead for Proton of Malaysia

It was an unenviable position in which any company could find itself. Proton's share of the domestic car market in Malaysia fell to 28 percent in 2010, sliding from 40 percent in 2005, 60 percent in 2002, and 73 percent in 1988. Tariffs on foreign-made cars were slowly being lifted under a regional free-trade pact called the ASEAN (Association of Southeast Asian Nations) Free Trade Area (AFTA).

Perusahaan Otomobil Nasional Sdn. Bhd. (known much better as simply "Proton") is one of Malaysia's two national car manufacturers. Like so much else in modern Malaysia, Proton was the brainchild of ex-Prime Minister Mahathir Mohamad. Proton was founded in 1983 as a joint venture with Japan's Mitsubishi Motors Corp., which ended its connection in 2004, after nearly 20 years. Mahathir is now an adviser to the board of the company and still retains an active interest.

Malaysia—The Country

Malaysia is generally regarded as one of the most successful non-western countries to have achieved a relatively smooth transition to modern economic growth over the last century. It is a country of nearly 28.7 million people and one of the most vibrant economies in Southeast Asia. Geographically, it consists of two regions separated by the South China Sea. Politically, it is a federation of 13 states and three federally administered territories. Most of the country's economic and industrial development is concentrated in the western part, known as Peninsular Malaysia, while the eastern part, which consists of the large states of Sabah and Sarawak, is comparatively less industrially developed.

Malaysia's multiethnic society comprises a majority Malay-Muslim population and a numerically lesser but economically more powerful Chinese population. The third racial segment is made up of the migrant Indians mostly in the working class apart from some who are medical and legal professionals. There are tribal groups, Eurasians, and a large pool of expatriate workers besides the three major racial groups. Malaysia has a well-earned reputation as a liberal, progressive, and modern Muslim country.

Trade, internationalization, and globalization are phenomena not new to Malaysia. It has a long history of being an important junction of major world trade routes. The indigenous population has been supplemented by an immigrant labor force mainly from China and India, allowing it to experience a diversity of cultures. Foreign capital has played a critical role throughout its economic development. Malaysia's exports comprise electronic equipment, petroleum and liquefied natural gas, chemicals, palm oil, timber and wood products, rubber, and textiles. It is among the world's biggest producers of computer disk drives, palm oil, rubber, and timber. In addition, it has a booming tourism industry.

Case prepared by Azhar Kazmi, Visiting Professor of Management at King Fahd University of Petroleum & Minerals, Dhahran, Saudi Arabia and formerly Professor of Business Administration at International Islamic University Malaysia, Kuala Lumpur. Reprinted with permission.

Car making in Malaysia

It's an enigma how a small country with such a small population could have the temerity to embark upon a large-scale project of manufacturing cars barely three decades after it attained independence from Britain in 1957. Most likely, it was an effort to put Malaysia firmly on the path of industrialization, as the automobile industry is considered a significant engine of industrial development. The history of the Malaysian automobile industry goes back to early 1960s, when the Malaysian government developed a policy to promote an integrated automobile industry to strengthen Malaysia's industrial base. The government's main objectives in promoting an automobile assembly industry were to reduce imports, save foreign exchange, create employment, develop strong forward and backward linkages with the rest of the economy, and transfer industrial technology.

Protective tariffs were announced in early 1966, when all distributors and dealers were required to obtain import licenses. In 1967, the Malaysian government approved the operation of six assembly plants. Initially, the assembly plants were mainly joint venture projects between European automobile manufacturers and local partners who had previously been their local distributors. Until the early 1980s, there were 15 assemblers that produced vehicles for European and Japanese manufacturers.

The big push toward a Malaysian automobile industry was led by the two national car projects, Proton and Perodua. The second national car manufacturer, *Perusahaan Otomobil Kedua Sdn. Bhd.* (Perodua), was established as a joint venture between Malaysian firms and Daihatsu in 1993. It started production of Kancil, a passenger car with a displacement volume of 660cc, modeled after the Daihatsu "Mira." While Proton offered larger-capacity cars, Perodua specialized in smaller-capacity, compact, and affordable cars.

Over the years, Malaysia has adopted a strong protectionist policy toward its automobile industry. Hefty tariffs on imported cars and car components have sought to protect the local car manufacturers from foreign competition. This protectionism has served as a double-edged sword. On the positive side, local car manufacturers have prospered, there have been reduced foreign exchange outflows, and higher government revenues have been realized from tariffs. There have also been spillover effects of the development of strong components and parts manufacturing and the development of original equipment manufacturers for other car companies. On the negative side, protections to local car manufacturers have made them complacent and inefficient, distortions of markets have taken place, customers have been deprived of high-quality cars at affordable prices, and the local car industry is not able to compete internationally.

Statistics show that Malaysia is the largest car market in Southeast Asia, with more than 560,000 new cars being registered in 2010 (see Table 1). Proton's share of this market is about 28 percent, and that has been steadily decreasing over the years.

Often it is said that the car is a product that evokes varying emotions. It is a house-on-wheels, a companion, a status symbol, and it offers security and safety besides being, of course, a means of mobility. For the Malaysians, car making has often been seen as a matter of national pride. It hurts terribly when suggestions are made to sell off stakes in the car companies to foreigners. Yet it is equally distressing that it is no longer possible to follow protectionist policies in a rapidly globalizing world that demands closer integration with the world economy. The choice is difficult indeed. For the typical globalization enthusiast, it is difficult to understand the emotions attached to motives for protectionism. For a person of nationalistic fervor it is not easy to visualize why "foreign marauders" should be allowed to gobble up hard-earned national wealth. There are strong arguments on both sides. As Mahathir Mohamed, the ex-prime minister said

TABLE 1: Number of Vehicles Registered in Malaysia		
Year	**Passenger Cars**	**Total Vehicles (including commercial and 4 × 4 vehicles)**
1980	80,420	97,262
1990	106,454	165,861
2000	282,103	343,173
2005	416,692	552,316
2006	366,738	490,768
2007	442,885	487,176
2008	497,459	548,115
2009	486,342	536,905
2010	563,594	605,156
YTD March 2011	142,546	158,433

Source: Adapted from: Malaysian Automotive Association's website at www.maa.org.my/info_summary.htm. Retrieved May 26, 2011.

in a *Businessweek* interview: "Korean and Japanese car makers were protected for 40 or 50 years. Why should we open our own small market after just 20 years?"

Foreign Connections

It is not as if Malaysia has a hands-off policy toward foreign capital, foreign technology, or foreign labor. Proton has had a good record of foreign collaborations over the years. It started operations in alliance with Mitsubishi and has sustained them for over 20 years. In February 2006, Proton and Mitsubishi Motors revived their alliance by signing a pact to develop new Proton vehicles.

Proton produced its first car, named "Saga," in 1985 mainly for the domestic market but made an initial export attempt the same year to Bangladesh. In 1989, it started exporting cars to United Kingdom. Although Proton has diversified export destinations since then, the UK has always been the main destination for its exports. On its website (www.proton.com/Corporate/About-Proton/Corporate-Information/History-of-PROTON.aspx#story), Proton claims to be exporting to 50 countries in Africa, Asia, Europe, the Middle East, and the Pacific. Export shipments stagnated during the 1990s and later (around 10,000 units annually), rising gradually to 25,000 units in 2010. Proton has consistently claimed to raise exports to 100,000 units, which may be unrealistic when looking at its past export performance.

Dissatisfied with the slow progress of the technology transfer from Mitsubishi and the rapid appreciation of the yen, Proton established an alliance with Citroen to produce a new model, "Tiara." Proton also established subsidiaries or related companies to assemble and distribute vehicles in the Philippines and Vietnam. In September 2006, PSA Peugeot Citroen signed an agreement with Proton to look at forming a strategic alliance in an effort to enter Southeast Asia. Earlier, Proton held talks on potential alliances with other car manufacturers, including Rover and Volkswagen, but they did not lead to partnerships. Proton also signed a memorandum of association in May 2006 with Chery Automobile Company of China on sharing production facilities, developing new vehicle models, and co-sourcing materials and components. Pushing toward the East, Proton entered into an agreement with Jinhua-Youngman of China to look for licensing opportunities for some of the group technologies it had developed. Overall, there have been strong signals that Proton was open to selling equity stake to a foreign partner. Yet, as one after yet another attempt at foreign tie-ups have come and gone, government as well as managers at Proton have balked at finalizing a deal.

Though the UK and Australia remain major export markets for Proton, it is developing markets in the Middle East and other Muslim countries as well as in the ASEAN countries. Currently, Proton has assembly plants in Iran, China, and India (with Hindustan Motors), and a joint venture between its subsidiary, Proton Edar and PT Ningz Multiusaha, to assemble and distribute Proton vehicles in Indonesia. This was its first effort to penetrate the regional Southeast Asian markets. Proton had plans to increase CBU (completely build unit) exports to the UK and Australia, as well as CKD (completely knocked down) assembly in Indonesia, Thailand, the Middle East, and Eastern Europe. Proton also considered the feasibility of CKD operations in China and India.

The difficulties ahead for Proton in its internationalization efforts could be seen in the context of predicted overcapacity in automobile manufacturing in several Asian countries. For instance, China, according to its eleventh five-year program (2006–2010), expected its 32 major automobile manufacturers to possess production capacity of 18 million by 2010. This figure is anticipated to rise to 30 million by 2015, creating a substantial surplus production capacity.

The Strategic Options: All Muddled Up?

Talking to *Asiaweek* magazine in 2000, Mahathir Mohamad, then-prime minister of Malaysia, said "It will be very difficult for (Proton) to penetrate the international car market with global car giants exercising mass production." He added, "We do not reject globalization or cooperating with the major players of the industry . . . but we want to retain (Proton) as ours because it identifies us as a nation on par with other automotive producing nations." It does, but at what cost? Today, Proton can barely utilize just half of its production capacity of 330,000 cars. Its exports are measly, barely touching 25,000 units in 2010, most of it to the UK. It has a very low brand power outside Malaysia and a weak customer loyalty and retention rate in addition to perceived quality problems in its cars. This is worsened by factors such as the lack of economies of scale, overcapacity, outdated technology, a limited product lineup, and other drawbacks as the Malaysian economy begins a slow recovery after a debilitating global recession. Competition from multinational corporations in the ASEAN area emanates from United States giants like Ford, General Motors, and DaimlerChrysler that are already present in neighboring Thailand. On the other hand, there is the formidable reputation of Mahathir as a person who defied the International Monetary Fund during the Southeast Asian financial crisis of 1997, from which Malaysia emerged relatively unscathed. Under his advisory tutelage, Proton may yet defy conventional wisdom and survive as a successful automaker.

Proton now finds itself at a crossroads. On the one hand, the government of present Prime Minister Najib Razak has to keep rolling back tariff protections as Malaysia honors its obligations under the AFTA. Tariffs on Southeast Asian-made cars sold in Malaysia were a stiff 50 percent in 2004 but were reduced to 20 percent in 2006, and had to be brought down to just 5 percent in 2008 and to zero percent in 2010. But the Malaysian Automotive Policy framework of October 2009 continued the discriminatory rebate policy on locally manufactured cars giving advantage to companies like Proton. On the other hand, the obligations to the ASEAN were likely to put Malaysia in jeopardy with regard to 10,000 jobs at Proton, plus 90,000 jobs in the parts and component plants that supply to it.

The supporters of Proton argue that with regional integration such as AFTA, Malaysia's car market is not limited to just its 27 million people but includes more than 500 million Southeast Asians. Critics of the company see no future for Proton as an independent company. Quoted in the July 2005 edition of *Businessweek*, Graeme

Maxton, Asia analyst for consultancy Autopolis in Hong Kong, says that "Proton is an anachronism in the automobile industry, and it's not going to survive over the long term." As a marginal producer with falling market share even in its home market, he says, Proton lacks the scale it needs to compete against bigger rivals. Strong words, but they may turn out to be true!

As the debate goes on, foreign suitor companies continually line up to either buy Proton or to use its facilities to increase their production in the hot Southeast Asian market. But they may have to fear the fate of Volkswagen AG, with which Proton had intermittent negotiations beginning in 2004, only to see that foreign company retreating, disappointed, in 2010.

CASE 1-2

Dabur—Developing Values in an Emerging Economy Through Value Chain and Product Line

Economy Overview

- The Indian economy has been on a strong growth trajectory, with real GDP growing at a CAGR of 7.5 percent over the last decade
- High rate of Gross Capital Formation of 35 percent and Gross Domestic Savings of 32.5 percent in 2009 is expected to drive GDP growth of around 8 to 9 percent going forward
- RBI's target for GDP growth is at 9 percent for the XI and XII five-year plans (till FY17)
- Per capita income in India is slated to triple in the next 10 years (Exhibit 1: Per Capita Consumption of FMCG products)

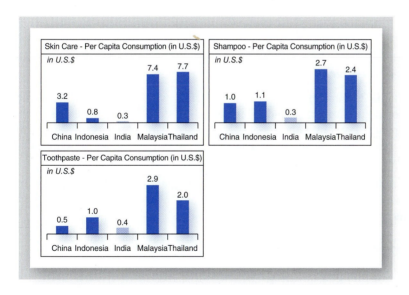

Exhibit 1: Per Capita Consumption of FMCG Products

FMCG Industry In India

- Indian FMCG industry size estimated at around U.S.$25 billion
- Personal care and food products dominate the sector
- Many categories are currently small and offer huge potential

Case prepared by Prashant Salwan, Indian Institute of Management. Reprinted with permission.

- Steady double-digit growth in the sector
- Rural India contributes c. 33% of the overall FMCG sector (see Exhibit 2: Penetration Levels (Urban & Rural))

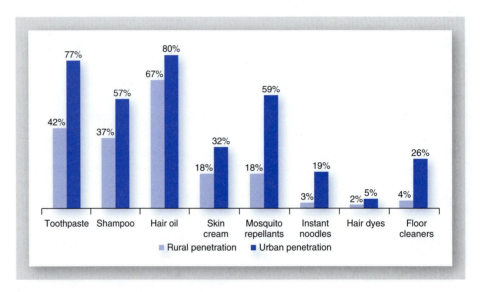

Exhibit 2: Penetration Levels (Urban & Rural)

Dabur at a Glance

Dabur India Limited has marked its presence with significant achievements and today commands a market leadership status. Its story of success is based on dedication to nature, corporate and process hygiene, dynamic leadership, and commitment to its partners and stakeholders. The results of its policies and initiatives speak for themselves:

- Leading consumer goods company in India with a turnover of **Rs 4110 Crore (FY 11)** with a profit of Rs 569 Crore in FY 11
- Three major strategic business units (SBU)—Consumer Care Division (CCD), Consumer Health Division (CHD), and International Business Division (IBD)
- Three subsidiary group companies (Dabur International, Fem Care Pharma, and Newu) and eight step-down subsidiaries: Dabur Nepal Pvt. Ltd. (Nepal), Dabur Egypt Ltd. (Egypt), Asian Consumer Care (Bangladesh), Asian Consumer Care (Pakistan), African Consumer Care (Nigeria), Naturelle LLC (Ras Al Khaimah-UAE), Weikfield International (UAE), and Jaquline Inc. (USA)
- 17 ultramodern manufacturing units spread around the globe
- Products marketed in over 60 countries
- Wide and deep market penetration with 50 C&F agents, more than 5,000 distributors, and over 2.8 million retail outlets all over India

The Consumer Care Division (CCD) addresses consumer needs across the entire FMCG spectrum through four distinct business portfolios of Personal Care, Health Care, Home Care, and Foods.

Its master brands:

- Dabur—Ayurvedic healthcare products
- Vatika—Premium hair care
- Hajmola—Tasty digestives
- Réal—Fruit juices and beverages
- Fem—Fairness bleaches and skin care products
- Nine billion-rupee brands: DaburAmla, DaburChyawanprash, Vatika, Réal, Dabur Red Toothpaste, DaburLalDantManjan, Babool, Hajmola, and Dabur Honey
- Strategic positioning of honey as a food product, leading to market leadership (over 75%) in branded honey market
- DaburChyawanprash—the largest selling Ayurvedic medicine with over 65 percent market share
- Vatika Shampoo has been the fastest-selling shampoo brand in India for three years in a row
- Hajmola tablets in command with 60 percent market share of digestive tablets category. About 2.5 crore Hajmola tablets are consumed in India every day.
- Leader in herbal digestives with 90 percent market share

The Consumer Health Division (CHD) offers a range of classical Ayurvedic medicines and Ayurvedic OTC products that deliver the age-old benefits of Ayurveda in modern ready-to-use formats.

- Has more than 300 products sold through prescriptions as well as over-the-counter
- Major categories in traditional formulations include:
  - AsavArishtas
  - RasRasayanas
  - Churnas
  - Medicated Oils
- Proprietary Ayurvedic medicines developed by Dabur include:
  - Nature Care Isabgol
  - Madhuvaani
  - Trifgol
- Division also works for promotion of Ayurveda through organized community of traditional practitioners and development of fresh batches of students

The International Business Division (IBD) caters to the health and personal care needs of customers across different international markets, spanning the Middle East, North and West Africa, the European Union, and the United States, with its brands Dabur Vatika.

- Growing at a CAGR of 33 percent in the last six years and contributes to about 20% of total sales
- Leveraging the "natural" preference among local consumers to increase share in personal care categories

- Focus markets:
  - GCC
  - Egypt
  - Nigeria
  - Bangladesh
  - Nepal
  - United States
- High level of localization of manufacturing and sales and marketing

Product Portfolio						
Category	**Products**					
Health care Personal care Home care Foods	Chyawanprash Amla Odonil Réal	Babool Vatika Odomos Activ	Meswak Gulabari Sani fresh Hommade	Glucose-D Fem	Honey Uveda	Hajmola

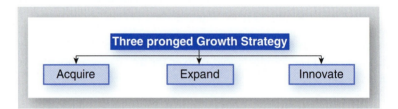

Strategy

Acquire:

- Acquisitions critical for building scale in existing categories and markets
- Should be synergistic and make a good strategic fit
- Target opportunities in our focus markets

Expand:

- Strengthening presence in existing categories and markets as well entering new geographies
- Maintain dominant share in categories where we are category-builders, like Health Supplements, honey, etc.
- Calibrated international expansion—local manufacturing and supply chain to enhance flexibility and reduce response time to change in market demands

Innovate:

- Strong focus on innovation. Have rolled out new variants and products which have contributed to around 5–6 percent of our growth per annum
- Renovation of existing products to respond to changing demands (toothpowder to toothpaste)

Dabur is an investor-friendly brand, as its financial performance shows. The company's growth rate rose from 10 percent to 40 percent between 2008–09 to 2009–2010.

Events	
Year:	**Event:**
1884	Dr. S K Burman lays the foundation of what is today known as Dabur India Limited. Starting from a small shop in Calcutta, he began a direct mailing system to send his medicines to even the smallest of villages in the whole of India.
1896	As the demand for Dabur products grows, Dr. Burman feels the need for mass production of some of his medicines. He sets up a small manufacturing plant at Garhia, near Calcutta.
Early 1900s	The next generation of Burmans take a conscious decision to enter the Ayurvedic medicines market, as they believe that it is only through Ayurveda that the healthcare needs of poor Indians can be met.
1919	The search for processes to suit mass production of Ayurvedic medicines without compromising basic Ayurvedic principles leads to the setup of the first Research & Development laboratory at Dabur. This initiates a painstaking study of Ayurvedic medicines as mentioned in age-old scriptures, their manufacturing processes, and how to utilize modern equipment to manufacture these medicines without reducing the efficacy of these drugs.
1920	A manufacturing facility for Ayurvedic Medicines is set up at Narendrapur and Daburgram. Dabur expands its distribution network to Bihar and the northeast.
1936	DaburIndia (Dr. S K Burman) Pvt. Limited is incorporated.
1940	Dabur diversifies into personal care products with the launch of its DaburAmla Hair Oil. This perfumed heavy hair oil catches the imagination of the common man and film stars alike and becomes the largest hair oil brand in India.
1949	DaburChyawanprash is launched in a tin pack and becomes the first branded Chyawanprash of India.
1956	Dabur buys its first computer. Accounts and stock keeping are one of first operations to be computerized.
1970	Dabur expands its personal care portfolio by adding oral care products. DaburLalDantManjan is launched and captures the Indian rural market.
1972	Dabur shifts base to Delhi from Calcutta. Starts production from a hired manufacturing facility at Faridabad.

Reference: Dabur Investor Analysis Report, Kotak India Corporate Day, June 2011, USA.
The author would like to thank Dabur India for their knowledge sharing and permissions.

The expected growth rate for two years was twofold. There is an abundance of information for its investors and prospective information including a daily update on the share price (something that very few Indian brands do). There's a great sense of responsibility for investors' funds on view. This is a direct extension of Dabur's philosophy of taking care of its constituents, and it adds to the sense of trust for the brand overall.

The company, through DaburPharma Ltd., does toxicology tests and markets Ayurvedic medicines in a scientific manner. It has researched new medicines that will find use in over-the-counter all over the country, therein opening a new market.

Dabur Foods, a subsidiary of DaburIndia, is expecting to grow at 25% growth in year 2011–12. Together its brands of juices, namely Réal and Active, make it the market leader in the Fruit Juice category.

Assessing the Global Marketing Environment—The Global Economy and Technology

If GM had kept up with technology like the computer industry has, we would all be driving $25 cars that got 1,000 mpg.

BILL GATES

LEARNING OBJECTIVES

After reading this chapter, you should be able to:

- Apply the PESTEL model to scan the global environment.
- Understand the characteristics of global companies.
- Evaluate the international trade position of the United States.
- Appreciate the power of transnational companies.
- Demonstrate the importance of high technology and global trade.
- Understand the arguments for and against globalization.

Many companies enter unfamiliar markets around the globe. The concept of doing business in these markets may require a significant change in the ways business is carried out in the home market. For example, risk managers have to make sure that overseas representatives do not offer bribes to obtain lucrative contracts. Or that engineers sent to carry out tests at a highway construction site in a developing country are covered with a kidnap and ransom insurance policy that includes a provision for a local crisis team trained to deal with such situations.

Marketers also have to be aware of subtle cultural differences between consumers. Social networks from abroad, such as Facebook, have had a hard time winning over Japan's 90 million web users. This is owing to a cultural misconception of Japan's users. They try to avoid inclusion of real names and photos, which is the way social networks are used in the United States and Western Europe.

Because of macro-environmental (Table 2-1) differences, doing business in foreign markets usually entails greater risks than doing business locally. Less familiarity and knowledge about foreign markets and business practices leads to greater uncertainty about how to operate abroad. Greater uncertainty in turn requires mechanisms for acquiring knowledge about foreign environments to manage risk.

In this and following chapters, we will learn about the global marketing environment, which includes *political, economic, social/technological, environmental/legal* determinants

TABLE 2-1 A PESTEL Analysis of the Macro-Global Environment	
Factor	**Possible Factors for Study**
Political	Local and national government structure, government stability, internal politics that affect business, international relations, terrorist activity, and political risk
Economic	Regional economic growth indicators, exchange rates, trade and trade policy, government intervention in the economy, taxation, consumption, employment/unemployment, inflation, balance of payments
Social	Demographics, lifestyle, education, living standards (health and welfare), immigration/emigration
Technological	Technological infrastructure,[1] including market opportunities in the electronics, high tech markets, development of bio-technology and information technology industries, and clean technology markets
Environmental	Environmental regulations, global warming, pollution, green marketing
Legal	Legal systems, business legislation, consumer protection, intellectual property issues

of global marketing strategy. These environmental factors form the acronym, **PESTEL,** which can serve as a framework for the audit of a company's external environment. Its findings can be used for strategic marketing planning. To help the decision maker, a PESTEL analysis should include examining these and similar factors included in Table 2-1. This chapter examines the environment of the global economy with an emphasis on high tech markets. Chapter 3 covers the social environment and Chapter 4, the political and legal environment.

THE GLOBAL ECONOMY

Economic Growth and World Trade

The major trends that occurred at the turn of the last century include increased economic liberalization (the **European Union** now has 27 members, with several more candidate countries waiting for admission), technological advances, and demographic shifts. An important fact to be considered is that the growth in global trade has far exceeded that of domestic growth. Figure 2-1 shows the trends in world trade. For example, the growth in world trade in 2007 increased from 10 to 30 percent until the economic crisis in 2008, while world industrial production averaged about 5 percent over the same time period. World trade is very intensive in manufacturing, and purchases of durable goods are most easily postponed when peoples' incomes fall and they feel less secure.

The United States is still the world's leading trader if both exports and imports of merchandise and services are considered. Table 2-2 shows trade figures of the ten leading countries. While Germany is the leading exporter of merchandise, it lags behind the United States in imports of merchandise and in the export and import of services. China is the second largest exporter of merchandise and the third largest importer of merchandise, but it is not a significant exporter or importer of services, although it will

1. Technological infrastructure includes the social and economic institutions that a nation relies on to develop and market new technology; e.g., the number of people employed in R&D, technical training schools, competence in high technology manufacturing, and capital markets.

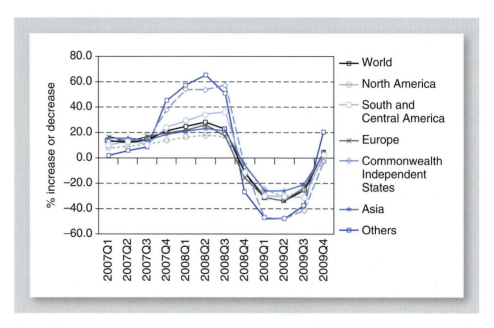

Figure 2-1 World Trade (2007–2009)

Source: Data from International Trade Statistics, WTO Secretariat, World Trade Organization, 2010.

TABLE 2-2 10 Largest Exporters and Importers (2008, $Billions)

	Merchandise						Services				
Rank	**Exporters**	**Value**	**Rank**	**Importers**	**Value**	**Rank**	**Exporters**	**Value**	**Rank**	**Importers**	**Value**
1	Germany	1462	1	US	2170	1	US	521	1	US	368
2	China	1428	2	Germany	1204	2	UK	283	2	Germany	283
3	US	1287	3	China	1133	3	Germany	242	3	UK	196
4	Japan	762	4	Japan	763	4	France	161	4	Japan	167
5	Netherlands	633	5	France	706	5	China	146	5	China	158
6	France	605	6	UK	632	6	Japan	146	6	France	139
7	Italy	538	7	Netherlands	573	7	Spain	143	7	Italy	132
8	Belgium	476	8	Italy	555	8	Italy	122	8	Ireland	106
9	Russia	472	9	Belgium	470	9	India	103	9	Spain	104
10	UK	459	10	South Korea	435	10	Netherlands	102	10	South Korea	92

Source: Adapted from: International Trade Statistics, WTO Secretariat, World Trade Organization, 2009.

probably increase its purchase of services, such as finance and insurance, in the near future. The United States has fallen into third place as an exporter of merchandise but is still the world's largest exporter (tied with Germany) if both exports of merchandise and services are included.

Who Are the United States' Major Customers?

Most trade is regional rather than global. Countries tend to trade with their neighbors, with whom they are likely to have preferential trade agreements. The United States is no exception; its exports to Canada and Mexico, with whom it has joined in the **North American Free Trade Association (NAFTA),** totaled $232 billion in 2010. The next largest customers of the United States were the European Union countries, followed

TABLE 2-3 United States Exports by Region (2010, US$ Billions)	
Region	**Exports**
European Union	135
Canada	142
Mexico	90
South/Central America	78
Newly Industrialized Countries	68

Source: Adapted from: Bureau of Economic Analysis, United States Department of Commerce, 2010.

by South and Central America and some of the newly industrialized countries (Hong Kong, South Korea, Singapore, and Taiwan). Canada is the single largest country-customer of the United States ($142 billion), followed by Mexico ($90 billion). In turn, the United States is the largest customer of both Canada and Mexico, as well (see Table 2-3).

While the United States is the world's largest trader, it has carried a deficit in its **balance of trade,** which is the difference between the value of exports and imports. As shown in Figure 2-2, the deficit narrowed by $30 billion between August 2008 and August 2009 owing to a larger decline in imports than exports, but it worsened somewhat in 2010. The improvement in the balance of trade was due mainly to the world economic crisis and a weakened dollar, which made United States exports cheaper and imports more expensive. A trade deficit needs to be corrected because the excess of imports over exports creates a net outflow of monetary payments from a country. An outflow of payments (e.g., dollars) further weakens their value. The deficit generates a decrease in **aggregate income** and its associated measures, especially consumption, saving, investment, and tax revenue. However, for some countries, an increase in economic growth and aggregate income will result in higher domestic consumption

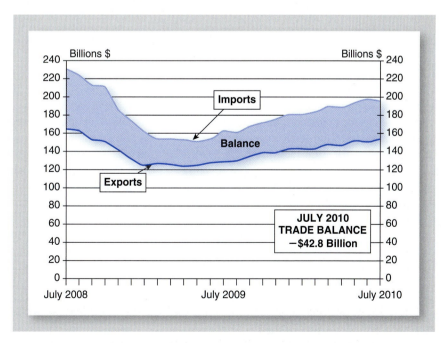

Figure 2-2 United States International Trade in Goods and Services

Source: International Economic Accounts, Bureau of Economic Analysis, United States Department of Commerce, 2010.

BOX 2-1   COMPANY IN FOCUS: BIO-MED DEVICES

Bio-Med Devices has received a 2009 Exporter of the Year award from ThinkGlobal Inc., publisher of *Commercial News USA*, the official export promotion magazine of the United States Commerce Department. The Guilford, Connecticut, company designs, manufactures, and markets a complete line of critical care and transportable respirators/ventilators, air-oxygen blenders, ventilation monitors, disposable and reusable breathing circuits, and accessories.

"We are very happy to receive this award as Exporter of the Year," said Dean Bennett, CEO. "Our international business has grown more than *400% in four years* thanks to the dedicated team at Bio-Med Devices and to our overseas distribution partners who are located in more than 75 countries around the world. Export sales and service has become an increasingly important part of our company."

Bio-Med Devices, Inc., has been a major manufacturer of ventilators and related equipment for the United States market since 1985. Export activities began in 1986, but the company launched an effort to increase export revenue in 2005 when exports represented less than 20 percent of total company revenue. In 2007, the company shipped products to more than 75 countries and hopes that exports will exceed 40 percent of total company revenue by 2011.

Source: Adapted from: United States Commercial Service, United States Department of Commerce.

expenditures, including the purchase of imports from foreign countries. In this case, the increase in imports, which may widen the trade deficit, is actually a result of a prosperous economy. Therefore, the trade deficit should not be labeled "unfavorable."

Export-driven companies are not limited to large, multinational companies. Small and medium-sized companies have succeeded in exporting significant shares of their total production output. In the United States, 95 percent of exporters are small- and medium-sized.[2] They account for about one-fourth of total exports. Similar patterns of export behaviour are present in other developed countries. Box 2-1 provides an example of such a company.

High Tech Products Lead World Trade

High tech products are produced by research-intensive industries using the most advanced technology available. These products include aerospace, pharmaceuticals, computers, electronics, and communications equipment. In both developed and developing economies, the high tech manufacturing sector has shown the fastest growth. The global market for high tech products has grown twice as fast as that for other manufactured goods. Nearly 65 percent of revenues for the leading United States high technology companies are generated from sales outside United States borders.

The rapid rate of **globalization** is made possible by the development and expansion of the Internet economy, which in turn is fueled by the unprecedented growth of high tech electronics manufacturing. In just one human generation, the high tech revolution has spread out from its birthplace in Silicon Valley, California, to encompass vast sections of the globe. Scotland, Ireland, Israel, and Taiwan are important producers of high tech products, most of which are exported. After the United States, which country is currently registering the largest number of new high tech companies? Great Britain? France? Japan? Germany? Wrong! It is Israel—and that's in terms of actual numbers, not as a proportion of the country's population. Although only half the size of Switzerland, Israel boasts over 3,000 high tech companies, four-fifths of which are less than 10 years old.

2. Trembley, C. (2008). Commentary: Internet resources for global business practitioners. *Daily Record*, p. A8.

Increased uses of technology will affect the way people interact with one another. Both global and domestic businesses are increasing their use of IT applications for knowledge generation and communication, and for producing and marketing finished products or services. Advanced technology and statistical control devices enable management to utilize sophisticated software programs to run their organizations. New developments in fields such as **nanotechnology** and **biotechnology** are being harnessed by business. Some of the industries that are most likely to be affected by nanotechnology are electronics (Kodak EasyShare providing brighter and less-energy-consuming displays), fashion (Maui Jim sunglasses having better anti-reflection capabilities) and cosmetics (L'Oreal having better skin moisturizing properties). It is expected that more industrial applications of nanotechnology will be forthcoming over the next decade. Illustrative of this view are the results of a survey undertaken by the European NanoBusiness Association reporting that most respondents expect that nanotechnology will have an impact on their business within a few years.[3]

Biotechnology has led to a wide field of industrial applications, ranging from health care, pharmacological products, and cosmetic materials to marine applications and medical imaging diagnostics. California, the birthplace of biotechnology, employed about 250,000 people in the life-science industry in 2006. However, more and more pharmaceutical companies are offshoring their research to China, India, and Eastern Europe. A survey of 186 global companies with a combined research and development budget of $76 billion found that three-quarters of R&D sites planned will be located in China and India. Moreover, these two countries account for almost a third of global R&D, an increase from 14 percent in 2004.[4]

Many high tech products are manufactured from components made in several countries. For example, a typical computer now contains components manufactured and assembled all over the world—semiconductor chips made in New Mexico, Scotland, or Malaysia; a disk drive made in Singapore or Thailand; a CRT (cathode ray tube) monitor made in Japan; circuit boards made in China and assembled in Mexico or Costa Rica.

From 2001–2006, total high tech exports grew by 4.7 percent. The electrical machinery industry, followed by scientific instruments and pharmacy (Table 2-4), had the highest growth rates among the leading high tech product categories. China and the United States had the highest world market share of high tech exports (16.9 and 16.8 percent respectively in 2006), followed by the 27 EU countries at 15.0 percent. The United States was the leading high tech product importer with a 17.3 percent world share, followed by the EU with 17.0 percent and China with 15.4 percent.[5] In relative terms, the share of high tech exports was highest in Malta, where they represented over 50 percent of total exports, followed by Luxembourg (41 percent) and Ireland (29 percent). In the United Kingdom, Cyprus, Switzerland, and Hungary, high tech exports accounted for more than 20 percent of national exports. By comparison, the United States had a 27 percent share and Japan had 22 percent. Developing and emerging countries also have high shares of high tech exports to total exports, as shown in Figure 2-3. The Philippines had the highest ratio (80 percent), followed by Malaysia (71 percent) and Singapore (62 percent).

How could a developing country be a top exporter of electronics despite having very limited technological capabilities? The basic idea is that electronics components—as intermediate inputs—can be imported for the assembly of final products to serve domestic and foreign markets or for processing in the country to be re-exported. Companies such as General Electric and Intel have large manufacturing plants in the

3. ENA. (2004). *The 2004 European nanobusiness survey: "Use it or lose it."* Research report, European NanoBusiness Association, Brussels.

4. Crabtree, P. (26 November 2006). Good old days gone for biotech. *The San Diego Union Tribune*, www.signonsaniego.com.

5. *Eurostat Statistics in Focus,* 25/2009, p. 3.

TABLE 2-4 World Market Shares of High Tech Products							
Business	*Total Exports of High Tech Products*			*Country (%)*			
	€ Million	Annual Growth Rate (2001–2006)	EU (27)	USA	Japan	China	Other
Aerospace	109,425	−2.5	33	47	1	0.7	19
Military	6,236	2.4	24	48	1	0.5	26
Chemistry	32,155	5.5	21	17	5	15	42
Computers/Office Machines	298,243	2.9	8	11	6	33	42
Electrical Machinery	46,328	9.7	10	13	15	9	52
Electronics/Communication	562,814	6.1	10	12	9	16	52
Non-Electrical Machinery	36,775	3.1	28	28	18	2	25
Pharmacy	49,802	8.2	44	21	2	4	29

Source: Adapted from: *Eurostat Statistics in Focus,* 25/2009.

Philippines, while IBM and Siemens have plants in China. Many lower-income countries have high imports of electronics components for the processing of components, or their assembly into final products is based on the employment of lower-wage workers rather than technological capabilities.

Characteristics of High Technology Markets

What characterizes high tech markets? High tech markets are:

1. Highly dynamic
2. Complex
3. Risky

As a result, markets tend to mature rapidly. They are fast moving and expensive, owing to technological advances, intense competition, and demanding consumers.[6] A major difference between high and low tech product markets is that the former are production- rather than consumer-oriented. Because these markets are very competitive, manufacturers rush to market, sometimes without proper preparation or consumer research.

In many cases, consumers cannot visualize future demand for high tech products. Supply determines demand for most consumer products, rather than the other way around. Therefore, high tech product developers must anticipate consumer needs even before consumers are aware of them. High tech marketers rely on a product focus, which is driven by technology rather than customer needs. However, there are abundant examples in which high tech consumer products could not generate sufficient demand. Among the well-known consumer product failures include Sony's Betamax videotape player and Philips's CD-I (compact disk home entertainment system). Steve Jobs, the CEO and co-founder of Apple, was asked what sort of market research the company did before launching the iMac. He answered that little was done because "for something this complicated, it's really hard to design products by focus groups. . . . people don't know what they want until you show it to them."[7] The disregard for consumer choice was also evident in the failures of the Betamax and CD-I products as well.

6. Rosen, D., Schroeder, J., & Purinton, E. (1998). Marketing high tech products: lessons in customer focus from the marketplace. *Academy of Marketing Science, 6,* 1–17.

7. Jobs, S. (1998, May 18). There's sanity returning. *Newsweek,* 48–52.

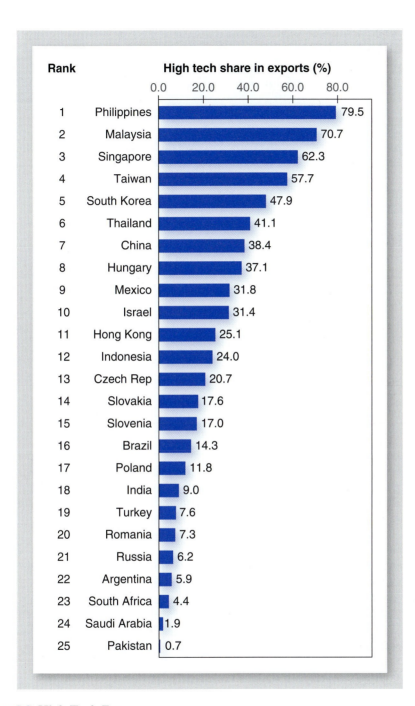

Figure 2-3 High Tech Exports

Measures the share (%) of "high tech" products in a country's exports of manufactures.
Source: Adapted from: "High Tech Exports," www.global-production.com, March 2008.

In order to reduce the risk of market failure in the introduction of high tech products, Rosen, Schroeder, and Purinton (1998) suggest that the following steps be taken:

■ Determine whether "first-mover" advantage is necessary, or whether it is best to be as sure as possible that there is sufficient interest in the product.

■ Rethink the value of market research before launching the product.

BOX 2-2   TECHNOLOGY IN FOCUS: GLOBALIZATION OF TECHNOLOGY

"Technology ventures, primarily those that are product-based, rather than service-based, cannot remain local. They must either globalize fast or they fade away. A high tech startup must be able to effectively compete with the market leaders in its field on their own turf; i.e., in major world markets. Otherwise, the large players will beat the startup across the board, including on *its own* turf, its native country. While it is possible to successfully market, say, a Turkish brand of beer in Turkey, it is far more difficult to succeed in local marketing of a Turkish-made computer modem. The product either needs to gain global market acceptance or it will gain none at all, not even in Turkey.

The rapid rate of innovation and the dynamics of technology flows mean that comparative advantage is short-lived. To maximize returns, arrangements such as transnational mergers and shared production agreements are sought to bring together partners with complementary interests and strengths. This permits both developed and developing countries to harness technology more efficiently, with the expectation of creating higher standards of living for all involved."

Source: Globalization of Technology: International Perspectives, The National Academies Press, 1988. Rptd. in "Globalization of Technology: Lessons from Israel," www.knowledge.wharton.upenn.edu; August 13, 2009.

- Target the market carefully, carefully identifying the consumers most likely to purchase the product.
- Exploit the innovators and early adopters.

Another critical issue in high tech marketing concerns the market entry choices of startup companies in high technology industries. Findings from surveys[8] show that preferred entry modes are characterized by relatively low resource commitment and are directed toward commercialization rather than production. The rush to commercialization may also explain the failure rate of startups, which is estimated at about 50 percent. The special issue of high tech startup company entry modes into foreign markets will be discussed in Chapter 7.

Global **supply chain** performance is also critical, especially as manufacturing expands beyond traditional locations into new regions and countries. As high tech manufacturers are subject to intense customer demands for service and delivery, the fact that component manufacture is performed in several countries, as pointed out above, complicates control over the supply chain. Therefore, manufacturers need to effectively manage global trade operations.

Technology and Global Financial Services

Global financial services are becoming more dependent on IT infrastructures in order to gain competitive advantage. While most of the investment in financial services originates from North America and Europe, institutions in the Asia-Pacific area are investing at a faster rate, as shown in Figure 2-4.

Technology-driven innovations in the financial services industry is focused on enhancing customer experience (see Box 2-3).

---

8. Burgel, O., & Murray, G. (2000). The international market entry choices of start-up companies in high technology industries. *Journal of International Marketing, 8*(2), 33–62.

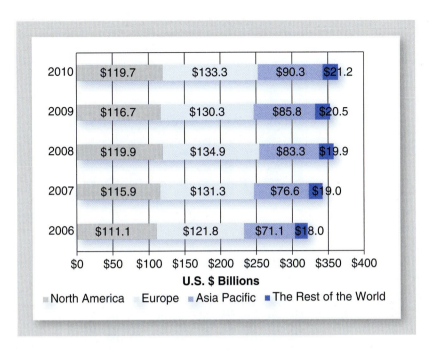

Figure 2-4 Global IT Spending by Financial Services Firms

Source: Adapted from: Jacob Jegher, "IT Spending in Financial Services: A Global Perspective," January 9, 2009. www.Celent .com/node/26595.

GLOBAL COUNTRIES AND GLOBAL COMPANIES

Both countries and companies can be typed according to the extent to which they are global. For example, *Foreign Policy* magazine, in association with the consulting company, A.T. Kearny, rates countries on factors such as economic integration, personal contact, technological connectivity, and political engagement. According to these indicators, Singapore was the most globalized country in 2006, followed by Switzerland and the United States. In 2007, Singapore was again number one, followed by Hong Kong, the Netherlands, Switzerland, and Ireland. At the bottom of the list of 20 countries in 2007 were Norway, Finland, the Czech Republic, and Slovenia. The United States was number seven on the list. Note that only three of the 20 are developing or emerging economies. Eleven of the 20 are members of the European Union. The list of 20 countries is shown in Figure 2-5.

BOX 2-3   COUNTRY IN FOCUS: SWITZERLAND

Credit Suisse sees an opportunity to provide service through technology to a mass-market clientele. "It'll give mass-market retail investors access to what is largely the domain of high-net-worth individuals . . . technology's the only mechanism to effectively and efficiently distribute that compared to face-to-face meetings. Technology is huge, and it's generally underutilized in the financial services industry. . . ."

Source: Global Financial Services Industry Outlook, Deloitte & Touche, USA, 2006.

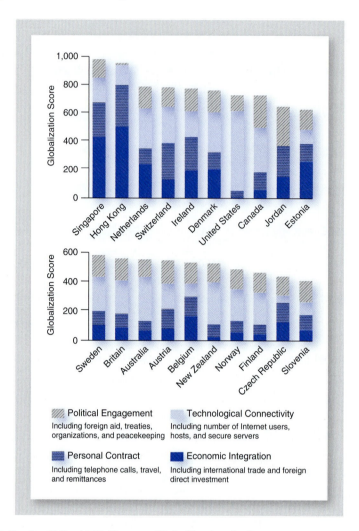

Figure 2-5 *Foreign Policy/*A.T. Kearny Globalization Index

Source: Data from "The Global Top 20," A.T. Kearney, November/December 2007.

The term *global economy* expresses the fact that most of the world's nations have become increasingly interconnected. Economies have expanded beyond national borders, and an increasing amounts of production is being accounted for by **transnational corporations (TNCs).** In short, production, finance, marketing, communications, and labor forces have become globalized. The number of transnational corporations in the world has increased from about 8,000 in 1975 to 40,000 in 2005. It is estimated that more than one-third of the world's private assets are owned by TNCs and that one-third of all international trade occurs in intra-TNC transactions. While global in reach, nearly all of these corporations' headquarters are concentrated in industrialized countries. More than half are headquartered in France, Germany, the Netherlands, Japan, and the United States. But despite their growing numbers, their resources are highly concentrated; i.e., the 300 largest corporations account for approximately one-quarter of the world's productive assets.

An indicator of globalization is the extent to which a firm's activities are concentrated outside of its home country. Table 2-5 lists the 10 most globalized companies. For example, the first firm listed in Table 2-5, General Electric, has 60 percent of

TABLE 2-5 The Top 10 Transnational Companies by Foreign Operations						
Company	Home Country	Industry	Foreign Assets/Total	Foreign Sales/Total	Foreign Employment/Total	TNI[a]
General Electric	US	Electrical & Electronics	59.9	37.3	46.3	47.8
Vodafone Group PLC	UK	Telecommunication	95.8	85.4	80.7	87.1
Ford Motor	US	Motor Vehicles	59.0	41.3	45.6	48.7
General Motors	US	Motor Vehicles	36.3	30.4	35.5	34.0
British Petroleum	UK	Energy	80.3	81.4	83.5	81.5
ExxonMobil	US	Energy	96.1	69.8	50.5	63.0
Royal Dutch/Shell	UK/Holland	Energy	67.4	64.2	84.2	71.9
Toyota Motor	Japan	Motor Vehicles	52.6	59.7	35.7	49.4
Total	France	Energy	86.1	80.9	55.9	74.3
France Télécom	France	Telecommunication	65.7	40.7	39.8	48.7

[a] TNI, the Transnationality Index, is calculated as the following three ratios: foreign assets to total assets, foreign sales to total sales, and foreign employment to total employment.

Source: UNCTAD/Erasmus University Database. www.ib-sm.org/ibr.htm. Reprinted with permission.

its assets, 37 percent of its sales, and 46 percent of its employees located outside the United States. It has a transnationality (TNI) index of 47.8. The most transnational corporation is Vodafone (TNI index of 87.1), followed by British Petroleum (TNI index, 81.5) and Total (TNI index of 74.3). Two of these three companies are in the energy industry, while others (not listed in the table) are concentrated in electronics, communications, pharmaceuticals, and automotive manufacturing. Of the 10 most globalized corporations, four are headquartered in the United States, three in the UK (Holland), two in France, and one in Japan.

Not only are TNCs highly globalized, they possess significant economic power. The economic strength or size of several transnational corporations equal that of many developed countries. This can be visualized by comparing transnational corporate sales with the GDP of countries; this comparison is shown in Table 2-6. For example, the largest of the Fortune Global 500 corporations in 2009 was Walmart Stores, with $408 billion in sales. Walmart's sales were higher than the GDP of many developed countries including Austria, Norway, and Denmark, to name several. The Bank of America's revenues were greater than the GDP of Denmark, Israel, Hungary, and New Zealand. Royal Dutch Shell's sales of $285 billion in the same year were greater than the GDP of Israel, Hungary, and New Zealand. In many cases, the economic power of TNCs has been used positively in the areas of capital formation, human resource

TABLE 2-6 A Comparison of Country and Company Size as Measured by Sales and GDP (2009)	
Country/Company	Sales or GDP (US$ billions)
Walmart Stores	*408*
Austria	382
Norway	383
Bank of America	*331*
Denmark	309
Royal Dutch Shell	*285*
Israel	195
Hungary	129
New Zealand	118

Source: Data from CNNMoney.com, Fortune 500 (Full List).

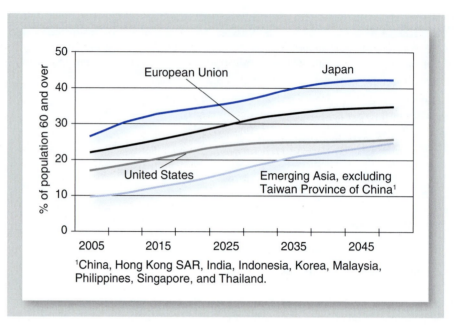

Figure 2-6 Aging Populations

Source: Adapted from: "Asia's Role in the World Economy," *Finance and Development IMF.* June 2006, 43.2.

development, technology transfer, international trade, and environmental protection. One of the most important contributions of TNCs, to developing countries in particular, is providing access to technology and distribution channels for trade.[9]

Global Demographics

Population demographics are also changing. As the twenty-first century began, the world population included approximately 600 million persons over 60 years of age—triple the number recorded fifty years earlier. By mid-century, there will be some two billion older persons—once again, a tripling of this age group in a span of 50 years. Population aging is profound, having major consequences and implications for all facets of human life. According to United Nations estimates, nearly one-third of Japan's population, one-fourth of the European Union's population, and one-fifth of the United States population will be over 60 years old by 2015. In the economic area, population aging will have an impact on economic growth, savings, investment and consumption, labor markets, pensions, taxation, and intergenerational transfers. Note that the relatively younger population of Asia means that these nations should have abundant labor necessary to sustain the high levels of growth recently attained (see Figure 2-6). Western European countries and the United States will have to maintain immigration from third world countries to provide the workforce needed to sustain economic growth. In the social sphere, population aging affects health and healthcare, family composition and living arrangements, housing, and migration.

The world population stands at about 6 billion. Of importance to global marketing is the estimate that nearly a billion new consumers will enter the marketplace in the next decade. Consumer purchasing power in emerging economies alone will increase to $9 trillion, nearly the spending power of Western Europe in 2006.[10]

9. World Investment Report (1992). *Transnational corporations as engines of growth.* New York: United Nations.

10. Davis, I., & Stephenson, E. (2006, January), Ten trends to watch in 2006, *The McKinsey Quarterly,* www.emergencemarketing.com/2006/01/19/ten-trends-to-watch-in-2006-according-to-McKinsey/.

THE GREEN ECONOMY

The **green economy** is an emerging marketplace that seeks to optimize the synergy among three sets of values: social, environmental, and financial. This is most commonly referred to as the "triple bottom line."

By definition, the green economy is:

- Environmentally sustainable, based on the belief that our biosphere is a closed system with finite resources and a limited capacity for self-regulation and self-renewal. We depend on the earth's natural resources, and therefore we should create an economic system that respects the integrity of ecosystems and ensures the resilience of life-supporting systems.

- Socially just, based on the belief that culture and human dignity are precious resources that, like our natural resources, require responsible stewardship to avoid their depletion. We should create a vibrant economic system that ensures all people have access to a decent standard of living and full opportunities for personal and social development.

- Locally rooted, based on the belief that an authentic connection to place is the essential precondition to sustainability and justice. The Green Economy is a global aggregate of individual communities meeting the needs of its citizens through the responsible local production and exchange of goods and services.

Increasing energy and commodity costs and consumer demands for a more sustainable environment have led to a push for a green economy in industries such as energy and utilities, construction, transportation, and manufacturing. Understanding the green economy and the opportunities it provides worldwide is of critical importance to global marketers. Part of the green economy entails the adoption of "clean technology." There is no standard definition of clean technology, but it is believed to comprise products, services, and processes that use renewable materials while conserving natural resources. Representative clean tech industries include wind power, solar energy, hydropower, and biofuels. As shown in Figure 2-7, South Korea and China are the major investors in clean technology, followed by the United States.

The Green Economy Market Size

How large is the green market? According to the Department of Commerce, green products and services account for about 1 to 2 percent of the total private business economy in the United States.[11] In monetary terms, the market size is estimated to be $371–$516 billion. The UK Department of Trade and Industry estimates that the world market for environmental goods and services will reach $688 billion in 2020.[12] There are 142 million consumers of organic food and drink in Europe, divided between loyal and occasional users. Loyal users account for 20 million people in Europe yet were responsible for 69 percent of spending. This suggests that a significant proportion of the organic market is not based on consumers who buy regularly. If production processes improve significantly in the conventional food market or organics lose their fashionable aspect, the market potential of organics will be considerably less than most analysts predict.

What do we know about consumer attitudes toward the purchase of green products and services? Because of the relatively higher costs to develop green products,

---

11. Economics and Statistics Administration. (2010, April). *Measuring the green economy.* Washington, D.C.: United States Department of Commerce.

12. Retrieved from www.dti.gov.uk/sectors_environment.html.

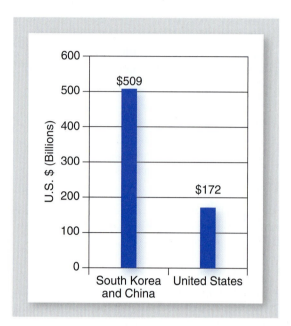

Figure 2-7 Public Investments in Clean Energy Technology, 2009–2013

Source: Data from "Rising Tigers, Sleeping Giant." Breakthrough Institute and the Information Technology and Innovation Foundation, November 2009.

it is essential to determine how consumers view environmental issues and how they behave, especially in their attitudes toward green and environmentally friendly products. Straughan and Roberts (1999) segmented college students based upon ecologically conscious consumer behavior and stated that the younger individuals were likely to be more sensitive to environmental issues.[13] The results of their study indicated that the demographic variables such as age and sex were significantly correlated with ecologically conscious consumer behavior when considered individually, and that income lacks significance. Green purchase intention correlates positively with age and income except for education.[14] Many studies have shown significant differences between men and women in environmental attitudes,[15] with men having more negative attitudes toward the environment compared to women.[16] Women are more likely to buy green products because they believe the product is better for the environment.[17] There is a general belief among researchers and environmental activists that through purchasing environmentally friendly or green products and products with recyclable packaging, or by properly disposing of non-biodegradable garbage, consumers can contribute significantly to improve the quality of the environment.[18]

13. Straughan, R. D., & Roberts, J. A. (1999). Environmental segmentation alternatives: A look at green consumer behavior in the new millennium. *Journal of Consumer Marketing, 16*(6), 558–75.

14. Soontonsmai, V. (2001). *Predicting intention and behavior to purchase environmentally sound or green products among Thai consumers: An application of the theory of reasoned action.* Unpublished doctoral thesis, Nova Southeastern University.

15. Brown, G. & Harris, C. (1992). The United States forest service: Toward the new resource management paradigm? *Society and Natural Resources, 5,* 231–245; Tikka, P., Kuitunen, M., & Tynys, S. (2000). Effects of educational background on students' attitudes, activity levels, and knowledge concerning the environment. *Journal of Environmental Education, 31,* 12–19.

16. Eagly, A. H. (1987). *Sex differences in social behavior: A social-role interpretation.* Hillsdale, NJ: Lawrence Erlbaum Associates.

17. Mainieri, T., Barnett, E., Valdero, T., Unipan, J., & Oskamp, S. (1997). Green buying: The influence of environmental concern on consumer behavior. *Journal of Social Psychology, 137,* 189–204.

18. Abdul-Muhmin, A. G. (2007). Exploring consumers' willingness to be environmentally friendly. *International Journal of Consumer Studies, 31,* 237–247.

**TABLE 2-7 Considerations When Purchasing Green Products
(% of Respondents Stating Extremely/Very Important)**

Is the right balance of quality and price	87
Contains no harmful chemicals	77
Is on sale	61
Is completely natural	40
Is organic	31
Has attractive packaging	10

Source: Adapted from: "Green Products and Services: A Viewpoint from Consumers and Small and Medium Business," Clearworks Green Resource Network, Fall 2009.

The quality of the environment depends critically on the level of knowledge, attitudes, values, and practices of consumers.[19] Consumers are more likely to buy organic goods or environmentally friendly products motivated by what makes them feel good about themselves, rather than for altruistic reasons. Some manufacturers have realized that putting self-interest first and altruism second makes for a successful product positioning. Café-Direct, for example, recently rebranded its fair trade coffee, marketing the quality of the product first and the fair trade aspect second. Attitudes are the most consistent explanatory factor in predicting consumers' willingness to pay for green products.[20] This means that price is not the *main* factor (although it's an important one) in motivating consumers to purchase green products if they are pro-environment. Consumers' perceived level of self-involvement toward the protection of the environment is another important factor.

A survey of American consumers found that quality and price were the most important motivations for buying green products (see Table 2-7). Other considerations were that the products were free of harmful chemicals. A segmentation study of consumers resulted in six segment categories: Alarmed (18 percent), Concerned (33 percent), Cautious (19 percent), Disengaged (12 percent), Doubtful (11 percent), and Dismissive (7 percent).

Those in the Alarmed category, or those most concerned about climate change and most personally active to reduce their impacts, want citizens, industry, and government to address the threat from climate change. These people would be the most likely to purchase products that had less of a negative or more of a positive impact on the environment and reduce greenhouse gas emissions. This group, the study reports, is also more likely to engage in consumer activism to encourage companies to increase action on climate change. They are more likely to reward companies that do act, more likely to have taken steps to improve energy efficiency in their own homes, or to "habitually engage in conservation activities" such as adjusting the thermostat. This demographic group is perhaps just what marketers are targeting when they are looking to sell their green products.

Communicating green solutions needs to focus not only on the environmental benefits of using a specific product or service, but also on the elements of cost savings, health benefits, and greater efficiency. Secondary messages should focus around the altruistic nature of buying green and demonstrating the benefits of the collective good. Marks & Spencer, a British retail company, is an example of how a green strategy can be integrated into an existing business. The company helped to educate 16 million customers about the environmental impacts of its products with its "Behind the Label" campaign, helped to green its suppliers by promoting biogas from ranchers, and promoted clothing recycling through a partnership with Oxfam.

19. Mansaray, A., & Abijoye, J. O. (1998). Environmental knowledge, attitudes and behavior in Dutch secondary school. *Journal of Environmental Education*, 30(2), 4–11.

20. Chyong, H. T., Phang, G., Hasan, H., & Buncha, M. R. (2006). Going green: A study of consumers' willingness to pay for green products in Kota Kinabalu. *International Journal of Business and Society*, 7(2), 40–54.

SUMMARY

- The PESTEL model is a useful framework for scanning the macro-global environment. A PESTEL analysis measures market potential, particularly indicating growth or decline, and market attractiveness, business potential, and whether market access should be attempted.

- Global trade has outpaced economic growth in most industrialized and emerging countries. Germany is the leading exporter of merchandise, but when both merchandise and services are combined, the United States is the world leader. Note that China may soon be the second largest exporter of merchandise, but not of services.

- Most world trade is regional. Most EU trade is internal, and the United States' largest customers are Canada and Mexico.

- Technological exports and imports dominate world trade, especially among developed countries. The global market for high technology goods is growing at a faster rate than that for other manufactured goods, and high technology industries are driving economic growth around the world. The United States and Japan lead the world in high tech exports.

- According to the *Foreign Policy*/A.T. Kearny index, the United States is the seventh most globalized country. However, four of the six largest transnational companies are American. The main reason for this is that the United States is less economically integrated (through multilateral trade treaties) than some of its European counterparts. Therefore, it is ranked lower on the globalization index.

- There is a large potential for employment and income creation in the green economy. Examples of green economy employment throughout the world include China, where 600,000 people are already employed in solar thermal making and installing products such as solar water heaters; Nigeria, where a biofuel industry based on cassava and sugar cane crops might employ 200,000 people; and India, which could generate 900,000 jobs in biomass gasification by 2025, of which 300,000 would be in the manufacturing of stoves and 600,000 in areas such as processing briquettes and pellets for the fuel supply chain. These figures show that the global market potential for green and clean tech products and services could become one of the fastest-growing economic sectors.

DISCUSSION QUESTIONS

1. It is argued that high tech products will dominate trade in the twenty-first century. Does this mean emerging market countries will be left out of this development?

2. Most developing countries have aging populations, and this trend is expected to intensify in the future. If you are the international marketing manager of a consumer products firm, how will these demographics affect your marketing mix over the next decade?

3. How would you differentiate an advertising campaign for the Alarmed market segment versus the Concerned segment?

EXPERIENTIAL EXERCISES

1. Select any country you wish (except your own) and apply the PESTEL model for an analysis of the environment for solar water heaters.

2. Go to the Internet and look up on *Newsweek's* website the "10 best countries to live in." Does this index have any relevance for global marketing? (Hint: Look at how the scores are calculated.)

KEY TERMS

Aggregate income, p. 39

Balance of trade, p. 39

Biotechnology, p. 41

European Union, p. 37

Global economy, p. 37

Globalization, p. 40

Green economy, p. 49

High tech products, p. 40

Nanotechnology, p. 41

North American Free Trade Association (NAFTA), p. 38

PESTEL, p. 37

Supply chain, p. 44

Transnational corporations (TNCs), p. 46

CASE 2-1

Fueling Indonesians: Window of Opportunity or Regret?

Kerosene is widely used as cooking fuel by Indonesian households, with an annual usage of 10 million kilolitres. It is a major subsidized fuel for household cooking, where its usage is over sixty percent of the 230 million population. The subsidy program costs the government heavily, where it amounts up to U.S.$4 billion a year. As the practice tends to bleed government expenditures quite heavily, the Indonesian government is embarking on a change in its current fuel subsidy involving kerosene. This is also due to the erratic price of crude oil, rampant smuggling of kerosene to unsubsidized markets, and rapidly increasing reported incidents of domestic fires triggered by kerosene. As a solution, the government decided that liquefied petroleum gas (LPG[1]) would be used to replace kerosene.[2] Though it is more expensive as compared to kerosene, LPG is efficient to use and manage. The Indonesian government is aware that many poor households would not be able to afford the required capital investment. The startup costs of buying a stove and paying a deposit for a fuel canister represents a serious barrier for many households.

Therefore, to encourage conversion, the Indonesian government will give each household a free stove, an LPG cylinder, and a first consignment of LPG, in addition to subsidizing[3] the 3kg cylinders LPG. As the demand for LPG is expected to rise dramatically, Indonesia's National Oil Company (PERTAMINA) has declared that it is not capable of meeting the market demand, which is expected at two million tons annually. Hence, the government is inviting foreign oil companies to venture into Indonesia's LPG market either as wholesalers or retailers—breaking PERTAMINA's monopoly[4] of the fuel market.

The government announcement, however, was received with absolute resentment from the public. Demonstrations were organized and people marched into the streets voicing their anger. Many were concerned about affordability and availability, as existing LPG supply is both expensive and limited, in addition to the potential loss of income of current sundry shops (sundry shops make up 90 percent of the kerosene distribution network). Others were worried about the potential change of lifestyle while a few claimed that food would never taste the same again.

The announcement, however, was anticipated by the foreign oil players considering the advancement of fuel consumption. Nevertheless, they were surprised with the

1. LPG stands for liquefied petroleum gas, a type of fuel used primarily for cooking and heating. It is gas in nature and needs to be stored either in steel container/cylinders or in specialized tanks.

2. Kerosene is liquid fuel extracted from crude oil. It is a traditional fuel normally used in developing countries. Kerosene is known as "minyak tanah" in Indonesia and Malaysia.

3. Subsidized means the price to end consumer is fixed. Government will compensate supplier the difference between actual product price and the fixed price. Price of LPG 3kg cylinders are fixed at Rp28,000 or U.S.$2.68 per cylinder.

4. PERTAMINA is holding a 80 percent market share of fuel production and marketing of fuel product in Indonesia. It is wholly owned by the government of Indonesia though there is a plan to list the company on the Indonesia Stock Exchange.

This case is based on a real-life company. In order to protect confidentiality, names of the company and people mentioned in the company have been changed. Case prepared by Abdul Rahim Abu Bakar and Fariza Hashim, Prince Sultan University, Saudi Arabia. The authors would like to thank Johari Jalil for his earlier contribution in the writing of this case.

government's aim of converting the current usage of kerosene to LPG in less than a year. It simply seems an impossible task to convert a population of 230 million—70 percent of whom have below-average national income—to a new product. Following this announcement, Blue Oil immediately called for an urgent meeting at its Indonesian office in Jakarta to discuss the Blue Gas potential entry into Indonesia LPG market. Blue Gas is the leading global player for LPG, with market presence in 80 countries. The parent company of Blue Gas, Blue Oil,[5] has already established a foothold in Indonesia in the Retail Service Station and Lubricants market. Vice President of Blue Gas, John Baily, Chairman of Blue Indonesia, Rodgier Van Cux, General Manager of Blue Gas—Southeast Asia, Johan Salleh, and Vice President of Corporate Communication-Blue Indonesia, Rudy Harianto, were huddled in an intense discussion.

"Surely you gentlemen agree that there is a strong business potential for Blue Gas to enter the Indonesian LPG market now," said Rodgier Van Cux, who was eager to seize any opportunity of expanding Blue Group presence in Indonesia. "For years, Indonesia's LPG market was monopolized by PERTAMINA. Foreign oil companies that attempted to enter the market faced government bureaucracy, hostile market conditions, and unprofitable return on investment. Now the window of opportunity opens by the invitation itself. Two million tons of annual market demand is too big of an opportunity to pass up. The demand is also the third largest after China and India," he commented.

To further demonstrate his points, Rodgier read aloud the preliminary report on Indonesia's LPG market. Indonesia houses a massive opportunity in an untapped LPG market. Armed with a population of 230 million and a steady growth of GDP, averaging 4.5 percent annually, it promises a huge market of LPG in Asia along with China and India. Under the leadership of the sixth president of Indonesia, Susilo Bambang Yudhoyona, Indonesia achieved credible economic growth over the backdrop of a stable political climate. Despite a market previously monopolized by PERTAMINA, LPG penetration in Indonesia is merely 15 percent, compared to neighboring countries that are 95 percent in Malaysia, 80 percent in Thailand, and 65 percent in the Philippines.

"There are a few fundamental factors at both the macro and micro level that need to be sorted out," Johan pointed out. "Our experience of new entries in countries like China and India taught us to be extra vigilant in injecting capital investment without adequately anticipating what the end game would be," he added.

Johan argued about the risk that the company would have to bear as he said, "The first factor is on subsidy; it appears that the government's motive to retrieve subsidy from kerosene was primarily driven to curb high product cost and smuggling. What will happen when the reverse trend occurs? I mean when the LPG base price is higher than kerosene? Will the government then reverse its policy when we have already invested millions of dollars in capital?"

At present, the government-set LPG cylinder price in Indonesia is around U.S.$0.45 per kg (U.S.$450 per ton) against an indicated full-cost price in relation to market LPG prices of U.S.$0.99 per kg (U.S.$990 per ton). This is a huge differential to subsidize, particularly as much of the LPG demand growth in the future will be supported by LPG imports, where Indonesia—specifically PERTAMINA—has to pay the full international market price. For instance, their most recent LPG import tender into Tanjung Uban for redistribution elsewhere in Indonesia saw PERTAMINA paying December CP plus U.S.$60 per ton for the CFR delivery. The subsidy cost that PERTAMINA will bear is estimated at U.S.$345 million in 2008 and could rise to U.S.$1.8 billion in 2012.

---

5. Blue is the second-largest oil company in the world with interest on upstream production and marketing of fuel products.

"I believe with the elections looming in 2009 and the Government awareness of the potential risk of social unrest in Jakarta and elsewhere, there would not be any major hike in LPG cylinder prices by the Government. However, what happens after that remains a concern," said Johan.

Johan continued, "The second factor is the uncertainty of a level playing field in Indonesia. Whether licenses issued will be fluid to foreign oil companies or whether there are restrictions of trade area and segments, etc. It is unlikely that PERTAMINA will allow its existing market share to erode with this invitation of entry to foreign oil companies. The government will likely devise some mechanism to protect the National Oil Company. Here the government's transparency is imperative," worried Johan.

"What would likely be the protection mechanisms available to the government?" asked John.

"Well, quite a few actually," replied Johan. "To start with, the government could restrict the area of trade on the foreign oil companies. It is generally known that the Island of Java houses 50 percent of the population and that's where the bulk of the demand growth is. It is also by far the most developed area in terms of logistics. Government may opt to restrict foreign oil companies to trade into Java Island and only permit trade on the rest of the islands like Sumatra, Kalimantan, Sulawesi, etc. That will pave the way for PERTAMINA to maximize its profit on existing infrastructure, while the foreign companies struggle to build infrastructures that translate to lower and longer return on investment."

"Can we seek confirmation on these potential implementations of restrictions before we decide to invest?" questioned John.

"We could, and even with the government assurance, there are risks that the policy changes when the new government is elected every four years. The sentiment of nationalism is high in Indonesia, thus issues like this will likely surface to win votes and support from the public," replied Johan.

"On the micro perspective, we have to be careful which segment we choose to invest in," Johan added. "There are two segments currently existing in Indonesia: the 3kg market, which is fully subsidized by the government and very popular, and the 12kg market,[6] which is not subsidized and is unregulated, where suppliers are free to position their price and is currently only targeted to the higher income group," he claimed. "The factor to consider is that the 3kg cylinders are not a standard Blue Gas package anywhere in the global market. Thus we would not be able to leverage on economies of scale if we need to adapt to this demand. If we ask our cylinder manufacturers to change their design, the plant carousel will need to be fitted with non-standard injection capacity and the whole R&D cost will increase to analyze the safety issues and enhancement related to the 3kg cylinders," he asserted.

"There is also the factor of imminent change of consumer preference in the future. The tendency is for the consumer to opt for a bigger package size once the domestic income improves. Our experience in China,[7] India, and even Malaysia proved the theory of evolving customer demand," John added.

"In addition to that, there are no guarantees that government will continue to subsidize the 3kg market in the future. The motivation of subsidy is clear for now to promote the conversion of the public from kerosene to LPG. Without the subsidy, no conversion can take place without triggering public anger," stated Rudy. "How the subsidy policy evolves beyond then is unknown. Should the government decide to

6. The 12kg cylinders are not subsidized. Its price changes on a monthly basis according to prevailing product price. Currently it sells at Rp148, 000 or U.S.$14.12 equivalent.

7. In China, consumer demand moves from 10kg to 14kg within four years in tandem with the gross domestic income. The 10kgs cylinders, due to drastic low demand, were forced to be scrapped.

discontinue the LPG subsidy, will consumers revert back to their old cooking fuel or look for new alternatives or substitutes?"

"So if we can put this into future perspective, should the subsidy no longer exist? There is little to differentiate on per kg basis between 3kg and 12kg. Consumers will soon realize that 12kg cylinders, though they have to fork out more money for them, are more convenient as they eliminate the hassle of frequent replenishment (it is estimated that the 3kg cylinder could last a week on normal cooking consumption)," stated Johan. "Are we then barking up the wrong tree, and should we focus our entry into the 3kg market now even though the demand is enormous?"

"May I add that there is also the nagging issue of the timing of subsidy repayment[8] from the government," added Johan. "It is easy to assume that preference of timely payment will be at PERTAMINA advantage. We need to be prepared to have a huge cash flow locked in Indonesia should the subsidy repayment be perpetually delayed."

"But it doesn't make sense for us to limit ourselves only to the 12kg market" said Rodgier in response. "To start with, the demand of the 12kg market is very small as compared to 3kg, thus we will not achieve the volume to satisfy our appetite. Secondly, the government may find that Blue Gas's proposal to limit to the 12kg market as unattractive, as they are focused on tackling the conversion mode which is targeted primarily on the lower income group. Thirdly, there is no guarantee that PERTAMINA will allow us to enter into the lucrative 12kg market without sharing the pain on the investment of 3kg market," added Rodgier.

"There is also one final factor that needs to be sorted out," said Johan. "We need to decide whether we should explore this entry independently or with other counterparts. In order to be a sustainable player in Indonesia, we must have absolute control over supply and not depend on third-party supply." (Depending on third-party sources would mean that product price would be dictated by the third party with absolutely no reliability of supply.) "An investment of an import terminal is huge, at U.S.$250 million. To mitigate such exposure we should consider the opportunity of joint venture with a local player, preferably a reputable one with strong financial standings and good government contacts that we can leverage," suggested Johan.

"Well, gentlemen, the issues are a lot more challenging than we expected. Anyway, let's recap our action points and agree on the timeline," said John. "We do not really have the luxury of time here, as the government of Indonesia is expecting a preliminary reply on our interest. Other players[9] will have similar interests in this market, and a first-mover advantage will bring some credibility to our proposal," he added.

The group agreed to meet in two weeks' time to finalize the proposal to the Blue Gas Investment Board. Would this be a successful opportunity or a regretted entry in the making?

Case Questions

1. Identify the opportunities and threats of the LPG industry in Indonesia. Should Blue Gas consider entering the Indonesian market?

2. Considering the characteristics of the Indonesian market, determine the Blue Gas product strategy. Which product market should it enter? Why?

3. Decide Blue Gas's communication strategy in view of Indonesian consumers and its product strategy.

---

8. On average, subsidy repayment from the government ranges between three months and 12 months.

9. Some of the big names that have shown interest are ExxonMobil, Caltex, and PETRONAS.

4. Should Blue Gas decide to focus on the 12kg cylinder, what should the pricing strategy be? Why?

5. What would be the best Blue Gas entry strategy? Why?

References

Nasution, B. (17 December 2008). Kerosene a luxury item in C. Java after conversion to LPG. *The Jakarta Post.*

Business in Asia Today. (17 February 2009). Retrieved from www.asiapulse.com.

Budya, H. (2008, September 24–26). Indonesia LPG kerosene conversion program, challenges and opportunities. *21st World LP Gas Forum.* Seoul, South Korea.

LPG in World Markets. (2007). LPG in Indonesia: Big plans, big problems.

CHAPTER 3

Evaluating Cultural and Social Environments

Ideally, as an international company we would like to think of ourselves as having one culture. But a company cannot transcend the cultures of nations. There are complex differences between East and West. We have had to accept and understand these differences. American companies doing business in China must learn about and understand Chinese culture. The same applies to the Chinese when they do business overseas.[1]

YANG YUANQING, CHAIRMAN, LENOVO GROUP

LEARNING OBJECTIVES

After reading this chapter, you should be able to:

- Recognize the importance of culture to global marketing
- Identify the components of culture
- Apply cultural frameworks to understand consumer behavior
- Segment countries by cultural similarities
- Employ cultural concepts to determine communication strategy
- Understand the difference between verbal and nonverbal communication

BIG BROTHER'S BIG CONTROVERSY[2]

"Racist Attacks Trigger Outrage" claimed *Hindustan Times*, "Big Brother India Backs Shilpa in UK" declared *The Asia Age*, and *The Economic Times* pronounced "Big Brother's Brown Shadow on Brown," referring to the visiting UK Chancellor of Exchequer Gordon Brown.

The event that spurred these headlines in the Indian press, and equally agitated ones in the UK press, was an episode of the *Big Brother* reality show aired on UK's Channel 4. What became known as a "race row" in Britain, India, and around the world started with a series of negative comments directed toward Shilpa Shetty, a Bollywood star, by some of the contestants on the show's "celebrity" edition, which followed the lives and interactions of 14 housemates as they were confined together

1. Quoted in PricewaterhouseCoopers. (2006, January). *10th annual global CEO survey*. Retrieved from www.pwc.com/extweb/insights.nsf/docid/A9FAF3E5965EED618525726B000B2109.

2. Sources: BBC News, Indiapress.org, Channel 4.com.

BOX 3-1   COMPANIES IN FOCUS: VITRO CORNING

Not all business alliances succeed, especially those made across borders. Such was the case with the Vitro and Corning joint venture contracted in 1992.

"Vitro and Corning share a customer-oriented philosophy and remarkably similar corporate cultures"—that was the conclusion made by Vitro executive Julio Escamez during the completion of the joint venture. Both companies had some organizational similarities; experience with joint ventures and global orientations and had founding family representation at the helm.

"The cultures didn't match," said Fransisco Chevez, an analyst with Smith Barney Shearson in New York. "It was a marriage made in hell." In spite of this background, the joint venture fell apart in less than three years.

The venture failed mainly because of cultural differences. Important decisions were not made in time (according to Corning's cultural timetable), and Vitro's sales approach was less aggressive, which was the opposite of Corning's competitive strategy.

The Vitro Corning failure was not a rare phenomenon between Mexican and American firms. Apparently, the NAFTA trade pact may have created unrealistic expectations about the cultural affinity between the two countries. While Mexicans have a different attitude toward time (Americans perceived Vitro executives as moving too slow, while Mexicans saw Americans as too direct and fast), they also have different attitudes toward work, running from people relations to decision making.

Source: Adapted from: DePalma, A. (26 June 1994). It takes more than a visa to do business in Mexico. *The New York Times.*

and isolated from the rest of the world for four weeks. Each week, at least one of the contestants, which included pop singer Jermaine Jackson (Michael's brother) and various other actors, singers, and models, was voted out of the house by the rest.

The housemates' comments, seemingly meant to insult Shilpa's race and culture, prompted street protests in India, a discussion on the floor of the British Parliament, an awkward press conference moment for Chancellor Brown, a pull-out from the show's main sponsor, and over 40,000 complaints by viewers.

An equally vigorous debate carried on in the global media on whether the housemates' comments were truly meant to disparage Shilpa's Indian heritage or if they were simply the angry outbursts of culturally ignorant people. Referring to Jade Goody, the model whose comments sparked the most outrage, Jermaine Jackson simply said, " . . . Shilpa is from another culture and they [Shilpa and Jade] don't fit."

While Shilpa went on to win the Big Brother contest that season and managed to rise above the social tumult, the issue of cultural differences and people's inherent difficulties with it is destined to remain a subject of discussion in our globalizing world.

Cross-cultural conflicts can result not only in poor management of international joint ventures and strategic alliances, but in the break up of a relationship, as demonstrated in Box 3-1.

Culture, and all its obvious and hidden implications, plays a critical role in the business world as well. International marketers in particular stumble upon it every time they try to market their product or service to a target audience that does not share their own cultural heritage. This chapter discusses the reasons why cultural differences play such a big role in international business and marketing, and the ways business professionals can learn about and cope in social and cultural environments that are different from their own.

An understanding of culture is important because it can give insight into international markets and provide competitive advantage to global business leaders. Being culturally mindful, international marketing leaders can better adapt their strategies to achieve business success in any society and culture. The concept of culture is complex. It has been the subject of extensive research in multiple fields of study that has added to the understanding of how cultural differences influence both business and consumer behavior.

CULTURAL DIVERSITY IN THE ERA OF GLOBALIZATION

Globalization has enabled us to overcome geographical and economic boundaries, creating borderless enclaves. Within this borderless world, the growth in the number of transnational corporations and the dissemination of information and ideas around the world have all had an impact on individual cultures. While globalization is a strong force for the spread of ideas around the world, there still exists a great deal of cultural diversity among regions and individual countries and even within countries. For example, Table 3-1 lists countries measured by language and religious diversity. While English is the dominant language in the United States, spoken by 82 percent of the population, there are some 150–300 additional languages in use (some used only in tribal rituals). The most widely spoken languages other than English are Spanish and Chinese. In some areas, such as California and Texas, Spanish speakers comprise 35 percent of the population. In Los Angeles alone, there are 22 Spanish-language radio stations, 17 audited weekly and daily newspapers, and eight TV stations. Chinese is the third most common language spoken in New York and the fourth most common language spoken in California and Maryland.

As well as the more obvious cultural differences such as language, eating habits, dress, and traditions, there are also significant variations in the way societies organize themselves, in their shared conception of ethics, and in the ways they interact with their environment. According to UNESCO, some five countries monopolize the world cultural industries trade. In the cinema industry, for example, 88 out of 185 countries do not have the ability to produce their own films.

Companies such as Starbucks, McDonald's and Kentucky Fried Chicken have changed eating habits in many countries. For example, McDonald's sells spicy French fries and a Shogun Burger (a pork bun served with Japanese teriyaki sauce and cabbage) in Hong Kong, while beef and pork products are not offered in India. Other variations are served in additional countries such as Japan and the Philippines. Kentucky Fried Chicken offers Sichuan pickle and shredded pork chops in addition to chicken in China.

TABLE 3-1 Countries with the Largest Cultural Diversity Indices	
Number of Languages	**Number of Religions**
India (several hundred)	India (40)
United States (150–300)	South Africa (30)
Philippines (170)	Taiwan (25)
Russia (100)	United States (20)
Mexico (62)	Canada (15)
China (10)	United Kingdom (10)

This chapter discusses the following issues: how useful is the study of culture in the determination of global marketing strategy? How have cultures been affected by globalization? To what extent have cultures remained diverse in the era of globalization? Before we tackle these questions, let us define what is meant by culture.

WHAT IS "CULTURE"?

A country's culture has been defined as a "shared meaning system"[3] or "the collective programming of the mind that distinguishes the members of one group or people from another."[4] A broad view of culture is that it encompasses all value systems of a nation. It is what defines a human community, its individuals, social organizations, and economic and political systems.[5] Culture is comprised of concepts such as:[6]

- National character
- Values
- Time orientation
- Space orientation
- Perception
- Thinking
- Language
- Nonverbal communication
- Behavior
- Social groupings and relationships

Figure 3-1 depicts many of these cultural elements as an "iceberg"; some are above the surface ("surface culture"), the tangible aspects, those that can be seen, heard, and touched. We can see how people behave, how they dress, and how they speak. However, most elements of culture are below the surface ("deep culture"), such as values, orientation toward time and space and **nonverbal communication,** such as facial expressions and posture ("body language"), many of which have hidden meanings and are understandable only to cultural insiders. The large area below the waterline can only be suspected, estimated, or intuited.

Knowing Your Iceberg

You are invited to someone's home in a foreign country for tea. Is "tea time" at the end of a dinner, or served alone, say, in mid-afternoon? You are invited for dinner at 7 P.M. in a Latin American country. Should you arrive promptly at the specified time, or somewhat after? How do you greet people in another country? Do you shake hands, embrace with a hug, or keep a respectful distance? Proper behavior in another culture depends upon understanding both the explicit and the implicit parts of culture. Making mistakes at the tip of the iceberg may not be serious, but mistakes below the surface can lead to communication failure, as the following example illustrates:

3. Sweder, R., & LeVine, R. (1984). *Culture theory: essays on mind, self and emotion.* New York: Cambridge University Press.

4. Hofstede, G. (2001). *Culture's consequences: comparing values, behaviors, institutions and organizations across nations* (2nd ed.). Thousand Oaks, CA: Sage.

5. Venkatesh, A. (1995). Ethnocentrism: a new paradigm to study cultural and cross-cultural consumer behavior. In Costa, J., and Bamossy, G. (Eds.), *Marketing in a multicultural world* (pp. 26–67). New York: Sage.

6. Maletzke, G. (1996). *Interkulturelle Kommunikation: zur Interaktion zwischen Menschen verschiedener Kulturen.* Opladen: Westdt. Verlage.

Figure 3-1 The Culture Iceberg

> A foreign company planned to enter the French market. . . . [T]he first several years were difficult . . . *We did not understand their mentality, and they had problems understanding us.* It was *a communications problem.* The French spoke English with us, but we soon realized that even though we were speaking the same language, we were not *communicating with* one another.

A marketing example of communication failure is illustrated by the case of a North American telephone company TV advertisement in a Latin American country. The ad portrayed a home with only one telephone located on the ground floor. As the phone rang, the wife was on the second floor and shouted to her husband to answer. The theme of the ad was that it would be more convenient to have a phone on each floor. The ad was a failure because in a masculine-oriented country, it was not the norm for the husband to be given what was perceived to be a command from his spouse.

Why is knowledge of culture important to global marketing? A country's culture has been identified as a key environmental characteristic underlying systematic differences in behavior.[7] As such, it is a powerful force that shapes consumer behavior. Moreover, ignoring cultural differences between countries has been cited as one of the causes of many business failures.[8]

Take the following incident, for example:

> An executive of Turbo Beer, a Scandinavian brewery, was sent on assignment to Eastern Europe as regional marketing manager. His task was to research the potential for, and then develop the market for his company's premium beer. Beer tastes and consumption are known to be influenced by culture. Therefore, the first step in the executive's plan was to determine whether the culture of the countries comprising the region were similar. Also, he wanted to know whether there were any similarities to beer drinking in these countries with his home country.

The executive in the above case needs some sort of model that can show which cultures are similar and which are dissimilar, and in what aspects are the similarities or

7. Steenkamp, J. (2001). The role of national culture in international marketing research. *International Marketing Review, 18*(1), 30–44.

8. Ricks, D. (1993). *Blunders in international business*. Cambridge: Blackwell.

Illustration 3-1 Early Conceptions of National Cultures

Source: Darton, W. (1790). *Inhabitants of the world.*

differences represented. In other words, what national cultural frameworks exist that can be relied on to provide the information that the beer executive needs for his project?

THE CONCEPT OF NATIONAL CHARACTER

One such framework is the concept of **national character.** The concept assumes that each country has its own character; i.e., people from a given nation share common behavioral patterns that are distinct from other nations. For example, President George W. Bush proclaimed "National Character Counts Week" in 2006. What values shape the American character? According to the president's proclamation they are supposed to be "integrity, courage, honesty, and patriotism." Are these perceptions of the American character generalizations based on personal experience or stereotypes that may have a "kernel of truth," or may they simply be inaccurate? How then may national character be determined?

Historically, the concept of national character or culture had its origins among philosophers beginning in the eighteenth century, among them d'Argens, Montesquieu, and Jean-Jacques Rousseau. They debated what constitutes the national character of a nation, such as physical and spiritual factors and political institutions. D'Argens, for example, averred that the inhabitants of each country constitute a nation with a unique set of characteristics.[9] Nevertheless, d'Argens' descriptions of "nations" were generally stereotyped.[10] The Spanish were described as being shrewd, proud, vain, and jealous, while the British were intelligent, fair, and industrious but rude. For another example, see Darton's portrayal of national culture in Ilustration 3-1, published in 1790.

Studies of national culture have been criticized for two main reasons. First, some national cultural studies lack rigorous foundations that result in stereotyped findings that have little basis in fact. People in all cultures have shared perceptions about the personality characteristics of the typical member of their own culture and of typical members of other cultures. Perceptions abound of national character, such as "the Germans lack humor," "the Italians are excitable," the British are "fair players," and the Swedes are "introverted." However, the reliability of these perceptions has been

9. Kra, P. (2002). The concept of national character in 18th century France. Retrieved from www.cromohs.unfi.it/7_2002/kra.html.

10. D'Argens, J. (1738). *Lettres Juives.* The Hague.

widely criticized by Peabody (1985).[11] He claimed that perceptions of national character are often based on indirect experience and therefore are inaccurate and clouded by racism, ethnocentrism, and discrimination.

National character may not reflect actual personality traits, as was found in a study of 49 cultures.[12] Terracciano (2005) and fellow researchers asked respondents to describe their "national culture." They found that perceptions of national culture differed significantly from personality scores (characteristics) of fellow nationals. Therefore, perceptions of national character may be based more on stereotypes than on reality, as the following illustrates:

> [A] characteristic of Swedish mentality is the urge to agree on things. Heated discussions are rare, and the best way to convince somebody in a matter is not to put maximum emotional energy into the discussion, but to give some good arguments. For this reason, foreigners sometimes think Swedish people [are] undercooled and formal. They probably have a point there, but it should be remembered that the tendency toward rationality and objectivity most of all is seen in public and professional life. Swedish people can be very emotional, too, especially after 2 A.M. in a bar.[13]

THE ROLE OF SUBCULTURES

Marketers should also develop an understanding of the differences between national cultures and the various subcultures that operate within them. **Subcultures** develop around a shared characteristic that is different and unique within the predominant national culture. This shared quality among the members of a subculture can be anything from a different ethnic background, religion, or language, to a demographic factor, such as age and gender, to a shared interest. For example, players of the popular online game Second Life form a subculture, as do fashionistas or vegetarians. What is often referred to as a company's "corporate culture" is also, in effect, a subculture that exists predominantly in the business world.

It is important to note that subcultures often transcend national borders and cultures, especially in today's interconnected world. Users around the world who adopt a subculture's values and rules often adapt them to their own national cultural values and, unwittingly, become a part of the ongoing paradox of modern society where national culture and globalization are inextricably mixed. Think of the MySpace user in Ukraine who has accepted the value of individual expression (culturally associated with the United States) by having a MySpace page, but who has also customized that page to her own culturally influenced values and sensibilities, and who, in turn, has connected with other MySpace users from around the world who share her interest in the online community but not necessarily her national cultural values or tastes.

Marketers who are trying to reach this hypothetical consumer should then ask themselves whether their product or service would appeal to their national cultural values, the values of the subcultures of which they are a member, or both.

The criticisms of attempts to develop national character frameworks can be addressed by referring to those research approaches that are valid and theory-based for studying *cross-cultural behavior*. These approaches consist of empirical studies of national character based on personality traits such as "openness," "agreeableness,"

11. Peabody, D. (1985). *National characteristics*. Cambridge, UK: Cambridge University Press.

12. Terracciano, A. et al. (2005). National character does not reflect mean personality trait levels in 49 cultures. *Science, 310*(5745), 96–100; McCrea, R., & Terracciano, A. (2006). National character and personality. Current *Directions in Psychological Science, 15*(4), 156–161.

13. Source: www.sverigeturism.se/smorgasbord/smorgasbord/culture/swedish/index.html. Retrieved 18 April 2007.

"conscientiousness," and other elements.[14] Examples of such frameworks include Hofstede (2001),[15] Schwartz (1994),[16] and GLOBE.[17] Second, some question the relevance of national character to international marketing because it cannot explain individual consumer behavior. However, the concept is important to international marketing because it can be useful in explaining *national* differences in marketing phenomena.[18] While national character studies do not explain or predict *individual* consumer behavior, they can explain *aggregate* consumer behavior, which can identify similar behavioral patterns cross-nationally. Moreover, there is evidence that national cultural moderates individuals' value priorities.[19] Identifying value similarities and differences has become a useful method to studying cultures. While these similarities and differences operate at the group level, they are often internalized by individuals. For example, Lee and Green (1991)[20] found that the degree of national culture individualism affects attitudes toward purchase intentions of both groups and individuals. This information can be used to shape market segments and to determine regional or global marketing strategy.

HOFSTEDE'S 5 DIMENSIONS OF NATIONAL CULTURE

Hofstede's framework is the most used and cited in international marketing research. Hofstede identified five dimensions that are inherent in cultures: individualism (relationship of individuals in a group), masculinity (implications of gender), power distance (social inequality), uncertainty avoidance (handling of uncertainty), and long-term versus short-term orientation. Each dimension is scaled on a continuum running from high to low.[21] The five dimensions are summarized in Table 3-2. His database consisted of 116,000 questionnaires filled out by managers and workers of IBM subsidiaries in 66 Western countries from 1967 to 1973 and replicated again during 1980 and 1983.

Considering employees of IBM subsidiaries as representative of a nation's culture is problematical,[22] but some researchers have replicated Hofstede's methodology more recently in various countries. A number of studies have revalidated Hofstede's dimensions[23] (Bochner, 1994; Sondergaard, 1994; Robertson & Hoffman, 2000). For example,

14. Terracciano, A. et al. (2005). National character does not reflect mean personality trait levels in 49 cultures. *Science, 310*(5745), 96–100.

15. Hofstede, G. (2001). *Culture's consequences: comparing values, behaviors, institutions and organizations across nations* (2nd ed.). Thousand Oaks, CA: Sage.

16. Schwartz, S. (1994). Beyond individualism/collectivism: new cultural dimensions of value. In Kim, U. et al. (Eds.), *Individualism and collectivism: theory, method and applications* (pp. 85–119). Thousand Oaks: Sage; _____ (1997). Values and culture. In Munro, D. et al. (Eds.), *Motivation and Culture* (pp. 69–84). New York: Routledge.

17. Javidan, M., House, R., Dorfman, P., Hanges, P., & de Luque, M. (2006). Conceptualizing and measuring cultures and their consequences: a comparative review of GLOBE's and Hofstede's approaches. *Journal of International Business Studies, 37,* 897–914.

18. Clark, T. (1990, October). International marketing and national character: a review and proposal for an integrative theory. *Journal of Marketing,* 66–79.

19. Steenkamp, J., Hofstede, F., & Wedel, M. (1999, April). A cross-national investigation into the individual and national cultural antecedents of consumer innovativeness. *Journal of Marketing, 63,* 55–69.

20. Lee, C., & Green, R. (1991). Cross-cultural examination of the Fishbein behavioral intention model. *Journal of International Business Studies, 21*(2), 289–305.

21. Appendix 1 shows scale values of Hofstede's five dimensions for a selected 19 countries.

22. McSweeney, B. (2002). Hofstede's model of national cultural differences and their consequences: a triumph of faith—a failure of analysis. *Human Relations, 55*(1), 89–118.

23. Sondergaard, M. (1994). Hofstede's consequences: a study of reviews, citations and replications. *Organization Studies, 15*(3), 447–456.

TABLE 3-2 A Summary of Hofstede's Dimensions	
Cultural Orientations	**Contrasts Across Cultures**
<u>Concepts of the self and others</u> Individualism vs. collectivism	The relationship between an individual and the group. Efforts and achievement are best accomplished by the individual or solved by the group.
<u>Interaction *with* others or *for* others</u> Masculinity vs. femininity	Assertiveness and personal achievement are favored (masculinity) versus caring for others, adopting nurturing roles, and emphasizing quality of life (femininity).
<u>Dealing with uncertainty</u> Uncertainty avoidance	Tendency to avoid risks (high uncertainty avoidance), to prefer stable situations, uncertainty-reducing rules and risk free procedures, which are seen as a necessity for efficiency. Or, conversely, a risk-prone attitude (low uncertainty avoidance) where people as individuals are seen as the engine of change, which is perceived as a requirement of efficiency.
<u>Equality or Inequality in Interpersonal Interactions</u> Power distance	Hierarchy is strong, power is centralized at the top (high power distance); power is more equally distributed and superior and subordinates have a sense of equality as human beings (low power distance).
<u>Virtue Regardless of Truth</u> Long-Term vs. Short-Term Orientation	Values associated with Long-Term Orientation are thrift and perseverance; those associated with Short Term are respect for tradition, fulfilling social obligations and protecting one's "face."

Sources: Adapted from: Usunier, J. (2000), *Marketing Across Cultures.* Harlow: Pearson Education Limited, p. 64 and http://www.geert_hofstede.com/.

Sondergaard's paper contains a review of over 60 replications of Hofstede's cultural model and concludes that Hofstede's dimensions are "largely confirmed." In addition, Hoppe (1990)[24] provided an update in 19 countries and concluded that there were few significant differences between his and Hofstede's scores of the countries studied.

To compensate for overemphasis on Western cultures, Hofstede added a fifth dimension to his original four—Long-Term versus Short-Term Orientation—which was developed from surveys of students in 23 mostly Asian countries using a questionnaire developed by Chinese researchers. Values associated with the Long Term are thrift and perseverance, and those associated with the Short Term are respect for tradition, fulfilling social obligations, and protecting one's "face." The concept of "face" means showing respect to someone in a way that acknowledges publicly his or her status. Berating a subordinate by a manager in front of other workers will cause the subordinate to lose face. Criticizing someone or pointing out mistakes or errors in public may make the person feel shamed or inferior. But a manager may also lose face because of the anger expressed in front of subordinates. For a person to maintain face is not unique to, but is very important in Asian social relations because face translates into power and influence and affects goodwill. Loss of face can result in a person losing honor and can cause serious embarrassment. Moreover, if one person loses face, the whole group loses face, so the consequences may be very serious. Consider the following example.

> An Israeli company established a wholly-owned subsidiary in China. After the completion of the factory buildings, local managers suggested that the home office consider constructing an expensive, monumental gate in front of the factory areas. Home office management in Israel considered the investment a waste of money. However, the Chinese believed that it was important to project a strong company image through such a

24. Hoppe, M. (1990). A comparative study of country elites: international differences in work-related values and learning and their implications for international management training and development. Doctoral dissertation, University of North Carolina.

TABLE 3-3 A Comparison of Western and Eastern Cultures Based on Hofstede	
Collectivist, Feminine	**Collectivist, Masculine**
Korea, Thailand, Chile, Costa Rica, Bulgaria, Russia, Portugal, Spain	China, Japan, Mexico, Venezuela, Egypt, Jordan, Syria, Greece
Individualist, Feminine	**Individualist, Masculine**
France, Netherlands, Scandinavian countries	Hungary, Poland, Slovenia, United States, UK, Australia, Germany, Austria
Small PD, Weak UA	**Large PD, Weak UA**
US, UK, Australia, Denmark, Sweden, Norway	China, India
Small PD, Strong UA	**Large PD, Strong UA**
Germany, Austria, Hungary, Israel	Egypt, Jordan, Syria, South Korea, Japan, Latin America

Note: PD = Power Distance, UA + Uncertainty Avoidance.

monumental gate. This incident is an example of "face culture," often critical in East-West negotiations. Many heated discussions over the gate were held, until finally the Israeli management realized that losing face was the main issue and approved the Chinese initiative.[25]

In the above example, continued confrontation between home and host management could have resulted in greater financial loss to the company in the form of decreased morale than the cost of constructing the gate.

Plotting countries using Hofstede's dimensions on two-dimensional maps or tables produces clusters or groups that are similar. As shown in Table 3-3, individualism is more pronounced in developed and Western nations, while collectivism is inherent in developing countries. Masculinity is high in Eastern European and German-speaking countries. Uncertainty avoidance is high in Latin American countries and Japan. Power distance is high in Latin American, Asian, and African countries. Fitting marketing strategies to each country cluster because of cultural distances is necessary for products that are culturally bound and for advertising messages, as we will see below and in further chapters.

APPLYING HOFSTEDE'S MODEL TO GLOBAL MARKETING

Cultural values affect many decisions inherent in the marketing mix, especially product and promotional considerations. For example, Steenkamp et al. (1999)[26] found that consumers in more individualistic and more masculine countries tended to be

25. Adapted from Zhu, Y., & Wagner, M. (2006). Cross-cultural management among foreign-owned subsidiaries operating in the People's Republic of China: The case of Sino-Israeli enterprises. *Journal of Transnational Management, 12*(1), 3–24.

26. Steenkamp, J., Hofstede, F., & Wedel, M. (1999, April). A cross-national investigation into the individual and national cultural antecedents of consumer innovativeness. *Journal of Marketing, 63*, 55–69.

more innovative. Innovativeness was also found in weak uncertainty avoidance countries. Because innovativeness is related to tolerance for ambiguity, members of weak uncertainty avoidance cultures tend to be more innovative. A cluster of high individualistic and masculine countries include Austria, Belgium, Czech Republic, Germany, Hungary, Italy, Poland, and the United Kingdom. Among those countries that have relatively low uncertainty avoidance scores are Austria, Germany, Italy, and the United Kingdom. Innovative consumers attach more importance to values such as stimulation, creativity, and curiosity. Therefore, these values should be used in communicating new products to consumers in low uncertainty avoidance countries. Häagen-Daz is an example of a product that is positioned as originating in Scandinavia (although produced in the United States by Unilever) in order to invoke novelty and credibility in the brand.

In another study, Steenkamp[27] calculated percentages of adoption categories for packaged goods in five European countries (France, Germany, Italy, Spain, and the United Kingdom). He found significant correlations between the adoption of these packaged goods and low uncertainty avoidance and high individualism cultures.

De Mooij (1998)[28] found that differences in product usage and buying motives are correlated with four of Hofstede's dimensions (not including the Long Term/Short Term dimension). Product categories in 13 European countries that were significantly correlated with most of the four dimensions included food and beverages, clothing and footwear, leisure, entertainment and recreation, and furniture and household equipment. Note that these categories are strongly culture-bound. A specific product highly correlated with the dimensions was mineral water. In France, Germany, Italy, and Belgium, all high uncertainty avoidance cultures, consumption of mineral water was higher than in Scandinavia and the United Kingdom, which are weak uncertainty avoidance cultures. The differences in consumption could not be explained by differences in income or the quality of tap water. The relationship became stronger when masculinity was added to mineral water consumption. These findings related to the years 1970, 1991, and 1996, showing a stable relationship between cultural values (Hofstede) and consumption over time.

THE SCHWARTZ VALUE SURVEY

Schwartz's research has provided insight into the development and consequences of a diverse range of behavioral attitudes and orientations, such as religious belief, political orientation and voting, social group relations, and consumer behavior, as well as the conceptualization of human values across cultures. His framework is based on four dimensions: openness to change (autonomy vs. conformity), self-transcendence (self-direction), conservation (tradition), and self-enhancement (achievement, power). Some similarities between the Hofstede and Schwartz theories can be detected. Smith & Bond (1998)[29] suggest that they overlap almost completely even though they were derived using different methods and, as a result, are close to reaching a universally applicable theory of values. Openness to change and self-transcendence are similar to Hofstede's individualism

27. Steenkamp, J. (2002). *Consumer and market drivers of the trial probability of new consumer packaged goods.* Working paper, Tilburg University.

28. De Mooij, M. (1998). *Global marketing and advertising, understanding cultural paradoxes.* Thousand Oaks: Sage Publications; De Mooij, M. (2000). The future is predictable for international marketers: converging incomes lead to diverging consumer behaviour. *International Marketing Review, 17*(2), 103–113; De Mooij, M. (2001). *Convergence and divergence in consumer behavior: consequences for global marketing.* Unpublished doctoral dissertation. Pamplona: University of Navarra.

29. Smith, P.B., & Bond, M. H. (1998). *Social psychology across cultures* (2nd ed.). London: Prentice Hall.

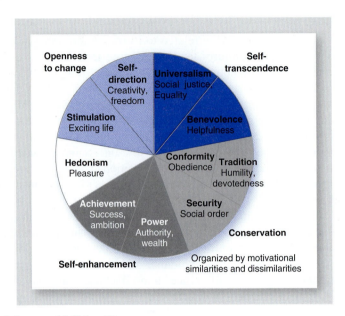

Figure 3-2 Schwartz 10 Value Types

Source: "The Structure of Value Relations," Norwegian Social Science Data Services, http://essedunet.nsd.uib.no. Accessed 6 June 2011. Reprinted with permission.

construct. The conservatism/autonomy value dimension bears considerable similarity to Hofstede's individualism/collectivism dimension. It also is closely linked to Hofstede's power distance dimension.[30] The Schwartz Value Survey has been replicated in many countries and validated for measurement equivalence.[31] Schwartz's human values scale identifies 10 motivationally distinct value orientations that are common to people in different cultures. The four dimensions and their values are shown in Figure 3-2.

An advantage to using the Schwartz Value Survey is that it can measure individual value differences. Schwartz and Bilsky (1990)[32] argued that the individualism–collectivism construct implies that different types of individualist values vary together consistently to form one type of value orientation that opposes that of collectivism. However, at the individual level personal and in-group interests may serve both individualist and collectivist values. Some values are collective, but not those of the in-group (e.g., equality for all and social justice). Heterogeneity of individuals within a society means that not all individuals in a collectivist culture necessarily share a collectivist orientation. To overcome some of these limitations, Schwartz proposes exploring value orientations at the individual level in greater depth. Individual values are concerned with hedonism, achievement, self-direction, social power, and stimulation; collective values are pro-social, restrictive conformity, security, and tradition, while maturity is classified as both an individual and collective value type. If the cultural values of participants had been measured in accordance with this paradigm, the importance of tradition for choice behavior could have been explored further and other relationships between value types and choice behavior may have been uncovered.[33]

30. Steenkamp, J. (2002). *Consumer and market drivers of the trial probability of new consumer packaged goods.* Working Paper, Tilburg University.

31. Spini, D. (2003). Measurement equivalence of 10 value types from the Schwartz Value Survey across 21 countries. *Journal of Cross-Cultural Psychology, 34*(1), 3–23.

32. Schwartz, S., & Bilsky, W. (1990). Toward a theory of the universal content and structure of values: extensions and cross-cultural replications. *Journal of Personality and Social Psychology, 53,* 550–562.

33. Jaeger, S. (2000). Uncovering cultural differences in choice behavior between Samoan and New Zealand consumers: A case study with apples. *Food Quality and Preference, 11*(5), 405–417.

A number of researchers have utilized the Schwartz Value Survey to study consumer behavior, especially for market segmentation and advertising. Kihlberg and Risvik (2007)[34] used the Schwartz Value Survey to determine if there are market segments among Scandinavian consumers of organic foods. They found that similar values were held by consumers segmented according to age and consumption frequency. For example, consumers aged above 30 emphasized values such as "freedom," "spiritual life," and "security," while those under 30 emphasized "hedonism," "friendship," and "success." The authors suggest that in order to increase consumption of organic food, marketers should offer products that have high sensory acceptance while communicating those values that are important for target markets. Likewise, a group of researchers found that value segmentation could be used to understand both differences and similarities across countries in Scandinavia, which some may consider to be homogenous.[35] A study[36] among Japanese respondents found that values play a significant role in segmenting those who choose to buy organically grown food products. These consumers are more altruistic and less egoistic than others, while females tend to be more environmentally conscious than males.

GLOBAL LEADERSHIP AND ORGANIZATIONAL BEHAVIOR EFFECTIVENESS[37]

The **Global Leadership** and Organizational Behavior Effectiveness (GLOBE) model uses a set of cultural values and practices to measure national culture. GLOBE was developed in response to Hofstede's call for good measurement and good theory in order to conduct rigorous cross-cultural research. The theory was developed from a proposition that attributes defining a specified culture are predictive of leadership styles and organizational practices. The theory also predicted that selected aspects of cultural practices will account for the economic competitiveness of nations as well as the physical and psychological well-being of their members.

The GLOBE research group has clustered countries on the basis of shared similarities among social and psychological variables such as attitudes, values and work goals. Sixty-one nations have been grouped into 10 clusters (Table 3-4) on the basis of nine cultural dimensions (Table 3-5), five of which have similar definitions to those of Hofstede. Like Hofstede, respondents included middle managers. However, unlike Hofstede, these managers were selected from 825 organizations (rather than focusing on one organization) in the 61 countries sampled.

Are the GLOBE and Hofstede clusters similar? Taking the Anglo cluster as an example, we can compare the individual country ratings of both frameworks. As shown in Table 3-4, Table 3-5, and Table 3-6, Anglo countries are similar as they are in the GLOBE survey. However, there are differences in scale ratings between the two frameworks. Power distance was rated higher in the GLOBE survey, while uncertainty avoidance and long-term (future) orientation was rated lower in Hofstede's sample than by GLOBE. Other cultural measures were similar in the two frameworks. These differences stem from sample selection and the way questions were worded on the questionnaires.

34. Kihlberg, I., & Risvik, E. (2007). Consumers of organic foods—value segments and liking of bread. *Food Quality and Preference, 18*(3), 471–481.

35. Bjerke, R., Gopalakrishna, P., & Sandler, D. (2005). Cross-national comparison of Scandinavian value orientations: From value segmentation to promotional appeals. *Journal of Promotion Management, 12*(1), 35–56.

36. Aoyagi-Usai, M., & Kuribayashi, A. (2001). Individual values and pro-environmental behavior: Results from a Japanese survey. *Asia Pacific Advances in Consumer Research, 4*, 28–36.

37. Javidan M., House, R.J., Dorfman, P.W., Hanges, P.J., & Sully de Luque, M. (2006). Conceptualizing and measuring cultures and their consequences: a comparative review of GLOBE's and Hofstede's approaches. *Journal of International Business Studies, 37*, 897–914.

TABLE 3-4 Societal Clusters of Countries	
Anglo	**Latin America**
England	Costa Rica
Australia	Venezuela
South Africa (White Sample)	Ecuador
Canada	Mexico
New Zealand	El Salvador
Ireland	Columbia
USA	Guatemala
	Bolivia
	Brazil
	Argentina
Latin Europe	**Sub-Sahara Africa**
Israel	Namibia
Italy	Zambia
Portugal	Zimbabwe
Spain	South Africa (Black Sample)
France	Nigeria
Switzerland (French Speaking)	
Nordic Europe	**Arab**
Finland	Qatar
Sweden	Morocco
Denmark	Turkey
	Egypt
	Kuwait
Germanic Europe	**Southern Asia**
Austria	India
Switzerland	Indonesia
The Netherlands	Philippines
Germany (East and West)	Malaysia
	Thailand
	Iran
Eastern Europe	**Confucian Asia**
Hungary	Taiwan
Russia	Singapore
Kazakhstan	Hong Kong
Albania	South Korea
Poland	China
Greece	Japan
Slovenia	
Georgia	

Source: Reprinted from Gupta, V. et al. (2002), "Cultural Clusters: Methodology and Findings," *Journal of World Business*, 37, 11–15. Permission from Elsevier.

CULTURE AND COMMUNICATION

An important component of culture is the way people communicate with each other. The spoken word, or verbal communication, is often believed to be the dominant form, yet it has been estimated that between 50 and 90 percent of communication is nonverbal. For instance, emotional subjects and expressions of attitude will contain a proportionately higher nonverbal content. Nonverbal communication consists of facial or

TABLE 3-5 GLOBE Cultural Dimensions	
Uncertainty avoidance	The extent to which members of an organization or society strive to avoid uncertainty by reliance on social norms, rituals, and bureaucratic practices to alleviate the unpredictability of future events.
Power distance	The degree to which members of an organization or society expect and agree that power should be unequally shared.
Societal collectivism	The degree to which organizational and societal institutional practices encourage and regard collective distribution of resources and collective action.
In-group collectivism	The degree to which individuals express pride, loyalty, and cohesiveness in their organizations or families.
Gender egalitarianism	The extent to which an organization or a society minimizes gender role differences and gender discrimination.
Assertiveness	The degree to which individuals in organizations or societies are assertive, confrontational, and aggressive in social relationships.
Future orientation	The degree to which individuals in organizations or societies engage in future-oriented behaviors such as planning, investing in the future, and delaying gratification. (Includes the future-oriented component of the dimension "Confucian Dynamism" of Hofstede and Bond [1988].)
Performance orientation	The extent to which an organization or society encourages and rewards group members for performance improvement and excellence.
Humane orientation	The degree to which individuals in organizations or societies encourage and reward individuals for being fair, altruistic, friendly, generous, caring, and kind to others. (Similar to the dimension "kind heartedness" by Hofstede and Bond [1988].)

Source: Adapted from: House, R. et al. (2002), "Understanding Cultures and Implicit Leadership Theories across the Globe: An Introduction to Project GLOBE," *Journal of World Business*, 37, 3, p. 6.

other body expressions and gestures, such as eye contact and the way space and time are utilized. Body language can be misunderstood, and gestures have different meanings in different cultures (see Figure 3-3). It is sometimes difficult to understand each other even with a common language, as the two examples of verbal communication shown below and in Box 3-2 illustrate.

The meeting, planned over a number of weeks, was over in less than an hour. The German team was annoyed that their hard work was not recognized, the French team was anxious that their lack of preparation for the meeting would not be revealed. The real problem was concealed in the translation of one word. The Germans wanted a discussion of their *Konzept*. The French translation used the apparently similar French word, *concept*. Unfortunately, the words have different meanings. To the Germans, *Konzept* means a detailed plan of a proposed new product; to the French, *concept* meant an opportunity to discuss, propose, and create a proposal that would eventually become the detailed plan. Unfortunately, the meeting never started with a firm mutually agreed upon framework. The result was a wasted meeting.[38]

38. *The Guardian* (15 March 1993).

TABLE 3-6 Hofstede's Dimensions of Culture					
Country	**PD**	**IND**	**UA**	**MAS**	**LT**
Australia	36	90	51	61	31
Canada	39	80	48	52	23
Germany	35	67	65	66	31
Great Britain	35	89	35	66	25
Netherlands	38	80	53	14	44
New Zealand	22	79	49	58	30
Sweden	31	71	29	5	33
USA	40	91	46	62	29
Brazil	69	38	76	49	65
China (mainland)	80	20	30	66	118
Hong Kong	68	25	29	57	96
Taiwan	58	17	69	45	87
Japan	54	46	92	95	80
South Korea	60	18	85	39	75
India	77	48	40	56	61
Philippines	94	32	44	64	19
Singapore	74	20	8	48	48
Thailand	64	20	64	34	56
West Africa	77	20	54	46	16

Source: Adapted from: Hofstede, G. (2001). *Cultures' consequences, comparing values, behaviors, institutions, and organizations across nations.* Thousand Oaks, CA: Sage Publications.

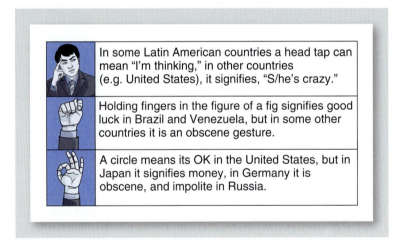

Figure 3-3 Examples of Nonverbal Communication

The anthropologist Hall (1966)[39] made a distinction between high and low *context* cultures. In low-context cultures (e.g., United States, Nordic countries, Germany), words are explicit and taken at face value. In high-context cultures (e.g., France, Latin American countries, Japan), the meaning of what is said is hidden in the way it is said, or in the background of the situation. One may have to "read between the lines" to understand what is meant. Moreover, members of high-context cultures tend to place more focus on nonverbal communication such as body language.

39. Hall, E. T. (1966). *The hidden dimension.* New York: Doubleday.

BOX 3-2   TECHNOLOGY IN FOCUS: LENOVO

A multicultural product design team met at Lenovo's North Carolina office to develop a concept that would give the computers a "unique look and feel." However, cultural differences were apparent. "The Western-based people said that the Lenovo product line should have a consistent look and feel, or what it described as a 'common icon.' The design team from China disagreed . . . The Western team used the word 'common' as a synonym for universal, while the team from China understood the word 'common' as a synonym for ordinary." This example shows that many words may have different meanings across cultures. For example, "boot" in British English, "trunk" in American English; "mess kit" to the British army means the smart bow tie gear worn to a formal mess dinner. To Americans, "mess kit" means a knife, fork, spoon, and tin plate. "Cheers" in South Africa means goodbye, while in the UK it means thanks; "just now" in South Africa means shortly, while in the UK it signifies right now.

Source: Adapted from: Rosenbusch, S. (2008, Spring). The developing world 101. *Wharton Alumni Magazine*, 15.

NONVERBAL COMMUNICATION

Both high- and low-context cultures can be distinguished by their relation to time. Low-context cultures are generally **monochronic** (doing one thing at a time); time is important and regulates how things are done. For example, it is more important to stick to the agenda of a meeting and use Gantt charts to plan and control projects. On the other hand, **polychromic** (doing a number of things at the same time) cultures are much less time-oriented and therefore less organized. Interrupting a speaker at a meeting is taken as a sign of interest rather than rudeness. Arriving 10–15 minutes late for a meeting in a monochronic culture requires a slight apology, while the same sort of apology in a polychromic culture would be the thing to do only if one arrives an hour after the scheduled time (see Table 3-7).

Some dimensions of time orientation for both monochronic and polychronic cultures are shown in Table 3-8. It should be kept in mind that in certain cultures, orientation to time may not be a dichotomy. For example, the Japanese tend to use both styles. In technology and dealings with foreigners they tend to be monochronic, while they may be polychronic for personal relations.

Another aspect of nonverbal communication is relation to space. Hall recognized two types of space, fixed-feature and semi-fixed, in the way in which people organize things, such as homes and offices. Some people demand large homes, big cars, and spacious offices. Even the location of a parking space adjacent to an office building may be an indication of status. "Big" in these cases may signal status, power, and importance. In other cultures, big may not be as important. University classrooms

TABLE 3-7 What to Do If You Are Late		
	If Late in a Monochronic Culture	**If Late in a Polychronic Culture**
Whisper some excuse time	5–10 minutes	45–60 minutes
Make an apology	10–15 minutes	60+ minutes
Prepare a good excuse	15+ minutes	Over one hour

TABLE 3-8 Some Differences between Monochronic and Polychronic Cultures		
Factor	**Monochronic Action**	**Polychronic Action**
Actions	Do one thing at a time	Do many things at once
Focus	Concentrate on the objective or task	Are easily distracted
Attention to time	Plan when things must be achieved	What will be achieved is more important than when
Priority	The task comes first	Relationships come first
Respect for property	Seldom borrow or lend things	Borrow and lend things often and easily

Source: Adapted from: Hall, E.T. (1959). *The silent language.* New York: Doubleday.

Ilustration 3-2 Culture Determines Distance between People

for example, can be organized so that students sit in an oval-shaped arrangement or in straight rows facing the lecturer. Moreover, classrooms can be level or banked, theater-style. The way in which the classroom is designed will affect the interaction between students with each other and with the lecturer.

Another form of space relates to distances between people, or personal space. According to Hall,[40] the distance required between people depends not only on the culture but also on the situation (see Ilustration 3-2). Situational distances depend upon whether people meeting each other are acquaintances or strangers, and whether the meeting is formal or informal. Generally, distances are greater between strangers during formal meetings. What is the permissible body contact in a given culture? In high-contact cultures such as those of Latin America and the Middle East, people maintain close distances between each other, as opposed to those of low-contact cultures, in which the opposite is true. An attempt by a Latin American salesperson to greet a potential German customer with a bear hug would not be conducive for starting a fruitful relationship.

These cultural distinctions largely explain why Western social networks such as Facebook and Twitter were not successful in Japan. Mixi, the country's largest social network, was positioned as a tool for communicating at a distance through the use

40. Hall, E.T. (1959). *The silent language.* New York: Doubleday.

of diaries and communities to meet like-minded members. It was not positioned like Facebook, to make new friends or for self-presentation.

GLOBAL CUSTOMERS

We learned above that culture is a key to understanding consumer behavior. This part of the chapter looks at the characteristics of some major regional markets of the world, including China and India. In studying these markets, we focus on the processes by which buyers learn, evaluate, and adopt products, and the factors that affect their decisions.

China

Many Western companies view China as the world's largest market. Companies often tend to think of China in terms of a simplistic, arithmetic calculation. For example, if each of the 1.3 billion people will use a product once in a year, that will bring enormous sales to companies. In fact, no one should be so naïve as to think of the market in these terms. However, many marketers have overestimated the market in China. There is a real need to understand the market prospects as well as the complexity of the Chinese market (Yong & Baocheng, 2003). An analyst from *Le Monde* (2003) underlined that entrepreneurs have to stop dreaming of the "Chinese Eldorado." China is a complex market which demands a lot of energy, as the Chinese are loyal consumers but hard to satisfy.

However, approaching China as one large, unified market is wrought with dangers. In fact, China is very similar to the European Union in terms of its subtle but important differences in culture, language, and tastes and the economic development of its different regional markets. First, there are differences between the urban, moneyed population in global cities such as Shanghai, Beijing, and Guangzhou and the interior of the country, which is much farther behind in development. China's outdated transportation infrastructure and shaky commitment to scheduling also give Western marketers, used to "just-in-time" operations, quite a challenge when it comes to distribution and logistics. Then there are the gender differences. According to one experienced advertising agency executive, Chinese women in the field are more honest, flexible, and quicker learners than the men, but they may often be in short supply as bigger and better offers from competing agencies often sway even the most loyal professionals. Finally, there's the most important difference for marketers: Chinese consumers rely on advertising for different information, depending on their level of marketing sophistication. The Chinese middle class, who are quickly acquiring the needs and wants of its counterparts around the world, is also more receptive to traditional product branding messages. The majority of the Chinese consumers, however, expect to learn more basic information about a product from its ads and labels. Therefore, localizing product packaging and marketing campaigns becomes more important than ever in China.[41] Another aspect of Chinese culture that influences buyers' behavior is the reluctance to pioneer. The typical Chinese consumer does not want to be among the first to try a new product, but the discomfort of being "behind the times" may make them think that if the neighbors have tried it, they had better follow suit soon. The strong collective characteristics may imply that informal channels of communication are important in Chinese society.

41. Anonymous. (2006, October/November). Don't think local, think locals. *FDI: Foreign Direct Investment*, 83.

BOX 3-3   PEOPLE IN FOCUS: THE CHUPPIES ARE HERE

Urban, young, and affluent Chinese professionals are dubbed "Chuppies." Many are successful entrepreneurs, business leaders, and employees of foreign companies based in China. While they comprise only a minority of the Chinese population (50 million), they are growing by 10 percent per year. Nevertheless, they comprise a significant potential consumer market. They are owners of iPods, use credit cards, are fashion conscious, dine out, and attend cultural events. They are much different than their parents when it comes to behavior and dress. They remain single longer, purchase their own home rather than rent, invest in stocks and bonds, and travel outside the country. Those born after 1960 did not experience the "Cultural Revolution" and its implications; they prefer the image of Mark Zuckerberg to Mao Zedong. Chuppies under the age of 30 dress the same as Chinese professionals living and working abroad.

Yet there are some differences between the Chuppies and their age class in Western countries. About half of the Chuppies save about 50 percent of their incomes, about 20 percent live with their parents, and a majority does not hesitate to buy fake branded products.

In short, Chuppies will continue to be an important consumer segment in China that exporters and those doing business in the country cannot afford to ignore.

Source: Adapted from: Robert Hsu. (2010). The Chuppie strategy. Phillips Investment Resources, LLC, newsletter to subscribers.

India

With a population of over one billion and a GNP of US$691 billion, India's per capita GNI of US$620 in 2004 was one of the lowest in the region. Some population experts predict that India will overtake China, which had a one child policy until recently, as the world's largest country by the middle of the century. Income within the country is polarized. India has hundreds of millions of poor people. Many of these people—an estimated 60 percent of the population—live close to or below the US$2-a-day poverty line.[42] But India also has pockets of prosperity in cities such as Bangalore, the Indian Silicon Valley where talented and computer-savvy young graduates are fueling the growth of the software industry in the country. Given this talent, the low salaries vis-à-vis the United States, and the availability of real-time communication links, many United States companies have sourced or opened offices in India for software development and export. In fact, India's software industry has been growing at over 30 percent in the last five years, and the electronics and technology sectors, which accounted for 20 percent of the country's total exports, are estimated to reach $80 billion by 2010.[43]

Based on this feverish economic growth, many compare India to the other emerging economic giant in Asia: China. However, there are some signs that India will have a harder time keeping pace with its rival. From signs of rising inflation to dismal infrastructure, a lack of public services, and corruption, India may be about a decade behind China in development.[44] Table 3-9 shows how India's infrastructure compares with China and the United States. China is rapidly catching up to the United States in roadways and airports, while India lags far behind. However, while China's growth

42. (3 February 2007). India on fire. *The Economist,* 69–71.

43. David, R. (9 February 2007). India IT industry faces competition. *Forbes.* Retrieved from www.forbes.com/markets/2007/02/09/nasscom-forum-india-markets-equity-cx_rd_0209markets20.html.

44. Hamm, S., & Lakshman, N. (19 March 2007). The trouble with India. *Businessweek.* Retrieved from www.businessweek.com/magazine/content/07_12/b4026001.htm.

TABLE 3-9 India's Infrastructure Compared to China and the United States			
	India	**China**	**United States**
Population	1.1	1.3	0.3
National expressways	3.7	25	47
Major airports	17	56	189
Electricity production	652	2,500	4,000
Internet penetration	3.6%	10.1%	69.3%
Port shipments	0.4	2.9	1.4

Source: Adapted from: Hamm, S., & Lakshman, N. (2007, March 19). The trouble with India: Crumbling roads, jammed airports, and power blackouts could hobble growth. *Businessweek Online.*

may seem impressive, do not forget the relative sizes (distances and populations) of the countries. Parts of China are still backward compared to the United States.

Nevertheless, given India's enormous market size and its current relatively small but growing middle class, marketers should consider its potential and the opportunities presented in this underserved market.

However, major challenges such as widespread corruption, a large informal economy (which accounts for a big portion of the Gross National Product in some Latin American countries), and the widest income disparity in the world between the poor majority and the rich elite, still threaten to derail the progress made in recent years in the region.

C. K. Prahalad claims in his influential book, *The Fortune at the Bottom of the Pyramid,* that these developing markets provide one of the biggest opportunities for companies. The four billion people that live on less than $2 a day represent tomorrow's four billion consumers if only they are offered the right products. Surprisingly, marketers control many of the factors that can make these products a reality and thus create the "capacity to consume" in these previously ignored target markets. According to Prahalad, the three principles for developing such products are based on the three A's:[45]

- Affordability: whether by designing smaller packets of shampoo, tea, matches, etc., or by devising innovative purchasing schemes that allow poor people to pay in smaller increments, marketers can develop products that are affordable for this market segment without being inferior in quality or efficacy.

- Access: by making their products available where the poor live and during the hours when they are not at work, marketers can take advantage of the distribution channels that will put their products within the reach of these consumers.

- Availability: the poor shop when and where they have cash in their hands. Therefore, by making their products easily available at more locations, marketers can increase their sales and market share at the "bottom of the pyramid" (BOP).

Developing markets in developing countries by designing products and services that fit the poor's special needs and purchasing patterns can mean opportunities not only for the underprivileged but also for the companies that are serving these markets.

Today, with the spread of mobile phones and the rise of user-generated content (UGC) on the web, early adopters and influencers have more ways than ever to communicate with their social circle and the world at large. Blogs, podcasts, websites, and all other interactive tools available through Web 2.0 make such interactions exceedingly simple.

45. Prahalad, C. K. (2002). *The fortune at the bottom of the pyramid.* Upper Saddle River: Pearson Education. Retrieved from www.whartonsp.com/articles/article.asp?p=389714&seqNum=4&rl=1.

SUMMARY

- Perhaps the most striking fact about world markets and buyers is that for the first time in modern history, the entire world is growing. According to World Bank estimates, every world region including Africa will continue to grow, and for the most part the developing countries will grow faster than the rich.

- There are various ways of dividing the countries of the world into different regional markets. In effect, defining regional markets is an exercise in clustering countries so that similarities within clusters and differences between clusters will be maximized.

- The shortage of goods and services is the central problem of transitioning economies and low income countries. While these countries may pose certain challenges for marketers, they represent potentially attractive markets for many consumer product companies. Marketers could apply basic marketing concepts to ensure that products are designed that fit the needs and incomes of these markets.

- All buyers go through a similar process in making a purchase decision. Thus, although buyers in different countries and world regions will go through a similar process in making their purchase decisions, they will make different purchases since they will respond to the unique economic, social and cultural, political and governmental, environmental, competitive, and personal factors that influence buyer decisions.

- The process that buyers go through is summarized in diffusion theory, a marketing universal. The pattern by which an individual adopts a new idea, described by sociologist Everett Rogers, comprises three concepts that are extremely useful to global marketers: the adoption process, characteristics of innovations, and adopter categories.

DISCUSSION QUESTIONS

1. Based on the information in Box 3-3 ("The Chuppies Are Here"), develop a market entry plan for a hypothetical wine label from Spain that is looking to enter the Chinese market.

2. Consumers in some countries, like Japan, are reluctant to accept "foreign" retailing institutions and imported products. Explain this behavior by using the models of culture contained in this chapter.

3. Do you agree with the statement "People do not buy products, they buy relationships"? Why or why not?

EXPERIENTIAL EXERCISES

1. Using the Hofstede framework, compare your home country with France. How would the framework help you to understand consumer behavior for culturally bound products like furniture?

2. Compare the Hofstede clusters of countries with those of the GLOBE model. Which clusters have a common group of countries? Which do not? How do you account for the fact that some of the clusters of both frameworks do not overlap?

KEY TERMS

CASE 3-1

Starbucks: Forbidden in the Forbidden City

Beijing's Forbidden City is China's top tourist attraction, holds UNESCO World Heritage site status, and hosts between six and eight million visitors each year. Covering 720,000 square meters, the Forbidden City consists of several buildings and over 10,000 rooms. Built in 1420, the Forbidden City served as the residence of 24 of China's Ming and Qing emperors until the end of imperial rule in 1911. It is a destination of choice for both Chinese and foreign visitors.

Coffee in China

With its strong tradition of tea drinking, many question the sustainability of the coffee market in China. Tea has a long history in China, is cheaper than coffee, and is believed to have health benefits that coffee does not possess. Coffee festivals were organized in both Shanghai and Beijing in 2001 by the International Coffee Organisation to familiarize Chinese consumers with coffee consumption and culture; still, for many Chinese, tea is considered a staple and coffee a fad.

As evidence of the potential of the coffee market in China, domestic and international companies are selling high-priced reports on demand forecasts, trends, and developments in the Chinese coffee market. Chinese consumers are typically more familiar with instant coffee, since it was introduced to the market before fresh brewed coffee.

Generally there are three groups of coffee consumers in China: young, affluent professionals; returnees (those who have studied or worked abroad, become coffee drinkers, and intend to continue to drink coffee on return); and foreign expatriates. Not surprisingly, coffee is consumed more frequently in large urban centers by those who are more familiar with Western tastes and lifestyles.

Starbucks

Starbucks, a Seattle coffee company started in 1971, is recognized worldwide as a highly successful North American company. The company was built on three tenets: hospitality, production, and education. The company went public in 1992 and opened its first international store in Tokyo, Japan, in 1996. In addition to the more than 11,000 locations operating in the United States, by 2008 Starbucks had over 4,500 stores located in 48 countries outside the United States. Stores are either company-operated, joint ventures, or licensed. President and CEO Howard Schultz's vision for the company was that it would occupy a "third place" in consumers' minds, after home and work.

Having saturated the North American market, Starbucks continues to look farther afield for potential markets. In its 2008 annual report, Starbucks highlights an international focus in its mission by stating: "Every store is part of a community, and we take our responsibility to be good neighbors seriously. We want to be invited in wherever we do business. We can be a force for positive action—bringing together our partners, customers, and the community to contribute every day. Now we see that our

Case prepared by William X Wei and Kimberley Howard, both of Grant MacEwan University. Reprinted with permission.

responsibility—and our potential for good—is even larger. The world is looking to Starbucks to set the new standard, yet again. We will lead."

In 2008, international activities accounted for 20 percent of Starbucks revenue. Starbucks is not naïve regarding the difficulty in entering and sustaining international markets. Some of the risks to their success internationally were listed in its 2008 annual report, including the global economic crisis, Starbucks' increasing dependence on the success of its international operations for growth, and the success of other international segments being determined by the financial performance of their three largest international markets—Canada, Japan, and Britain.

Starbucks' Experience in China

Starbucks launched a Taiwanese store in 1998 and registered both the name "Starbucks" as well as a Chinese version of its name, "Xingbake." Xingbake is a literal and phonetic rendering of the Starbucks name; "xing" means "star," and the Chinese phonetic pronunciation of "bake" is similar to "bucks." In 1999, a coffee shop called the Shanghai Xingbake Coffee Shop Ltd. opened. Its logo was similar to Starbucks—a circle with white words on a green background; however, instead of a picture of a mermaid in the center, there was a picture of a cup of coffee.

After unsuccessful attempts to settle out of court, Starbucks sued Xingbake, and in December 2006, a landmark decision by the Shanghai Municipal Higher People's Court ruled in favour of Starbucks. Shanghai Xingbake was ordered to stop using the name Xingbake, apologize publicly to Starbucks, and pay 500,000 yuan (U.S.$62,500) to Starbucks. The case was considered by many multinationals operating in China as a breakthrough in deterring trademark infringement.

Believing that Chinese consumers want a Western experience when they patronize Starbucks, there were only minor changes made to the products served and sizes offered in China. The décor of Starbucks' Chinese locations is typically a mix of Eastern and Western styles. Starbucks often include a fireplace, a foreign concept in Chinese homes, but also incorporates many familiar components such as bamboo and Chinese symbols, designs, and artifacts.

Starbucks is generally viewed as an exotic, Western-style place for young Chinese professionals and provides a place to meet, talk, see, and be seen. Many see it as a bridge between East and West. Starbucks provides an experience as well as a product, and for many patrons it's the atmosphere as much as the coffee that attracts. The environment and the fresh-brewed coffee process is interesting and exciting for these young Chinese.

Opportunities exist to better educate potential consumers. Unfamiliar with the coffee drinking culture, some Chinese report not knowing what to do or how to act in a Starbucks. One customer said, "The first time I come to Starbucks, I don't know what this [sugar, stirrers, milk] was for, I want to use this but I don't know if this [is] simple for me to use…I like to come to Starbucks, I like the environment and atmosphere, but I don't like the coffee very much here because I think this is a cultural [sic], you need to try to explain this culture to me more in detail, but they don't do this."

At the invitation of Beijing administrators, Starbucks opened a store in the Forbidden City in 2000, near the Hall of Preserving Harmony. City officials envisioned the opening of Starbucks as contributing to municipal funds. Some of the initial media coverage questioned whether Starbucks belonged in the Forbidden City, but eventually the discussion subsided. Occasionally the debate would reoccur, and in response, Starbucks removed its sign in 2005 but continued to operate.

In January 2007, the debate heated up when Chenggang Rui, a popular CCTV anchor, argued on his blog that Starbucks' presence in the Forbidden City was "not globalizing but trampling over Chinese culture." He went on to say, "The Forbidden City is a symbol of China's cultural heritage. Starbucks is a symbol of lower middle class culture in the West. We need to embrace the world, but we also need to preserve our cultural identity. There is a fine line between globalization and contamination." These statements triggered an online campaign for the removal of Starbucks from the Forbidden City, which collected more than 500,000 signatures supporting the closure of Starbucks.

When Jim Donald, Starbucks president and CEO at the time, received a letter from Chenggang Rui reiterating his belief that Starbucks should leave the Forbidden City, Donald responded, "When Starbucks was invited by museum officials to open a store six years ago, we did so with great sensitivity to, and respect for, the historic and cultural heritage of the Forbidden City. We have shown and continue to show our respect for local history, culture, and social customs, and have made serious efforts to fit within the environment of the Forbidden City."

In response to the protests, Starbucks executives worked with the administration of the Forbidden City to come up with a solution acceptable to both parties. One of the proposed options included continuing to operate in the Forbidden City, only without the Starbucks name. In the end, Starbucks' VP for Greater China stated: "We decided that it is not our custom worldwide to have stores that have any other name, so therefore we decided the choice would be to leave." Starbucks' Forbidden City location closed in July 2007. Starbucks' officials described the decision as "very congenial." A traditional Chinese café has since replaced Starbucks.

Starbucks closure may have sparked a trend of diminishing the commercial presence in the Forbidden City. Since the Starbucks closed, the number of shops in the Forbidden City has been cut in half.

As of September 2008, Starbucks has 448 company-operated and licensed stores in China.

CASE 3-2

Hong Kong Disneyland: Chinese Tourists' Behavior and Disneyland's Internationalization Strategy

Mainland China has been making unprecedented economic growth in the previous three decades, and one of the major contributors is its tourism industry. The mainland Chinese tourists are a major force in world tourism. Considering its proximity to mainland China, the Hong Kong Special Administrative Region (HKSAR) has all the benefits to gain from the increasing demand by mainland Chinese for traveling abroad and for shopping. To enhance Hong Kong as a first choice for mainland Chinese tourists, the Hong Kong government successfully sealed a joint venture with Walt Disney Company for the establishment of a Hong Kong Disneyland Park. However, the Hong Kong government also gave Ocean Park, its local theme park, all the needed support to rejuvenate itself in the wake of impending competition from Disneyland, and to give a boost to attract more tourists to Hong Kong.

Hong Kong Disneyland Park, owned and managed by Hong Kong International Theme Parks, is an incorporated company jointly owned by The Walt Disney Company and the Hong Kong Government. Located on reclaimed land in Penny's Bay, Lantau Island, it opened for visitors on September 12, 2005, after protracted negotiations and construction hassles. The Walt Disney Company dealt with a lot of cultural backlash and therefore had to incorporate Chinese culture, customs, and traditions into the design and construction of the resort, including following the principles of Feng Shui. The park was designed to handle 34,000 visitors per day. The park attracted 5.2 million visitors in its first year of opening, compared to its expectations of 5.6 million. In the second year, the visitors fell by 20 percent to four million, and in the third year increased by 8 percent to 4.5 million visitors. Since the opening of Hong Kong Disneyland in 2005, the theme park has attracted 15 million guests.

Hong Kong Disneyland Park's competitor, Ocean Park, was Hong Kong's only homegrown theme park, which opened in 1977. It was Asia's largest marine-based theme park and claims to be the only Asian park accredited by the American Zoo and Aquarium Association. It features a giant panda exhibit, a butterfly garden, a shark tank, and a three-story aquarium, as well as numerous rides. It has an area of 870,000 square meters and currently has over 40 rides and attractions. With the opening of Hong Kong Disneyland Park, Ocean Park expected a 25 percent decrease in visitors.

Disney Theme Parks and Resorts

The Walt Disney Company is a brainchild of Mr. Walt Disney, after whose name the theme park and its related entertainment businesses were named. The first Disneyland in Anaheim, California, opened its doors for the first time in 1955. Since then the company has become an icon of children's entertainment and more. Sixteen years after opening the first Disneyland theme park in Anaheim, the Walt Disney Company opened its second theme park in Florida in 1971. Its first foray into foreign land was

This case was written by Joseph Sy Changco,University of Macau, and Ramendra Singh, Indian Institute of Management Calcutta, and is an abridged version of the Hong Kong Disneyland case. Reprinted with permission.

with the development of Tokyo Disneyland in 1983. Tokyo Disneyland turned out to be a huge success with mostly Japanese visitors. In fact, it is one of the world's most popular theme parks. However, because of the licensing agreement, the royalties stipulated in the agreement limited the Walt Disney Company's earnings. In Europe, Euro Disney opened in 1992, and was the second Disney theme park built outside the United States It performed very badly due to a combination of factors, including cultural disparity between the United States and Europe; high interest rates; low tourist spending as a result of the European recession; and a strong franc currency. In late 1994, it required a huge restructuring effort to get Euro Disney back on track. Its lenders agreed to suspend interest payments on debts for 24 months and to delay payment of principal for three years. From 1992 to 1998, the Walt Disney Company agreed to forgo management fees and sold its equity to raise funds. Its recovery was also backed by a U.S.$500 million investment from a Saudi Arabian prince. A last ditch effort was made to attract more European visitors by renaming the park as Disneyland Paris, which connotes magic and romance.

Hong Kong Disneyland

The sheer size and continued strong economic performance of the Mainland China market lured the Walt Disney Company. Other locations vying for a Disney park were Shanghai, Zhuhai, and Singapore. Shanghai was a very interesting option for Disney since it was one of the most progressive and strategically located cities in China. However, its inferior infrastructure, lack of a Western legal system, lack of easily convertible currency, and less accessibility to the rest of Asia, among other reasons, made it less attractive than Hong Kong. Zhuhai fared poorly compared with both Hong Kong and Shanghai considering its less-developed infrastructure and lower GDP. Although Singapore has the basic conditions to make it a feasible location for the third Disney outside the United States, its location did not help it achieve the Walt Disney Company's ultimate goal of clinching a foothold on the China market (Chan and Wang, 2000). Negotiations with the Hong Kong government ended up with a joint venture agreement between the Hong Kong government and The Walt Disney Company in a 57 percent to 43 percent equity structure (Hong Kong Government, 1999). Hong Kong Disneyland was supposed to serve as springboard for The Walt Disney Company's future operations in Mainland China. The Hong Kong government, on the other hand, saw it as a means of revitalizing its sagging tourism industry and of signaling to the international business community that Hong Kong is still the place to be.

In addition to its financial woes, Hong Kong Disneyland was also beset with an unhappy workforce clamoring for equal treatment to their counterparts abroad. This is in stark contrast to the success that Ocean Park experienced in the process of its reinvention. Ocean Park aspired to be the world leader in providing excellent guest experiences in a theme park environment connecting people with nature. Ocean Park's mission to connect people with nature through conversation, entertainment, and education is what truly differentiates them within the market. It believes that its cutting edge is this "edutainment" experience, which enables visitors to get up close and understand how animals behave in the wild. As a bridge to the natural world, the park awakens respect for the beauty of animal and marine life and, in the process, also an awareness of the importance of conservation. As a result of the commitment to this ethos, Ocean Park's popularity grew ever stronger. Essentially a homegrown park with a local heart, Ocean Park has reached global markets through innovative products that ignite and inspire its guests' imaginations. Its recent ranking in 2006 by Forbes.com as one of the world's 10 most popular theme parks was a proud moment for both

Ocean Park and Hong Kong, reinforcing the quality of Ocean Park and its ability to compete at the global level while remaining relevant to the local needs. Most people may view Hong Kong Disneyland as the only competitor to Ocean Park. However, the latter sees theme parks all over the world—particularly marine parks—as competition.

Factors Leading to Hong Kong Disneyland's Woes

Cultural Adaptation

Although Hong Kong Disneyland tried its best to understand the culture of its market, the company failed to culturally adapt the theme park in prelaunch stages. The Mainland Chinese market was very unfamiliar with the Disney characters. Those in their middle age did not grow up watching American television shows or movies. The younger generation, who were born after China's opening in 1978, were brought up with Japanese cartoons rather than American heroes. Japanese pop culture exerted a lot of influence on the younger generation. In short, Mickey Mouse and Donald Duck were foreign products to the Chinese market. Thus, when the Mainland Chinese tourists visited Hong Kong Disneyland, they did not easily connect with the characters in the park. They were unfamiliar with the product. Even though Hong Kong Disneyland tried to address this by introducing the Disney characters even before it officially opened, and even introduced a short program at the entrance of the park to introduce the Disney stories to those unfamiliar with them, these efforts seemed insufficient to attract the Mainland Chinese to the park. Hong Kong Disneyland perhaps assumed, given its global brand and despite lessons in Paris, that unlike Western tourists—for whom vacations are very experiential—the Chinese enjoy focusing on what they can buy, eat, and bring home. Furthermore, taking pictures and bringing them back home to show friends and relatives of their trip abroad seem to be more important to Chinese tourists than the experience of being in the place itself. For example, when Chinese go to the beach, many of them do not actually swim in the water. Being there and seeing the place would be enough. Actually swimming in the sea and sunbathing are not necessary. In fact, many Chinese avoid the sun since they want to keep their skin fair. For them there is a saying: "The whiteness of your face can cover its ugliness."

Chinese Tourist Behavior

For Western tourists, going abroad for vacation is a good time to relax and experience the foreign culture. However, for the tourists from Mainland China, going to Hong Kong means a shopping experience, and so they choose the cheaper alternative to Hong Kong Disneyland, which is Ocean Park. In fact, for many local tourists, Ocean Park provides a perceived better experience at a lower price. Thus Hong Kong Disneyland might have anticipated this local demand by reducing entry costs or going for innovative pricing so as to increase the foothold in the theme park first and to generate revenue subsequently. Hong Kong Disneyland could not successfully handle the pressures of local demand in terms of the need to travel for shopping and the price-sensitive nature of Chinese shoppers and tourists. In apparent management hubris, Hong Kong Disneyland believed that Chinese tourists would love the Disney brand (case writers' assessment) because of its global appeal, without realizing that they were culturally more closely connected with Ocean Park and its theme.

In general, the Chinese people also put a premium on education, and look at it as a means of social mobility to provide them with financial security. Thus a typical Chinese family would make sure that their children will go to the best universities in the country and even abroad. The educational slant provided by Ocean Park would seem to have a stronger pulling power than the fantasy experience Hong Kong Disneyland provides. Hong Kong Disneyland again failed to look at or overlooked this local cultural nuance.

Relationship with Travel Agents

Unlike Western tourists, the Mainland Chinese tourists depend a lot on travel agents for their trips abroad. The travel agents are gatekeepers of information and they exert great influence on the decisions made by mainland tourists. Hong Kong Disneyland failed to spot this practice and did not heed too much attention to building a relationship with the travel agents. Meanwhile Ocean Park, being a pioneer in the region, gave a lot of concessions to the travel agents, who then promoted visits to Ocean Park over Hong Kong Disneyland.

Some Afterthoughts

In hindsight, The Walt Disney Company's decision to develop its third Disneyland park outside the United States seems to have been a big lesson for the company. As The Walt Disney Company's intention was to gauge the Mainland Chinese market through its operation in Hong Kong, it may find its experience a record of its success, though it may be an apparent failure. This experience has taught Walt Disney to carefully watch its step when the time comes for it to enter Mainland China. The success of Ocean Park affirms the importance of a visionary leadership in an organization, exemplified in the case of Ocean Park by its tandem of entrepreneurial talent in Mr. Zeman and technical expertise in Mr. Mehrmann.

On the other hand, Hong Kong Disneyland failed despite its global competitive advantages because it failed to meet the pressures of local demands. Multinational corporations or MNCs with strong corporate controls and powerful global brands often fail to adapt to local markets, either because they are worried that brands would be diluted locally through adaptation, or because of a simpler case of oversight in understanding or implementing consumer insights. This also resulted in several instances of negative publicity.

Discussion Questions

1. What led to the eventual woes experienced by Hong Kong Disneyland in its first year of operation? How should Hong Kong Disneyland rectify its market situation?
2. To what extent could Hong Kong Disneyland adapt its product to Chinese consumers without diluting its image?
3. How should Hong Kong Disneyland address competition?

Sources

Anonymous. (2003). Ocean Park. *Hong Kong Chamber of Commerce*, Member's Profile, Ocean Park.

Chan, S. H. and Wang, K. (2000). Hong Kong Disneyland (A): The Walt Disney perspective. *Asia Case Research Center*, University of Hong Kong.

Crawford, B. (2006, July 31). Mr. Enthusiasm. *South China Morning Post*.

Doz, Y. (1976). *National policies and multinational management*. Unpublished doctoral dissertation. Boston: Harvard Business School.

Emmons, N. (2002). Hong Kong Disneyland on time, on budget. *Amusement Business, 114*(13), 6.

Fan, M. (2006). Disney culture shock. *Washington Post*. Retrieved from www.thestandard.com.hk/news_detail.asp?pp_cat=20&art_id=32372&sid=10991562&con_type=1&d_str=20061122&sear_year=2006.

Hong Kong Disneyland (Accessed from http://en.wikipedia.org/wiki/Hong_Kong_Disneyland) (accessed on July 9, 2009).

Hong Kong Government. (1999). Background information on Hong Kong Disneyland. Press release.

Hong Kong Institute of Marketing. (2004). Lan Kwai Fong—Over two decades of success. Retrieved from www.hkim.org.hk/event_20041211.html and http://www.chamber.org.hk/info/member_a_week/member_profile.asp?id+32&P=3&KW=&search_p (accessed 24 March 2009).

Lau, J. (21 March 2005). HK theme park plans revamp to compete with Disneyland. *Financial Times*, p. 6.

Leung, W. (2005). Wong under fire as Disney escapes action in FEHD case. *The Standard*. Retrieved from www.thestandard.com.hk/news_detail.asp?pp_cat=11&art_id=25410&sid=5401592&con_type=1&d_str=20051110&sear_year=2005.

Liu, E., & Wong, E. (1999, November 10). Information note—Disneyland Paris: Some basic facts. *Legislative Council Secretariat*.

Miller, P. M. (2007, January/February). Disneyland in Hong Kong. *The China Business Review, 34*(1), 31–33.

Murphy, J. (2006, May 19). Morale Crisis Shakes HK's House of Mouse. *Media*, 1.

Ocean Park Corporation. (2003). Annual report.

Pierson, D. (2007, June 30). Hong Kong theme park outsmarts the mouse. *Los Angeles Times*.

Prahalad, C. K. (1975). *The strategic process in a multinational corporation*. Unpublished doctoral dissertation, Harvard Business School. _____, & Doz, Y.L. (1987). The multinational mission: Balancing local demands and global vision. New York: The Free Press.

Reckard E. (19 December 1999). Disney discovering it's a small world after all. *Los Angeles Times*.

Reuters. (9 September 2006). Disneyland struggles to make magic in Hong Kong.

Roberts, G. (27 February 2004). HK park gears for battle with Disney. *Media*, 8.

Roth, K., & Morrison, A. J. (1990). Empirical analysis of the integration-responsiveness framework in global industries. *Journal of International Business Studies, 21*(4), 541–564.

Whaley, F. (2001, May). Move over Mickey. *Asian Business, 37*(5), 28.

Yim, B. (2007). Ocean Park: In the face of competition from Hong Kong Disneyland. *Poon Kam Kai Series*. Asia Case Research Center, Hong Kong University.

Yim, C. K. (2004). Hong Kong Disneyland: Where is the magic. *Poon Kam Kai Series*. Asia Case Research Center, University of Hong Kong.

Analyzing Political and Legal Environments

Let every individual and institution . . . think and act as a responsible trustee of Earth, seeking choices in ecology, economics and ethics that will provide a sustainable future, eliminate pollution, poverty and violence, awaken the wonder of life and foster peaceful progress in the human adventure.

JOHN MCCONNELL, FOUNDER OF INTERNATIONAL EARTH DAY

LEARNING OBJECTIVES

After reading this chapter, you should be able to:

- Understand some of the legal barriers to using a global, standardized marketing mix.
- Identify legal issues of international marketing.
- Relate how the use of the Internet for the international sale of goods raises legal problems.
- Discuss how intellectual property disputes can be resolved.
- Understand the forms of political risk and how political risk can be managed.
- Discuss the efforts of the WTO to liberalize trade.

LEGAL/GLOBAL POLITICAL SYSTEMS

Global trade and marketing are subject to laws, rules, and regulations formulated by diverse legal systems. As shown in Figure 4-1, there are five different legal systems in the world. No one system dominates the world's legal landscape, but common, civil, and Muslim law are dominant. Only about 30 percent of the world's gross domestic product is generated in countries governed by civil and common law systems. **Civil law** systems are based mainly on Roman law heritage and are found in Europe, Asia, and Central and South America. They consist of a comprehensive system of rules or legislation, usually codified, that are applied and interpreted by judges. **Common law**, adopted in North America, is based on English custom, where court adjudications are the primary source of law, although governments pass statutes and legislation that are only seen as incursions into the common law and thus interpreted narrowly. Each case that raises new issues is considered on its own merits, and then becomes a precedent for future decisions on that same issue. Exceptions include the state of Louisiana in the United States, whose legal system is based on the *Napoleonic Code*, and Quebec, which adheres to civil law.

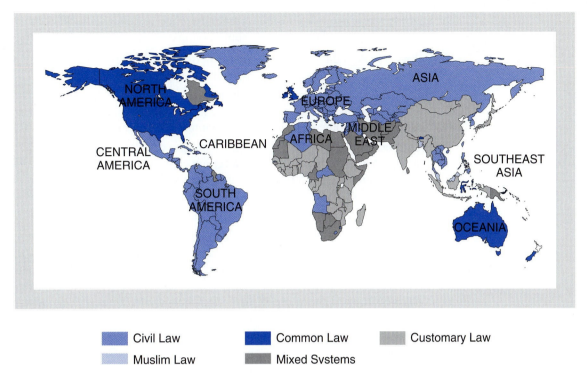

Figure 4-1 World Legal Systems

Source: Adapted from: JuriGlobe World Legal Systems Research Group, University of Ottawa. Accessed 6 June 2011.

Both the common and civil law systems are fundamentally different with regard to concepts and legal method. However, common law countries such as the United States also have civil law and learn how to work with statutes. Also, Scots law is civil-based, such that UK attorneys are often exposed to a more European environment. However, today there are sufficient legal advisors who are versed in both systems.

Muslim Law

One of the problems in dealing with Islamic law in the realm of international business is that Islamic law has many inconsistencies that make predictability in business matters a major concern. Additionally, the inconsistencies often vary between different sects of Islam, such as between Sunnis and Shi'ites, for example. Indeed, the lack of uniformity and consistency can be confusing and disconcerting. *Sharia*, which is Islamic law, proceeds by way of example rather than principle. While this does present issues to international business dealings, each of the Islamic states in the Gulf region currently has a set of codified corporate laws.

LEGAL ISSUES FOR GLOBAL MARKETING

Global marketers should be familiar with certain aspects of the legal systems in which they operate. Specifically, sales agent, distributorship agreements, and other forms of doing business abroad, customs and international trade regulation, export incentives and controls, arbitration, intellectual property rights, and international technology transfer should be consulted. Consider some examples:

- Buyers in Peru didn't pay for a shipment of bearings from a small supplier in Houston, Texas. What is the recourse for the supplier?
- Consumers in France ordered books from a supplier in another country who falsely advertised the goods on the Internet. Where can the buyers file their complaint, at home or in the seller's country (if identifiable)?
- Your branded products (for example, Samsung cellular phones) are sold through authorized distributors in a certain country. You receive a call from one of your dealers informing you that these same products are being imported and distributed by an unauthorized distributor. What can you do about it?
- Is your product politically vulnerable in the target market?

As the global marketing manager for your company, you and your legal advisors must be able to answer these questions. In the first case above, breach of contract violations may be adjudicated under the United Nations Convention on Contracts for the International Sale of Goods (1980), to which both the United States and Peruvian governments are signatories. In the case of cross-border consumer fraud, the redress is dependent upon cross-border agreement and cooperation. The growing use of the Internet has led to fraud on a large scale across national borders. Fraudulent companies often set up shop in one country to target consumers in another. Most likely, consumers should turn to the country in which the fraud was committed. However, the ease of doing so is dependent upon whether the country in question has the evidence (the alleged fraud was committed in another country) necessary to prosecute and is willing to do so in the first place.

A sale of products through unauthorized distributors is a practice that is called **parallel importing** or gray market distribution. It occurs when identical products are sold without authorization from the owner of the brand and trademark, usually the manufacturer. In some countries parallel importing is illegal, in others it is legal.

The sale of politically vulnerable products should be avoided. Cigarettes and alcohol are examples. However, even food products may be vulnerable to political influence. Countries whose populations suffer from "over nutrition," i.e., who have significant numbers of overweight people, may ban products that contain high amounts of trans fats. Some defense-related products may be designated as crucial to the economy and their exportation limited or prevented altogether. The exportation of computers and peripheral equipment to Communist countries was banned by the United States and some Western countries who were members of NATO (the North Atlantic Treaty Organization). Military aircraft produced today by several countries, including the United States and France, are not exported with the latest electronic technology in use. It is wise to determine the political status of products before introducing them into foreign markets. This determination is part of political risk analysis. Additional legal issues include patents, trademarks and intellectual property protection, marketing mix regulations, consumer protection employment practices, and environmental regulations.

INTELLECTUAL PROPERTY ISSUES: TRADEMARKS, PATENTS, AND COPYRIGHTS

Trademarks and patents, like all **intellectual property,** are based on the principle of territoriality. Each state or country determines for its own territory what is to be protected, who should benefit from such protection and for how long, and how the protection should be enforced.

BOX 4-1   COUNTRY IN FOCUS: CHINA

China has a first-to-file trademark system that requires no evidence of prior use or ownership, leaving registration of popular foreign trademarks open to anyone, including some well-known global brands such as Sony-Ericsson and even the coat of arms of Britain's royal family! The above means that a company planning to establish a franchise in China must take immediate action to register its trademark, domain names, and brands. If patents are involved they should be registered also. Failure to do so can have devastating consequences and may result in a lengthy court battle. Another option would be to buy back the trademark from its owner.

Companies, particularly those that sell goods or services direct to the public, regard their trademarks (whether brand names or pictorial symbols) as being among their most valuable assets. Trademarks protect words, names, symbols, sounds, or colors that distinguish goods (™) and services (SM); in other words, a brand name or an advertisement.[1] Trademarks, unlike patents, can be renewed forever as long as they are being used. The rights to a trademark are gained by registration in most countries ("first to file") or by their use ("first to use"), depending on country legislation. While globalization implies global recognition of trademarks, this is not necessarily the case. International trademark disputes may arise from a number of causes. For example, the same term regarded as distinctive in one country may not be in another because of different consumer perceptions of a brand. Another cause of disputes is the mistaken belief that a trademark covers similar products or services. For example, a Lenovo computer trademark may not cover Lenovo "sunglasses" in some countries, assuming the manufacturer extends its product line from its main line, for example, computers to dissimilar categories as in the sunglasses example.

Changing international relations between states may present legal problems relating to intellectual property. Take the case of Cuba. Normalizing relations between the two countries, if and when it occurs, may open a Pandora's Box of legal problems.

The General Cigar Co., Inc., of Richmond, Va., has sold Cohiba brand cigars in the United States since the 1990s. Cohibais is also Cuba's premier brand and was reportedly a favorite of Fidel Castro before he stopped smoking in the mid-1980s. But Habanos S.A., the state-owned tobacco company, never registered Cohiba as the trademark in the United States. Even so, when General Cigar marketed its own Cohiba brand in 1997, Habanos sued. After a nine-year court battle, the United States Supreme Court ruled in 2006 that the United States trade embargo against Cuba barred such a trademark challenge.

Trademark Protection

A global arrangement for trademark protection is exemplified by the Madrid agreement administered by the International Bureau of the World Intellectual Property Organization (WIPO) in Geneva, Switzerland. Registration of a trademark under the agreement provides for the legal equivalent of registration in member countries designated by the mark owner and affords the owner protection in all member countries for a 10-year period. Moreover, registration in one language is sufficient for all countries.[2]

---

1. The familiar symbol ® designating a trademark can only be used in the United States following registration.

2. However, some legal experts suggest registration in the local language as well, e.g., China, Muslim countries.

BOX 4-2   COMPANY IN FOCUS: MCDONALD'S

An Indian restaurant in Malaysia used the name "McCurry." McDonald's claimed its trademark was infringed and sued the restaurant, in spite of the fact that the only thing common to both trademarks is the prefix "Mc." Nevertheless, McDonald's believes that the prefix is its intellectual property. A precedent occurred in Malaysia when McDonald's won a court case against two restaurants that called themselves "McBagel's" and "McDhama's." However, in this case, the court ruled in favor of the local restaurant, enabling it to continue using the name "McCurry." Craig Fochler a, trademark lawyer, reflecting on this ruling, said "When you get a [trade] mark like McDonald's or Coca-Cola or 7-Eleven, it's a constant policing effort."

In Australia, the situation was different. There the court held that the prefixes "Mac" and "Mc" are the intellectual property of McDonald's. A small business in Tasmania used the "McBaby" brand for its children's clothing line. The court ruled that "McBaby" was too close to the trademark "McKids" sold in Walmart stores under license by McDonald's.

Sources: Adapted from: DKD Trade. (7 May 2009). Trademark battle lost by McDonald's. *Trademark News*; Eviatar, D. (2005). It takes a global village to protect McDonald's trademark. *IP Law & Business*.

Despite the advantages of registration through the agreement, the United States and several other major countries (e.g., Australia, Denmark, Finland, Greece, Iceland, Ireland, Japan, the Netherlands, Republic of Korea, Sweden, and the UK) are signatories only to the Protocol. This means that international registrations based on application for trademark registration, say, in the United States, would be limited to protection only in those countries that are members of the Protocol.[3]

Regional recognition of trademarks is exemplified by the Community Trademark Registration, which affords unitary rights to their mark in all EU countries. Trademark protection is available throughout the EU by using the mark in only one EU country.

PATENTS

A patent is a form of protection that provides a person or legal entity with exclusive rights for making, using, or selling a concept or invention, and excludes others from doing the same for its duration. There are a number of international patent agreements, including the Patent Cooperation Treaty (PCT), the Eurasian Patent Office (EAPO) and the African Regional Industrial Property Organization.

The PCT is administered by the World Intellectual Property Organization. It addresses procedural requirements for obtaining a patent and aims to simplify filing, searching, and publication of international patent applications. The Patent Cooperation Treaty provides the possibility to seek patent rights in a large number of countries by filing a single international application with a single patent office. All EU countries are members of the treaty, but there is no EU-wide patent available. Generally, applicants first apply in their home country before applying elsewhere. The European Patent Convention (EPC) allows the filing of a single European patent application in one of three languages (English, French, and German); it is possible to obtain patents in all EPC countries. However, as it is in the case of trademarks, the decision to grant or reject a patent rests with each country's authority. As of 2009, there were 36 member countries of the European Patent Organization, with several more pending for admittance. Patents can be maintained for a maximum period of 20 years.

3. For a list of members of the Agreement and Protocol, see www.wipo.int.

TABLE 4-1 Patent Grants by Country (2008)				
Country		**Number of Patents**	**Patents per Million People**	
U.S.	1	92,000	289	3
Japan	2	36,679	994	1
Germany	3	10,086	235	4
South Korea	4	8,731	779	2
Taiwan	5	7,779	–	
UK	6	3,843	82	8
France	7	3,813	205	5
Canada	8	4,125	31	11
Italy	9	1,916	13	12
China	10	1,874	1	13
Netherlands	11	1,724	189	6
Australia	12	1,614	75	9
Israel	13	1,312	74	10
Finland	14	908	187	7
India	15	672	1	13

Source: United States Patent & Trademark Office; WIPO (World Intellectual Property Organization). (2009). Intellectual Property Statistics. Publication A. Geneva.

The Eurasian Patent Organization (EAPO) members include Armenia, Azerbaijan, Belarus, Kazakhstan, Kyrgyzstan, Moldova, the Russian Federation, Tajikistan, and Turkmenistan. Under the Eurasian Convention, a single patent application designating all of the member countries is filed in a single language (Russian) in a central patent office in Moscow. Administration of that application is similar to that of the European Patent Office. Maximum duration of a patent is 20 years.

Of all countries, the United States grants the most patents (Table 4-1), followed by Japan and Germany. There are a number of factors that account for the number of patent filings in a given country. Some of these are the amount of money invested in R&D and education. Other indices measure the relative success of a country in producing patent applications. One such index is the number of patents per million people, which takes the size of country into consideration. Using this index, the United States was in third place after Japan and South Korea. In contrast, the Netherlands was ranked eleventh in number of patents but sixth per million people, while Finland ranked fourteenth in number of patents but seventh per million people.

Most patent filings in the United States, Japan, and Europe are for high technology applications. The United States Patent Office had the highest share of patent applications in the high technology fields, with 39 percent of all applications occurring in this area. Of this number, 55 percent were from domestic applicants (Figure 4-2). At the Japanese Patent Office, the share of high technology applications decreased to 22 percent in 2007, and 86 percent of such applications were from domestic applicants. At the European Patent Office, the share of high technology applications remained stable at 23 percent, with 37 percent coming from 39 member states and three applicants (Albania, Bosnia and Herzegovina, and Serbia).

In Africa, there are two intellectual property organizations, the African Regional Intellectual Property Organization (ARIPO), whose members are mainly English speaking, and the African Intellectual Property Organization, for French-speaking nations. Each organization has 16 members. In ARIPO, membership is open to members of the United Nations Economic Commission for Africa or the African Union (AU).

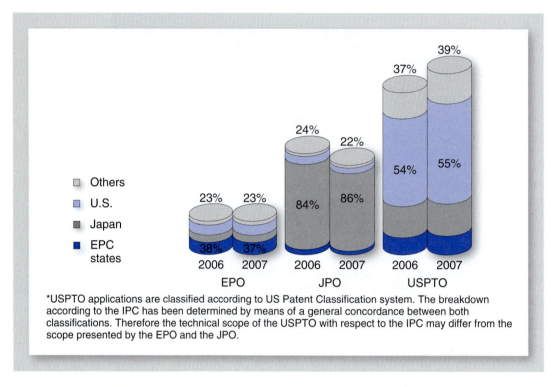

Figure 4-2 Proportion and Origin of High Tech Applications

Sources: United States Patent & Trademark Office; WIPO (World Intellectual Property Organization). (2009). Intellectual Property Statistics. Publication A. Geneva.

Both organizations centralize the registration of applications for patents and trademarks for all member countries, which are then submitted to member states for consideration.

COPYRIGHTS

A copyright is a law that gives ownership to "original works of authorship," such as literary works, paintings, music, video games, and drama. In the United States, the Library of Congress registers copyrights for the life of the author plus 70 years, as is the case in the EU. Copyrights extend to other countries as long as the country in question is covered by an international copyright treaty, convention, or organization. In Canada, copyrights extend 50 years after the life of the author. One of the most contentious issues is the question of databases, digital recordings, and websites. The TRIPS agreement ensures that computer programs will be protected as literary works under the Berne Convention and outlines how databases should be protected.[4] The agreement also states that performers must also have the right to prevent unauthorized recording, reproduction, and broadcast of live performances (bootlegging) for no less than 50 years. Producers of sound recordings must have the right to prevent the unauthorized reproduction of recordings for a period of 50 years.

4. The TRIPS Agreement is annex 1C of the Marrakech Agreement Establishing the World Trade Organization, signed in Marrakech, Morocco, on 15 April 1994.

BOX 4-3   TECHNOLOGY IN FOCUS: TRADE SECRETS

Many technology companies rely on trade secret law to protect their intellectual property. A trade secret is any confidential business information that provides an enterprise with a competitive edge. Companies may require nondisclosure agreements from employees or business associates who may have access to trade secrets. An example occurs when an employee leaves a company in the midst of a major software development for a company working on a similar process. In this case, the first company can ask for an injunction preventing the use of its trade secret. Nevertheless, the law does not protect against legitimate reverse engineering efforts.

TRADE SECRETS

Trade secrets are information that companies keep secret to give them an advantage over their competitors; however, they are not protected by intellectual property law in the same way that trademarks or patents are. Protection for trade secrets is done by using nondisclosure agreements to ensure that the information will be kept confidential. For example, a firm demands that its employees sign such an agreement not to disclose designs, instruments, or whatever is classified as a trade secret. The lack of formal protection, however, means that a third party is not prevented from independently duplicating and using the secret information once it is revealed.

Trade Regulations

From 1947 to 1994, the **General Agreement on Tariffs and Trade (GATT)** was the main international organization that codified rules for trade liberalization. It put order into a world trading system that had broken down during World War II. Its major goal was to work toward agreement to lower tariff restrictions. During the tenure of the organization, about half of all world trade was covered by subsequent agreements. One of the major problems of the GATT agreement was that services were not included even though they had become a significant component of overall world trade. Another problem was an increasing protectionist policy among many nations in order to subsidize their agricultural exports. These and other problems led to a decrease in the effectiveness of the GATT and to the formation of a new organization called the World Trade Organization. In 1995 the GATT was replaced by the World Trade Organization, which functions to this day.

In its formative years (1947–1973) the WTO concentrated on reducing tariffs through multilateral negotiations in so-called trade rounds (see Table 4-2). The Tokyo Round, held intermittently during 1973–1979 with 102 countries involved in the negotiations, was the first major attempt to deal with trade barriers other than tariffs. However, the Tokyo Round met with mixed success because few industrialized nations could agree to the many of the proposals. The eighth, the Uruguay Round of 1986–1994, was the last and most extensive of all. It led to the WTO and a new set of agreements including services, agriculture, and intellectual property, resulting in an average one-third reduction in customs duties in the world's nine major industrial markets, bringing the average tariff on industrial products down to 4.7 percent. Another round took place in Doha, Qatar, in 2001, and negotiations have continued in Cancun (2003), Geneva (2004), Hong Kong (2005), Geneva (2006), Potsdam (2007),

TABLE 4-2 GATT Trade Rounds			
Year	**Place/name**	**Subjects covered**	**Countries**
1947	Geneva	Tariffs	23
1949	Annecy	Tariffs	13
1951	Torquay	Tariffs	38
1956	Geneva	Tariffs	26
1960–1961	Geneva Dillon Round	Tariffs	26
1964–1967	Geneva Kennedy Round	Tariffs and antidumping measures	62
1973–1979	Geneva Tokyo Round	Tariffs, nontariff measures, "framework" agreements	102
1986–1994	Geneva Uruguay Round	Tariffs, nontariff measures, rules, services, intellectual property, dispute settlement, textiles, agriculture, creation of WTO, etc.	123
2001–	Doha, Qatar	Needs of developing countries, nontariff barriers, agriculture and industrial tariffs	

Source: Data from International Trade Statistics, WTO Secretariat, World Trade Organization (2009).

and Geneva again (2008). The negotiations in 2008 reached an impasse because of disagreement between developed and developing countries on the liberalization of agricultural trade, especially between the United States, India, and China. In particular, there was considerable disagreement between India and the United States over the special safeguard mechanism (SSM), a measure designed to protect poor farmers by allowing countries to impose a special tariff on certain agricultural goods in the event of an increase in imports or a fall in prices.

Like the GATT, the **World Trade Organization (WTO)** is a forum for governments to negotiate trade agreements and settle trade disputes. Some 150 nations are members of the WTO. About 75 percent of them are developing countries. Developing countries have been given some preferential treatment, such as a longer period of time to meet tariff reductions required under the agreement. Unlike the GATT agreement, the WTO covers services, including intellectual property. In addition, nontariff barriers such as discriminatory **product standards** are also included in the agreement.

ARBITRATION AND MEDIATION

Trade disputes rise often as exemplified by the examples on page 92. Disputes can arise between private parties such as businesses, between two countries, or between an individual and a country. There are three ways to settle a dispute: (1) litigation through a court, (2) arbitration, or (3) mediation. Litigation can be very costly and time consuming. Therefore, many prefer other alternatives.

What is the difference between arbitration and mediation? **Arbitration** is a course of action by which a dispute is submitted by the parties to one or more arbitrators whose decision is binding. This procedure is an alternative to going through the courts. Once arbitration commences, the parties cannot withdraw. The arbitrators' ruling is therefore binding on the parties and must be carried out within a reasonable amount of time. The advantages of arbitration are enforceability, confidentiality, technical expertise of the arbitrators, and lower expenses than litigation.

Mediation, on the other hand, is nonbinding. It is a process where two parties agree on a mediator who tries to guide them to a satisfactory settlement of the dispute. Even if mediation does not result in an agreement, the process itself defines the issues of a dispute that can later be used to prepare for arbitration if needed. Mediation may be the preferred procedure to take when the parties hope to preserve or renew their commercial relationship. Another advantage of mediation is the shorter amount of time it takes.

There are a number of international organizations that provide arbitration, mediation services, or both. Examples of arbitration centers include the International Center for Settlement of Investment Disputes (ICSID), the World Intellectual Property Organization (WIPO), the Arbitration and Mediation Center, the London Court of International Arbitration, and the International Chamber of Commerce (ICC). The following are examples of arbitration cases.

A French pharmaceutical research and development company licensed know-how and patented pharmaceuticals to another French company. The license agreement includes an arbitration clause that provides that any dispute will be resolved under the WIPO Arbitration Rules by an arbitral consisting of three members in accordance with French law. Faced with the licensee's apparent refusal to pay the license fee, the R&D company initiated arbitration proceedings.

A United States company providing data processing software and services and an Asian bank concluded an agreement regarding the provision account processing services. The parties agreed that the United States company was to be the exclusive service provider for certain of the bank's affiliates in North America and Europe. The agreement stated that any dispute arising out of or in connection with the agreement would be resolved under the WIPO Expedited Arbitration Rules.

Four years after the conclusion of their agreement, the United States company alleged that the bank had violated the agreement by using processing services offered by third parties in the countries covered by the agreement. When the parties failed to settle the dispute, the United States service provider commenced WIPO-expedited arbitration proceedings, claiming infringement of the agreement and substantial consequential damages.

The parties agreed upon a sole arbitrator who held a two-day hearing in New York City. Three months after the request for expedited arbitration, the arbitrator rendered a final award finding partial infringement of the agreement and granting damages to the United States service provider.[5]

INTERNATIONAL CENTER FOR SETTLEMENT OF INVESTMENT DISPUTES (ICSID)

Headquartered in Washington, D.C., the ICSID arbitrates investment disputes between nations and nationals of other nations (e.g., *Continental Casualty Company v. Argentine Republic, EDF (Services) Ltd.* v. *Romania)*. A filing fee for arbitration is $25,000, which is nonrefundable. There are 156 signatory states to the ICSID convention.

WORLD INTELLECTUAL PROPERTY ORGANIZATION (WIPO) ARBITRATION AND MEDIATION CENTER

Based in Geneva, the center provides arbitration and mediation services for settling disputes between private parties. The center specializes in disputes involving technology, intellectual property, the Internet, and electronic commerce. The center has handled disputes involving sums ranging from $20,000 to several hundred million

5. www.wipo.int/amc/en/arbitration/case-example.html. Retrieved 10 October 2009.

United States dollars. Two examples of arbitration cases conducted under WIPO rules are given in the appendix.

THE LONDON COURT OF INTERNATIONAL ARBITRATION (LCIA)

The LCIA provides arbitration and mediation services for contractual disputes in international commerce, including telecommunications, insurance, oil and gas exploration, construction, shipping, aviation, pharmaceuticals, shareholders agreements, IT, finance, and banking. It is a nonprofit organization and covers its expenses by charging £1,500 for filing a request for arbitration and thereafter an hourly fee. It is managed by the City of London, the London Chamber of Commerce and Industry, and the Chartered Institute of Arbitrators. Its court of arbitrators has up to 35 members from major world trading areas, of which no more than six members are citizens of the UK.

MARKETING MIX REGULATIONS

Product Standards

Consumers all over the world expect that the products they buy will be safe and healthy and conform to the claims of the manufacturer. In order to ensure these expectations, product and promotion regulations have often been necessary. The impact of worldwide legislation and regulations is a primary concern to both manufacturers of consumer and industrial products. The concern is owing to the possibility of different product regulations and standards on a global, regional, or national level. These differences mean that multinational manufacturers must plan product strategy on a global or regional basis, adapting products whenever necessary to fulfill required standards.

Product planning is of three major types. First, end products must meet standards in each target country. Can a manufacturer design the product to allow acceptance by all the regulatory agencies? Second, how does a company efficiently and cost-effectively accomplish this task? How can you ensure that new products or new generations of older products will satisfy all of the regulations necessary to qualify for sale? The third challenge relates to the standards themselves. Do they represent an achievable goal, or will conformity cause undue hardship to manufacturers and customers alike? And how can changes to regulations be anticipated before the product is marketed?

While nearly all products are subject to some sort of regulation, industries such as pharmaceuticals, cosmetics, food, and electronics are more closely supervised. For example, the pharmaceutical industry has become one of the most legislated and regulated industries in the world. The worldwide regulations, although differing in scope and intensity, all target pharmaceutical development, testing, and manufacture of drug products. For a multinational electronics manufacturer, selling products to countries all over the world means contending with an array of conformance standards that can vary significantly from one country to the next. The production, processing, distribution, retail, packaging, and labeling of food products are governed by a mass of laws, regulations, and codes of practice and guidance that differ from one country to another.

Achieving a worldwide or regionwide agreement for product standardization is a difficult task. Many of you have traveled abroad with a laptop. Going from the UK to France and then to Switzerland requires three plug adapters. While this is a minor annoyance, there are more serious barriers, such as safety requirements for cars and trucks and, in some cases, machinery. All require adaptation of products to meet the specific requirements of a given country. In some cases, differentiating product standards is done to gain a competitive edge. Sony introduced its Betamax system in 1975. A year later, JVC launched its VHS (Video Home System). Manufacturers were divided between the two competing systems, with Japanese companies adopting either one or the other. However, a major difference between the two was recording time. Betamax could record only up to 60 minutes while VHS lasted up to three hours. By 2002, Betamax was history and today both systems have been replaced by digital technology.

There is no such thing as a worldwide standard for products. The EU has begun a process of harmonization of standards that will apply to all its members. The term "harmonization" refers to a process by which the technical requirements of various standards have been made equivalent or identical. An exception is the "principle of mutual recognition" of the EU. This principle holds that a product lawfully marketed in one member state should be allowed to be marketed in any other member state, even when the product does not fully comply with the technical rules of the member state of destination. However, a member state may refuse entry to any product that it considers a threat to public safety, health, or the environment.

The International Organization for Standardization (ISO)

The ISO is an NGO headquartered in Geneva, Switzerland, consisting of a network of national standards institutes of over 160 countries. Its primary task is to develop international product standards based on consensus with its members. Compliance with ISO standards is voluntary. Member organizations may apply for certification of ISO's Quality Management System (QMS), which includes top management commitment to quality, employee competence, process management (for production, service delivery, and relevant administrative and support processes), quality planning, product design, review of incoming orders, purchasing, monitoring, and measurement of processes and products. Most well-known brands are ISO certified as complying with international standards; e.g., Adobe Systems' PDF (Portable Document Format), Bang & Olufsen, Samsung, Nokia, and HP.

REGULATION OF COMMUNICATION

Advertising regulations are nationally and locally determined. Every country determines how to regulate advertising that is perceived to be fraudulent or misleading. In the European Union, advertising is self-regulated. According to the European Standards Advertising Alliance, self-regulation (SR) is "a system by which the advertising industry actively polices itself. The three parts of the industry (advertisers, advertising agencies, and media) work together to agree to standards and to set up a system to ensure that advertisements which fail to meet those standards are quickly corrected or removed." While attempts have been made to harmonize especially sensitive advertising, such as alcohol and advertising to children, little has been accomplished. However, all EU countries have enacted legislation that regulates advertising in these areas.

Cyberlaw

Most people today have an e-mail account or access the web on a daily basis. If you have an e-mail account, you have no doubt been inundated with "junk mail" (unsolicited commercial e-mail), commonly known as *spam*. These messages offer products for sale, some that you may want in your home but others that you may not. In any case, you can filter some but not all of the spam mail that comes your way. E-mail is not filtered is not only a nuisance but also has a cost, a higher monthly service fee resulting from the time it takes to delete unwanted e-mail. Unwanted e-mail also uses memory on both ends and can result in slowing down traffic on the web. While unsolicited commercial e-mail is an international problem, there are difficulties in the regulation of cyberspace. A single transmission may involve regulations in three countries: (1) regulations if the country in which the recipient resides, (2) regulations of the country where the server is located, and (3) regulations of the country in which the transaction takes place. It is not out of the ordinary that these regulations may be at odds. Take for example, the *Yahoo!* v. *France* case.

> In 2001, Nazi memorabilia was offered for sale on the Yahoo! auction website in France. As the sale of such products was banned in France, a number of groups took legal action to have the memorabilia removed from the company's website. The French court ordered Yahoo! to remove the memorabilia from its website and failing to do so would incur a fine of F100,000 for each day of noncompliance. The company in turn held that as it was incorporated in the United States, the French court did not have jurisdiction over it. It requested the District Court of California to overrule the French court's decision. The American court held that the French court's order was not enforceable in the United States and was in violation of the First Amendment of the United States Constitution. Thus, this case shows that the jurisdiction of a court in one country may not necessarily be enforceable in another country.

A step in the attempt to harmonize computer crime laws on the international level is the Council of Europe's Convention on Cybercrime, signed by 38 countries including the United States. The convention is intended to outlaw computer intrusion, child pornography, commercial copyright infringement, and online fraud. In the words of United States Attorney General Alberto Gonzales, the "treaty provides important tools in the battles against terrorism, attacks on computer networks and the sexual exploitation of children over the Internet, by strengthening United States cooperation with foreign countries in obtaining electronic evidence." Both European and nonEuropean countries are signatories of the treaty, such as the United States, Canada, Japan, and South Africa.

POLITICAL RISK

Political risk may be defined as the probability that a set of unwanted events may occur. "Unwanted events" are those that can impact upon a firm's performance to the extent that they threaten the firm's value. Examples (see Table 4-3) of such events include **firm-specific** risks (micro risk) that are directed at a particular company and **country-specific risks** (macro risk) that are not aimed at a particular firm, but are nationwide, impacting all firms in a given industry. Examples of firm-specific risks

TABLE 4-3 Categories of Political Risk		
	Government Risks	**Instability Risks**
Firm-Specific Risks	■ Discriminatory regulations ■ "Creeping" expropriation ■ Breach of contract	■ Sabotage ■ Kidnappings ■ Firm-specific boycotts
Country-Specific Risks	■ Mass nationalizations ■ Regulatory changes ■ Currency inconvertibility	■ Mass labor strikes ■ Urban rioting ■ Civil wars

Source: Wagner, D. (2000). Defining "Political Risk," *International Risk Management Institute*. Retrieved March 21, 2007, from www.irmi.com/IrmiCom/Export/Articles/2000/Wagner10.aspx. Reprinted with permission.

include expropriation of the firm's assets, kidnapping employees, limits on the transfer of certain technologies, and breach of contract.

Country-specific risks include limiting the repatriation of profits, civil unrest, currency inconvertibility, forced local shareholding, and nationalization of an industry (e.g., the government taking over the assets of all firms in a given industry, such as electricity production). For example, after Fidel Castro's government took control of Cuba in 1959, hundreds of millions of dollars worth of American-owned assets and companies were expropriated. Unfortunately, most, if not all, of these American companies did not receive any compensation for their financial losses.

Assessing political risk should be a major concern for companies that have:

- High ratios of international to domestic revenues
- Significant amounts of capital invested abroad
- Dependence on a global supply chain
- Significant concentration of assets or operations in a single region or country
- Dependence on international growth

The major issues that concern political risk are its measurement and management. Most observers of political risk agree that it is determined by the exercise of political power, either by government or groups such as unions and activists. The use (or misuse) of political power is usually an outgrowth of unrest caused by economic downturns, religious strife, etcetera. Therefore, the probability that political risk may occur can be measured by monitoring whether political unrest and instability may occur and eventually threaten the firm's performance. Political risk assessment is done by risk management experts employed in transnational firms, banks, or by consulting firms. Methods for assessing political risk range from comparative techniques of rating and mapping systems to analytical techniques such as expert systems and probability determination.

There are two approaches to measure political risk: (1) qualitative, based on expert (economists, union officials, politicians, local businessmen) analysis using Delphi-type techniques and (2) quantitative, which begins with the identification of quantifiable factors that affect political risk. Then a formula is used to determine numerical scores for each factor. A weighted average of the factors' numerical scores is the final score for the country. While the second technique seems more objective, it may not be more accurate than qualitative methods. It all depends upon the reliability and validity of the models and the databases used.

Two well-known providers of political risk assessment using quantitative methods are the Economist Intelligence Unit (the EIU model) and the Business Environment Risk Intelligence (BERI) model. The EIU composite risk rating includes political risk (22 percent of the composite), economic policy risk (28 percent), economic structure risk (27 percent), and liquidity risk (23 percent). The political risk component measures political stability (war, social unrest, orderly political transfer, politically motivated violence, and international disputes). The BERI model includes a Profit Opportunity Recommendation, which is a macro risk measure based on an average of three ratings:

- Political Risk Index composed of ratings on political and social variables
- Operations Risk Index, composed of political, financial, and structural (economic) variables
- R Factor (Remittance and Repatriation), a weighted index of the country's legal framework, foreign exchange, hard currency reserves, and foreign debt

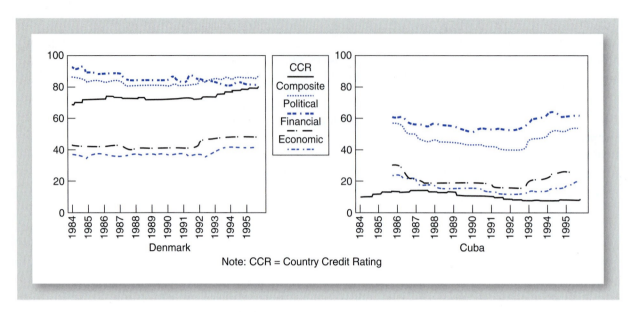

Figure 4-3 Country Risk Measures

Source: Campbell A. Harvey, Duke University. Reprinted with permission.

An example of the results of a quantitative assessment of political risk (also economic and financial risk) of Cuba and Denmark is shown in Figure 4-3. The higher the score on the y-axis, the lower the risk. Note the relatively high political risk (bold line) for Cuba compared to that of Denmark (hardly any risk at all). On the basis of the composite index (an average of the political, financial, and economic indices) shown in the charts, doing business in Cuba would be highly risky for the included years.

It is imperative for each company to conduct risk assessment, keeping in mind unique, industry-specific micro-political risks, while at the same time taking into consideration the general macro-political risks. Table 4-4 proposes a simplified risk-assessment model using critical variables that have been discussed in this chapter. This table can serve as a matrix that every company can start within its endeavor to model a comprehensive political risk-assessment strategy. Firms should add the appropriate country-/industry-/project-specific variables to the microvariables section. Assigning a weighting factor to each critical variable should reflect the respective firm's industry, location, risk tolerance, and general political-economic environment. Scores should then be assigned for each country in each category and multiplied by the weighting factor. The country scores are added, and the total scores for each country are then easily compared to assess the relative risk of each country.

The above discussion also drives home another very significant factor: the existence of country-specific or region-specific risks. For instance, while companies seeking to operate in the Middle East, South Asia, and certain parts of Africa face a heightened threat of terrorism and corruption, companies seeking to expand into the Scandinavian countries do not face a similar threat. Each nation or region must be looked upon as a unique operating environment. This suggests that companies must resort to risk-assessment strategies at multiple levels.

It is recommended that every company adopt political risk assessment at two or three levels. The assessment team at the corporate headquarters can be assigned the task of creating a general model that identifies broad macro-variables applicable for all international operations such as exchange-rate fluctuations, GDP growth rate, threat

TABLE 4-4 Risk Assessment Model						
	Macro-Variables	**Weight**	**Country -1-**	**Country -2-**	**Country -3-**	**Country -4-**
Political/ Governmental	War & Security Issues	0–10				
	Regime Stability	0–10				
Economic	Inflation	0–10				
	Exchange Rate Volatility	0–10				
	Economic Stability	0–10				
	GDP per capita	0–10				
	Balance of Payments	0–10				
	Real GDP Growth Rate	0–10				
	Currency Convertibility	0–10				
Social	Social Revolutions	0–10				
	Corruption	0–10				
	Micro-Variables	**Weight**	**Country -1-**	**Country -2-**	**Country -3-**	**Country -4-**
Political/ Governmental	Industry Regulatory Bodies	0–10				
	(Appropriate Political/Government Micro-Variables)	0–10				
Economic	Energy Vulnerability	0–10				
	(Appropriate Economic Micro-Variables)	0–10				
Social	(Appropriate Social Micro-Variables)	0–10				
		TOTAL				

Source: Alon, I, Gurumoothy, R., Mitchell, M., & Steen, T. (2006). Managing micropolitical risk: A cross-sector examination. *Thunderbird International Business Review, 48*(5), 623–642.

of war, and broad, industry-specific micro-variables. On the other hand, assessment teams at each international location can create sub-models that incorporate country-specific macro- and micro-variables. Large multinational corporations can take it a step further in creating region-specific models as well. In conclusion, every global company in today's world must consider adopting a comprehensive political risk-assessment strategy to ensure it invests in the right places and continues making the decisions necessary to outperform its competitors.

Figure 4-4 Is the World Becoming Safer or More Dangerous for the American People?

Source: Adapted from: Bittle, S., Rochkind, J., & Ott, A. (2010, Spring). *Confidence in United States Foreign Policy Index*, vol. 7.

The Case of Terrorism

Terrorism has become a major threat to the stability of entire regions of the world (Middle East, Africa, and parts of Latin America and Asia). Terrorism poses both direct and indirect threats to the operations of the firm. It represents a market imperfection that increases transaction costs and creates barriers to the free flow of goods, affecting potential gains that would occur in the presence of unhindered exchange. Terrorism reflects the risk or actual encounter of violent acts whose goal is to engender fear, coercion, or intimidation.[6] Terrorism has impacted tourist travel as well as overall trade. For example, a national probability sample of 1,002 adults living in the continental United States by the Public Agenda organization found that Americans see the world as a dangerous place for the United States and its interests (see Figure 4-4). The number who say the world is becoming "more dangerous for the United States and the American people" was virtually the same in 2010 as in 2008: 72 percent, compared with 73 percent in 2008. These perceptions are also held by the general public, as evidenced by cancelations of travel plans whenever a threat of terrorism arises.

Nitsch and Schumacher (2003)[7] studied bilateral trade flows of more than 200 countries over the period 1960 to 1993 and found that terrorist actions reduced the volume of trade. A doubling in the number of terrorist incidents was associated with a decrease in bilateral trade by about 4 percent. Costoiu (2006) also found a relationship between increased terror and a reduction in trade.[8] Given the association between terror and trade, the latter has become an important component of political risk analysis.

Managing the risk of terrorism is a special issue. Terrorism can impact many forms of business activity, including attacking tourists, kidnapping personnel, and damaging infrastructure, to name a few. Terrorism risk can be viewed as having three components: the *threat* to a target, the target's *vulnerability* to the threat, and the *consequences* should the target be successfully attacked. People and organizations represent threats when they have both the intent and capability to damage a target. The *threat* to a target can be measured as the probability that a specific target is attacked in a specific way during a specified period. Thus, a threat might be measured as the annual

6. Czinkota, M., Knight, G., Liesch, P., & Steen, J. (2005). Positioning terrorism in management and marketing: Research propositions. *Journal of International Management, 11*(4), 581–604.

7. Nitsch, V., & Schumacher, D. (2003). Tourism and trade. *European Journal of Political Economy*, 353–366.

8. Costoiu, A. (2006). *The reciprocal effect of terrorism and international trade, 1975–2002.* University of Illinois at Chicago.

probability that a city's football stadium will be subject to attack with a radiological weapon. *Vulnerability* can be measured as the probability that damage occurs, given a threat. Damages could be fatalities, injuries, property damage, or other consequences; each would have its own vulnerability assessment. *Consequences* are the magnitude and type of damage resulting, given a successful terrorist attack. Risk is a function of all three components: threat, vulnerability, and consequences.[9]

In testimony before the United States congress, Professor Czinkota (2005) discussed the results of a survey undertaken to determine the perception of terrorism and readiness of managers in American business firms who were involved in some sort of international marketing.[10] The vast majority of respondents felt that there had not been a specific terrorism threat against their business, even though many more believed that their firm might be directly affected by a terrorist attack in the next 10 years. However, many managers reported that their firms had no contingency plans to deal with terror. On a cost-benefit basis, many believed that the risk did not justify the investment required to manage it. Nevertheless, domestic companies having subsidiaries abroad should consult with one of the many terrorism risk management firms to determine whether a threat exists and, if so, what is the extent of vulnerability. The United States government, in particular, has enacted a Terrorism Risk Insurance Program (TRIP) which compensates insurance companies that have losses due to a recognized terrorism act.

Managing Political Risk

Given that there is significant political risk in some countries, it cannot be ignored. However, while political risk cannot be eliminated, it can, in some cases, be reduced or managed. For example, insurance against some political risks is offered by both governmental and private agencies. The Overseas Private Insurance Corporation (OPIC), an American government agency, offers insurance covering currency inconvertibility, expropriation, and political violence, and is available for investments in new ventures and expansions of existing enterprises. Similar insurance coverage is available from the Canadian government agency Export Development Canada. Many other governments, and some private insurance carriers such as AIG, offer similar insurance policies.

Apart from insuring risk, there are other ways to manage it. One way is to share ownership with host country nationals. This alternative has a number of advantages. First, governments are less likely to take action that would be detrimental to local economic interests. Second, participation of local nationals can be a good bridge to host government and union representatives. Another method in which risk can be reduced is through participating in community projects such as promoting social welfare (schools, medical facilities) and rural development projects. An example of participation in social-welfare projects is the case of Nike's micro-development project in Indonesia. In a five-year period, the Nike-funded project has provided nearly $1.8 million in small business loans, called micro-credit, to 11,500 Indonesian entrepreneurs. These collateral-free loans have enabled them to launch their own enterprises, lifting them out of chronic poverty.[11]

9. Willis, H, Morral, A. Kelly, T., & Medby, J. (2005). *Estimating terrorism risk*. Santa Monica, CA: Rand Center for Terrorism Risk Management Policy, p. xvi.

10. Czinkota, M. (1 November 2005). *International marketing and terrorism preparedness*. Testimony before the House of Representatives Committee on Small Business.

11. Frank, W. (2007). *Successful partnership for CSR activities in Thailand: The NIKE village development project.* Retrieved from www.pda.or.th/pdf/CSR-Thailand.

SUMMARY

- Although there are five different legal systems in use around the world, common and civil law countries account for about 30 percent of the world's gross national product.

- Global marketers must be aware of the legal problems that can arise when doing business abroad. Specifically, these problems center on marketing issues such as the "4Ps": product, place, price, and promotion.

- Intellectual property includes patents, trademarks, copyright and related rights, geographical indications, industrial designs, know-how, and trade secrets. Intellectual property is an integral part of international trade, and its importance is increasing as the effective use of knowledge contributes ever more to national and international economic prosperity.

- Trade disputes can occur between countries, between countries and business firms, and between business firms. The major agency dealing with trade disputes involving two or more countries is the World Trade Organization. However, while it deals with settling trade disputes, its main aim is to liberalize trade through the reduction or elimination of trade barriers such as tariffs and quotas.

- Doing business abroad may entail political risk. There are two types of risk: macro, or country risk that threatens an entire economic sector, and micro, or firm risk that threatens individual companies. Political risk cannot be eliminated. Therefore, it is imperative for global firms to forecast what sort of risk they face and how it can be managed.

DISCUSSION QUESTIONS

1. How can intellectual property rights be protected in China?

2. Explain some of the pitfalls faced by a multinational manufacturer when trying to have its products conform to a universal standard.

3. You are responsible for risk management in your firm. How would you go about forecasting the political risk for investment in emerging markets? How can a small–medium enterprise (SME) assess and manage political risk?

EXPERIENTIAL EXERCISES

1. Using whatever sources you can find, prepare a political risk analysis for China.

2. Select four EU countries. Explain how the advertising of alcoholic beverages is regulated in each.

KEY TERMS

Arbitration, p. 98

Civil law, p. 90

Common law, p. 90

Country-specific risk, p. 102

Firm-specific risk, p. 102

General Agreement on Tariffs and Trade (GATT), p. 97

Intellectual property, p. 92

Mediation, p. 99

Parallel importing, p. 92

Political risk, p. 102

Product standards, p. 98

World Trade Organization (WTO), p. 98

CASE 4-1

Serious Problems Creating a Partnership in Russia

In the mid-1990s a medium-sized Baltic food producer BaltFoodEx (founded in the early 1990s)[1] decided to enter Russia because it felt that, although its products were quite popular among its customers and it had reached a relatively high market share in its home market and also the other two Baltic countries and managed even to outcompete some well-known Western brands, the Baltic market did not offer it enough growth opportunities. The firm decided to enter Russia, not Scandinavia or Poland, because Baltic food had been quite popular among Russian and other ex-Soviet customers in the Soviet time (especially in the St. Petersburg and the Moscow regions); there, many people saw the three Baltic countries as "almost real Western Europe," and the fact itself that a product originated from the West was a symbol of high quality. At the same time, Baltic food was not very familiar to Polish or Scandinavian customers, as in the Soviet time, Baltic food had not been actively exported there (at that time, Soviet companies—including Baltic firms—could not select export markets themselves: the Planning Committee made such decisions, and the main task given to Baltic firms was to supply the northwestern part of Russia and other Soviet Republics). Moreover, although the living standard was lower in Russia than in the three Baltic countries, its larger population (around 150 million at that time) made it an attractive market. Russia also had a larger market and a higher living standard (especially in the Moscow and St. Petersburg regions) than Belarus and the Ukraine, which were also geographically close to the Baltic market and whose customers were quite well familiar with Baltic products. Thus, Russia was preferred to these two countries. The geographically more distant countries—other Western European countries and other former Soviet Socialist Republics—were excluded almost from the start because of high transport costs, unfamiliarity with Baltic products (the former group of countries), or low incomes (the latter group). BaltFoodEx's managers' good Russian language skills[2] and their belief that Russian business practices should not be very different from their own (after all, they shared a common history) also influenced the firm's market selection.

BaltFoodEx could not enter Russia successfully by exporting because the country had high import duties on Baltic food products and the firm could not successfully compete with Russian lower-cost producers (it had tried to export there a year earlier but without considerable success: Russian consumers were quite price conscious,

---

1. The Baltic market consists of three small countries: Estonia, Latvia, and Lithuania, with populations of 1.3, 2.2, and 3.5 million, respectively, that all joined the European Union in May 2004. These countries restored their independence in 1991 when the Soviet Union dissolved (they were also independent for about two decades before the start of World War II). Because of the sensitive nature of this case story, the names of the two case enterprises were completely changed (so the real names of these enterprises have nothing in common with Rusfood, Baltfood, Baltex, Rusprod, or any other names of this type) and their exact area of activity and financial data were concealed in order to retain their anonymity.

2. Although in each of the Baltic countries a different language is spoken, in the Soviet time, all children studying in local-language schools had to learn Russian as their first foreign language; usually English or German came next. Now the first foreign language is usually English in local-language schools and the local language is taught first in Russian-language schools.

Case prepared by Tiia Vissak, Faculty of Economics and Business Administration, University of Tartu, Narva Rd. 4-A211, 51009 Tartu, Estonia. Reprinted with permission.

while some of those who were not preferred well-known "real" Western brands that had been inaccessible for them in the Soviet time). Even without the duties, the firm's products would have been more expensive than the Russian ones because of transportation costs and higher salaries in Baltic countries. So, BaltFoodEx decided to establish a production unit in Russia. The firm lacked funds for establishing such a unit in the country alone. Establishing its own subsidiary would have been also difficult because the company's owners and managers had not established close ties there, and they also feared Russia's strict bureaucracy; moreover, they did not have enough knowledge of the Russian market, as the firm was founded after the dissolution of the Soviet Union, and the owners and managers had no business experience from this area of activities from that time. So, they decided to cooperate with a local enterprise. At a food fair, the company found a rather small Russian enterprise, RusFoodProd, already producing similar types of products with quite a high market potential, but that had relatively outdated technology. RusFoodProd lacked funds for updating its technology and increasing its production capacity on its own, so it was interested in a partnership with the Baltic food producer. The two firms discussed their future plans: they wanted to expand the Russian plant, add some Baltic products to its portfolio, increase its market share in Russia, start exporting to some neighboring countries in the near future, and even consider opening a new plant in the Ukraine in the more distant future.

In the contract, BaltFoodEx and RusFoodProd agreed that the former would provide the latter with technology (it had recently acquired more modern machinery with a higher production capacity, so it did not need some of its old machinery anymore, but it also agreed to acquire some additional machinery for the Russian partner), and with that, obtain a considerable share in the Russian enterprise. The Russian partner advised BaltFoodEx to save on customs duties by not declaring the machinery correctly on the Russian border. The Baltic firm agreed to follow the suggestion because the cost savings seemed to be substantial and the control at the Russian border was not very strict, so the risk of getting caught and paying the resulting fine was low; moreover, the Russian partner assured that they knew some of the right people at the border, so, even if the machinery were discovered, paying the fine could be also avoided at "just a little extra cost."

The machinery successfully crossed the border without anybody checking it and arrived at the Russian enterprise on time. When BaltFoodEx contacted its Russian partner and asked when it would obtain the share in RusFoodProd, as was agreed to in the contract, the Russian firm claimed that the Baltic firm could not prove it had ever sent the machinery to RusFoodProd, as there were no documents showing that the machinery had crossed the Russian border or reached the enterprise at all. They also made some vague threats to their Baltic partners about knowing where their families lived and suggested that they send the machinery again or forget about the partnership. The owners of the Baltic firm decided to follow the latter suggestion, although they could not be sure how realistic these threats were.

So BaltFoodEx lost a considerable amount of money without managing to obtain any share in RusFoodProd or getting the machinery back (it did not wish to admit to the authorities that it had not paid the customs duties properly and it also did not want to contact any "unofficial structures," as this could have caused even more serious problems; moreover, it was afraid that making the problem public would harm its image in the Baltic market and decrease its chances to enter other countries in the future). The only consolation for them was that they had not shared their recipes with their Russian partners yet. BaltFoodEx never completely recovered from this experience and it never entered Russia again. It also could not expand further in the Baltic market as it had planned: for example, it lacked funds for buying a local enterprise that it had promised to buy before facing problems in Russia. Because of financing problems, the company also failed to enter other foreign countries. Some years later, the firm was taken over by a larger Baltic food producer. This firm has not become active in Russia, either: it has decided to enter Scandinavia instead.

Questions for Discussion:

1. Was Russia the logical choice as a new target market for the Baltic firm?
2. List the reasons why BaltFoodEx was interested in cooperating with RusFoodProd and the other way around.
3. Explain why the cooperation between the two case firms failed.
4. Do you think that BaltFoodEx made the right decision to exit Russia without trying to get a compensation for the machinery or getting its share in the Russian enterprise? Was it a reasonable decision never to reenter this country? Why?

Recommended Literature

- CIA—The World Factbook (https://www.cia.gov/library/publications/the-world-factbook/index.html /); this site provides information about the countries' current economic state, etc. (the data are periodically renewed).
- Doing Business 2011, Russian Federation (http://www.doingbusiness.org/~/media/fpdkm/doing%20business/documents/profiles/country/db11/RUS.pdf).
- Doing Business in Russia: 2011 Country Commercial Guide for United States Companies (http://www.buyusainfo.net/docs/x_6323090.pdf).
- International Trade Administration, United States Department of Commerce. (2004). *Business ethics: A manual for managing a responsible business enterprise in emerging market economies.* Retrieved from www.ita.doc.gov/good-governance/adobe/bem_manual.pdf.
- PricewaterhouseCoopers. (2010). *Doing business and investing in the Russian Federation.* Retrieved from http://www.pwc.ru/en/doing-business-in-russia/assets/Doing-Business-Russian-Federation-2010.pdf.
- The Library of Congress Country Studies (http://lcweb4.loc.gov/frd/cs/list.html); this source provides information about the countries' earlier history, society, economy, etc.
- World Business Culture Cultural Compatibility Test (www.worldbusinessculture.com/compatibility/test/); answering the 25 questions in this test allows you to measure cultural similarities and differences with people from other countries (including Russia) along seven dimensions.

CASE 4-2

An Expanding Dilemma: Between Mubarak and a Hardliner?

Case Overview

Carter James has always been adventurous. However, his next decision will be the most risky and most potentially rewarding he's ever made. Last year his United States-based automotive technology company, WowTech, Inc., developed a new carburetor that increases the efficiency of older vehicles by 10 to 20 percent. Increased sales have outgrown his domestic shop's production capacity. Therefore, he has decided to outsource the production capabilities to meet global demand. Now he needs to choose exactly where to build this new facility. Competition in this new, ultra-efficient green automotive business is tough, and he can't afford any disruptions as a result of the transition. He has to choose the right location the first time.

Carter James and WowTech

Working on cars is in Carter's blood. From an early age he watched his family work on cars to save money, and he was always there helping and learning. When he graduated from college, Carter never imagined that in a few short years he would be managing his own rapidly expanding startup company. WowTech was founded as the automotive equivalent to Silicon Valley's high tech research and development labs. Its main business was creating visionary designs for the new generation of automobile engines, but by chance the company's most popular product had become the Greenuretor, which replaces the carburetor on older vehicles to increase fuel efficiency by 10 to 20 percent. This revolutionary product has become an overnight success due to the high profile social media treatment it had received from green industry activists. The federal government had also proposed tougher emissions regulations and tax credits for efficient vehicles, which only increased public interest.

Carter quickly realized that demand for the Greenuretor would outstrip the company's current production capacity within six months, so he needed to act fast. In order to maintain WowTech's emphasis on research and development, he decided to outsource the production of the Greenuretor. To help him make the difficult transition, he hired an international consulting firm with a track record of working with the Big Three: General Motors, Ford, and Chrysler. Their principal task was to find potential locations for the new facility and negotiate incentive packages with host country governments. After months of work and fact-finding trips, the consultants narrowed the decision down to two countries: Egypt and Venezuela. These two governments are looking to lure automotive manufacturers away from East Asia and have therefore offered attractive incentives to secure WowTech's foreign direct investment (FDI). They are both located near large potential markets with fleets of aging cars, and they have developed domestic automotive manufacturing capabilities.

The similar offers made by the governments of Egypt and Venezuela look very attractive on paper, but there is more to the decision than what appears on paper.

Case prepared by Matthew Mitchell, Assistant Professor of International Business at Drake University. Reprinted with permission.

Carter knows he must consider the wider sociopolitical environment for doing business in both of these countries. Will WowTech be able to operate smoothly in these foreign markets with very different economic, social, and governmental institutions? To help him systematically address these questions, the risk management team has put together two summary sheets (see Market Summaries below) and a scorecard to compare the two possible locations. The consultants have provided him with the necessary information, but ultimately Carter must make the decision for himself.

Market Summary—República Bolivariana de Venezuela

General Information: The Bolivarian Republic of Venezuela, located on the northern coast of South America, is one of the most urbanized countries in Latin America, with more than 26 million inhabitants. Venezuela prides itself on its racial and cultural diversity, which includes influences from the original American Indians as well as Spanish, African, Italian, and Portuguese immigrants. Venezuela has been one of the more stable regimes in Latin America throughout much of the last century. However, since 1989, the country has witnessed deadly riots, two unsuccessful coup attempts, and general political unrest that ushered in a new era of political leadership and uncertainty. In 1998, Hugo Chavez won the country's presidency by campaigning on a socialist platform of economic redistribution and radical political reform. Over the last decade, Chavez has systematically implemented his reform program (known as the "Bolivarian Revolution") in spite of criticism, strikes by government and oil workers, and failed coup attempts. Chavez has also sought to export his brand of "Twenty-first Century Socialism" to the rest of the world, taking every opportunity to publically denounce globalization, free-market principles, and his favorite scapegoat: The United States of America.

Economic Factors: In spite of the harsh anti-United States rhetoric from Chavez, there are real commercial opportunities in Venezuela that should not be overlooked. The United States continues to be Venezuela's most important trading partner, accounting for 52 percent of the country's exports and 25 percent of its imports. This relationship is due largely to Venezuela's proximity to the United States market. Furthermore, Venezuela has enjoyed a long tradition of foreign direct investment from the United States in a variety of industries, including petroleum, automotive manufacturing, paper, and textile products. Venezuela's economy is dominated by the government-run oil industry, which is subject to significant price fluctuations. Recent government spending—made possible by high oil prices—has contributed to inflation rates of over 30 percent in 2008. In 2008 the country adopted the "Bolivar Fuerte" as its new government-controlled currency, and all foreign exchange transactions require official approval. Furthermore, it is widely believed the currency is overvalued and will come under pressure if oil prices were to decline. Decreased oil prices will also create balance of payment problems and inhibit the government's ability to pay for necessary imports. Finally, increased government spending on social programs is increasingly financed by raising the "social responsibility" requirements of firms, increasing the effective tax rate.

Social Factors: Venezuela is largely a relationship-based rather than a rules-based society, which means that firms must understand the local cultural complexity in order to succeed. According to the cultural guru Geert Hofstede, Venezuela is categorized by extreme scores on all four cultural dimensions. First, the large Power Distance Indicator (PDI = 81) would suggest that the inequality in the population has historically been tolerated. This however has not been the case since Chavez's populist government came to power. Second, the high Uncertainty Avoidance Indicator (UAI = 76) indicates a low tolerance for uncertainty, which could lead to comprehensive regulation regimes to ensure security and reduce risk. Next, the low Individualism score (IDV = 12) indicates a strong preference for collective goals that benefit the relevant "group," which could include family, community, or even the entire nation. Chavez seems to have capitalized on this cultural trait given his strong socialist policy orientation. Finally, the high Masculinity score (MAS = 73) indicates a high degree of gender differentiation. While the society is predictably male-dominated, the high MAS score indicates that the female population will also be more assertive and competitive. In this type of environment it is crucial to identify and work closely with a local partner who can navigate all the potential cultural pitfalls.

Political Factors: As described in the introduction, the political environment in Venezuela is dominated by the character and policies of Hugo Chavez. The government's implementation of the anti-market-oriented "Bolivarian reforms" has profound implications for any firm considering an investment in the country. First, private property rights are threatened by nationalizations and expropriations. In recent years the government nationalized the entire domestic cement and steel industries as well as select banks, food processors, and manufacturers. Second, the protection of intellectual property rights (IPR) is marginal at best. Due to poor legislation and weak enforcement, the government is under continual pressure by international activists and rights holders to provide greater IPR protection. Next, the persistent problems of corruption and inadequate transparency continue to deter foreign investment. Venezuela ranks 162nd out of 180 countries on Transparency International's 2009 Corruption Perceptions Index. Finally, the tensions both between Venezuela and the United States and within Venezuela necessitate a full consideration of the risks and rewards of any firm's investment in the country.

Firm/Industry Related Factors: In 2008, Venezuela's manufacturing sector contributed 16 percent to the national GDP and has experienced steady growth since the economic crisis of 2002–2003. The automotive sector is generally highly developed and coordinated with production facilities for most of the major automakers and parts suppliers. However, recently the industry has suffered disruptions in production due to labor disputes. The sector has also experienced slow growth due to a lack of private investment and an overvalued currency that reduces the competitiveness of exports. Under the newly instituted political reforms, the Ministry of Light Industry and Commerce (MILCO) has assumed complete licensing authority to set strict quotas for imports, exports, and production for all automotive industry manufacturers. Furthermore, companies are required to submit detailed yearly operational targets for governmental approval, which only serves to slow production.

Market Summary—Arab Republic of Egypt

General Information: The Arab Republic of Egypt forms a transcontinental land bridge between northeastern Africa and southwestern Asia. Egypt's strategic location at the crossroads of Africa, Asia, and Europe has made it an economic, political, and cultural power in the region for millennia. Egypt is also the most populated country in the Middle East, with an ethnically homogenous population of 79 million inhabitants. Egypt's population is concentrated primarily in Cairo, Alexandria, and in less populated regions along the Nile River and Suez Canal. Since the 1950s, Egypt has been a republic in name; however, the late president—Mohamed Hosni Mubarak—held power for more than 28 years. Mubarak's long tenure was characterized by a tenuous peace with Israel, persistent accusations of political corruption, frustratingly slow democratic reforms, slow economic growth, and consistently high unemployment. In the last five years, Mubarak's government had shown a serious commitment to market-oriented reforms by cutting customs and tariffs. Nevertheless, the public was increasingly restless because the reforms seemed to have benefitted the well connected at the expense of average Egyptians. This widespread social discontent could easily generate significant political unrest.

Economic Factors: Egypt's economy has long been characterized by unfulfilled potential and frustration. For most of the past 50 years, the economy of Egypt was centralized and dominated by the public sector. However under the leadership of former President Sadat and President Mubarak, the economy had begun to liberalize. In 1991, a comprehensive economic reform program was initiated but was quickly abandoned, dooming the economy to 14 years of continued slow growth. However, in 2005, these processes were restarted with promising results: stalled privatizations were completed, tariffs and barriers to trade were reduced, transparency of governmental decision-making was increased, and legislation was passed to improve economic competitiveness. In spite of this progress, much more still needs to be done: bureaucratic obstacles remain, persistent corruption reduces efficiency, and a complex system of legislation and regulatory policies can confuse potential investors. The United States continues to be Egypt's main economic partner, accounting for 10 percent of imports and 7.1 percent of exports. Furthermore, to support the Middle East peace process, the United States contributes more than U.S.$2 billion annually to Egypt (and Israel) and has arranged for zero tariffs for Egyptian products with a certain percentage of Israeli components.

Social Factors: The Egyptian civilization has a 5,000 year history and culture. In order to succeed in Egypt, a firm must (1) learn as much as possible about this complex culture, (2) remain flexible and patient in the face of a frustrating bureaucracy, and (3) develop an understanding of the role that Islamic faith plays in business. According to the cultural guru Geert Hofstede, Islam is the dominant influence on the culture of the Arab World (which includes Egypt and Saudi Arabia among others). First, the large Power Distance Indicator (PDI = 80) suggests that the population generally accepts the unequal distribution of power in society. Therefore, the separation of leaders from the general population is generally accepted and endorsed as part of the local cultural heritage. Second, the high Uncertainty Avoidance score (UAI = 76) indicates a risk-adverse society that does not welcome the prospect of change. In countries with high UAI scores, one can expect to encounter extensive bureaucracies and regulations. Societies with high Power Distance and Uncertainty Avoidance scores are characterized by strong leaders like Mubarak, who were supported and perpetuated by the large bureaucracies under their control. Third, the moderate Individualism (IDV = 38) score indicates a preference for collective goals of the group and a cultural emphasis on loyalty. Finally, the moderate Masculinity index (MAS = 52) is very near the global average (MAS_{avg} = 50). This score indicates that the Egyptian society as a whole balances the assertive and competitive traits of masculinity with the modest and caring characteristics of femininity.

Political Factors: Egypt plays a leading role in African and Arabic politics and culture. Cairo, Africa's largest city, has long been a center for learning, culture and education and has wielded significant influence throughout Europe, Africa, and the Middle East. Along with the recent economic reform program Mubarak had also shown an interest in political reform to achieve greater freedom and democracy for Egyptians. First, Egypt's legal system is based on Islamic and civil law with the courts recently demonstrating greater autonomy. Furthermore, for the first time in 2005 the election law was changed to allow a multi-candidate election. However, he also initiated an impossible series of requirements to *file* for candidacy—effectively guaranteeing his victory. After the election, Mubarak's main opponent, Ayman Nour, was imprisoned five years for forgery. These continued offenses had made the

Egyptian people and the United States government very skeptical of Mubarak's commitment to democracy, freedom, and the rule of law. The international community had also been critical of Egypt's persistent corruption and human rights violations. Egypt ranks 118th out of 180 countries on Transparency International's corruption index, and in 2009 Freedom House described the society as "Not Free." All of these factors have contributed to widespread social and political discontent. The possibility of political revolution in Egypt is very real and the general sentiment is that social, political, and economic freedoms would increase as a result. This could be very beneficial for foreign firms investing in Egypt, but it doesn't come without significant risks.

Firm/Industry Related Factors: Egypt's strategic location, strong domestic market, and recent government initiatives have helped the country develop into a regional manufacturing hub for the automotive industry. Much of this success is attributable to the economic reform program that lowered tariffs for the automotive industry from a range of 5 to 12 percent to 2 to 5 percent, and slashed the corporate tax rate from 40 percent to 20 percent. This progress is expected to continue based on the strategic plan laid out by the Ministry of Industry and Technological Development. As a result, United States foreign direct investment into Egypt has grown more than tenfold over the five-year period ending in 2008. However, serious concerns remain: The recent appreciation of the Egyptian Pound and the relatively high local cost of production will make exports less competitive. Furthermore, widespread unskilled labor and terrorism remain as long-term challenges for the Egyptian government to address for continued growth.

Political Risk Analysis

Use the two market summaries and the political risk scorecard given below to compare the two suggested locations for WowTech's new production facility.

The columns in the political risk scorecard are organized as follows: Column 1 lists the important political risk dimensions discussed in this case. Depending on the specifics of the project or history of the firm being addressed, some items may be deemed as less relevant, while others might need to be added still. In Column 2, a prioritization is assigned to each factor to reflect how important it is for company objectives; ranging from 0 to 5, "0" indicates no importance (or irrelevance) for the potential risks faced, while "5" would indicate extreme importance. In Column 3, each factor's potential impact is assessed, through a rating that ranges from −4 to +4. A "−4" assessment should suggest that factor alone could affect the firm both significantly and negatively; "0" means the factor has no bearing on the unit at this time; "+4" would suggest a factor with major and favorable impact on the unit. In Column 4, each factor is assessed for the likelihood that it will occur, with that assessment being assigned within a range of 1 to 4, representing less likely to practically certain, respectively. In Column 5, the results in Columns 3 and 4 are multiplied to create an index; how good/bad a factor might be for the firm is multiplied by its likelihood of occurring. Finally, Column 6 provides the culmination of the analysis and assessments performed in the rest of this framework. This step integrates them into a single set of outputs ranging from 0 to 100; one may then compare the overall relative impacts of the separate political risk dimensions on the firm, as well as assess the overall profile of the risks faced by the firm. Use the market summaries and the political risk scorecard to compare the two locations.

POLITICAL RISK SCORECARD

Column 1	Col. 2	Col. 3	Col. 4	Col. 5	Col. 6
Factor Description	Factor's importance rating [0 to 5]	Factor's impact on firm: Very bad to very good [−4 to 0 to +4]	Factor's occurrence likelihood [1 to 5]	Factor's risk assessment [Col. 3 × Col. 4]	Overall potential effect [Col. 2 × Col. 5]

ARAB REPUBLIC OF EGYPT SCORECARD

I. Economic Factors
(e.g., labor conditions, economic policies, regulation, balance of payments effects, currency stabilty, trade agreements, etc.)

A.					
B.					
C.					
D.				Economic Total:	

II. Social Factors
(e.g., cultural scores, cultural distance, public opinion, activists, etc.)

A.					
B.					
C.					
D.				Social Total:	

III. Political Factors
(e.g., level of governmental control, degree of nationalism, transparency & corruption, diplomatic & economic relations, etc.)

A.					
B.					
C.					
D.				Political Total:	

IV. Firm/Industry Related Factors
(e.g., contribution of firm/project to local economy, level of technology, size of operation, bargaining power of firm, dependence of firm on local market, etc.)

A.					
B.					
C.					
D.				Firm Total:	
				GRAND TOTAL:	

REPUBLICA BOLIVARIANA DE VENEZUELA SCORECARD

I. Economic Factors
(e.g., labor conditions, economic policies, regulation, balance of payments effects, currency stabilty, trade agreements, etc.)

A.					
B.					
C.					
D.				Economic Total:	

II. Social Factors
(e.g., cultural scores, cultural distance, public opinion, activists, etc.)

A.					
B.					
C.					
D.				Social Total:	

III. Political Factors
(e.g., level of governmental control, degree of nationalism, transparency & corruption, diplomatic & economic relations, etc.)

A.					
B.					
C.					
D.				Political Total:	

IV. Firm/Industry Related Factors
(e.g., contribution of firm/project to local economy, level of technology, size of operation, bargaining power of firm, dependence of firm on local market, etc.)

A.					
B.					
C.					
D.				Firm Total:	
				GRAND TOTAL:	

Integrating Global, Regional, and National Markets

[G]lobal multinationals have . . . viewed developing Asia [countries] . . . as an offshore-production platform. The offshore-efficiency solution is still an attractive option. But what really could be powerful [is] a growing opportunity to tap the region's 3.5 billion consumers.

STEPHEN ROACH, CHAIRMAN, MORGAN STANLEY ASIA

LEARNING OBJECTIVES

After reading this chapter, you should be able to:

- Differentiate between regional and global trade agreements.
- Understand the difference between various types of regional economic blocs.
- Understand the key issues and concepts associated with emerging markets, especially the BRIC countries.
- Discuss why there is more regional than global trade.
- Make an argument for "fair trade."
- Determine which emerging markets have the most potential and why.

As Rapiscan Systems prepared to bid on a security-equipment contract last year, Vice President of Government Affairs Peter Kant thought he deserved an edge over his two competitors because only his company was based in the United States and was set to manufacture the equipment domestically. Rapiscan, a manufacturer of baggage- and cargo-screening systems in Hawthorne, California, was up against a British-based company and a United States company that had paired with a Chinese firm and planned to manufacture its equipment in China. But Chemonics, the prime contractor managing the United States. Agency for International Development's $40 million contract to screen cargo, awarded the subcontract to the American-Chinese team. USAID had opted not to include a clause in the contract that would have required the supplier to assemble the equipment in the United States. That decision, and Kant's ensuing disappointment, illustrates the growing debate over "Buy American" regulations as agencies struggle to comply with the complicated, decades-old legislation in a world driven by global supply chains (see Figure 5-1). As agencies and contractors grow increasingly frustrated with the high costs of compliance, industry groups are pushing to liberalize the regulations.[1]

1. Palmer, K. (22 November 2006). 'Buy American' compliance tricky in increasingly global economy. Retrieved from http://GovernmentExecutive.com.

Figure 5-1 "Buy American" Advertisement

Source: Logo reprinted with permission from How Americans Can Buy American.

Not a day goes by without an article in the newspaper or a briefing on television about world trade issues. In times of economic crises, there is increased pressure to buy domestic-made products rather than imports. While most consumers are free to choose between locally made and imported products, in reality most international commerce involves some sort of government intervention to protect domestic industry.

Protectionist policies include **tariffs** (taxes on imports), **quotas** (limits on the quantity of imports), and **non-tariff trade barriers** such as mandates on the quality or the content of imported goods. It is the latter type of constraint that is most prevalent today. Sales to government agencies in many countries are restricted by "buy local" legislation. The American 1979 Trade Agreements Act requires government agencies (as exemplified by the Rapiscan case above) to buy products that undergo "substantial transformation," or final assembly, in the United States or one of 30 approved countries that have trade agreements with Washington. However, it is difficult to enforce such legislation in a globalized world.

Even among European Union member states, who have agreed to free trade and the free movement of labor and capital, there are signs of protectionism. The British Prime Minister, Gordon Brown, was quoted as saying "British Jobs for British Workers," ostensibly encouraging preference for British employees over other EU citizens. In a non-related incident, the French government was considering subsidizing its struggling automobile industry. Both actions contravene EU policy.

Most economists support trade liberalization in a globalized world. The idea is to get as many nations as possible into multilateral agreements that will increase trade among them, especially between developed and developing nations. The question is whether agreements to do so can be globalized or not.

This chapter discusses the issue of regional versus global trade agreements. Next, the major types of trade agreements will be explained. Significant growth in domestic markets as well as in trade has taken place in emerging markets, especially the so-called **BRIC** countries (Brazil, Russia, India, and China). The last section of the chapter presents a market analysis of the BRIC countries.

REGIONALISM OR GLOBALISM?

While globalization has led to greater interdependence among economies, regional trade agreements have outpaced global arrangements. In theory, a global trade agreement is an ideal solution in terms of resource allocation, economic welfare, and economic prosperity. Such an agreement would allow many countries to enjoy trade with each other free from most restrictions. The next best solution is the regional trade agreement, which lowers trade barriers among members without having to lower barriers for non-members. The difficulties experienced in attempting to achieve multilateral or global trade agreements have led many countries to focus on regional trade arrangements as the primary means to expand international trade. An example of the difficulties inherent in multilateral negotiations was the failure of the Cancun Ministerial Conference (held in Mexico during 2003 under the auspices of the World Trade Organization) to conclude agreement on most of the trade issues on the agenda.

Free trade blocs such as the North American Free Trade Agreement (NAFTA) and customs and monetary unions, like the European Union (EU), resulted in the removal of trade barriers between member countries, while at the same time retaining flexibility over which sectors of industry to liberalize and which issues to negotiate. Trading blocs have resulted in a concentration of trade within regions rather than globally.

The formation of regional blocs also influences market entry. First, preferential trading terms reduce the cost of exporting to member country markets. Locating within a trading bloc provides lower cost access to member country markets than does exporting to member countries from outside of the bloc. Second, the costs of serving multiple countries within a trading bloc may differ depending on the base of operations. Strategically locating in one country can lead to greater efficiencies than investing in another country outside of the bloc. It may be easier to harmonize marketing standards on a regional level than globally; thus the rise of regional integration movements.

Regional Trade

The formation of regional economic groups such as the European Union has accelerated international trade flows of goods and services. Foreign trade flows are concentrated in developed countries, especially by the **Triad nations** of the United States, the European Union, and China (see Figure 5-2). Until recently, Japan was considered a member of the Triad, but it has been surpassed by China. These nations accounted for 50 percent of all world trade in 2009. About one-third of total United States and Chinese merchandise trade is within the Triad, and 10 percent of EU trade. Moreover, intra-EU trade (trade only between EU member countries), accounts for about 10 percent of world trade. Much of world trade increasingly occurs within regions and between three major economic areas: NAFTA, Asia, and Europe.

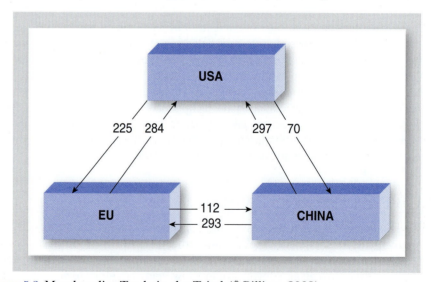

Figure 5-2 Merchandise Trade in the Triad ($ Billion, 2009)

Sources: United States Census Bureau, Foreign Trade Division, Washington, D.C. European Commission.

TABLE 5-1 The World's Largest Exporters and Importers (Merchandise and Services, US$ Billions—2009)	
1. United States	3,462
2. China	2,522
3. Germany	2,495
4. Japan	1,402
5. European Union	12,123

Source: Data from International Trade Statistics, Secretariat, World Trade Organization, 2010.

While the United States is still the largest exporter and importer in the world, it lost this distinction to China, in 2011 (see Table 5-1). China has already outdistanced Germany and Japan as a major trading country, so the Triad includes the United States, the European Union, and China.

The rapid increase in China's trade has created opportunities for many countries, but suppliers of textiles and electronic goods now face a major competitor, which has resulted in increased price competition see Box 5-1. Now that quotas have been removed from Chinese textiles there has been a major increase in imports to the United States. Textile mills in the Southeast will more than likely shrink in number as a result. Not only have American manufactures been impacted, but those in Asia, as well. Garment industries in Japan, Taiwan, and South Korea also face increased competition from China.

Chinese competition also affects other emerging economies, such as India. About one-third of the products manufactured by Indian bulk drug, small manufacturing enterprises (SMEs) are also available from China, but at a price lower than the cost of raw materials needed to produce them in India.

On a regional basis, Asia has experienced relatively high growth rates. Asia's share of world GDP is rising, thanks to its economic dynamism. Indeed, the region's economy, having fully recovered from the 1997–1998 financial crisis, is now the fastest growing in the world, contributing close to 50 percent of world growth. As of 2005, Asia's share of world GDP (35 percent) on a purchasing power parity (PPP) basis (see Figure 5-3) exceeded that of the United States (20 percent) and the European Union (20 percent). **Purchasing power parity** reflects differences in the cost of living

BOX 5-1   COUNTRY IN FOCUS: CHINA

Economics is one thing, but politics is another. During 2006, nearly half of the United States administration's cabinet, led by Hank Paulson, the United States Treasury Secretary, and accompanied by the Federal Reserve's chairman, Ben Bernanke, paid an official visit to China to discuss the first of a continuing "strategic economic dialogue" with Chinese officials. The most critical item of the agenda was (and still is) China's growing trade surplus with the United States, which reached nearly $200 billion at the time of the visit. Expectations that China would import more goods from the United States, while revaluing the yen upwards, were not very realistic. By 2009, the trade surplus had risen to $227 billion.

Source: Adapted from: Big guns, small prizes. (2006, December 19). *The Economist.* Retrieved from www.Economist.com/node/8450185.

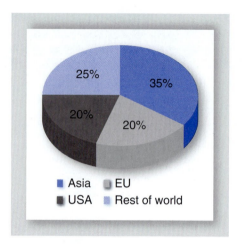

Figure 5-3 Share of World GDP (2005)

Source: Adapted from: International Monetary Fund. (2006, June). Asia's role in the world economy. *Finance and Development, 43*(2). Retrieved from www.imf.org/external/pubs/ft/andd/2006/06/picture.htm.

TABLE 5-2 Most Attractive Global Business Locations: Responses of Experts and TNCs*	
Responses from experts	**Responses from TNCs**
1. China (85%)	1. China (87%)
2. United States (55%)	2. India (51%)
3. India (42%)	3. United States (51%)
4. Brazil (24%)	4. Russian Federation (33%)
5. Russian Federation (21%)	5. Brazil (20%)
6. United Kingdom (21%)	6. Mexico (16%)
7. Germany (12%)	7. Germany (13%)
8. Poland (9%)	8. United Kingdom (13%)
9. Singapore (9%)	9. Thailand (11%)
10. Ukraine (9%)	10. Canada (7%)

*Countries are ranked according to the number of responses that rated each as the most attractive location.

Source: UNCTAD, *Global Investment Prospects Assessment* (www.unctad.org/fdiprospects), 2005–2008. Reprinted with permission.

between countries equalizing the purchasing power of countries' currencies to better reflect a country's wealth than if market exchange rates were used.

The anticipated future growth of Asian markets has made them more attractive to potential investors. As shown in Table 5-2, expert respondents and executives of **transnational corporations (TNCs)**[2] ranked developing countries such as China and India as most attractive for foreign investment (United Nations Conference on Trade and Development [UNCTAD]). China is considered an attractive location by 87 percent of TNC executives and 85 percent of the experts, about 30 percentage points above the next attractive country, the United States. These results imply that investment will shift from more developed countries that have saturated markets and high production costs to emerging economies, such as Asian countries.

2. A *transnational corporation (TNC)* is generally regarded as an enterprise comprising entities in more than one country which operate under a system of decision making that permits a common strategy. (United Nations Commission for Trade and Development). Other terms that are used to describe these firms are Multinational Corporations (MNC) and Multinational Enterprises (MNE).

Changes in relative shares of economic growth between regions will be significant, but changes within regions will be no less important. For example, real GDP growth averaged 6.5 percent during 1999–2005 in Ireland and 4.5 percent in Luxembourg, but only 1.5 percent in Denmark and Italy (EU Commission, 2006). The economic and financial crisis of 2008–2009 led to negative growth of GDP. Most developed nations experienced negative growth. However, China (+8.7%) and India (+8.8%) were among the only exceptions to negative growth. The way in which member states of economic groupings perceive themselves also differs. A **single market** such as the European Union may mean different things to different people. For example, the biggest piece of European Union legislation in years; a renewed attempt to enforce a maximum working week across Europe; and a recent opinion poll suggesting that a majority of businessmen in Europe think the cost of EU rules exceed the benefit. All reflect changing attitudes toward Europe's single market, and different philosophies about what it is for.[3]

There is ample evidence that a regional rather than a global strategy prevails among countries and businesses. For example:

1. Triad and regional trade are dominant; e.g., 67 percent of the EU members' exports are to other EU countries.

2. Most multinational corporations pursue regional, not global, strategies; e.g., approximately 90 percent of all cars manufactured in Europe are sold in Europe.

In order to understand these developments, we begin by examining regional trade arrangements and then answer the question of whether a global or regional response is the preferred international strategy.

REGIONAL ECONOMIC BLOCS

The economic and political forces of globalization have led to the regionalization of societies thorough the establishment of integrated economies such as the European Union, NAFTA, and MERCOSUR, so-called markets united by harmonized regulatory standards and common levels of social protection. These markets have provided the framework through which firms, including manufacturers, distributors, and service providers act under a new set of rules: those of the economic region in addition to those of the nation state. These new rules have led to the formation of supranational firms that attempt to globalize marketing operations on a world-wide or regional basis.

Regional trading blocs such as the EU, NAFTA, and Mercusor were established to liberalize trade between countries and facilitate the flows of goods, services, investment, and communication. A central tenet of these groups is that they have trading and investment policies that are favorable for members. They also have common policies regarding trading arrangements with non-members. There are three main forms of cooperative agreements, short of full monetary and political union among members. These are free trade areas, customs unions and common markets (see Appendix 1 at the end of this chapter).

Free Trade Areas

Free trade areas (FTAs) are arrangements in which countries give each other preferential treatment in trade by eliminating tariffs and other barriers on goods. Each

3. Single market blues. (5 February 2009). *The Economist*. Retrieved from www.Economist.com/world/Europe/PrinterFriendly .cfm?story_id=8134936.

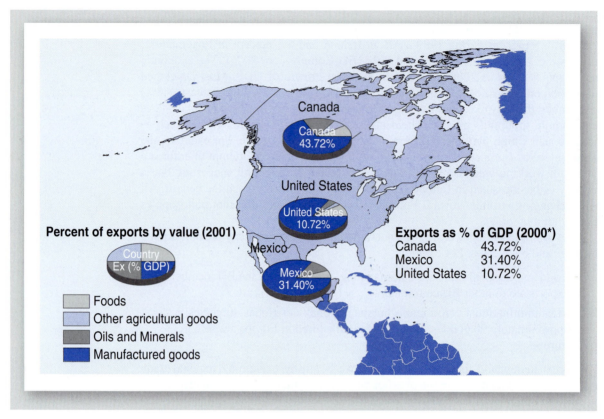

Figure 5-4 NAFTA Export Composition

* Export (% GDP) data for the United States and Canada for year 1999.
Sources: NAFTA Export Composition data from UNCTAD. Used with permission. Exports (% GDP) data from World Bank, World Development Indicators, 2002.

country continues its normal trade policies with other countries outside the FTA agreement. An example of a free trade area is the North American Free Trade Agreement (NAFTA), signed between the United States, Canada, and Mexico in 1994 (see Figure 5-4). It resulted in the elimination of customs duties between the three countries on most industrial products traded among them. Free trade area agreements aim to reduce or eliminate tariffs and non-tariff barriers among member countries. However, each member country may determine the extent of **external tariffs** it wishes to maintain with non-member countries.

In Figure 5-5, countries B and C are members of a free trade area. As a result, there are no customs duties levied on trade between them. Suppose, a manufacturer in country A, a non-member country, wishes to export building materials to country B. Country B levies a 15 percent tariff on building materials from non-member countries, which may make country A's products higher priced than local competitors. In order to be more competitive, the manufacturer can export instead to country C, pay the lower 8 percent *external tariff* and then re-export to country B (no tariff between C and B). In reality, most countries have domestic content legislation, which requires that products must contain a minimum value added in the country of origin in order to be free of customs duties.

Because the building materials were produced in country A, and not in country C, they would not enjoy relief from customs duties. Therefore, they would be subject to

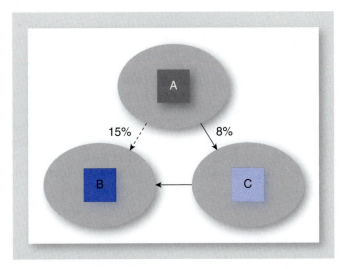

Figure 5-5 An Example of Trade Diversion

TABLE 5-3 The EFTA Network: FTA Agreements			
Eastern Europe	**Balkans**	**Middle East & Africa**	**Americas & Asia**
Bulgaria	Croatia	Israel	Chile
Romania	Macedonia	Morocco	Mexico
		Jordan	South Korea
		Lebanon	Singapore
		Tunisia	
		Turkey	
		Palestinian Authority	
		Southern African Customs Union (Botswana, Lesotho, Namibia, South Africa, Swaziland)	

an additional 7 percent tariff of country B, eliminating any possibility of circumventing customs duties by first exporting to country C.

There are many FTAs, some involving more than two countries, but there are **bilateral agreements** as well, as between the United States and Israel and the United States and South Korea. The **european free trade area (EFTA)** (Iceland, Liechtenstein, Norway, and Switzerland) includes those countries that did not opt to join the EU in its inception. However, residents in the EFTA countries are more than twice as wealthy as those in the EU. They also enjoy lower inflation, higher employment, healthier budget surpluses, and lower real interest rates. Interestingly, they also export more per capita than EU countries. In 1994, the EU and EFTA established the **european economic area (EEA),** thereby creating a european single market.[4] While not members of the EU, EFTA countries have free movement of goods, capital, services, and people, but without a common monetary and agricultural policy or the same social welfare policies as the EU. Each country is free to negotiate free trade agreements with other countries. All EFTA countries have a vast network of free trade and bilateral agreements. Table 5-3 shows those countries with which EFTA has concluded an FTA agreement.

4. Switzerland is not a member of the EEA, but it has a separate agreement with the EU.

Of the countries listed, the United States has bilateral agreements with Israel, Jordan, Mexico, Morocco, South Korea, and Singapore. Mexico has the most bilateral trade agreements, including countries in Latin America, the EU, and EFTA.

Customs Unions

A **customs union** contains the same provisions as a free trade area with one major addition—a common external tariff. In the building products example earlier, countries B and C would have a common external tariff against imports of building materials and other products from non-member countries. In this case, the lower tariff advantage of country B would be eliminated. The Common external tariff of countries B and C would probably fall between the original tariff rates of 8 and 15 percent.

Common Markets

The most advanced form of trade bloc is the **common market.** This type of organization combines the provisions of a free trade area and a customs union with two additional criteria, the free movement of people and capital. The largest of the common markets is the European Union, established as the **European Economic Community** in 1958 with six member countries, which increased to 27 member countries in 2007. The EU has two additional goals: the establishment of a monetary and political union. A monetary union requires at least a common currency and a central bank. Eleven countries of the EU—Austria, Belgium, Finland, France, Germany, Ireland, Italy, Luxembourg, the Netherlands, Portugal, and Spain—initially qualified to participate in the monetary union. This required them to adhere to criteria established by the **Maastricht Treaty** regarding price stability, public finance (especially government deficits), and interest and exchange rates. Following this initial agreement, a European Central Bank beg an functioning in 1998 and a **Euro area** in 1999. Euro notes and coins were introduced in 2002, replacing national ones. By 2007, 13 EU countries adopted the Euro in addition to six non-EU members: Andorra, Kosovo, Monaco, Montenegro, San Marino, and the Vatican City. Including both users of the Euro and those countries whose currencies are pegged to it makes the Euro the largest currency area in the world, with about 500 million people.

A final stage in the integration of countries belonging to a trade bloc is political union. While this stage is included in the Maastricht Treaty, it is far from fruition. Political union means relinquishing some if not all national sovereignty to the union, which many countries are unwilling to do, especially Great Britain, Germany, and France. Some forms of political cooperation are possible, such as a common defense and foreign policy, as exemplified by membership in NATO. However, formal political union remains a distant goal to be achieved.

How "Free" Is Intra-EU Trade?

While internal tariff barriers within the EU have been removed, non-tariff trade barriers still remain, especially in the form of narrow technical standards that companies use to keep their products out of national markets. In an effort to put an end to such barriers, the EU has proposed legislation that would require governments to accept goods approved for sale in another EU country, a principle called **mutual recognition.** However, the **harmonization** of product standards in the EU and between other countries is far from completed, as the following case illustrates.

A Dutch food producing company is subject to trade barriers because of a lack of harmonization. For example, there is no European harmonized definition of a sauce, which results in differences in interpretation. A product that in one country is considered a sauce can in another country be described as "vegetables based on solids." Apart from that, different techniques are being used to determine the composition of a product, which creates inconsistencies. Consequently, different import levies are charged in various countries for the same product.[5]

Of all the common markets in the world, the EU is the largest and most well known in every respect, by the number and size of its members, by their economic strength, and by the institutions (Parliament and Central Bank) that govern the union. However, there are other trade arrangements in every region of the world. See Table 5-4 for some examples. Most do not have a single currency as in the EU (the GCC is planning for a common currency), nor do they actively seek political union, but they have removed barriers to cross-country investment and services.

MERCOSUR

MERCOSUR is South America's largest trading bloc, with a combined GDP of $1.1 trillion. It was established in 1991 by the Treaty of Asuncion and the Treaty of Ouro Preto, which formalized a customs union that provides for the free movement of goods, capital, services, and people among its member states. The bloc's combined market encompasses more than 250 million people and accounts for more than three-quarters of the economic activity on the continent.

Brazil and Argentina have the greatest national income and trade of bloc members. Bolivia, Chile, Colombia, Ecuador, and Peru are associate members; they can join free trade agreements but remain outside the bloc's customs union. MERCOSUR tariff policies regulate imports and exports and the bloc can arbitrate trade disputes among its members.

In the future, MERCOSUR aims to create a continentwide free trade area, and the creation of a MERCOSUR development bank has been suggested. However, there have been tensions among members. For example, the bloc's smaller members, Paraguay and Uruguay, have complained of restricted access to markets in Argentina and Brazil and have sought to enact bilateral trade deals outside the bloc, even though such agreements are not permitted. Talks to secure a trade accord with the EU have stalled, with farm subsidies and tariffs on industrial goods being among the stumbling blocks. Negotiations on a planned, United States-backed Free Trade Area of the Americas are similarly mired, with some MERCOSUR leaders rejecting United States free market policies.

TABLE 5-4 Trade Arrangements	
Organization	**Members**
Association of Southeast Asian Countries (ASEAN)	Brunei, Cambodia, Indonesia, Laos, Malaysia, Myanmar, Philippines, Singapore, Thailand, Vietnam
East African Community (EAC)	Kenya, Uganda, Tanzania, Burundi, Rwanda
Gulf Cooperation Council (GCC)	Bahrain, Qatar, Kuwait, Oman, Saudi Arabia, United Arab Emirates
Southern Common Market (MERCOSUR)	Brazil, Argentina, Paraguay, Uruguay

5. Confederation of European Business Associations. (2004). *It's the internal market, stupid: A company survey on trade barriers in the European Union,* p. 13.

EAST AFRICAN COMMUNITY (EAC)

Much smaller than MERCOSUR, the **East African Community (EAC)** bloc has a combined population of 120 million people, a land area of 1.85 million sq kms, and a combined gross domestic product of $41 billion. The EAC was formed in July 2000 with the establishment of an FTA and later a customs union in 2005. It is working to form a common market and a monetary union, and ultimately a Political Federation of the East African States. The rules of the community and trade issues are handled by a legislative assembly and court of justice.

ASSOCIATION OF SOUTHEAST ASIAN NATIONS (ASEAN)

The **Association of Southeast Asian Nations (ASEAN)** free trade association was established in 1967 by the five original member countries: Indonesia, Malaysia, Philippines, Singapore, and Thailand, which were later joined by Brunei, Vietnam, Lao PDR, Myanmar, and Cambodia. The ASEAN region has a population of about 560 million and a combined gross domestic product of US$ 1,100 billion. The bloc's objective is to create a stable, prosperous, and highly competitive economic region in which there is a free flow of goods, services, skilled labor, investment, and capital.

GULF COOPERATION COUNCIL (GCC)

The **Gulf Cooperation Council (GCC)** charter states that the basic objectives are to effect coordination, integration, and interconnection between member states in all fields, strengthening ties between their peoples, formulating similar regulations in various fields such as economy, finance, trade, customs, tourism, legislation, and administration, as well as fostering scientific and technical progress in industry, mining, agriculture, water and animal resources, establishing scientific research centers, setting up joint ventures, and encouraging cooperation of the private sector. In essence, the GCC is both a customs union and a common market, allowing for the free movement of goods, capital, and people among member countries. The GCC members have some of the fastest-growing economies in the world, mostly due to oil and natural gas revenues along with a building and investment boom financed by decades of accumulated petroleum revenues. The GCC has an economic and technical cooperation agreement with the EU in the fields of energy, industry, agriculture, fisheries, and science.

Free versus Fair Trade

We have learned that free trade means removing barriers to international commerce among nations. On the other hand, there is a concept known as "fair" trade. **Fair trade** is an approach to international commerce that aims to ensure that producers in developing countries receive a fair price for goods and services, decent working conditions, and a commitment from buyers so that there is reasonable security for the sellers.

There are a number of non-governmental organizations (NGOs) that aim to promote fair trade, including the Fairtrade Foundation (www.fairtrade.org.uk), Oxfam International (www.oxfam.org), Traidcraft (www.traidcraft.org.uk), and the International Fair Trade Association (IFAT, www.ifoam.org/partners/partners/ifat.html). These organizations have defined fair trade as "an alternative approach to conventional international trade. It is a trading partnership which aims at sustainable development for excluded and disadvantaged producers. It seeks to do this by providing better trading conditions, by awareness raising, and by campaigning."

There are about 300 fair trade organizations in over 60 countries associated with IFAT, including producers, export marketing companies, importers, retailers, and financial institutions. For example, Organic Partners is a UK-based organization affiliated with the IFAT that is associated with more than 100 producers and suppliers in 40 countries covering over 1,000,000 hectares of certified land, specializing in the provision of plant-based raw materials and ingredients to international manufacturers and traders of food, beverages, medicines, and cosmetics. The organization establishes partnerships with farmers and collectors of plants, assisting them in crop production and handling its sale. Organic Partners has developed a profit share structure whereby producers are offered a financial stake in the company based on a share of annual profits. A major contribution to producers is supply chain management, which enables them to obtain "fair" prices for their crops.

Global marketers should be aware of the growing importance of these organizations. Their market share has become significant in some countries: 47 percent of all bananas, 28 percent of the flowers, and 9 percent of the sugar sold in Switzerland are fair-trade labeled. In the UK, a market with eight times the population of Switzerland, labeled products have achieved a 5 percent market share of tea, a 5.5 percent share of bananas, and a 20 percent share of ground coffee. The annual net retail value of fair trade products sold worldwide is estimated at €2.9 billion, and in Europe, approximately €660 million.

EMERGING MARKETS

The term *emerging market* was coined by Antoine W. Van Agtmael, then-Deputy Director of the Capital Markets Department of the International Finance Corporation of the World Bank. He included all low- and middle-income countries as "emerging." The term's meaning has since been expanded to include more or less all developing countries. Yet what is a "developing" country? The General Agreement on Tariffs and Trade (GATT) defined developing countries as those having low standards of living but did not designate how low the living standard should be. The World Trade Organization leaves it up to a country to designate whether it is developed or developing. Others claim that the degree of development should be the money value that people can produce or earn, such as gross national income per capita.[6] More often than not, some measure of national income is the most-used indicator of a country's development. However, although measures of national income in emerging markets are lower than that of developed countries, market potential for many products is substantial as demonstrated in Box 5-2.

BOX 5-2   TECHNOLOGY IN FOCUS: EMERGING MARKETS

Future technology growth will be driven by emerging markets rather than Europe, North America, or Japan. Consumers in these emerging markets will probably use handheld devices like smartphones and iPads rather than desktop or laptop computers that have been the mainstay to cyberspace communication.

Emerging markets provide sales potential for companies like Nokia, Samsung, and Ericsson because they have not had the time or money to expand cable communication. However, the wireless communication companies will have to adapt their products to meet consumer requirements and purchasing power.

Source: Adapted from: Abate, T. (2007, August 31). Emerging markets in BRIC nations are focus of technology firms. *The San Francisco Chronicle.* Retrieved from http://articles.sfgate.com/2007-08-31/business/1725917_1_ emerging-markets-technology-firms.

---

6. Cui, F. (2008). Who are the developing countries in the WTO? *Law and Development Review, 1*(1), 144.

Kvint suggests that an emerging market country can be defined as a society transitioning from a dictatorship to a free-market-oriented economy, with increasing economic freedom, gradual integration within the global marketplace, an expanding middle class, improving standards of living and social stability and tolerance, as well as an increase in cooperation with multilateral institutions.[7] Following this definition, emerging economies include Eastern European countries such as Hungary, Poland, and Romania, the Baltic States, Estonia, Latvia, and Lithuania, and Asian countries such as China, Indonesia, and Malaysia.

As emerging markets, these countries implement economic reform programs that result in stronger and more responsible performance levels, as well as transparency and efficiency in capital markets. If reforms are successfully implemented, emerging countries are more likely to receive aid from developed countries and from organizations such as the World Bank and the International Monetary Fund.

Referring to the CAGE model discussed in Chapter 2, there are a number of distances between developed and emerging markets. **Cultural distances** are evident, including wide gaps when it comes to corporate social responsibility and ethical issues. Political risk is also an important consideration when considering investment in emerging markets. **Administrative distances** are most prevalent in the absence of membership of some countries in multilateral groupings such as common markets and the World Trade Organization. Administrative distance also results from institutional weakness and a lack of managerial talent and experience. There is also more government regulation and control over elements of the economy, such as requiring the use of domestic distributors. **Geographic distances** are both inter-country and intra-country. For example, take the case of distribution in a large country such as India (Box 5-3). Infrastructure and facilities are key issues for companies distributing in India. In many parts of the country it is difficult to deliver a damage-free product to the consumer, owing to poor roadways and poor handling of the merchandise.

In rural areas, the distribution infrastructure is much more inefficient than in developed areas such as Delhi. Therefore, supply chain management may be fraught with difficulty and lead to high costs. **Economic distances** are represented by underdeveloped financial institutions, lack of a developed communication and transportation infrastructure and of course, lower incomes and domestic investment.

An emerging market economy must weigh local political and social factors as it attempts to open up its economy to the world. Businesspeople and consumers in

---

BOX 5-3 COMPANY IN FOCUS: WHIRLPOOL

In India, a major issue for Whirpool is the delivering of its many products over large distances without sustaining damage. A poor transportation infrastructure, especially in rural areas, provides a serious challenge to the company in overcoming unmaintained roads and the need for a number of interfaces between rail, truck and small vehicles carrying the products. In addition, the many interfaces results in lost time in supplying products from the manufacturer to consumer.

---

7. Kvint, V. (28 January 2008). Define emerging markets now. *Forbes.* Retrieved from www.forbes.com/2008/01/28/kvint-developing-countries-oped-ex_kv_0129kvint.html.

emerging markets have been accustomed to being protected from the outside world, and can often be distrustful of foreign investment. National pride may also be an issue, because citizens may be opposed to having foreign ownership of parts of the local economy. Liberalizing the economy during transition also means that people are exposed to different consumption cultures such as fast food, Western movies, and work cultures such as standards and ethics.

BRIC Countries

Among the fastest-growing groups of emerging economies are the so-called BRIC countries. The BRIC countries (Brazil, Russia, India and China) were first designated as such by the investment firm Goldman Sachs in 2001 as those that offer high consumer potential and that could overtake the economies of the developed world by 2050. China could become the largest economy in the world by that time, and India the third largest after the United States. The combined GDP of the BRIC countries could exceed that of the G6 (United States, EU, Australia, Japan, India, and China) countries combined. China, especially, is at the forefront of world economic development. As shown in Table 5-5, China has the largest population in the world, the second largest GDP (by purchasing power parity), is first in exports, third in imports, and first in foreign reserve holdings, ownership of mobile phones, and the number of Internet users.

All BRIC countries had experienced real GDP growth until the financial crisis of 2008–2009. As shown in Figure 5-6, China had the highest growth, reaching over 10 percent in 2007. India had growth of nearly 10 percent in the same year, followed by Russia (8 percent) and Brazil (6 percent). All of these GDP figures were impressive when compared to developed countries over the same time period.

BRIC countries are not only a major source for manufacturing, but are also consumers of basic products like food and clothing and high technology products. Consumer products have to be adapted to local requirements and be priced to make them accessible to a large number of people. As incomes are lower in emerging markets, a product that appeals to middle-income people in a developed country will have to be positioned to upper-middle-income consumers in developing countries or be adapted so that it can be sold at a lower price.

TABLE 5-5 BRIC Countries

Categories	Brazil	Russia	India	China
Area	5th	1st	7th	3rd/4th
Population	5th	9th	2nd	1st
GDP (nominal)	10th	8th	12th	3rd
GDP (PPP)	9th	6th	4th	2nd
Exports	21st	11th	23rd	1st
Imports	27th	17th	16th	3rd
Current account balance	47th	5th	169th	1st
Received FDI	16th	12th	29th	5th
Foreign exchange reserves	7th	3rd	4th	1st
External debt	24th	20th	27th	19th
Public debt	47th	117th	29th	98th
Electricity consumption	10th	3rd	7th	2nd
Number of mobile phones	5th	4th	2nd	1st
Number of internet users	5th	11th	4th	1st

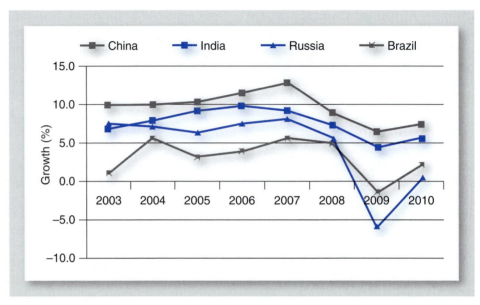

Figure 5-6 BRIC Real GNP Growth—2003–2010

Source: Adapted from: Assis, L. (2009, June 25). Special report: diverging demographic prospects for BRIC consumer markets. *Euromonitor.*

Local shopping habits also differ across BRIC countries. A McKinsey survey[8] found that clothing shoppers in China have small budgets, and hence small wardrobes, and that in Brazil consumers are fashion conscious, whereas in India, shopping is a family affair with all taking part in the decision of what to buy. In addition, only one-fourth of Chinese consumers prefer Western brands, whereas in India the proportion is 50 percent. Chinese shoppers base their perceptions of product quality on price more than consumers in Brazil, India, and Russia. In India and Brazil, about 80 percent of consumers look forward to shopping for clothing, but in China and Russia only about one-fourth of consumers look forward to a shopping experience.

Table 5-6 summarizes the key strengths and weaknesses of the BRIC countries. One of the major strengths common to all four countries is economic reform. Russia has privatized many industries and businesses, and India and Russia have encouraged foreign investment, while Brazil has implemented economic reforms and liberalization measures in its economy. Russia and India possess skilled labor, while Brazil and China are investing in education in order to upgrade human resources, especially skilled managers. On the downside, all BRIC countries must improve their infrastructures in order to achieve economic progress. Bureaucracy is a problem in many emerging countries, and the BRIC group is no exception. For example, the time to register a business takes much longer in the BRIC countries, as shown in Table 5-7. While in other emerging countries, such as Poland and Belarus, registration takes longer, it is still higher in the BRICs compared to industrialized countries like the United States, the UK, and Australia.

THE FUTURE POTENTIAL OF EMERGING NATIONS

GlobalEDGE at the International Business Center of Michigan State University has constructed a market potential index based on a number of accepted economic and market indicators such as market size, potential, growth, and others, as shown in Table 5-8. According to the index, the 10 countries with the most potential are Hong Kong,

8. How half the world shops: apparel in China, Brazil and India. (2007). *McKinsey Quarterly*, p. 4. Retrieved from www .mckinseyquarterly.com/how_half_the_world_shops_Apparel_in_Brazil_China_India_2075.

TABLE 5-6 Strengths and Weaknesses of BRIC Countries		
Country	**Key Strengths**	**Key Weaknesses**
Brazil	South America's leading economic power. Brazil is increasing investment in higher education. Abundant natural resources and a diversified economy.	GDP growth and consumer spending power is declining. More investment needed in the infrastructure.
Russia	Abundant natural resources and a skilled labor force.	The only BRIC country undergoing a population decline, reducing the labor market and increasing the number of pensioners.
India	27% of the population will be younger than 15 in 2020, an important future consumer market. Economic growth averaged about 8% since 2003. Large population of world-class competitive industries, IT-competent workforce. Stable financial institutions and strong legal system.	Limited foreign investment, inadequate infrastructure. Inadequate domestic savings that could fuel investment.
China	Annual economic growth of 10.7% between 2003–2008. Large population of 1.3 billion can provide growing domestic consumption. Market-oriented reforms continuing (e.g., accession to the WTO).	Weak financial system, growing income gap could lead to social instability. There is a shortage of skilled management. Weak intellectual property laws.

TABLE 5-7 Time Needed for Property Registration and Execution in Selected Countries				
	Ownership registration		**Contract execution**	
Country	**Period (days)**	**Costs (% of property value)**	**Period (days)**	**Costs (% of property value)**
Russia	37	0.8	330	20.3
China	32	3.1	241	25.5
India	67	13.9	425	43.1
Brazil	42	2.0	566	16.5
Portugal	83	7.3	320	17.5
Poland	204	1.6	1,000	8.7
Hungary	79	6.8	365	8.1
Kazakhstan	52	1.8	400	8.5
Azerbaijan	61	0.5	267	19.8
Armenia	18	0.9	195	17.8
Belarus	221	0.2	250	20.77
UK	21	4.1	288	15.7
Germany	41	4.2	184	10.5
Italy	27	1.3	1,390	17.8
Australia	7	4.3	157	14.4
United States	12	0.5	250	7.5
DR Congo	106	10.1	909	256.8

China, Singapore, Taiwan, South Korea, Czech Republic, Hungary, Mexico, Israel, and Poland. India and Russia are ranked 11 and 12, and Brazil is 23rd on the list. By looking at the individual indices, you can see why a country is ranked as it is. For example, China is ranked second in potential mainly because of its large market and high growth (weighted heavily on the overall index) and moderate country risk. Brazil, on the other hand, ranked far behind China because of lower market growth and intensity.

TABLE 5-8 Market Potential Index (MPI) for Emerging Markets–2009

Overall Rank	Country	Market Size	Market Growth Rate	Market Intensity	Market Consumption Capacity	Commercial Infrastructure	Economic Freedom	Market Receptivity	Country Risk	Overall Score
1	Singapore	1	28	73	57	94	77	100	100	100
2	China	100	100	1	60	34	1	4	55	97
3	Hong Kong	1	27	100	48	100	93	69	89	93
4	South Korea	10	12	64	100	92	77	15	67	69
5	Czech Republic	1	17	45	94	94	85	14	77	61
6	Israel	1	12	68	74	70	77	23	74	54
7	Poland	4	27	63	78	78	70	6	61	53
8	Hungary	1	1	67	90	82	81	16	43	48
9	Russia	25	38	29	75	65	7	3	48	40
10	Malaysia	3	26	27	73	64	45	24	55	36
11	India	38	54	25	60	2	44	3	24	36
12	Turkey	7	38	66	58	49	51	4	35	33
13	Chile	2	27	49	24	49	100	13	63	33
14	Mexico	10	16	58	38	46	63	15	51	31
15	Saudi Arabia	4	39	12	75	59	19	12	72	31
16	Brazil	21	29	44	20	47	54	1	46	26
17	Egypt	4	40	54	75	32	19	6	34	24
18	Argentina	4	53	47	42	56	46	3	14	23
19	Thailand	4	31	22	52	46	38	15	40	18
20	Pakistan	6	52	61	79	4	28	1	1	17
21	Peru	2	56	42	39	1	61	5	40	16
22	Indonesia	11	26	37	55	30	43	3	27	15
23	Philippines	5	12	59	48	26	38	6	25	8
24	Venezuela	3	24	37	60	41	5	7	13	3
25	South Africa	6	21	45	1	13	65	6	47	3
26	Colombia	3	17	46	9	41	47	3		2

SUMMARY

- Intra-regional trade accounts for 10 percent of all world trade. About half of total United States trade is with its neighbors, Canada and Mexico. Nearly three-fourths of EU trade is within Europe and half of Asian trade is within Asia. The growth of intra-regional trade is owing to regional trading blocs such as NAFTA and the EU.

- China has become a major economic power. It has more exports and imports than Japan and Germany that are increasing at a higher rate than all developed nations. China is also one of the most attractive countries for investors.

- Most of the world's economic growth is shifting to emerging nations. While not limited to, they are usually represented by the BRIC countries: Brazil, Russia, India, and China. The BRIC countries have experienced rapid economic growth and have large consumer markets and an abundance of skilled human resources. However, other emerging markets like South Korea, Taiwan, and Eastern European countries such as Poland, Hungary, and the Czech Republic are also developing rapidly.

DISCUSSION QUESTIONS

1. Look up export statistics for your state. Are there exports to emerging markets? If so, what is the proportion of exports compared to developed countries?

2. Do you agree that there is little difference between emerging markets and developing countries? Why or why not?

3. You are asked for advice by the owner of a medium-sized firm manufacturing digital alarm clocks. He thinks there is a market for his product in the BRIC countries. How would you advise him on what to look for first?

EXPERIENTIAL EXERCISES

1. Using the CAGE Model (Chapter 2), discuss the distances between the four BRIC countries.

2. Using Table 5-8, discuss why the market potential for China is greater than that of India.

KEY TERMS

Administrative distances, p. 130

Association of Southeast Asian Nations (ASEAN), p. 128

Bilateral agreements, p. 125

BRIC countries, p. 119

Common market, p. 126

Cultural distances, p. 130

Customs union, p. 126

East African Community (EAC), p. 128

Economic distances, p. 130

Emerging market, p. 129

Euro area, p. 126

European Economic Area (EEA), p. 125

European Economic Community, p. 126

APPENDIX 1

Comparison between Regional Blocs

Activities

Regional bloc	Free Trade Area	Customs Union	Economic and Monetary Union		Free Travel		Political Pact	Defense Pact	Other
			Single Market	Currency Union	Visa-free	Borderless			
EU	in force	in force	in force	in force	in force	in force (Schengen and CTA)	in force	in force (NATO and CFSP/ESDP)	ESA, Euratom
EFTA	in force	in force	in force		in force	in force (Schengen treaty)		in force (NATO)	ESA
CARICOM	in force	in force	in force	in force and proposed common	in force	proposed	proposed		
CSN — MERCOSUR	in force	in force			in force		proposed for 2014		
CSN — Can Common	proposed for 2014	proposed for not after 2019	proposed for 2019	proposed for 2019	in force		proposed for 2019		
ECOWAS	in force	in force		in force and proposed for 2009 and proposed common	in force	proposed	proposed	in force	
CEMAC	in force	in force	proposed	in force	proposed				
EAC	in force	in force		proposed for 2009	proposed		proposed for 2010	in force	
SACU	in force	in force	proposed for 2012	de-facto in force and proposed common for 2016	proposed				
COMESA	in force	proposed for 2008		proposed for 2025					
Agadir	in force								

138

Activities

Regional bloc	Free Trade Area	Customs Union	Economic and Monetary Union		Free Travel		Political Pact	Defense Pact	Other
			Single Market	Currency Union	Visa-free	Borderless			
GCC	in force	in force	proposed for 2007	proposed for 2010					
NAFTA	in force			proposed				in force (NATO and Security and Prosperity Partnership of North America)	
ASEAN	in force	proposed	proposed for 2015	proposed	in force		proposed for 2015	proposed for 2020	
SAARC	in force		proposed						
EurAsEC	proposed *in effect*, proposed	in force	proposed	proposed	in force		proposed	in force	
PARTA	*in effect*, proposed	proposed							
CACM	proposed	proposed							
AEC *(for reference)*	proposed for 2019	proposed for 2019	proposed for 2023	proposed for 2028			proposed for 2028		

Area, Population, and GDP by Regional Bloc

Regional Bloc	Area (km²)	Population	GDP (PPP) ($US)		Member States
			in millions	per capita	
EU	4,325,675	496,198,605	12,025,415	24,235	27
EFTA	529,600	12,233,467	471,547	38,546	4
CARICOM	462,344	14,565,083	64,219	4,409	16
CSN	17,339,153	370,158,470	2,868,430	7,749	10
ECOWAS	5,112,903	251,646,263	342,519	1,361	15
CEMAC	3,020,142	34,970,529	85,136	2,435	6
EAC	1,763,777	97,865,428	104,239	1,065	3
SACU	2,693,418	51,055,878	541,433	10,605	5
COMESA	3,779,427	118,950,321	141,962	1,193	5
Agadir	1,703,910	126,066,286	513,674	4,075	4
GCC	2,285,844	35,869,438	536,223	14,949	6
NAFTA	21,588,638	430,495,039	15,279,000	35,491	3
ASEAN	4,400,000	553,900,000	2,172,000	4,044	10
SAARC	5,136,740	1,467,255,669	4,074,031	2,777	8
EurAsEC	20,789,100	208,067,618	1,689,137	8,118	6
PARTA	528,151	7,810,905	23,074	2,954	14
CACM	422,614	37,816,598	159,536	4,219	5

CASE 5-1
Walmart in Japan

Walmart's Expansion into the Japanese market

Walmart is, in many ways, the quintessential American retailer, though this hasn't stopped the company from expanding aggressively to overseas markets in recent years. Already the number one retailer in the three North American markets, Walmart began aggressive international expansion a few years ago. Walmart bought ASDA Group in Great Britain, making it one of the largest retailers in the UK, while also expanding in Asia, placing stores in Hong Kong, and setting up a successful joint venture in Mainland China. However, Walmart has not been able to achieve success with the Seiyu Group, a Japanese general merchandise and grocery store chain that came into the Walmart family in 2002. Walmart has spent a fortune in both time and money to turn around the once-dominant retailer and become a force in the Japanese market. Due to mistakes and missed opportunities, Seiyu's market share has shrunk and losses have mounted. Walmart's Japanese protégé has become a favorite target for shareholder criticism and a blot on the company's international reputation. How did this happen?

Seiyu (The Seiyu Co., Ltd.) is older than its partner, Walmart. Founded after World War II as part of the Saison Group, the company was linked up with the Seibu railway company, helping to provide a ready stream of customers to its stores. While not a well-known conglomerate like Mitsubishi or Nissan, Seiyu was part of a group of linked firms with Sumitomo Bank as the primary shareholder. This arrangement ended only when Walmart bought out Sumitomo's equity in Seiyu.

Seiyu expanded heavily in the 1980s, but when the bubble economy burst in the mid-90s, and land values dropped at the same time, Seiyu started to have financial problems. Even before Walmart bought a stake in Seiyu, the retailer had been struggling, though its core grocery business was profitable.[1] In an attempt to reach new markets, Seiyu was expanding into newly built residential areas and experimenting with new types of stores such as The Mall, Mizuho 16, a mall complex with a Seiyu-managed store as the anchor and numerous other retailers renting space, and Livin, a department store with groceries on the bottom floors, a common practice in higher-end Japanese retailing. Seiyu was also rebuilding and remodeling several stores a year, though it simply did not have the capital to move as fast as it needed to. Seiyu was a firm that had expanded too much in the heady days of Japan's bubble economy. The company had lost sight of its core business and was no longer nimble enough to fight off rivals. Seiyu was suffering declining sales, declining profits, and declining brand prestige. Many consumers seemed confused as to what exactly Seiyu offered them. It was just one more name in a crowded retail field, a name that many consumers did not feel a particular draw to. In a recent poll, only 5 percent of those asked responded that the reason they shop at Seiyu was quality.[2]

1. Smith, C. (13 December 2002). Walmart stocks up on Seiyu. *The Daily Deal*. Retrieved from "http://www.lexisnexis.com"www.lexisnexis.com.

2. Ibid.

Case prepared by Aaron Toussaint and Parissa Haghirian, Sophia University, Tokyo. Reprinted with permission.

While Seiyu was struggling, competitors were moving up in the industry. In 1990, Seiyu was the third largest retailer in Japan.[3] The top two spots were occupied by Daiei and Ito Yokado, respectively, both grocery and general merchandise stores like Seiyu. By 2003, Seiyu had been knocked out of the top five, while Daiei, Jusco/AEON (another grocery and general merchandise store), and Ito Yokado remained. The first and fifth spots, respectively, were held by convenience store chains Lawson and Seven-Eleven (Seven and I holdings owns both Seven-Eleven convenience stores and Ito Yokado).[4]

In 2002 Seiyu was thrown a lifeline in the form of capital investment from Walmart. After some years of financial trouble, a tie-up with the biggest retailer in the world must have seemed like a windfall. Indeed, looking at media reports from the time, there were many voices urging caution but predicting that with the right moves, Walmart and Seiyu could make money in Japan.[5] Seiyu's financial troubles also gave Walmart more of a free hand to make drastic yet necessary changes.[6]

The two companies seemed to be a good fit. Both were general merchandise stores. Both had built extensively in the suburbs. Seiyu and Walmart both tried to undercut the competition on price. Walmart had what many were seeing as a golden chance to enter Japan with a well-established partner. It could thus forgo the risks that plagued firms like Ikea and Carrefour, who had decided to go it alone in Japan.

Japanese Consumer Behavior—A Greater Challenge than Expected

Japan and the United States are very different places. Japanese shoppers behave differently, have different preferences for goods, and have different attitudes about what they want from a retailer than their American counterparts. For the Japanese consumer, price is not the sole determinant of value. For the Japanese consumer, fresh fish is as important as bulk toilet paper, and packaging is nearly as important as product. It seemed that Walmart understood the financial risks of its tie-up with Seiyu,[7] but looking at its actions over the next few years, it is far less clear that it understood the fundamentals of the Japanese retail market.

Everyday Low Prices in Japan?

Japan has often been called a mass luxury market. Louis Vuitton, the famous French purveyor of purses and fancy shoes, makes nearly one third of its total sales in Japan.[8] Japanese consumers have a taste for the luxurious, though it has also been shown that on some goods Japanese consumers are practically giddy about saving money. This fact must be mentioned with a caveat; though Japanese consumers like saving money, they are still picky about quality. They will not buy cheap goods, especially if the goods are perceived as an inferior substitute. As the old saying goes, "*yasukarou, warukarou*"—"if it's cheap, it's bad." With Japanese cuisine, how the

3. Aoyama, Y. (2006, July17–18). *Why foreign retailers fail in Japan, Carrefour vs. Walmart.* Paper presented at the Globalizing Retail Seminar, Surrey, UK. Retrieved from www.sorn.surry.ac.uk/research/groups/globalizingretailseminar/Aoyama.pdf.

4. Ibid.

5. Troy, M. (25 March 2002). Walmart invests in Japan, buys 6% share of Seiyu—*DSN Retailing Today*. Retrieved from http://findarticles.com/p/articles/mi_m0FNP/is_6_41/ai_84183445/.

6. Kumakura, T. (27 October 2007). Walmart seeks full ownership of Seiyu; Business Asia by Bloomberg. *International Herald Tribune*. Retrieved from www.bloomberg.com/apps/news?pid=newsarchive&sid=a4LJlkfK12FI.

7. Smith, C. (13 December 2002). Walmart stocks up on Seiyu. *Daily Deal.* Retrieved from www.lexisnexis.com/us/Inacademic/delivery/PrintDoc.do?.

8. Japan is the World's Most Concentrated Source of Revenue for Luxury Brands. (2006, May). *Japan External Trade Organization*. Retrieved from www.jetro.org/content/361.

food is presented is as important as what it tastes like, perhaps even more important because bad-looking food will not be consumed. Pricing is one aspect of presentation.

In contrast to this, Walmart has thrived on a low-cost image since its inception. Warehouse stores and Walmart's deep discounts on national brands are key to the company's success in the United States. It is important to ask whether this low-cost leadership strategy is fundamentally sound in Japan. Management slips and consumer misunderstandings may have played a part in Walmart's eventual woes. But perhaps the most important question to ask is "Will 'Everyday Low Prices' work in Japan?"

The Japanese attitude toward price and quality carries over to groceries, but it applies to other goods as well. Walmart carried a serious risk in Japan by being too cheap. Seiyu and its new partner were spending huge amounts of money to rebuild and renovate stores, making them more attractive to Japanese consumers, but they still had to convince consumers that they were getting a great deal, namely the best products for a price that they cannot believe. This has been a problem for the retailer. As former Seiyu president Masao Kiuchi lamented, "The lower price on *sashimi* doesn't mean that it's a few days old, but that Walmart got a better price on it." Sadly, many Japanese consumers cannot help but be suspicious of items, especially food items, priced in the bargain range.

Reading Japanese Customers

One of Walmart's first mistakes was to step on the toes of a powerful stakeholder group in Japan: housewives. One of the reasons for Walmart's spectacular success in the suburbs of America is the car society and the shopping habits it engenders. Suburban Americans will drive the car to the nearest strip mall or supercenter and stock up on goods and groceries for the week. They have the space in their homes to stock cheap goods in bulk, as well as cars to transport heavy loads. In Japan, especially in urban areas, shopping is spread throughout the week and is often done by bicycle or on foot. For several items, especially fresh grains and vegetables, Japanese consumers go shopping an average of once every other day.[9] Housewives compare prices before they go out by looking at daily newspaper inserts called *chirashi*.

In 2004, citing its famous slogan "Everyday Low Prices," Walmart had Seiyu cut out the *chirashi*. In the United States, consumers associate Walmart with lower prices (15 to 20 percent lower) than the competition.[10] In Japan, consumers still wanted to see the deals in print—they did not trust Seiyu to deliver the lowest prices without some sort of authentication.[11] Without being able to compare prices, housewives were confused and simply went elsewhere.[12] After a marked drop in sales, Walmart was forced to resurrect the *chirashi*.

Private Brands

Another major arm of Walmart's Japan strategy is the aggressive introduction of private brands. In the United States, Walmart is famous for exclusive store brands, like Sam's American Choice Cola, that are inexpensive and perceived as a good value by United States consumers. Seiyu is putting more and more Walmart goods on its

9. Aoyama, Y. (2006, July17–18). *Why foreign retailers fail in Japan, Carrefour vs. Walmart.* Paper presented at the Globalizing Retail Seminar, Surrey, UK. Retrieved from www.sorn.surry.ac.uk/research/groups/globalizingretailseminar/Aoyama.pdf.

10. Rowley, I. (28 February 2005). Japan isn't buying the Walmart idea. *Businessweek*, Retrieved from www.businessweek.com/magazine/content/05_09/b3922073.htm.

11. Ibid.

12. Holstein, W. J. (27 July 2007). Why Walmart can't find happiness in Japan. *Fortune*. Retrieved from http://money.cnn.com/magazines/fortune/fortune_archive/2007/08/06/100141311/index.htm.

shelves in the hope of attracting price-conscious consumers.[13] Other Japanese retailers have also started down this path. Seven and I Holdings (Ito Yokado and Seven-Eleven's parent company) and Jusco/AEON have begun to offer many generic items like laundry detergent and snacks. The recent economic downturn has provided further impetus to Japanese retailers to speed the introduction of private brands. According to a recent article in the *Nikkei Marketing Journal,* nearly 70 percent of Japanese retailers now stock private brands, including more than 90 percent of supermarkets.[14] This is a dramatic increase from even a few years ago. Since Walmart has introduced its private brands all over the world, the firm should be clearly ahead of the game in developing its own brands. But will these global Walmart brands fit Japanese tastes? If Seiyu misreads recent consumer trends concerning private brands, it may wind up attracting fewer shoppers, not bringing in new ones.

Saying Yes to Japan

To its credit, Walmart has stayed the course in Japan, believing that it can make Seiyu work. This is not simply stubbornness; Walmart has shown in both Germany and South Korea that it knows when to quit. Walmart has also shown that it knows how to adapt.[15] In Seiyu, Walmart sees real opportunity. However, the company has not had full operational control for its entire sojourn at Seiyu. It was not until 2006 that the Japanese chairman of Seiyu stepped down and Walmart was able to place its own man, Edward Kolodzieski, at the helm. Walmart did not even make the company a wholly owned subsidiary until 2007. Looking at these facts, Walmart has been in full control of Seiyu for a relatively short period of time. Since gaining a free hand at Seiyu in the last two years, Walmart has moved aggressively to perform triage on Seiyu as the red numbers continue to add up. Yet many of the problems outlined above remain. Questions still remain about Walmart's understanding of the Japanese shopper and the Japanese market. Walmart has raised eyebrows by pressing forward in remaking Seiyu in the American Walmart's image and by adopting many radically different strategies from its rivals.[16]

Walmart continues to rebuild and remodel Seiyu stores, hoping to make them more attractive to Japanese consumers. However, many of the remodeled stores look like Walmart stores back in the United States. It remains to be seen if this is a style that will appeal to picky Japanese consumers. Another big change at Seiyu reflecting Walmart's influence is the introduction of private brand goods.

Going back to *chirashi*, Walmart finally embraced the paper leaflets. Showing its continued desire to be the lowest priced retailer and to make sure that "Everyday Low Prices" survive in Japan, Seiyu announced that it would now honor the *chirashi* of its competitors, as well[17]—a marketing coup designed to make sure that when customers think of low prices, they think of Seiyu.

13. Seiyu to boost store-brand goods to lure bargain hunters. (2 May 2008). *The Nikkei Friday Morning Edition.* Retrieved from www.nni.nikkei.co.jp/cgi-bin. See also: Seiyu to import 100 Walmart store brand items by year's end. (7 June 2008). *The Nikkei Saturday Morning Edition.* Retrieved from http://e.nikkei.com/bti-ntn.

14. PB wo tokubai 17%—7wari dounyuu, hyakattennmo hannsou. (17% give sales on PB items—70% of Japanese firms stock PBs, including 50 percent of department stores). (24 June 2009). *Nikkei Marketing Journal.* Retrieved from www.shopbiz.jp/rt/news/35872.html. Translated by authors.

15. One small example: in Canada, Walmart's Super Centers are spelled "Super Centre." Also, in numerous markets, Walmart has kept from making huge changes to acquisitions' names and logos. Walmart's China stores have also provided ample opportunities for adaptation to local markets.

16. Seiyu adopts contrarian strategy. (19 March 2007). *The Nikkei Weekly.* Retrieved from http://e.nikkei.com/e/fr/tnks/Nni20110820D.htm.

17. Seiyu 'tamise chirashi nebiki OK' supa—kakaku sennsou hakusya. (Spurring on the supermarket wars—Seiyu announces competitors' coupons are OK.) (12 May 2008). *Fuji Sankei Business/Bloomberg Global Finance.* Translated by authors. Retrieved from http://www.business-i.jp/article/200812040018a.nwc.

What about the Future?

Seiyu again failed to post a profit in 2008, though some stores were starting to show an increase in year-on-year sales.[18] There was a new CEO at the helm and the company seemed optimistic. However, the fact remained that Walmart had embarked on year seven of its tie-up with Seiyu and still had not made money from its investment.

The Japanese economy, though still the second largest in the world, is not as affluent as it once was. Consumers may be willing to accept cheaper substitutes, assuming they still meet a basic standard of quality. It would seem that the global recession and Japanese consumer's appetite for saving may still mesh well with Walmart's private brand strategy. Walmart is America's low price leader. It has worked hard to transplant this image to Japan, as well, even going so far as to honor competitors' coupons. With the current financial troubles hitting consumers hard, Walmart and its "Everyday Low Prices" should be in an optimum position to gain on its rivals in the coming years.

However, Japan is a fickle market, and although rising prices on well-known national brand foods and consumer goods was the story in the first half of 2008, the second half of the year seemed set to be dominated by the much cheaper private brands.[19] Only time would tell if this was a long-term trend or a temporary reaction to the global recession.

We have seen Walmart and Seiyu make mistakes and miss opportunities. The economic crisis has given the company a good chance to increase sales and market share, assuming that it has learned from its mistakes. In a company that increasingly sees itself as a global entity, failure in Japan would be a huge blow. Staying the course in Japan longer before admitting defeat would be even more painful.

Questions

1. Which market entry strategy did Walmart choose to enter the Japanese market?

2. What challenges did Walmart meet in Japan?

3. How does Japanese consumer behavior differ from Western consumer behavior?

4. Can private brands be internationalized?

5. Should Walmart change its pricing policy?

6. What effect will economic downturn have on Walmart's business in Japan?

7. Are there other American retailers that are successful overseas? Please name some and point out their international marketing strategies.

8. What future strategies should Walmart apply in the Japanese market?

---

18. Holstein, W. J. (27 July 2007). Why Walmart can't find happiness in Japan. *Fortune.* Retrieved from http://money.cnn.com/magazines/fortune/fortune_archive/2007/08/06/100141311/index.htm.

19. PB wo tokubai 17%—7wari dounyuu, hyakattennmo hannsuu. (17% give sales on PB items—70% of Japanese firms stock PBs, including 50 percent of department stores). (24 June 2009). *Nikkei Marketing Journal.* Retrieved from www.shopbiz.jp/rt/news/35872.html. Translated by authors.

CASE 5-2

Understanding Global Consumer Behavior in Aesthetic Surgery

News and trend analyses all over the world indicate that the importance of physical appearance is highly recognized, and there is an accompanied rise in demand for aesthetic surgery. Today, the beauty industry is a multibillion dollar business that influences the viability of cosmetics companies, pharmaceuticals, plastic surgeons, department stores, salons, spas, beauty parlors, magazines, and books. Identity reflected in the body itself becomes a saleable commodity in modernity, creating a link among self, body, and consumption. The body becomes saleable because the image of an ideal body is largely displayed through the consumer culture.

Aesthetic (or cosmetic) surgery remains a very effective beautification tool, which includes surgical operations on the face (such as rhinoplasty and face lift) and on other parts of the body (such as abdominoplasty, breast reduction, breast augmentation, and liposuction). In the area of plastic surgery, major developments took place after World War II, in order to cure the traumatic body dysfunctions of soldiers in particular. Since then, major developments have occurred in plastic surgery knowledge and technology, accompanied by changing needs and desires of plastic surgery patients. By definition, this medical branch is perceived as elective and luxurious.

Although it is risky and painful and requires time, energy, and money, aesthetic surgery has exploded in popularity over the past decade. People all around the world are having a greater number of surgeries. Patients are no longer just patients. They are patient–consumers with unique demands and different expectations. Many doctors are now utilizing advertising to increase demand for their work. If the body can be perceived as another consumption item, and patients as patient–consumers, this medical branch becomes an area of global marketing and consumer behavior. The effects of producers (doctors, medical companies, and the media) and consumers (patients of aesthetic surgery) can be discussed on an international basis.

Promotion of a Global Ideal Image

How an ideal physical appearance is globally promoted remains a topic of hot debate among academic scholars as well as practitioners in different contexts. Medicine is one of the areas where healthy body is defined by numbers. Consumer culture may encourage people to discipline their bodies in the name of health. The language used in ads for beauty products can be quite technical and scientific, making the claims more believable. Hence, the inclusion of physicians as medical authorities contributes to the "medicalization of appearance." Since the body now can be measured in terms of height, weight, skin color, and proportions of body parts, it becomes easier and more feasible to communicate it globally in the form of statistical averages and medical facts.

Medical discourse around the world neutralizes requirements for a "fit" body, while the media reinforces this view through healthy and fit images of men and women. One of the most important arguments is that the advertising system establishes, proposes,

Case prepared by Assistant Professor Dr. Berna Tarı Kasnakoğlu of the TOBB University of Economics and Technology. Reprinted with permission.

and promotes an ideal appearance both for men and women. Other than the media itself, fashion, through large-scale mediums such as fashion shows, fashion magazines, and fashion models, influences the way people establish a standard about what is (fashionably) beautiful. Film and music represent other areas where consumers in different parts of the world might be exposed to "prevailing" norms of beauty through its practitioners; i.e., movie stars, singers, and other celebrities. Beauty pageants are another area of a visual discourse of identity and otherness that serves as a model for the way global and local cultural institutions articulate beauty.

In a globalizing world, therefore, people may establish similar or different—and most of the time hybrid—standards of beauty for themselves. Another cultural ideal, different from their own, may be interpreted as a look that is aesthetically pleasing. This look may become so fashionable across many cultures that it might create a collective mood and thus a preference for a particular style or appearance.

Aesthetic Tourism

Just like an individual is defined in a national society in relation to other societies, an individual's body is also exposed to images taken from other communities around the world. At the same time, aesthetic tourism; i.e., traveling outside one's own country to go through cosmetic surgery, is on the rise. The ease of seeking medical treatment and services overseas contributes to worldwide spending on aesthetic tourism. This rise is supported by the existence of a global market for international hospital chains. Planning for aesthetic tourism trip is similar to planning a vacation using a travel agent. Due to lower costs, even with the cost of travel, aesthetic tourism provides an economic benefit. It also offers a social benefit since decisions are relatively autonomous and do not become a community affair. Lastly, it offers a legal benefit because some clinics apply procedures that are illegal in patient–consumers' home countries, such as a sex change.

Further, these clinics market themselves as romantic gateways, where patients can enjoy having fun in an exotic city. Sometimes the whole package is customized for the individual, including the visa procedures, traveling, being picked up from the airport, or having the surgery preceded or followed by a holiday at the destination. It is usually possible to talk to the doctors over the Internet, request an approximate price for the total package, and ask for financing options in the host country. International healthcare accreditation of the plastic surgery clinic or the hospital becomes a major concern for patients. Many of the hospitals in developing countries advertise themselves as equivalent to hospitals in the United States and Western Europe, usually by being accredited by the Joint Commission International, because it suggests that the hospital has earned the same quality and reliability.

Global Co-Creation of a Medical Consumption Experience

With many sources of information about plastic surgery and an increasing number of people going through these operations, plastic surgery patients can now make comments about their problems or deformities, criticize the physician for his or her treatment, and interfere with technical details since they are more readily available in the media, although they are not necessarily correct. They sometimes "test" the surgeon's knowledge by asking questions that they learned from the Internet. One of the differences in language appears when the patient wants to see the exact result before the operation. Doctors may try to make sure that the patient understands that the results of the operation may not coincide with what they imagine in their minds, and operation results depend on the patient's physical characteristics and healing factors.

Importance of communication between the patient and the doctor is demonstrated, especially when the doctor is perceived as a friend rather than a medical doctor. It is generally much less common for a doctor and a patient to become friends in other medical spheres, but since plastic surgeons are seen as experts on beauty, they are also seen as companions along the way toward ideal physical appearance. Trust is established when patients feel that the doctor understands their needs and expectations. Almost all informants state that it is very important to trust the doctor because your new appearance will "depend on" the doctor's knowledge and abilities. Besides medical knowledge and experience, doctor's individual characteristics, such as honesty and friendliness, play a very important role in building trust.

Similar to doctors, machinery, technology, and software can move around the globe very easily. All kinds of medical knowledge, equipment, pharmaceuticals, and tools can be imported and exported with minimum trouble across different countries. Hence "beauty" becomes the universal language for all people, and we can talk about a special kind of interdependence among these firms, doctors, and patients all around the world.

Discussion Questions:

1. Can medicine and doctors be included in a discussion of marketing? How? What are the marketing tools?
2. Who are the global patient–consumers of aesthetic surgery? What is their consumer behavior? What are the cultural similarities and differences?
3. How is tourism defined in terms of a global phenomenon in the context of aesthetic surgery?
4. What are the ethical issues concerning medical marketing?

Sources:

Appadurai, A. (1990). Disjuncture and difference in the global cultural economy. *Theory, Culture & Society, 7*(2/3), 295–310.

Bocock, R. (2001). *Consumption*. London: Routledge.

Burkett, L. (2007). Medical tourism: concerns, benefits, and the American legal perspective. *Journal of Legal Medicine, 28,* 223–245.

Featherstone, M. (1982). The body in consumer culture. *Theory, Culture & Society, 1*, 18–33.

Howson, A. (2004). *The Body in Society: An Introduction*. Cambridge: Polity.

Parasuraman, A., Zeithaml, V. A., & Berry, L. L. (1985, Fall). A conceptual model of service quality and its implications for future research. *Journal of Marketing, 49,* 41–50.

Global Marketing Functions and Strategies

Conducting Marketing Research

The need for information, the need for sharper, smarter, timelier, quicker information is just increasing.

SANGEETA GUPTA, DIRECTOR OF CONSUMER INSIGHTS, PEPSICO INDIA

LEARNING OBJECTIVES

After reading this chapter, you should be able to:

- Explain why global marketing research is important to multinational firms.
- Understand the differences between marketing research and marketing intelligence.
- Understand the importance of information technology for managerial decision making.
- Determine how to use a marketing intelligence/information system.
- Explain how firms can anticipate marketing crises.
- Know why some marketing research techniques may not be used in all countries.

Marketing managers at an American company were shocked when they discovered that the brand name of the cooking oil they were marketing in a Latin American country was translated into Spanish as "Jackass Oil." An American company that manufactures heating systems was trying to determine whether its products would be attractive to both industrial and household consumers in Sweden. In order to consider entering the Swedish market, management needed information about the ecological, cultural, technological, economic, political/legal, and competitive environments in Sweden. Specifically, management needed to determine whether its products could be sold as is, or whether they had to be adapted. Moreover, other aspects of the marketing mix had to be determined, such as pricing, distribution, and communication strategies. Finally, if there is sufficient demand for the products, what entry mode would be best for the American company?

It is the task of marketing research employees to determine, along with management, the sort of information that is needed to help answer questions like the one above. Therefore, the role of global marketing research is primarily to act as an aid to the decision maker by collecting and analyzing information relevant to solving a given problem.

IMPORTANCE OF GLOBAL MARKETING RESEARCH

In the midst of the global economic meltdown of 2007–2009, many marketers had a glum view of the near future; one of the few areas of marketing that retained some of its growth was market research. Global market research revenues reached $32 billion in 2008—an overall growth of 4.5 percent (net 0.4 percent) according to the ESOMAR Global Market Research Report. More importantly to global marketers, the highest growth rates in the research field continued to be in emerging markets, particularly in the Asia Pacific and Latin America regions.[1] Performance in North America was poor, with absolute growth of 1.5 percent and a decline of 2.1 percent after inflation, while growth in Europe slowed to 4.7 percent year-to-year and just 0.9 percent after correcting for inflation. Europe accounted for about half of total research expenditures, while the North American share was one-third of the total.

Another industry survey, Marketing Trends, also showed that only about 22 percent of market research executives expected a decrease in their budgets for the next year while 39 percent expected an actual increase in their budgets.[2] Their optimism was not unfounded, considering the importance of market research to the global success of an organization.

Although many use the terms market research and marketing research interchangeably, market research is considered a part of the larger marketing research field. The American Marketing Association (AMA) defines **marketing research** as any information used to discover marketing opportunities and problems, give directions to marketing actions, track performance, and contribute to a better marketing process overall.[3] This definition clearly includes **market research,** which usually studies market sizes and trends, but also encompasses competitive research, price or product research, and other research related to the marketing mix and the customer.

ESOMAR, the global trade organization for the market and opinion research industry, distinguishes market and social research activities from other forms of marketing, such as advertising or selling, by emphasizing that market researchers do not use or disseminate the personal information gathered about research participants for commercial purposes. There are many cultural, methodological, and other considerations for conducting global market and marketing research, as you will learn later in this chapter.

When managed correctly, the process of and insights collected through marketing research can yield undeniable results for a company. For example, the European grocer Tesco was able to increase sales of its baby products by 8 percent after monitoring its loyalty card data and combining that with survey research on products that were not popular at some of its stores. Through this research, Tesco found out that young mothers were not buying as many baby products at certain stores because they perceived pharmacies as more trustworthy sources for them. In response, Tesco launched BabyClub, a program that provided expert advice and baby product discounts to that consumer segment. By winning young moms' trust, Tesco was also able to claim a larger share of their wallets.[4]

Another example is the case of LG Electronics. According to the manager of their Insight Marketing Team, the company's success in Western countries is a result of market research undertaken to understand how product's fit into people's lives. For example, cultural differences between Asian and Western countries determine the design of appliances. In some Asian countries, washing machines are displayed where visitors will see them as a sign of affluence. In the West, appearance is less important. This difference led to a line of red wine-colored appliances; in the West a metallic, industrial look is preferred.[5]

1. ESOMAR. (8 September 2009). *ESOMAR global market research report—slowdown in market research revenues confirmed*. Press release. Retrieved from www.esomar.org/index.php?mact=News,cntnt01,detail,0&cntnt01articleid= 211&cntnt01returnid=1894.

2. Anderson, T. (2009, March). Back to basics. *ESOMAR's Research World,* 12–14.

3. American Marketing Association. Definition of marketing. Retrieved from http://www.marketingpower.com/AboutAMA/ Pages/DefinitionofMarketing.aspx.

4. Forsyth, J. E., Galante, N., & Guild, T. (2006). Capitalizing on customer insights. *The McKinsey Quarterly, 3*, 43–53.

5. Bowman, J. (2009, April). Made in Asia. *Research World*, 17.

SCOPE OF GOBAL MARKETING RESEARCH

Acquiring marketing insights is critical for marketers who are looking for the best strategies to enter a new market, gain competitive advantage, or increase market share, for example. A simple definition of **international marketing research** describes it as marketing research performed with the purpose of informing marketing decisions that have to be made in more than one country. The research could be performed in all markets simultaneously or sequentially.[6] Smart companies (and marketers) conduct some form—and many conduct several forms—of global marketing research before they engage in any of the above mentioned activities.

Some of the most important reasons to perform marketing research include:

1. Risk management
2. Competitive advantage
3. Strategic decision making
4. Tactical decision making
5. Performance tracking and reporting

Listening to customers through various research methodologies and acting on the collected insights is one of the most important distinguishing characteristics of high-performing businesses, both in Europe and the United States. Firms that successfully use marketing research by sharing their findings throughout the organization and aligning them with the organization's priorities tend to have better product innovation, more effective customer communication, and superior return on marketing investment.[7]

Conducting Global Marketing Research

Global marketing research is responsible for gathering, analyzing, and summarizing the information needed to make decisions about potential new markets and marketing opportunities worldwide. On a continuous basis, marketing research is also used to monitor and evaluate marketing performance and recommend changes, if needed. In global marketing, research should inform market entry decisions and any changes marketing managers make to the company's products, pricing, placement, and promotion strategies in order to gain and maintain market share in new markets.

TYPES OF RESEARCH

Market research is conducted in a variety of ways. The most broadly defined techniques are quantitative and qualitative research.

Quantitative Research. **Quantitative research** relies primarily on the collection and analysis of numerical data, usually gathered via standardized surveys or questionnaires. Quantitative researchers then use statistical analysis methods to draw out insights into particular area—be it customer behavior, market trends, or pricing discrepancies. Many executives prefer the quantitative research technique because it provides "hard numbers" based on larger audience samples, and thus offers a stronger base for decision making. According to ESOMAR, quantitative research accounted for 80 percent of the global research budgets in 2008.[8]

---

6. Aaker, David A., Kumar, V., & Day, G. (2004). *Marketing research* (8th ed.). Hoboken, NJ: John Wiley & Sons, Inc.

7. Holscher, A., & Grogan, A. (2008, April). Breaking the mold. *Research World*, 12–15.

8. ESOMAR. (8 September 2009). *ESOMAR global market research report—slowdown in market research revenues confirmed*. Press release. Retrieved from www.esomar.org/index.php?mact=News,cntnt01,detail,0&cntnt01articleid= 211&cntnt01returnid=1894.

BOX 6-1 TECHNOLOGY IN FOCUS: ONLINE RESEARCH TOOLS

Web Analytics

Web analytics is a new research field that grew out of the increasingly sophisticated uses of the Internet for commerce and marketing. Specifically, web analytics is defined by the Web Analytics Association as the measurement, collection, analysis, and reporting of Internet data for purposes of understanding and optimizing web usage. Web analytics tools can track a plethora of data associated with visitors' interactions with a company's website (onsite analytics) or with the company's brand elsewhere on the web (offsite analytics)—for example, on social media sites, and third party vendors. The web analytics market remains highly polarized between free tools, such as Google Analytics, WebTrends, StatCounter, Woopra, Nielsen, and Omniture, which was recently acquired by Adobe.

Researchers may use web analytics tools to assess the general performance of a website by tracking visitors' paths through it, the links they clicked on, the length of time spent on specific pages, etc. Others may combine this information with online surveys or traditional research to explore questions such as visitors' satisfaction, and the effectiveness of different marketing offers. By observing and analyzing the application usage over a certain period of time, it is possible to extract users' behavior patterns.

Before using web analytics technologies in countries other than the United States, it is best to first determine their legal status. For example, in 2011, German authorities declared that the use of web analytics tools such as Google Analytics is illegal without the consent of the person being tracked. Restrictions over use may be in place in other countries as well.

The international shipping company UPS commissioned two surveys for the Chinese market that provided its customers with the information needed to increase their sales (and therefore ship more products) to China and established UPS as a valuable knowledge resource on the Chinese market. The first survey of 1,000 urban, middle-class citizens established what American products are attractive to the Chinese consumers. CDs, DVDs, beauty products, athletic shoes, and washing machines topped the list. The second survey, comprising 1,200 residents of six of the largest cities in China, sought to find out why these products have appeal in the local market. It confirmed the notion that Chinese consumers are about as individualistic as United States consumers when it comes to personal preferences and product choices. UPS made its research findings available to customers who are not yet exporting to China, to customers who don't export at all, and to potential clients. Given the richness of the information provided in the surveys about this high-profile but challenging market, UPS's research received wide coverage across all media. More importantly, the impact on the company's bottom line has also been significant, according to UPS.[9]

Of course, quantitative research is useful only when it measures the "right" things. This is why survey design—from deciding what to measure to asking the questions that prompt relevant responses to correctly interpreting the data—is so crucial. The importance of properly designing and conducting quantitative research only grows in international markets, where differences in language, culture, and social norms can render research results completely useless if they were derived from surveys and questionnaires that were not designed with that particular market in mind. Box 6-1 highlights some of the considerations researchers must keep in mind when conducting marketing research abroad.

---

9. Fielding, M. (1 February 2007). Special delivery. *Marketing News*, 13.

Quantitative research has other limitations, as well. Some experts, like Scott Anthony, the Managing Director of the international investment firm Innosight Ventures, maintains[10] that quantitative research is very useful to perform in well-defined, existing markets, where the marketing issue may be increasing market share, for example. The technique is less useful in discovering original ways to improve customer satisfaction or to spur innovation in new product design. Furthermore, executives who rely too much on quantitative research may generate a false sense of security by basing their strategy simply on the confines of the gathered data and failing to notice faint market signals that may represent new markets of opportunity.

Qualitative Research. Unlike quantitative research, **qualitative research** has a much more subjective, free-form format. Qualitative research techniques usually include face-to-face interviews, focus groups, and observational methods such as ethnography and, increasingly, online focus groups and interviews. These research techniques are designed to bring researchers a better understanding of their customers and their needs and desires.

By its very nature, qualitative research relies on the researchers' own interpretations of the world around them and their reading of the meaning behind people's words and actions.[11]

Qualitative research is typically used when the objective is to improve the customer experience with the company's products or services, to discover unmet needs, or to get inspiration for new product design, for example. Branding and customers' relationships with brands are frequent topics in qualitative research studies. Because qualitative research focuses on a certain topic in-depth, its results are not presented in the highly structured, numbers-driven format that quantitative research reports usually are.

The types of issues usually explored in qualitative marketing research are reflected in McDonald's Global Moms Panel, comprised of nine mothers from six countries. McDonald's Global Chief Marketing Officer, Mary Dillon, explained that the company's goal was "to listen and learn from our Global Moms Panel with the goal of providing the best possible experience for families in our restaurants around the world. We want to become the best ally we can for moms and a true partner in the well-being of families everywhere."[12] Intended to focus on topics such as healthy lifestyle initiatives, restaurant communications, and children's well-being, the panel's input has helped McDonald's develop new products and marketing campaigns that promote a balanced diet. One such initiative was the global campaign associated with the movie "Shrek the Third," which extended to over 100 countries, offered toys created in eight languages, and amounted to McDonald's single biggest promotion of fruit, vegetables, and milk to date, according to the company.[13] Another example involved a large IT firm with small- and medium-sized affiliates worldwide. Headquarters wanted to know how the needs of the smaller affiliates differed from those of its larger companies. Areas of interest were communication channels used and portfolios of services provided by each. In-depth interviews with almost

10. Anthony, S. (2 September 2009). In market research, use numbers with caution. [Web log post]. Retrieved from http://blogs .hbr.org/anthony/2009/09/in_market_research_use.html.

11. Denzin, N. K., & Lincoln, Y. (Eds.). (2005). *The Sage handbook of qualitative research* (3rd ed.). Thousand Oaks, CA: Sage Publications, Inc.

12. McDonald's. (9 May 2006). McDonald's announces global moms panel. [Press release]. Retrieved from www.mcdonalds .com/corp/news/corppr/2006/corp_05162006.html.

13. McDonald's. (8 May 2007). McDonald's brings the joy of Shrek to customers around the world. [Press release]. Retrieved from http://mcdepk.com/shrek/mediadocs/McDonalds_Shrek_LeadRelease.pdf.

500 CEOs, CFOs, and other IT executives were conducted internally to provide the information needed.

Qualitative research, which accounted for 14 percent of global research spending in 2008 according to ESOMAR, is often used in conjunction with quantitative research. This practice is growing in popularity, as marketers attempt to gain an ever more complete and detailed view of their customers and markets.

Types of Research Data. Data is the lifeblood of marketing research. Researchers have two primary methods of obtaining data: collecting original, first-hand responses from research participants in the marketplace, called **primary research,** or collecting and analyzing existing data from sources such as statistical abstracts, media reports, and previous research studies, called **secondary research.**

The majority of quantitative and qualitative research conducted today collects data from direct or primary sources, such as interview respondents and focus group participants. Secondary research (also called desk research) has its place however, holding about 6 percent of the global research budgets, according to ESOMAR.

When researchers conduct empirical marketing research in multiple countries, the questions of data quality and metrics consistency are two of the most difficult to confront. Yet they are of key importance to ensure that any cross-national market study produces valid results when comparing and contrasting responses to the same issues from different markets. Some studies have found that cultural differences may play a role in how respondents interpret the questions asked[14] or how they perceive the scales offered for formulating their answers.[15] Since these conditions may bias the final analysis of the data, researchers are often urged to assess the consistency of the study's questions, scales, and metrics across markets. But a recent survey found that the process, called measurement invariance assessment, is rarely performed, due to researchers' limited knowledge of it and the perceived complexities of the different measurement invariance methods.[16]

Online Research

Increasingly, marketing research of all types is performed online today. **Online research** encompasses marketing research conducted via online panels, social media channels, online surveys, polls, and other research methods implemented over an Internet connection. Although estimates of how much of total research is performed online range anywhere from 10 to 20 percent, it is clear that online research will only continue to grow as the technologies and methods to perform it will become more and more sophisticated. Lower costs and faster project cycles are two of the most obvious appeals of online research. Easier access, at least in countries with high Internet penetration and increasingly tough conditions for collecting data via traditional methods, also tips the scales in favor of conducting marketing research online.

As with any emerging practice, however, online research still has plenty of issues to work out before it can become an established, mainstream method for conducting marketing research, especially on a global scale. One of the main questions is whether the quality of online research can match that of traditional methods. For issues such

14. Myers, M. B., Calantone, R. J., Page Jr., T. J., & Taylor, C. R. (2000). An application of multiple-group causal models in assessing cross-cultural measurement equivalence. *Journal of International Marketing, 8*(4), 108–121.

15. Riordan, C. M., & Vandenberg, R. J. (1994). A central question in cross-cultural research: Do employees of different cultures interpret work-related measures in an equivalent manner? *Journal of Management, 20*(3), 643–71.

16. Yi, H., Merz, M. A., & Alden, D. L. (2008). Diffusion of measurement invariance assessment in cross-national empirical marketing research: perspectives from the literature and a survey of researchers. *Journal of International Marketing, 16*(2), 64–83.

verifying the identity of respondents (to duplication or fraud), using consistent metrics, or crafting questionnaires appropriate for the online environment, researchers are still struggling to come up with quality standards and practices that are widely accepted. Of particular interest to global marketers is the issue of translating online surveys into one or more languages—a practice where shortcuts, such as using machine translation, often lead to highly inaccurate results.[17]

Another big issue is the inherent bias in using only online populations for any kind of research that aims to reveal insights from the general public. Even in countries with deep Internet penetration rates, it is likely that any online-only research sample would remain unbalanced if it excludes the offline population. The bias would be particularly apparent in emerging markets, where Internet connectivity is much lower and the majority of the population has sporadic, if any, access to the Internet.

An ongoing study of global online panels that has collected data from 150 panels across 35 countries highlights the importance of measuring the consistency and validity of sample sources from which respondents are drawn, particularly for multinational marketing research. Using consistent metrics that can be transferred across multiple markets without significant changes to their meaning is also crucial to conducting high-quality global marketing research.[18]

Online audience metrics suffer from an almost universal lack of credibility, especially when it comes to international research. A recent survey of marketing researchers in the UK found that, although 96 percent of them agreed that having consistent audience measurements is "extremely important," only 23 percent of them thought that such standards have been established. The research professionals cited inconsistencies in cross-national and regional markets as the biggest issue.[19]

Despite some of these issues, online research continues to evolve, with new, more advanced trends and emerging forms such as web analytics, mobile research, and social media research becoming increasingly common. For a quick overview of some of these forms of online research, see Box 6-1.

The Role of Social Media in Global Marketing Research

The enormous appeal of using social media networks such as Facebook, LinkedIn, and Twitter, or their global competitors such as Viadeo (France), Xing (Germany), or Tianji (China), is the sheer volume of unfiltered consumer data available to marketing researchers from these networks' hundreds of millions of users. The fact that most of this data is freely available is another advantage, as are its perceived authenticity and the diversity of the online population providing it.

The possibilities for offering valuable services to marketing researchers are not lost on the social media leaders. For example, Facebook provides targeted information about its users and user preferences in order to enable marketers to create better, more relevant ads. LinkedIn has partnered directly with research firms for specific B2B research projects covering topics such as customer satisfaction, market outlook, and brand perceptions. Offering population samples directly to researchers is another service considered by some networks. Currently, the most widely used methods by social media researchers continue to be pop-ups and banner ads for sample sourcing for surveys and text search, sometimes using natural

17. Day, D. (2009, December). Online research grows up. [Special supplement]. *Research*.

18. Gittelman, S., & Trimarchi, E. (2009, November). The value of consistency auditing of online panels. *Quirk's Marketing Research Review*. Retrieved from http://www.quirks.com/articles/2009/20091107.aspx?searchID=53982536.

19. Online metrics get thumbs down. (2009, June). *Research*, p. 6.

BOX 6-2   COUNTRY IN FOCUS: CONDUCTING RESEARCH IN INDIA

India has become a focal point for global markets, but they are uncertain as to the extent to which social and interactive media can reach target markets. Traditional media is still the best way to reach most Indian consumers. Interactive media is aimed mainly at highly educated young men in upper income brackets. However, while a minority of Indians uses the Internet, those who do are also users of social media. Advertisers that are aiming at India's growing middle class should use an integrated marketing strategy based on interactive and social media as well.

Source: Adapted from: Steven Noble, "Social Technographics in India: While Few Indians Are Online, Most Who Are Use Social Media." *Forrester.* Updated October 6, 2010.

---

language processing tools for data mining or consumer sentiment research such as brand perception studies.[20]

Many researchers caution, however, that with the advantages of social media research come some pitfalls. In order to meet the basic standards of the marketing research industry, researchers using social media tools should rigorously test their search and source parameters, properly categorize and map the researched content, adjust their some of their metrics used for trend identification and, ultimately, summarize all their findings in reports that provide actionable intelligence to executives.[21]

An example of the use of social media to reach consumers in India is shown in Box 6-2.

The growth of online research technologies has also sparked a vigorous debate over online consumer privacy in many countries. Marketing researchers should stay aware and vigilant about observing the local laws and policies regarding this hot topic.

Differences in Conducting Global Marketing Research

Conducting reliable, high-quality global marketing research also means that both clients and vendors (if vendors are used) must understand and agree on the special conditions often imposed on the research methodologies by the particular local culture, social customs, or other contextual factors. For example, United States research clients must realize that international phone interviews may take longer and cost more, due to an obligatory extended introduction and small talk with the interview subjects. Such interview style is required by the social norms in most other countries, where the direct approach used in the United States is considered rather rude. Some other examples of such international differences in conducting global marketing research are shown in Table 6-1.

THE GLOBAL MARKETING RESEARCH PROCESS

The best way to ensure optimal results in any marketing research project is to start with a well-defined plan of action and clear understanding of the steps needed to be taken to accomplish the task. Whether the project concerns a single national market

---

20. Poynter, R. (2009, October). The rise of observational research. *Research World*, 29–31.

21. Evans, R. S. (2009, December). Promises and pitfalls of social media. [Special supplement] *Research.* Retrieved from www.research-live.com/magazine/promises-and-pitfalls-of-social-media/4001830.article.

TABLE 6-1 Differences in Conducting Global Marketing Research in Selected Countries
Country/Area

China

Personal interviews are the preferred method for surveys in China, where the subjects are business executives, doctors, or government officials. Professionals and government officials must be shown respect by sending an advance invitation to participate in a survey.

While phone interviews may have some use in China, language differences, for example, between Mandarin and Cantonese, or differences in brand name pronunciations, may hamper understanding and skew research findings.

India

Indian consumers are often willing to discuss their shopping preferences and motivations in personal interviews. Observational research at shopping points such as stores and markets is a good way to determine shopping behavior.

Latin America

Most marketing research in Latin America is conducted with respondents in the middle and some upper socioeconomic classes. One cannot generalize about research methods used in the area because of country differences; however, personal interviews are preferred in most countries because of the importance of social contact between people. Cost differences also dictate the research method used. For example, in Panama it is cheaper to use personal interviewers in homes than to interview the same person on the phone because of very high local phone tariffs.

Middle East

The preferred data collection method in the Middle East is the personal interview. However, the preferred place of interviewing is outside the home. In most Middle East countries, women may be interviewed if accompanied by a male family member, generally in the home. Focus groups, in-depth interviews, paired friendship interviews, and several other qualitative techniques have become widely used, as well.

entry or a global competitive analysis, it will require the researchers involved in carrying it out to take a number of smaller steps and make independent decisions along the way. To ensure that all of their actions add up to the desired final product, it is crucial for all parties to understand the purpose and objectives of the research and follow the agreed upon steps in the research process.

The typical marketing research process can be defined in the following six steps:

1. Defining the research purpose and objectives
2. Deciding on the research methodology
3. Designing the research
4. Collecting the data
5. Analyzing the data
6. Reporting the data

Defining the Research Purpose and Objectives

Developing a well-defined research purpose and objectives creates a clear target for the research team and makes subsequent decisions—from what sources to use for primary and/or secondary research to composing survey questions and choosing sample sizes—much easier.

The most natural topic of research that comes to mind in global marketing is the identification and evaluation of new markets. Indeed, whether a company is making its first foray into international markets or is an established player in the global scene, it is likely that it will often need new market research.

Despite the common theme, the purpose and the objectives of each research project could be quite different. For example, a small firm may decide to conduct an initial **foreign market opportunity analysis,** where the purpose is to find out what international markets may be most suitable for their product or services. The objectives then can be defined as assembling profiles of the top 10 potential markets with basic information such as population, per capita income levels, sales of specific product categories, trade restrictions, and other relevant indicators, and developing a scoring criterion on which these 10 markets can be ranked.

A company with some experience in global markets may be more interested in assessing the competitive landscape in a particular world region. In this case, the purpose of the research could be to identify the main rival firms in the region and their strengths and weaknesses in the market place. Objectives could include performing a SWOT analysis on each competitor, analyzing their marketing strategy and effectiveness, or conducting a product line review aimed at pinpointing gaps in the coverage or underserved market areas.

Determining the Research Methodology

Once the information requirements for the research are established in the initial phase, it is time to decide on some of the basic elements that will constitute this project.

The foremost decision to be made here is how to obtain the information needed. Is it worth conducting primary research or is there enough data available from secondary sources to answer the questions? To make this decision, marketers have to consider additional factors such as the level of data customization desired, data reliability, the costs associated with obtaining it, and the time frame for the project.

Another important factor is the preferred method of project administration: is this project going to be run by the company's headquarters or (in the case of MNCs) is the implementation going to be left to the local offices? Furthermore, is the company going to use in-house resources or outsource the work to a marketing research firm?

The answers to each of these questions hinge not only on the company's internal structure, resources, and culture, but also on the markets' characteristics. The more the researched market is different and unfamiliar to the company, the wiser it is to use market research providers specializing in that market. This strategy may eliminate many potential issues down the road, regarding sampling, translation, data quality, findings interpretation, and others.

Designing the Research

This step of the research process adds more specifics to the project. Now is the time to decide whether qualitative or quantitative data would be more useful (or a combination of both). This decision is best made by referring back to the purpose and objectives of the project and asking whether they can be met by convening focus groups or online panels, by conducting a survey, by using published reports, or a combination of these or other approaches. Other factors that influence the research design have to do with local conditions. If phone interviews seem to be the most suitable technique but local laws restrict phone access to consumers or such market research methods are unfamiliar to consumers in that country, the research design may have to be modified.

Regardless of the technique used, researchers charged with designing the research project should try to avoid being affected by the **self-reference criterion (SRC),** the often unconscious tendency to assume that people everywhere perceive the world the same way one does and hold similar cultural values or personal attitudes. SRC is most likely to creep up in the process of developing questionnaires for global research

TABLE 6-2 Selecting Research Instruments

Interview—Questioning respondents in order to collect information for market research purposes. Interviews may be face-to-face, by phone, fax, or online. They can take place at different locations: in the home, office, street, shopping malls, or at entertainment arenas.

Consumer Survey—A survey to determine the demographics of a target audience, why people make certain purchasing decisions, when and where people shop, market potential, and buying habits.

Omnibus Study—A periodic survey conducted on a variety of subjects for more than one client. It allows clients to share the costs of research by pooling questions. All the questions for a given wave are then put to a representative sample, as part of a single questionnaire. Each individual

client's questions are of course confidential, and results are processed in such a way as to ensure that each party only sees their own data.

Focus Group—A focus group involves encouraging an invited group of participants to share their thoughts, feelings, attitudes, and ideas on certain subjects.

Observation Study—A research study where data is collected by watching consumer behavior in a shopping situation. The researcher (observer) records the behavior without making contact with the subject being observed.

Questionnaire—A questionnaire is a research instrument consisting of a series of questions and other prompts for the purpose of gathering information from respondents.

projects and in interpreting (wrongly) the answers of survey respondents from other cultures.

Another important element to decide on is sample size. How big a sample is required to collect meaningful data? The answer may depend on the company's requirements for accuracy, level of certainty in the results, and project budget, among other things.

COLLECTING THE DATA

The process of collecting the data also has a number of dimensions that should be well established before the actual collection begins in order to ensure consistent and valid research results. Protocols for all steps of the process, from obtaining permissions to the types of data sources used and the standards for record keeping, should be clearly understood and followed by all researchers. Ensuring such consistency, whether collecting quantitative or qualitative data, is essential to avoid introducing bias into the process.

The researchers' capability to collect data in diverse research environments while maintaining the integrity of the research design is of key importance during this stage of a global research project. Using local staffs that speak the language and can make research respondents feel at ease by interacting with them according to the established cultural and social mores are more likely to maximize responses and collect meaningful, reliable data, while using some of the primary research methods listed in Table 6-2. Professionally trained staffs are also more likely to adhere to the quality and ethical standards established in the marketing research field.

IN-HOUSE VERSUS OUTSOURCING

A critical decision for a global marketing organization is whether to conduct market research using internal staff and resources or to use outside agencies. Even for firms that have internal market research departments in their affiliates overseas, it may be more efficient to outsource the work to professional market research organizations. A case in point is when the firm plans to conduct regional or worldwide research. In this case, it is critical to ensure that equivalency is maintained in all the research conducted. A basic issue in cross-cultural research is the determination of whether the concepts used have similar meaning across the social contexts surveyed. Concepts used in cross-cultural market research predominately come from a particular source culture (e.g., the United States) and were developed in a particular linguistic context (e.g., American English). Conceptual equivalence with target contexts should be assessed before using a United States source or another country source because they may lose some of their meaning in translation and therefore may not be equivalent. A major issue in cross-cultural marketing research is the so called *emic* versus *etic* dilemma, which focuses on whether or not the measure is culture bound (*emic*) or can be used across all cultures (*etic*). Behavioral-type measures or scales must be examined within each cultural domain to determine if the construct and its measure is relevant in the specific cultural context and that there are equivalent measures. Using local research agents or global agents that have branches in many countries but use local staff who are familiar with the culture will go a long way to ensure that equivalency is maintained. Table 6-3 shows the major global marketing research agencies that have affiliates in many countries. Using such agencies helps to ensure equivalency and the coordination of marketing research projects undertaken in many countries, especially when the research is conducted at the same time frame.

ANALYZING THE DATA

Interpreting the data collected during the previous step and molding it into actionable sets of findings is the main purpose of the data analysis phase. However, the processes used to analyze and interpret qualitative and quantitative data are as different as the two approaches used to collect it.

In qualitative data analysis, researchers usually review recordings of the actual data collection session—for example, from in-depth interviews or focus group sessions— or they may rely on their own notes and recollections from the sessions. Such conditions naturally introduce subjectivity and personal bias into the process and leave much of the final interpretation and analysis of the findings to the skills and experiences of the individual researchers.[22]

Analyzing quantitative data is a much more structured, multi-step process. It begins with a thorough "scrubbing" of the data to ensure that only properly completed, error-free questionnaires are sent for further processing. The processing then may involve running the properly coded and aggregated answers through a number of analytical methods, such as correlation analysis, regression analysis, and other measurement methods designed to establish the relationship between the numbers. Usually, these complex calculations are done by specialized software programs, directed by the researchers. By interpreting the results of the analyses, researchers find the underlying meaning of the data and identify potential trends, hidden tendencies, or other factors that may influence consumer behavior, competitive pressures, or market performance.[23]

For example, a Bank of America study recently found that China outpaced the United States in the production of passenger cars for the first time in 2006. However, on more closer examination, it noted that China includes light vans in its definition of passenger cars, whereas the United States does not. If light vans are not counted, the United States remains ahead in passenger car production, with the difference growing even more significant if light trucks, such as sport utility

22. Crouch, S., & Housden, M. (2003). *Marketing research for managers*. Oxford: Butterworth-Heinemann, p. 223.

23. Ibid.

TABLE 6-3	Top 25 Global Marketing Research Organizations						
Rank 2008	Company	HDQTS	Parent Company	Number of Countries with Affiliates	Research Only Full-Time Employees	Global Research Revenue (US$ Millions)	Percent of Global Revenue Outside of Home Country
1	The Nielsen Co.	New York	U.S.	108	34,516	4,575	51.2%
2	The Kantar Group	London & Fairfield CT	UK	80	21,510	3,615	75.3
3	IMS Health Inc.	Norwalk, CT	U.S.	76	7,500	2,330	63.9
4	GFK SE	Nuremberg	GERMANY	57	9,692	1,797	77.3
5	Ipsos Group, S.A.	Paris	FRANCE	64	9,094	1,442	89.0
6	Synovate	London	UK	61	6,746	961	85.1
7	IRI	Chicago	U.S.	8	3,600	725	37.4
8	Westat, Inc.	Rockville, MD	U.S.	1	1,998	470	–
9	Arbitron, Inc.	Columbia, VA	U.S.	2	1,116	369	1.2
10	INTAGE, Inc.	Tokyo	JAPAN	3	1,779	332	1.1
11	J.D. Power & Assocs.	Westlake Village, CA	U.S.	9	850	272	30.7
12	Maritz Research	Fenton, MO	U.S.	4	756	230	14.4
13	Opinion Research Corp.	Princeton, NJ	U.S.	5	485	228	36.2
14	The NPD Group, Inc.	Port Washington, NY	U.S.	13	1,090	226	25.5
15	Harris Interactive, Inc.	Rochester, NY	U.S.	7	899	222	38.2
16	VideoResearch Ltd.	Tokyo	JAPAN	3	393	188	0.1
17	IBOPE Group	Sao Paulo	BRAZIL	12	1,884	159	22.5
18	Comscore Inc.	Reston, V	U.S.	5	581	117	14.1
19	Cello Research & Consulting	London	UK	2	451	99	39.8
20	Market Strategies International	Livonia, MI	U.S.	3	307	92	15.9
21	Lieberman Research Worldwide	Los Angeles, CA	U.S.	4	324	90	18.2
22	Mediametrie	Paris	FRANCE	1	515	85	11.0
23	BVA Group	Paris	FRANCE	4	742	84	10.7
24	You Gov PLC	London	UK	9	474	83	71.0
25	Dentsu Research Inc.	Tokyo	JAPAN	1	16	68	0.3

Source: Adapted from: *Marketing News*, American Marketing Association, August 30, 2009.

vehicles (SUVs), are included. Nevertheless, China's growth rate in this industry remains impressive, surging 16 times higher since 1997, when it comprised only 5.4 percent of United States production.[24]

24. Simon, B. (8 March 2007). China speeds past the United States in passenger car production. *Financial Times*, 25.

BOX 6-3   COMPANY IN FOCUS: PERRY ELLIS

Perry Ellis Deploys a Valuable Tool for Growth and Integration

To deliver products based on customers' needs, grow its stores, and integrate its brick-and-mortar operations with its e-commerce business, were three of the main goals for Perry Ellis International, Inc., a Miami-based fashion house that manages a portfolio of 27 established brands such as Perry Ellis, Nike Swim, and Jantzen. The company sells its products at 12,500 locations, including its own boutiques and luxury department stores such as Nordstrom and Neiman Marcus in the United States.

Maintaining relevancy in the fast-moving fashion industry across so many brands and so many channels of distribution requires paying close attention to customers' needs and tastes, according to Perry Ellis' CIO Luis Paez. "We do this by mining point-of-sale data collected from each location. We also use geographic information system [GIS] software and custom programs to predict trends and analyze POS [point-of-sale] down to the SKU [stock keeping unit] at store level," he says, adding, "These strategies enable us to target the right product to the right market."

Using specialized software from Oracle Corp., Perry Ellis is able to filter POS data and import it into another software module that calculates markdown recommendations and almost immediately send these back to the retail stores. This process reduces unnecessary markdowns and increases sales at the same time. Most importantly, the same system can be integrated into the company's new online stores, where it will help calculate demand and design promotions in direct response to trends seen in its customers' purchasing behavior. Thus, a single stream of customer data can be used across the organization to plan marketing and pricing strategies almost in real time—a much needed competitive edge in the crowded fashion retail industry.

Source: Adapted from: Amato-McCoy, D. M. (2007, February). Perry Ellis' IT priorities. *Chain Store Age, 83*(2), 33.

REPORTING THE DATA

Many researchers find nothing more frustrating than to see their final reports—the fruits of their weeks- or months-long research efforts—sit on an executive's shelf unused. The best way to ensure that research reports are read, understood, and utilized is by making them accessible and relevant to business executives who may not be steeped in research industry jargon or practices.

Following the order and structure of the research objectives in the final report is a reliable strategy to engage executives who are invested in knowing the answers to the questions that prompted the study in the first place. By making a direct connection between the original questions and the study's findings, researchers can make it easy for those not involved in the process to understand the report's logic and conclusions. Researchers who can present these conclusions in an easy-to-follow story format, rather than in a dry, numbers-driven analysis, may generate even greater interest in their reports and create more significant impact in the rest of the organization.[25]

Today's researchers can rely on more than just the written word to educate executives. Multimedia tools such as video or sound recordings can sometimes communicate in minutes what may take hours to read in a report. Such methods of presentation may fit better with executives' own styles of consuming information, and now they can be easily incorporated into presentations or as audiovisual aids to final reports.[26]

25. Widemann II, R., & Fitzgerald, A. (2008, April). By the numbers: mastering the art of writing quantitative research reports. *Quirk's*. Retrieved from www.quirks.com/articles/2008/20080410.aspx?searchID=65182389&msg=3.

26. Johnston, G. (2005, December). Thoughts on the role of video and ethnography in marketing research. *Quirk's*. Retrieved from www.quirks.com/articles/a2005/20051206.aspx?searchID=65180541&sort=9.

Global Marketing Intelligence/Information Systems

"I never dreamed this would happen to us," exclaimed the CEO of a large American pharmaceutical company. The company was unaware that it would be investigated by a Senate subcommittee on health, involving charges that the company mishandled research on two of its best-selling products.

Another example involved Toyota's slow response to safety problems that ultimately led to recalls of 8.5 million vehicles worldwide in 2010. The question is how a Japanese global company like Toyota could have failed to anticipate the problem and not have had a readymade contingency plan for dealing with it. Some blamed Japan's consensus culture, where the lengthy decision-making processes hinder quick responses.

These scenarios show that these companies, like others, did not have an adequate "early warning" capability or intelligence system which could have enabled management to anticipate the crises.

Marketing intelligence is not synonymous with marketing research. Marketing research usually focuses on a specific problem or project that has a definite beginning, middle, and end. Marketing intelligence/information systems involve the continual collection and analysis of marketing information. Moreover, intelligence is evaluated information; i.e., information whose credibility, meaning, and importance has been established, so that the intelligence has application to a present or *potential* marketing situation.

The American Marketing Association (AMA) defines a marketing information system (MIS) as a "set of procedures and methods for the regular, planned collection, analysis, and presentation of information for use in making marketing decisions." In other words, the purpose of the MIS is to not only aggregate data but also to help change the data into meaningful information and help present it in a manner that facilitates decision making. A proper MIS should also help integrate marketing information with other pertinent information that may reside elsewhere in the organization—in accounting or operations, for example—since today most organizational functions rely on up-to-the-minute global market information to stay competitive. When viewed in this context, marketing research, which is usually project based, solving one defined issue at a time, becomes a part of the broader marketing intelligence system, which is intended to collect, interpret, and organize marketing information from a variety of sources on an ongoing basis. Some of these sources may include:

- Secondary data analysis
- Human resources
- Executives based abroad, company subsidiaries, and affiliates
- Traveling and building contacts
- Database analysis (internal/external)
- Industry experts
- Formal market research

Moreover, an MIS should provide not only snapshots of the current state of the markets, but also forecasts that can be used for future or potential marketing initiatives. A model of a marketing intelligence/information system appears as Figure 6-1.

The model has five interrelated dimensions: (1) marketing decisions, (2) management functions, (3) marketing environment, (4) information constraints, and (5) system evaluation factors. The first two dimensions of the model are derived

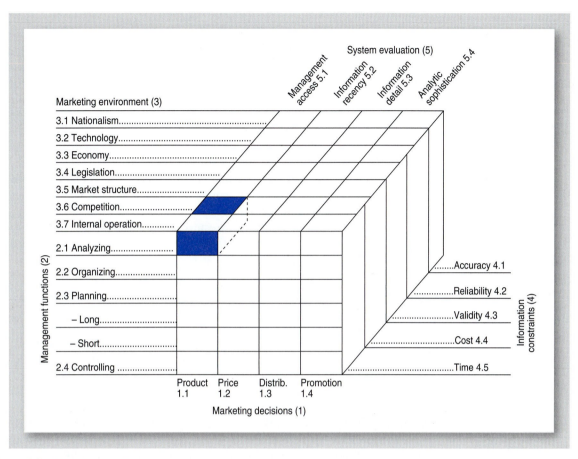

Figure 6-1 A Marketing Information Requirements Model

from the tasks a marketing manager performs, namely (1) analyzing, (2) organizing, (3) planning,and (4) controlling. These efforts are in four marketing decision areas: (1) product, (2) price, (3) distribution, and (4) promotion. For example, analyzing ongoing product strategies requires knowledge of the marketing environment, dimension be the coordinates 1.1, 2.1, 3.5, again product analysis, but this time involving market structure; market share, market segmentation, and so on. Each cell therefore becomes a page or section in a plan book including all information needed for the marketing decision and managerial function represented by the cell.

For any cell, two additional dimensions; for example, time and cost, and intelligence system evaluation. When collecting data, it must be examined for validity and reliability as in dimension 4. Evaluation of the system can be accomplished by applying four criteria: (1) management access, the time interval between a request for information and its receipt, (2) information recency, the time interval between the occurrence of an event and its information storage in the system, (3) information aggregation, the desired detail with which information is stored in the system, and (4) analytic sophistication, the structure of the data in the system, ranging from description of events to statistical evaluation and model building.

One of the factors making the MIS function doable is the democratization of information; its availability on the Internet and other free and easily accessible sources has shifted the control over the marketing fate of a product or company from the marketers to the consumers. Today, international marketers have to scan and monitor not only what competitors are doing, but also what kind of information bloggers post about their products, how YouTube videos feature it, and what rating it gets on consumer review sites such as Epinions.com. This explains the increasing popularity of features such as customizable information filters and electronic agents at information portals like Yahoo!, MSN, and Google and the rise of Really Simple Syndication (RSS) tools called "aggregators" or feed readers.

New technological tools are also at hand to help marketers. Data management programs, specialized software tools for data mining, text retrieval and classification, patent searching, web page tracking, and Internet monitoring are becoming more and more popular at leading firms in highly competitive industries such as pharmaceuticals, computer technology, telecommunications, defense, and aerospace, among others. They also make it much easier for executives to cover a wider array of media sources, hone in on the most pertinent information for their company, and share that information across the organization.

SUMMARY

- The role of global marketing research in formulating marketing strategy takes on increased importance because of the cultural, social, and economic differences between countries. Expanding into new markets requires special expertise to deal with market differences and to coordinate research activities regionally. Companies that operate globally and regionally have to decide whether research should be conducted on a country, regional, or global basis. In most cases, how research is conducted will depend on the company's global organization of operations. Moreover, global companies have to decide whether marketing research should be done in-house or outsourced to multinational research agencies and local firms who may have a better grasp on survey techniques that are required in a given area or country.

- Advances in technology such as the Internet have made significant contributions to global marketing research. Before the advent of the Internet, global (and domestic) marketing research was only affordable to large companies. Today, a substantial amount of international marketing research can be done on a PC within a matter of hours. In addition, data collection devices based on computer technology such as scanners, CATI (computer assisted telephone interviewing), and CAPI (computer assisted personal interviewing) are used frequently in developed countries and are beginning to be used in emerging markets. Of course, multinational corporations still have much more research resources at their disposal, but small and medium-sized firms can download a substantial amount of research at an affordable cost.

- There is a growing recognition among global firms that in addition to marketing research, marketing intelligence/information systems are necessary in order to acquire a future-focused perspective on competitors and market structures for long-term planning. They also provide an early warning capability to avoid missed market opportunities or to forecast threats that, if they occur, can be very costly to the firm.

DISCUSSION QUESTIONS

1. How can you determine which data collection method (personal interview, telephone, etc.) would work best in a survey of household consumers in Kenya, Nigeria, Ghana, and South Africa? See Table 6-2.

2. You are requested by the VP Marketing to determine consumer preference for restaurants in Paris and New York City. What sources would you use to determine this?

3. Would the imports of consumer goods into a given country be a good indicator of the size of the internal market for those products? Why or why not?

4. What sort of information is critical to the global firm that is not often necessary for a firm operating in the home market only? Detail the sorts of information critical to the global firm.

EXPERIENTIAL EXERCISES

1. Visit www.acnielsen.com and pick one consumer report from the "Trends and Insights" section. Based on the findings reported, recommend a strategy for entering a new geographic market with a specific product category. Justify your recommendations.

2. The mid-sized consumer products company that you work for has decided to expand into China. As the marketing manager, you were tasked with hiring a market research firm to conduct primary research to help you determine which of your product lines you should first offer in this new market. Formulate the research problem that you face and the questions you would like answers to at the end of the research project.

3. Using the Marketing Information Requirements model on page 165, state which cells should be used to obtain information about the following:

   a. Suppose that your operations in Country X may be threatened by a change in government. How could you go about determining the probability that this will happen?

   b. You are informed that your competition in Country Y is in the process of developing a new product that, if successful, can prove to be superior to your product that is currently on the market. How can you obtain information about your competitor's stage of development of this product?

KEY TERMS

Foreign market opportunity analysis, p. 159

International marketing research, p. 152

Market research, p. 151

Marketing research, p. 151

Online research, p. 155

Primary research, p. 155

Qualitative research, p. 154

Quantitative research, p. 152

Secondary research, p. 155

Self-reference criterion (SRC), p. 159

CASE 6-1

Rio Tinto: Can the Concept of "Strictly Business" Be Applied in the Chinese Market?

The Anglo-Australian mining company Rio Tinto (Rio) is the world's third-largest and Australia's second-largest mining company. It has been a major iron ore supplier to steel and aluminum producers in China and has established long-term relationships with numerous Chinese commercial and government agencies (Lo, 2007).

In response to the country's strategic goal to increase its presence in the world's mineral resource market to support its internal demand, the world's second-largest and the largest state-owned aluminum corporation of China (Chinalco) formed a strategic partnership with Rio by acquiring 9.3 percent of its ordinary share in February 2008. Since then, Chinalco has become Rio's single largest stakeholder and largest customer (Leggatt, DeGeer, & Makin, 2009). Simultaneously, China's extension into the Australian resource market, which threatened Australia's national interest, has become a hot political debate (*ChinaStakes*, 2009).

Just prior to a February 6, 2009, deadline for the world's largest Anglo-Australian mining company (BHP) to firm up a takeover bid of the financially ill Rio, Chinalco teamed up with the world's third-largest United States aluminum producer, Alcoa, to form a joint venture (with Chinalco owning 91.45 percent and Alcoa owning 8.54 percent) in an attempt to buy a 9 percent stake in Rio, thus blocking BHP's action. They signed a U.S.$19.50 billion conditional contract subject to the approval of Rio's shareholders and various government authorities (*ChinaStakes*, 2009). If this agreement was successfully implemented, it would allow Chinalco to secure its mineral supply from Rio in order to largely satisfy China's huge domestic demand for the next 20 years and at the same time increase its shareholding in Rio to 18 percent. Leveraging Chinalco's offer, Rio was concurrently awaiting a higher bid from all parties concerned. "BHP Billiton's offers, while improved, still fail to recognize the underlying value of Rio Tinto's quality assets and prospects," Rio's chairman Paul Skinner said in a news conference (*BBC News*, 2008).

On June 5, 2009, Rio signed a joint venture agreement with BHP, valued at U.S.$5.8 billion, to jointly exploit the mine in Western Australia, and instantaneously scrapped Chinalco's offer with a break fee of U.S.$195 million, which was stated in the "letter" of the conditional contract (Zhu, Wu, & Ma, 2009). According to Fortgang, Lax, and Sebenius (2003, p. 66), a "letter" of contract is concerned with the terms and conditions written explicitly in a contract. The reason that drove Rio Tinto to reject Chinalco's proposal might be "something other than economic concern," said Zhang Yansheng, director of the Institute of Foreign Trade of the National Development and Reform Commission (Zhu, et al. 2009). In fact, cooperation between the two mega mining companies would be "what the Australian government wanted to see," said Hu Kaian, an analyst at Umetal (Zhu, et al. 2009).

However, Rio's unfriendly action aroused anger from Beijing (*BBC News*, 2009). Chen Yanhai, an official at the Ministry of Industry and Information Technology, responded publicly that the Rio–BHP iron ore alliance had a "strong monopolistic

Case prepared by Dr. Thomas K.P. Leung of the Department of Management & Marketing, The Hong Kong Polytechnic University, Hung Hom, Kowloon, Hong Kong. Reprinted with permission.

color" (Powell, 2009). The combined production from the two mega-mining companies contributes one-third of the world's iron ore supplies that substantially worsened the already weak bargaining power of major Chinese steel and aluminum makers (*BBC News*, 2008).

On July 9, 2009, China confirmed that the top Chinese executive with Australian nationality, Stern Hu, and his three Chinese subordinates of Rio Tinto, who were mainly responsible for price negotiation of iron ore supply with the China Iron and Steel Association, had been detained on suspicion of spying and stealing state secrets that might stem from how the four employees collected information concerning pricing from Chinese steel producers to formulate negotiation strategies with these steel producers (Barboza, 2009a).

On August 12, 2009, Chinese officials revealed to Australian diplomats that they had decided not to pursue the initial state secret charges against the four Rio employees, but were replacing them with much lighter charges of suspicion of commercial bribery and trade secret infringement, after weeks of pressure from Australia and growing concern in the international business community about a lack of transparency in the case (Barboza, 2009b). The initial state secret charges carried a potential sentence of life imprisonment, while the commercial bribery charge could be punished with as little as a fine or a fixed-length prison term (Galani, 2009). It was now up to the Chinese investigators whether to send the case to prosecutors to seek a trial or to abandon it (Kang & Norton, 2010).

When the above evidence is considered, the arrests of the four Rio Tinto employees indeed reflected that the political and economic relationships between the Australian and the Chinese government were on the verge of a dilemma. In saying that, the AFIRB was highly unlikely to approve Chinalco's U.S.$19.5 billion investment in Rio because of internal political pressure and the possible control of national interests by the Chinese state-owned company, Chinalco. Therefore, Rio may have very little choice but to leverage Chinalco's offer to bargain with another Anglo-Australian mining company, BHP, for a better deal to solve its urgent short-term financial problem. The alliance between two Anglo-Australian companies sensibly avoids the intervention of AFIRB. However, Rio's alignment with BHP would be an act of betrayal to its old friend Chinalco, because its reason for rejecting Chinalco's offer was to form a joint venture with BHP in order to avoid the disapproval of its shareholders and the AFIRB.

In response, Chinalco openly denounced Rio as a "dishonorable woman" (Nagpal, 2009), because Rio's treachery pushed its long-term relationships with Chinalco and the Chinese government to the edge of a cliff, and also caused Chinalco to lose its *mianzi* in front of the Chinese government. Meanwhile, Beijing was enraged about the unfriendly actions of a long-term trading partner who used the ploy with Chinalco to eventually dance with BHP. "Causing the Chinese business partner who brought you to the table to lose *mianzi* is no mere faux pas; it's a disaster" (Graham & Lam, 2003, p. 9). The pricing negotiation of iron ore, in fact, added fuel to this relationship dilemma. Tung (1982) warned Western firms long ago that sincerity and a long-term prospective are the attitudes needed to negotiate with their Chinese partners. West Australian Premier Colin Barnett concurred: "It was not proper that Australia's diplomatic, political and economic relationships with China were determined by a private company, Rio, and its boardroom in London" (Anonymous, 2009).

The downgrade of the charges from state secrets to commercial bribery, and the consideration of dropping or proceeding with the bribery charge, are actually signs given by the Chinese government to Rio and the Australian government regarding the possibility of mending the political and economic relationships between the two countries. Jerome Cohen, a specialist in Chinese law at New York University, commented: "That (the downgrade of the case) puts it in the business context rather than the realm of state secrets... This would seem to be a lowering of temperature somewhat" (Garnaut, 2009). To conclude, the Chinese government will use relevant laws to punish a company that upset its plan in response to a betrayal from an old friend and a collapse of a long-term relationship with that company. Indeed, legal scholars noted that China's state secrets law is vague (Cohen & Daum, 2009) and is often used to punish political opponents or those Beijing considers a threat to national interests. Therefore, the key to a company doing business in China is to maintain a harmonious relationship with the Chinese government and all parties concerned if the project is negotiated in accordance with Chinese national interests, which is vital to avoid a company falling into a political precipice. The harmonious relationship perspective is supported by Ho (1979), Wilson (1974), and others (Kirkbride, et al. 1991). Also, Ghauri and Fang (2001) and others (Fayerweather & Kapoor, 1976; Ghauri, 1996) noted that Chinese politics has an all-pervasive influence on every aspect of Chinese life. Chinese business and politics can hardly be separated under the Chinese economic planning mechanism. Therefore, a foreign company or its executive must be aware of the political standing of its Chinese partner and not get caught in the crossfire of Chinese power struggles (Anonymous, 1995).

Concerning the second issue, the Chinese government, in fact, has very stringent regulations concerning state employees giving or receiving gifts to and from foreign companies in official functions. According to the *Regulations of the State Council of the People's Republic of China on Giving and Receiving Gifts in Official Functions Involving Foreigners 1993*, no state employee shall give or receive gifts in terms of cash or negotiable securities without authorization, nor shall he solicit gifts from foreign firms either explicitly or implicitly (Article 2 & 8) (China Legislative Information Network System, 1993). Also, the *Supplementary Provisions of the Standing Committee of the National People's Congress Concerning the Punishment of the Crimes of Embezzlement and Bribery* (Order 63) promulgated on Jan. 21, 1988 (http://www .lawinfochina.com.ezproxy.lb.polyu.edu.hk/law/), state that whoever conspires with state personnel, personnel of collective economic organizations, or other personnel in public service to accept bribes shall be punished as an accomplice in the crime (Article 4). Article 7 also says that whoever, in economic activities, violates the relevant provisions of the state, gives property of a large quantity or value to state personnel, shall be punished for the crime of bribing.

Steidlmeier (1999) noted that throughout the Chinese history, Chinese authorities have been using laws and regulations to condemn corruption and bribery rather than advocating them. In fact, they will continue their pressing of companies that violate them. In this context, the Chinese laws, indeed, work against a foreign company's presentation of gifts, specifically in terms of cash or negotiable securities to state employees, because the boundary between bribery and monetary gifts is blurred. According to an unconfirmed piece published in the *Fairfax Press,* Rio Tinto-employed PR firms regularly distribute bulky cash envelops to Chinese journalists who normally are state employees to gain media coverage in China (Crook, 2009). If this is true, the four Rio employees may indirectly and unintentionally have infringed upon the Chinese laws in gift-giving or bribery, because company managers are considered legal representatives (Fu, 1993) of a company in China and are liable for what their employees are doing. As such, the arrests of the top Rio Tinto legal person and his three employees appeared to be in compliance with the legal system in China.

In summary, the managers of MNEs must be very sensitive to its social and political environment when they enter the important Chinese market.

Discussion Questions

1. Should an MNE manager emphasize the letter of the contract only when he/she negotiates with his/her Chinese partner? If no, what else should he/she be aware of when he/she forms a contractual relationship with his/her Chinese partner?

2. Should an MNE manager purely follow the local customs, such as the practice of gift-giving, when he/she negotiates with his/her Chinese partner? If no, what should he/she do?

3. Besides the economic factors, what other potential factors should an MNE manager consider?

References

Anonymous. (6 February 2008). Anglo-Australian mining giant BHP Billiton has formalized a hostile bid to buy its rival Rio Tinto in a deal worth about U.S.$147bn (£74.8 bn). *BBC News*. Retrieved from http://news.bbc.co.uk/2/hi/business/7229516 .stm on January 21, 2010.

Anonymous. (11 July 2009). Australia not handle well relation with China: West Australian Premier. *People's Daily*. Retrieved from http://english.peopledaily.com .cn/90001/90776/90883/6698338.html on January 19, 2010.

Anonymous. (14 February 2009). Chinalco eyes assets and board seats in Rio Tinto deal. *ChinaStakes*. Retrieved from http://www.chinastakes.com/2009/2/ chinalco-eyes-assets-and-board-seats-in-rio-tinto-deal.html.

Anonymous. (25 February 1995). The perils of connections. *The Economist*, 64–65.

Anonymous. (2009). Rio Tinto–Chinalco U.S.$19.5B deal now dead. *China Daily*. Retrieved from http://www.chinadaily.com.cn/china/2009-06/05/contents_8252601 .htm on January 21, 2010.

Anonymous. (6 February 2009). Mining firm Rio Tinto has rejected a U.S.$147 bn (£74.8bn) takeover offer from rival BHP Billiton. *BBC News*. Retrieved from http://news.bbc.co.uk/2/hi/business/7230670.stm on January 21, 2010.

Anonymous. (14 July 2009). China's Rio Tinto inquiry widens. *BBC News*. Retrieved from http://news.bbc.co.uk/2/hi/business/8149061.stm on January 21, 2010.

Barboza, D. (9 July 2009a). China says Australian is detained in spy case. *The New York Times*. Retrieved from www.nytimes.com/2009/07/10/world/asia/10riotinto .html on January 28, 2010.

Barboza, D. (12 August 2009b). 4 on Rio Tinto's China staff won't face spying charge. *The New York Times*. Retrieved from www.nytimes.com/2009/08/13/ business/global/13riotinto.html on January 28, 2010.

China Legislative Information Network System. (1993). *Regulations of the State Council of the People's Republic of China on giving and receiving gift in official functions involving foreigners*. Retrieved from www.lawinchina.com/laws/list.asp on January 1, 2010.

Cohen, J.A., & Daum, J. (2009, August 6). China's draft state secrets law: revision without reform. *United States Asia Law Institute*. Retrieved from http://www.usasialaw .org/?p=1491 on February 5, 2010.

Crook, A. (16 July 2009). The envelope please: Rio's winning way with public relations. *Crikey*. Retrieved from http://www.crikey.com.au/2009/07/16/the-envelope-please-rios-winning-way-with-public-relations on February 3, 2010.

Fayerweather, J., & Kapoor, A. (1976). *Strategy and negotiation for the international corporation: Guidelines and cases*. Cambridge, MA: Ballinger Pub. Co.

Fortgang, R.S., Lax, D.A., & Sebenius, J.K. (2003, February). Negotiating the spirit of the deal. *Harvard Business Review*, 66–75.

Fu, T. (1993). Legal person in China: Essence and limits. *American Journal of Comparative Law, 41,* 261–272.

Galani, U. (12 August 2009). China steps back in Rio Tinto 'spy' case. *The Telegraph.* Retrieved from http://www.telegraph.co.uk/finance/breakingviews-com/6016800/China-steps-back-in-Rio-Tinto-spy-case.html.

Garnaut, J. (12 August 2009). Rio 'spy' case: Stern Hu officially charged. *Sydney Morning Herald.* Retrieved from http://www.theage.com.au/business/rio-spy-case-stern-hu-officially-charged-20090812.

Ghauri, P., & Fang, T. (2001). Negotiating with the Chinese: A socio-cultural analysis. *Journal of World Business, 36*(3), 303–325.

Ghauri, P. (1996). Introduction. In P. N. Ghauri & J. C. Usunier (Eds.), *International business negotiations* (pp. 3–20). Oxford: Pergamon.

Gundlach, G. T., & Murphy, P. E. (1993). Ethical and legal foundations of relational marketing exchanges. *Journal of Marketing, 57,* 35.

Graham, J.L., & Lam, M.N. (2003, October). The Chinese negotiation. *Harvard Business Review*, 82–91.

Kang, B., & Norton, J. (8 January 2010). Rio Tinto spy saga set to move forward next week. *Mineweb.* Retrieved from www.mineweb.com/mineweb/view/mineweb/en/ on January 27, 2010.

Kirkbride, P.S., Tang, S.F.Y., & Westwood R.I. (1991). Chinese conflict preferences and negotiating behavior: cultural and psychological influences. *Organization Studies, 12*(3), 365–386.

Leggatt, H., DeGeer, C., & Makin, J. (2009, March). *Rio Tinto Review*, Issue 89.

Lo, A. (2007, August 27). *Rio Tinto in China.* Speech and presentation in Beijing. Retrieved from www.riotinto.com/media/speeches_6693.asp on January 28, 2010.

Nagpal, S. (4 September 2009). Rio Tinto toughens China iron ore stance. *TopNews.in.* Retrieved from www.topnews.in/rio-tinto-toughens-china-iron-ore-stance-2210537 on February 1, 2010.

Powell, B. (24 August 2009). Rio Tinto—China strikes back. *CNN News.* Retrieved from http://money.cnn.com/2009/08/24/news/companies/china_rio_tinto.fortune/index.htm. on January 28, 2009.

Steidlmeier, P. (1999). Gift giving, bribery and corruption: Ethical management of business relationships in China. *Journal of Business Ethics, 20,* 121–132.

Tung, R.L. (1982, Fall). United States China trade negotiations: Practices, procedures and outcomes. *Journal of International Business Studies, 13*(2), 25–37.

Zhu, Y., Wu, Q., & Ma, S. (2009). Chinalco confirms deal breakup with Rio Tinto, expresses disappointment. Retrieved from www.chinaview.cn on January 21, 2010.

CHAPTER 7

Selecting International Markets

It was the best of times, it was the worst of times. . . .
CHARLES DICKENS, *A TALE OF TWO CITIES*

LEARNING OBJECTIVES

After reading this chapter, you should be able to

- Understand what motivates a firm to expand abroad rather than in its domestic market.
- Identify the drivers of international market expansion.
- Understand the fundamentals of internationalization theories.
- Apply various models used to select an entry mode strategy.
- Apply theories of internationalization to case studies of business firms.
- Use the tools for international market screening.

Nuvotronics (pseudonym) has a current sales volume of about $4.5 million per year and employs 65 people. While about 80 percent of sales are to the United States government and military, 20 percent are to commercial buyers, including the oil and gas industries, aerospace, and satellite manufacturers. The company's core competency is in manufacturing capacitors, modules, and assemblies of high quality and reliability that can work in extreme environments. This has helped the company differentiate itself from competition. International sales account for approximately 15 percent of total sales. To lessen the domestic business and political cycles inherent in its industry, the company wants to increase foreign sales to about 30 percent of total sales within five years. Thus, the objective of the firm is to significantly increase the internationalization of the firm.

Internationalization occurs when a firm makes a strategic decision to enter foreign markets and adapts its operations to international environments by committing both tangible and intangible assets, experiential knowledge, learning, and human resources to this effort. Management must realize that foreign or international markets are more competitive than domestic markets owing to the complexity of consumer demands across different countries and because of intensive rivalry from both domestic and international firms. On the one hand, international markets provide firms like Nuvotronics with an opportunity for expansion and profitability, but on the other hand, represent a tough competitive environment. Thus management's choice of which markets to enter, the mode of entry, and timing are of critical importance.

This chapter deals with the alternatives open to the firm and the motivation for internal (domestic) versus external (foreign) expansion. In the example of Nuvotronics, the first decision management must take is whether to concentrate on the domestic market, to expand abroad, or both.

Suppose that it is decided to expand abroad. The next step is to locate specific market opportunities. Once promising markets are located, then an expansion strategy must be decided upon, to enter one market (concentration) or to enter several markets over a short period of time (diversification). Following this decision, an entry mode must be selected (e.g., export, franchising, or some other alternative). An excellent framework for understanding expansion alternatives is a model developed by Ansoff (1965).

THE ANSOFF EXPANSION MODEL

It is axiomatic that in order to be competitive and profitable, firms must expand their operations. According to Ansoff, they can do this in four ways: market penetration, market development, product development, and diversification. The following matrix (Figure 7-1) illustrates these possibilities. Note that commercial risk increases as the firm introduces new products and or penetrates new markets.

PRESENT MARKETS/PRESENT PRODUCTS

Firms choosing this strategy attempt to gain higher market share in existing markets using existing products. More resources are dedicated to marketing effort through adjusting the marketing mix, such as more aggressive advertising and sales promotion. Penetration can also be accomplished by offering price discounts and better relationship with customers. Of the four growth strategies, market penetration has the lowest risk. Fuller's London Pride is an example of this strategy.

Have you heard of, or better yet tried, Fuller's London Pride, initially a regional ale selling in the Southeast of the UK, but later becoming the best selling national draught ale? The market penetration of Fuller's Ale was accomplished by improving the product and investing in better advertising and merchandising.

PRESENT MARKETS/NEW PRODUCTS

This strategy entails offering new products to current markets. It requires developing or acquiring new products or line expansion. A good example of this strategy is the

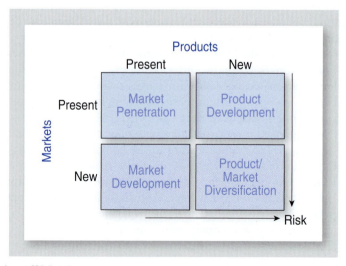

Figure 7-1 Ansoff Matrix

Source: Adapted from: Igor Ansoff, "The Firm of the Future," *Harvard Business Review,* September–October 1965.

German company, Mont Blanc, best known for its fountain pens. However, once you purchase one of their pens or sets, you are set for life. Only a few collectors will purchase additional pens or pencils. In order to expand sales among existing customers, Mont Blanc expanded into accessories, such as wallets and cuff links.

NEW MARKETS/PRESENT PRODUCTS

New markets may be solely domestic or both domestic and global. Dress Barn, one of the largest retail women's clothing chains (about 1,500 stores in 48 states and the District of Columbia) operated initially in the eastern part of the United States from its founding in 1962, but purchased the Maurices chain in 2005 to expand to the Midwest and western United States. They do not have stores outside the United States, but most of their clothing is contract-manufactured in Asia, the Middle East, and Africa.

On the other hand, Tesco, the UK's largest food retailer has diversified globally, with most of its floor space outside of the UK (Figure 7-2). Tesco PLC operates over 2,300 stores in the UK, Ireland, Hungary, Poland, the Czech Republic, Slovakia, Turkey, and Asia. Tesco's operations include convenience (Tesco Express), small urban stores (Tesco Metro), hypermarkets (Tesco Extra), financial services, and a telecom business. Tesco is also a leader in online grocery sales through its online store at www.tesco.com.

NEW MARKETS/NEW PRODUCTS

Apple Computers started out by targeting the graphic design market. Today they market to the final consumer not only computers, but also consumer electronics as exemplified by the iPod and iPad. They also expanded globally. As of 2008, they operate

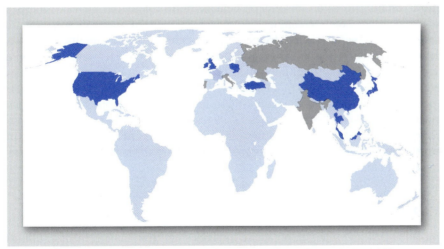

● Countries in which Tesco currently operates (United States, Ireland, UK, Czech Republic, Poland, Slovakia, Hungary, Turkey, China, Japan, South Korea, Malaysia, Thailand)

● Countries with planned or speculated future Tesco operations (Portugal, Italy, India, Russia)

● Countries from which Tesco has withdrawn (France, Taiwan)

Figure 7-2 Global Presence of Tesco

Source: Adapted from: www.tescopoly.org/index. Retrieved June 20, 2011.

19 stores in the UK (their largest store is not in New York but on Regent Street in London), nine in Canada, seven in Japan, three in Australia, two in Switzerland, and one each in China, Israel, and Italy. In 2008, Apple's world share of the PC market was about double that of its share in the United States.[1]

INTERNATIONALIZATION AND THE ANSOFF MATRIX

Internationalization has been defined as the process of adapting a firm's operations (strategy, structure, resources) to international environments. Therefore, only a market development strategy—entering foreign markets—would fit this definition. However, most of the firms described above have expanded their operations both domestically and internationally by adopting most, if not all, of Ansoff's suggested strategies. Looking at the matrix again (Figure 7-1), this time using the Tesco Company as an example, we see that they have adopted all four strategies at one time or another.

Tesco has increased its market share both domestically and internationally by using all elements of the marketing mix, including line extension and differentiation (e.g., financial services to existing customers and consumer electronics to both current and new customers). It has also expanded internationally (new markets). What are some of drivers that have motivated the above and other companies to internationalize their operations?

MOTIVATION TO INTERNATIONALIZE

The idea or urge to internationalize may be internal or external to the firm. It may occur internally by the realization of management that there is more potential for growth overseas than in the domestic market. Or the motivation can be an external source, resulting from an unsolicited contact from a potential buyer overseas who heard something about the company's products by word of mouth or a news write-up on the Internet. The unsolicited trigger to follow up and investigate markets abroad is a **reactive motive.** It is similar to motivation fostered by the occurrence of a domestic event not under the control of the firm such as a recession at home. On the other hand, there are **proactive motives** to internationalization such as the desire of management to become global players. Generally, these motives fall into one of four classes, as shown in Table 7-1 (Albaum, et al).

Jompponen, et al. (2004)[2] used the Albaum, et al. classification to survey the internationalization motives of Estonian and Russian banks. Many of the motives found are similar to those in Table 7-2.

PROACTIVE MOTIVES

Generally speaking, internal, proactive motives stem from management's beliefs that there are firm-specific assets that can be exploited abroad. For example, idle capacity that can be exploited by exporting products abroad, international experience possessed by top managers that has not been sufficiently utilized, and utilizing the advantage of a strong brand identity.

1. From http://apple20.blogs.fortune.cnn.com/2008/05/19/report-apples-market-share-of-pcs-over-1000-hits-66/. Retrieved October 15, 2008.

2. Jumpponen, J., Liuhto, K., Sörg, M., & Vessel, V. (2004). *Banks' internationalization: Estonian and Russian banks' expansion to the foreign markets*. School of Economics and Business Administration, Tallinn University of Technology, p. 88.

TABLE 7-1 A Classification of Internationalization Motives		
	Internal	**External**
Proactive	■ Managerial Urge ■ Growth and Profit Goals ■ Preempt Competition ■ Economies of Scale ■ Unique Product/Technology	■ Foreign Market Opportunities ■ Change Agents ■ Location Advantages
Reactive	■ Risk Diversification ■ Extend Sales of Seasonal Products ■ Excess Capacity	■ Unsolicited Orders ■ Small Home Market ■ Stagnant or Declining Home Market

Source: Adapted from: Albaum, G., Strandskov, J., Duerr, E., & Dowd, L. (1994). *International marketing and export management* (2nd ed.). Reading, MA: Addison-Wesley.

TABLE 7-2 Motives of Internationalization of Estonian and Russian Banks		
	Internal	**External**
Proactive	■ Search for Market Power, Increase Market Share ■ Distinctive Service and Brand ■ Extend Product Range and Life Cycle ■ Visionary Leadership	■ Increasing Concentration through M&As ■ Improvements in Information Technology ■ Improvements in Physical Infrastructure (Communication Networks)
Reactive	■ Improve Levels of Business Performance ■ Suitable Situation to Obtain Foreign Bank by Default ■ Excess Capacity	■ Intensity of Competition ■ Service Existing Customers Who Have Gone International ■ Stagnant or Declining Home Market

A survey of SMEs in Poland found the internationalization motives found in Figure 7-3, which are largely proactive.

John Dunning (1993)[3] observed four categories of proactive internationalization motives: market seeking, resource seeking, efficiency seeking, and strategic resource seeking.

Market seeking firms search for opportunities to expand and may enter new markets to preempt competition or to better serve their customers. Another reason is to exploit competitive advantages. Filipescu[4] (2007) gives three case studies of internationalizing firms in the baking, optical, and toy industries. In all three, the main motivation for beginning international activities was the necessity to survive in a global world. All three firms were innovative, introducing new products. Thus they had a strong asset with which to compete internationally. Child and Rodrigues (2005)[5] give four case studies of market-seeking Chinese firms. The studies indicate that the firms sought technology and brand assets to create a competitive position in foreign markets. In these cases, Chinese firms were motivated in order to internationalize in order to address competitive *disadvantages*. Their internationalization strategies were "inward" in the sense that they engaged in original equipment manufacture (OEM)

3. Dunning, J. (1993). *Multinational enterprises and the global economy.* Reading, MA: Addison-Wesley

4. Filipescu, D. (2007). *Innovation and Internationalization: A Focus on the Spanish Exporting Firms.* PhD Dissertation, Universitat Autònoma de Barcelona.

5. Child, J., & Rodrigues, S. (2005). The internationalization of Chinese firms: A case for theoretical extension? *Management and Organization Review, 1*(3), 381–410.

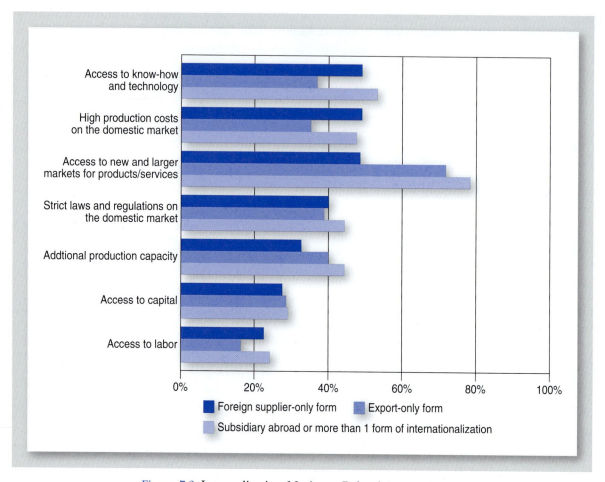

Figure 7-3 Internalization Motives—Poland

Note: The percentage that rated a motive to internationalize "important" or "very important."

Source: Data from ENSR Enterprise Survey, 2003.

and joint ventures and also "outward" internationalization through acquisition of assets abroad.

Resource seeking companies invest abroad in order to obtain resources. Perhaps the wanted resource can be acquired at a lower comparative cost, or simply does not exist at all in the home country. Examples are the acquisition of raw materials, and the use of low wage employees especially for production of labor intensive products. The motivations of SMEs in Poland shown in the above diagram are mainly resource seeking.

Efficiency seekers are usually firms that are already established abroad but look to rationalize their operations by gaining economies of scale and scope through common governance and knowledge sharing.

Strategic resource seekers are firms that try to attain competitive advantage by acquiring assets that are essential for its long term strategic objectives. Such assets include knowledge, patents, and skills embedded in human resources.

A major external motive or initiator is the change agent. These may be resident buyers for foreign companies such as department store chains. They seek out products for sale in the chain and initiate contact with the domestic supplier. They may suggest how to modify the product for sale in the foreign market.

Another sort of change agent is the so-called roving export manager (ROV) employed by the Israel Export Institute. These agents are retired export managers who have amassed significant experience and knowledge in a variety of industries. They act as the representative of SMEs who wish to internationalize but lack the knowledge and skills for doing so. The ROV negotiates on behalf of the local firm, concludes the sale, and arranges for the exportation of the goods. He is compensated partly by the Institute and by the firm.

Trade agreements are also motives for internationalization. An agreement that serves to reduce trade barriers will certainly encourage domestic firms to take advantage of lower tariffs in order to export. Similarly, the removal of barriers such as banking and investment regulations in host countries may motivate these institutions to establish branches or affiliates abroad. Also, higher prices abroad may be a strong incentive to export.

REACTIVE MOTIVES

Reactive motivated firms view internationalization as a necessary response to unfavorable conditions in their current markets. Such conditions may be increased competitive pressures, excess capacity given domestic market conditions, or a declining domestic market. Ersson and Tryggvason (2007)[6] found that a major internationalization motive of Nordic banks was a saturated home market. In addition, management can react to negative changes within the firm by choosing internationalization as a method for improving or overcoming internal problems. However, their motives in these examples may be more tactical than strategic or short term rather than long term.

Much of the literature reflects reactive motives as negative, while proactive ones are positive. There is some evidence to show that firms that engage in proactive planning are more successful than those that do not (reactive).[7] Small firms with limited resources and lack of international experience are more prone to reactive expansion. However, even larger companies may be reactive in the beginning stages of internationalization but become proactive later. A case in point is Heineken (see Box 7-1).[8]

BOX 7-1   COMPANY IN FOCUS: HEINEKEN

In the 1950s and 1960s, Heineken concentrated on export markets in which maximum financial reward could be gained with relatively little effort. These included markets in Africa, the United States, the Caribbean, the Persian Gulf region, and the duty-free markets. Heineken did not devote many resources to penetrate the developed, complex beer markets in Europe that were characterized by heavy competition. Only after the "easy" markets had been penetrated did management switch its attention to the more difficult developed markets in the 1970s and 1980s.

Source: Adapted from: www.annualreport.Heineken.com. Retrieved, December 20, 2010.

---

6. Ersson, M., & Tryggvason, J. (2007). *Internationalization of two Nordic banks* [master's thesis]. Luleå University of Technology.

7. van Gelder, J., Reinout, E., de Vries, M. F., & Goutbeek, J. (2007). Differences in psychological strategies of failed and operational business owners in the Fiji Islands. *Journal of Small Business Management, 45*(3), 388–400.

8. From www.heineken.com/annualreport, 2010.

Heineken switched from a mainly reactive expansion strategy to a proactive one because of competitive pressures. Nevertheless, it has become one of the largest breweries and distributors in the world. It has utilized different entry strategies and modes (licensing, joint ventures, and acquisitions). Heineken beer is sold in 170 countries, with over 100 breweries in 50 countries.

THEORIES OF INTERNATIONALIZATION AND MARKET ENTRY

Internationalization theory tries to explain the conditions under which it is more efficient for a firm to create an internal, domestic market rather than enter foreign ones. The criterion for determining whether to expand in an internal, rather than a foreign market, is based on the transaction costs of information, opportunism and asset specificity. Generally speaking, the cost of information acquisition in foreign markets is far more expensive than acquiring information in internal markets. Control over agents abroad may be more difficult resulting in opportunistic behavior (agents operating in their own interest rather than that of the principal, or where one party to an agreement tries to better his/her position at the expense of the other). Examples of opportunistic behavior include not reporting all sales, disregarding codes of conduct required by headquarters and outright fraud. Also, a firm with technological or marketing know-how advantages is better able to protect them in its home market. If transaction costs of operating abroad are higher they cause market failure and serve as a barrier to internationalizing the firm.

Nevertheless, firms do internationalize in spite of higher transaction costs. They do this by *internalizing* firm specific advantages such as technological know-how by using entry modes such as direct investment rather than licensing the know-how to an agent, which carries the risk of losing it. Internalization theorists suggest that foreign direct investment occurs when the benefits of internalization outweigh its costs.

A typical foreign entry pattern is by exports through local agents in new markets followed later by licensing and a wholly owned subsidiary/manufacturing plant (see Figure 7-4). The progression from one stage to another is dependent upon the acquisition of experiential knowledge which is gained over time as a result of learning.

INTERNATIONAL PRODUCT LIFE CYCLE

Raymond Vernon (1966)[9] developed the **International Product Life Cycle (IPLC)** model (see Figure 7-5), which explained how an innovating United States manufacturer (and similar producers in other developed countries) internationalized their operations. According to the model, the American firm developed new products essentially for the home market. As demand for the product emerges in overseas markets, the firm exports the product. Production at home and exporting comprise the first (new product) stage in the IPLC.

In the second, maturity stage, the product becomes more of a commodity, and loses much of its competitive advantage. It is easily produced by manufacturers abroad. Now the American firm has competition from both developed and developing countries in

9. Reymond Vernon (1966). International investment and international trade in the product cycle. *Quarterly Journal of Economics*. 80, 190–207.

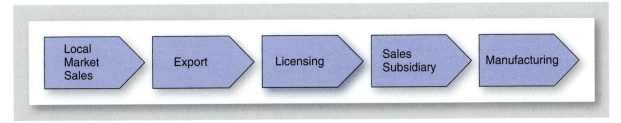

Figure 7-4 Typical Foreign Entry Pattern

its overseas markets, which are able to produce the product at lower cost. In this situation, the American manufacturer cannot hold on to its overseas markets by exports alone and so must find other locations to produce the product, especially in low-cost developing countries.

As the product becomes more standardized, and its home market becomes saturated, the manufacturer must either find ways to "re-invent" the product, reduce process costs, or take the product off the market. Or, the product is produced offshore by the company in low-cost countries and exported back to the home market.

A good example of the IPLC is the case of IBM laptops, developed and produced first in the United States. In the second stage, a few R&D centers were located abroad, as well as production facilities. In the third stage, production was shifted to Asian countries, such as Singapore and later China, when the product was sold to Lenovo in China.

Critique

Vernon's main assumption was that the diffusion process of a new technology occurs slowly enough to generate temporary differences between countries in their access and use of new technologies. By the late 1970's, he recognized that this assumption was no longer valid. Income differences between advanced nations had dropped significantly, competitors were able to imitate products at much higher speeds than previously envisioned and MNCs had built up an existing global network of production facilities that enabled them to launch products in multiple markets simultaneously.

UPPSALA MODEL

According to the Uppsala model, firms first enter into markets that are close psychically (psychic distance)[10] to their home base and later enter more distant markets as their experiential knowledge increases.[11] Most researchers agree that decision makers are most likely to explore first those markets that they perceive to be similar to their domestic market. The principle of similitude[12] suggests that foreign entrants will

---

10. Evans, J., Treadgold, A. & Movondo, F. (2000). Explaining export development through psychic distance. *International Marketing Review,* 17 (2), 164–174. These authors define psychic distance as the "mind's processing, in terms of perception and understanding, of the cultural and business differences." between the home and foreign market.

11. Bilkey, W. & Tesar, G. (1977).The export behavior of smaller-sized Wisconsin manufacturing firms. *Journal of International Business Studies,* 8 (1), 93-98; Cavusgil, S. (1980). On the internationalization process of the firm. *European Research,* (November), 273–281; Johanson, J & Vahlne, L. (1977). The internationalization process of the firm—a model of knowledge development and increasing foreign market commitments. *Journal of International Business Studies,* (Spring/Summer), 3–32.

12. Jaffe, E. D. (1974). *Grouping: an international marketing strategy,* New York: American Management Association.

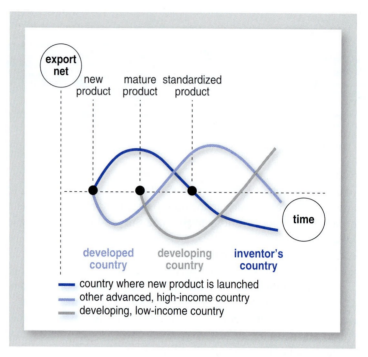

Figure 7-5 Vernon's International Product Life Cycle

Source: International Product Life Cycle. Retrieved from www.provenmodels.com/583 on June 7, 2011. Reprinted with permission.

employ that strategy which needs a minimal degree of product adaptation to foreign markets.

Johanson and Weidersheim-Paul (1975)[13] investigated the internationalization of Swedish companies and found four different stages of entering international markets (see Figure 7-6). This theory explained why the firms studied initiated internationalization strategies later in their development. Basically, firms remained domestic unless some internal or external driver motivated them to expand, such as an unsolicited export order. Over time, firms gradually progress through a series of stages based on experiential learning and commitment of resources. Each stage represents a higher degree of international market commitment and geographic diversification as shown below. In the first stage there are only sporadic exports, mostly from unsolicited orders. Regular exporting is accomplished in the second stage, via contracts with established, independent distributors and sales representatives abroad. In the third stage, a foreign sales subsidiary is organized. Finally, in the fourth stage, a manufacturing subsidiary is established. According to the model, geographic diversification involves greater psychic distance as the firm enters new markets. Following this assumption, Swedish firms would first enter low psychic distant markets such as Finland and Denmark and then later more distant ones. However, Nordström (1991)[14] found that the Swedish companies that

13. Johanson, J. & Weidersheim-Paul, F. (1975), "The internationalization of the firm—four cases," *Journal of Management Studies,* 8, 23-32.

14. Nordström, K. (1991). The internationalization process of the firm—searching for new patterns and explanations. Stockholm: Institute of International Business, Stockholm School of Economics.

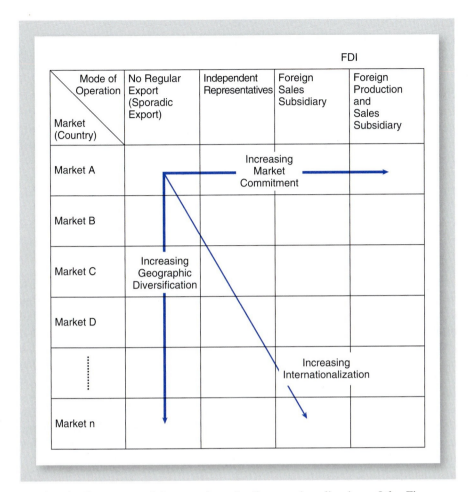

Figure 7-6 An Incremental Approach to the Internationalization of the Firm

Sources: Adapted from: Forsgren, M., & Johanson, J. (1975). *Internationell företagsekonomi (International business economics).* Stockholm: Norstedts; Dervilée, F., Rieche, M., & Zieske, A. (2004). *Internationalization and foreign market entry choice: An alternative approach to the Kristianstad 30 Model* [MBA thesis]. Högskolan: Kristianstad.

he investigated entered Germany, the USA and UK before Denmark, Finland and Norway.

Critique

There are a number of criticisms of the stage models. Why can't firms leapfrog stages? Acquisition of knowledge is faster than indicated by the stage model. Knowledge may be acquired by hiring experienced international managers, by attending seminars sponsored by export institutes and from consulting organizations. Another explanation may be that since the exposition of such models, the world has become flat and integrated, facilitated by rapid dissemination of information.

Another criticism of the model is that it is uni-directional; it does not consider the possibilities of changing strategies at a given stage, e.g. divestment or choosing a cooperative mode such as a strategic alliance.

BOX 7-2   TECHNOLOGY IN FOCUS: BORN GLOBAL

Infomedia, Ltd., is a publicly listed Australian company that has become a leading supplier of electronic parts catalogues for the global automotive industry. The company is headquartered in Sydney and has support centers in Melbourne, Europe, Japan, Latin America, and North America.

This born-global company first expanded into international markets by partnering with other businesses before distributing more of its product itself through wholly owned subsidiaries. As is typical for born-global enterprises, Infomedia was dragged into the world market by its customers. Today, Infomedia's electronic parts catalogs have become the global standard for the automotive industry, shipping to more than 50,000 dealers in over 160 countries and 25 languages.

Critics of the early version of internationalization theory have objected that it is too simplistic. They cite cases such as the Italian and Israeli paradoxes where, they argue, these countries' exporters have not progressed sequentially into deeper modes of foreign penetration (such as creating branches or subsidiaries or manufacturing plants) but have instead increased their communications efforts with their distributors as a means of more efficient diffusion (see Rosson and Reid [1987][15] and Bonaccorsi and Dalli [1990])[16] These so-called **born global** companies were established at the outset, not to serve the local market, but to do business abroad. Internationalization theorists have defended themselves by stating that while the simple evolutionary theory was appropriate to the internationalization of firms until the mid-seventies when markets were not as globalized and integrated, they do not regard it as an adequate theory for our times.

THE NETWORK APPROACH

One more often used and cited part of the theoretical framework of internationalization processes is the work by Mattson & Hertz (1998),[17] who discuss the occurrence and importance of having **international networks** (see Figure 7-7). Network participants are governed by exchange relationships rather than through the market. Because many small companies do not have infinite resources, network collaborations are seen as an important internationalization strategy. "[I]nternationalization . . . is a cumulative process in which relationships are continually established, developed, maintained, and dissolved in order to achieve the objectives of the firm."[18] An industrial network normally includes different players involved in production, distribution, and usage of services and products (Johanson & Mattson, 1988).[19] Financial networks are important for SMEs since these companies normally need to finance their expansion with external capital. In some cases it might be easier to find financing in the country

15. Rosson, P. & Reid, S. (1987). *Managing export entry and expansion: concepts and practice,* New York: Praeger Publishers.

16. Bonaccorsi, A. & Dalli. D. (1990). Internationalization process and entry channels: Evidence of small Italian exporters. Iin H. Mulbacher, & C. Jochum (Eds.), *Proceedings of the European Marketing Academy Conference,* Innsbruck.

17. Mattson, L., & Hertz, S. (1998). Domino effects in international networks. *Journal of Business-to-Business Marketing, 5*(3), 3–32.

18. Ahokangas, P. (1998). Internationalization and resources: An analysis of processes in Nordic SMEs [unpublished dissertation]. Retrieved from http://worldcat.org/oclc58312841.

19. Johanson, J., & Mattson, L. (1988). Internationalization in industrial systems—a network approach. In N. Hood (Ed.), *Strategies for global competition*. London: Croom Helm.

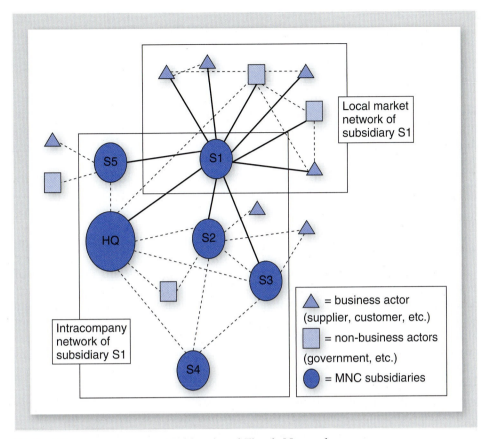

Figure 7-7 Illustration of a Multinational Firm's Network

Source: Rian Drogendijk, "The Development of Network Relations of MNC Subsidiaries: How Internal MNC and External (Local) Relations Evolve," Department of Organizational Strategy, Tilburg University, December 2005. Reprinted with permission.

TABLE 7-3 Network versus Market Based Relationships	
Shared Knowledge	Knowledge Serves Competitive Advantage
Interdependent	Independent
Consent	Contracts
Trust	Price
Learning	Power
Partners	Customers
Scandinavia	UK, U.S., Australia

of expansion instead of on the home market. This has to do with the fact that some venture capitalists prefer to invest in their own home region, where they have a better understanding of the market.

Table 7-3 shows some of the differences between network and market-based relationships. In a network, knowledge is shared, not only by wholly owned subsidiaries (e.g., best practices), but also with suppliers. For example, buyers and suppliers may be connected via computer to each others inventory system, which will automatically inform global suppliers who are partners in the network when to ship goods to their related customers. Therefore, both subsidiaries and suppliers are interdependent. Finally, the network model is more prevalent in Scandinavian countries than in the United States and the UK. Note that this partly stems from the fact that the Scandinavian countries have more collective cultures on Hofstede's scale, while the United States and the UK are more individualistic.

During the internationalization process a company can form new networks in three ways: by creating new relations to networks in the country of expansion that were previously unknown to the company, by creating new relations to actors in networks that were previously known to the company, or by using existing contacts in order to connect to new networks (Johanson & Mattson, 1988).

Indeed, Johanson and Mattson[20] have argued that the stage and network theories complement each other. We would agree that today the theories complement each other, since organizational learning takes place within multinational corporations and this intangible, firm-specific advantage is common to both theories.

The figure below illustrates a network configuration of a multinational corporation. The network is made up of the MNC's corporate headquarters along with five subsidiaries in, let us assume, different countries. The figure details the network of Subsidiary S1 with its headquarters, other subsidiaries in the network, and interdependent agents. In addition, it shows that each subsidiary is networked with headquarters and with one or more of the additional subsidiaries. MNC subsidiaries are not only part of the network, they also develop relations with network actors, such as suppliers, distributors and regulatory agencies, and competitors. Firms interact and build relations with local network actors in order to exchange resources, including goods, services, knowledge, and information. By building network relations, subsidiary management learns how to function in the local environment.

A central point in network theory is that different processes within a company cannot be explained without analyzing the networks that a company directly or indirectly is a part of. The roles of networks have attracted a lot of attention in the last decades. It is often said that having a good network is one of the keys for success. For an SME, both industrial and financial networks play an important role when internationalizing.

For those firms choosing to develop new markets abroad, one of the most crucial decisions that have to be made is what entry mode to use. The remainder of this chapter deals with what motivates firms to internationalize, when is it more advantageous to expand internationally, how to select foreign markets, and what expansion strategy and entry mode to use.

TRANSACTION COST ANALYSIS

The decision of whether or not to internationalize the firm is also based on transaction costs. A **transaction cost** is a cost of making an economic exchange. All forms of market entry incur transaction costs. Basically, there are three sorts of costs:

1. Search and information costs. Market research, research to find suitable distributors or partners abroad.

2. Bargaining costs. Once a potential distributor or partner is located, bargaining on the terms of an agreement follows. The bargaining process incurs costs such as legal and consultant fees, travel expenses, and telephone and other communication expenses.

20. Ibid

3. Monitoring (governance) costs. Once an agreement has been concluded, it has to be enforced to make sure that both sides are living up to the terms of the contract. In the case of suspected breach of contract, these costs can be substantial when arbitration or legal action has to be taken.

We can discern at least three scenarios of transaction costs by mode of entry. Production at home for export involves local manufacturing costs, search and bargaining costs for distributors, and governance costs. Licensing includes search and bargaining costs for a licensee, governance costs, and the risk of dissemination. Dissemination risk occurs when control over an asset such as brand name, a patent, and knowledge is low.

The loss of such assets carries a cost to the firm that can be considerable. A classic case occurred with the American firm Radio Corporation of America (now known as the RCA Corporation, owned by Thomson SA, France). In 1939 RCA unveiled its electronic TV system at the World's Fair in Flushing Meadows, New York. The company began manufacturing TV sets for sale in the United States after World War II. In 1953, its color TV system became the standard (NTSC) approved by the government. Sets were marketed to the public in 1955. Later, the company sold its proprietary knowledge to Japanese companies, who succeeded in taking over the American market.

Production abroad involves manufacturing costs in the foreign country, possible bargaining costs if the subsidiary is not wholly owned, and some governance costs. According to transaction cost theory, a firm will tend to export or license when transaction costs are low or shift production abroad when transaction costs are high.

Hirsch (1976)[21] viewed exporting and foreign direct investment (FDI) as alternative strategies for market entry. Producing at home for export bears costs of (1) domestic production costs, P_d, (2) export marketing costs, M_d, and (3) domestic governance costs, C_d. Producing abroad incurs costs of (1) foreign production, P_f, (2) local marketing, M_f, and (3) foreign governance, C_f. The difference between export marketing and domestic marketing costs (M) is defined as:

$$M = M_f - M_d$$

The difference between foreign and domestic governance costs (C) is defined as:

$$C = C_f - C_d$$

The decision to export or produce abroad (FDI) is determined as:

$$\text{If } P_d + M < P_f + M + C, \text{ then export}$$
$$\text{If } P_d + M \geq P_f + M + C, \text{ then FDI}$$

Critique

Transaction cost theory assumes that exporting and production are substitutes. In reality there are many examples where a firm both manufacturers abroad *and* exports from its home market, as well. Of Honda's total car sales in the American market, about 84 percent is manufactured in the United States, while the remainder is exported from Japan. There are similar examples of other car manufacturers producing abroad and exporting from their home market such as Toyota and Volkswagen.

A firm may invest abroad in order to gain raw materials or know-how that are not available at home. This behavior is not explained by transaction costs. Another criticism of the theory is that it is difficult to measure transaction costs, especially in advance of choosing an entry mode.

21. Hirsch, Z. (1976). An international trade and investment theory of the firm. *Oxford Economic Papers, New Series, 29*(2), 258–270.

Small and medium enterprises (SMEs) tend to reflexively rely on non-equity modes of entry (exporting, licensing) because they would rather preserve capital and avoid high risks when moving into international markets. However, recent research suggests[22] that using transaction cost analysis to select an international mode of entry—a method usually associated with large corporations—can actually improve their chances of selecting the most efficient method for their specific organization. The authors of the study recommend that SMEs evaluate three specific transaction cost criteria:

- Level of investment required for each asset. If no particular asset requires a large investment, non-equity modes such as licensing or franchising may be suitable for market entry. If such entry requires a high level of specific-asset investment, equity modes of entry, such as IJVs or fully owned subsidiaries, may be more appropriate.

- Environmental factors of the target country. A more stable and economically and politically secure country would be more inviting to an equity mode of entry, whereas a country with political or social turmoil and frequent economic crises would be suitable for non-equity modes of entry.

- Status of internal control systems and processes. A business that is built on strong internal culture and regulations would be more comfortable upholding them in their new markets by entering through equity modes. On the other hand, a more open and flexible firm may be comfortable with relying on the controls of partners such as exporting agents or licensees.

SME decision makers can rely on transaction cost theory to make more informed decisions about the most appropriate mode of entry for their company. Decisions made using this method seem to lead to a better performance abroad, according to this study. Whether a firm uses transaction cost analysis or any other accepted method to evaluate its international market strategy, the choice of entry mode should be carefully considered and planned to ensure smoother, more profitable operations abroad.

DUNNING'S ECLECTIC OLI MODEL

John Dunning (1981)[23] posited that entry mode decisions are based on three conditions or advantages: Ownership (who is going to produce abroad), Location (where to produce), and Internalization (why to produce rather than license someone else to produce for you using your assets and know-how). Foreign direct investment (FDI) will be the preferred mode when three conditions are fulfilled:

1. The firm must have net ownership advantages over competing firms. These advantages must be sufficient to offset the additional costs of operating in a foreign environment.

2. It must be more profitable for the firm possessing these unique assets to use them itself rather than transfer the rights to others.

3. It must be advantageous for the firm to exploit its unique assets through production outside its home country rather than by exporting.

22. Brouthers, K. D., & Nakos, G. (2004). SME entry mode choice and performance: A transaction cost perspective. *Entrepreneurship: Theory and Practice, 3,* 229–247.

23. Dunning, J. (1981). *International production and the multinational enterprise.* London: George Allen & Unwin; Dunning, J. (1998). The eclectic paradigm of international production: A restatement and some possible extensions. *Journal of International Business Studies,* 1–31.

FDI is possible when a firm has some monopolistic advantage over local firms. This advantage can be in the form of assets (the firm's size, which gives it economies of scale, an advantage of common governance over a number of operations abroad) and skills (the marketing of differentiated products, managerial experience). The monopolistic advantage must be greater than the costs of establishing and operating a foreign subsidiary. Taken together, these are the ownership advantages of the model.

Locational advantages stem from the attractiveness of a given country. A firm interested in investing abroad chooses the most favorable location where it can control financial risk and achieve sufficient returns. In this case it is the country that possesses specific advantages in the form of raw materials, low production costs, good infrastructure, and the like. Location advantage may also be a function of spatial market failure where trade barriers make imports prohibitive or very expensive to local consumers.

Internalization advantages accrue when the firm can overcome risk and uncertainty through the choice of a hierarchal mode of organization where subsidiary organizations are subordinate to headquarters. Such an organization structure results in the integration of different activities of the chain (see the example in Chapter 1) in different countries. Such an organization structure can protect property rights and ensure quality control of the production process. However, the higher the costs of governing a hierarchical organization, the more likely management will prefer a shared equity form such as a joint venture. Transaction costs can be reduced by finding a local partner in the foreign market who is familiar with the territory and the company's products. Such a partnership can result in faster penetration of the market, while at the same time managing risk and uncertainty.

Critique

In the eclectic framework, location advantages are treated independently from ownership advantages. However, the decision of where to expand internationally is not

---

BOX 7-3   PEOPLE IN FOCUS: JOHN DUNNING

Professor Dunning was awarded honorary doctorates from the University of Uppsala in Sweden, the Autonomous University of Madrid, and the University of Antwerp. He was also honorary Professor of International Business at the University of International Business and Economics at Beijing. He was past president of the International Trade and Finance Association, and of the Academy of International Business. A book edited by Peter Buckley and Mark Casson was published in his honor in 1992, and a second book was published in 2003 embracing his work at Rutgers University. A volume edited by John Cantwell and Rajneesh Narula entitled *International Business and the Eclectic Paradigm* was devoted to his theoretical contributions to international business. In August 2002, Professor Dunning was honored as Distinguished Scholar in International Management at the Academy of Management's annual meeting at Denver. In December 2004 he was presented with a Lifetime Achievement Award at the annual meeting of the European Academy of International Business in Ljubljana, Slovenia.

independent of ownership advantages or of the route by which these advantages will be used. In other words, there is a constant interplay between O, L, and I.[24]

MARKET SELECTION

Market Expansion Screening

The purpose of screening is to select those markets that have the best potential for expansion in foreign markets. The first step is to define the criteria that are relevant to the firm's environment. Some of these include political and economic risks, cultural diversity or convergence, product match, size of market demand and growth rates, and the intensity of competition. Each firm must decide for itself which criteria are relevant to its performance. According to Maranda (2001),[25] one can postulate that decision makers have, a priori, a perceptual space of market possibilities that can be considered for foreign entry whether they subsequently do so or not. Market selection can thus be seen as a decision process that involves narrowing down from a considered set of markets for entry that can be regarded as part of the total market space available for future export activity. This narrowing down can be done quantitatively by the use of multiple factor indices and decision matrices.

MULTIPLE FACTOR INDICES

The first step involves identifying those factors that determine demand for the firm's product or service. In Table 7-4, demand for dairy product containers is a function of the number of population under the age of 15 (P15), average population growth (APG), gross national product per capita (GNP/N), and an overall index of economic indicators (EAI). The final rating for each country is given by the multiple factor index (MFI). The higher the MFI, the greater the market potential. The results show that the

TABLE 7-4 Multiple Factor Index and Political Activity Index						
Country	P15	APG	GNP/N	EAI	MFI	PAI
USA	.081	.016	.428	.288	.813	.800
Canada	.090	.024	.333	.267	.714	.793
Bahamas	.129	.092	.207	.039	.467	.218
Jamaica	.138	.030	.060	.007	.235	.384
Puerto Rico	.111	.028	.149	.086	.374	.712
Sweden	.063	.006	.364	.225	.658	.697
UK	.072	.006	.204	.228	.510	.789
France	.075	.012	.279	.219	.585	.668
W. Germany	.075	.000	.264	.240	.579	.706
Switzerland	.069	.020	.299	.093	.481	.728
Mexico	.138	.066	.060	.065	.329	.408
Libya	.132	.062	.159	.024	.377	.002
Italy	.072	.014	.158	.186	.480	.441
Australia	.087	.038	.254	.255	.634	.702
Japan	.072	.024	.173	.258	.527	.742

24. Cantwell, J., & Narula, R. (2001). The eclectic paradigm in the global economy. *International Journal of the Economics of Business, 8*(2), 155–172; Dunning, J. (2001). The eclectic (OLI) paradigm of international production: Past, present and future. *International Journal of the Economics of Business, 8*(2), 173–190.

25. Maranda, Z. (2001). Market and channel preferences for manufacturing exporters: A study of Zimbabwean companies. *Zambizia, 28*, 70–82.

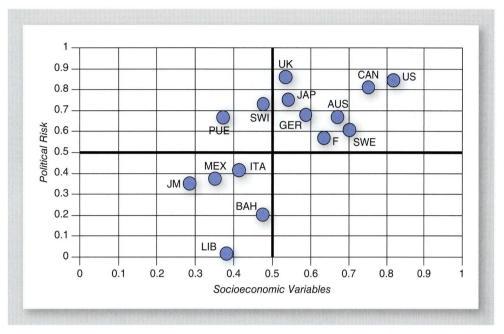

Figure 7-8 A Plot of the Multiple Factor and Political Activity Indexes

United States, Canada, Sweden, and Australia have the highest potential for the firm given the criteria in the demand function.

In addition, a political risk measure (PAI) shown on the y-axis in Figure 7-8, was made for each country. The higher the PAI coefficient, the lower the political risk. The countries with the highest MFI potential also have relatively low political risk. Both indices can be plotted (Figure 7-8) on the above matrix, which assumes they have the same weight. There seem to be two relevant clusters of countries: the United States and Canada (North American cluster), and Australia, Sweden, Germany, France, the UK, and Japan.

DIRECTIONAL POLICY MATRICES

Directional policy matrices have been used to plan strategy for strategic business units of the firm. However, they can also be used in the screening stage of market entry. In this case, countries replace strategic business units as the objects of analysis. Two major matrices have been used; the Boston Consulting Group matrix (market growth and market share are the parameters) and the McKinsey/General Electric matrix, wherein market attractiveness replaces market growth and competitive strength replaces market share. The McKinsey/General Electric matrix is more appropriate for selecting countries for market entry, since the company has no market share in these potential markets. Also, market growth is only one indicator of a country's attractiveness; others include market size, barriers to entry, political risk, competitive intensity, and distribution structure. Competitive or business strength may be measured by brand awareness/image, other firm-specific assets, cost structure compared to competition, and international experience. Such a matrix is shown as Figure 7-9.

In Figure 7-9, assume that the size of the circles represents a value for market attractiveness and business strength in a number of countries. In this example, the larger the circle, the higher the value of both attractiveness and business strength. Therefore, the UK would be the most attractive country and also one in which the company's competitive/business strength is greatest. It certainly would be the first choice for entry.

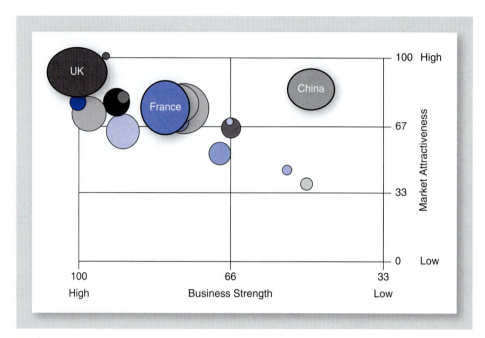

Figure 7-9 McKinsey/General Electric Matrix

Next, France is highly attractive and its competitive/business strength is moderate. China, on the other hand, represents a highly attractive market, but the company is not competitive. In this case, the question for the company is whether it has the potential to improve its competitive strength either before or soon after entry. If not, China would not be a good choice.

Should the company enter both the UK and France at the same time and perhaps one or two of the other countries positioned in the high–high quadrant? These questions represent two possible entry strategies: concentration and diversification. A concentration strategy is the selection of one or a relatively few countries with the objective of intensive penetration of their markets. It is preferable when first-mover advantages are apparent.

CONCENTRATION VS. DIVERSIFICATION

Expansion into markets abroad requires management to decide on two main strategies: concentration or diversification. Both strategies require different levels of marketing effort and resources. A **concentration strategy** involves focusing marketing effort and resources on one or a few key markets in the short run and gradual expansion into other markets in the long run. A **diversification strategy,** on the other hand, requires investing marketing effort and resources into a larger number of markets in the short run. In both cases, the amount of resources required depends on the entry mode. For example, fewer resources are required for exporting than for direct investment in subsidiaries. Given a fixed amount of resources, the amount assigned to each market in a diversification strategy would be less than for concentration. Therefore, for SMEs, an export concentration strategy would be preferable. Concentrating marketing effort and resources in one or a few markets should gain larger market share and, subsequently, higher profits. However, if competition is intense, then small firms should avoid direct

TABLE 7-5 Concentration versus Diversification Strategies		
Market/Product Factor	**Concentrate**	**Diversify**
Sales response function	S-curve	Concave
Growth rate in each market	High	Low
Sales stability in each market	High	Low
Competitive lead time	Long	Short
Spillover effects	Low	High
Need for product adaptation	High	Low
Need for promotion adaptation	High	Low
Distribution economies	High	Low

Source: Adapted from: Ayal, I., & Zif, J. (1979). Market expansion strategies in multinational marketing. *Journal of Marketing*, 84–94.

competition with larger firms. In this case, it would be preferable to have small market shares in a larger number of markets. Therefore firm size and market factors (such as competition) are factors that influence expansion strategies. In addition, there are market factors such as growth rates and sales stability in each market and the need for standardization or adaptation of products and advertising messages. Table 7-5 lists the market-product factors that have to be considered when choosing an expansion strategy.

The costs of penetrating a market are among the most important considerations in choosing an expansion strategy. One of the tools available, the sales response function, is a calculation that relates the value of investment in marketing effort to the revenue generated (or profit, units sold, etc.). If the sales function is S-shaped, a concentration strategy of seeking a large market share is preferred. In the first stage, market entry is based on building brand awareness and demand. Afterwards, further investment in marketing effort results in growing market share and marginal revenue, much like the growth stage in the product life cycle. This is based on studies that show that high market shares are associated with higher profitability. If the markets for a company's products have a concave sales function, further investment in one or a few markets would result in low or no marginal revenue. Therefore it pays to diversify into a larger number of markets. Additional factors that point to a diversification strategy (and opposite for a concentration strategy) are low growth rates and sales stability (e.g., seasonality), short competitive lead time (which makes it important to enter markets quickly), high apillover effects between countries (e.g., the use of the same patents), little need to adapt products and promotion, and little gain from distribution economies of scale. In reality, these factors are not dichotomous (either high or low), but somewhat in between.

Figure 7-10 demonstrates the different functions of both curves. Expanding into one market and investing at point a will yield a return of c sales if the curve is s-shaped, and a return of e sales if the curve is concave. However, an additional marketing investment in the same market of f will yield sales of j if the curve is s-shaped, but only h if the curve is concave. Therefore, if the market is characterized by an s-shaped curve, it would pay to select a concentration strategy. However, the decision maker has to consider the other factors listed in Table 7-5, as well.

Table 7-6 lists again the market/product factors that determine an expansion strategy. In the first column (W), management of a given firm has weighted the factors by importance. The most important factors are the growth rate, sales response function and sales stability in each market. The least important are spillover effects and

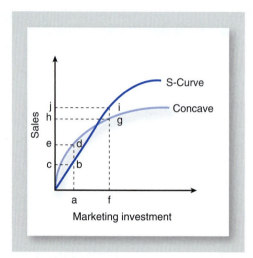

Figure 7-10 Sales Response Function

W	Market/Product Factor	X	W(X)
.2	Sales response function	5	1.0
.4	Growth rate in each market	6	2.4
.2	Sales stability in each market	4	.8
.02	Competitive lead time	2	.04
.01	Spillover effects	2	.02
.07	Need for product adaptation	7	.49
.09	Need for promotion adaptation	5	.45
.01	Distribution economies	2	.02
1.00	X = low 1 – 7 high		Σ(wx) = 5.22

TABLE 7-6 Concentration versus Diversification Strategies

distribution economies. Next, for a given market that is being considered for expansion, management rates each factor on a scale of 1 to 7 (X). For example, the growth rate and need for product adaptation in this market are considered to be very high. Competitive lead time and distribution economies are low (not important). The final rating is based on the sum of the factor weights multiplied by management's rating (W[X]). The outcome is Σ(wx) = 5.22 , which on a scale of 1 to 7 is high, resulting in a concentration strategy.

SUMMARY

- The decision to expand a firm is necessary for its survival. Firms can expand domestically or internationally. Choosing the internationalization option must be done for the right reasons. If not, the foreign entry may be only a temporary one, resulting in a loss of valuable resources. Once management of a firm decides to internationalize, it must determine the best route to do so. Choosing a best route begins with a market search. Following our internationalization model, the first step is identifying a pool of potential markets.

- **Market screening** involves choosing a method that can identify those markets that have the best potential for the firm's products and services. Country grouping is one example of a method that can be used in the market screening stage. Once these markets are identified, the next step is to select an entry strategy.

- Two possible entry strategies are available: concentration or diversification. In the former, the firm enters one or a few markets at the first stage of expansion. The other possibility is simultaneously entering a larger number in the short run. The market and internal factors that determine which strategy to select along with a deterministic framework were discussed above.

- The final stage in internationalization involves choosing an initial entry mode. This initial mode is critical because it locks the firm into a particular strategy over the short run. However, as the firm internationalizes, it may change its mode of operation as it expands into additional markets. This expansion is explained by models such as the Uppsala and Dunning models. The advantages and disadvantages of specific entry modes are the subjects of Chapter 8.

DISCUSSION QUESTIONS

1. Explain the difference between directional policy matrices and multiple factor indices.

2. What monopolistic advantages does a multinational firm have over domestic firms?

3. How does the Uppsala Model take into consideration dynamic countries (disinvesting)?

4. Can the Uppsala Model explain the actions of large MNCs?

5. How can a manager make use of the eclectic decision framework?

6. Will the Uppsala Model be useful or relevant in 30 years? What do you think?

EXPERIENTIAL EXERCISES

1. Interview a top executive of a small or medium-sized firm in your area that has international operations. Determine the steps that were taken to analyze foreign markets. Do they resemble what has been recommended in this chapter? Why or why not?

2. Choose another firm that has international operations in more than three countries. Determine whether management chose a concentration or diversification strategy. Detail the reasons for the selection of either.

KEY TERMS

Born-globals, p. 184

Concentration strategy, p. 192

Efficiency seekers, p. 178

Diversification strategy, p. 192

International networks, p. 184

International Product Life Cycle (IPLC), p. 181

Internationalization, p. 173

Market screening, p. 195

Market seeking firms, p. 177

Dunning's OLI Model, p. 188

Proactive motives, p. 176

Reactive motives, p. 176

Resource seeking companies, p. 178

Strategic resource seekers, p. 178

Transaction cost, p. 186

Uppsala IP Model, p. 180

CASE 7-1

Archer Daniels Midland (ADM)
Agricultural Processing Industry

The agricultural processing industry can be segmented into four primary segments: Oilseed Processing, Agricultural Services, Corn Processing, and Other. The Other segment is composed primarily of food and feed ingredients. Table 1 shows the position of ADM business segments within the agricultural processing industry life cycle.

Oilseed Processing

The Oilseed Processing segment is a mature segment within the agricultural processing industry. The Oilseed Processing segment includes activities related to processing oilseeds, such as soybeans, cottonseed, sunflower seeds, canola, peanuts, and flaxseed. These are made into vegetable oils and meals for the food and feed industries. In addition, oilseeds may be resold into the marketplace as a raw material for other processors. Crude vegetable oil is sold "as is" or is further processed by refining, bleaching, and deodorizing into salad oils. Salad oils can be further processed by hydrogenating into margarine, shortening, and other food products. Partially refined oil is sold for use in chemicals, paints, and other industrial products. Oilseed meals are primary ingredients used in the manufacture of commercial livestock and poultry feeds.

Table 2 shows the sales and profit by segment for ADM's business segments. The Oilseed Processing segment represents approximately 33 percent of ADM's sales and 22 percent of its profits. This segment is a price-sensitive market.

As shown in Figure 1, the Oilseed Processing segment is a cash cow for ADM. This segment generates significant cash to fund ADM's growth business segments.

In 2005, ADM's Oilseed Processing experienced some growth. European processing results improved, principally due to strong demand in Europe. This strong demand in Europe came from increased European vegetable oil demand and resulted in improved oilseed processing financial results. North American processing results improved principally due to increased demand for soybean meal.

TABLE 1 Agricultural Processing Industry Life Cycle & ADM Business Segments

ADM Business Segments	Stage of Industry Life Cycle			
	Introduction	Growth	Maturity	Decline
Oilseed Processing			*	
Agricultural Services			*	
Corn Processing				
–Sweeteners & Starches		*		
–Bioproducts	*			
Other				
–Food & Feed Ingredients		*		
–Financial			*	

Case prepared by Michael L. Pettus and J. Mark Munoz. Reprinted with permission.

TABLE 2 Agricultural Processing Segments (2005)					
Segments	**Sales**	**Profit**	**% Sale**	**% Profit**	**ROS**
Oilseed Processing	11,803,309	344,654	32.84%	22.22%	2.92%
Corn Processing	4,363,924	530,233	12.14%	34.19%	12.15%
Agricultural Services	15,198,831	261,659	42.28%	16.87%	1.72%
Other	4,577,746	414,394	12.74%	26.72%	9.05%
Total	35,943,810	1,550,940	100.00%	100.00%	4.31%

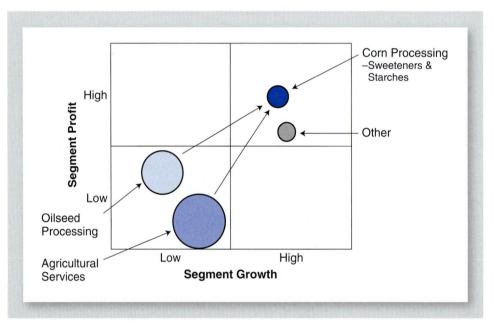

Figure 1 Segment Growth and Profit
Note: Circle size refers to ADM's revenue per business segment

Agricultural Services

The Agricultural Services segment utilizes the company's extensive grain elevator and transportation network to buy, store, clean, and transport agricultural commodities, such as oilseeds, corn, wheat, oats, and barley. It then resells these commodities primarily as feed ingredients and as raw materials for the agricultural industry. Agricultural Services' grain sourcing and transportation network provides reliable and efficient services to the company's agricultural operations.

This is another segment of the agricultural processing industry that generates a great deal of cash to support ADM's growth segments (Table 2). In addition, this is ADM's largest segment from a revenue perspective. This segment accounts for 42 percent of the sales and 17 percent of the profits. From an industry perspective, the Oilseed and Agricultural Services segments represent maturity business segments (Table 1).

Agricultural products are now being used to satisfy more needs than ever before. One reason is that the need for quality foods is increasing as the population increases. Enhanced nutrition is demanded by health conscious people throughout Europe and North America. As a result, nutritional feed ingredients for livestock are used more today than ever before.

Corn Processing

The Corn Processing segment includes activities related to the production of sweeteners, starches, dextrose, and syrups for the food and beverage industry. It also includes activities related to the production and fermentation of bioproducts such as alcohol, amino acids, and other specialty food and feed ingredients.

Corn processing consists of harvesting raw grains, corn, soybeans, wheat, cocoa, sunflower seeds, canola, peanuts, and flaxseed. These are then processed and delivered to customers around the world as products such as protein meals, oils, sweeteners, ethanol, biodiesel, and flour. These products are growing in demand because of the increasing buying power of the world's middle class.

The Corn Processing segment consists primarily of two divisions: (1) sweeteners and starches and (2) bioproducts. It is in the bioproducts segment that ADM is focusing the bulk of its growth. The production of ethanol is one principle aspect of bioproducts. As alternative sources of fuel continue to be in large demand, ADM may invest significant resources within this business segment.

Other Segment

The Other segment consists primarily of food and feed ingredients. This segment represents 13 percent of revenue and 27 percent of the profit.

The products produced by corn, agricultural, and other oilseed processors require global distribution and transportation networks. Processors must develop a dependable network to procure a steady supply of raw materials into their plants. They must have the means to store grains and seeds until they can be processed and they must have a transportation system that is flexible enough to meet market conditions. It is not enough that grain processors be competent at the procuring, transporting, storing, and processing of grain; these firms must also be good at merchandising their products.

Financial Position of Competitors

Table 3 provides a financial overview of the competitors in the agricultural processing industry. Companies within this industry offer products that have little differentiation from their competitors. Therefore, products are primarily bought because of their competitive price levels. Commodity-type producers can control their selling price only to the extent that they can control their costs.

As shown in Table 3, Archer Daniels Midland (ADM), Cargill, and Bunge Ltd. are three companies that control the majority of the agricultural processing industry. All have established substantial market share within the industry, and they are positioned to take advantage of the industry's future growth. Cargill is a privately owned business with revenues in 2005 of U.S.$71 billion. ADM is the largest of the publicly held companies, with 2005 revenue of over U.S.$36 billion.

ADM's Financial Position

ADM is the worldwide market leader in oilseed processing and corn processing. ADM is also a leader in the United States market for the production of ethanol. Table 4 provides a 10-year financial history of ADM. ADM has seen significant growth both in revenue and profit in the last five years.

ADM set an earnings record of over U.S.$1 billion in 2005. This was achieved with domestic sales of U.S.$19 billion and international sales of U.S.$17 billion. Most of the corn

TABLE 3 Financial Position of Competitors

	ADM	BG	Pvt1	CAG	Industry
Market Cap:	28.98B	7.02B	N/A	11.82B	18.11B
Employees:	25,641	23,495	124,000[1]	38,000	88.18K
Rev. Growth (ttm):	7.50%	2.80%	N/A	4.40%	5.90%
Revenue (ttm):	36.47B	24.43B	71.07B[1]	14.67B	16.82B
Gross Margin (ttm):	7.48%	6.17%	N/A	21.21%	39.95%
EBITDA (ttm):	2.42B	820.00M	N/A	1.61B	2.42B
Oper. Margins (ttm):	4.31%	2.15%	N/A	8.60%	14.79%
Net Income (ttm):	1.10B	490.00M	2.10B[1]	730.00M	1.10B
EPS (ttm):	1.674	4.096	N/A	1.124	1.93
PE (ttm):	26.34	14.37	N/A	20.24	19.18
PEG (ttm):	2.31	1.49	N/A	3.70	2.31
PS (ttm):	0.82	0.29	N/A	0.81	1.29

BG = Bunge Ltd.
Pvt1 = Cargill, Incorporated (privately held)
CAG = ConAgra Foods Inc.
Industry = Food–Major Diversified
B = Billions of dollars

processing is done domestically and is much more profitable than the oilseed processing or agricultural services. ADM is focusing upon using free cash flow from the corn processing division to strengthen its international position. ADM is focusing upon supplying India, China, and the Commonwealth of Independent States with protein products.

Transportation and distribution consists of a large portion of cost of goods sold for the agricultural processing business. ADM's investment in transportation and distribution has proven to be an effective way of managing costs. This network has contributed to efficiencies that add both flexibility and cost control.

ADM is a giant in the world of agricultural processing. This kind of success has come about by concentrating on the strengths of the company and the ever-changing opportunities created by market forces. Distribution, transportation, its financial position, global positioning, and renewable fuels are strengths of ADM.

Discussion Questions

1. Should ADM take a stronger position in the development of alternative sources of fuel?
2. Develop a global expansion plan for ADM.

TABLE 4 ADM Financial History

Archer Daniels Midland ADM

| 10-Yr Income | 10-Yr Cash Flows | 10-Yr Balance Sheet | 5-Yr Restated | Quarterly Results |

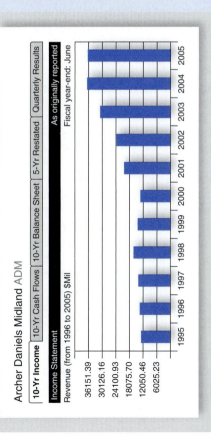

	1996	1997	1998	1999	2000	2001	2002	2003	2004	2005	TTM
Revenue	13,314.1	13,853.3	16,108.6	14,283.3	12,876.8	20,051.4	23,453.6	30,708.0	36,151.4	35,943.8	35,833.8
COGS	11,949.6	12,552.7	14,727.7	13,051.3	11,657.2	18,619.6	21,770.1	28,980.9	34,003.1	33,512.5	33,368.4
Gross Profit	1,364.4	1,300.5	1,381.0	1,232.0	1,219.6	1,431.8	1,683.5	1,727.1	2,148.3	2,431.3	2,465.4
Operating Expenses $Mil	**1996**	**1997**	**1998**	**1999**	**2000**	**2001**	**2002**	**2003**	**2004**	**2005**	**TTM**
SG&A	450.0	675.1	660.7	701.1	729.4	731.0	826.9	947.7	1,401.8	1,080.8	1,158.4
R&D	—	—	—	—	—	—	—	—	—	—	—
Other	0.0	0.0	0.0	0.0	0.0	0.0	0.0	0.0	0.0	0.0	0.0
Operating Income	914.4	625.4	720.3	531.0	490.2	700.8	856.5	779.4	746.5	1,350.5	1,307.0
Other Income and Expense $Mil	**1996**	**1997**	**1998**	**1999**	**2000**	**2001**	**2002**	**2003**	**2004**	**2005**	**TTM**
Net Int Inc & Other	140.0	19.0	(110.3)	(111.1)	(137.0)	(178.9)	(137.6)	(148.5)	(28.5)	165.9	149.5
Earnings Before Taxes	1,054.4	644.4	610.0	419.8	353.2	521.9	718.9	631.0	718.0	1,516.4	1,456.5
Income Taxes	358.5	267.1	206.4	138.6	52.3	138.6	207.8	179.8	223.3	472.0	437.9
Earnings After Taxes	695.9	377.3	403.6	281.3	300.9	383.3	511.1	451.1	494.7	1,044.4	1,018.6
Acctg Changes	—	—	—	—	—	—	—	—	—	—	—
Disc Operations	—	—	—	—	—	—	—	—	—	—	—
Ext Items	—	—	—	—	—	—	—	—	—	—	—
Net Income	695.9	377.3	403.6	266.0	300.9	383.3	511.1	451.2	494.7	1,044.4	1,018.6
Diluted EPS, Cont Ops$	1.00	0.54	0.59	0.41	0.45	0.58	0.78	0.70	0.76	1.59	1.55
Diluted EPS$	1.00	0.54	0.59	0.39	0.45	0.58	0.78	0.70	0.76	1.59	1.55
Shares	702	690	686	685	669	664	656	646	647	656	655

Entering Global Markets

*[S]ome foreign companies have tired of waiting and retreated from China,
hoping to return at a more opportune moment . . . the Chinese may well consider
such a retreat as typical of . . . self-interested outsiders and never let them back.*

ANDREW WILLIAMSON, *THE CHINESE BUSINESS PUZZLE*

LEARNING OBJECTIVES

After reading this chapter, you should be able to:

- Distinguish between the various options a firm has for establishing a presence overseas.
- Understand the factors that influence the overseas market entry decision.
- Compare the advantages and disadvantages of equity and non-equity entry modes.
- Explain why joint ventures are prone to failure.
- Distinguish between joint ventures and strategic alliances.
- Know the risks involved with different modes of international market entry.

Introduction

This chapter examines the various modes of entry that are available to small or medium enterprises (SMEs) although much of the material is relevant for larger firms as well. In particular, it discusses entry modes such as exporting, licensing, franchising, contract manufacturing, turnkey operations, management contracts, international joint ventures, and fully owned subsidiaries.

The entry into foreign markets is very frequently accidental for entrepreneurs. One likely scenario is that the first export order from abroad came as a result of the company's exposure on the Internet, or mention of the company's products in a chat room or a blog. If a company is taking full advantage of its Internet presence, it should virtually expect to gain international cyber clients within months.[1]

Whether a firm takes more deliberate action to enlarge its international market share after the first few successful exports is up to top management's vision for the company. However, business owners today should not think that just because they are well entrenched in their home market, they are immune to the competitive pressures of globalization. It is likely that, even if a business does not pursue international strategy,

1. This assumes that the company is conducting an active Internet marketing campaign with emphasis on search engine placement, website advertisements, affiliate marketing strategy, and other marketing methods. Also, to be appealing and understandable to international visitors, a website should use (at a minimum) common English language, simple navigation signs and graphics, and clear pictures and descriptions of the products/services offered.

BOX 8-1   FOCUS ON TECHNOLOGY: SHARPENING TOOLS

Diamond Machining Technology Inc. (DMT) makes manual sharpening tools that are used by the United States Olympic speed skating team and endorsed by PBS' *American Woodshop* host Scott Phillips.

The Marlborough, Massachusetts, company has been in business 27 years with sales of $10 million and has established itself as a leader in the tool-sharpening industry. Soon after the company launched a line of industrial sharpening products using diamonds, it faced significant competition from lower-priced sharpeners from Israel.

The company responded to the competitive threat by developing a competing product called Diamond Whetstone, a small, handheld sharpening tool. "We had to come up with a different product that would keep us alive," a senior executive said.

The firm introduced the Diamond Whetstone at the Gourmet Product Show in San Francisco in 1979. That same year, the Diamond Whetstone was also featured in the Brookstone catalog.

The company changed its distribution strategy by marketing directly to consumers, quickly establishing a niche among hunters, cooks, athletes, gardeners, and woodworkers, all of whom wanted tools that wouldn't eat away the metal edges of their blades.

The company is currently facing competition from diamond-based sharpeners in China, which can cost up to 20 percent less than DMT's products, so executives are emphasizing their brand's quality and looking to expand their market to the more casual consumer. Although DMT had no plans to compete in international markets, foreign competition on its own turf forced this 30-employee company to improve its products.

Source: Adapted from: Archambeault, B. (2004, February 19). Sharpening its focus. *Boston Business Journal* [electronic version].

---

international competitors, suppliers, buyers, etc., would eventually pursue it (see "Sharpening Tools"). A company that decides to limit itself to a single domestic market is likely to be much less competitive and successful than its internationalized counterparts.

Some of the many reasons for going international include:

- Expand beyond a saturated domestic market
- Find new source of profits
- Add to the firm's competitive edge
- Diversify and enlarge markets to hedge against economic crises
- Follow customers who are going abroad

The remainder of this chapter is divided into three sections. The first discusses the factors that motivate the mode of entry decision from the standpoint of the company and the environment in which it operates. The second section is the heart of the chapter, which analyzes the advantages and disadvantages of the different modes of entry. Within this section, several illustrations and SME practices are provided. Finally, the conclusion reflects on approaches that an SME can utilize in expanding its business abroad.

FACTORS THAT INFLUENCE THE MODE OF ENTRY DECISION PROCESS

Once a decision has been made to go international, a deliberate consideration of the mode of entry should ensue. The decision process is influenced by a number of factors that may often pull the decision makers in opposite directions. Management goes through a successive decision-making process that includes answering the following questions:

- Can our product be marketed abroad?
- What are the key success factors for our products?
- Is secondary data available for those markets/products?
- What additional data is needed and how can we get it?
- Which of our products have the highest potential abroad?
- Which markets have the greatest potential for our products?
- Do we have excess production capacity?
- What are the characteristics of our target market?
- What are the international capabilities of the firm?

Answering these questions is the first step in a preliminary market analysis for market and mode of entry selection.

To enable the discussion of all the different forces involved in the entry mode decision process, we categorize these factors into two major groups: internal and external factors. The **internal factors** have to do with the firm's resources, overall strategy, management mindset, time commitment and, very importantly, types of products or services considered for international markets. For most entrepreneurial firms, the key issues discussed during this initial stage of the decision process revolve around:

- Financial resources—how much can we spend on international market expansion; should we borrow funds or use accumulated financial assets; are the potential rewards of this initiative worth the financial risks, etc.

- Human resources—should we hire new staff or use existing personnel to lead the expansion effort; what would be the compensation for the new position; how would the new management role be defined; where would the position be located, etc.

- Type of product and/or service—which of our products/services should we market internationally; how adaptable are they; what is required to make them ready for the target market, etc.

- Time horizons—how much time can we dedicate to the international expansion effort; are we willing to accommodate longer receivables cycles, etc.

- Risk tolerance—are we prepared to absorb the higher risks inherent in dealing with currency exchange rates, unfamiliar political, legal and market environments, economic cycles, etc.

Recent studies have focused on the accelerated timeframe in which small and medium-sized firms move from domestic to internationalized operations, leading academics to question the stage model for the internationalization process. The question "Are some firms born global?" has been raised. A recent study of 677 small and medium companies in France, Denmark, and Norway finds that "going global" sooner depends in large part on the companies' internal makeup, developed at the initial stages of their creation. The most important indicator of how quickly a firm would be ready and willing to export depended on the early development within the firm of resources beneficial to international market competitiveness.[2] These findings further underscore the importance of internal evaluation before moving into international business.

2. Deresky, H. (2000). *International management: Managing across borders and cultures* (3rd ed.). Upper Saddle River, NJ: Prentice Hall.

In addition to the internal factors, many external factors also need to be considered before a final decision on the mode of entry can be made. Factors that affect the company's choice to enter a foreign market but are independent of management's decisions are called **external factors.** External factors fall under two categories: target country factors and domestic country factors.

Target country factors that should be considered when choosing a mode of entry include:

- Market—its size, competitive environment, marketing infrastructure, etc.
- Production conditions—everything from the cost, quality, and quantity of local materials and labor to the transportation, communications, energy supply and other similar economic infrastructure components.
- Environmental conditions—this broad category includes most of the political, economic, geographic, and social factors that make one country more attractive for international commerce than another. Examples include government policies toward foreign trade, the overall rate of foreign investment, the gross national product, the diversification level of the local economy, the country's corruption ratings, and cultural and language barriers.

Some **domestic country factors** also strongly influence the foreign market entry mode. For example, if a company has a large enough domestic market, it can grow to a significant size before it chooses or needs to expand internationally. The choices of market entry methods can differ significantly for small and large companies, depending on their capitalization, production capacity, and marketing resources, among other issues. Conversely, a large domestic market can make some companies disinterested in expanding internationally due to the significant growth opportunities at home, while a small domestic market may spur even small companies to seek international expansion sooner. Other domestic country factors that might spur a company to seek international markets include competitive pressure at home, high domestic production costs, and favorable government policies toward exporting (tax incentives, trade support programs), for example.

The Dynamics of Market Entry

Market entry is not static, and entry modes may have to be restructured as environmental conditions change. These conditions include economic factors, competition, market structure, consumer characteristics, and government regulations. A case in point is India, which is illustrative of other emerging markets. Many international companies in India have structures different from those at the time they entered the market. For example, in 1977, the Indian government passed a law that required foreign companies to dilute their equity stake in subsidiaries to 40 percent if they wanted to continue operating in the country. This regulation required wholly owned foreign subsidiaries to share ownership with Indian nationals, or cease operations, which Coca-Cola and IBM did. However, the law was changed in 1996, allowing 100 percent voting control, even though the home corporation owned only 51 percent of the equity shares.

Several multinational companies and brands have changed their operating modes in India over time. VF Corporation[3] entered India in the 1980s by licensing its brand to Dupont Sportswear. Since then it has launched a variety of brands in different product categories with a number of Indian partners over a period of 20 years and finally formed a joint venture, called VF Arvind Brands Pvt. Ltd. (India).

---

3. VF is an American corporation headquartered in North Carolina. Its brands include Nautica, Wrangler, Lee, and others.

Another example of a company that has evolved its presence is Benetton, which first entered India through a licensee (Dalmia). Benetton then transitioned in 1991 into a 50–50 joint venture, and finally in 2004 took over the Indian business completely. However, it adopted the franchising route in 2006 for its premium fashion brand, Sisley, appointing Trent (a Tata Group company) as the national retail franchisee.

Each of these changes in strategy has cost the brands time, management effort, money, and occasionally market share. In many cases the original entry mode was restructured because of changing market conditions, including the growth of modern retailing in India and increased consumer buying power. Those companies anticipated these changes had the advantage of making strategic changes to their mode of operation and thus gain a competitive edge over competition. This is another example of why environmental scanning is so important to global marketing planning.

METHODS OF ENTRY TO INTERNATIONAL MARKETS

Because most entrepreneurial businesses are small to medium in size, their initial choices for international market entry tend to include low- to moderate-risk strategies, such as exporting, licensing, and franchising. As the companies become bigger and more successful internationally, some may decide to deepen their presence and commitment to particular foreign markets by entering into contract manufacturing, turnkey operations agreements, or management contracts and even forming international joint ventures (IJVs) or investing in fully owned subsidiaries. Figure 8-1 is a graphic representation of these most common market entry methods, ranked by the increase in risk for the entering firm. Another form of international market entry, the international strategic alliance, is discussed later.

Exporting The most common and low-risk method of entering overseas markets, exporting is also the one requiring the least investment in financial, marketing and human resources, and time. Because of its low commitment requirements, exporting is the preferred mode of entry of most small and entrepreneurial businesses. It is an

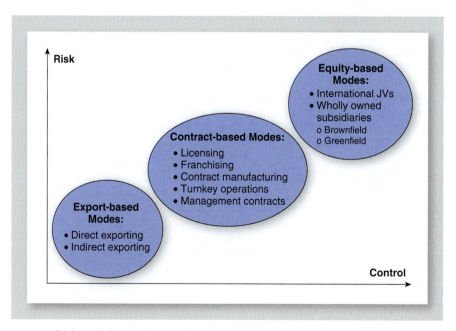

Figure 8-1 Risk and Control Considerations in Selecting an Entry Mode

especially well-suited method for initial market tests due to the relative ease of pulling out of a market if it turns out to not be profitable.[4]

The main difference between exporting and the other entry modes is that exporting is limited to actual physical products that are produced outside the target country market. By nature, service companies cannot perform their services domestically and then ship them to another country; thus they are required to use contractual or investment entry modes. Exported products, on the other hand, can be sold overseas by intermediaries who specialize in this activity from the home base—**indirect exporting**—or they can be distributed directly through agents and/or distributors in the target country—**direct exporting.** An alternative that falls under the direct exporting method is to export products to a direct branch or subsidiary of the company, which assumes that some form of direct investment in the target market has already been made.[5]

One small electronics firm's experience with direct exporting started after the company decided to actively pursue international markets for its specialized products. The management of the company took a deliberate, analytical approach to selecting its first international target markets, while remaining mindful of the limited resources they could dedicate to the expansion. First, with the help of the United States Department of Commerce, they researched product exports based on commodity numbers taken directly from the export documentation's Schedule B. This is an excellent indicator of market export potential because it is directly related to the company's products.

Next, they analyzed the hits on their website to see where most of their visitors were coming from. While this measure can be volatile, over time it can provide a rich source of data on the countries that show most interest in the company's products. Third, management looked at the company's customers and/or competitors to find relevant foreign markets. Since its competitors tend to be other small firms, not publicly traded or known, little information existed. However, examining the internationalization of the industry as a whole or the internationalization of large multinational companies proved to be helpful. Finding the local buying centers of the multinational companies was the most challenging part of this research. After settling on several potential markets, the company ranked them first by their market potential and next by the ease of entry. The firm evaluated and prioritized the most promising markets before moving on to the decision of the actual mode of entry.

The company decided to use direct exporting as mode of entry due to the specialized nature of its products and the specific industries that held the largest market potential. The next step in the process centered on deciding whether it would be more advantageous to divide its target markets by geographic or industry-specific criteria and, consequently, whether to look for distributors whose network covered a wide geographic area or for distributors who were well established in the specific industries chosen as target markets. The company decided industry-specific knowledge and relationships were more important than geographical coverage of the market. Therefore, the following indicators were used to select the appropriate distributor:

- Does the distributor have established connections in the targeted industries?
- Is the distributor familiar with the type of products manufactured by the company?
- Does the distributor have experience working with American companies?

4. Deresky, H. (2000). *International management: Managing across borders and cultures* (3rd ed.). Upper Saddle River, NJ: Prentice Hall.

5. Ibid.

- What are the distributor's size, current product lineup, and revenues?
- Will the distributor allow the company to conduct independent marketing and sales within the country?

The company's search for the right distributor started with a visit to the United States Commercial Service's industry specialists located in the target countries. These international trade professionals were instrumental in providing in-depth analysis and contact information for the first stage of the selection process. After several meetings and evaluations of a few potential partners, the company was able to form an agreement with a distributor based on mutual business objectives, interest, and compatibility.

As with all others forms of market entry, an entrepreneur who is considering exporting should do plenty of research and planning before committing to a market or a distributor. Despite the advance of global free trade, some countries remain hostile to imports and impose many barriers on them such as high tariffs, taxes, or currency exchange restrictions. Learning about the importing environment of one's target country market or hiring a country specialist who knows the local government's import requirements for the specific product is essential. Also a must is researching and hiring a reputable and trusted distributor, whether at home or abroad.

Some of the ways to ensure that an exporting partner meets the company's criteria for doing business in the target market is by researching the company's market reach and infrastructure, ethical standards, financial statements, and track record. References and current client interviews are an excellent way to ensure that an intermediary in the international market maintains and enhances the company's good brand by providing equivalent levels of service, pricing, and ethical behavior. Lastly, to ensure that the importing company's legal rights and privileges are protected, one should review the country's laws and regulations regarding import/export partnerships. The laws and regulations of some countries make it problematic to pull out of a distribution or an agent contract even when that party is not performing its contractual duties.

A 2001 study[6] published in the *Journal of International Marketing* sought to extract the definitive factors contributing to harmonious or problematic exporting partnerships. Based on their interviews with 201 United States exporting manufacturers, the researchers developed the following export management guidelines for other firms looking to excel in international business relationships:

- Treat exporting as a bundle of evolving business relationships that are not defined just by the financial terms of the agreements but are dynamic and evolving. Therefore, each one should be monitored and cared for both individually and as a part of the overall international business portfolio.

- Relationships with people from other countries are most successful when conducted by skilled relationship management professionals who have cross-cultural experience and language proficiency. The training in international business skills of the rest of the company's staff is also important for smooth relationships with overseas customers.

- A proactive approach that assigns strategic importance to the firm's international operations and is supported by all departments and staff is essential. It is important for the firm to conduct systematic market analysis and appraisal of the exporting operations and the international customer base.

- Dealing with customers that are thousands of miles away physically and psychologically creates certain barriers to developing proper customer

6. Adapted from Leonidou, L. C., Katsikeas, C. S., & Hadjimarcou, J. (2002). Executive insights: building successful export business relationships: a behavioral perspective. *Journal of International Marketing, 3,* 96–15.

relationships. Exporters should make concerted efforts to reduce the distance by learning about their international clients through specialized literature, economic data, field trips, cross-cultural training and simulations, etc.

- Continuously building and enhancing the trust between the partners is essential to a sustained and prosperous international relationship. Being a trustworthy business partner is especially important in certain cultures and an exporter should take deliberate steps to gain and retain that trust even through the inevitable problems that arise in the course of any long-term business relationship.

- Reducing the uncertainties inherent in international business is a crucial factor in creating a hospitable environment for a cross-border partnership. Establishing communication, organizational, financial, and operational processes that ensure the reliable dissemination and acquisition of long-distance information is critical.

- It is challenging enough to come to a mutual understanding even between domestic partners, but when different cultural, political, environmental, and economic factors come in, the challenge is even greater. Open-mindedness, goodwill, and reciprocity are essential for a long-lasting international partnership.

- Being flexible and willing to accept small sacrifices, costs, restrictions, etc., in an international business relationship fosters commitment and long-term view. When this flexibility and commitment is mutual, the relationship can truly blossom.

- As in any relationship, open and continuous communication is the key. To facilitate communication across national, organizational, and personal differences, both parties should invest in cross-cultural training, onsite visits, and interactive communication technologies.

- Conflict is inevitable and healthy for an international business partnership, when managed properly. Exporters should ensure that conflict is kept functional, overt, and controllable in order to be dealt with and resolved quickly.

- Just as all companies strive for intra-company cooperation, the goal of greater inter-firm cooperation, goal compatibility, and information dissemination should be a priority for any exporter-importer relationship.

Licensing Another popular method for market entry is through licensing. International **licensing** is the process of transferring the rights to a firm's products to an overseas company for the purpose of producing or selling it there. For a set royalty fee, the *licensor* allows the *licensee* to use its technology, trademarks, patents, and other intellectual property in order to gain presence in the markets covered by the licensee.

Licensing is an attractive mode of entry for many entrepreneurial firms because, like exporting, it involves smaller upfront risks and expenditures. Since most of the costs of developing the licensed products have already been incurred, the royalties received often translate into direct profits for the licensor.[7] This form of market entry is most appropriate for countries that impose barriers to imports such as high tariffs and profit repatriation restrictions, and for mature products with relatively standardized production.[8]

---

7. Griffin, R. W., & Pustay, M. W. (2003). *International business: A managerial perspective* (3rd ed.). Upper Saddle River, NJ: Prentice Hall.

8. Deresky, H. (2000). *International management: Managing across borders and cultures* (3rd ed.). Upper Saddle River, NJ: Prentice Hall.

Licensing is not without its drawbacks, however. As with export partners, a firm considering licensing is advised to thoroughly research its potential licensees and their professionalism standards and to devise detailed legal contracts specifying the agreement's constraints, compensation rates, duration, and other similar issues. Such a cautious approach is important especially for countries where the legal protection for intellectual property is weak or not strongly enforced by the government. All too often, licensing companies have found themselves competing against their very licensees, who have copied their know-how and entered the markets with little or no R&D expenses. High tech firms considering licensing should be especially wary of the dangers of technology expropriation.

Franchising A form of licensing that eliminates some of the concerns described in the previous section is international **franchising.** International franchising gives more control to the *franchisor* company over the *franchisee* that has licensed the company's trademarks, products and/or services, and production and/or operation processes. Control is exerted through the franchise fee, which can be expropriated if contracts are not adhered to, and elaborate contracts that govern the relationship between the franchisor and the franchisees. On the flip side, the franchisor is also required to provide more materials, training, and other forms of support to the franchisee. A well-functioning franchise provides a win-win arrangement for both parties: the franchisor gets to expand into new markets with little or no risk and investment and the franchisee gets a proven brand, marketing exposure, an established client base, and management expertise to help it succeed.

Although franchising in most developed countries of North America and Europe has reached a saturation point, many emerging markets are experiencing phenomenal growth in international franchising. To succeed in developing countries, an entrepreneur who is considering this mode of market entry should consider several important environmental factors such as the level of economic development, the economic growth rate of the country, and its market governance policies before starting to look for potential franchisees there. While franchising has been the domain of mostly large, multinational corporations (MNCs) such as McDonald's, Dunkin' Donuts, and Holiday Inn, international franchising is opening unprecedented opportunities for smaller companies to enter new markets and compete successfully.

Contract Manufacturing (Outsourcing) Contract manufacturing or outsourcing has garnered much attention recently for its economic and business benefits as well as for its controversial but inherent trend to move production jobs across borders. Contract manufacturing's growing popularity is due to the large savings it can produce in the financial and human resources areas of a business.

The arrangement of using cheaper overseas labor for the production of finished goods or parts by following an established production process is called **contract manufacturing** or **outsourcing.** Companies using this mode of entry benefit not only from lowering their production costs but also from an entry to a new market with small amounts of capital and with no ownership hassles. One of the drawbacks of using outsourcing methods is the loss of control over the manufacturing process and the working conditions in the facilities, which can potentially lead to lower quality of the goods and/or human rights abuses and result in bad publicity and financial damages to the company's brand. Nike, Timberland, and several other high-profile American firms have served as unintentional examples of this undesirable scenario.

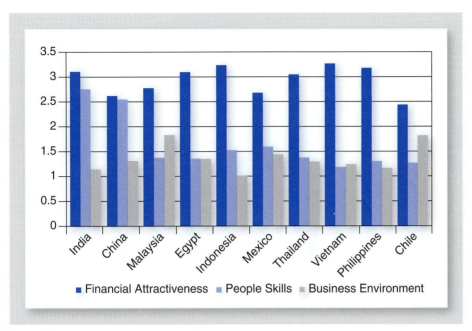

Figure 8-2 Leading Outsourcing Recipients

Source: Data from A. T. Kearney Global Services Location Index 2011.

In recent years, multiple firms from emerging markets such as China and India have emerged to help SMEs lower their costs by sourcing products, manufacturing, and services abroad. While India is reported to be the leading outsourcing recipient (see Figure 8-2), SME outsourcing is directed not only to developing countries. Wax Info Ltd., a leading UK-based developer of secure distributed content management software, chose a New Zealand firm, Black Coffee Software, Ltd., to develop a complex and large-scale secure application in record time.

As shown in Figure 8-3, IT companies are the heaviest users of outsourcing, followed by human resources and marketing and sales. About 40 percent of all Fortune 500 companies utilize outsourcing in one form or another, but as illustrated above, it is also an opportunity for SMEs to level the battlefield in competition with larger rivals.

Turnkey Operations

Another contractual entry mode to a new market is participation in a turnkey project. **Turnkey operations** typically involve the design, construction, equipment and, often, the initial personnel training, of a large facility by an overseas company which then turns the key to the ready-to-run facility over to the purchaser.

Most often the province of the largest specialized construction and manufacturing companies, turnkey operations projects are usually contracted out by governments for enormous projects such as the building of dams, oil refineries, airports, energy plants, etc. Nevertheless, opportunities exist for the participation of smaller entrepreneurial firms as subcontractors for turnkey projects.[9]

Because of their extraordinary size and scope, many such projects require long-term commitment of personnel, financial reserves, supplies, and other resources. Before a small company decides to participate in turnkey operations, it should carefully examine

9. Daniels, J. D. & Radebaugh, L. H. (2001*). International business: Environments and operations* (9th ed.). Upper Saddle River, NJ: Prentice Hall.

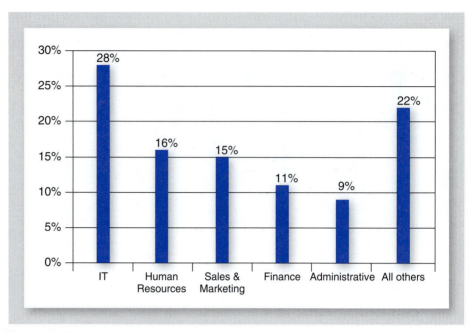

Figure 8-3 IT Leading as Most Active Area of Outsourcing

Source: Data from A. T. Kearney Global Services Location Index 2011.

whether it is ready to absorb the long-term currency exchange fluctuations, the extended drain on its resources and the other elevated political, economic, and financial risks that are likely to come up in such complex undertakings. Some SMEs providing specialized services can sell their service/product through turnkey operations. One such company in Orlando, Florida, markets airport development services to developing countries' governments using regional joint venture partners for the construction and financing of the project through major international banks. There is always a risk that the last payment for the project upon completion will not be paid as the incentives to pay decrease.

Management Contracts

A mode of entry into new markets that is most widely used in the hotel and airline industries is management contracting. Under a **management contract,** a company in one country can utilize the expertise, technology, or specialized services of a company from another country to run its business for a set time and fee or percentage of sales. For example, many owners of hotel buildings contract with well-known hotel management firms such as the Ritz-Carlton Hotel Company, LLC, to develop and manage their properties.

While the management company is responsible for day-to-day operations, it cannot decide on ownership, financial, strategic, or policy issues for the business. Such an arrangement is suitable for companies that are interested in earning extra revenues abroad without getting entangled in long-term financial or legal obligations in the foreign market.

International Joint Ventures

As part of the larger category of international business alliances international joint ventures (IJVs) have been one of the most popular methods for entering international markets. A form of foreign direct investment (FDI), **joint ventures** are created when two or more companies share ownership of a third commercial entity and collaborate in the production of its goods or services. IJVs are attractive to businesses because of the relative ease of market entry they offer, their shared risk, shared knowledge and expertise, and the potential for synergy and competitive advantage in the global marketplace.[10]

International joint ventures are formed for different reasons, such as to continue the expansion of an existing business, to introduce the company's products to new markets, to introduce foreign products to the company's existing markets, and to branch out into new business. For entrepreneurs, joint ventures are a fitting way of entering into new markets with little or no international business experience, and for entering some specific countries where people tend to value trust as a cultural characteristic and are more open to international collaboration.[11]

IJVs can also take many different forms.

- Two or more companies from the same country form an alliance to enter another country
- An overseas company joins a local company to enter its domestic market
- Firms from two or more countries band together in a JV formed in a third country
- A foreign private business and a government agree to join forces in a pursuit of mutual interests
- A foreign private firm enters into a JV with a government-owned firm to enter into a third national market

There are many different forms of JVs; however, let us consider the difference between **upstream joint venture** and **downstream joint venture** arrangements. An example (Figure 8-4) of a downstream JV occurs when two or more partners form a company

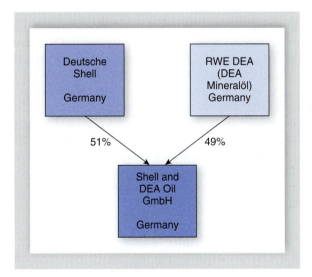

Figure 8-4 Downstream JV

10. Griffin, R. W., & Pustay, M. W. (2003). *International business: A managerial perspective* (3rd ed.). Upper Saddle River, NJ: Prentice Hall.

11. Daniels, J. D., & Radebaugh, L. H. (2001). *International business: Environments and operations* (9th ed.). Upper Saddle River, NJ: Prentice Hall.

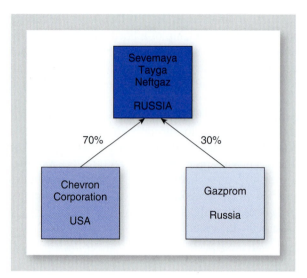

Figure 8-5 Upstream JV

(the joint venture) to produce a final or intermediate product or to integrate wholesale and retail activities. In the case of Example 1, a JV was formed in order to integrate supply and refining including the retail sale of both partners' oil products. All downstream activities of both companies were integrated, including dual branding of their products. In addition, the JV consisted of 3,000 service stations, making it the largest retail supplier of oil products in Europe.

An upstream JV may be formed to exploit raw materials needed by each of the partners to produce intermediate products. In this case (Figure 8-5), a JV is established to mine and/or process raw materials that are then supplied to the partners for further processing. Example 2 shows a JV between Chevron Corporation and the oil unit of the Russian gas monopoly OAO Gazprom, both of which established the JV entity for the purpose of oil exploration. The initial ownership was 70 percent Chevron and 30 percent Gazprom.

Much has been written about the factors contributing to the success and (more often) failures of cross-border strategic alliances such as joint ventures. To summarize, the most general issue with such an arrangement is maintaining the delicate balance between the partners' goals and objectives, management requirements, contributions, organizational and national cultures, and the myriad other factors that make some collaborations successful and others not. Many failed JVs can be attributed to the so-called Prisoner's Dilemma. It is a situation in which both partners have a chance to benefit from collaboration. However, due to lack of trust, both parties end up competing with each other and so get lower benefit. Following is an example of a failed joint venture and one that succeeded.

The Wadia–Danone JV (1995)

The Wadia Group (India) is a conglomerate that has investments in textiles, aviation (Go Airlines), plantations, health care, food, and electronics. Groupe Danone, based in Paris, claims world leadership in fresh food products. The company derives about half of its sales from dairy products and is well known for its yogurt brands. About 30 percent of its sales are from emerging markets, mainly through joint ventures. Both Wadia and Group Danone (Figure 8-6) held equal shares in a holding company, Associated Biscuits International, which in turn owned 50 percent of Britannia, the largest

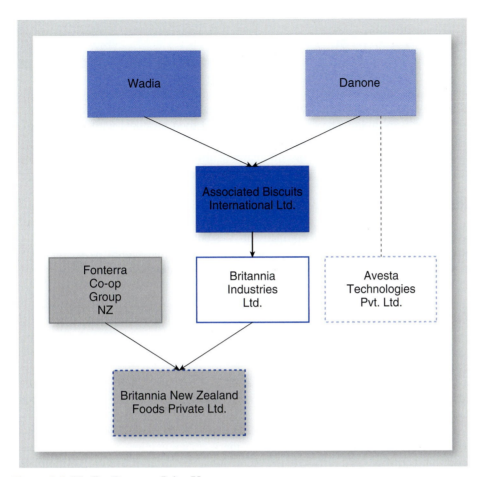

Figure 8-6 Wadia–Danone Joint Venture

biscuit firm in India, with a 38 percent market share. Britannia is well known for its Britannia and Tiger brands. The Tiger brand alone is reported to account for 20 percent of Britannia's total sales.

Trouble between the JV partners began in 2001 when Britannia formed a joint venture with the Fonterra Co-operative Group of New Zealand. Each partner held 49 percent of the JV, with a strategic investor holding the remaining 2 percent. Under the agreement, Britannia would market in India milk products produced by Fonterra, while Britannia's dairy business would be run by the JV. However, the JV was in conflict with Danone, which had established its own dairy business. Later, Danone bought 4.6 percent of Avesthagen, an Indian biotech company whose subsidiary, Avesta Good Earth Foods, produces health foods (see Box 8-2).

Sources reported that Wadia Group was not buying Groupe Danone's stake in Britannia Industries Ltd. for now, as it was not able to raise funds in the current scenario. Negotiations between both sides failed to resolve the issue. In 2009, Danone sold its share in the JV to Wadia, which put an end to the partnership.

Goodyear–Sumitomo Joint Venture

In 1999, Goodyear Tire and Rubber Company and Sumitomo Rubber Industries Ltd. formed several joint ventures integrating many of their plants and sales operations

BOX 8-2   COMPANY IN FOCUS: WADIA GROUP

The Wadia Group, an Indian-based conglomerate, owns food giant Britannia Industries, and had a joint venture with Wadia–Danone BSN India. The Wadia Group objected to the Danone investment in Avesthagen, citing violation of Press Note 1 (PN 1). It alleged that the biotech company's subsidiary, Avesta Good Earth Foods, had a similar line of business. Avesta Good Earth Foods manufactures health foods.

PN 1 makes it mandatory for a foreign joint venture partner to have the domestic partner's consent before making any new investment in the same business segment. Avesthagen's vice-chairperson and managing director contested the claim that there was a violation of PN 1, claiming that his

company was involved in biotechnology research, which is in the highly niche, emerging segment of clinically validated food products with therapeutic benefits. It has to be distinguished from a glucose biscuit manufacturing company.

"We are not in the same business and therefore, there is no question of Groupe Danone requiring to [have] any other party's consent before investing in our company. In fact, there is no research-based company in the entire world that has a strategy or product line of the same nature as we have," claimed Avesthagen's vice-chairperson.

Source: Adapted from: Prasad, G. (2007, September 24). Avesthagen contests Wadia claim on Groupe Danone. *The Economic Times*.

located in the United States, Europe, and Asia. The annual sales of the combined operations of the joint ventures totaled about $15.5 billion at the time. What were the motivations for the joint ventures?

During the end of the 1980s, the United States tire industry contracted, owing to mergers and acquisitions. The largest American companies, such as Firestone, Goodrich, Uniroyal, and Armstrong were acquired by foreign tire corporations. By 1991, Goodyear remained as the only major United States tire manufacturer, while all United States tire manufacturers accounted for only 17 percent of world production. Goodyear's world market share declined from 24 percent in 1971 to 17 percent in 1993. Although Goodyear was the dominant tire manufacturer in the United States, it ended 1998 with about $2 billion in debt and was third to Bridgeton and Michelin in terms of world market share. Michelin especially was threatening to strengthen its position in the North American market at the expense of Goodyear.

Advantages of the Goodyear–Sumitomo JVs

The joint ventures gave Goodyear access to Sumitomo's Dunlop brand and a bridge to the Japanese market. In Europe, the JV gave Goodyear and Sumitomo an edge over Bridgeton, but Michelin remained the market leader. However, the combined market shares of Goodyear and Sumitomo (see Table 8-1) put them slightly ahead of both Bridgeton and Michelin. Another motive for the JVs was cost savings as a result of eliminating inefficient plants, while combining purchasing and other functions. The main motivation for Sumitomo was the reduction of mounting debts owing to problems with its Dunlop operation and the recession in Japan. Access to Goodyear's superior technology was another motive.

The joint ventures consisted of four operating companies: one in North America, one in Europe, and two in Japan, and two synergy-focused support ventures based in the United States: one for global purchasing and one for sharing tire technology. Goodyear's share in the North American and European JVs is 75 percent, while Sumitomo

TABLE 8-1 Global Tire Market Shares (%)			
1997		**2009**	
Bridgeton	18.6	Michelin	19.2
Michelin	18.3	Bridgeton	18.8
Goodyear	17.1	Goodyear	16.8
Sumitomo	5.5	Sumitomo	3.7
Total World Sales $69 Billion		Total World Sales $127 Billion	

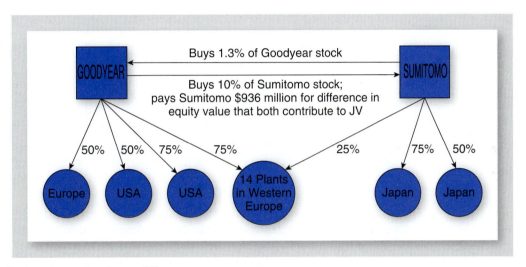

Figure 8-7 Goodyear–Sumitomo JVs

controls 75 percent and 50 percent of the two Japanese JVs. As part of the agreement, Goodyear acquired a 75 percent interest in Dunlop Tyres (Japan) and in the Dunlop Tire Corporation. Goodyear and Sumitomo also made investments in each other. As shown in Figure 8-7, Goodyear acquired 10 percent of Sumitomo's equity, while Sumitomo received a 1.4 percent stake in Goodyear. In addition, Goodyear payed Sumitomo $936 million for the difference in equity value that both contributed to the joint venture, a sum that helped Sumitomo to reduce some of its debt. Goodyear's North American tire group, including Kelly-Springfield and Canada, and its operations in Poland, Slovenia, Turkey, Morocco, and South Africa were not included in the joint venture. Within five years of the JVs, Goodyear's Dunlop became Europe's second-largest tire maker (after Michelin), while a financially strengthened Sumitomo remained the second largest tire maker in Japan (after Bridgeton).

By 2009, the combined global market share of Goodyear and Sumitomo was 20.5 percent, giving the joint venture the largest global market share.

INSURING AGAINST JV FAILURE

A number of studies[12] have shown that about half of all JVs fail. An extreme view is that JVs last for only five to seven years, only a little longer than the average career of

---

12. Turowski, D. (2005). The decline and fall of joint ventures: How JVs became unpopular and why that could change. *Journal of Applied Corporate Finance, 17*(2), 82; Bamford, J., Ernst, D., & Fubini, D. (2004, February). Launching a world-class joint venture. *Harvard Business Review*, 1.

a National Football League running back![13] What are the reasons for the high rate of JV failure and what can be done to prevent it? Here are a number of causes and suggested remedies:[14]

- *Bad ideas.* In the classic JV situation, companies form a joint venture because neither of them has adequate resources to undertake the venture on its own. Increasingly, JVs are motivated less by resource sharing than by risk sharing. Unfortunately, "risky" is often a code word for not worthwhile or commercially viable. If a project is not worth undertaking alone, it may not be worth undertaking.

- *Insufficient planning.* One of the most prevalent reasons for a failed joint venture is a lack of sufficient planning. Joint venture "plans" consisting of nothing more than a statement of each party's intended contributions to the JV and their respective share of profits seldom work. The parties have nothing to shape their expectations or to govern their disputes. Parties of the joint venture should agree to a comprehensive written plan including the form of the JV, each party's contribution, logistical issues (who will be doing what and where), governance, and ownership of jointly developed assets, dispute resolution, and the terms for winding up the JV if such a need arises.

- *Inadequate capitalization.* Joint ventures are typically allocated a fixed amount of capital based on the estimated funds necessary to accomplish the JVs goals. It is critical that any plan provide for not just the current capital needs, but for future or excess requirements.

- *Lack of leadership.* Too often, joint venture partners insist on sharing the leadership role. The parties should agree from the beginning that will have day-to-day operational control of the project (or different parts of the project). Agreement should only be required in cases of fundamental decisions; for example, a sale or other disposition of the JV or its assets, the incurrence of debt, or the admission of a new partner. Even in those situations, the governing document should provide for a method of dispute resolution in the event of a stalemate.

- *Lack of commitment.* Many companies enter into JVs looking for a quick profit. When that profit is not realized, or is not realized as quickly as expected, they lose interest.

- *Cultural and ideological differences.* In evaluating JV partners, companies should perform the same compatibility and integration analyses they would do for an acquisition, including a thorough evaluation of corporate culture, management style, personnel, and employee benefits and IT systems. In international JVs, where the partners originate from two countries or more, cultural differences may impede a good working relationship much more than differences in corporate culture. Opposites may attract each other, but unless a way is found to blend differences, the joint venture is likely to be unstable.

International Business Alliances[15]

International alliances are defined as "relatively enduring inter-firm cooperative arrangements, involving flows and linkages that use resources and/or governance structures from autonomous organizations, for the joining accomplishment

---

13. From www.1000ventures.com/business_guide/jv_main.html. Quoted in MacMillan, T. (2006). *CIBC Mellon: A joint venture success story.* [Speech to the Financial Services Institute.]

14. Spranger, D. (2004). *Why joint ventures fail.* Retrieved from www.saul.com/common/publications/pdf_29.pdf.

15. Alon, I. (2003). International business alliances: A practical perspective from the packaging industry. *Proceedings, Annual Academy of International Business, Southeast Meeting.*

of individual goals linked to the corporate mission of each sponsoring firm." International strategic alliances are becoming a fast-growing method of foreign market entry. Compared to foreign direct investment, international strategic alliances embody a lower level of financial investment and risk, and allow for the pooling of resources, skills, and abilities across multiple firms with the goal of achieving a joint purpose. International strategic alliances, however, are not risk-free. The different decision style of the alliance companies, the loose association that exists among the alliance firms, and the sharing of strategic resources exposes firms to potential failure and an unstable business environment in which one partner may take advantage of another.

Strategic Alliances

A **strategic alliance** is a formal, contractual relationship between two or more firms that share resources to pursue a common goal. In short, these are non-equity agreements in which partners to the alliance share some strategic assets, such as technology, in order to create synergy or to gain access to resources that one or both firms do not possess. For a general description of such alliances, see Box 8-3.

Strategic alliances are vertical or horizontal. In a vertical alliance, firms from different industries cooperate. For example, a construction company can form an alliance with an interior design firm to provide finished apartments that are completely furnished. In a horizontal alliance, firms are from the same industry. An advertising agency handling political candidates may form an alliance with a marketing research firm that specializes in political polling. In both cases, these arrangements are contractual and do not form a new entity. The Fujitsu and Cisco example (see Box 8-3) is also an example of a horizontal alliance.

What makes an alliance "strategic"? According to Director of Operations of Global Alliances at Hewlett Packard Company in California, there are five criteria that determine whether an alliance is strategic:[16]

- It is critical to a core business goal or objective
- It is critical to the achievement of a competitive advantage
- It is necessary in order to preempt competition
- It can be vital for future strategic options of the company
- It can help manage risks that threaten strategic objectives

Despite the risk factors associated with strategic alliances, this mode of entry into foreign markets has its advantages. For example, strategic alliances have the potential to lower the transaction costs, hedge against strategic uncertainty, acquire needed resources, allow firms to evade international barriers to entry, protect a firm's home market from international competition, broaden a firm's product line, enter new product markets, and enhance resource use efficiency. Tallman argued that firms utilizing strategic alliances could enhance their firm-specific resources (physical assets, intangible property, patents and trademarks, human resources, complementary resources), technical capabilities (R&D, manufacturing, marketing, sales, market knowledge), and managerial competencies (management skills and abilities, value-added activities).

The advantages gained by using international strategic alliances depend on the type of industry and the way in which the alliance is structured. For example, some researchers contended that firms in a mature industry are more likely to benefit from

---

16. Wakeam, J. (2003, May–June). The five factors of a strategic alliance. *Ivey Business Journal*, 1–4.

BOX 8-3   COMPANY IN FOCUS: FUJITSU AND CISCO

Fujitsu and Cisco Expand Strategic Alliance to Deliver Unified Communications Solutions in Japan

Both Companies Combine Expertise and Deliver Collaboration Solutions That Help Enterprises Become More Productive

TOKYO—On April 16, 2009, Fujitsu and Cisco announced the expansion of their strategic alliance to deliver unified communications in the Japanese market. In adition, Fujitsu and Cisco have agreed to work together to develop unified communications solutions and collaborate on services and marketing activities.

This expansion of the Fujitsu and Cisco strategic alliance combines Cisco's industry-leading Unified

Communications advanced technology and proven global experience with Fujitsu's Information and Communications Technology (ICT) product development capabilities. The strategic alliance will enable both to provide a set of comprehensive collaboration tools and unified communications solutions for customers in the Japanese market.

Based in Tokyo, Fujitsu is a leading provider of IT-based business solutions for the global marketplace. It has approximately 160,000 employees supporting customers in 70 countries. The company combines a worldwide corps of systems and services experts with highly reliable computing and communications products and advanced microelectronics to deliver added value to customers.

Source: Adapted from: Cisco press release, April 19, 2009.

strategic alliances, whereas others proposed that technology-based alliances tend to benefit high-tech industries more than traditional industries.

Many different frameworks have been developed for the proper formation and execution of an international business alliance, including conducting SWOT analysis, goal compatibility, and value-added analyses for participating firms, and/or examining their market power, efficiency, and competencies. Nevertheless, the most vital issues for a successful international business alliance remain selecting the right partner, developing trust, and developing the appropriate contractual framework.

Wholly Owned Subsidiaries

As the most capital-intensive mode of entry, fully owned **subsidiaries** are usually considered viable only for large, internationally experienced corporations that can afford the great risks associated with ownership and operation of a business in a foreign country. Entering a market through a wholly owned subsidiary involves buying an existing business (also called *Brownfield strategy*) or building new facilities (also called *Greenfield strategy*) in a new target country. While both of these scenarios allow companies to exercise maximum control over their operations and to decisively enter the target country's markets, they also expose the company to the highest level of political, environmental, legal, and financial risks.

Advantages and Disadvantages of Alternative Entry Modes

Table 8-2 summarizes the advantages and disadvantages of alternative entry modes. Many of the advantages or disadvantages relate to financial and/or political risk, speed of market entry, control over operations, and the acquisition of market knowledge.

TABLE 8-2 Advantages and Disadvantages of International Modes of Entry

Mode of Entry	Advantages	Disadvantages
Exporting	Low risk Easy market entry or exit Gain local market knowledge Bypass FDI restrictions	Tariffs and quotas Transportation costs Possible distributor relationship issues
Licensing	Low risk Fast market access Bypass regulations and tariffs Gain local market knowledge	Less control over market and revenues Intellectual property concerns Potential problems with licensees/future competitors
Franchising	Low financial risk Bypass regulations and tariffs Keep more control Gain local market knowledge	Less control over market and revenues Some loss of control over operations Potential franchisee relationship issues
Contract manufacturing	Low financial risk Save on manufacturing costs Flexibility of short-term commitment Emphasis on marketing/sales	Less control over operations Less knowledge about local market Potential damage to brand/finances if human rights issues arise
Management contracts	Insider access to market Emphasis on firm's expertise Low financial risk	Limited profits and market access Potential copyright and intellectual property issues
Turnkey operations	Access to FDI-unfriendly markets No long-term operational risks Emphasis on firm's expertise	Some financial risks Potential issues with partners/ infrastructure/ labor/ profit repatriation
Joint ventures	Insider access to market High profit potential More control over operations Shared risks Gain knowledge from partner(s)	High investment of resources Potential issues between partners over control/ contributions/goals, etc. More management levels Potential intellectual property issues
Wholly owned subsidiaries	Full market access/acceptance Full control over operations/profits Bypass tariffs Diversify operations	High financial/resources investment High political and environmental risks Potential profits repatriation issues More management levels

SUMMARY

- We have examined the various alternative entry strategies a firm can take during its internationalization. It should be emphasized that when a firm enters more than one market at a time, it may choose different entry modes for each market. Such a strategy is most often used for two reasons: to enter several markets at the same time or to leverage the advantages of one entry mode before transitioning to another. As global communications, travel, and trade have become increasingly easier and more wide-spread, many companies have found it possible and even beneficial to use more than one entry mode simultaneously.

- If no particular asset requires a large investment, non-equity modes such as licensing or franchising may be suitable for market entry. If such entry requires a high level of specific-asset investment, equity modes of entry, such as IJVs or fully owned subsidiaries, may be more appropriate.

- A more stable and economically and politically secure country would be more inviting to an equity mode of entry, whereas a country with political or social turmoil and frequent economic crises would be suitable for non-equity modes of entry.

- A business that is built on strong internal culture and regulations would be more comfortable upholding them in its new markets by entering through equity modes. On the other hand, a more open and flexible firm may be comfortable with relying

on the controls of partners such as exporting agents or licensees.

- SME decision makers can rely on transaction cost theory to make more informed decisions about the most appropriate mode of entry for their company. Decisions made using this method seem to lead to a better performance abroad, according to a limited study.

- Whether a firm uses transaction cost analysis or any other accepted method to evaluate its international market strategy, the choice of entry mode should be carefully considered and planned to ensure smoother, more profitable operations abroad.

DISCUSSION QUESTIONS

1. What in your opinion are the most difficult challenges facing SMEs deciding to outsource?

2. In your opinion, are there any differences facing SMEs and larger firms when dealing with an entry mode decision?

3. Joint ventures in emerging countries have higher failure rates than in more developed countries. Why do you think this is so?

EXPERIENTIAL EXERCISES

1. You are going to advise a small to medium-sized service firm considering expanding to the UK. None of its managers have any international business experience. How would you go about determining their readiness to consider such a move?

2. Search United States Department of Commerce sources to determine which market entry strategy has been used most frequently over the last decade by American firms in emerging countries. Explain the reasons for this trend.

KEY TERMS

Contract manufacturing, p. 210

Direct exporting, p. 207

Domestic country factors, p. 205

Downstream joint venture, p. 213

External factors, p. 205

Franchising, p. 210

Indirect exporting, p. 207

Internal factors, p. 204

Joint ventures, p. 213

Licensing, p. 209

Management contract, p. 212

Outsourcing, p. 210

Strategic alliances, p. 219

Subsidiaries, p. 220

Target country factors, p. 205

Turnkey operations, p. 211

Upstream joint venture, p. 213

CASE 8-1

GOL: Evaluating the Entry of a Brazilian Airline in the Mexican Market

GOL (www.voeGOL.com.br) was one of the most profitable low cost airlines in the world, with net revenue of U.S.$1,778 million, a net income of U.S.$266 million, and U.S.$131 million in cash in December 2006.

The success of the Brazilian company was centered on its low-cost strategy in the domestic market and some Latin American countries. The company reached 37.1 percent share in the home market and 13 percent share of the Brazilian international market share in December 2006.

GOL flew 530 daily flights to 55 destinations in five Latin American countries at the end of 2006.

At the beginning of 2007, the company's challenge was to launch new destinations in Latin America. Following this objective, the company was evaluating entry into the Mexican market. Mexico was the second most important market in Latin America behind Brazil, with a market value of U.S.$5.5 billion and more than 40 million passengers. Mexico's two big companies, Mexicana and Aeromexico, were competing in domestic and international markets. In addition, five new local low cost carriers were also competing for the local market. These issues showed some difficulties that had to be evaluated for a successful entry in this market.

The Company

The company was the most profitable low-fare, low cost airline operating in Brazil, providing frequent service on routes connecting all of Brazil's major cities and select South American cities.

GOL began its operations in January 2001 with six single-class Boeing 737–700 Next Generation aircraft serving five cities in Brazil. It carried one million passengers in less than a year of operation.

The company's origins were based on the founders' experience in land transportation: the Aurea Group. They were the owners of 36 companies dedicated to land transport.

The miracle worker was Constantino de Oliveira Jr., CEO and President of GOL. When Oliveira decided to introduce in Brazil the low cost model that had done so well for Southwest in the United States and Ryanair in Europe, few thought he had much chance to succeed. Oliveira was barely 32 and had no experience in commercial aviation. However, Oliveira did have some managerial experience with the Aurea Group, his family-owned land transportation company, which has been in the business for more than 50 years.

In 2004, GOL began the internationalization process, flying to different top destinations in South America: Buenos Aires, Montevideo, and Asunción, and the last destination was Santiago de Chile in September 2006.

The long-term business objective was to bring affordable air travel to all significant destinations in South America. By the end of 2006 GOL was operating 530 flights per

---

Case prepared by Marcelo Barrios, EDDE-Escuela de Dirección de Empresas, Argentina. Reprinted with permission.

day to 55 domestic and international destinations. GOL showed a ROE of 25.8 percent during the 2006 fiscal year.

In March 2007, GOL bought for U.S.$320 million the rights to control the almost extinct Brazilian airline company, Varig. This company still had market value because of its name, which was still known in many countries of the world as the most traditional airline brand name in Brazil.

GOL made the purchase through its subsidiary company, GTI S.A. By doing this, GOL tried to protect its finances against the billions Varig had in debt. Through this, GOL also made clear that it would try to lift Varig independently from its main company.

The two companies were completely distinct, with different executive staff, and in theory were competitors. GOL continued the focus on low cost domestic flights while Varig was prioritizing international and non-stop flights, which were more expensive for the passengers.

GOL was second place in the Brazilian airline market for national and international flights. In February 2007, the company made almost 19 percent of international flights, while TAM was the leader with 61 percent. For domestic flights, the competition was tighter, with GOL making 40 percent of the flights compared to 47 percent from TAM.

The Mission

To provide safe and high-value passenger and cargo transportation through innovative solutions for its customers, shareholders, employees, and society.

The Vision

To be recognized by 2010 as the airline that popularized high-quality, low-fare air transportation in South America.

Values

To continue to improve the company's business model based on original, creative, ethical, and fair initiatives that are focused on sustainable and long-lasting results and based on high-quality service and low fares for its clients. For its employees—respect, professional recognition, and career opportunities, coupled with a spirit of solidarity and an attitude of social and environmental responsibility.

The Business Model

The company's operating model was based on a highly integrated, multiple-stop route network that was a variation on the point-to-point model used by other successful low cost carriers worldwide. The high level of integration of flights at selected airports permitted GOL to offer frequent nonstop flights at low fares between Brazil's most important economic centers and South American interconnections through its network, linking city pairs through a combination of two or more flights with little connecting or stopover time. The company's network also allowed it to increase its load factors on its strongest city pair routes by using the airports in those cities to connect its customers to their final destinations.

In addition to offering low fares, its strategy was to make flying a simpler, more convenient experience. The company had achieved this objective largely through the elimination of unnecessary extras and common-sense applications of technology.

GOL encouraged its customers to use the Internet not only to make reservations, but also to make many of the arrangements from the comfort of their home or office that they would otherwise have to make at crowded airports or airline ticket offices, such as checking in and changing their seat assignments.

Tarcision Gargioni, the marketing vice president, attributed the success to technical factors. "Our planes fly more than other airlines' planes do. They carry more people, and spend less time on the ground, on average. That makes a difference. Basically, our work is more focused on costs, and we have a record of achievement that translates into higher productivity than other companies."

GOL's competitive advantage was not simply expertise at managing costs and optimizing its operational efficiency. "GOL has always been a low cost company, but it was never a low fare airline. Its ticket prices are lower than other Brazilian companies' prices but if you compare them with Europe and the United States, GOL's prices are not low," noted Sampaio Gilso de Lima Garofalo, a professor at the Pontifical Catholic University of São Paulo.

The company boosted productivity by increasing aircraft utilization, which reached an average of 14 block hours/day—the highest in the Brazilian industry and above the best international standards.

In addition, GOL's record turnaround time of 25 minutes was one of the lowest among its international peers. Low turnaround meant more time in the air, with higher productivity, in turn allowing lower fares.

The Marketing Strategy

GOL deployed aircraft in a highly efficient manner to maintain industry-leading aircraft utilization and concentrated heavily on Internet-based distribution channels and sales. The strong promotion of Internet-based distribution channels and sales was an integral element of its low-cost structure and efficiency and had made the company one of the largest and leading e-commerce businesses in Brazil.

The sales channels were concentrated in 82 percent on Internet and 15 percent through the call center and airport. Close to 70 percent of sales were indirect and commissionable through travel agencies.

GOL believed it effectively employed technology to make its operations more efficient, using real time sales and operating information, Internet-based sales and ticketless traveling, advanced yield management systems, and intelligent outsourcing.

Simplified on-board service was part of GOL's strategy. GOL worked in a niche unexplored by other airline companies that offer industrialized meals that are not always appreciated. On short-haul flights, GOL offered snacks and cereal that are healthy, nutritious, and considered "fashion," according to research from the Brazilian magazine *VIP*.

The company believed that through its low fares and high-quality services, GOL provided the best value in its international and domestic markets and created demand for air travel services. GOL's average fares were lower than the average fares of its primary competitors. The company identified and stimulated a demand among both business and leisure passengers for air travel that is safe, convenient, and simple and is a reasonably priced alternative to traditional air, bus, and car travel.

By combining low fares with simple and reliable service that treats passengers equally in a single-class environment, GOL had successfully increased its international and domestic market share, strengthened customer loyalty, and attracted a new group of air travelers in its markets. These new travelers had not previously considered air travel due to the higher prices and more complicated sales procedures that preceded GOL's entry into the market.

The company believed that the GOL brand had become synonymous with innovation and value in the Brazilian domestic airline industry.

In 2005, GOL was named one of Brazil's most valuable brands by *Isto é Dinheiro* magazine in its fourth annual Most Valuable Brazilian Brands Ranking, with a brand value of U.S.$326 million. The company was also named Best Airline in Latin America by *Global Finance* magazine in 2005. In addition, GOL was recognized among Brazilian and international investors as a company with a very high level of disclosure and transparency, releasing financial information simultaneously in Brazilian GAAP and United States GAAP. The company ranked first in the category of "Disclosure Procedures" in Latin America and top five in the category of "Corporate Governance" in Brazil at the Eighth Annual IR Global Rankings in February 2006.

In particular, GOL expected to increase its focus on business travelers from medium-sized companies—a growing customer base that tends to be more price sensitive—by closely monitoring the routes and flight frequencies that best serve their travel needs and by increasing marketing efforts directed at this segment of its customer base. By offering international flights with stops integrated in its network, GOL created opportunities for incremental traffic, feeding its network and increasing its competitive advantage and supporting its strategy of stimulating demand for its service. The addition of routes between Brazil and cities in neighboring South American countries had been based upon an extension of its existing network using the same growth strategy that had proven to be successful for the company at the end of 2006.

The International Development

In 2004 GOL started flying to Buenos Aires, Argentina, as the first international destination. Eight months after the inauguration of the Brazil–Buenos Aires route, GOL verified an exceptionally high satisfaction ratio among Argentinean passengers, with 83 percent of interviewees approving of the company's services. The survey, carried out between April and July 2005 by Databrain Pesquisas Inteligentes, also highlighted extremely strong customer loyalty: 89 percent said they would not hesitate to use GOL again, while no less than 92 percent affirmed that they would "certainly" recommend the company to friends and acquaintances and 62 percent said it was their favorite airline. It was worth pointing out that 56 percent of the passengers using this route were from Argentina.

These figures encouraged GOL to continue expanding its routes in the region and it added two more Argentinean destinations—Córdoba and Rosario—in the first two weeks of January 2006. No other Brazilian airline was flying to as many destinations in that country. It continued the international development, adding flights to Montevideo (Uruguay), Asunción (Paraguay), and Santiago (Chile).

The Mexican Market

In 2005, the Mexican government decided to privatize two state-owned airlines—Aeromexico and Mexicana—and allowed several low-cost airlines to enter a market with a population of 103 million.

The Mexican airline industry generated total revenues of U.S.$5.5 billion in 2005, representing a compound annual growth rate (CAGR) of 4.2 percent for the five-year period spanning 2001–2005. Industry passenger volumes increased with a CAGR of 5 percent from 2001–2005, to reach a total of 46.6 million passengers in 2005.

In 2006, more than 70 percent of Mexican in-and-out international flights were dominated by foreign airlines; in that year, only seven Mexican carriers flew to foreign destinations. These airlines represented 27 percent of the total international traffic. According to the Mexican Direction General of Civil Aeronautics (DGAC), since October 2005 there were more commercial flights from the United States to Mexico than in earlier years. Just seven United States airlines carried 40 percent of the international Mexican passengers. These airlines represented 34 percent of the flights between Mexico and their countries. American Airlines had 11 percent of the international Mexican market.

The performance of the industry was forecast to accelerate, with an anticipated CAGR of 5 percent for the five-year period 2005–2010 expected to drive the industry to a value of U.S.$7 billion by the end of 2010. The industry's volume was expected to rise to 54 million passengers by the end of 2010, this representing a CAGR of 3 percent for the 2005–2010 period.

Main Mexican Players

Mexicana was one of the leading airlines in Mexico with 20 percent of total market share. This company had lost close to 20 percent market share in the previous years and presented financial problems.

In its international operations, Mexicana had a large portfolio of codeshare agreements with other airlines, which gave customers access to a wide range of destinations. The company operated services in close to 800 world destinations and had locations in many different countries, including New Zealand, Hong Kong, South Africa, the UK, Singapore, Argentina, and the United States. Mexicana was headquartered in Mexico City, Mexico.

Mexicana was hoping to grow 12 percent in 2007. The company had 30 percent of the domestic market, 25 percent of the United States–Mexican market, and 52 percent of the Latin America market.

Aeromexico, another important player, had approximately 300 daily departures, and its maintenance base had been certified as the workshop authorized for airplane repairs by the FAA in the United States and the DGAC in Mexico.

The company operated primarily in Mexico, North America, South America, and Europe. In South America the main destinations were: São Paulo (Brazil), Buenos Aires (Argentina), Santiago (Chile), and Lima (Peru). It was headquartered in Colonia del Valle, Mexico, and employed about 7,900 people.

The company recorded revenues of U.S.$3,662.8 million during the fiscal year ended December 2005, an increase of 8.8 percent over 2004. The net profit was U.S.$135.2 million in fiscal year 2005, as compared to U.S.$55.3 million in fiscal year 2004.

Mexicana and Aeromexico were also exploring other strategies besides price discounting from low cost carriers to retain customers.

To strengthen services offered to domestic passengers, in 2005 Mexicana launched the low cost carrier Click Mexicana. The service offered value fares on domestic flights via the airline's hubs in Mexico City, Guadalajara, and Veracruz.

Both airlines were undergoing cost cutting measures, again, like their United States counterparts, and looked to international routes where low-cost carriers did not fly.

The Mexican Low-Cost Carriers

Air transportation in Mexico, historically limited to upper and middle class households, was aiming for the masses with the influx of new low-cost carriers in 2005 and 2006.

The lack of a strong low-cost competitor, a young population, and recent economic stability created an environment ripe for investment. The large bus transportation market provided opportunities for low-cost carriers to divert people from road travel to air travel.

Most of the potential passengers were part of the 33 percent population between 20 and 40 years old.

Click, a subsidiary of Mexicana, was the first to arrive in July 2005. Avolar was next to fly in September followed by Interjet. Volaris began flying in March 2006, and in June, Aerolineas Mesoamericanas started as well.

Of the airlines flying in 2006, Click served the most cities (19 in Mexico, plus Havana, Cuba, and soon Miami), followed by Avolar (17), Interjet (7), and Volaris (5). There were also Vuela and Viva.

For most airlines, passengers were expected to be Mexican nationals attracted by cheaper fares and better connections than those offered on the older carriers. But the opportunities did not lie just within the domestic market.

The open skies agreement with the United States made it easier for Mexican airlines to fly there. With a large immigrant population in the United States, these airlines had the opportunity to expand internationally and catch people visiting friends and family across the border.

Some of these new airlines were interested in developing a marketing strategy to target the 26 million Mexicans that live in the United States in order to increase their growth in the next decade.

Many routes also made sense for United States travelers as well, especially people interested in hopping around or tacking on an extra city or beach to their getaway.

One of the challenges for the low-cost carriers and United States passengers was the booking systems. Most websites were in Spanish only. Also, prices were generally given only in pesos. Travelers accustomed to getting around on bumpy, crowded Mexican buses, however, preferred the new headaches to the old ones.

Low-cost carriers priced their fares slightly higher than the price of a bus ticket along the same route, with the expectation that people were willing to pay a small premium for a shorter travel time.

Developing Internet sales was crucial to keep distribution costs low. To become a significant player, a low-cost carrier had hourly departures to compete against national carriers for business travelers. The brand was also expected to compete against United States carriers along routes to the United States

Evaluating the Entry in the Mexican Market

One of the key 2007 issues that GOL presented to its investors was its growth strategy. This point was focused in launching eight new markets: five in Brazil and three international and to add over 130 new flight frequencies.

Mexico was the market selected, although some regulations complicated the entry, like the share of foreign investments in local companies.

GOL had entered the previous international markets with the same entry strategy: alone and with low fares. But Mexico was a special market. It was necessary to fight two strong domestic and international players: Mexicana and Aeromexico. The first one had also launched a low cost carrier named Mexicana Click a few months earlier. At the same time, the big challenge was the five new low-cost carriers that invested, in total, close to U.S.$800 million to launch their companies. Each company invested between U.S.$90 and U.S.$200 million.

These companies were trying two future objectives: first, develop the domestic market during the following years, and second, try to be international or Latin American players. One important point was that there was not any low cost Latin American carrier competing in the international Latin American routes.

Another challenge was centered in the possibility that the big United States players that dominated more than the 40 percent of the Mexican international flights would decide to compete in a more aggressive way in the international Latin American routes.

With these scenarios, what was the best strategy to enter the Mexican market? Was the traditional GOL low cost model the best way? Was it the best option to evaluate the entry in the domestic market with a local partner? Or was it enough to go alone like the other GOL international destinations? Recently GOL had bought Varig in Brazil. Was the same strategy the best way to enter Mexico? What were the pros and cons of each decision? Was there another option to enter the Mexican market?

Segmenting, Targeting, and Positioning for Global Markets

We are saying you've got to understand and choose the customers you want to serve. Don't just go after everyone. Define the target market carefully through segmentation and then really position yourself as different and as superior to that target market. Don't go into that target market if you're not superior.

PHILLIP KOTLER[1]

LEARNING OBJECTIVES

After reading this chapter, you should be able to:

- Segment global markets.
- Understand how globalization affects market segmentation.
- Apply the criteria for targeting markets.
- Understand the difference between differentiated and undifferentiated marketing.
- Demonstrate how customized marketing can be applied globally.
- Show how to gain competitive advantage through positioning.
- Select a global target market strategy.

Making Apples and Cherries "Cool" in Taiwan[2]

Two organizations representing the apple and cherry growers of Washington state in the United States were aiming to increase consumer demand for their fruits in Taiwan, which has been one of their top five markets for the last three years. These fruits have long been a prestige purchase in the country because of their higher prices and positive association with the region in which they're grown. Cherries in particular are special occasion fruits in Taiwan—often saved for birthday parties and holidays—and are popular as personal and business gifts.

The organizations wanted to build on that prestigous image while also focusing on the youth market. "In the past, we've focused (marketing efforts) on mothers who are . . . buying the fruits," says Eric Melton, vice president of international marketing for the commissions. "But 70 percent of the people in Asia are under the age of 35.

---

1. Five steps to marketing success. (30 June 2005). *Global Office*, CNN.com. Retrieved from www.cnn.com/2005/BUSINESS/06/29/guru.kotler/index.html?section=cnn_latest.

2. Andruss, P. L. (4 Dec. 2000). Groups make fruits apple of Taiwan's eye. *Marketing News.* Retrieved from www.marketingpower.com/content16144S0.php.

We decided no one's going to buy it if no one wants to eat it, so we wanted to catch the attention of the young people."

The growers decided that the right positioning for their fruits was as "hip" and "cool"—to appeal to their younger audience and to maintain the elevated status of their apples and cherries. To maximize the impact of their rather limited, $2 million media budget, the organizations created their own TV shows that followed the winners of two beauty pageants—for Ms. Washington Apple and Ms. Washington Cherry—as they traveled through Washington state during the three-month cherry-growing season. The two new beauty queens became the stars of lifestyle shows, entertainment programs, travel segments, and cooking shows and generated much additional publicity through other media coverage.

The fruit growers' organizations successfully used segmentation, targeting, and positioning strategies to market their products in Taiwan. **Segmentation, targeting, and positioning** (STP) are concepts that are easy to understand for marketers and often hard to put into practice effectively. Even in domestic markets, where critical factors such as culture, customer preferences, and marketing channels are well known, marketers often fail to segment their markets properly, which in turn leads to off-the-mark targeting and positioning, and ultimately to unrealized potential for the given product or service.

The challenges are even greater in global markets, where the variety and complexity of segments, target audiences, and positioning options grow exponentially.

THE NEED FOR STP STRATEGY IN GLOBAL MARKETS

Segmentation, targeting, and positioning are some of the most fundamental concepts in marketing strategy and practice today. In fact, Philip Kotler, one of the leading marketing experts in the world today, lists segmentation, targeting, and positioning as the three most important concepts in marketing in his classic book *Marketing Management*.

Simply put, STP allows marketers to determine the value their product or service can deliver to specific types of customers (segmentation), to identify the methods through which they can reach these customers (targeting), and to communicate the said value in appealing ways to them (positioning).

In global markets, where heightened competition, pricing pressures, and cultural adaptation needs are just a few of the challenges facing marketers, crafting the right STP strategy becomes even more vital to the success of their marketing campaigns.

Segmentation, in particular, allows marketers to simplify their decision-making process by using the same set of guidelines for segments that exist across national and cultural markets. This marketing standardization process—from product development to marketing communications—can save operational costs for the company. On the other hand, segmentation also can identify target market groups across the world that differ from the standard parameters and require a completely new marketing approach.

The continuous fragmentation of both audiences and marketing channels in global markets creates a number of additional challenges for marketers. As new technologies allow consumers to communicate their interests and preferences to marketers, and congregate (especially online) with people who share those interests and preferences, they have in essence created an infinite number of customer segments that demand relevant, customized communications from the brands that are trying to reach them. Otherwise, those brand communications are likely to be ignored.

Figure 9-1 Traditional Marketing Communications Are Giving Way to Customized Marketing Messages That Strive to Engage Specific Target Segments and Position Brands to Their Particular Needs

Source: © image100/Corbis

This shift toward the need to engage customers across a number of specialized channels versus simply broadcasting a standard marketing message through traditional print, TV, or radio channels requires global marketers to pay even greater attention to their STP strategy. The goal becomes to not only identify and engage the right customer segments, but also to preserve the true identity of the brand while answering the need to position it in very customized, segment-specific communications (see Figure 9-1).

It is also worth noting that while Web 2.0 technologies, for example, have brought a new level of complexity to the segmentation, targeting, and positioning efforts of global marketers, it has also given them unprecedented access to their customers. The amount of information from online panels, cookies, search engine statistics, blog comments, and the myriad other consumer behavior tracking tools has provided a veritable treasure trove to marketers, who can now find everything from the browsing habits and preferred shopping methods of their customers to their opinion of specific brands and products, to name a few examples. What's more, marketers can get instant feedback on how their campaigns resonate with their target segments.

Armed with all this instantaneous and detailed knowledge about their customers, marketers should be able to correctly identify their target markets and communicate with them effectively, right? Unfortunately, as we'll see in this chapter, this is not always the case.

GLOBAL MARKET SEGMENTATION STRATEGIES

Segmentation is defined by the American Marketing Association as "the process of subdividing a market into distinct subsets of customers that behave in the same way or have similar needs."[3]

3. Market segmentation. *AMA Dictionary*. Retrieved from www.marketingpower.com/_layouts/Dictionary.aspx? on July 6, 2008.

Getting market segmentation right is not an easy or quick process in any market. In global markets, where segments, especially in developing countries, may shift with each social, political, or economic change, the task of identifying the right segments is even harder. Despite the many challenges inherent in market segmentation analysis and implementation, however, when done well, the practice can give a company a substantial competitive advantage.

The key to good segmentation is selecting useful dimensions by which to identify each customer segment. Five criteria have to be present to make any group of customers a true market segment. Each segment must be:

1. Measurable
2. Different enough to warrant changes in the marketing mix
3. Accessible through marketing and distribution channels
4. Large enough to be profitable
5. Stable enough to allow for proper targeting and measurable response[4]

Only segments that have all of the above dimensions can help marketers design appropriate marketing campaigns that address real customer needs, reach customers through effective channels of communication, and have a measurable financial impact on sales.

Globalization and global markets have had a polarizing effect on segmentation. On one hand, as globalization brings the world closer, certain segments of similar consumers are becoming easier to identify across the world. Think of the tech gadget fans that lined up outside Apple stores in 22 countries around the world on July 11, 2008, for the launch of the iPhone 3G, for example. On the other hand, as more global markets are becoming accessible, marketers find it increasingly difficult to contend with the variety of segments spurred by the difference in cultures, social habits, regional and national preferences, and other factors.

Given the wide variety of segmentation methods used in the field today, it is easier to distinguish them first by the entity used as a basis for segmentation. In this sense, the two broad categories that emerge are country-based segmentation and individual-based segmentation (or company-based, in the case of B2B marketing).

Country-Based Segmentation (Macro-Segmentation)

The country-based segmentation approach incorporates some of the most basic segmentation methods, but their simplicity often underlies their limitations. This approach uses geographic, demographic, and socioeconomic variables such as location, GNP per capita, population size, or family size to group countries into market segments. For example, a company may decide to market its product only in countries where population size is over 100 million and per capita income is above $10,000. Or it can decide to market the same product in all countries of the Middle East or in all Spanish-speaking countries.

Such an approach enables a company to centralize its operations and save on production, sales, logistics, and support functions.[5] But such country-based segmentation doesn't take into consideration consumer differences within each country and among the country markets that are clustered together. It also fails to acknowledge the existence of segments that go beyond the borders of a particular geographic region.[6]

4. Ibid.

5. Steenkamp, J. E. M., & Hofstede, F. T. (2002). International market segmentation: Issues and perspectives. *International Journal of Research in Marketing, 19,* 185–213.

6. Hassan, S. S., & Kayanak, E. (Eds.). (1994). *Globalization of consumer markets: Structures and strategies.* New York: Haworth Press.

Consumer-Based Segmentation (Micro-Segmentation)

Using the individual consumer as the basis for segmentation introduces many more variables into the analysis and increases its complexity. It too can include certain geographic and demographic variables, but the most value can be found in the more sophisticated psychographic and behavioral-based segmentation methods which allow for a finer "slicing and dicing" of the markets and therefore more precise targeting and positioning strategies.

An approach where consumers are grouped based on common characteristics such as cultural preferences, values, attitudes, or lifestyle choices also offers greater flexibility to marketers in terms of geographic focus. Certain segments identified to have the same characteristics may be present on a truly global scale, while others may be particular to a specific country or region.

For example, a study by RoperASW measuring values and attitudes between the different generations in Asia discovered that young consumers have much more individualistic values than their parents. Individualism, ambition, and freedom were valued considerably more by those of 13 to 19 years of age than by 40- and 65-year-old adults in Asia, confirming that, thanks to globalization, young people from different cultures often have more in common with each other than with older generations in their own cultures.[7]

Euro RSCG Worldwide conducted another study among young consumers that compared attitudes toward eating. It found that, while American teens prefer their food on the go, most other youngsters in the world enjoy a meal that is consumed in no hurry in a calm atmosphere.[8]

Analyses of other segments, such as the retiring baby boomers in the United States (see Box 9-1) reveal other insights that can help marketers better understand and segment their audiences.

BOX 9-1   PEOPLE IN FOCUS: THE PSYCHOGRAPHIC PORTRAIT OF A GENERATION

C&R Research conducted a study designed to shed some light into the values, thoughts, and habits of the aging American baby boomers—a market segment that is still considered misunderstood, despite its large size and considerable market clout.

Based on these and other findings, the study segmented boomers into four groups: Looking for balance (27%), confident and living well (23%) at ease (31%), and overwhelmed (19%).

Adapted from: Business is booming. (2005, March/April). Marketing Management, 4.

Baby boomers daydream about

Money/financial freedom: 34%
Vacations/travel: 21%
Spending time with family: 15%
Retirement: 14%
Health: 6%

Baby boomers worry about

Money/financial issues: 39%
Family: 20%
Health/diet: 16%
Job security: 6%

Baby boomers' favorite activities include

Athletics/sports: 65%
Movies/theater: 65%

Baby boomers spend the most time

At work: 75%
With family: 64%
With grandchildren: 58%

---

7. Parmar, A. (28 October 2002). Global youth united. *Marketing News*, 49.
8. Ibid.

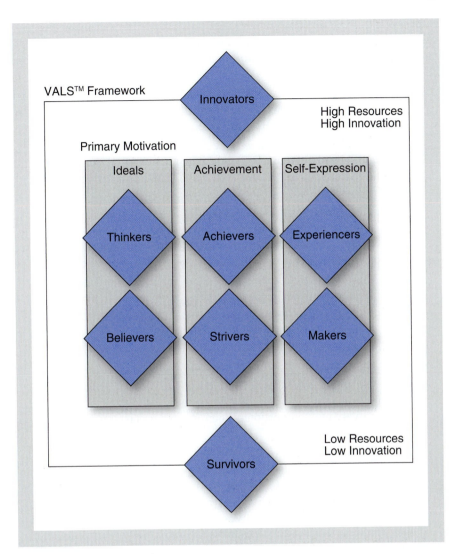

Figure 9-2 VALS Framework

Source: Strategic Business Insights (SBI); www.strategicbusinessinsights.com/VALS. Reprinted with permission.

One of the most long-lived and authoritative systems that segment people on the basis of personality traits is **VALS**, owned and operated by Strategic Business Insights (SBI), an SRI International spin-out. (VALS was originally known as the Values and Lifestyles program).[9]

The basic tenet of VALS is that people express their personalities through their behaviors. VALS specifically defines consumer segments on the basis of those personality traits that affect behavior in the marketplace.

While its beginnings can be traced to the late 1970s, the VALS model was redefined in 1989 to allow it to predict consumer behavior on the basis of enduring personality traits rather than social values that change over time. The current VALS system for the U.S. consumer marketplace contains the following segments (also shown in Figure 9-2). VALS systems have also been developed for other countries. SBI's research shows that similar psychological traits drive similar kinds of consumer

9. SRI Consulting Business Intelligence (SRIC-BI); www.sric-bi.com/VALS.

behavior no matter what culture you are in, but the expression of the trait varies by culture. For example, every culture has consumers who are motivated to buy goods based on the status the good confers to them. However, the specific status symbols vary by country and culture.

Innovators are successful, sophisticated, take-charge people with high self-esteem. Image is important to Innovators, not as evidence of status or power but as an expression of their taste, independence, and personality.

Thinkers are motivated by ideals. They are mature, satisfied, comfortable, and reflective. They tend to be well educated and actively seek out information in the decision-making process. They favor durability, functionality, and value in products.

Believers are strongly traditional and respect rules and authority. Because they are fundamentally conservative, they are slow to change and technology adverse. They choose products they are familiar with and established, well-known brands.

Achievers have goal-oriented lifestyles that center on family and career. They avoid situations that encourage a high degree of stimulation or change. They prefer premium products that demonstrate success to their peers.

Strivers are trendy and fun loving. They have little discretionary income and tend to have narrow interests. They favor stylish products that emulate the purchases of people with greater material wealth.

Experiencers appreciate the unconventional. They are active and impulsive, seeking stimulation from the new, the offbeat, and the risky. They spend a comparatively high proportion of their income on fashion, socializing, and entertainment.

Makers value practicality and self-sufficiency. They choose hands-on constructive activities like building a deck or outdoor grill and spend leisure time with family and close friends. In product selection, they prefer value over luxury and usability over style.

Survivors lead narrowly focused lives. Because they have the fewest resources, they purchase fewer products than other groups and therefore do not exhibit a strong primary consumer motivation. While the past often seems fuller to them than the future (i.e., when their spouse was living or when the kids were at home), they are not necessarily sad or hopeless about the present but are accepting of life's smaller pleasures. They are concerned about safety and security, so they tend to be brand loyal and buy discounted merchandise.

Compare this fairly straightforward U.S. model to the much more complex and layered Japanese VALS model shown in Figure 9-3.

The Japanese VALS model shown in Figure 9-3 classifies consumers into 10 consumer segments ranging from a high to a low degree of innovation strength. The segment having the highest degree of innovation strength is classified as "integrators" (4 percent of the population). They are highly educated and modern, highly social, high up on the income scale, read and travel frequently, and follow the latest trends. Traditional innovators (6 percent) and adapters (10 percent) follow religious customs and are socially conservative. These beliefs color their purchasing behavior that favors familiar products. Self-innovators (7 percent) and adaptors (11 percent) are positioned relatively high on the innovative strength scale. As the term implies, these consumers regard self-expression as an ideal. Self-expression can be realized through

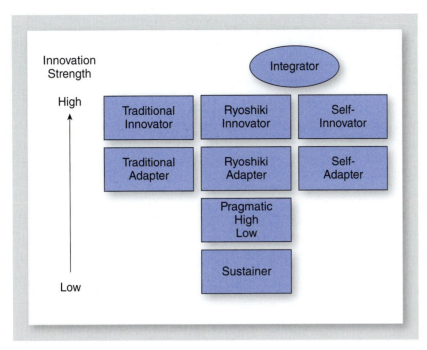

Figure 9-3 VALS Japan Framework

consumption of products that broadcast self-image, such as fashion clothing, or that provide personal experiences. Ryoshiki ("social intelligence") innovators (6 percent) are middle-aged and career-oriented, and adapters (10 percent) are concerned about both personal advancement and family and social status. High pragmatics (14 percent) are withdrawn, while low pragmatics (17 percent) are uncommitted to lifestyles and prefer inexpensive products. Sustainers or realists (15 percent) are resistant to change and have minimal education and income. They are lowest on the innovation scale and are past-oriented.

Backer Spielvogel & Bates Worldwide (BSB) has created Global Scan, an ongoing psychographic survey undertaken mostly in the Triad and Pacific Rim countries. Global Scan measures a wide variety of attitudes and consumer values, as well as media use and buying patterns. Values like self-sufficiency and self-esteem and personality characteristics are included in the survey, as are political opinions and attitudes about social issues. Consumers are also questioned on their use of more than 1,000 brands and products. The agency claims that 95 percent of the combined population of all countries surveyed can be divided into five segments: (1) adopters (18 percent), older consumers who hold on to time-honored values; (2) traditionals (16 percent), who follow traditional, cultural values and prefer familiar products; (3) pressureds (13 percent), mainly women who are responsible for the family with little time for employment or recreation; (4) achievers (22 percent), opinion leaders with relatively high incomes who are concerned about style and quality; and (5) strivers (26 percent), younger people who seek instant gratification.

B2B Segmentation

Several major differences become apparent when one compares the segmentation process in the consumer marketplace and the business-to-business environment. The most apparent one is the size of the markets. While consumer marketers often have to contend

BOX 9-2 COMPANY IN FOCUS: DEALING WITH SEGMENT SHIFTING

In today's quickly globalizing world, market segments often shift, change, or disappear altogether with the pace of global, social, and cultural changes that affect every society in the world. Global companies and marketers have to be able to quickly identify the new or shifting segments and adjust their product and marketing strategy accordingly. Consider the response of Hans Stråberg, the CEO of Electrolux, the Sweden-based international mid-market appliances company, to a question by *The McKinsey Quarterly* about market polarization trends: "Given the differences in what consumers value, we have abandoned the traditional industry segmentation based on price and a 'good-better-best' hierarchy . . . "

As a result, the company's segmentation strategy has 20 product positions that relate directly to the lifestyle and purchasing patterns of different consumers. To illustrate, steam ovens are now successfully marketed to health-oriented consumers. Compact dishwashers, which were initially developed for smaller kitchens, are now marketed to a broader consumer segment interested in washing dishes more often.

Source: Adapted from: Trond Riiber Knudsen, "Escaping the Middle Market Trap: An Interview with the CEO of Electrolux," *The McKinsey Quarterly*, no. 4, 2006.

with a market that reaches in the many thousands and even millions of individual consumers, the B2B marketplace for a company rarely exceeds several hundreds of companies and only a few very large firms can claim a business client base of many thousands.

However, when purchasing capacity is considered, the scenario is reversed. Business purchasing volume far outstrips individual consumer purchasing, especially when compared on a single transaction basis.[10]

Another differentiating point is the dynamics of the actual purchasing process. From motivation to selection to execution, business purchasing is a distinctly more complex affair, given the number of people, factors, and systems involved, than steps involved in an individual consumer's purchasing decision and ultimate action.

That said, the ultimate goal of the segmentation for both consumer and B2B marketers is the same: to divide the market into defined, like-minded chunks. Dun & Bradstreet (D&B), for example, points out these few ways of segmenting business customers based on their similar behaviors:

- Industry
- Geography
- Decision maker demographics and lifestyle
- Surveyed data (companies with similar aspirations, preferences, complaints, etc., behave similarly)
- Firmographics and payment behavior (companies with similar business characteristics, payment data, supplier base, risk, amount of experience, growth, etc., behave similarly)[11]

A more inside-out perspective may be to classify customers based on their importance to the marketer's business—the most active, repeat, high-volume clients would be considered most important, smaller ones would be considered less so, and so on.

10. Hague, P., Harrison, M. (n.d.). Market segmentation in B2B markets. *B2B International, Ltd.* Retrieved from www.b2binternational.com/whitepapers3.htm.

11. Janis, T., & Singson, M. (15 November 2005). Leveraging cluster analysis in the B2B world: Motivations, applications & successes. *AMA webcast.* Retrieved from www.b2bsalesandmarketing.com/ama/.

TABLE 9-1 Segmentation Strategies for Advertising and New Products		
	Advertising	**New Products**
Target market	Product and service users	Consumers having similar needs
Data sources	Attitude surveys	Purchase frequency, product usage, store loyalty, purchasing power
Results	Segments differentiated by their response to a message	Segments differentiated by buying behavior and income

Source: Adapted from: Yankelovich, D., & Meer, D. (2006, February). Rediscovering market segmentation. *Harvard Business Review*, 3.

Current Thinking on Segmentation Methods

In recent years, segmentation methods based on values, lifestyles, and other individual traits have come under criticism for becoming more of a tool for advertising and branding than for truly effective segmentation that guides marketers in finding meaningful groups of consumers likely to buy their product. As Daniel Yankelovich, one of the earliest proponents of non-demographic segmentation, put it in the *Harvard Business Review,* "Psychographics may capture some truth about real people's lifestyles, attitudes, self-image, and aspirations, but it is very weak at predicting what any of these people is likely to purchase in any given product category. It thus happens to be very poor at giving corporate decision makers any idea of how to keep the customers they have or gain new ones." The author then goes on to describe the qualities that define good segmentation today—it should identify the groups most worth pursuing, it would stay dynamic, and it would lead companies to design products that relate to customers' needs—and distinguishes between the type of segmentation needed to develop advertising vs. the segmentation that helps product development. Table 9-1 explains the main characteristics of the two types.

Another critical look at segmentation[12] brings up the point that despite marketers' ability today to define ever narrower segments and launch more and more new products for them, over 90% of those products are unsuccessful because they fail to meet the one most important test—they're not helpful to the customer for the tasks that they need to perform. In other words, marketers today are spending more effort trying to understand customers—their self-image, aspirations, and tastes—when they should be trying to understand the "jobs" that customers need done and bring to market products that help with those jobs. To quote the late Theodore Levitt, "People don't want to buy a quarter-inch drill. They want a quarter-inch hole!"

One brand that has faithfully followed Levitt's advice to use people's desires to accomplish certain tasks as a basis for segmentation is Church & Dwight, with its line of Arm & Hammer baking soda products. In the late 1960s, marketers for the company began observing how and in what circumstances customers used baking soda during their daily routines. Surprisingly, they discovered that some customers used it in their laundry, others in their toothpaste, and yet others employed it as odor eliminator in their refrigerators or for their carpets. Using this research, Arm & Hammer devised several lines of products to serve the customer segments that needed these specific jobs done:

- Clean my mouth—Arm & Hammer toothpaste
- Clean my home—Arm & Hammer cleaning products

12. Christensen, C. M., Cook, S., & Hall, T. (2005, December). Marketing malpractice: The cause and the cure. *Harvard Business Review*, 74–83.

- Clean my pool—Arm & Hammer pool pH stabilizers
- Deodorize my refrigerator—Arm & Hammer odor absorbers
- Deodorize me—Arm & Hammer deodorants
- Deodorize my carpets—Arm & Hammer carpet deodorizer
- Deodorize my pets litter—Arm & Hammer cat litter
- Deodorize my clothes—Arm & Hammer laundry detergents
- Help me cook—Arm & Hammer baking soda

Thus, by focusing on the practical applications of its one basic product, the company was able to exponentially extend its markets, increase the value of its brand, and gain the loyalty of its customers.[13]

SEGMENTATION IN THE WORLD OF UNLIMITED CHOICES

In his groundbreaking book, *The Long Tail: Why the Future of Business Is Selling Less of More*, Chris Anderson takes on the profound shift that is occurring in the marketplace, writing that "Technology is turning mass markets into millions of niches." To prove his point, Anderson gives the examples of Amazon, eBay, Google, Rhapsody, iTunes, Netflix, and other Internet-based media and retail companies who, thanks to technology, are able to offer not only the hit products in music, film, books, etc., but also the obscure, the underground, the specialized, and homemade creations of individuals from around the world. Expressed visually, this phenomenon is creating a "long tail" graph where hits and sales represent the bulkier, steeper trend line, followed by a long, thinning "tail" that represents the millions of unknown products that previously had no chance of exposure in the marketplace but are now available to create their own customer segments, thanks to the democratizing power of the web.

In this world of limitless choices and limitless numbers of customer segments, how can marketers succeed? As Chris Anderson puts it, "In traditional media, we used to compete with giants, now we compete with an army of minnows."[14] In the online world of unlimited shelf space, the way products can succeed is by catering to the specific niche or niches created by these millions of minnows. They are the new tastemakers, the new filters to which consumers choose to listen and base their purchasing decision on. Table 9-2 provides Anderson's comparison of some of the old and new channels through which today's "marketing" messages reach their intended audiences. Clearly, marketers are still searching for effective ways to select and address their target segments through these new channels of communication.

The debate over the theory described in *The Long Tail* was rekindled by an article in the *Harvard Business Review*[15] that agrees with the assertion that digital markets create a long-tail effect, but disagrees with the conclusion that long tails will permanently change markets by creating millions of niche market segments. In fact, according to the author, "[H]it products remain dominant, even among consumers who venture deep into the tail." The statement is based on the observation that the largest segments of consumers (for music and video, at least) are "light" consumers, who tend

13. Sources: "Marketing Malpractice: The Cause and the Cure"; www.churchdwight.com, Hoover's.

14. Comments made during "The New Economy: Long Tail vs. 80/20" presentation by Chris Anderson at the MPlanet 2006 conference, American Marketing Association, Walt Disney World Dolphin Resort, Orlando, Florida, Nov. 30, 2006.

15. Elberse, A. (2008, July/August). Should You Invest in the Long Tail? *Harvard Business Review*. Retrieved from http://harvardbusinessonline.hbsp.harvard.edu/hbsp/hbr/articles/article.jsp?ml_action=get-article&articleID=R0807H&ml_issueid=BR0807&ml_subscriber=true&pageNumber=1&.

TABLE 9-2 Can Every Customer Be a Segment?	
The Old Filters	**The New Filters**
Marketers	Consumers
Advertisers	Customers
Editors	Bloggers
Record Label Scouts	Recommenders
Studio Executives	Playlists
Department Store Buyers	Reviewers

Source: Adapted from: Chris Anderson, *The Long Tail: The New Economics of Culture and Commerce*, New York: Hyperion, 2006, p. 123.

to purchase already established hit products, while "heavy" consumers may experiment with obscure offerings from time to time, but they also purchase hits regularly. The author's advice to businesses: continue marketing your most popular products to stay profitable, but broaden your portfolio, if you can do it cost-effectively, to attract the long-tail audiences.

TARGETING

Once all viable segments have been identified in the targeted markets, the process of selecting the most promising segments—those with the highest potential to generate sales and profits for the company—and deciding how to address their needs begins.

Criteria for Targeting

Just as in segmentation, the criteria used for selecting the best potential target segments (or markets) are extremely important. Some of the basic and most widely used targeting criteria are:

- *Market size*—the larger the segment, the more sustainable and profitable it is likely to be
- *Growth rate*—the faster a segment is growing, the more sales it is likely to generate
- *Competitive position*—the less competitive offerings are available for the target segment, the more likely the company is to gain large market share
- *Market accessibility*—the more cost-effectively and quickly a segment can be reached, the more attractive it will be
- *Customer fit*—the more compatible the segment is with the company's brand and resources, the more likely it is that sales will follow

The question of customer fit—whether the pursuit of a particular segment is compatible with the company's overall goals and established sources of competitive advantage—is illustrated with the example below of a small soft drink producer that was able to challenge the global conglomerates thanks to a good targeting strategy.

Although Pepsi and Coca-Cola are firmly entrenched in the Latin American market, a small Peruvian competitor, Kola Real, was not afraid to take them on. At the time of Kola Real's entry, the two soft drink giants had nearly 100 percent of the Peruvian cola market. This would appear to be a difficult position to challenge, but because Kola Real used a no-frills, minimal advertising and low price strategy that was appealing to its target segments, it was able to quickly capture almost 20 percent of the Peruvian market and successfully carve out a place for itself in Ecuador, Venezuela, and Mexico.[16]

Often, several criteria are used simultaneously to develop a detailed analysis of the most attractive segments. For example, China is an attractive market based on its huge market size and fast-growing middle class, especially in large metropolitan areas.

Russia is another large and growing market where, after a couple of decades of economic and political frustrations, a sizable middle class is emerging. In just six years, Russia's middle class has grown from merely 8 million to 55 million, accounting for some 37 percent of the population. Flush with newly found affluence, this large new market segment is beginning to demand the types of products and services available to other well-off nations, and global businesses are happy to comply. Everybody from the Dutch brewer Heineken and Swedish retailer IKEA to more than a dozen carmakers, such as Ford, General Motors, and Toyota, and retailers such as Zara, Nike, and The Body Shop, are entering or expanding their presence in Russia. Banking is also a booming industry—in 2006, Citibank reported that it nearly doubled its branches in the country and its business there is growing at 70 percent annually.[17]

SELECTING A GLOBAL TARGET MARKET STRATEGY

How are these global companies targeting their new markets? Are they simply transferring their existing products to Russia or are they developing new or modified products in order to reach specific segments within this market? The strategies used to target attractive global markets can vary, but their difference can always be traced back to the age-old question in global marketing of standardization vs. adaptation.

Undifferentiated Approach

Also called **mass marketing** or **standardized marketing,** at the center of the undifferentiated approach to target marketing is the assumption that customer segments across the world will accept the same product or service regardless of their cultural, behavioral, or socio-economic differences. In other words, when using an undifferentiated approach, a company is basing its marketing on the common needs of its customers, instead of on the differences.

Very few brands have managed to be successful on a global scale by using a standardized, global strategy. As a result, however, most of them are recognized as the premier brand names and marketers around the world. According to John Quelch, a director at the renowned WPP Group marketing services company, those global brands share the following characteristics:[18]

1. **The same positioning worldwide.** This provides a combination of functional product quality and innovation with emotional appeal. Think Coca-Cola and Disney.

2. **A focus on a single product category.** Think Nokia and Intel.

3. **The company name is the brand name.** All marketing dollars are concentrated on that one brand. Think GE and IBM.

16. Luhnow, D., & Terhune, C. (27 October 2003). Latin pop: A low-budget cola shakes up markets south of the border. *Wall Street Journal*, A1.

17. Bush, J. (18 December 2006). Russia: How long can the fun last? *Business Week*, 50.

18. Quelch, J. (16 October 2007). How to build a global brand. *Harvard Business Review*. Retrieved from http://discussionleader.hbsp.com/quelch/2007/10/how_to_build_a_global_brand.html.

4. **Access to the global village.** Consuming the brand equals membership in a global club. Think IBM's "solutions for a small planet."

5. **Social responsibility.** Consumers expect global brands to lead on corporate social responsibility, leveraging their technology to solve the world's problems. Think Nestlé and clean water.

For some products, especially commodities such as gasoline or sugar, or for brands that dominate the global B2B market, such as Boeing and Airbus, this standardized marketing approach is more viable. However, even in the most commoditized markets, the undifferentiated marketing strategy is beginning to fade away as competition intensifies around the world. For example, Jim Stengel, the global marketing officer for P&G—one of the traditional giants of mass marketing with global brands such as Tide, Wella, Zest, Vicks and others—recently announced that "[T]he end of the era of mass marketing is a very positive thing for our company, for our brands and for the industry."[19] At the same time, Stengel acknowledged that in many of the 140 countries in which P&G markets, television is still the primary (mass) channel of connecting with its customers.

Some studies have found empirical evidence that standardized marketing in similar target markets may have a significant positive effect on the performance of a brand over time. However, this positive effect is often distorted by the simultaneous tendency to centralize decision making when undifferentiated strategy is pursued.[20]

Differentiated Approach

In contrast to undifferentiated marketing, the differentiated approach aims to adapt the product and the marketing mix to each target market segment. Most global brands today use a version of this approach to stay competitive and expand their appeal to more market segments through products and advertising designed specifically for their needs and tastes.

The mobile phone manufacturer Nokia has become one of the leading global companies that have mastered the differentiated targeting approach. A few years ago, the company conducted a massive marketing research study across 21 countries that aimed to discover who its customers are and what role the mobile phone plays in their lives. The results of the study helped the company identify 12 global market segments of mobile phone users, depending on their lifestyle needs and the role the mobile phone played in meeting them. From there, Nokia devised four key targeting categories through which it can reach these global segments: live, connect, achieve, and explore.

- The "live" category is comprised of fashion-forward, urban hipsters who care about design, style, and trends. The phone targeted to them is the Brian Eno-designed Sirocco 8800.

- The "connect" category defines consumers who are looking for an easy way to stay in touch with their family and social circles via voice or text messaging and who may appreciate the elegant and easy-to-use Nokia model phone 6131.

- The consumers in the "achieve" category are business executives looking to maximize their productivity without sacrificing home life. They are likely

19. Colvin, G. (17 September 2007). Selling P&G. [C-Suite series]. *Fortune*. Retrieved from http://money.cnn.com/magazines/fortune/fortune_archive/2007/09/17/100258870/.

20. Özsomer, A., & Prussia, G. E. (2000). Competing perspectives in international marketing strategy: Contingency and process models. *Journal of International Marketing, 8*(1), 27–50.

to enjoy the calendar, e-mail, and web browsing tools of the E61 Nokia model.

■ In the "explore" category are those tech-savvy consumers who lead the trend toward electronic convergence gadgets that can receive and produce multimedia content. They are likely to be attracted to the Nokia N-series phones.

According to Jo Harlow, senior vice president of global marketing at Nokia, these four target consumer markets exist across all countries, but the need for marketing differentiation becomes evident when regional attitudes are considered. For example, Nokia's marketing may change in Asia, where status is an important consideration for consumers. In contrast, Nokia's messaging may emphasize functionality in North America, which resonates more with the consumers there.[21]

Customizing marketing offers based on the targeted segments increases the cost of doing business for companies but it has proven to also increase branding effectiveness and sales. For a graphic comparison of the three approaches, see Figure 9-4.

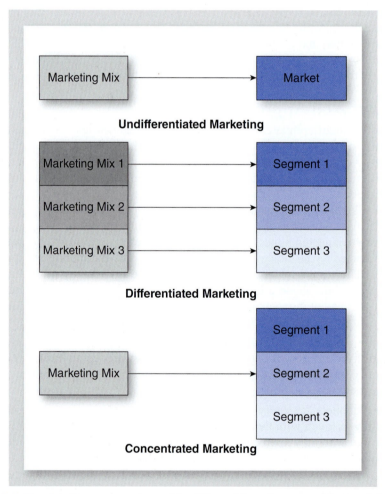

Figure 9-4 Graphic Representation of the Three Most Common Market Selection Approaches Used in Targeting

21. Harlow, J. (18 December 2006). Segmenting for success. *Brand Strategy,* 11.

Concentrated Approach

Sometimes called niche targeting, the concentrated approach is used when a company focuses intensely on one segment of the market and designs its marketing efforts with that segment in mind. Think of the company that targets skateboarders across the world or the services firm that focuses on attracting government contracts only.

Royal Bank of Canada (RBC) discovered a few years ago that a significant number of its more affluent customers spent the cold winter months in their second homes in Florida. Being Canadian, they frequently found it difficult to establish credit, purchase a house, or conduct other complex financial transactions in the United States In addition, the personalized, long-term relationship that they had created with their home-country bank was not available in Florida. So, RBC targeted these "snowbirds" by recreating the "Canadian experience in their branches in Florida." The bank organized social gatherings at its branches and strived to make the transition as smooth as possible to its Florida-bound customers by offering them no-fee traveler's checks, U.S. dollar accounts, customized mortgage services, and other products designed specifically for this niche group.[22]

Focusing on a single segment can have its benefits, such as decreased competition and (if successful) dominant market share. However, when executives end up "putting all of their eggs in one basket," the risk of losing all is also a possibility. If skateboarding declines in popularity, for example, or global economic crisis forces governments to decrease spending, the companies servicing those markets exclusively are likely to suffer.

Customized Approach

With the advent of the Internet age and social media networks, a new approach to marketing has been gaining success and popularity. Called the customized or micromarketing approach, it entails an even deeper segmentation of the target market and the creation of even more nuanced and specialized products and marketing campaigns aimed at very specific sub-segments of consumers.

As Thomas Ranese, the CMO at the New York office of the government agency responsible for attracting tourists to New York State, notes, "In marketing today, you're trying to find the market of one." To do that, his agency recently re-launched the famous "I ♥ New York" campaign. In contrast to previous years, about half of the campaign budget will be spent on the Internet for customizable brochures and videos, as well as for search engine marketing and targeted banner ads. In addition, the geographic reach of the campaign will also be much more targeted, with specific messaging and designs for the audiences in nearby states and Canadian provinces only.[23] Such a tailored approach to marketing to individuals with very specific needs and near very specific places has been available to marketers only in most recent years.

The online environment has played a key role in the growth of the marketing customization trend, particularly since sophisticated data analysis programs have made it easy to track and report return on marketing investment (ROMI) for online campaigns. According to some experts, targeted online ads, such as those Ford used in 2007 to push its Lincoln Mercury line of cars to "women online age 25 to 54 who are independent and business-minded," can cost twice as much, but they can also be twice as effective as untargeted ads.[24]

22. Selden, L., & Selden, Y. S. (10 July 2006). Profitable customer: The key to great brands. *Advertising Age, 77*(28), S7. Also: United States banking for Canadians. *RBC Bank website.* Retrieved from www.rbcbankusa.com/specialtybanking/cid-96799.html.

23. Elliott, S. (6 May 2008). Calling on tourists to come for New York City, but stay for the state. *The New York Times.* Retrieved from www.nytimes.com/2008/05/06/business/media/06adco.html.

24. Behind those web mergers. (21 May 2007). *Business Week.*

BOX 9-3   TECHNOLOGY IN FOCUS: BEHAVIORAL TARGETING: MARKETERS' NEW ONLINE FRIEND

The increasing sophistication and effectiveness of behavior-targeted online advertising is appealing to a growing number of marketers who are attracted to its easily measured return on marketing investment (ROMI), and the opportunity it provides for customer insights. According to a recent report from eMarketer, the behavioral targeting trend will grow exponentially in the United States, soaring from an estimated $775 million in 2008 to over $4.4 billion in 2012.

But behavioral targeting, which involves tracking the sites visited by often unsuspecting Internet users and displaying ads related to their interests, has also come under fire by privacy advocates who consider it too intrusive and unethical. In addition, marketers are concerned over the loss of control, given that ads are displayed independent of context and can show up on any site, even those considered inappropriate for their brand. Marketers also wonder whether ads could be too targeted, creating consumer segments too small to be viable.

Nevertheless, the promise and the potential growth of behavioral targeting has spurred a number of industry deals, as large Internet players such as Google, Yahoo!, and Microsoft are jockeying for market share in this new and fast-growing marketplace. In just over a month in 2007, four such deals were forged, each including the acquisition of a company offering behavioral targeting tools or know-how.

David Hallerman, a senior analyst with eMarketer, cites three main reasons for the growing popularity of behavioral targeting: marketers can use fewer impressions to attract a more interested audience, Internet publishers get to populate more of their pages with ads that "monetize" them, and users see more ads that they may actually find interesting. eMarketer predicts that the fast-growing online video sites such as YouTube are likely to attract the most behavioral marketing clients in the next four years.

In many countries where online privacy laws are more stringent, it is still questionable whether behavioral targeting will ever become a viable online marketing strategy. If it does, marketers would have a new challenge: finding a way to navigate the legal, cultural, and ethical considerations of each country or region they advertise in online. But given the borderless online environment, there's little doubt that behavioral targeting online is already a global phenomenon.

Sources: "Behavioral Targeting Poised for Growth," press release, eMarketer, June 16, 2008; "Behavioral Targeting Goes Online," *Marketing Matters Newsletter*, July 2, 2007; "Behind Those Web Mergers," *Business Week,* May 21, 2007.

While micro-marketing can become expensive, advancements such as mobile marketing, embedded global positioning systems (GPS), behavioral tracking (via cookies) on the Internet, and digital printing for direct mail continue to make it easier and more cost-effective to implement for smaller and smaller target segments of the market.

Positioning

Positioning is a process that is, for the most part, out of the hands of marketers. In fact, positioning is something that happens mainly in the mind of the consumer, who, by comparing similar brands and products, creates a sort of mental map of how each of them relates to his or her individual needs and wants. Thus, as marketers devise their positioning strategies, the goal is to influence the position their brands have in the minds of consumers in relation to competitor brands.

Successful positioning should result in strong, long-term emotional ties to the brand for the consumer. Such connection can only be built by consistently sending marketing messages that resonate on a personal level with the consumer and following through with products and services that deliver on the promises made.

Guinness, the popular and distinctive Irish stout, uses a virtual community to position and reinforce its marketing to a devout fan base that spans the globe. From selling product-related items in their Internet store, to their 1759 Society for "true Guinness Draught lovers," to the collectors community site and the free downloadable screensavers, different segments of Guinness drinkers are consistently reminded of what the product is all about while forging emotional connections with it and with other Guinness drinkers. Thanks to the web, Guinness has found a way to connect with drinkers around the world and encourage its members to stay in touch with the company, with fellow consumers, and with the brand, dramatically increasing its "real estate" in the consumers' minds, and remaining consistent in its positioning across the globe.[25]

Can such positioning consistency work on a global basis for most brands? Much depends on whether the brand can appeal to universal human needs and desires or whether it is suitable for more limited audiences with specific lifestyles, cultural preferences, or particular tastes. Certain positioning themes, such as quality, price, or performance can transition easily from local to global scale and back. Think of Nestlé's "Good Food, Good Life," Walmart's "Everyday Low Prices," or Nike's "Just Do It" positioning statements—they represent broad and broadly appealing sentiments to which people from around the world can relate.

Cultural preferences or traditions also can have a lasting effect in the global positioning strategy for a brand, however. For example, a recent study comparing marketing strategies of firms in 18 Western and Eastern European countries demonstrated that companies from the old, developed Western European countries tended to use attributes such as quality and distribution to distinguish their products in the minds of consumers, whereas companies from the less-developed Eastern European countries relied more on associations with price and quality to position their products.[26]

Some brands reposition their products based on the benefits considered most appealing to the local market. Nokia mobile phones, for example, are positioned as elegant and high quality in the West, while consumers in developing countries see them as easy to use as well as reliable. Even between countries, Nokia advertising is not standardized. For example, in Denmark a theme recently used was "Connecting People." The same phone was advertised in the United States as "Designed for the Way We Live." And in Argentina, an ad read "You Will Get to the Event with Nokia." Also, while Nokia does not compete on price in developed countries, its aggressive pricing in markets such as China, the Middle East, and Africa has helped it gained over a third of the global market for mobile phones. [27]

25. Flavián, C., & Guinalíu, M. (2005). The influence of virtual communities on distribution strategies in the Internet. *International Journal of Retail & Distribution Management, 33*(6/7), 405–425.

26. Golob, U., & Podnar, K. (2007). Competitive advantage in the marketing of products within the enlarged European Union. *European Journal of Marketing, 41*(3/4), 245.

27. Fielding, M. (1 September 2006). Walk the line: Global brands need balance of identity, cultural respect. *Marketing News,* 9–10.

SUMMARY

- Through global market segmentation, the similarities and differences of potential buying customers can be identified and grouped.

- Marketers can use macro-scale segmentation based on a country's or a region's demographic and economic statistics, or a micro-scale segmentation method based on individuals' demographic, psychographic, and behavioral patterns to define market segments.

- To target the appropriate consumer segments, marketers must evaluate and compare them on the basis of market size, growth potential, market accessibility, competitive position, and compatibility.

- In selecting the right market targeting strategy, marketers must decide whether to use an undifferentiated, differentiated, concentrated, or customized approach. Each requires a different degree of standardization or adaptation of the product and the marketing mix for each segment.

- Positioning occurs in the mind of the consumer, who, by comparing similar brands and products, creates a mental map of how each of them relates to his or her individual needs and wants. Marketers strive to influence the position their brands have in the minds of consumers in relation to competitor brands.

DISCUSSION QUESTIONS

1. Explain the difference between differentiated and undifferentiated marketing.

2. Explain the difference between segmenting and positioning.

3. Apply country-based segmentation to the European Union. Use whatever sources are necessary, such as the Internet.

4. Illustrate how Fiat is targeting its cars in the United States.

5. China is characterized by regional differences. Describe how retailers in China market to these differences.

EXPERIENTIAL EXERCISES

1. Visit the World Bank's World Development Indicators (WDI) site, accessible from www.worldbank.org. Learn more about the different categories of indicators used and make a list of the ones that can be particularly helpful to marketers looking to enter new international markets with products related to the consumer-side of the telecommunications industry.

2. List your favorite clothing brands and try to guess the targeting and positioning strategies used by the company that made it appealing to you. Would you do anything differently if you were the marketing executive in charge of that brand?

KEY TERMS

CASE 9-1

Moda Textile Factory: Bishkek, Kyrgyzstan

Sergei Ivanov and his wife Olga faced some important decisions regarding the future of their small sewing business in downtown Bishkek. The company, founded eight years before and now employing 15 people besides themselves, produced made-to-order women's suits, dresses, skirts, and raincoats for local wholesalers that supplied the raw materials and designs and sold the finished goods to retailers across the country and region. Sergei and Olga had long dreamt of producing quality, fashionable cashmere coats, and they now sought partners and financing to move their company in this direction.

In 1985, Sergei Ivanov and Olga Ivanova thought their entire life was planned out. They lived in a closed Soviet town in southern Kyrgyzstan created under Stalin as the site of the Soviet's key electric light bulb factory and center for uranium mining and processing. They had reliable jobs at the electric bulb factory that supplied the entire Soviet Union. Their salaries were modest, but they were well respected and life was stable and predictable. They lived in a close-knit community with the other factory workers, and the social welfare system took good care of their basic needs. Food, housing, education, and healthcare were practically free. They thought they would have their jobs for life.

After the breakup of the Soviet Union, followed by the independence of the Kyrgyz Republic in 1991, the country suffered a major economic downturn as it began the transition to a market-based economy. Industries and factories shut down completely or began operating at minimal capacity. Sergei described the collapse of the Soviet Union as an earthquake because it was so unexpected and happened so quickly. People struggled financially and psychologically to deal with the massive changes.

In 1992 Sergei and Olga lost their once-secure jobs. Desperate to survive the difficult transition, they moved to the capital, Bishkek, 800 kilometers away, in search of a new life. "Perhaps my entrepreneurial spirit is part of a family tradition. My grandfather in Russia was a merchant. Many people in my family now have private businesses. Olga is from a family of merchants." Trade was the easiest business to get into. They started selling clothes at an outdoor market in Bishkek. The biggest problem was finding the start-up capital to purchase inventory. They borrowed U.S.$650 from family and friends, and Olga left for her first buying trip to India. She returned and within a short period of time sold the goods and earned a profit of U.S.$300. Olga's buying trips for clothes continued to India and China, and Sergei began buying jeans apparel in Turkey for retail sale in Bishkek. Over the next 10 years (1994–2003), Sergei made over 80 buying trips to Turkey to purchase wholesale jeans apparel. Eventually the government closed down the outdoor market where Sergei sold his jeans, not compensating stall owners for the disruption. He then rented a stall in the city's largest department store, where the rent was high (U.S.$400 per month) compared to the outdoor bazaar (U.S.$50 per month) and inventory turnover was slower. There were 200 vendors in that retail space. Nonetheless, the business was profitable because his prices were competitive.

This case was written by Sherry Sposeep and Professor Richard Linowes of the Kogod School of Business at American University in Washington, D.C. It was produced in conjunction with the Emerging Markets Development Advisors Program (EMDAP) under the sponsorship of the United States Agency for International Development (USAID) and managed by the Institute of International Education (IIE). Reprinted with permission.

Opening of the Sewing Factory

Though the wholesale jeans business was profitable and stable, Sergei and Olga dreamed of something bigger. In the mid-1990s, they started a family-owned sewing factory of high-quality apparel. They produced made-to-order women's suits, dresses, and raincoats. All clients were wholesale traders who sold their goods to retailers in Kazakhstan, Russia, and other parts of Kyrgyzstan. Clients brought required material and patterns at order time, but paid for the goods only when delivered, never in advance.

There were about 500 sewing workshops in Bishkek of varying size. Many of them operated illegally out of people's homes. The intense competition meant a high turnover among workshops. New shops opened often and old small shops closed.

Sergei worked to establish a solid and loyal customer base. He had known many of his clients for 10–15 years. They were old personal friends with whom he had traveled during buying trips to Turkey. Recently the company had added some new customers, but they were also old personal friends.

Moda still wanted to make cashmere coats and raincoats for export to the United States, Europe, or Russia. They dreamed of making fashionable Italian-imported cashmere coats, but the market demand was too small in Kyrgyzstan alone. They needed good partners and access to foreign markets. In addition, they needed capital to purchase equipment. They had few business contacts abroad and government customs and tax regulations were undefined or difficult to maneuver. Sergei knew that finding honest, stable partners would be difficult. Last year he tried to establish a business partner in Russia, but in the process he spent over U.S.$900 on transportation, telephone, and fax expenses. Sergei wanted to make a marketing trip in the summer and distribute a winter clothes catalog. However, he did not have capital to produce a catalog or make the trip. Recently he bought a computer to create a web page, hoping this medium would help him reach new partners and buyers.

Crossing the borders overland to transport goods was a major problem for all trade operations. When Sergei and Olga were only involved in the import business, they were afraid to cross the borders overland carrying goods even with the correct trade documents because custom officers commonly demanded bribes. When Olga went to China, she registered her goods through a travel agency to prevent problems. One time Sergei tried to transport goods through Uzbekistan, but the goods were almost confiscated by customs officers. There were additional risks at the borders because they could suddenly close due to unexpected political disruptions and security concerns, especially in light of the violent conflicts taking place in other countries in the region.

Sergei and Olga wanted to diversify their client base and somehow capitalize on the fact that current clients had their customer bases in Russia. The challenge now was to find better ways to reach potential customers and secure the financing required to move in new directions.

Discussion Questions

1. How have Sergei and Olga's lives changes since Soviet days? Are their lives better?
2. What is Moda Textile Factory's competitive advantage? How can it be used to expand the business?

3. What kind of people should Sergei and Olga look for as business partners to help them expand their market outside Kyrgyzstan? How should they find a partner they can trust? What can they do to build trust with this person?

4. How can Sergei and Olga begin producing fashionable women's cashmere coats in their factory? Is this feasible or should they give up this dream? Propose an action plan to move their business in this direction.

CASE 9-2
Marketing Corona in Japan

It had been an interesting year, thought Export Brands International's (EBI) marketing manager as he looked out his corner window. In the late 1990s, EBI had partnered with Nippon Spirits (NS) to market Corona beer in Japan. Over the last decade it had managed to build a solid export business. However, the business environment was changing and it was time for EBI to start thinking about some potential next steps.

Grupo Modelo

Cervecería Modelo started operations in 1925 in Mexico City. Corona was one of its first beers. By the 1950s Modelo had become Mexico's top brewery. Through a series of acquisitions Modelo continued to grow, becoming a large public consortium with breweries throughout Mexico. Grupo Modelo currently has a portfolio of 12 beer brands, which in addition to Corona include Modelo, Victoria, Pacífico, Estrella, Leon, and Tropical, among others. Together, Modelo brands command 63 percent of the Mexican beer market, with Corona with the top selling beer in Mexico.

Corona Exports

Corona exports to the United States, its most significant foreign market, began in 1933. Initially sporadic, they grew in response to increasing demand for Mexican beer, associated by Americans with fun and relaxing sunny beach vacations "south of the border." By 1986, thanks to aggressive sales and marketing, Corona managed to become second among United States imports. By 1997, it had achieved the number one position, surpassing Heineken and hundreds of other international brands, including top European beers with centuries of tradition. Today, Corona continues to be by far the number one import beer in the United States. It commands roughly 28 percent of the import market, over Heineken's distant second 18 percent. A recent Facebook survey confirmed Corona's popularity; it was voted favorite beer, surpassing Heineken, Guinness, Stella Artois, and even local brew Budweiser. Corona is also the top Mexican beer sold around the world, available in over 150 countries, with a leadership position in over 20 of them. Corona is one of the top five beers worldwide, considered one of biggest success stories of the last 30 years.

Interest in Japan

Modelo had already exported Corona to Japan in the mid-1980s. However, in line with its 1990s push toward proper globalization, Modelo wanted to formally consolidate its presence in that market. There were several reasons why Modelo was interested in Japan. To start, the country had a substantial population. Its 127 million people made it the eleventh most populated country in the world. But it was the characteristics of its population that made Japan attractive: densely concentrated in a country slightly smaller than California, 66 percent urban, and 64 percent aged 15 to 64, with 35 million people in the 20 to 40 age bracket. All of this would allow for easy access, volume, and economies of scale. Furthermore, Japanese were affluent consumers with a

Case prepared by Francisco Conejo, Department of Marketing, University of Otago, Dunedin, New Zealand. Reprinted with permission.

253

high purchasing power. Like consumers from other developed economies, they looked for new and different product experiences, with a particular affinity for imports. In addition, beer was by far the most widely consumed liquor. Finally, Japanese were Asian trendsetters, meaning that strategically the market could be used as a stepping stone for subsequent incursion into other Asian markets.

Japanese Entry Options

Modelo had several options for entering Japan. The first was to set up its own local production facility. This would capitalize on the company's extensive brewing and beer marketing experience, reduce transport and importation costs, and provide nearly total control. However, it would be tremendously expensive, complicated, and time consuming, distracting Modelo from its core business and markets. To avoid these complications, a second option would be for Modelo to enter into a joint venture with a local brewer and licence Corona production and distribution. While much more practical, and substantially reducing effort, time, and costs, this option also had important drawbacks. From a strategic perspective it would mean relinquishing control, exposing Corona to suboptimal marketing, and even risk being purposely neglected or shelved by the partner to protect other interests. More importantly, just like setting up a local brewery, this option would still completely undermine Corona's foreign and genuine nature, critically important for consumers. A third option was to export directly, which would capitalize on Modelo's production experience, capabilities, and low costs, without the detrimental control issues. Coming directly from Mexico would also keep Corona genuine and exotic, a big plus with consumers. While exporting in itself was not really complicated, setting up its own Japanese sales and marketing office, with the necessary management, sales force, and fleet, would be expensive, time consuming, and cumbersome. Most importantly, being a *gaijin* meant not having the appropriate connections, requiring Modelo to set up distribution from the ground up, an extremely difficult proposition. Of the three options, exporting was by far the most viable. However, in order to reap the benefits while minimizing the costs, marketing in each country would need to be handled by the importer. Leaving this task to local specialists would not only optimize efforts, but also allow Modelo to focus on its core brewing and sales business.

Export Brands International

After careful consideration, Modelo chose to work with EBI/NS for its Japanese exports. EBI was a United States-based full-service export management company. There were several factors that made EBI a suitable partner. EBI covered all aspects of exporting in-house, from shipping and finance to sales and marketing, making it a convenient one-stop solution. But what set EBI apart from its competitors were a series of unique competencies: a specialty in food and beverage exports, making it familiar with delicate logistical and regulatory issues; long experience exporting to Japan, which meant familiarity with market's cultural nuances; an established Japanese network, critically important in a market operating largely on personal relationships; and a long-term focus on international brand building, opposed to mere short-terms sales.

Nippon Spirits

NS was a Japanese specialty liquor wholesaler. Founded in the late 1970s, NS had since grown to become Japan's second-largest independent spirits importer/distributor. It handled over 40 brands of beer and welcomed Corona as part of its portfolio diversification and growth. There were several factors that made NS an attractive partner: immediate access to an established and successful beer marketing system; solid resources to support initiatives; decades of experience; a broad network of connections; national coverage with sales offices in key cities around the country; and an impressive roster of clients, consisting of over 20,000 convenience stores, supermarkets, liquor shops, discount stores, department stores, and bars and restaurants, all ready to sell product. In addition, NS had two unique capabilities. First, it could also supply tax-free beer to United States military bases and foreign embassies, increasing Corona sales and visibility even further. Second, it owned an upscale pub franchise, whose 23 key locations could be used to promote and focus brands and educate Japanese consumers.

Corona's Japanese Target Market

Corona's target market consisted of mid- to high-income 20-to-40 year old Japanese with active and trendy lifestyles. While they sought consumption experiences, they were also value-oriented, looking for affordable or reasonably priced quality. In line with its successful American positioning and its Japanese target market, Corona was presented as an upper-end import with character. While high quality and sophisticated, it was also to be perceived as a young, fun, and accessible beer, different from other stodgy imports.

Strategy, Tactics, and Results

Corona's strategy was thus one of differentiation. This was reflected in its marketing, based on cheeky beach vacation imagery highlighting the beer's exotic and relaxed Mexican origin. The positioning also reflected the physical product. Unlike most other beers, Corona came in a transparent bottle with a long neck. While this increased spoilage due to UV exposure, and made shipping, storing, and displaying bottles more difficult, it was an important point of differentiation. Another source of distinction, and a crime to beer purists, was the suggestion of Corona being drunk with a lime slice. This association with tequila, the quintessential Mexican drink, further reinforced its exotic and exciting nature. In line with its differentiation positioning, Corona was priced at the upper end but on par with other major imports. This kept the purchase decision from being price-based, instead being led by brand image, one of Corona's strengths.

Given the intense competition within the Japanese beer market, Corona was backed by aggressive sales and marketing. Sales efforts covered both off- and on-premise retail outlets all over Japan, including Mexican restaurants and high-profile franchises such as the Hard Rock Café and TGI Friday's, among others. Advertising was regularly placed in local newspapers, magazines, and on public transport, covering a large and broad consumer base. Special promotions were organized, both at the retail and consumer levels, to stimulate interest in the product. Eye-catching point of sales materials were set up at retail outlets to spur interest even further and to stimulate trial and repurchase. NS also organized fun Mexican theme nights in its pubs to introduce patrons to Corona, sustain interest, and generate word of mouth. It also capitalized on the tens of thousands of American troops stationed in Japan, selling them a familiar and welcome piece of home. As a result of all these efforts, Corona sales in Japan started to climb.

In 2002, the Soccer World Cup was jointly held by Japan and Korea. Most importantly, the Mexican team participated. EBI/NS seized the opportunity and organized a special World Cup promotion in which consumers could win, among others, highly coveted and nearly impossible to get match tickets. The World Cup promotion was a tremendous success. Not only did it boost Corona sales, but most importantly, it positioned the brand within the big leagues. Corona sales continued to grow. By 2008, Corona sales were almost a million cases a year, on the verge of being the top imported beer in Japan, surpassing competitors such as Carlsberg, Guinness, Miller, and Coors.

Looming Changes

Corona's success in Japan was partly attributable to how clearly the Modelo/EBI/NS partnership had been structured. Essentially, Modelo produced the beer, EBI coordinated delivery and developed the Japanese marketing strategy, and NS distributed and implemented marketing tactics. However, it had been almost a decade since the partnership was formed, and it was now feeling the pressures of globalisation. That is, Modelo was now pushing to consolidate marketing communications throughout the Asia-Pacific region. This change would allow Corona to develop a more standardized brand image while reaping economies of scale. However, it also meant restructuring operations, with Modelo becoming more involved while EBI and NS lost some of their functions and autonomy.

Markets were also evolving. While in the late 1990s, United States import beer had been the rage, top-end consumers were increasingly shifting away from mass-produced beers toward higher quality, classier, and locally produced craft micro brews. The trend, albeit weaker and later than in the United States, was also being seen in Japan. The bottom end of the Japanese market, hardest hit by the current world recession, was switching back to more affordable domestic brands, particularly lower priced low- or no-malt beers. Either way, sales of import beers were slowing, with market share slowly eroded from both sides. Another important issue was how consumers now perceived Corona. According to some analysts, the brand had reached maturity in its lifecycle. Unlike in the 1980s and 1990s, when the brand was still relatively new and different, it had started to become stale, now one of several beach or vacation beers, not changing or reinventing itself with the times.

Competition had also increased. Unlike a decade earlier, when Corona was virtually the only Mexican beer in the Japanese market, it was now under direct attack by a series of other Mexican beers such as Tequiza, Sol, Tecate, and Dos Equis. Also troubling was the fact that these new rivals were quickly gaining awareness and market share thanks to healthy marketing budgets. Furthermore, while not directly a Mexican beer, Anheuser-Busch's new Bud Light Lime, which was selling extremely well in the United States, was directly attacking Corona's lime and Mexican positioning. Finally, the number of beers available in Japan from all over the world had also increased.

The corporate landscape had also changed. Large beer conglomerates, once fierce rivals, were now working together. Modelo was now 50 percent owned by United States giant Anheuser Busch, makers of Budweiser, one of Corona's main rivals in Japan. Carlsberg, another of Corona's Japanese competitors, now had the exclusive rights to import and sell Corona across Eastern Europe. However in China, Carlsberg was helping Sol against Corona. The lines between competition and cooperation had blurred. The functions and capabilities of different players had also become ambiguous. That is, Modelo was not just brewing and selling anymore, it had also become the exclusive Mexican importer and distributor of Budweiser and other AB beers. This not only changed the fundamental nature of Modelo's core business, but gave it an entire new set of core competencies, potentially transferable to other markets.

All these changes made seeing the big picture extremely difficult, making the mid- to long-term future of the Japanese Corona business quite uncertain. It was thus time for EBI to think to how to consolidate or further grow its business.

Discussion Questions

1. How aligned are Modelo's, EBI's, and NS's short and long-term interests?
2. What dangers does EBI potentially face?
3. How can EBI consolidate its Corona business?
4. What alternatives does EBI have?

Sources

Beer Marketers Insights online (www.beerinsights.com/); Beer Business Daily online (www.beernet.com/); Beverage World online (www.beverageworld.com/index .php); Bernstein, M. (2005, September). Leased railcars lower beer maker's overhead. *World Trade*, 48–52; Marketing by the neck. (2001, September). *Beverage Industry, 92*(9), 42; CIA World Factbook online (www.cia.gov/library/publications/the-world-factbook/geos/ja.html); Corona official website (www.corona.com/home/index.jsp); Crainer, S., & Dearlove, D. (2003, Winter). Windfall economics. *Business Strategy Review, 14*(4), 68–72; FIFA official website (www.fifa.com/); Grupo Modelo official website (www.gmodelo.com.mx/intro_es_4.html); Harrell, B. (30 June 2002). Beers all round! *The Japan Times*; Hoovers online (www.hoovers.com/company/Grupo_ Modelo_SAB_de_CV/htryif-1.html); Asahi says cheers to cheap beer. (24 January 2009). *Japan Today*; Malkin, E., & Melcher, R. A. (17 July 1995). Can Corona beer hang onto its crown? *Business Week, 3433*(90B); Can Sol take Mexican beer battle to Corona? (2006). *Media: Asia's Media & Marketing, 9*(8), 19; Corona calls pitch to raise Asia profile. (2008). *Media: Asia's Media & Marketing, September 4*, p. 2; Mullman, J. (24 March 2008). Corona losing its golden glow. *Advertising Age, 79*(12), p. 3; Mullman, J. (15 September 2008). Thanks to Bud, Corona has bummer of summer. *Advertising Age, 79*(34), p. 3; PC World online; Sandstrom, G. (2009). Carlsberg will market Corona in Eastern Europe for Modelo. *The Wall Street Journal* (Eastern Edition), February 25, p. B.2. Tejada, C. (8 March 2000). Corona beer emerges as key model for United States importers. *The Wall Street Journal* (Eastern Edition), 1; Trevino, L. J. (1998, May/June). Strategic responses of Mexican managers to economic reform. *Business Horizons, 41*(3), 73–80.

PART 3

The Four Ps of Global Marketing

Developing Global Products and Brands

People ask me what has driven the resurgence of the Levi's brand and my answer is always: "product, product and more product." Among all the initiatives we are pursuing to strengthen the company, creating great products is the most critical to our success.

JOHN ANDERSON, PRESIDENT AND CEO, LEVI STRAUSS & Co[1]

LEARNING OBJECTIVES

After reading this chapter, you should be able to:

- Define global products and services.
- Understand what is meant by "international product life cycle."
- Discuss the standardization versus adaptation alternative.
- Describe product features and perception in a global context.
- Discuss why many differences in product attributes are found in emerging markets.
- Explain the key approaches to branding decisions in global markets.
- Identify and discuss the main international product strategies.

Once the target markets and the international entry modes have been chosen, the company's first and most critical decisions to face are those relative to product management in foreign markets. This applies both to products and services. As a matter of fact, it is important to note that while most people think of a tangible object when they hear the word "product," services such as insurance and financial advice, or experiences such as vacations or shows, are also included in this definition.

Some of the variables that a company has to take into consideration in order to reduce the risk of failure in a foreign market are differences in product use and expected benefits; product and brand perception; and preferences in style, color, and design, just to name a few.

It is not enough to think that if a product is successful in one market, it will necessarily be as successful in other markets. A company that is introducing a product to a target country often has to wonder if it should modify it to make it more appealing to that market.

---

1. Quoted in Levi Strauss & Co. (n.d.). *Annual Financial Report 2007*. Retrieved November 8, 2010 at www.levistrauss.com/sites/default/files/librarydocument/2010/4/AR_2007.pdf, p. 6.

The German carmaker Volkswagen A.G., for example, learned too late the consequences of not analyzing in depth American preferences in terms of product. In a market that is more interested in minivans, compact sport utility vehicles, and convertibles and that best knows VW as a low- to mid-market brand, the company's "strategy of moving the brand more up-market was flawed," said one industry observer.[2] VW was forced to withdraw its luxurious and expensive new model, the Phaeton, from the United States market less than three years after first introducing it there, due to poor sales.

Costa Cruise, the Italian brand of Carnival Corporation, the world's number one cruise operator, is very successful nowadays in the American market. What is the reason for success? Design, elegance, style and . . . first of all . . . Italian food . . . seven, eight, 15 days of world-famous Italian cuisine? Well, not exactly, because one of the main reasons why American clients were not satisfied with the first editions of Costa Cruises was in fact the food, which was not in line with their expectations. Costa was serving real Italian dishes, while the American clients were used to and liked the recipes of Italian restaurants in the United States—two ways of cooking that have grown apart. The company had to take this into consideration and adapt the recipes to create a successful product and service.

On the other hand, there can also be a different approach to a foreign market. The alternative is that a company should try to change the market's view of the product. The gourmet coffee company Starbucks is certainly betting on this strategy in China. Faced with the fact that the majority of China's population drinks tea as a taste preference and centuries-old tradition, Starbucks' coffee products and culture are not things the Chinese flock to naturally. Therefore, the company has targeted the Chuppies—the young, brand- and status-conscious professional class, open to Western culture and products—and has begun introducing them to coffee and the coffeehouse culture's intricacies. From stocking its stores with educational brochures to holding frequent tasting sessions and passing out free samples, Starbucks is on a mission to change Chinese tastes from tea to coffee. Nevertheless, the company has also adapted in order to gain market share in this market with enormous potential. It has changed its stores to offer more food and seating and has altered its product offerings to include green tea cheesecake and Chinese moon cakes during the mid-autumn festival. The give-and-take approach seems to be paying off. Despite a slow start, Starbucks is continuing its expansion in China.[3]

This approach, however, is not so simple. Often it doesn't even depend on the consumer but can be influenced by other variables like competition and system structure. For example, according to Datamonitor,[4] a larger number of high-definition TV sets (HDTV) are sold in the United States compared to Europe. On first glance, this may indicate to marketers of HDTV sets that Europe presents a great untapped market. However, the market may not seem nearly as attractive when considered that, unlike the United States, where 87 percent of households are serviced by a cable operator that offers HD services, very few European cable operators offer it. In addition, because of the different TV broadcast technologies in the two markets, the improvement in the picture quality with HD programming is not nearly as noticeable in Europe as it is

2. Stoll, J. D., Rauwald, C., & Power, S. (15 November 2005). VW to withdraw luxury sedan from United States market. *The Wall Street Journal*, A8.

3. Adamy, J. (29 November 2006). Different brew: Eyeing a billion tea drinkers, Starbucks pours it on in China; Its big challenge: creating a new taste for coffee, and charging top prices; wooing the "little emperors." *The Wall Street Journal*, A1.

4. 187 million digital TV households expected across Europe and the United States by 2010. (23 August 2006). *Datamonitor*, Accessed through ProQuest:http://dbic.datamonitor.com.ucfproxy.fcla.edu/news/article/?pid=925350F2-C1F9-4000-8060-AA33F12D23F6&type=ExpertView.

in the United States. Given these factors related to the differences in the HD service system, it is clear why the demand for HDTV in Europe is not that high.

This chapter discusses product decisions in international marketing strategy. The goal is to underline the importance of the more complex variables that need to be taken into consideration before offering a product in a foreign country. We don't pretend to be comprehensive, also because every product or service has its very distinctive characteristics in relation to its classification based on the category it belongs to (industrial vs. consumer, durable vs. non-durable, convenience/preference/shopping/specialty, etc.). Furthermore, in each country, consumer characteristics and behavior can vary, the situations and the way in which they use a product change over time, and competition can be different. As a result, marketing strategies need to be reevaluated. The company may need to redefine a product that represents the key of its success in global markets.

LOOKING FOR NEW GROWTH OPPORTUNITIES: THE PRODUCT LIFE CYCLE ACROSS COUNTRIES

The course a product's sales and profits takes over its lifetime, from its introduction to its final withdrawal from the market, is described by the **product life cycle (PLC)** which is divided into five different stages (Figure 10-1).

The **research and product development stage** occurs when the company identifies and develops a new product idea, with high research and development costs. If marketing research demonstrates that the idea could be successful, the product is launched in the market.

In the **introduction phase,** sales pick up very slowly and the company may incur a loss if it does not manage to compensate for high product development costs with new sales. The potential consumers aren't aware of the product benefits yet, because it is targeted for an emerging potential need. Demand is limited and is mainly led by the country's innovative segment. The product offered is still in its early stages and marketing communication is mainly informative. In this phase, given the limited availability of information related to product benefits, the company can easily influence the consumer's cognitive system and therefore the purchase decision process.

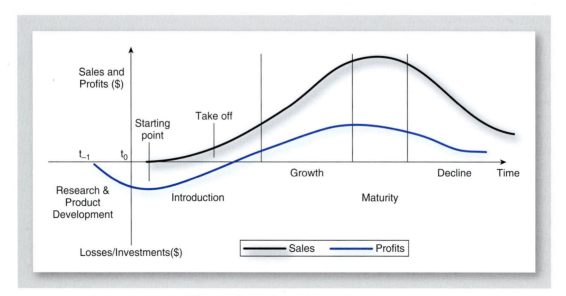

Figure 10-1 The Product Life Cycle (PLC)

The third stage is the **growth phase,** characterized by a swift increase in sales. Now it is time for the company to begin to offer a wider selection to stimulate demand for the specific brand.

The **maturity phase** is defined by a demand slowdown that settles on a steady growth rate, usually equivalent to the GDP growth rate or population growth. The product is well known, price competition is high, and marketing communication has shifted from an information to a persuasion tool, more often playing on the product's emotional characteristics.

The last stage is the **decline phase,** where a structural decrease in demand occurs and consequently a decrease in sales and profits.

The PLC can significantly vary across different countries. We can find differences in:

- The shape of the PLC curve
- The product phase in the life cycle

In relation to the shape of the PLC curve, there are three differences in the diffusion process among various countries:[5]

- The starting point
- The take-off point
- The rate at which acceptance occurs (depicted by the slope of the diffusion pattern after take-off)

As indicated in Figure 10-1, the timeframe from when a new product is introduced into the market (time 0), to the time of adoption of a specific product by "innovating" consumers (starting point), can vary in length depending on the degree of receptiveness in the target foreign market.

Also, the timeframe between the starting point and the take-off point, or rather between when the new product is adopted and then grows steadily in the market, can vary depending on the number of "innovators" in the segment or country analyzed.

Finally, the increase of the adoption rate after the **take-off point** is mainly due to the **interpersonal communication** development (**word-of-mouth**) among the members of the foreign target segment, which can vary from country to country.

Tellis et al. (2003)[6] analyzed 137 new products across 10 categories in 16 European countries. Their main results suggest that sales of most new products display a distinct take-off in various European countries and that the take-off time varies substantially not only across product categories but also across countries. For example, it is almost half as long in Scandinavian countries compared to Mediterranean ones. In a second study, Stremersch and Tellis (2004)[7] found that growth patterns across the same countries differ significantly, explained mostly by economic wealth.

Even the life cycle phase that the product goes through can be different in a given country. As pointed out in Figure 10-2, a specific product, at a certain time t_x, can be in the decline stage in the domestic market, in the maturity stage for country X and in the introduction stage for country Y. Managing the PLC across different countries can guarantee to the company the maintenance of a constant level of profits.

For example, in Western countries, disposable diapers are a commodity (maturity phase). However, it's not the same in the Chinese nursery market, where the culture is different: disposable diapers were only introduced a few years ago and even if recently

5. Parthasarathy, M., Jun S., & Mittelstaedt, R. A. (1997). Multiple diffusion and multicultural aggregate social system. *International Marketing Review, 14*(4), 233–247.

6. Tellis G. J., Stremersch S., & Yin, E. (2003, Spring). The international take-off of new products: The role of economics, culture, and country innovativeness. *Marketing Science, 22*(2), 188–208.

7. Stremersch S., & Tellis G. J. (2004). Understanding and managing international growth of new products. *International Journal of Research in Marketing, 21*, 421–438.

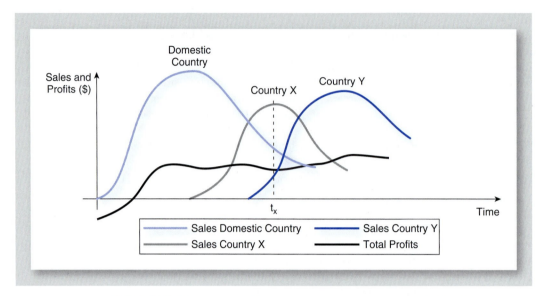

Figure 10-2 PLCs Across Different Countries for a Specific Product

Figure 10-3 A Chinese Child with *kaidangku* at the 2010 Shanghai Expo

there has been rapid growth, today many mothers still use open pants called *kaidangku* (Figure 10-3).

The PLC model can be defined from different perspectives. For example it can be related to the whole product category or to a specific brand. In all cases, in order to identify the phase occupied by a product/brand in the PLC, it is possible to analyze the market demand. The existence of wide disparities in the demand for a product or brand from one market to the next can be a good indication of the possible potential for that product in the low-saturation-level market. Ready meals (a product category) and Nivea (a brand) are two representative examples. Ready meals is a product category that was first introduced in the U.S. market and only later, as a result of life style changes (working women, singles, fast food, no time to cook), to European countries that today have high potential for these products. In 2008 the global market for ready meals reached a value of $63.8 billion, and it is set up to grow to a value of $77.2 billion by the end of 2013. While in the past the American market had the largest ready meals market, it was recently overcome by the European market. Today Europe has a market share by value of 38.7 percent, followed by Asia Pacific (31.3 percent) and the Americas (29.90 percent). From 2008 to 2013, annual revenues are expected to grow by only 3 percent in the American market and 4 percent in Europe.[8]

In the case of the Nivea brand, the biggest skin and beauty care brand worldwide, the German company Beiersdorf is focusing, in addition to Western Europe, on regions with above-average growth rates and low per capita sales, such as Asia, South America, and Eastern Europe, where Beiersdorf's substantial growth potential emerges. Target countries where sales are still limited can represent a good market opportunity. For example, in 2010 Beiersdorf recorded growth of more than 15 percent in Latin America, led by excellent performance in Deo Men's, and Sun Care.[9] Nivea provides an example of a successful brand that occupies the mature phase of the PLC in Western Europe and the introductory or growth phase in emerging markets.

The potential difference in the product or brand life cycle obviously requires differentiation in the company's marketing choices. In the case of illy coffee, a household brand for premium Italian coffee marketed in more than 140 markets worldwide, the concept of illy espresso coffee is presented differently in each country depending on the lifecycle phase the product is going through (Figure 10-4). Where the espresso and the illy

Figure 10-4 Product Life Cycle and Advertising across Different Countries

Source: Reprinted by permission from illycaffè©.

8. Global ready meals. (2009). Datamonitor. Retrieved from www.datamonitor.com; Mescam, S. (2008). Innovation and NPD in ready meals. *Business Insights Ltd.*, 51.

9. Company presentations. (4 November 2010, and September 22–23). Retrieved from www.beiersdorf.de/Investor_Relations/Kalender_Präsentationen/2010.html.

brand are in the introduction phase, it is necessary to explain and provide information on the product characteristics ("Perfection in 50 beans"). In countries like Italy, where espresso is in its maturity phase, the marketing message is not about the product but about lifestyle ("Siamo quello che beviamo" equals "We are what we drink").

It is important, however, to always evaluate when defining marketing strategies the product knowledge level that consumers have achieved. We could be talking about a product unknown to the majority of consumers, known only generically, or known to the majority of consumers but with limited commercialization, for example, because of insufficient disposable income in the country.

Various choices can be made in the growth phase and, subsequently, in the maturity phase. A global company, for example, begins by offering a differentiated product assortment addressing the various demand segments that it identifies on a transnational level, with potential adaptations to the specific characteristics of each country. The company's offer, in fact, may be made more attractive through the adaptation of some of the product's characteristics to consumers needs. In the decline stage, companies usually choose a standardized product strategy, because they cannot sustain high costs in a contracting market.

THE STANDARDIZATION VERSUS ADAPTATION DILEMMA

The choice between **standardization** and **adaptation** of marketing strategies and policies that define the positioning of the company's product or brand in international markets has always played a central role in the business literature. This choice, in fact, is often held responsible for the effectiveness and the efficiency of marketing campaigns or for the company's chances to successfully enter a market.

A simplified approach to the standardization and adaptation dilemma points out five alternatives (Vianelli, 2001):[10]

- The domestic product is exported abroad without modifications: in this case a company standardizes the domestic product to enter foreign markets.

- The domestic product is exported abroad with some adaptations.

- A global standardized product is created to target a transnational segment across different foreign markets.

- A global product is created to target a transnational segment across different foreign markets, but some adaptations are required to meet local country differences.

- A new product is created to target a foreign market.

The debate in favor of or against standardization in international markets began in the 1960s. The first studies dealt with communication strategy (Roostal, 1963; Ryans, 1969).[11] Then, with Buzzel (1968) and Bartels (1968),[12] attention shifted to marketing strategy analysis. A recent study[13] has shown that multiple factors influence the standardization–adaptation decision. The phenomenon is in fact very complex, because it

10. Vianelli, D. (2001). Il posizionamento del prodotto nei mercati internazionali., Franco Angeli, Milano.

11. Roostal, I. (1963, October). Standardization of advertising for Western Europe. *Journal of Marketing, 27,* 15–20; Ryans, J. K., Jr. (1969, March/April). Is it too soon to put a tiger in every tank? *Columbia Journal of World Business, 4*(2), 69–75.

12. Bartels, R. (1968, July). Are domestic and international markets dissimilar? *Journal of Marketing, 32,* 56–61.

13. Chung, H. (2007). International marketing standardisation strategies analysis: A cross-national investigation. *Asia Pacific Journal of Marketing and Logistics, 19*(2), 145–167.

has to simultaneously take into consideration the relationship among market, industry, and company factors.[14]

The logic behind a standardization strategy assumes the existence of a global or regional market and calls for the development of similar marketing activities across national boundaries. The adaptation school, on the other hand, suggests opting for a differentiated strategy that allows for adapting to the specific material, social, cultural, and symbolic characteristics of foreign markets and to competition. Therefore relevant cost savings using a standardization strategy often outweigh the disadvantages of not being perfectly adapted to the consumers' requirements. On the other hand, with adaptation a company can increase customer satisfaction by tailoring products to the specific needs to consumers.

Standardization and adaptation are two extremes of a continuum, inside of which it is possible to identify an infinite number of alternative options. As pointed out by Johansson (2000),[15] costs of manufacturing are high in the case of adaptation and decrease when a company moves toward full standardization. However, in the case of standardization, customer satisfaction risks being low because the company doesn't meet local needs, therefore resulting in lost sales in the foreign market (high cost of lost sales). In the case of adaptation, consumer satisfaction is high and the company can increase sales in the foreign market (low cost of lost sales): the optimal level of standardization and adaptation is found (it is not very easy in practice) when the combined costs of manufacturing and lost sales are at a minimum (Figure 10-5).

To evaluate the ideal combination of standardization and adaptation, we have to take into consideration the advantages and disadvantages of the two alternatives. A synthesis is proposed in Table 10-1.

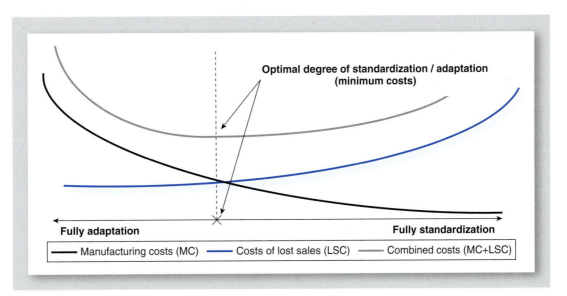

Figure 10-5 The Standardization/Adaptation Trade-Off

Source: Adapted from: Johansson, J. (2000). *Global marketing: Foreign entry, local marketing & global management* (p. 367). Reprinted by permission of The McGraw-Hill Companies.

14. Powers, T. L., & Loyca, J. J. (2007). Market, industry, and company influences on global product standardization. *International Marketing Review, 24*(6), 678–694.

15. Johansson J. K. (2000). *Global marketing: foreign entry, local marketing and global marketing* (2nd ed.) (pp. 366–367). New York: McGraw-Hill.

TABLE 10-1 Advantages and Drawbacks of Standardization and Adaptation

Variables	When standardization is favorable	When adaptation is favorable
Environmental factors	Homogeneous	Non-homogeneous
Costs	Cost reduction	
Image	Global image	Local image
Planning and control	Easier	
Innovations	Diffusion of innovation	
Motivation		Motivation of local managers
Consumers	Consumers are homogeneous	Benefits for local consumers
Legal issues and differences in technical standards	No differences	Many differences
Distribution costs, coordination, and personal client services	Low costs	High costs that can be reduced with adaptation
Competition	Global competition	Local competition
Customers	Global customers	Local customers

ENVIRONMENTAL FACTORS

Differences in the environment are perhaps the first factors that have to be taken into consideration when evaluating standardization or adaptation. As already pointed out in Chapter 2, elements such as the physical characteristics of the country, socioeconomic and demographic differences, religion, political aspects, language, and culture can significantly influence marketing decisions. South Africa's Standard Bank Group recently launched its first Islamic banking product in Tanzania, aware that half of the Tanzanians are Muslims and that most of them remain without banking services because conventional banking conflicts with their faith: in fact, earning interest is viewed as usury under Islamic law, and speculation and investments in non-Sharia-compliant industries are prohibited by Islam.[16]

Another example is represented by Nutella, the chocolate cream manufactured by the Italian company Ferrero, famous everywhere for its taste and appreciated in many countries all over the world. Also in the case of Nutella, adaptation is required. In some countries the hot climate has imposed upon the production of a cream chocolate that has to be resistant to high temperatures to avoid the alteration of ingredients. Furthermore, due to different food cultures, the taste of Nutella is not the same everywhere. For example, in Italy it's richer with nuts, while in Germany the taste of chocolate is dominant.

COST REDUCTION

The standardization of marketing activities favors cost reduction thanks to the accomplishment of economies of scale in R&D, production, marketing, and managerial and organizational processes.[17] These last factors become extremely important if evaluated in relation to the company's resources (human, financial, productive resources, etc.), income potential, and the development costs of a feasible adaptation strategy.[18]

16. Standard bank launches Islamic banking product. (2010, May 5). *AfricaTimesNews*. Retrieved on May 26, 2010 from www.africa-times-news.com/2010/05/standard-bank-launches-islamic-banking-product/.

17. See: McGrath, M. E., & Hoole R. W. (1992, May/June). Manufacturing's new economies of scale. *Harvard Business Review, 70*(3), 94–102; O'Donnell, S., & Jeong, I. (2000). Marketing standardization within global industries: An empirical study of performance implications. *International Marketing Review, 17*(1), 19–33; Özsomer, A., & Simonin, B. L. (2004, December). Marketing program standardization: A cross-country exploration. *International Journal of Research in Marketing, 21*(4), 397–419.

18. See Yorio, V. M. (1983). *Adapting products for export*. New York: The Conference Board.

Cost reduction can be determined not only by economies of scale but also by experience economies both from the point of view of the product's concept engineering and of the technical and productive efficiency obtainable from the cumulative experiences deriving from mass production.[19] Moreover, the company can exert greater contractual power both with suppliers (lower supply costs) and with customers (lower distribution costs). Lower production costs allow the company to achieve greater competitiveness in price determination than the competition in order to obtain higher margins that can be reinvested to effectively promote the product in foreign countries.

GLOBAL IMAGE

A homogenous strategy also contributes to the strengthening of the corporate image and the brand on an international level. The company communicates one message that is recognizable all over the world. Such a message not only takes its form from the product's tangible characteristics or its advertising, pricing, and distribution policies, but also in the post-sale assistance and consumer warranty policies. The creation of a global image is particularly favorable when the company's offer fits with the emergence of global customer segments. Brands like Nike, Coca-Cola, McDonald's, Lego, and Sony are only a few examples of products and brands targeted to transnational segments characterized by a high level of homogeneity.

EASIER PLANNING AND CONTROL

The development of a standardized approach can also benefit the company with greater control over the development and implementation of strategies and marketing mix policies. A company that commercializes products with a standardized positioning is definitely easier to manage in terms of organization and procedures control than a company that adapts its positioning in international markets.[20]

DIFFUSION OF INNOVATION

If standardization is applied, development costs can quickly be reabsorbed thanks to the minimal adaptations of the product's commercialization and promotion on an international level. The possibility to obtain a quick return on investment with standardization, therefore, favors the spread of product innovations. In fact, delays in the international new product roll-out due to the necessity of adaptation can have a negative impact on new product performance.[21]

MOTIVATION OF LOCAL MANAGERS

Adaptation can be advantageous for the company as an innovation stimulus. Hibbert (1990)[22] affirms that standardization often discourages creativity and innovation, especially in the management of local branches. If their role is limited to product commercialization, they end up gradually losing motivation to contribute to improving products, contracting the company's development process. On the other hand, opting for adaptation can create stronger staff commitment, thus favoring a continuous search for the solutions that can strengthen the competitive potential of the company abroad.

19. See: Hout, T., Porter, M. E., & Rudden E. (1982, September/October). How global companies win out. *Harvard Business Review,* 60. Levitt, T. (1983, May–June). The globalization of markets. *Harvard Business Review,* 92–102.

20. Hibbert, E. P. (1990). *The principles and practice of export marketing.* Portsmouth, NH: Heinemann Professional Publishing.

21. Chryssochoidis, G. M., & Wong, V. (2000). Customization of product technology and international new product success: Mediating effects of new product development and rollout timeliness. *Journal of Product Innovation Management, 17,* 268–285.

22. Hibbert, E. P. (1990). *The principles and practice of export marketing.* Portsmouth, NH: Heinemann Professional Publishing.

BENEFITS FOR LOCAL CONSUMERS

Various researchers have underlined how contextualizing marketing activities has a positive impact on the company's performance.[23] As a matter of fact, consumers often tend to refuse to purchase standardized products, preferring instead a product that values their traditions, uses, and customs. The logic of adaptation to demand is an essential requirement to increase the company's competitive potential in those countries where customers have differentiated needs.

The example of Gibson Guitar Corporation in the Japanese market highlights this critical variable that positively influences the adaptation choice for the product. The company, headquartered in Nashville, TN, is known worldwide for producing classic models in every major style of fretted instrument, including acoustic and electric guitars, mandolins, and banjos. Gibson makes a range of guitar models that are available only in Japan—its largest international market. The Tak Matsumoto's limited edition Les Paul model, for example, is sold exclusively there and is offered in special shades such as canary yellow and sunburst. The company's Japanese image conveys coolness and authenticity and inspires reverence that is not matched in its domestic market. Its fans are predominantly Japan's baby boomers, who witnessed music legends such as Jimi Hendrix, play Gibson guitars in the 1970s and are now able to indulge their nostalgia by collecting this quintessentially American and quintessentially rock-n-roll instrument.[24]

LEGAL ISSUES AND DIFFERENCES IN TECHNICAL STANDARDS

A standardized product strategy cannot be adopted when individual country requirements are different in terms of technology, standards, and approval procedures. In all these cases managers have to make a significant effort to customize the product in order to satisfy local differences.[25] In other cases, like in the telecommunications, office equipment, or consumer electronics sectors, customers do not buy a product but rather select a system. From the company's point of view, this implies an offer that consists of locally differentiated, more flexible systems. The video game industry is a good example. The three different video game systems that dominate the world today—Microsoft Xbox, Sony's Playstation, and Nintendo's Wii—require different standards for video games that can be played on their consoles. In addition, different United States, European, and Japanese video signal standards also prevent a game that plays on one brand's console in the United States from playing in the same brand's video game system sold in Germany, for example. As a consequence, video game companies are forced to design products that comply with every single type of technical requirement in each regional market.

COSTS OF DISTRIBUTION, COORDINATION AND PERSONAL CLIENTS' SERVICES

Standardization obtained with centralized production, operating on a global scale, involves production cost reduction. On the other hand, there are consistent increases in shipping costs, global demand coordination costs, and customer service costs[26] that can be overcome with adaptation and also offer localization advantages.

23. See: Anderson, C., & Zeithaml, C. P. (1984). Stage of product life cycle, business strategy and business performance. *Academy of Management Journal, 27*, 5–24; Venkatraman, N., & Prescott, J. E. (1990). Environment–strategy coalignment: An empirical test of its performance implications. *Strategic Management Journal, 11*, 1–23.

24. Kageyama, Y. (15 September 2006). The Japanese dream: Japan market warmly welcomes Gibson Guitars. *Marketing News*, 48.

25. Chryssochoidis, G. M., & Wong, V. (2000). Customization of product technology and international new product success: Mediating effects of new product development and rollout timeliness. *Journal of Product Innovation Management, 17*, 268–285.

26. See Bartlett, C. A., & Ghoshal, S. (1989). *Managing across borders: The transnational solution*. Boston, MA: Harvard Business School Press.

GLOBAL VERSUS LOCAL COMPETITION

If the company is confronted with global competition, the rules of the game tend to be similar on an international level, favoring standardization. On the other hand, if the company has to compete with very strong localized brands defending their competitive (and often only) territory, adaptation is necessary in order to meet local consumer needs. It is accomplished working closely with local intermediaries and offering personalized services. In some countries the only way to compete with local brands is to buy a local competitor's brand.

GLOBAL VERSUS LOCAL CUSTOMERS

When the company's target is based on global clientele that often have purchasing functions centralized on a global basis, standardization is necessary because consumers in every country demand products and services of similar quality. This is valid not only in relation to the product but, for example, also for pricing policies. In fact, if there are significant price differences, a global retailer can easily buy in the country where the prices are cheaper and sell in the others.

Therefore, identification of the best solution comes from careful examination of all the costs and benefits for the company. The company must focus on the goals it wants to pursue in foreign markets and on the material and non-material resources it wants to assign to the internationalization process. Nowadays we can see from experience that the optimal solution in terms of performance comes from a careful equilibrium between standardization, and adaptation.[27] This requires the centralization of some activities and decentralization of others and the coordination of marketing activities on an international level in order to:

- Replicate the solutions that have been successful in some countries by sharing information and allowing for adaptation of marketing strategies and policies if necessary.
- Integrate marketing activities developed by managers of different countries (or clusters of countries) through a company's communication network that creates transnational synergies that maximize the benefits of both standardization and adaptation models.

The impact of an adaptation strategy on organizational decisions is not insignificant. As described by Ghemavat (2007),[28] when choosing adaptation a company usually creates local units in each national market that completes all the steps in the supply chain, whereas when choosing standardization, a company tries to group the development and production processes; this aggregation attempts to deliver economies of scale by creating regional or sometimes global operations. An intermediate strategy is arbitrage, which is the exploitation of differences between national or regional markets. This is often achieved by locating separate parts of the supply chain in different strategic locations, such as call centers in India, factories in China, and retail shops in Western Europe. In all cases, the choice between the three strategies—adaptation, standardization and arbitrage—is difficult and managers have to accurately evaluate their companies' needs and market priorities.

27. See: Samiee, S., & Roth, K. (1992). The influence of global marketing standardization on performance. *Journal of Marketing, 56*, 1–17; Carpano, C., & Chrisman, J. J. (1995). Performance implications of international product strategies and the integration of marketing activities. *Journal of International Marketing, 3*(1), 9–27; O'Donnell, S., & Jeong, I. (2000). Marketing standardization within global industries: An empirical study of performance implications. *International Marketing Review, 17*(1), 19–33; Takeichi, H., & Porter, M. E. (1986). Three roles of international marketing in global strategy. In M. E. Porter (Ed.), *Competition in global industries.* Boston, MA: Harvard Business Review Press.

28. Ghemavat, P. (2007, March). Managing differences: The central challenge of global strategy. *Harvard Business Review*, 58–68.

In order to create the sought-after balance between standardization and adaptation, product decisions can only be made after the target market has been analyzed. Some fundamental questions can be raised at this point. What is the use for the product? What are the expected benefits? What are the style, design, packaging, and service preferences? Which are the best product and branding strategies and policies? What is the role of management orientation?

PRODUCT USE

Differences in **product use** can influence the company's marketing strategies and policies because they are closely tied to consumer behavior. To speak of product use in a foreign market means to consider:

- The use function
- The use situation
- The use conditions
- The product utilization level

Let's consider, for example, the product's *use function,* with the case of Vicks Vapor Rub. This cough and cold over-the-counter medicine is still used to fight mosquitoes in some countries.[29] But there is a long list of examples. In Peru, for instance, powdered milk is still used to paint house walls, since casein, the protein found in milk, makes a durable binder for pigments to adhere to porous surfaces.[30] And Whirlpool managers discovered that it is not wise to sell top-load washing machines in India because many families used them for stirring curd and making buttermilk: compared to electronic stirrers, they are cheaper and more suitable.[31]

The analysis of the *use situation* is also particularly critical because it can frequently vary according to the foreign market considered. Use situation means considering all the factors that define a "time" and a "place" that have a proven and systematic effect on the consumer's behavior.[32] More specifically, "place" can refer to the communication setting, the product purchase, or consumption. Numerous researches demonstrate that a different use situation can modify:[33]

- The importance consumers give to the product's characteristics
- The number and the type of brands taken into consideration in the purchase process
- The acceptable price threshold
- The time dedicated to information search
- The information resources used

29. Retrieved from www.ehow.com/how_5026133_use-natural-insect-repellent.html.

30. Assael, H. (1998). *Consumer behavior and marketing action*. Cincinnati, OH: South-Western College Publishing.

31. Retrieved from www.1000ventures.com/business_guide/new_product_devt_design_observing-people.html.

32. See Belk, R. (1974, May). An exploratory assessment of situational effects in buyer behaviour. *Journal of Marketing Research, 11*, 156–163; Quester, P. G., & Smart, J. (1998). The influence of consumption situation and product involvement over consumers' use of product attributes. *Journal of Consumer Marketing, 15*(3), 220–236. Differences in usage situation are numerous. As an example, Askegaard and Madsen (1998) report that internationalization in the food industry is mainly taking place at the ingredient level, but not in the usage situation. Both Italians and Danes drink cappuccino, but not in the same way. The Danes have happily adopted cappuccino and drink it at all times of the day, while in Italy, the native country of this special coffee, it is consumed only in the morning. Askegaard, S., & Madsen, T. K. (1998). The local and the global: Exploring traits of homogeneity and heterogeneity in European food cultures. *International Business Review, 7*, 549–568.

33. See: Lai, A. (1991). Consumption situation and product knowledge in the adoption of a new product. *European Journal of Marketing, 25*(10), 55–67; Bonner, P. (1983). Considerations for situational research. *Advances in Consumer Research, 10;* Chow, S., Celsi, R., & Abel, R. (1990). The effects of situational and intrinsic sources of personal relevance on brand choice decisions. *Advances in Consumer Research, 17*, 755–759.

For example, rich Chinese families often have two kitchens in their houses, one "to be shown" to friends and guests and one "for cooking": for the first one they buy luxury kitchen cabinet brands with European design, while for the second one they buy locally made and less expensive furniture.

Also, product *use conditions* often have different characteristics depending on the country. When Coca-Cola tried to introduce its two-liter bottle in Spain, it was not successful due to local storage conditions: in fact, few Spaniards have refrigerator doors large enough to accommodate the large two-liter bottle.[34] Hibbert (1990)[35] emphasizes how use conditions can even influence the product's technology, imposing modifications on a technical–functional level. Let's take the example of refrigerator manufacturers in Western countries. They had difficulty selling their products in Japan; the refrigerator motors were too noisy to be suitable for the traditional Japanese houses where the walls were thin and made of paper. It was therefore necessary to adapt technology to local requirements, modifying, at the same time, positioning criteria in order to adapt the product to that country's consumer needs.

The *utilization level* is another variable that needs to be taken into consideration in order to define the characteristics of the product and of the marketing mix. The use of a laundry dryer in Mediterranean countries, for example, is very limited in comparison with countries like the United States. This is due to various reasons other than climate. On one hand, there is the idea that it's healthier to let the laundry dry naturally outside; on the other hand, there is fear that laundry can get ruined in the dryer because of high temperatures and fast spinning (American cotton clothes are also thicker and stronger then European ones). The dryer is therefore a niche product in Europe; there are few models available at a higher price in comparison to the American standard.

PRODUCT PERCEPTION AND EXPECTED BENEFITS

The culture and environment of the consumer can greatly influence **product perception,** and consequently consumer needs and expectations. If the expected benefits change, the importance given by consumers to the product's different attributes will also vary, thus influencing the company's choices in terms of product decisions.[36]

Much research has studied product perception, its **expected benefits,** and the evaluation system of product characteristics on an international scale. These analyses are based mainly on consumer goods. According to Jain (1995),[37] industrial products typically satisfy specific needs that don't vary too much from country to country. An interesting study is one cited by Askegaard and Madsen (1998)[38] that looks at different food cultures in Europe. The identification of 12 European clusters underlines how many different product choices companies can have in the food industry depending on the European region considered.

Heineken has been successful in the United States because it was able to adapt product characteristics to the market's expected benefits. In fact, the Dutch brewer knew that it had to get the taste of its new Premium Light lager just right in order to make inroads with American consumers, who prefer pale and less flavorful beer than Heineken's traditional offerings. After 20 trial versions and a successful marketing campaign that highlighted the new, attractive bottle design of Heineken Premium

34. Bennet, A. G. (Ed.) (2010). *The big book of marketing.* New York: McGraw-Hill.

35. Hibbert, E. P. (1990). *The principles and practice of export marketing.* Portsmouth, NH: Heinemann Professional Publishing.

36. Collesei, U. (2006). *Marketing.* Padova, Italy: Cedam.

37. Jain, S. C. (1995). *International marketing management.* Boston, MA: PWS-Kent.

38. Askegaard, S., & Madsen, T. K. (1998). The local and the global: Exploring traits of homogeneity and heterogeneity in European food cultures. *International Business Review, 7,* 549–568.

Light, the company launched the new product: sales were 50 percent higher than projections. "We've been able to deliver a beer that plays in the light beer sandbox but is true to the Heineken brand," noted Andy Thomas, Heineken USA's CEO.[39]

In some instances, the company must meet the consumer's specific requirements and must develop products with highly innovative characteristics that are specifically targeted for the consumers of that country. For example, German skin and beauty care company Beiersdorf is continuing to expand the distribution in India of its Nivea For Men brand, focusing on whitening products. Inviting men to "Join the Whitening Revolution," the launch is part of a concerted effort to strengthen Nivea as the leading face care brand in the geographical area. Statistics are encouraging, revealing that men in Asia have a higher usage rate of face care products than their European counterparts. But needs are also completely different. While in the United States and Europe people buy sunless self-tanners to give a healthy image to their skin, for both Asiatic men and women, fairness of skin that is unblemished and untouched by the sun is an ideal of beauty. Many years ago sunburned skin was associated with people of a lower class who had to make their living working outdoors. That ideal for pale skin has stuck, and now even men aspire to it.[40]

On top of the expected benefits, the importance given to product characteristics can also vary, depending on the country. In research focused on behavior analysis of consumer choices and purchase of products like milk, washing machines, and deodorants, significant differences have been identified in the importance attributed to product characteristics.[41]

More often, differences in the evaluation of product characteristics depend on the way in which the product is perceived across cultures. For example, consumers consider airline services from different perspectives in different countries. In contrast with the United States, where many people take airplanes for a variety of reasons and tend to treat airline travel as a commodity, in other countries the situation is different because consumers have many alternatives. Europeans often compare airline travel to trains such as TGV in France and ICE in Germany. In Korea, people also use automobiles or trains more often than airplanes. Thus taking the plane is still considered somewhat special in those countries, which determines a different perception and evaluation of the characteristics of the product or service considered.[42]

PRODUCT ATTRIBUTES

One of the main issues defining the international product offer is to determine which **product attributes** can be standardized and which have to be adapted. Physical characteristics, color, shape, style, design, packaging, country of origin, branding, and service attributes are all elements of the total product offer which need to be examined accurately before entering a foreign market. Some of these elements—for example, color or style—can be a physical characteristic and convey a symbolic meaning at the same time.

Product attributes that have to be analyzed include the following:

- Regulations and standards
- Style and design, color, and product quality
- Packaging

39. Retrieved from www.businessweek.com/magazine/content/07_03/b4017070.htm.

40. Pitman, S. (2005). Biersdorf hails men's skin whitener a success in Asia. *Data Monitor.* Retrieved from www.cosmeticsdesign-europe.com/Products-Markets/Biersdorf-hails-men-s-skin-whitener-a-success-in-Asia; Nivea launches male whitening products in India. *Data Monitor.* Retrieved from www.datamonitor.com/industries/news/article/?pid=914A3E5F-A4FD-451F-977F-89EA1DA7A430&type=NewsWire.

41. Sriram, V., & Forman, A. M. (1993, Fall). The relative importance of products' environmental attributes: A cross-cultural comparison. *International Marketing Review, 10*(3).

42. Cunningham, L. F., Young, C. E., Lee, M., & Ulaga, W. (2006). Customer perceptions of service dimensions: Cross-cultural analysis and perspective. *International Marketing Review, 23*(2), 192–210.

BOX 10-1   COUNTRY IN FOCUS: AFRICA

When International Marketing Struggles with In-Nation Diversity: The Case of Africa and Its Passion for Sports

According to the World Bank 2010 Doing Business report, 14 of the world's 15 worst places to do business are in Africa. Despite the difficulties plaguing the region, many global companies find it interesting to penetrate these countries, adapting their marketing decisions to local needs. But what are "local needs"? The answer is not simple when one realizes that Africa is not a single place, and that not even a single African country is homogeneous for marketers.

Take the example of Nigeria. The religion, which can influence consumer behavior, is Christianity in the south and Islam in the north, while Traditional religion is transversal in the two areas. The result is that, for example, beer and other alcoholic beverages are sold everywhere in the south, but they are forbidden in the north. Another element of in-country diversity is language, which represents a vehicle of culture: with 374 ethnic languages and groups in

Nigeria alone, it becomes very complex to promote a product using the same brand, packaging, advertising, etc. In both cases, product and promotion adaptation is required, affecting marketing performance of global and multinational companies.

But there is another face of Africa, where fragmentation is overcome by their sport culture. As pointed out by Enzo Scarcella, executive manager of Vodacom, the leading telecommunication brand in South Africa and other important African markets, the people of South Africa and Bafana Bafana, the national soccer team are one, inseparable, and indivisible. In a country of cultural diversity, football is a common culture, and brands who want to speak to the African consumers as a whole can use the common language of the passion for sports.

Sources: World Bank Group. (2010). *Doing Business 2010*. Retrieved from www.doingbusiness.org/EconomyRankings/; Ekerete, P. P. (2001). The effect of culture on marketing strategies of multinational firms: A survey of selected multi-national corporations in Nigeria. *African Study Monographs, 22*(2), 93–101; Show Dem Bafana Bafana! (2010, May 27). *Vodacom press release*. Retrieved from www.vodacom.com/news_article.php?articleID=614; Manqele, S'bu. (2009, March/April). Tapping Africa's passion for sports. *Communication World*.

- Branding
- Country of origin
- Service attributes

Especially when considering emerging markets such as Africa, China, or India, the challenge for a company is to take into consideration not only differences between countries but also diversities within a specific country itself. As shown in Box 10-1, Africa, as a country, is so heterogeneous in culture and values that identifying commonalities in African culture becomes very complex for a marketer willing to introduce a product to the country: the coexistence of many different sub-cultures significantly influences the adaptation of marketing activities.

Regulations and Standards

We have already pointed out how a standardized product strategy cannot be adopted when individual country **regulations** are different in terms of technology, **standards,** and approval procedures.

The process of standards harmonization, carried out, for example, with the ISO standard (International Organization for Standardization) or on a European level with the objective of supporting the creation of a global market,[43] will reduce the need

43. The European standards bodies CEN (European Committee for Standardization), ETSI (European Committee for Electrotechnical Standardization), and CENELEC (European Telecommunications Standards Institute) are the most important organizations in terms of standards unification; they are based in Brussels, Belgium.

to modify the product characteristics depending on the country, thus facilitating the achievement of higher efficiency thanks to the economies of scale attainable in the production process.[44]

Country laws and standards for various products have always strongly influenced company policies, sometimes imposing radical modifications on the product and its marketing in general. In particular, such laws proliferated because of two specific phenomena:[45]

- The development of an environmental conscience that brought the passage of numerous laws that support environment protection
- The reduction of tariff barriers all over the world has resulted in the creation of substitutive entrance barriers in the form of laws and standards that make it difficult, if not quite impossible, for a foreign company to enter their market.

Companies that want to enter a market in a given country must fulfill specific requirements concerning quality, safety, size, ingredients composition, and detail. In some cases such requirements can act as a barrier when they are used in order to prevent or hinder international trade.[46] European Union countries are interested in international harmonization of product standards to encourage internal trade through the elimination of technical barriers, increase market access, and promote and disseminate technologies. Product changes that need to be made in order to adapt to another country's laws can in fact strongly affect product cost, therefore making it not very competitive when exported abroad.

There are still significant differences in different business sectors on an international level. For example, different countries are still using different types of broadcast TV systems. The NTSC system was originally developed in the United States by the National Television Standards Committee and is generally used in the majority of 60 Hz based countries. A modified version of NTSC is known as PAL (Phase Alternate Lines) and is mainly used by countries based on 50 Hz systems. Moreover, the French designed a system of their own, SECAM (SEquential Couleur Avec Memoire), primarily to protect their domestic manufacturing companies.

The definition of different standards is often also linked to competitive targets. An example can be the recent software joint venture, Soft At Home, between three leading French telecommunications technology groups—France Télécom, Sagem Communications, and Thomson—created with the goal of competing against Microsoft. Soft At Home is software designed to help improve communications between Internet set-top boxes, televisions, phones, and other electronic devices. Its ambition is to create the industry standard and license the software to telecom operators around the world. The company is taking aim at the Microsoft standard, which has made a big push in Internet Protocol-based television over the past two years and licensed its Mediaroom software to operators like AT&T, BT Group, Deutsche Telekom, and Bell Canada.[47]

Nevertheless, mandatory adaptations are often less frequent in comparison to physical adaptations that are required to meet differences in consumer behavior and national marketing environments.[48] As already pointed out above, the differences in local product usage, consumer preferences, needs, and so forth impose adaptations

44. Saghafi, M. M., & Sciglimpaglia, D. (1995, May 16–19). Marketing in an integrated Europe. *Proceedings of the 24th Annual Conference of the European Marketing Academy.* Cergy-Pontoise, France.

45. Czinkota, M. R., Ronkainen, I. A., & Tarrant, J. J. (1995). *The global marketing imperative.* Lincolnwood, IL: NTC Business Book.

46. Bertoli, G., & Valdani, E. (2010). *Mercati internazionali e marketing.* Milan, Italy: EGEA.

47. French telecommunication companies seek to challenge Microsoft. (2008, February 21). Retrieved from www.iht.com/articles/2008/02/20/business/ftel.php.

48. Usunier, J., & Lee, J. A. (2005). *Marketing across cultures.* Harlow, England: Prentice Hall, Pearson Education Ltd.

among countries. In the case of Levi's,[49] even if jeans are targeted worldwide at the mid-teen to mid-twenties generation, the product has to be adapted to local perceptions creating different standards. Still today in the United States and Europe, jeans denote casualness and rebelliousness. In Russia, jeans have connotations of sophistication and high status, and in Spain their high price turns them into a fashion item. But a different perception is not the only thing that can hamper a global standard. Product perceptions aside, there are also physical, environmental, and demographic factors that determine a different standard. For example, European markets prefer a standard weight denim, but hotter climates in other countries require a lighter weight and brighter colors. Moreover, people are not the same size all over the world; for example, the Far East Asian market demands much shorter inside leg measurements.

Also, the food market is far from standardized. Take for example Asian countries. Japan is one of the most innovative countries when it comes to soft drinks. Ito En, for example, is a new and successful vegetable-based drink with no added sugar or salt that contains 25 different vegetables: carrots, celery, moroheiya, broccoli, kale, tomatoes, sweet potato, red bell peppers, green beans, kidney beans, pumpkin, lettuce, green bell peppers, asparagus, Chinese cabbage, sweet potato stalk and leaf, green peas, mustard spinach, angelica, parsley, cress, cabbage, radish, spinach, and Japanese wild chervil.[50] How could it be successful in regions such as the United States and Europe, where the high vegetable content is not as appreciated as in other countries?

Similarly, in the United Arab Emirates dairy market, there is an increasing interest in camel's milk products (cheese, flavored drinks, and ice cream).[51] Camel milk is said to have an improved nutritional profile over cow's milk, but these characteristics will probably not be enough in order to market this product successfully in other countries. On the other hand, this is not an exception; the same thing happens with products that are already considered global and that are commercialized all over the world: Nestlé, for example, markets more than 200 blends of Nescafé to cater to the differences in tastes in different markets.[52] The same happens to Coca-Cola.

Style and Design, Color and Product Quality

In international marketing, product design, style, color, dimensions, and quality variations occur frequently (Vianelli, 2001).

Design often holds an essential role because it allows the creation of a link between technological and market innovation. Managers are required not only to be creative, but also to take advantage of creativity in order to meet market demands. Many products are purchased because of their unique design and style; think about Danish furniture or Italian fashion, for example.

However, design preferences can vary considerably from country to country. Research by Yamaki and Kanehisa (1995)[53] examined consumer preferences in different countries in relation to some basic characteristics that define product design. The countries analyzed were the United States, France, Korea, China, Japan, England, and Thailand. The results showed very similar tastes between Japan and Korea and

49. (2005). *Strategic Direction Journal, 21*(6), 14–15; Q, Emerald Group Publishing Limited, ISSN 0258-0543; Vrontis, D., & Vronti, P. (2004). Levi Strauss: An international marketing investigation. *Journal of Fashion Marketing and Management, 8*(4), 389–98, ISSN: 1361-2026.

50. Retrieved from www.itoen.co.jp.

51. Van de Weyer, C. (2007). Emerging food and drinks markets: Growth opportunities in Brazil, Russia, India, China and the UAE. *Business Insights Ltd.*, 102.

52. Salvatore, D. (9 November 2006). *Globalization, international competitiveness, and European regions.*
General Assembly of the Assembly of European Regions (AER), Palma de Mallorca. Retrieved from
www.aer.eu/fileadmin/user_upload/Governing Bodies/General Assembly/Events/AG2006/speeches/Dominick-Salvatore.doc.

53. Yamaki, T., & Kanehisa, T. (1995, May 16–19). International comparison of images for basic design patterns. *Proceedings of the 24th Annual Conference of the European Marketing Academy.* Cergy-Pontoise, France.

between the United States and France. Strong similarities between the United States and China have also been pointed out. Thailand turned out to be very similar to France and England in some design aspects, while for others it was closer to Japan and Korea.

Obviously, every product is a case in itself when planning its design, as illustrated in the case of Nokia (Box 10-2). The challenge for the company is how to successfully adapt a product to local needs and technology requirements while at the same time minimizing developmental costs.

BOX 10-2 TECHNOLOGY IN FOCUS: NOKIA

Nokia's Design Research Is Facing a Technology Challenge in Emerging Markets

Nokia is continually expanding its services in emerging markets such as China, Africa, Brazil, India, and Indonesia. For example, Africa's cellular market is one of the fastest growing in the world because mobile technology can be very useful to the local population. In rural Togo, information on agricultural market prices in the capital are checked in real time by local farmers. In Ghana, entrepreneurs can easily connect using Internet telephony, a technology that enables phone calls through the Internet. One of the key issues is design, which has to take into consideration local technology while satisfying specific needs and tastes.

Nokia is one of the most active companies in this emerging market. For example, Nokia Life Tools allow consumers to access to agricultural information, education, and entertainment services without the use of GPRS (General Packet Radio Service) or Internet connectivity. Nokia operates through a group of psychologists, industrial designers, materials experts, and anthropologists, analyzing local needs that can inspire innovative products for which technology and design are the key issues, and they are strongly connected.

As pointed out by Antti Kujala, a design director at Nokia's headquarters in Finland, "This means localized colors, surface textures, and user-interface content such as wallpaper, services, or ring tones."[54] For example, in rural areas, mobile phones are shared among villages or families. For these areas, Nokia designed two models, the Nokia 1200 and Nokia 1208, which have shared use as

the top priority. Since the mobile phone is used by many people, they have physical features that guarantee higher robustness, such as a seamless keypad to protect them from dust and a special grip areas to make them easier to hold in hot conditions. They have a shared address book so that each member of a family or village can save their own contacts and numbers separately from others. They also provide a call tracker that allows people to preset a time or cost limit on each call, which allows for lending the mobile phone while maintaining the control of the cost of the telephone call.

Nokia London Design Studio. Photo reprinted by permission from Nokia

Sources: Lakshman, N. (2007, August 10). Nokia's global design sense. *Business Week.* Retrieved from www.businessweek.com/innovate/content/aug2007/id20070810_686743.htm; Nokia's Design Research for Everyone. (2007, March). *Business Week.* Retrieved from www.businessweek.com/innovate/content/mar2007/id20070314_689707.htm; Africa Recovery. (2010). Africa takes on the digital divide. Retrieved May 30th 2010, www.un.org/ecosocdev/geninfo/afrec/vol17no3/173tech.htm; Nokia in 2009. Retrieved from http://phx.corporate-ir.net/External.File?item=UGFyZW50SUQ9NDE1NDZ8Q2hpbGRJRD0tMXxUeXBlPTM=&t=1.

---

54. Lakshman, N. (10 August 2007). Nokia's global design sense. *Business Week.* Retrieved from www.businessweek.com/innovate/content/aug2007/id20070810_686743.htm.

Design differences are often necessary in order to reduce the product's final price so that it becomes affordable to the final consumer. In India, motorcycle companies are redesigning bikes to sacrifice speed for mileage and sell these models at very low prices to millions of customers. As pointed out by Bharadwaj et al. (2005),[55] the design-to-cost approach can reduce the product's cost by 30 percent without any deterioration in the consumer experience. Local consumers positively accept the trade-offs between performance and price. Meanwhile the companies have the guarantee of a better cost margin.

Another very critical element is **color,** which may be interpreted differently by consumers in various countries. There are numerous examples: in the Ivory Coast, dark red is associated with death and witchcraft;[56] the color white, while in many countries a symbol of purity, in some Asian countries is the color of death and bad luck.[57] In Mexico, yellow flowers represent death or disrespect (Cateora & Graham, 1998).[58] Jacobs, Keown, Worthley, and Ghymn (1991)[59] carried out in-depth research on the meaning that consumers associate with color in different countries. They claim that the highly symbolic content of color requires careful analysis of its consistency with positioning choices. For example, in China and Korea, the color gray is associated with the idea of a low cost product; the color purple is associated with an expensive product. American consumers, on the other hand, associate opposite meanings with these two colors.

A particularly meaningful element is **quality.**[60] A product that in one country is considered to be of high quality can be considered low quality in another country that is similar in purchase behavior and consumer characteristics.[61] This has significant implications for international marketing strategy formulation, product and service development, distribution, pricing, and communications. The case of white goods sold by the Italian Merloni Group in France is a good example. In Italy, their Ariston brand was positioned in the middle-upper-level market. In France, because it was "made in Italy," it was perceived to be low quality. Therefore, Italian producers would have had to offer their product at a price from 10 to 30 percent lower than French competition; instead German-made household appliances that were perceived to be of high quality could be sold at a price at least 20 percent higher than French products. The development of a marketing plan consistent with product positioning that required a low price was the only possible strategy to succeed in the French market, but this approach could not easily be accepted by Italian managers.[62]

Quality perception becomes even more critical for services. Recent research (Malhotra et al. 2005)[63] carried out in the banking sector of three different countries—the United States, India, and Philippines—underlined systematic differences between developed and developing countries based on service quality dimensions, pointing out how a common marketing strategy for these two kinds of countries may not be appropriate.

55. Bharadwaj, V. T., Swaroop, G. M., & Vittal, I. (2005, September). Winning the Indian consumer. *The McKinsey Quarterly*, 42–51.

56. Kahler, R. (1983). *International marketing*. Mason, OH: South-Western Publishing Co.

57. Keegan, W. J., & Green, M. C. (2008). Global marketing (5th ed.) (p. 388). Upper Saddle River, NJ: Pearson International.

58. Cateora, P. R., & Graham, J. L. (1998). *International marketing*. Burr Ridge, IL: Irwin, Inc.

59. Jacobs, L., Keown, C., Worthley, R., & Ghymn, K. (1991, Fall). Cross-cultural colour comparisons: Global marketers beware! *International Marketing Review, 8*(3), 21–30.

60. Vernon-Wortzel, H., & Wortzel, L. H. (1990). *Global strategic management*. New York, NY: John Wiley & Sons.

61. Cateora, P. R., & Graham, J. L. (1998). *International marketing*. Burr Ridge, IL: Irwin.

62. Barre, C. (1983). Merloni Group. *Harvard Business School*, Case No. 9-383-152.

63. Malhotra, N. K., Ulgado, F.M., Agarwal, J., Shainesh, G., & Wu, L. (2005). Dimensions of service quality in developed and developing economies: Multi-country cross-cultural comparisons. *International Marketing Review, 22*(3), 256–278.

For example, in developing countries, quality perception depends on core service aspects; hence attributes such as savings and checking accounts should be emphasized. On the other hand, in developed countries, a bank should put more emphasis on augmented services, such as credit card services or Internet banking, that are more intangible. In Manila, the Bank of America focuses on competitive interest rates and extended banking hours, while its facilities in the United States offer Internet account access and transaction capability. Also, service delivery expectations and evaluations are very different. In developing countries, customers tend to have higher tolerance levels for ineffective services and lower quality expectations. In developed countries, service defects may lead to loss of customer patronage. Technology level, "breakthrough" service, timely response, a pursuit of continuous improvement, and a proactive effort are crucial to be able to establish reliability and responsiveness.

It is important to specify how the quality concept is strongly linked to perceived product characteristics. Therefore, marketing mix variables assume a meaningful role, and not only those tied to the product (for example, packaging, brand, or country-of-origin). The company's price and distribution policies also play prominent roles.

PACKAGING

The role of **packaging** is of primary importance to product innovation. Of all the innovative soft drinks launched worldwide between 2004 and 2007, 70.8 percent were innovative because of their formulation, while 13.2 percent were due to a packaging benefit.[64] One-quarter of the innovative confectionery products launched between 2004 and 2006 offered a packaging benefit.[65] Packaging represents a form of protection, but at the same time it is a relevant and essential marketing and communication vehicle. It determines differentiation on the supermarket shelf. Furthermore, it is able to convey a product's ethical and sustainability position.

There are four elements to packaging analysis:[66]

- Labeling
- Packaging style and design
- Packaging dimensions
- Functional characteristics

Each of these elements must be carefully analyzed in order to evaluate not only whether the packaging is in line with the norms of the foreign country, but above all whether it conveys the meaning and the company's product values to the final consumer, and whether these are in line with the company's positioning choices. In spite of the advantages obtainable with standardized packaging (for example, lower production and distribution costs), companies rarely succeed in standardizing their products' packaging on an international level.

In general, **labeling** needs to be modified according to the country in which the product is sold; the language is different, and in the great majority of cases, regulations impose specific informative and descriptive content. In some countries, the label must be bilingual, for example, in Canada, where French and English are official languages of the country; in Belgium (French and Flemish); and in Finland (Finnish

64. Horton, N. (2008). Next generation soft drinks: Innovation in natural, functional and premium beverages. *Business Insights Ltd.*

65. Lewis, H. (2007). Growth opportunities in confectionery: Emerging flavors and new added value segments. *Business Insights Ltd.*

66. Vianelli, D. (2001). Il *posizionamento del prodotto nei mercati internazionali*. Franco Angeli, Milano.

and Swedish).[67] Packaging plays an important promotional role as well. It is important therefore to consider how the package looks. The wrong choice of color, style, design, or size runs the risk of creating a distorted consumer perception of the product.

Often it is the law that regulates; for example, dimensions of cans or the use of bottles or specific containers for different types of products.[68] Other times it is the consumer that imposes significant modifications. The reasons can be connected to symbolic aspects characterizing the country's culture. In Japan, for example, some consumer products are sold in three-packs instead of the usual four-pack, because the Japanese symbol for the number four is very similar to the symbol for the word "death."[69] Or different product usage in different cultures can influence its characteristics. When analyzing the options for a global market strategy development for The Hershey Company, the largest North American manufacturer of quality chocolate and sugar confectionery products, it has been pointed out that in countries like China, where chocolate is still primarily used for gift giving, Hershey's traditional brown and silver paper packaging could not be successful. The current perception of Hershey's chocolate is in fact that of a snack. By changing the use function, the appearance should be more luxurious, refined, or sophisticated.[70]

Moreover, the cultural and historical differences that characterize some countries can strongly influence a company's choices. A manager of Brandexcel, a branding and design agency based in Athens, Greece, states that cultural differences between Western countries and emerging markets such as Romania, Bulgaria, and Russia are so profound that Western trends, in particular in the food industry, cannot work. Minimalistic, modern package design and retro or nostalgic motifs, which are so appreciated in Western economies, do not work in Eastern Europe. Instead, they want to see something realistic and something that doesn't remind them of their past.[71]

The education level of a country is also a factor that needs to be taken into consideration. In Kenya, Malaysia, and Singapore, products come in standard size; for example, bottles and cans. The aim is to be able to compare prices and avoid confusion that can come with variety.[72] A recent contribution by Hermann and Heitmann (2006)[73] also pointed out that benefits and costs associated with perceived variety seem to differ significantly across countries. While consumers in individualistic cultures appreciate choice and variety seeking, it is not the same in collectivistic cultures.

The type of distributive channels can also affect product packaging.[74] If the channel is very long and goods take a long time to transport from the producer to the distributor, packaging must guarantee a higher protection level and allow a much longer shelf life. These considerations are also valid for those countries where climatic characteristics influence the products' preservation techniques.

Finally, variations in a product's package also depend on the country's economic development level. Sometimes this influences the way a product is purchased; for example, with no packaging, single packaged, or multiple units.

67. Czinkota, M. R., Ronkainen, I. A., & Tarrant, J. J. (1995). *The global marketing imperative*. Lincolnwood, IL: NTC Business Book.

68. Onkvisit, S., & Shaw, J. J. (2004). *International marketing: Analysis and strategy* (4th ed.). London, UK: Routledge.

69. Czinkota, M. R. & Ronkainen, I. A. (2007). *International marketing*. Mason, OH: Thomson South-Western.

70. Frost, R. (2007). Hershey's chocolate dips into foreign markets. Retrieved from www.brandchannel.com/print_page. asp?ar_id=397&section=main

71. de Mesa, A. (2007). Europe: A branding dichotomy. Brandchannel.com. Retrieved from www.brandchannel.com/print_page. asp?ar_id=384&section=main.

72. Mühlbacher, H., Leihs, H., & Dahringer, L. (2006). *International marketing: A global perspective*. London: Thomson Learning.

73. Hermann, A., & Heitmann, M. (2006). Providing more or providing less? Accounting for cultural differences in consumers' preference for variety. *International Marketing Review, 23*(1), 7–24.

74. Paliwoda, S. J. (1992). *International marketing*. Portsmouth, NH: Heinemann Professional Publishing.

In all these cases, when packaging modifications incur higher costs, a company could decide to increase the product's final price. On the other hand, especially in countries where purchasing power is limited, it is more likely that the company will decide to leave its price policies unchanged, instead reducing production costs through the introduction of a much simpler product to the foreign market.

Branding

A brand identifies the manufacturer or seller of a product or service. It can be built through the development of a name, term, sign, symbol, design, or a combination of these.[75] The role of **branding** in international marketing strategy is underlined by the vast literature on the subject.[76] In general, branding is even more important when the emotional dimension prevails in the product positioning strategy.

Brand development managers have to make challenging decisions that become even more critical and complex when facing global markets. The most important decisions in an international context are the following:

- Brand strategy (global versus local brands)
- Brand positioning
- Brand selection (name and logo)

BRAND STRATEGY

Brands have acquired such an important position that they are considered an essential part of the company's intangible knowledge assets contributing added-value. In some cases, the **brand value** of a company is greater than its revenue. For example, based on Interbrand brands ranking,[77] the brand value of Coca-Cola in 2009 was $70.4 billion compared to revenue the same year of $31 billion. Microsoft's brand value was $60.9 billion compared to $60 billion revenue. While in the opposite direction, IBM's brand value was $64.7 billion, its revenue was $96 billion. Those companies that have managed to obtain a strong brand value are more prone to exploit this advantage through **global branding.** This way, in fact, they manage to defend more easily their product position in the market, keeping a high level of perceived quality that is guaranteed by the brand on a global level while at the same time enhancing the company's financial performance abroad.[78] This is also possible thanks to the standardization of other marketing activities, particularly communication, that are feasible because of the brand's uniqueness. Companies like IBM whose brand value is much lower than revenue must invest more in activities that will enhance their brand image.

On the other hand, we can identify other motivations that could induce a company to develop different **local brands** in the countries or geographic areas where it markets its product. Adapting products to target segment needs, homogeneous branding policies could constitute a serious limitation, especially if competition in the foreign country is local and therefore has better knowledge of its consumers and adapts better to their needs. If this is the case, it is preferable for the company that wants to

75. Kotler, P., Wong, V., Saunders, J., & Armstrong, G. (2005). *Principles of marketing* (4th European ed.). Harlow, England: Pearson.

76. Whitelock, J., & Fastoso, F. (2007). Understanding international branding: Defining the domain and reviewing the literature. *International Marketing Review, 24*(3), 252–270.

77. Best Global Brands 2010. (2010). *Interbrand*. Retrieved from www.interbrand.com/en/best-global-brands/best-global-brands-2008/best-global-brands-2010.aspx.

78. Wong, H. Y., & Merrilees, B. (2007). Multiple roles for branding in international marketing. *International Marketing Review, 24*(4), 384–408.

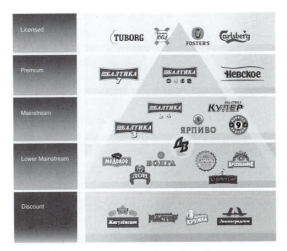

Figure 10-6 The Carlsberg Group: Russian Brand Portfolio

Source: www.carlsberg.com. Reprinted by permission from Carlsberg.

penetrate the market on an international level to operate with local brands instead of a single global brand.[79]

The choice of a local brand, moreover, introduces other advantages. In the first place, it eliminates the risk of acquiring negative connotations. Potential mistakes made in a country could in fact have repercussions in the other countries in which the enterprise operates with the same brand.

Finally, it can be difficult for a company to guarantee uniform product quality on an international level, especially if it is not centralized. In this case, local brands should be considered. Otherwise the risk is that consumers will perceive the products as totally differentiated and, therefore, non-comparable.

In conclusion, the utilization of multiple local brands promotes the development of customized marketing that creates a strong appeal in individual markets. On the other hand, adoption of a single global brand allows for a standardization strategy. In practice, market leadership is obtained through the development of a portfolio of products characterized by both global and local brands that allow the maximization of market share in every target segment. The case of the Carlsberg group in Russia is a representative example (Figure 10-6).

As in every national context, there are different sponsors behind this high number of brands. Options that can be identified include the following:

- Manufacturer's own brand: it occurs when a brand is owned by a producer of a product or service. Dove, San Pellegrino, and Armani are some examples.

- Private brand: the brand owner is the retailer. H&M, Carrefour, Zara, Amazon.com, and Toys 'R' Us are all examples of retail brands. From the manufacturer's perspective, in many countries it is possible to export a product through modern distribution producing only for a local or global retailer.

- Co-branding or ingredient branding: the established brand names of two different companies are used on the same product. It becomes ingredient branding when one of the two brands is an ingredient or component of the final product. A recent example of co-branding is Martini Gold, the alcoholic drink developed by Martini

79. Onkvisit, S., & Shaw, J. J. (1989). The international dimension of branding: Strategic considerations and decisions. *International Marketing Review, 6*(3), 22–34.

and Dolce & Gabbana. On the other side, the Dell computer with an "Intel core" is an example of ingredient branding, because the Intel processor is a component of the laptop.

- Licensed brand: it occurs when a company uses a brand name offered by the brand owner for an agreed fee or royalty. An example is the brand Benetton, licensed to the Allison Group until 2013 for the production and worldwide distribution of eyewear.

GLOBAL BRAND POSITIONING

It is not easy to define how a company can create value through global **brand positioning.** Interbrand (2006)[80] suggests six guidelines that can be critical for the success of global brand: recognition, consistency, emotion, uniqueness, adaptability, and management.

Recognition is typical of leading brands and is based on a strong awareness that enables rapid penetration into new markets. An example is the BMW car, which is the symbol of "performance" in engineering and design and identifies the owner as a "high in career" person.

Consistency is reached when a brand is able to deliver a consistent customer experience worldwide, creating a visual, verbal, auditory, and tactile identity across borders, often due to a global marketing investment. McDonald's is an example. Not only does it have a global message, but at the same time it appropriately modifies its approaches in store appearance and the menu to satisfy local consumers.

The *emotional* dimension is strongly connected with human values and aspirations, and must have a common appeal despite cultural differences. An example is Nike, which was able to target the mass market worldwide around the passion for different sports.

Great global brands need to express their *uniqueness* not only through product features, but also through communication. Apple has created its brand uniqueness worldwide around the concept of innovation, becoming the symbol of technology solutions that can be used in everyday life.

Adaptability is reached when a global brand demonstrates that it is able to respect local needs, desires, and tastes, communicating a "global" advantage. An example is the HSBC Group, the "world's local brand," which pursues local adaptation while fulfilling a global mission.

Finally, global brand success is not possible without *management* commitment, which is always involved in ensuring that the corporate culture will put the brand at the center of every activity.

Brand positioning is hard to implement also because of the markets' progressive fragmentation. This has become a critical factor, especially for companies that operate on a transnational level, because they face the necessity of identifying significant horizontal segments at a regional or global level. Companies can offer their product in a standardized way, but at the same time have to keep in mind the symbolic differences associated with the product by consumers of the different countries. This is why the brand is important, because it reflects the uniqueness of the product image and therefore allows coordination of the company's positioning choices in the identified transnational segments, respecting at the same time the differences from country to country in relation to the product, distribution, and communication. These differences, if sometimes minimal, play a determinant role in local consumer choice processes, and

80. Lessons learned from global brands. (4 July 2008). *Interbrand.* Retrieved from www.brandchannel.com/papers_review. asp?sp_id=1260.

at the same time constitute an element of differentiation from local competition. The example of the Ritu Kumar Designer Wear brand—a leading Indian designer brand which sells in markets like the United States, the UK, and the Middle East, highlights a transnational segment that managed to develop unique product positioning even as it had to take into consideration the differences between the various countries when implementing the marketing mix (see Box 10-3).

Finally, a global brand's positive and strong image can allow companies not only to achieve the goals mentioned above, but also to overcome potential negative attitudes toward a foreign product, or, on the other hand, to highlight the positive elements of the country to which the product is associated. We will elaborate on this "in the country of origin" section later on.

BOX 10-3   COMPANY IN FOCUS: RITU KUMAR: AN EXAMPLE OF BRAND POSITIONING

The Company and the Brand

Ritu Kumar Designer Wear is a leading Indian designer brand that merges contemporary Indian creativity with traditional local roots and identity. The company began its activity 40 years ago in a small village near Calcutta. Ritu, the founder, became the first woman to introduce "boutique" culture in India. Today she has outlets all over the country and sells internationally in markets in the United States, the UK, and the Middle East, representing a sign of India's reach in the world of fashion.

Brand Positioning Vision Statement

Vision—to be the leading Indian designer brand for the modern, upscale, urban woman aged 30+.

Strategy—to offer a range of clothing and accessories to meet her every wardrobe and lifestyle need.
  Target Audience:

- Upscale, urban women, aged 30+
- Women who want designer wear for everyday and for occasions, in order to make a style statement
- Women who want to be fashionable and glamorous yet elegant and chic
- Women who like the "ethnic Indian look" and particularly appreciate the finer nuances of traditional Indian craftsmanship

Brand Proposition

Benefits/Reasons to Want: Ritu Kumar Designer Wear makes an authentic Indian style statement like no other brand can, so that you are set apart and stand out from the crowd.
  Reasons to Believe:

- As a designer, Ritu Kumar has unparalleled knowledge and expertise in the history and heritage of Indian textiles and craftsmanship.
- She has invested in training and reviving the skills of hundreds of craftsmen across the country.
- She is the designer of choice for India's contestants at the Miss World and Miss Universe pageants, creating personalized lines for them.
- Hers was the first (the original) designer boutique in the Indian market.

Values & Personality

Values—Ritu Kumar believes in authenticity, superior quality, being world class, in Indian heritage.

Personality—She embodies timeless elegance, style, and a meticulous perfectionism.

Sources: www.ritukumar.com; Shivkumar, H. (2006, January). Managing global brand advertising. *AdMap,* 42. Reprinted with permission. www.warc .com/admap.

A brand's image plays a fundamental role not only for products that have a strong emotional dimension, but also in the opposite case, for high-technology products. In these cases, the consumer overcomes difficulties connected with the inability to adequately evaluate complex product characteristics and trusts only the brand. In fact, the brand can convey the perception of functional and performance characteristics that for high-technology products can constitute a beneficial competitive element against competition. The case of Toyota is an example of this. Thanks to one of its latest models, the Prius, Toyota managed to strengthen its brand image, extending the perception of a manufacturer of environmental-friendly and fuel-efficient vehicles to all its models.[81]

BRAND NAME AND LOGO SELECTION

The **brand name** and **logo** are an integral part of the company's product. Their relevance is significant because they are part of the communication strategy created for target clientele. Therefore they cannot be randomly chosen, as often happened in the past; instead, the choice has to be carefully evaluated in order to avoid mistakes, either symbolic or legal, that sometimes can be irreparable.[82] The importance of the brand name is demonstrated, for example, by the recent choice made by Apple on a global level; faced with the global success of its non-computer products, such as the iPod, Apple Computers recently changed its name simply to "Apple" to better reflect its transformation as a "media-interpretive-device company."[83]

The main questions a company needs to answer when defining its brand and logo for selling abroad are:

- Can we use the same brand name in all our potential foreign markets?
- Can we standardize our logo on an international level?

There are various choices that can be made in reference to the brand name and logo.[84] One possibility is entering the market with the original brand name. For imported products with a strong image, this strategy can be successful. Consider, for example, luxury brands and fashion labels in India. Luxury brands already established in India include Hugo Boss, Chanel, Louis Vuitton, Versace, Salvatore Ferragamo, Bulgari, Christian Dior, Cartier, Piaget, Tiffany, Moschino, Tag Heuer, and Dolce & Gabbana. Also, fashion labels such as French Connection (FCUK), La Perla, Tommy Hilfiger, and Calvin Klein (CK) have marked their Indian presence.[85] All of these brand names, even if sometimes pronounced differently, are kept homogeneous because they represent status symbols on an international level.

Another possibility is to use a completely different brand name. This strategy is often used by multinationals that entered a foreign market by acquiring local brands. These companies, in order to standardize their brand image in the various countries,

81. Kiley, D. (29 January 2007). How the hybrid race went to the swift. *Business Week*, 58.

82. There are numerous examples of mistakes in the translation of brand names or simply of their application in a foreign market. Ricks (1983) provides a vast review in Ricks, D. A. (1983). *Big business blunders: Mistakes in multinational marketing.*, Homewood, IL: Dow Jones-Irwin. To analyze more in-depth the legal implications, see Onkvisit, S., & Shaw, J. J. (1987, Fall). Standardized international advertising: A review and critical evaluation of the theoretical and empirical evidence. *Columbia Journal of World Business, 22,* 43–55.

83. Fujii, R. (2007). Steve Jobs introduces iPhone, TV at weeklong Macworld. *Knight Ridder Tribune Business News*. Retrieved from Proquest on September 16, 2008.

84. See: Mühlbacher, H., Leihs, H., & Dahringer, L. (2006). *International marketing: A global perspective*. London: Thomson Learning; Hong, F. C., Pecotich, A., & Schultz, C. J. (2002). Brand name translation: Language constraints, product attributes, and consumer perceptions in East and Southeast Asia. *Journal of International Marketing, 10*(2), 29.

85. Srivastava, S. (25 September 2007). Indians in the lap of luxury. *Asia Times Online*; The underwear market in India. (2010). Retrieved from www.export.by/en/?act=s_docs&mode=view&id=6706&type=by_country&country_id=48&mode2=archive&doc=64.

TABLE 10-2   Heartbrand Ice Creams in Unilever: A Unique Logo for Different Brand Names

Brand name	Country
Algida	Serbia, Greece, Italy, Poland, Slovak Republic, Turkey, Hungary, Czech Republic, Romania
Bresler	Chile, Bolivia
Eskimo	Croatia, Austria, Slovenia
Frigo	Spain
Frisko	Denmark
GB Glace	Finland, Sweden
Good Humor	United States
Holanda	Mexico
Kibon	Brazil
Kwality Wall's	India, China
Langnese	Germany
Lusso	Switzerland
Miko	France
Ola	Belgium, South Africa, Netherlands
Olá	Portugal
Pingüino	Ecuador, Colombia
Selecta	Philippines
Streets	Australia, New Zealand
Tio Rico	Venezuela
Walls	Ireland, UK

Source: Author's elaboration based on Unilever country sites.

often link different brand names with a homogeneous logo that makes it possible to recognize the product on a global level. The Unilever ice cream brand has different names but they are all united by the famous hearth shaped logo (see Table 10-2).

The Coca-Cola case represents a brand example that has been phonetically translated in various local languages. In different countries, Coca-Cola appears as Coca-Cola, Coke, 可口可乐 and other translations, but it is always recognizable as the Coca-Cola brand. The translation, on the other hand, is not always necessary. In Italy, foreign brands like Nike, Levis, Adidas, or Colgate, to name a few, are pronounced differently, but this doesn't have a negative impact on the product image; therefore changing the brand name would be completely useless.

In other instances, when the brand name has a different meaning, translation can become necessary in order to relay a homogeneous meaning to the final consumer. Think about Danone low-calorie products: Vitalinea, Vitasnella, Taillefine, and Silhouette are all translations of the brand name conveying the same meaning for the same product.

In most cases, even if the brand name is different, the logo offers a chance for standardization.[86] Research has demonstrated how different national cultures react similarly to logo designs.[87] Moreover, as underlined by Henderson et al. (2003),[88] the logo

86. Kapferer, J. (1992). *Strategic brand management: New approaches to creating and evaluating brand equity.* London: Kogan Page.

87. Pittard, N., Ewing, M., & Jevons, C. (2007). Aesthetic theory and logo design: Examining consumer response to proportion across cultures. *International Marketing Review, 24*(4), 457–473.

88. Henderson, P. W., Coteb, J. A., Leongc, S. M., & Schmitt, B. (2003). Building strong brands in Asia: Selecting the visual components of image to maximize brand strength. *International Journal of Research in Marketing, 20*, 297–313.

is always highly recognizable and therefore offers interesting benefits to the companies, especially those whose names are not understood because of language differences. Pictures are recognized faster than words, and even the briefest exposures can result in some message being received. Memorization can be high for a brand name even if pictures do not interact with the accompanying word; any picture can create an association with a target word. Volkswagen has pushed a global naming strategy for decades, and at times has come up with controversial names as a result. There was the Bora, which is also a strong wind that blows north by northeast across the Adriatic Sea. After complaints from dealers that the name Bora sounded like "boring," VW eventually renamed the car the Jetta (as in Jet Stream) in the United States. For the updated Fiesta, Ford executives were not all of one mind: some of the people interviewed in focus groups said "Fiesta" sounded cheap. A few executives preferred the name the car was given for the auto shows: Verve. CEO Alan R. Mulally and James D. Farley, the head of marketing, had the last word. They heard the dissent, but still decided Fiesta made sense. "It's crazy to walk away from the enormous equity in our names," said Mulally.[89]

COUNTRY OF ORIGIN

Country of origin, or **made-in effect,** represents the extension of the perception of a specific country to its products or brands, because consumers react differently depending on the country where the product has been manufactured. In general, the attitude toward the made-in label is linked to the perception of the representative products for that country and to its historical, socioeconomic, political, and cultural characteristics. In other instances, instead, attitudes are linked more specifically to the general perception on the quality of the products manufactured in that country.

Since the 1970s, numerous studies have investigated the effect that perception of the made-in country has on the consumer evaluation process.[90] Reierson (1966)[91] had already demonstrated how American consumers perceived products in a different way depending on their country of origin. He later pointed out that such perceptions, if not strongly rooted in the consumer's memory, could be influenced and therefore modified with an appropriate communication campaign.[92] This is what most countries have been trying and are still trying to do, both to overcome negative perceptions that can undermine their products, and therefore their economy, and to reinforce an image that is sometimes indefinite. They deliberately work on changing a negative image into a positive, or, at least a neutral one. This strategy is far from easy to implement. Research results suggest that country-of-origin images are significantly predicted by human values, which are factors beyond a company's control and cannot be easily changed.[93] Taiwan-based Acer Group, starting as a behind-the-scenes original equipment manufacturer (OEM), has been able to build a brand that stands for quality and globalization. However, Acer hasn't been able to establish itself successfully in the United States and Japanese consumer markets—the two largest PC markets. After some initial successes, it has abandoned these highly competitive markets and repositioned itself as a high-quality OEM supplier in those

89. Kiley, D. (24 March 2008). One world, one care, one name. *Business Week,* http://www.businessweek.com/magazine/content/08_12/b4076063825013.htm.

90. Chattalas, M., Kramer, T., Takada, H. (2008). The impact of national stereotypes on the country of origin effect: A conceptual framework. *International Marketing Review, 25*(1), 54–74.

91. Reierson, C. (1966, Fall). Are foreign products seen as national stereotypes? *Journal of Retailing, 42,* 33–40.

92. Reierson, C. (1967, November). Attitude changes toward foreign products. *Journal of Marketing Research, 4,* 385–387.

93. Balabanis, G., Mueller, R., & Melewar, T. C. (2002). The human values lenses of country of origin images. *International Marketing Review, 19*(6), 582–610.

countries. Its entry into China, the market it attempted to penetrate next, has been more successful, although it risked being a failure from the beginning because of the rising national animosity during the heated political dispute between Taiwan and China in 2000. Stan Shih, Acer's founder, strongly believes that the main reason for the company's difficulties in establishing its own identity has been "The stereotype of 'Made in Taiwan' ".[94]

An important aspect of country-of-origin analysis is the ethnocentrism phenomenon—the perception that locally made products are more valuable then imported products. Ethnocentrism has been confirmed by many researchers, and its analysis will become more relevant and complex in view of the evolution of ethnic composition of nation states.[95] Suh and Kwon (2002),[96] for example, have claimed that consumer ethnocentrism influences consumers' negative preference for foreign products, hence demonstrating that consumers can be reluctant to buy even if they have been exposed to the massive globalization phenomena. These results didn't always match, because the conclusions drawn have very often been strongly influenced by the type of product considered, by the characteristics of the analyzed country, by the interaction with other variables of the marketing strategy, by the analysis methodology employed, etc.[97]

If it is important to recognize the high generalization risks, it is also important to highlight how the made-in effect, positive or negative, can exist and that it needs to be evaluated by the company every single time it plans to penetrate a foreign market.

The product nationality perception can be influenced by the following elements (Usunier & Lee, 2005, pp. 286–287):[98]

- The national product's image versus imported or international products
- Generic products perceived country of origin: yogurt is associated with the Balkans, perfume evokes France, jeans the United States, pasta is linked with Italy, etc.
- The manufacturing company's national image
- The image diffused by the brand name
- The label's "made in" image, indicating the manufacturing origin, mandatory in international trade

All of these dimensions of the made-in concept define the product image, and the company has to build the marketing mix around it. This is not an easy task. Very often, in a globalization context, we find hybrid products, which are products with more than one country of origin.

In some cases, the company must be able to define the best marketing decisions that will allow compensating for a negative made-in image. The previously mentioned case of Acer demonstrates how this is a very complex process that doesn't always bring the desired results. In the majority of cases, products manufactured in a foreign country have perceived risk, especially if the company's image is not globally

94. Amine, L. S., Chao, M. C. H., & Arnold, M. J. (2005). Executive insights: Exploring the practical effects of country of origin, animosity, and price-quality issues: Two case studies of Taiwan and Acer in China. *Journal of International Marketing, 13*(2), 114–150.

95. Vida, I., Dmitrović, T., & Obadia, C. (2008). The role of ethnic affiliation in consumer ethnocentrism. *European Journal of Marketing, 42*(3/4), 327–343.

96. Suh, T., & Kwon, I. G. (2002). Globalization and reluctant buyers. *International Marketing Review, 19*(6), 663–680.

97. See: Thorelli, H. B., Lim, J. S., & Ye, J. (1989). Relative importance of country-of-origin, warranty and retail store image on product evaluations. *International Marketing Review, 6*(1), 35–46; Al-Sulaiti, K. I., & Baker, M. J. (1998). Country of origin effects: A literature review. *Marketing Intelligence & Planning, 16,* 150–199.

98. Usunier, J., & Lee, J. A. (2005). *Marketing across cultures.* Harlow, England: Prentice Hall, Pearson Education Ltd.

established. The ideal tools to have in order to be able to win over consumer reticence about a foreign product and to strengthen the brand image include:

- The company's products are guaranteed by independent manufacturers
- The company's products have been examined by external labs tests[99]
- The company offers warranties on the products[100]
- The company partners with prestigious distributors

The positioning needs to be able to underline these aspects about the product in order to neutralize negative perceptions. This usually implies the development of different choices from the ones adopted in the country of origin.

For example, a potential negative country-of-origin effect can be reduced or nullified if there is a shift of the consumer attention from the manufacturer to the distributor. For this reason, when a company makes an agreement with a foreign distributor, it has to be chosen carefully, because the point of sale is one of the factors that greatly influences the consumer choice, especially for specific types of products.

In other instances, the company can catch the competitive advantage of a positive country image. For Louis Vuitton (LVMH), it has been a winning move to enter foreign markets as a French company in the fashion and luxury industry.

But let's take, for example, the Barilla company. Who should have been able to sell pasta in a foreign market better than an Italian company? Well, the internationalization of the premium segment hasn't been so obvious and easy, and the reason, surprisingly, is the perception of "made in Italy" that came with the product (see Box 10-4).

Service Attributes

Service attributes can be of significant importance for the evaluation of product quality. Services include installation, after-sales services, warranties, repair and maintenance, spare parts, returns, instruction manuals, and so forth. Product image can be seriously damaged if a proper after-sale service is not guaranteed.[101] This consideration can be valid not only in relation to the company's image and the product image in the eyes of the final consumer (*business to consumer*) but also for companies that work in the *business to business* segment.

In business to consumer marketing, the guarantee of an after-sale service can be essential not only if the product ends up being faulty after it is bought, but also before the sale in order to reduce potential customer reticence toward a foreign product, especially when the product evaluation is difficult, incomplete, or if there is a negative made-in image. This phenomenon, pointed out by numerous studies on the subject,[102] persists even in the context of growing globalization. Tan and Leong (1999),[103] for example, described how the purchase-perceived risk of a product, if influenced by a negative made-in country image, can be partially reduced thanks to the warranty quality and the reputation of the companies that offer the assistance service. Similarly,

99. Bilkey, W. J., & Nes, E. (1982, Spring/Summer). Country-of-origin effects on product evaluations. *Journal of International Business Studies, 13*(1), 89–99.

100. Schooler, R. D., Wildt, A. R., & Jones, J. M. (1987, Fall/Winter). Strategy development for manufactured products of third world countries to developed countries. *Journal of Global Marketing, 1*(1/2), 53–68.

101. Czinkota, M. R., & Ronkainen, I. A. (1993). *International marketing.* Chicago: Dryden Press; Terpstra, V., & Sarathy, R. (1999). *International marketing.* Chicago: Dryden Press.

102. Numerous authors pointed out the importance of warranty and post-sale service as a client reassurance tool. Ahmed and d'Astous (1995) have noticed, for example, that in the case of household appliances, the warranty can be even more important then the brand and the country of origin. Ahmed, S. A., & d'Astous, A. (1995). Comparison of country of origin effects on household and organizational buyers' product perceptions. *European Journal of Marketing, 29*(3), 35–51.

103. Tan, S., & Leong, W. (1999). Warranty strategy: A solution to hybrid product woes? *International Marketing Review, 16*(1).

BOX 10-4   COMPANY IN FOCUS: PASTA BARILLA

When we think about pasta, it's natural to think that Italian pasta would "sell itself." "Made in Italy" has always been a winning strategy. But when Barilla, the world's number one pasta, started going international in the 1970s, it soon realized that the concept had already been used by other companies in other countries where pasta, although an Italian specialty, was loved and eaten in big quantities. Panzani in Marseilles had already launched his pasta in France, letting people believe he was Italian. Panzani became a leader in the market using communication that mixed Don Camillo, an Italian-French character, with the smile and good appetite of Fernandel. In Spain, the leading pasta brand was Gallo, an Italian name again, perceived as Italian, and on top of that, the word "Gallo" means rooster in both languages, and the rooster in Spain is a symbol of national pride. In Germany, the market leader was Birkel, a German company that consumers appreciated for product quality.

Therefore, in this context, can we believe that the use of the "made in Italy" label alone to represent the high quality of Barilla could be enough to be successful in the global food industry? Can the consolidated image of Italian cuisine in Europe with macaroni, bread, pasta, chefs with long mustaches, moms with big smiles, and the background of the Naples bay, match with the high positioning at which Barilla was entering the market?

No, it wasn't possible. If Barilla wanted to be perceived as a premium product, it had to match the perception of its pasta with a different "made in Italy" association. The marketing choice was to link the Barilla brand with the "made in Italy" of the luxury, fashion, and jewelry industries. Presenting Pasta Barilla as a "collection of jewels" proved to be successful, underlying once again how product management in a foreign market always needs to come to terms with different cultures and multifaceted and complex competitive contexts.

Source: Adapted with permission from Gonizzi, G. (2003). 125 anni di pubblicità e comunicazione.

Germany:

"Das ist Fusilli, ein Stück aus meiner Lieblingskollektion"

France:

"La collection préférée des italiens"

Photos reprinted by permission from Archivio Storico Barilla—Parma, Italia.

findings from a study by Tan et al. (2001)[104] show that a more reputable warrantor resulted in more favorable consumer product assessment for hybrid products resulting in lower consumer perceived risk. It is not a coincidence that *market follower*

104. Tan, S. J., Lee, K. S., & Lim, G. H. (2001). Warranty and warrantor reputations as signals of hybrid product quality. *European Journal of Marketing, 35*(1/2); 110–132.

companies, whose image hasn't yet been established on a global level, tend to offer better warranties and the best post-sale service.[105]

On the other hand, warranty extension is not always possible. Some countries lack a consumer culture, and customers do not behave as a company would have expected. As pointed out by Mahajan et al. (2000),[106] examples of this are attempts made by companies like Domino's Pizza and Amway, which offered the same services they provide in the United States to other countries. In one Latin American country, Domino's Pizza customers took advantage of its 30-minute delivery guarantee in order to receive a free pizza by ordering from complex and confusing addresses which slowed down the driver. Also, the money-back guarantee offered by Amway Worldwide didn't work well in China. The company told customers that if they were not satisfied, they could return the product back for a full refund, no questions asked, even if the bottles were already empty. Soon after, the company realized that refunds amounted to $100,000 per day and had to rescind the policy.

If a company operates in the business to business sector, the evaluation of services offered to customers is more complex and needs to be considered together with the level of standardization and the type of warranties offered in the country of origin and abroad.

The manufacturer itself doesn't have specific advantages in offering a standardized service. But client companies are the ones hoping for standardized post-sale assistance and a warranty policy on an international level. This can be due to multiple factors.[107] First of all, any difference needs to be justified (for example, for climatic or political reasons or, in general, for different use conditions). Otherwise, the company's different branches would end up using the same product but would benefit from different types of warranties and post-sale services depending on the branch location. Second, if the product is purchased by a subsidiary in a country and then moved to another subsidiary abroad, as often happens, the lack of a homogeneous warranty would make the product assistance service confusing and difficult. Finally, standardization is usually mandatory for products that can be hazardous to human life. For example, products like lifts, airplanes, and medicine. For these types of products, a diversified warranty would run the risk of undermining the company's reputation and reliability (Vianelli, 2001).

Nevertheless it is important to note, especially for the business to consumer market, that post-sale service is not relevant in all countries. In some countries, the concept of ordinary and extraordinary maintenance is totally unknown, or there is lack of personnel available to offer the service. Services, in some cases, used to play a significant role as an entrance barrier for some products. Bartlett and Ghoshal (1989)[108] pointed out that often, a sector's globalization can be facilitated by the progressive decrease of the need and the importance of local assistance. Therefore, there must be a minimal risk of faulty items for the commercialized products so that maintenance becomes minimal and secondary (Cateora and Graham, 1998).[109] Nowadays, especially in the electronics industry, for example, the use of new components and manufacturing processes allows the companies to improve product reliability and reduce the need for post-sale service and therefore the need for specialized labor.

105. Vianelli, D. (2001). *Il posizionamento del prodotto nei mercati internazionali*. Franco Angeli, Milano.

106. Mahajan, V., Pratini De Moraes, M. V., & Wind, J. (2000, Winter). The invisible global market. *Marketing Management*, 30–35.

107. Terpstra, V., & Sarathy, R. (1999). *International Marketing*. Chicago, IL: Dryden Press.

108. Bartlett, C. A., & Ghoshal, S. (1989). *Managing across borders: the transnational solution*. Boston, MA: Harvard Business School Press.

109. Cateora, P. R., & Graham, J. L. (1998). *International marketing*. Burr Ridge, IL: Irwin.

PRODUCT STRATEGIES IN INTERNATIONAL MARKETS

Potential differences in consumer characteristics and competition in company strategies determine whether a company can replicate its marketing strategy on an international level or must opt for adaptation. Sometimes the company can disregard these choices when it launches a new product that is created from the start for a global target. The advantages and disadvantages of these choices have already been considered above. From a strategic point of view, even if it is true that the adaptation/standardization issue concerns all of the marketing mix variables, it is important to underline how the most critical decisions are those relative to the product and its communication. As pointed out by Keegan (1969) and Keegan and Green (2008),[110] the company is faced with five strategic alternatives:

- Strategy 1: Product–Communication Extension (Dual Extension)
- Strategy 2: Product Extension–Communication Adaptation
- Strategy 3: Product Adaptation–Communication Extension
- Strategy 4: Product–Communication Adaptation (Dual Adaptation)
- Strategy 5: Product Invention

Dual extension occurs when a company is selling the same product with the same communication strategy across different countries. This strategy is usually easier to carry out for industrial rather than consumer products. The latter are too often linked with local culture characteristics to allow a total product and communication extension.

Take, for example, the McDonald's strategy. Its burgers are sold all around the world (sometimes with modifications and additional items) and its communications emphasize its family-friendly brand, which has been well received in virtually every country. This is an example of dual extension, but not in its purest form. In fact, McDonald's pro-family values underlie its global marketing campaigns, but they are often positioned in varying contexts across countries. For example, in the United States the context may be convenience; in India it's "bang for the buck"; in Russia, it's a uniquely American experience; and in Asia, it's togetherness for the young and trendy.[111]

Some marketers have learned the hard way that a dual extension approach does not work in every market. The global retailer Walmart was recently forced to pull out of the German market, where its standard retail model, used invariably in all new geographic markets, simply did not work. Walmart's traditional practices for team building and customer service—the Walmart cheer and the use of bag-packers at checkout—were never fully accepted by German employees and consumers. In addition, Walmart's standardized global positioning as the low-price leader did not distinguish it enough from established German discount retailers. The ensuing price wars and a damaged reputation eventually convinced the global giant to sell its remaining 85 stores to Metro AG, another global retail chain.[112]

Product extension–communication adaptation is a strategy that can be pursued by those companies that, when offering a product with homogeneous features, are faced

110. Keegan, W. J. (1969, January). Multinational product planning: Strategic alternatives. *Journal of Marketing, 33,* 58–62; Keegan, W. J., & Green, M. C. (2008). Global marketing (5th ed.) (p. 388). Upper Saddle River, NJ: Pearson International Edition.

111. Fielding, M. (1 September 2006). Walk the line: Global brands need balance of identity, cultural respect. *Marketing News,* 8–10.

112. Wiesmann, G. (29 July 2006). Why Wal-Mart decided to pack its bags in Germany. *The Financial Times,* 21.

with consumers who perceive the product's quality and value differently, or who are using it for a different purpose and are looking for different benefits to satisfy different needs. This is the case of De'Longhi. De'Longhi is an Italian Group world leader in the portable heating, air-conditioning, and air-treatment appliances market. Its goal is to achieve European leadership in cooking, ironing, and floor care appliances. With Group revenues of €1,491 million and 77 percent of Group sales coming from international markets, the company has grown a lot during the last few years, especially thanks to the communication adaptation that took into consideration consumers' product perception and expected benefits. In fact their product is the same in Europe and the United States, but the communication is different. In Europe, the product value of the De'Longhi fryer is linked mainly to the technical and aesthetic characteristics and attention to detail. "Cleverly made by those who really know what they are doing," associated with the image of a woman's hand that represents precision, is the slogan used on a European level. This positioning is also necessary to compensate a potentially negative image of the "made-in" linked to Italian technology. In the United States, the most important characteristic is that the product must be easy to use. Therefore, the company presents itself with the pay-off: "Turn one on and you will understand," pointing out that it is very easy to make the product work!

The product adaptation–communication extension strategy targets a market that can be similar in the communication approach but needs adaptation to meet the needs, customs, and characteristics of a local context. Product adaptation–communication extension may be easier and more natural for online businesses. For example, as the popular social networking site MySpace has expanded globally, Tom Anderson, the company's co-founder, has always been portrayed as Friend #1 to every new registrant in markets ranging from Australia to Ireland. However, as the "place for friends" entered the Japanese market, MySpace was wise to adapt its product by handing the role of Friend #1 to Ozzie Inoue, a Japanese native. The move, which went beyond the simple language translation and localized content strategy used in the other country-specific sites, is intended to make MySpace more culturally relevant for the notoriously hard-to-enter Japanese market.[113]

Product and communication adaptation is a mandatory choice for companies that need to enter markets that are totally different, both in the offer that satisfies their needs, and in the communication that conveys the message efficiently to the target client. For example, the mobile phone giant Nokia is using a dual adaptation strategy to gain traction in India, the fastest growing market for wireless phones. The company is implementing innovations such as dust-proof keypads to make the phones usable in India's hot countryside, where dusty, unpaved roads are the norm. It is also changing the way it advertises and sells its products. To avoid losing control over its marketing and advertising by distributing its phones through India's tens of thousands of small vendors, the manufacturer has hired a number of Nokia-branded vans and minivans that visit remote villages across the country on market or festival days. Nokia representatives traveling in these vans educate the customers about the phones and sell directly to them on the spot. "You have to work with local means to reach people— even bicycles and rickshaws," says Kai Oistamo, Nokia's executive vice president and general manager for mobile phones.[114]

The product and/or communication adaptation represents a choice that in some cases will not be enough for growth in a foreign market. In emerging markets it is

113. Hempel, J. (4 December 2006). Japan's friend no. 1. *Business Week*, 14; Angwin, J., & Alabaster, J. (2006, November 8). MySpace adds a friend in Japan. *The Wall Street Journal*. Retrieved from http://online.wsj.com/article/SB116290234314615478.html.

114. Ewing, J. (4 May 2007). First mover in mobile: How Nokia is selling cell phones to the developing world. *Business Week*.

often necessary to enter in a totally different way to satisfy needs that are not present in other parts of the world. Therefore, the new product conceptualization (product invention) is often linked to satisfy existing needs with products accessibly priced to mass markets. But in industrialized countries, where products are in the maturity phase of their life cycles and where competition doesn't easily leave room for growth, the development of a company is also based on the launch of new products. It is in this perspective that innovative ideas develop like the ones pursued by Intel, OLPC, and Ford.

In fact, both the microprocessor giant Intel and the nonprofit initiative One Laptop Per Child (OLPC) are developing simplified, cheap portable electronics that can be distributed in the third world. While OLPC is focusing on developing notebooks with a unique architecture and interface that can be sold for US$100, Intel is pouring its energies into making its microchips compatible with all different types and sizes of electronic devices, so that PDAs, mobile phones, and PCs will all have the same full functionality and Internet access capabilities regardless of where they are sold.[115]

The Ford case is different. Forced by competitive and financial pressures, as well as consumer trends, Ford Motor Co. has been at work on a global small car. And, since coming on board, CEO Alan Mulally has been a strong proponent of the project. He recently merged several far-flung development teams into a global program team tasked with developing such a product that will be sold in the European, North American, and Asian markets. Ford plans to start selling the cars, which use a Mazda-developed platform, in the three markets.[116] While the engineering side of the project is hoping to eliminate unnecessary structural changes, reduce costs, and slim down the number of team members, a separate design team will be working to develop a global design theme that will resonate with Ford customers around the world. According to J. Mays, Ford Motor's group vice president of design, the ultimate goal, which may take as long as seven years, is to ". . . be able to get off a plane anywhere in the world and say, 'Oh, yeah, there's a Ford.' "[117]

MANAGEMENT ORIENTATION

In many cases, management orientation (ethnocentric or global oriented) is an aspect that can make the difference in the choice between standardization or adaptation. Take the example of Lenovo, the first Chinese quasi-private enterprise founded in 1984, today the fourth largest PC company in the world, number one in China, ahead of foreign competitors like HP and Dell and domestic rivals like Founder and Tongfang. Lenovo is a perfect example of a global/local company, with no fixed headquarters, leadership meetings in Paris one month and Cambodia the next, marketing decisions made in Bangalore (India) and design work done in Beijing (China), Raleigh (North Carolina), and Yamato (Japan). With this global culture, managers are aware of the cost advantages of standardization, but are also open to adaptation, understanding the local needs especially of faster-growing but also low-income markets such as India, Russia, Brazil, and Turkey on which the company is focusing.[118]

Alternatively, other companies can reveal a completely different culture. It was the case with an Italian company producing a rather famous brand of underwear and

---

115. Kirkpatrick, D. (11 May 2007). Intel on $100 laptops, smartphones and the Net. *Fast Forward* [newsletter]. Retrieved from http://money.cnn.com/2007/05/11/technology/fastforward_inteltiny.fortune/index.htm?postversion=2007051112.

116. Wilson, A. (12 March 2007). Ford will have 1 team for global small car. *Automotive News*, 8.

117. Wilson, A. (22 January 2007). Ford brand plans a global design theme. *Automotive News*, 4.

118. Buckman, R. (2008). Not East or West. *Forbes, 182*(13), 50–52.

swimwear. The company was strongly involved in exporting, but the entrepreneur always refused to make any kind of adaptation to meet local needs: for example, in Germany, distributors and retailers were asking for women's swimwear in sizes from one to six, not only for classic bikinis but also for sexy ones. For the latter, the entrepreneur never agreed to produce all the sizes, arguing that it was not coherent with the Italian style where "aggressive" models tend to be offered only in sizes one to three. The company recently failed and was acquired by an international fashion group that maintained the brand but changed the company's culture, eliminating any ethnocentric thinking and teaching managers that there can be some communalities across countries but that the reality is the "differences," especially when considering fast-growing emerging markets that are the future for Western companies.

SUMMARY

- The product is the most important element of a marketing program. Global marketers face the challenge of formulating a coherent global product strategy for their companies.

- Product strategy requires an evaluation of the basic needs and conditions of use in the company's existing and proposed markets.

- When defining the marketing strategy, a company should take into consideration the stages of the product life cycle across countries.

- The market potential for products is determined by many factors such as product saturation levels, national income levels, technology standards, and cultural conditions.

- Marketers should be able to identify the optimal level of standardization or adaptation of their products

according to the countries they serve in order to define the opportunities for each product in different markets. Marketers must consider four factors when designing products for global markets: product use, product perception and expected benefits, adaptation or standardization of product attributes, and management orientation.

- Five strategic positioning alternatives are open to companies pursuing global market expansion for their products: product–communications extension; product extension–communications adaptation; product adaptation–communications extension; dual adaptation; and product invention. Choosing a strategy for global market expansion should be based on analysis of the factors that would make the product most profitable in each market.

DISCUSSION QUESTIONS

1. How can you define a global product or service? Discuss and give some examples of local products and global products.

2. List and briefly describe the main product features. Considering a product that is representative of your country and is marketed abroad, define the stage of the product life cycle in your country and in other countries and discuss the standardization/adaptation alternative. Which features are standardized? Which are adapted?

3. What are the most important branding decisions managers have to take in international markets?

4. How can a company manage a negative country-of-origin perception? What are the opportunities associated with a positive country of origin? Discuss some examples of negative and positive countries of origin in your country.

5. What are the advantages and disadvantages of different product expansion strategies?

EXPERIENTIAL EXERCISES

1. Listen to the NPR story "Video Game Pioneer Kutaragi Leaves Sony," about Sony's Playstation 3 and its struggles against rivals such as Microsoft's Xbox 360 and Nintendo's Wii (www.npr.org/templates/story/story.php?storyId=9884088).

   a. Based on the comments of the young gamers, what, besides the high price, were Sony's biggest misses in launching this product?

   b. Do you believe that Sony can recover after its initial stumble in the U.S. market? If so, what steps do you recommend that it takes?

2. Select a product from your daily life that is very useful, but costs over US$100. Recommend design, production, and functionality changes that would not reduce its usefulness but would make it more affordable and practical in poorer countries. Develop a marketing strategy for this product in one third world target market of your choice.

KEY TERMS

Adaptation, p. 266

Brand name, p. 286

Brand positioning, p. 284

Brand value, p. 282

Branding, p. 282

Color, p. 279

Country of origin, p. 288

Decline phase, p. 263

Design, p. 277

Expected benefits, p. 273

Global branding, p. 282

Growth phase, p. 263

Interpersonal communication, p. 263

Introduction phase, p. 262

Labeling, p. 280

Local brands, p. 282

Logo, p. 286

Made-in effect, p. 288

Maturity phase, p. 263

Packaging, p. 280

Product attributes, p. 274

Product life cycle (PLC), p. 262

Product perception, p. 273

Product use, p. 272

Quality, p. 279

Regulations, p. 275

Research and product development stage, p. 262

Service attributes, p. 290

Standardization, p. 266

Standards, p. 275

Take-off point, p. 263

Word-of-mouth, p. 263

CASE 10-1
Lux: The Art of Cross-Cultural Branding

Lux is called 力士 (Strong Man) in China, a name contradicting the image of a young lady on its package. When the brand first entered the Chinese market in the early 1980s, a Hollywood actress was employed in one of earliest Western TV commercials. While bathing herself in a large bathtub (certainly an exotic scene to Chinese viewers at the time), she said in a soft, seductive voice, "I only use *Strong Man*. How about you?" This proved to be a huge success, and Lux became a household name within weeks.

In Taiwan, Lux is called 麗仕 (Beauty), a name that matches the image of a young woman. Both names are pronounced with the exactly same sound and tone. This means that Lux has two different names with totally different images in the same language and culture. An explanation can be found in the ideological differences existing in the two parts of China. While 麗仕 (Beauty) would be a perfectly acceptable name in mainland China today, it was certainly a problem back in the 1980s. Under the orthodox communist doctrine, "beauty" was related to decadent bourgeoisie aesthetics.

Renaming brands in a foreign market is no straightforward process. As a language and culture loaded with symbolism and imagery, a direct translation can often lead to comical or negative results. For many international companies entering the Chinese market, the first barrier they encountered was the language. As the Chinese use characters based on ideograms, and the majority of people are unfamiliar with the Roman alphabet, the international brand has to choose a proper Chinese name. This is a complicated task that requires a thorough understanding of Chinese culture as well as linguistic skills.

A study on brand renaming (Fan, 2002) has found that there are three common renaming methods: mixed translation is used most often (46 percent), followed by free translation (29 percent) and direct translation (25 percent). Direct translation maintains the phonetic link between the two names—i.e., the new name sounds like the original—but it has no specific meaning in Chinese. Free translation, on the other hand, gives a meaningful Chinese name but loses the phonetic link with the original. The mixed method seems to be the most popular among the three, as it creates a new name that both sounds like the original and has a meaning in Chinese.

Other things being equal, a brand name that has some meaning to the consumer will be more easily recalled. In addition to linguistic issues, other factors that affect the translation or naming process are identified as follows:

- Reflecting product benefits or industry characteristics
- Quality and brand positioning
- Links to logo or packaging
- Country-of-origin effect
- Traditional values
- Beliefs and customs

Case prepared by Ying Fan, Northampton Business School, University of Northampton, NN2 7AL England. Reprinted by permission.

Reflecting product benefits and brand positioning are the two largest groups. It is interesting to compare Coca-Cola with Pepsi Cola. In their Chinese names—可口可乐 (Palatable and Enjoyable) and 百事可乐 (Hundred Things Enjoyable)—the last two characters are the same. However, the difference between the first two characters sets them apart. Coca-Cola's name has a clear link with product benefits (可口); the repetition of character 可 makes the name rhythmic and enhances the name recall. In contrast, Pepsi's name is a poorer imitation without any distinctive feature.

Out of 100 brands, three-quarters are given a meaningful new name. Chinese names place more emphasis on meaning than sound. A meaningful name is crucial in developing both a mental image and favourable associations. Mercedes Benz is 奔驰 (Speed On). The sound and visual image of two characters (particularly, 驰 with a horse as radical) generate associations of speed, dynamism, performance, and capability—the exact attributes that the German brand symbolizes. Brand positioning is another important consideration. In the case of Canon, consider its old name, 卡侬 (based on direct translation), with its new name, 佳能 (based on mixed translation). 卡侬, though sounding very close to Canon, has no meaning in Chinese. In contrast, 佳能 (meaning Best Calibre in Chinese) is strategically desirable: it sounds appealing and generates an association of high quality.

A poorly conceived name could cause confusion for the consumer or harm the brand's equity. Although no simple rule can guarantee a good name, an understanding of the issues will help a company prevent the costly blunder of choosing the wrong one. The translation process gives an international brand not only a new name in Chinese, but also a distinctive local image. Take BMW as an example. To millions of Chinese consumers, BMW is 宝马 —a "Precious Horse" rather than "the ultimate driving machine." A horse is generally perceived as a heroic creature in Chinese culture: there are dozens of idioms and legends describing its feats, and it is a popular subject in traditional Chinese paintings. By adopting such a name, the brand can tap into the rich cultural deposits and create a favourable mental image in the consumer's mind.

The dilemma faced by the international brand is not about whether to choose a suitable Chinese name (it is a necessity in the majority of cases), but whether to maintain a Western image or create a more localised image. For example, Nike and Reebok have adopted very different brand image strategies. Nike maintains a standardised "fitness and performance" image in all of the markets it serves. Nike is translated into Chinese directly as 耐克, a name that has no specific meaning (though the first character means "durable") but has a distinctive foreign or western image and sounds more appealing. Its rival Reebok, on the other hand, customises its image on the basis of national differences. It is rendered as 锐步 (Dashing Step), a meaningful name that lacks a foreign image.

The challenge for international branding is to find a fine balance between the two strategies, as there are risks at both extremes. A pure global image that is alien to the national culture will not appeal to local consumers. On the contrary, a totally localised image will not benefit from brand assets of the original and will find it hard to differentiate itself from the local competition. Unilever is a good case in point. A global brand, according to its chairman Michael Perry, is simply "a local brand reproduced many times." For many years, the company has been actively pursuing a localised branding strategy in China, localising all its international brands and acquiring successful local brands. Most Chinese consumers probably have no idea about Unilever's origin; it is perceived as a multinational company with a Chinese identity, as its name suggests: 联合利华 (United Benefit China).

Renaming a brand in a foreign market can be a creative and value-added process when cultural issues and brand positioning are taken into consideration along with linguistic factors. It provides the international brand with a rare opportunity to recast the brand in the new market, creating a unique global–local image with built-in positioning attributes that enhance the brand equity of the original.

Discussion Questions

1. Global branding is a paradox. There may be global brands, but their image, positioning, and perception are influenced by the local market conditions, especially by cultural differences. Discuss with examples. How do you define a global brand given the fact that its image varies in different markets?

2. Choose three global brands to investigate. For each brand, study two websites (one in your own country and the other in the home country of the brand) to find whether there are any differences in terms of brand identity (name, logo, and brand associations) and brand positioning (slogan, marketing communications, etc).

3. Try to explain those differences you have identified above. What are the implications of these differences on the firm's marketing strategy in your own country?

Further Readings

Fan, Y. (2002). The national image of global brands. *Journal of Brand Management,* 9(3), 180–192. This paper presents a study of 100 international brands, focusing on the key factors that affect the meaning of these brands in the Chinese market. The paper can be downloaded free from http://bura.brunel.ac.uk/handle/2438/1289.

De Mooij, M. (2005). The global–local paradox in global branding. In *Global Marketing and Advertising* (2nd ed.). London: Sage Publications.

CHAPTER 11

Setting Global Prices

We have invested more behind brand equity and in product quality. This today gives us the pricing power we need to pass on cost increases while maintaining market competitiveness.

JIM LAWRENCE, UNILEVER CHIEF FINANCIAL OFFICER[1]

LEARNING OBJECTIVES

After reading this chapter, you should be able to:

- Understand the centrality of pricing in the international marketing mix.
- Identify the main competitive, consumer, product, and country factors influencing pricing decisions.
- Understand how to define objectives, strategies, and pricing policies.
- Distinguish between cost versus market-based pricing approaches.
- Learn how to manage new product pricing.
- Discuss the standardization versus adaptation alternatives.
- Recognize pricing strategies prototypes.
- Understand how to manage transfer pricing.
- Describe terms and methods of payment.
- Understand the concept of countertrade.

A Challenging Decision

When considering pricing strategies and policies, there are complex decisions that the company has to make. There are countless factors that need to be taken into consideration. Many of them depend not only on internal company variables such as corporate strategy or product cost, but also on external factors such as the characteristics of the target market, global and local competitors, and a country's economic and legislative structure. A manufacturer's pricing policy is also influenced by the relative power of distributors in the channel of distribution. It is not coincidental that research based on a sample of 45 industrial exporters[2] demonstrated that pricing decisions are preferably made centrally, under the supervision of top-level managers. This seems to be mainly related to the perceived importance of international pricing for the financial success of the company abroad.

Price, together with other marketing mix variables, must reflect the value that the consumer is willing to pay for the company's product, taking into consideration competitive

1. Quoted in the presentation by Jim Lawrence, Unilever Chief Financial Officer, at the 2008 Consumer Analyst Group of New York (CAGNY) Conference, February 20, 2008, retrieved from www.unilever.com/Images/ir_CAGNY_Conference_2008_Speech_tcm13-120416.pdf.

2. Stottinger, B. (2001). Strategic export pricing: A long and winding road. *Journal of International Marketing*, 9(1), 40–63.

products as well. For many consumers, price acts as an evaluation index for the product's quality. As pointed out by Gianluigi Buitoni, former president and CEO of Ferrari North America, if a company is selling a commodity type of product or service, then price will be the driving factor determining sales. Prices have to be competitive because many customers look for cheaper deals not only in traditional retailing but also through the Internet. If a company is not able to reduce its costs, it will go out of business. A company needs to be efficient because even luxury items can no longer be unreasonably priced.[3]

Price is a tangible value of an offer created through product, distribution, and communication decisions. Therefore, pricing decisions are intrinsically tied to other marketing mix variables. Nintendo, for example, was a brand that seemed to be losing its consumer appeal. The launch of the Wii console, with its physically active and convincing interface and DS range, sparked consumers' interest. Nintendo differentiated itself from competitors through its "enjoyment of gaming" theme and repositioned its brand to attract new consumers, not only in the teenage male segment but anybody who enjoys playing. Wii's sales grew beyond expectations. In the launch phase, lines forming outside stores were not uncommon, and consoles were selling on eBay for twice the retail price.[4]

In a global context, the price that a product can gain in the market often determines its development. In low-income countries, price must be in line with purchasing power. A company must first evaluate the price that the consumer is willing to pay for the product. Only then will it be possible to define the most suitable product features and distribution and communication policies.

Take P&G, for example. To be price competitive in the Chinese market, the company introduced a new product with lower manufacturing costs. Benefits such as stain removal and fragrance were absent, and the product contained less advanced cleaning enzymes. A 320-gram bag of Tide Clean White laundry detergent was sold for $0.23, compared to $0.33 for 350 grams of Tide Triple Action.[5]

Another example is Microsoft. It is working with governments in emerging countries to price software in a way that is relevant to those markets. The choice to make its products affordable, particularly to companies in the Pacific Rim, is fully justified, because consumers have low purchasing power. But how is this pricing strategy explained to clients in established markets such as North America and Western Europe? The solution is to coordinate pricing strategies across countries and geographical areas, in order to not only avoid losing revenue and profitability but also to avoid ruining the company's image and its brands.[6]

This chapter explores the main issues that need to be faced when making pricing decisions in international markets. After analyzing the numerous influencing factors, we will discuss pricing strategies and policies. Next we will focus on some specific problems that need to be managed by the global company, such as price escalation, transfer prices, terms of payment, and countertrade.

FACTORS INFLUENCING PRICING DECISIONS

There are several factors influencing international **pricing decisions** that can be categorized into four groups:

- Competitive factors
- Consumer factors

3. Gian Luigi Buitoni explains his theory of "Dreamketing," HSM global.com, http://us.hsmglobal.com/notas/36000-gian-luigi-buitoni-explains-his-theory-of-dreamketing.

4. Interbrand. (2007). *Best Global Brands 2007*. Retrieved from www.interbrand.com/surveys.asp on March 2, 2009.

5. Madden, N., & Neff, J. (23 February 2004). P&G adapts attitude toward local markets. *Advertising Age, 75*(8), 28.

6. www.infoworld.com/article/04/03/01/HNrethinks_1.html.

- Product factors and distribution channels
- Country factors

Also, company factors are important elements to consider, especially at a strategic level. Their role will therefore be underlined when considering international pricing strategies and objectives.

COMPETITIVE FACTORS

The structure and intensity of competition varies significantly from country to country and therefore affects pricing strategy. For example, Unilever, which is usually the leading brand in many emerging markets, has to face the competition of Nirma in India. This local brand, which started out 35 years ago selling soap powder at a third of the price of Western competitors, now dominates the market with a market share of 35 percent.[7] There is a similar case of aggressive pricing strategy with Arvind Limited, an Indian company that makes denim jeans for Lee, Wrangler, Arrow, and Tommy Hilfiger—brands that sell for the equivalent of $60 or more in the West. This local company is also the owner of the biggest-selling Indian jeans brand, Ruff & Tuff, which sells its products at just $6 via tailors in the form of a complete "sew it yourself" kit.[8] The situation in the retailing sector is no different. In China, for example, foreign retailers in the market face fierce price competition from local rivals. Not only do Chinese retailers frequently discount goods deeply, they also send their own employees to buy up limited supplies of promotional, specialty-priced items from their rivals and use other aggressive methods to out-price newcomers.[9]

All of these elements determine the level of competitive pressure that strongly influences pricing decisions. A survey by McKinsey & Co. of top global executives found that the greater the intensity of competition, the more difficult it is for an individual firm to price competitively. Executives in highly competitive markets such as North America and Europe were more apt to agree with that statement than those in fast-growing markets such as China and India, who still have some flexibility in price setting.[10]

It is important to emphasize how the power to determine a given price is strongly linked to the value that the company is able to create around its offer through different marketing mix variables. Companies that have a weak brand image relative to competition are the ones that are often subjected to price pressures. This happened, for example, to one of the most famous brands in the apparel industry: Gap (see Box 11-1).

CONSUMER FACTORS

Factors linked to the consumer that can influence price policies are very complex. From the company's point of view, product unit price represents a clearly defined numeric value; however, from the consumer point of view, the concept of perceived price comes into play. It is important to distinguish between two dimensions regarding

---

7. www.equitymaster.com/research-it/compare/compare_comp.asp?symbol=NRMA-HLL&value=compare-NIRMA-LTD-HIND-UNILEVER; Jordan, M. (11 December 1997). Indian soap maker steps up battle with big firms. *The New York Times*. Retrieved from www.nytimes.com/1997/12/11/business/worldbusiness/11iht-nirma.t.html.

8. The bottom of the pyramid is where the real gold is hidden. (8 February 2007). *Marketing Week, 18*. Retrieved from Proquest on August 8, 2008.

9. Ready for warfare in the aisle. (5 August 2006). *The Economist*, 60.

10. McKinsey global survey of business executives: Inflation and pricing. (2007, April). *McKinsey Quarterly*. Retrieved from www.mckinseyquarterly.com/article_page.aspx?ar=1999.

BOX 11-1   COMPANY IN FOCUS: GAP

Fighting Against Price Pressure

Stylish clothing at affordable prices sold through specialty retail chains was the basis for Gap's success in the 1990s. Was it possible to maintain product differentiation in the long term? The answer is negative. In an industry with low entry barriers and minimal switching costs, its business model was easily replicated. The brand has become compressed between different trends in the fashion market, unable to identify the correct positioning for its target customers.

Considering the competitive environment, on one side there are consumers looking to mix low-priced basics. Today, the same American staple of T-shirts, jeans, and chinos are offered by other companies, but at a lower price, generating a price pressure that Gap is not able to meet. Zara and H&M are examples of this. On the other side, there are premium brands offering unique and expensive signature pieces. Also, with the opening of hundreds of competing stores during the last 10 years, the company has lost its original perception of uniqueness. Numerous attempts to define a more fashionable positioning have failed, leaving the brand with an irrelevant positioning and an overpriced product line.

The brand portfolio has created further problems. In the United States, Gap has further confused its consumers by proposing alternative stores, Old Navy and Banana Republic, which have worsened the situation and cannibalized Gap's sales. The first one, Old Navy, which offers fun-oriented and less expensive options, has gained popularity during the economic recession; the other, Banana Republic, which sells higher quality and more up-market items, is expected to increase sales following the economic slowdown, when sales will start again.

Considering the internal and external difficulties together with the necessity to determine a new correct price-quality ratio coherent with a distinctive positioning, it is clear that a turnaround is needed to guarantee the future of Gap's company.

Sources: Best global brands. (2008). *Interbrand.* Retrieved from www.interbrand.com/surveys.asp; Retail competition could hurt Gap stock. (23 June 2010). Retrieved from www.trefis.com/company?article=17701#; M. Duff. (11 February 2010). Gap's comeback strategy: Jeans for life. Retrieved from http://industry.bnet.com/retail/10007070/next-move-in-gap-comeback-is-kids-stuff/.

the perceived price: monetary and non-monetary. **Monetary price** represents the idea that a consumer has regarding a product's price, for example, expensive or cheap. This idea often depends on the consumer's past experience, on the information he or she has had access to, and competitive offerings (Monroe, 1990).[11] **Non-monetary price** represents the sacrifice that a consumer must face when purchasing a product: taking into consideration, for example, the time necessary for the purchase, the effort necessary to learn how to use it, and the risks involved.[12] Also, in this case, perception of the non-monetary price will tend to vary significantly from country to country; for example, in cultures that can be defined as "time saving" rather than cultures where time economy is not important. Or it can depend on the importance the consumer attributes to the product, and therefore to the effort that he or she is willing to expend in order to be able to acquire it. The final price perception, therefore, will depend on a careful evaluation of costs (monetary and non-monetary) and benefits (tied to the obtainable advantages linked with the purchase of a product or service). Finally, the perceived functional and other product benefits will be balanced against costs of

11. Monroe, K. B. (1990). *Pricing. Making profitable decisions.* London: McGraw-Hill.

12. See: de Chernatony, L., Harris, F., & Dall'Olmo, R. F. (2000). Added value: Its nature, roles and sustainability. *European Journal of Marketing, 34*(1/2); Gronroos, C. (1997). Value driven relational marketing: From products to resources and competences. *Journal of Marketing Management, 13*, 407–419; Zeithaml, V. A. (1988, July). Consumer perception of price, quality and value: A means end model and synthesis of evidence. *Journal of Marketing, 52*, 2–22.

acquisition, internal costs (learning to use new product, lost time, disposal of previous product, etc.), and purchase risks (financial, social, and physical).[13]

There are many studies demonstrating how cultural factors influence the relationship between price and quality.[14] Tellis and Gaeth (1990),[15] for example, identify three choice strategies consumers may use under uncertainty: best value, price-seeking and price-averse. The *best value* strategy occurs when consumers make rational decisions, choosing the brand with the best value or lowest total expected cost. Nevertheless, buyers may associate higher prices with better quality with the result that they tend to ignore objective quality information and make a *price-seeking* choice. On the other hand, consumers may be overpowered by uncertainty and prefer a *price-averse* choice; in this way they minimize immediate losses by choosing the cheapest brand. Companies must take into consideration these differences not only to be able to define price strategies, but also to identify specific operational policies. A study on the price-ending practices in low context (Western countries) and high context cultures (non-Western countries) suggests that the perception of retail prices ending in 0.5 (even ending) and 9 (odd ending) is not homogeneous. Non-Western cultures seem to be less deceived by the cheapness or gain that an odd ending price wants to convey. In some cases they feel that someone is attempting to "fool" them.[16]

Globalization has not yet resulted in convergence of consumer perception, not even in specific geographical areas. A research study by Kotabe and Jiang (2006),[17] for example, underlines how, in general, American and other Western multinational companies tend to lump together Japanese, Korean, and Chinese markets. They assume that Asian consumers have similar tastes and preferences moderated by different income levels. Instead, this is far from the truth, especially referring to the price-quality relationship, as shown in Box 11-2.

Price and the Internet

The growing use of the Internet has definitely given a push toward consumer rationality. In fact, on a global scale, the Internet is helping shoppers throughout the world to compare prices of similar products. Sites such as NexTag.com, which has German, French, and British versions as well as its United States site, not only allow consumers to compare prices for everything from diapers to online education degrees, but also offer tools such as historic price charts, product reviews, vendor ratings, and more.

Even though there are tools that can help consumers rationalize purchasing decisions, social context and customs are still very influential. This is demonstrated by the results of the "name your price" strategies that some companies have implemented in the past few years in various cultural contexts (see Box 11-3).

Product Factors and Distribution Channels

An important variable to consider in pricing decisions is the stage of the product life cycle (PLC) that exists in different countries. As discussed in Chapter 10, each stage

---

13. Blythe, J. (2006). *Principles and practice of marketing*. London: Thomson Learning.

14. Usunier, J., & Lee, J. A. (2005). *Marketing across cultures*. Harlow, England: Prentice Hall, Pearson Education Ltd.

15. Tellis, G. J., & Gaeth, G. J. (1990, April). Best value, price-seeking, and price aversion: The impact of information and learning on consumer choices. *Journal of Marketing, 54*(2), 34–45.

16. Nguyen, A., Heeler, R. M., & Taran, Z. (2007). High-low context cultures and price-ending practices. *Journal of Product & Brand Management, 16*(3), 206–214.

17. Kotabe, M., & Jiang, C. (2006, March/April). Three Dimensional: The Markets of Japan, Korea, and China are Far from Homogeneous. *Marketing Management, 15*(2), 39–43.

BOX 11-2   COUNTRY IN FOCUS: JAPAN & CHINA

Price-Quality Perception Differences in Japan and China

Japan. Clear needs and desires and high expectations for products for which they are willing to pay premium prices: this is the picture of Japanese consumers, which can be classified among the highest product-quality seekers in the world. In fact, they view information other than price (e.g., brand, packaging, advertising) to assess product quality and make a decision. Even the Walmart "Everyday Low Prices" philosophy doesn't seem to attract many Japanese consumers, because they often associate low price with low quality; i.e., *yasu-karou, warukarou,* or "cheap price, cheap product."

Some companies quickly understand this. Procter & Gamble sought the best available materials for product formulations and packaging. In order to become the country's largest fast food chain, McDonald's opened its first store in Tokyo's Ginza district, which is identified with luxury brand-name goods. And Levis are sold at very high prices because they are perceived as the designer's elite brand product and representative of the American lifestyle. Nevertheless, there is also another segment of young people displaying alternative consumer behavior. On one side, they prefer very low-priced products for their everyday uses. On the other hand, they are still willing to pay premium prices for select quality products—especially those from Europe—to achieve self-satisfaction and social status. The outcome is that products that fall in the middle of the price range (for example, local designer products) generate limited profits.

China. This country is evolving and facing contradictory behaviors. Many consumers are price sensitive and money savers. In most cases, affordable prices are necessary if a company wants to penetrate the market. This explains why P&G needed three years before it was able to become profitable in China, why, L'Oreal took nine years, and why the world's most popular chicken restaurant chain, KFC, spent 10 years improving its business model and successfully running restaurants in 450 Chinese cities.

Nevertheless, Chinese consumers also report significantly high prestige sensitivity, and the younger generations are especially attracted by Western and luxury brands. If it is true that they frequently end up buying pirated versions and creating enormous anti-counterfeiting control problems, it is also a matter of fact that the luxury market is constantly growing. This growth is interesting also for some Chinese companies that are increasingly attracted by the premium segment. Take the example of Shanghai Tang, a Chinese brand in the fashion market that promotes high-quality innovative design and high prices yet does not hide its "made in China" label, but rather emphasizes its "proud to be Chinese" image. The perceived value of the brand is demonstrated by the fact that the company was bought by the Richemont Group, known all over the world for its Cartier brand. This led to growth not only in China but also internationally.

Sources: Adapted from: Kotabe, M., & Jiang, C. (2006, March/April). Three Dimensional: The Markets of Japan, Korea, and China are Far from Homogeneous. *Marketing Management, 15*(2), 39–43. Meng, J., & Altobello Nasco, S. (2009). Cross-cultural equivalence of price perceptions across American, Chinese, and Japanese consumers. *Journal of Product & Brand Management, 18*(7), 506–516; Analysis of Japanese consumers. (2010). *Intelligent Bridges.* Retrieved from www.intelbridges.com/japaneseconsumer.html; www.shanghaitang.com.

needs different management of marketing mix policies, including price choices in each country.[18]

Another aspect that needs to be taken into consideration is the company's ability to convey to consumers the real quality of the product, a goal that is not always easy to implement if the company operates in industries where competition relies mostly on the price variable rather than on differentiation strategies. It is in these circumstances that it

18. Theodosiou, M., & Katsikeas, C. S. (2001). Factors influencing the degree of international pricing strategy standardization of multinational corporations. *Journal of International Marketing, 9*(3), 1–18.

BOX 11-3   COMPANY IN FOCUS: RADIOHEAD

All music purchases are based on the honor system, since music purchased in stores or from iTunes could be easily downloaded for free. But the United States rock band Radiohead turned the marketing world upside down by allowing its fans to "name their own price" to download its album "In Rainbows." In other words, "the price is up to you," and the difference in Radiohead's approach was that they allowed buyers to self-price. This policy, which also included the possibility of getting the album for free, was definitely successful from the communication point of view, bringing them more global awareness than a conventional album release ever could, with virtually free marketing and publicity, increased demand for tour tickets, and a flood of fan marketing data. But what about sales? Over the first 29 days, 62 percent of global downloaders paid nothing, while 38 percent voluntarily paid for it. Among the latter, the worldwide average was $6, with a significantly higher expenditure of U.S. consumers paying an average of $8.05 versus non-U.S. consumers paying an average of $4.64.

Nevertheless, the profitability was interesting, and a music magazine found that the rock band gained much higher profits relative to selling the music through music companies or retailers.

The Radiohead approach wasn't the first or only one to apply this type of pricing policy. It is certain however, that this approach works better in cultures like North America, where the tipping culture is diffused and accepted and consumers are willing to reward a good experience, but it is unthinkable it could work everywhere. In many cultures, consumers would end up paying nothing. In other countries—for example, Northern Europe and Scandinavia—people really seek the clarity of a fixed price, and this price strategy might not be appreciated at all.

Sources: Pricing strategies: The price is right? (10 December 2007). *Brand Strategy*, 14, retrieved from Proquest database; Mohammed, R. (3 October 2007). How much is Radiohead's new CD? Whatever price you want to pay! Retrieved from www.pricingforprofit.com/pricing-strategy-blog/how-much-radiohead-s-new-cd-whatever-price-you.htm; Anonymous. (1 October 2007). Putting a price on Radiohead. *The Economist*. Retrieved from www.economist.com/blogs/freeexchange/2007/10/dollars_and_cents.

often becomes important to support price with appropriate communication leveraging on product or company attributes that can be recognized on an international level, with the objective of transferring the product value to the target client. GranitiFiandre, for example, is a leading Italian company in the business-to-business luxury ceramic tiles industry. It distinguishes itself by premium price positioning. The company conveys the perception of its products' value in an international context through the image of some of its customers who have used GranitiFiandre tiles for their luxury stores or their company sites. Among these are Ferrari, Armani, Benetton, Givenchy, and Porsche, all companies whose brand and reputation are well known by potential international clients. The company has been able to develop a high-quality perception coherent with a high price. Value creation is the focus of their communication, as it emerges also in the slogan of a recent advertising campaign where *"Valore è anche la capacità di trasformare la materia in un sogno"* ("Value is also the ability to transform raw materials into dreams") (see Figure 11-1).

When determining the final price of a product in international marketing, expenses for adapting, manufacturing, and selling a product, as well as export-related costs and a profit margin, are all essential elements for the product's final price definition. Costs to be taken into account are:[19]

- ■ Variable costs (raw materials, labor, energy, agents' commissions, etc.)
- ■ Marketing expenses (analysis, promotion, and product management)
- ■ Finance charges

19. Demers, J. (2003, June/July). Enhanced export pricing strategies. *CMA Management, 77*(4), 52–54.

Figure 11-1 GranitiFiandre: An Example of Value Creation in an International Business-to-Business Context

Source: Advertising reprinted by permission from GranitiFiandre

- Bank charges (currency operations, exchange rate risk, etc.)
- Export-related charges (translation, labeling, country-of-origin marking, export banding and packaging, containerization, documentation, forwarding fees, customs brokerage, etc.)

Who controls the pricing decision? The pricing decision is particularly critical when emerging markets are taken into consideration. As pointed out by Keith Pardy, Nokia's senior marketer, "It's one thing to build and design a phone for €500, but it takes really innovative thinking to deliver the same Nokia promise of trust, reliability, quality, and connectivity for €(50) or €(60)."[20]

The export process operational costs are also strongly related to distribution channel length (the number of intermediaries) and channel characteristics, which can determine a relevant increase of the final export price if compared to the domestic price.[21] This phenomenon, known as **price escalation,** can be seen in Table 11-1, where two export scenarios are compared to a typical domestic situation. In the first case (Italy), only the retailer is present in the channel, allowing the company to charge a higher margin (70 percent instead of 50 percent). In the second case (United States), the distribution channel has been lengthened with a foreign importer. The third scenario adds a wholesaler. Even if both the United States and Russia's manufacturing margin is lower, the escalation is significant 40.34 percent and 82.35 percent, respectively.

In order to avoid the risk that the final price ends up being out of the market, the company must implement some alternatives that would allow avoiding or limiting price escalation.[22] The first alternative would be to reduce the length of the distribution channel. This is the case of Nokia. After assessing India's notoriously fragmented retail marketplace, management decided to bypass retailers and distributors altogether and

20. Knudsen, T. R. (2007, May). Confronting proliferation . . . in mobile communications: An interview with Nokia's senior marketer. *The McKinsey Quarterly Web exclusive*, 1–9.

21. Becker, H. (1980). Pricing: An international marketing challenge. In H. B. Thorelli and H. Becker (Eds.). *International marketing strategy*. Elmsford, NY: Pergamon Press.

22. Cavusgil, T. S. (1988). Unravelling the mystique of export pricing. *Business Horizons, 31*(3), 54–63.

TABLE 11-1 Export Price Escalation: An Example for Coffee in the Retail Channel

	Italy Domestic channel with retailer (*Manufacturer margin: +70%*)	USA Foreign channel with importer and retailer (*Manufacturer margin: +50%*)	*Russia* Foreign channel with importer, wholesaler, and retailer (*Manufacturer margin: +50%*)
Manufacturer's cost	5.00	5.00	5.00
Manufacturer's margin (%)	+70%	+50%	+50%
Manufacturer's margin ($)	3.5	2.5	2.5
= Manufacturer's price	8.50	7.50	7.50
+ Insurance and shipping cost (2%)	–	0.15	0.15
= Landed cost	–	7.65	7.65
+Tariff (20%)	–	1.53	1.53
= Importer's cost	–	9.18	9.18
+ Importer's margin (30% on cost)	–	2.75	2.75
= Wholesaler's cost	–	–	11.93
+ Wholesaler's margin (30% on cost)	–	–	3.58
= Retailer's cost	8.50	11.93	15.51
+ Retailer's margin (40% on cost)	3.40	4.77	6.20
= Consumer's cost (= retailer's price)	11.90	16.70	21.70
Price escalation over domestic		+40.34%	+82.35%

began selling its phones directly to consumers via its own fleet of specially marked and equipped vans.[23] Alternatively, it is possible to lower the producer's net price eliminating, for example, expensive features or shifting production of the product or of some of its components to low-cost countries. Finally, it is evident that the possibility of limiting price escalation will strongly depend on the company's power to control final prices, also imposing lower margins on channel members of each target country.

Chaco Footwear, a United States manufacturer of high-end sandals exporting to 28 countries, adopts a different pricing approach. In markets where its staff is not fluent in the local language, such as Japan, it leaves final pricing up to distributors. In other countries—for example, Canada—Chaco has its own sales network and negotiates prices directly with buyers, retaining control over retail and marketing strategy.[24]

As described by Myers and Harvey (2001),[25] control of pricing decisions in the distribution channel is particularly critical in international marketing. Control is exercised when the exporter is able to influence the distributor's behavior with the aim to set desirable prices in foreign markets or when the exporter has autonomy to set prices directly. In order to be effective in monitoring, managing, and regulating prices throughout the channel, a company requires a significant amount of information as well as financial and human resources. However, the results are valuable. A company can coordinate prices across countries reducing the possibilities of gray-market

23. Ewing, J. (4 May 2007). First mover in mobile: How Nokia is selling cell phones to the developing world. *Business Week*.

24. Kolodny, L. (2005, February). The price might be wrong. *Inc*. Retrieved from http://www.inc.com/magazine/20050201/going-global.html.

25. Myers, M. B., & Harvey, M. (2001). The value of pricing control in export channels: A governance perspective. *Journal of International Marketing, 9*(4), 1–29.

imports.[26] Second, the price–quality relationship is controlled and protected. Finally, manufacturers can guarantee the coverage of underlying production costs associated with individual products.

Country Factors

Socioeconomic and political country characteristics are among the elements that can influence a company's pricing strategies and policies. These factors are not controllable by the company, so it must adapt to them when selling its products to a specific country. Per capita income, for example, is an important factor to consider in emerging economies where many global companies want to penetrate to not only a minority of relatively rich consumers, but also target the mass market. Many premium brand owners adopted the strategy of introducing second brands or product lines to access the low-priced markets of Eastern Europe, Middle East Africa, and Asia. In these cases, care must be taken to not cannibalize sales of existing brands or cheapen the brand's image. A successful case of a two-tier pricing strategy is 3M, which employs a two-brand strategy in the office products market with its Tartane brand in Eastern Europe, a cheaper product than its 3M Post-It brand. This strategy enables 3M to expand its price range and product portfolio to meet different end user segment needs.[27]

CURRENCY CONSIDERATIONS

One of the key elements in international trade is the **currency** used for invoicing. Exchange rate risk could be transferred to buyers if they agree to pay using the exporter's currency. However, in many transactions there is no choice, as trade conventions are standard. For example, crude oil trading is done in United States dollars only. Quite often, small or medium-size companies refuse to pay for imports in any currency other than their own. This behavior is often related to excessive exchange rate volatility and the associated risk. In the international monetary system, there are several exchange rate arrangements which allow countries to set up an anchor on which to base exchange rate price expectations (IMF, 2006).[28] With a conventional exchange rate, governments are committed to maintaining a target rate within a narrow margin of at most ±1 percent around the central rate, as in the Bretton Woods era. If the arrangement is stable, pricing in foreign markets is no longer an issue. Even when horizontal bands are larger, maximal gain (loss) can be easily calculated. For instance, Denmark has not introduced the euro, but the Danish kroner is pegged closely to the Euro in ERM II, the EU's exchange rate mechanism. Due to its high degree of convergence, Denmark has entered into an agreement with the European Central Bank on a narrower fluctuation band of ±2.25 percent, but actual fluctuations have been smaller than 1 percent since 2002. Hence, pricing in kroners or euros is almost equivalent.

A credible floating exchange rate cannot be a threat to international trade. In this framework, the currency is adjusted periodically in small amounts at a fixed rate or in response to changes in selective quantitative indicators, such as past inflation differentials vis-à-vis major trading partners, differentials between the inflation rate target, and expected inflation in major trading partners. When the floating rate is known, pricing in foreign markets is easy. In the 1990s, several Latin America countries pegged their currencies to the U.S. dollar, but due to the significant inflation differentials compared to the United States it was evident that local currencies would need to be severely

26. Gray markets or parallel imports occur when channel members located in low price markets, not under the strict control of the manufacturer, resell their products to market areas for significantly higher prices.

27. The price is right? (2005, January/2004, December). *Brand Strategy,* 32.

28. IMF 2006, *De Facto Classification of Exchange Rate Regimes and Monetary Policy Framework,* at www.imf.org/external/np/mfd/er/2006/eng/0706.htm.

devalued. Because a rapid devaluation would create instability, local currencies were slowly devalued toward a more appropriate exchange rate.

However, financial and currency crises are frequent, typically in emerging countries. Exchange rates, such as the $/€ or yen/$, are flexible and not easily predictable, even in the short run, and often there is a lack of a nominal anchor. Moreover, floating exchange rates are believed to be excessively volatile with respect to money supply, price levels, and current account balances, and exhibit a similar magnitude of financial asset prices.[29] In these cases the choice of the currency is equivalent to the choice of who is bearing the currency risk burden. Changes in exchange rates alter the firm's ability to compete, therefore affecting international pricing strategies.

A weakening of a domestic currency can stimulate exports and also create new market opportunities. As the dollar began to weaken in the early 2000s, a small United States boat sail manufacturer saw it as an opportunity to enter the competitive European market with its new-found price advantage. Hampered by 14 percent tariffs, Neil Pryde Sails International had not been able to compete in this large market. However, with the dollar losing nearly 25 percent of its value against the euro, the company's products became about 10 percent cheaper than those of their European rivals, allowing it to nearly double its sales in that region.[30]

Purchasing power parity theory can shed some light on exchange rate movements. The theory states that the very same good or basket of tradable goods should sell for the same price in different countries when measured in a common currency, taking into account transaction costs as well. *The Economist*'s Big Mac Index represents a practical example (see Table 11-2).

The basket consists of a similar product produced in about 120 countries: a McDonald's Big Mac. According to Table 11-2, Chinese producers enjoy a comparative advantage, as they can sell the Big Mac for 12.5 yuan or $1.83, according to the actual exchange rate of 6.83 (12.5Y/6.83 = 1.83$), while the price in New York is $3.57. In case of PPP (i.e., same price of Big Mac in the United States), the yuan should have been changed at 3.50 (12.5Y / 3.57$); that is, 49 percent less when compared to the actual exchange rate ((6.83–3.50)/6.83). Chinese exports to the United States would change both local prices, via demand and supply, appreciating the yuan versus the U.S. dollar. Actually, the local price in China entails an undervaluation of the yuan by 49 percent and an overvaluation of the U.S. dollar.[31]

TABLE 11-2 *The Economist*'s Big Mac Index: Some Examples					
	Big Mac prices		Implied PPP of the dollar	Actual exchange rate	Under (−) / over (+) valuation against dollar (%)
	In local currency	In $			
United States	$3.57	3.57			
China	Yuan 12.5	1.83	3.50	6.83	−49
Norway	Kroner 40.0	7.88	11.2	5.08	+121
Russia	Ruble 59.0	2.54	16.5	23.2	−29

Note: PPP = Purchasing Power Parity.

Source: Adapted from: Sandwiched. (24 July 2008). *The Economist.*

29. MacDonald, R. (1988). *Floating exchange rates: Theories and evidence.* London: Unwin-Hyman.

30. Wahlgren, E. (2003, November). Trade winds. *Inc.* Retrieved from www.inc.com/magazine/20031101/casestudy.html.

31. The Big Mac Index. (2008, July 24). *The Economist.* Retrieved from www.economist.com/markets/bigmac/about.cfm.

However, empirical analysis points to a failure of the PPP theory. There is evidence showing exchange rates fluctuating with little or no tendency to move toward a long run equilibrium level.[32] Moreover, Meese and Rogoff (1983)[33] and Mark (1995)[34] found that open economy models failed to outperform a simple random walk model. Hence the best forecast of any future exchange rate is the spot rate. If the seller does not want to bear a currency risk, hedging is needed. Hedging allows companies to avoid some or all of the risks associated with foreign-currency transactions by eliminating much of the guesswork about currency exchange rates at the time of the actual transaction. Large companies can perform in-house hedging when many transactions in foreign currencies are performed.

Let's assume a Canadian Company will collect £50,000 in 10 installments each at the end of each month next year and will pay out £1 million after six months. Taken together, only the difference between actual cash flows must be covered. Ignoring interest rates, while there is no risk, unknown exchange rate movements can still affect the company's profit. To manage its exposure, this Canadian company could acquire forward contracts or options that basically lock in a currency-conversion rate for a specified future date. Forward exchange rate quotations are for prices agreed on today for future delivery, typically 30, 60, or 90 days ahead up to one or more years. These quotations are usually made by commercial banks, and customized maturities may be negotiated at given fees. If the future exchange rate for six months' delivery is 1.5 Canadian dollars per pound, the sure cost of a £1 million payment after six months is 1.5 million Canadian dollars (plus commissions). If the Canadian company buys the foreign currency due in six months and holds an offsetting foreign currency liability, its position is "closed," and there is no risk in both transactions. By the same token, this company can offset risk associated with its 10 future exports. However, if exchange rates are free to float, it's very unlikely that the same rate at the time the agreement was made will prevail at maturity, but the bank will bear the risk.

INFLATION AND PRICE DECISIONS

Inflation should be taken into account when pricing. The challenge is to manage different inflation rates in multiple countries while maintaining a price position. As pointed out by Mühlbacher et al. (2006)[35], if inflation is high in the production country, a company may not be able to adjust prices as necessary in order to cover rising costs. The company may be forced to absorb the added costs resulting in a decrease of margins. On the other hand, if inflation is high in the customer's country, a price increase may be necessary, taking into consideration customer reaction, government controls, and operative costs related to price changes such as updating price tags, and reprogramming cash registers. In price negotiations, the company must also cover the risk of payment delay if the customer is located in an inflationary market, because the real price paid would be lower.

GOVERNMENT REGULATIONS, TARIFFS, TAXES, QUOTAS, AND VARIOUS NON-TARIFF BARRIERS

Government regulations, tariffs, taxes, quotas, and various non-tariff barriers are further elements a company has to take into consideration. It is rather common to have

32. De Grauwe, P. (1989). *International money: Pat war trends and theories*. Oxford: Oxford University Press.

33. Meese, R. A., & Rogoff, K. S. (1983, February). Empirical exchange rate models of the seventies: Do they fit out of sample? *Journal of International Economics, 14,* 3–24.

34. Mark, N. C. (1995, March). Exchange rates and fundamentals: Evidence on long-horizon predictability. *American Economic Review, 85,* 201–218.

35. Mühlbacher, H., Leihs, H., & Dahringer, L. (2006). *International marketing: A global perspective*. London: Thomson Learning.

to deal with government intervention introduced to maintain trade balances, develop domestic industries, and defend local employment and national security. Some interference in the market can also be due to political reasons. In 2005, coffee merchants in Venezuela encountered strict government price controls over some of their fresh ground coffees. As a result, they focused on providing only the more expensive types of coffee, such as aromatic and flavored ones, that were not regulated by the government. Their actions caused significant shortages of certain coffee products but also a dramatic rise in prices of value-priced coffee, which—if found in stores—were selling at a price almost 86 percent higher than the price set by the government.[36]

Taxation is another instrument of local protection, used to increase the domestic price of an imported product. The Mercosur area, for example, introduced a taxation system on imports so high as to make it almost compulsory for many companies that wanted to operate in Latin America to opt for foreign direct investment. And despite efforts on an international level to develop fair agreements that encourage free commerce guaranteeing competition, there have been many attempts to evade them. A clear example is the new "green tax" introduced in China in the automobile industry. With the aim to encourage foreign car manufacturers to use more local suppliers and reduce imports, China has imposed a special 25 percent tariff on imported car parts, in addition to the usual 25 percent tariff requested for imported new cars. The tariff was eliminated by the WTO, but less than a month later China introduced a new 40 percent tax on sales of cars exceeding an engine capacity of 4.1 liters. The official scope was to reduce fuel consumption and pollution, but it seems not to be a coincidence that this characteristic is typical of foreign cars.[37]

In general, government subsidies are introduced to reduce local prices to increase domestic companies' local or global competitiveness. For example, after the Chinese government increased its energy subsidies to the steel industry, the country's local production and exports rose significantly. In some cases, exports of government-subsidized products are considered a form of dumping in the importing country.[38]

Nevertheless, government subsidies can also force a company to make strategic product modifications in order to be price competitive. For example, both Ford in Europe and General Motor's Saab division quickly converted some of their cars destined for the Swedish market to use the modified E85 fuel, which is made of 85 percent ethanol and 15 percent gasoline, because Sweden began subsidizing ethanol fuel in 2001.[39] When the United States government offered a $1 per gallon subsidy for ethanol fuel, car manufacturers and oil companies began focusing their efforts in that area, too.

OBJECTIVES, STRATEGIES, AND PRICING POLICIES

In planning international pricing strategies, differences between countries and company objectives have to be taken into consideration. Strategy decisions will therefore be influenced by variables as short- versus long-term internationalization objectives, entry modes, competitive strategies, and profit and cost factors. A company's ability to efficiently choose and pursue specific strategies that are considered more suitable to its objectives will strongly depend on the possibility to control the final product price. The pricing control level is positively correlated with

36. Coffee—Venezuela: Market Insight. (2006, July 7). *Euromonitor International* [industry report].

37. Taking another road. (21 August 2008). *The Economist*. Retrieved from www.economist.com/node/11967001.

38. Dumping takes place when products are sold in other countries' markets below cost or below domestic prices, with the objective of obtaining relevant market shares in the foreign countries.

39. Edmondson, G. (2007, April 27). Europe looks beyond ethanol. *Business Week*. Retrieved from www.businessweek.com/print/globalbiz/content/apr2007/gb20070427_164153.htm.

internal organizational factors. As pointed out by Cavusgil (1996),[40] centralized decision making in international pricing leads to higher control of final prices and of their coordination across different countries. Other organizational variables, such as international experience, size, channel independence, and manufacturer asset specificity in the business relationship become important in export pricing control.[41] More experienced firms understand the complexity of foreign operations and prefer to internalize pricing decisions. Larger firms have the human and financial resources necessary to support foreign distributors, monitor prices, and acquire the information necessary to control prices in export channels. Channel dependence is another relevant variable affecting price control. Finally, asset specificity in the export country (i.e., specialized investments supporting the distribution function in a specific foreign market) increases the degree of pricing control. In fact, dedicated investments increase distributor dependency on the manufacturer, enabling it to reduce opportunistic behaviors and impose authority in order to exercise a high degree of control in price setting.

Becoming a profitable exporter does not depend on one particular pricing strategy but on a combination of the strategies listed above. What is important is the existence of a rational and consistent strategy that fits the company's goals as it expands in foreign markets.[42] For example, in a survey of over 400 mid-sized United States exporters from the manufacturing sector,[43] the authors found that the cost-based pricing method, accompanied by centralized decision-making and a product standardization strategy, is still predominant. Nevertheless, in terms of profitability, this method was closely followed by a more market-oriented approach, where price-setting decisions, decentralization, and reliance on market intelligence were the defining characteristics.

This proliferation of prices and pricing strategies across channels, geographies, and brands, can cause problems. In some cases, consumer packaged goods companies are forced to deal with as many as 20 million price points every year. A manufacturer of lighting equipment selling in the business-to-business marketplace was estimated to manage over 450,000 stock-keeping units (SKUs) for its 10 brands sold internationally to direct-sales representatives, key-account management teams, and third-party agents.[44] Clearly, achieving profitable pricing in all of these instances is a challenge for even the most disciplined companies.

There are a number of strategic alternatives or approaches to setting international prices:

- Cost versus market-based approach
- New product pricing: skimming versus penetration pricing
- Standardization versus adaptation approach
- Centralized versus decentralized approach
- Preparedness for internationalization and industry globalization: pricing strategy prototypes

40. Cavusgil, T. S. (1996, Winter). Pricing for global markets. *Columbia Journal of World Business, 31,* 67–78.

41. Myers, M. B., Cavusgil, T. S., & Diamantopoulos, A. (2002). Antecedents and actions of export pricing strategy. *European Journal of Marketing, 36*(1–2), 159–188.

42. Ibid.

43. Cavusgil, S. T., Chan, K., & Zhang, C. (2003). Strategic orientations in export pricing: A clustering approach to create firm taxonomies. *Journal of International Marketing, 11*(1), 47–72.

44. Bright, J. K., Kiewell, D., & Kincheloe, A. H. (2006, August). Pricing in a proliferating world. *The McKinsey Quarterly* [web exclusive]. Retrieved from www.mckinseyquarterly.com/article_page.aspx?ar=1841.

Cost versus Market-Based Approach

The **cost-based method** focuses on setting prices by fixing a profit margin over established product costs and thus ensures a more stable, predictable profit. This method, based on the equation *cost + margin = price,* has a serious weakness because it ignores demand and competition in foreign markets.

The **market-based method,** on the other hand, requires a much more dynamic approach that takes into consideration competition and customer demand. A recent study[45] finds that, given the competitive environment in global markets, the latter approach is much more appropriate for exporting firms.

The cost-based method includes three alternative options:[46]

- Full-cost pricing
- Incremental-cost pricing
- Profit-contribution pricing

Full-cost pricing represents the sum of total unit costs attributed to a product (direct production costs, direct marketing costs, allocated production, and other overheads) plus a profit margin. It is very easy to determine, and it guarantees that each sales transaction is profitable. However, indirect costs are arbitrarily allocated. Furthermore, ignoring demand and competition, it does not consider the price influence on sales volume. As a consequence, it fails to take into consideration the effect of price on production volume and therefore on total unit costs. Finally, if the determined price is not competitive, profit margins may be cut, with the result of obtaining a less-than-full-cost price.

Incremental-cost pricing distinguishes between variable costs and fixed costs. Based on this distinction, this approach takes into consideration production and marketing costs that the company must face when exporting. Incremental production and marketing costs plus a profit margin will determine the final price. Through this method, a company defines a floor price that cannot be lowered or it will result in a loss.

Profit-contribution pricing takes into consideration demand elasticity. The demand curve shape and demand elasticity abroad can significantly differ from the domestic market due to different preferences, buyer behaviors, and competition. A company must determine how total sales revenue will fluctuate in relation to price changes. Profit contribution represents the difference between incremental revenues and incremental cost of exporting in a foreign target market. The best price occurs when the highest profit contribution is generated (Table 11-3).

TABLE 11-3 Profit-Contribution Pricing: An Example for Wine in the German Food Market for a French Company				
Price (€/liter)	Estimated sales volume (liters)	Incremental revenue (000 €)	Incremental cost (000 €)	Profit contribution (000 €)
8,00	0	0	0	0
7,50	220.000	1650,00	990,00	660,00
6,60	380.000	2508,00	1635,00	**873,00**
6,25	400.000	2500,00	1700,00	800,00

45. Cavusgil, S. T., Chan, K., & Zhang, C. (2003). Strategic orientations in export pricing: A clustering approach to create firm taxonomies. *Journal of International Marketing, 11*(1), 47–72.

46. Root, F. R. (1994). *Entry strategies for international markets*. San Francisco, CA: Jossey-Bass.

Market-based pricing takes into consideration target market characteristics and, in particular, competitive prices. It can therefore be utilized for products that are already known and present in the foreign market. Take, for example, the automobile industry. Fiat launches the new Fiat 500 in Europe, copying BMW's premium pricing strategy. The company is in fact convinced that the Fiat 500, like the Mini, can charge a high price thanks to its distinctive characteristics. Automotive research points out that there is a market for retro, nostalgic small cars and that those customers are willing to pay a premium price for them.[47] It is therefore the market and competition that drive the company in its price decisions.

This method is based on the equation *affordable unit price – margin = target cost*. In this way, a company can calculate backwards, starting from market demand and then determining a suitable profit margin. For example, a Belgian manufacturer selling beer found that the affordable unit price for Polish consumers was 3€ per bottle. Considering the margins due to the importer and the retailer, the manufacturer's price should have been 1€ per bottle. Since the company margin was 55 percent, the target cost could not exceed 0.64€, otherwise the Polish market would have been unprofitable.

New Product Pricing: Skimming versus Penetration Pricing

A **skimming strategy** is based on the concept that a company can charge some consumer segments higher prices for a product. Starting from the high end of the market, which represents the "cream" (i.e., consumers who are willing to pay more), price is successively lowered to reach all other segments, achieving maximum profitability from different target consumers. This strategy results in high margins, but there are numerous risks. High prices should be justified by distinctive product features, while competitors should not be aggressive. Furthermore, the company has to take the risk of creating a market easily conquered by other competitive products. Finally, if price is lower in the domestic market, there is always the possibility of favoring parallel imports (gray market).[48] The example of Sony underlines how some of the risks cited above are inherent, while its management is not easy. In fact, when Sony launched its PlayStation 3 video game console, it gave it a sticker price of $600 in the United States market and over $800 in the European market. This price was well above its competitors, Microsoft and Nintendo, who were selling their new consoles, the Xbox 360 and the Wii, at about $400 and $150, respectively. Sony's price-skimming strategy may have backfired, however, because, despite its superior technology and features, the PS3 quickly lost market share in the United States to the lower-priced Wii. Despite multiple factors contributing to the failure, the initial high price was definitely a determinant, because only a million of PS3's most loyal fans may be willing to pay the market-skimming price.[49]

On the other hand, **penetration pricing** sets a low price for the new product in order to enter a foreign market, and often tends to base its communication campaign on this same strategy. Penetration pricing allows the company to quickly penetrate the market and obtain a significant market share, hence gaining market awareness and economies of scale related to production and distribution. This strategy is efficient when

47. Fiat charges premium price for new 500. (5 July 2007). *Automotive News*. Retrieved from www.egmcartech .com/2007/07/05/fiat-copies-bmw-charges-premium-price-for-new-500/.

48. Gray markets or parallel imports occur when channel members located in low price markets, not under the strict control of the manufacturer, resell its products to market areas for significantly higher prices.

49. Taylor, C. (27 April 2007). Where Sony went wrong. *Business 2.0* [Future Boy e-newsletter]. Retrieved from http://money. cnn.com/2007/04/27/magazines/business2/sony_playstation.biz2/index.htm; Palmer, M. (29 March 2007). European fans help Sony PS3 to a record-breaking launch. *Financial Times*, 1.

consumers are price sensitive, enabling the company to gain a competitive advantage against competition. The attractiveness of a penetration price must be evaluated not only as a strategy to gain market share, but also how it affects the company's overall global business strategy. For example, in its battle against PayPal, Google tried to win clients and gain market share in online payment processing, offering its Google Checkout service at a break-even price or at a loss: the company viewed this strategy "not as a standalone business, but as a driver of the Google network."[50]

Standardization versus Adaptation

When entering foreign markets, a company can set the same price in different markets or adapt pricing policies to local market conditions.

Price standardization implies the same price positioning strategy across different markets. As pointed out by Theodosiou and Katsikeas (2001),[51] factors that are potentially important in influencing the price standardization level are the economic and legal environment, distribution infrastructure, customer characteristics and behavior, and product life cycle stage. Basically, a standardization strategy is possible when the company operates in global sectors. It often becomes necessary when the company sells to global retailers. The retailers expect the product to be delivered at the same price in each country. If this does not happen, they would concentrate their purchases in the country where the product is offered at the lowest price. For example, multinational company discovered that one of its most important brands of deodorant had a price difference between Switzerland and Portugal of 80 percent and that European retailers could very conveniently buy the product in Portugal and sell it in other countries. The company immediately reacted, reducing the price gap to a maximum of 20 percent. This difference doesn't enable opportunistic behavior, because the price advantage for the retailer is eliminated by higher transportation costs. In general, it is necessary to negotiate a global-pricing contract between the supplier and the customer.

Price adaptation occurs when a company is compelled to adopt a different price positioning strategy, owing to heterogeneities in consumers' preferences, product perception, the intensity of competition, and country-of-origin effect. Global giants such as IBM and Coca-Cola have been adamant about maintaining consistent pricing for their distributors across the world. However, they and many other large companies have modified their strategy in low-income but emerging markets such as India and China, much to the dismay of their distributors in developed countries.[52]

Adaptation can be evaluated not only in relation to the final listed price, but also in reference to the entire transaction. Managing transaction pricing means determining which discounts, allowances, payment terms, bonuses, etc., should be applied to single transactions (see Table 11-4).[53]

PRICE DUMPING

When adaptation requires exporting at lower prices than those quoted in the importer's country, **dumping** may occur. Dumping is defined as selling products in other countries' markets below cost or below domestic prices, with the objective of obtaining relevant market shares in the foreign countries.[54] However, dumping is controlled by

50. A battle at the checkout. (5 May 2007). *The Economist*, 87.

51. Theodosiou, M., & Katsikeas, C. S. (2001). Factors influencing the degree of international pricing strategy standardization of multinational corporations. *Journal of International Marketing, 9*(3), 1–18.

52. The price is wrong. (23 May 2002). *The Economist*. Retrieved from www.economist.com/node/1143622.

53. Marn, M. V., Roegner, E. V., & Zawada, C. C. (2003). The power of pricing. *The McKinsey Quarterly*, (1), 27–36.

54. Mühlbacher, H., Leihs, H., & Dahringer, L. (2006). *International marketing: A global perspective*. London: Thomson Learning.

TABLE 11-4 A Hole in Your Pocket: Many On- and Off-Invoice Items Can Easily Lead to Price and Margin Leaks	
Annual volume bonus	An end-of-year bonus paid to customers if preset purchase volume targets are met.
Cash discount	A deduction from the invoice price if payment for an order is made quickly, often within 15 days.
Consignment cost	The cost of funds when a supplier provides consigned inventory to a wholesaler or a retailer.
Cooperative advertising	An allowance paid to support local advertising of the manufacturer's brand by a retailer or wholesaler.
End-customer discount	A rebate paid to a retailer for selling a product to a specific customer—often a large or national one—at a discount.
Freight	The cost to the company of transporting goods to the customer.
Market-development funds	A discount to promote sales growth in specific segments of a market.
Off-invoice promotions	A marketing incentive that would, for example, pay retailers a rebate on sales during a specific promotional period.
On-line order discount	A discount offered to customers ordering over the Internet or an Intranet.
Performance penalties	A discount that sellers agree to give buyers if performance targets, such as quality levels or delivery times, are missed.
Receivables carrying cost	The cost of funds from the moment an invoice is sent until payment is received.
Slotting allowance	An allowance paid to retailers to secure a set amount of shelf space.
Stocking allowance	A discount paid to wholesalers or retailers to make large purchases into inventory, often before a seasonal increase in demand.

Source: Excerpted from Marn, M. V., Roegner, E. V., & Zawada, C. C. (2003). The power of pricing. *The McKinsey Quarterly,* (1), 27–36. Retrieved from www.mckinseyquarterly.com. McKinsey & Company. All rights reserved. Reprinted by permission.

many rules developed both at national (to hedge local companies against dumping) and international levels. Since the creation of the WTO in 1995, anti-dumping activities have been strongly reduced (see Figure 11-2). Nevertheless anti-dumping investigations are still numerous, with China being the biggest target.

GRAY MARKETING AND PARALLEL IMPORTS

A standardized pricing strategy, reducing price disparities across markets, is actually preferable if a company wants to minimize the risk of **gray marketing** and **parallel imports**.[55] A parallel import occurs when channel members located in low price markets, not under the strict control of the manufacturer, resell its products to market areas for significantly higher prices.[56] In another type of gray marketing, a company manufactures a product in its home country market as well as in foreign markets. In this scenario, products manufactured by the company's foreign affiliate for sales abroad are sold by foreign distributors to gray marketers, who bring the products into the producing company's home-country market to compete with the domestically produced goods. In both cases,

55. Myers, M. B., Cavusgil, T. S., & Diamantopoulos, A. (2002). Antecedents and actions of export pricing strategy. *European Journal of Marketing, 36*(1–2), 159–188.

56. Muhlbacher, H., Leihs, H., & Dahringer, L. (2006). International marketing: A global perspective (3rd ed.). London: Thomson Learning.

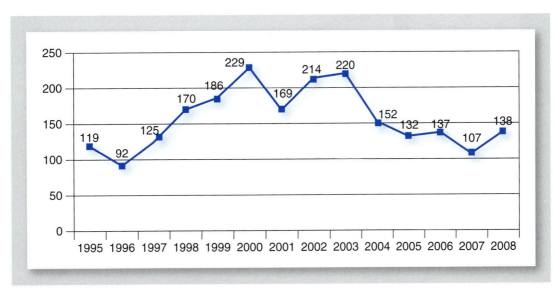

Figure 11-2 Global Anti-Dumping Initiations from 1995 to 2008

Source: Data from WTO Secretariat reports increase in new anti-dumping investigations. (2009, May 7). *World Trade Organization.*

the marketing opportunity that presents itself requires gray market goods to be priced lower than goods sold by authorized distributors or domestically produced goods.[57]

The launch of the iPhone is an example of how gray markets are created and how difficult it is to manage them even for companies like Apple (see Box 11-4).

Another example occurs in the European Union (EU) market for pharmaceuticals, where prices for the same medications are much cheaper in Hungary, Poland, and the Czech Republic than in Germany, France, or Italy. In fact, a research study estimated that parallel trade accounted for $3.8 billion between Eastern and Western Europe, with the largest flows moving from East to West. Some international pharmaceutical companies tried to solve the problem by imposing restrictions on wholesalers, while others attempted to reduce the price differentials for their products across the EU, and yet others, such as Schering AG, applied consistent pricing policies for the region. The most effective measure, however, may be the ongoing process of market unification in the EU, in which all pricing, currency, and regulatory fluctuations are slowly disappearing.[58] In Box 11-5, some gray marketing issues are pointed out, showing how difficult yet critical it is to manage the problem of parallel imports across countries.

Centralization versus Decentralization

Centralized versus decentralized decision making in international pricing is a rather critical issue in a company's strategies, especially in the case of multinational companies (MNCs). The conditions that can push MNCs toward a centralized pricing choice or toward decentralized pricing are numerous. Reasons that favor centralization can be summarized as follows on page 320.[59]

57. Tedeschi, B. (3 July 2006). A gray market in furniture spawns a feud in Europe. *The New York Times*. Retrieved from www.nytimes.com/2006/07/03/technology/03ecom.html?pagewanted=all.

58. New EU countries represent both market and manufacturing opportunities. (2005, March). *Pharmaceutical Business Strategies* [online newsletter]. Retrieved from www.pbsmag.com/Article.cfm?ID=181.

59. See: Cavusgil, T. S. (1996, Winter). Pricing for global markets. *Columbia Journal of World Business, 31*, 67–78; Bertoli, G., & Valdani, E. (2010). *Mercati internazionali e marketing.* Egea, Milano; Hollensen, S. (2010). *Global marketing* (5th ed.). Essex, UK: Pearson Education Limited.

BOX 11-4 COMPANY IN FOCUS: APPLE

Gray Market Sales of the iPhone

By the time the Apple iPhone officially went on sale in the United States, Great Britain, France, and Germany, where Apple has signed exclusive contracts with cellular carriers, 800,000 to 1,000,000 iPhones had already been "unlocked" by software hackers and were able to run on networks other than those of Apple's exclusive partners.

However, the marketing strategy developed since 2007 by Apple for the iPhone created the perfect conditions for a parallel or gray market. What are the main reasons for this?

The first one was the attempt to maintain exclusivity and control of the market. In the United States, the iPhone was locked to the AT&T network, allowing Apple to not only maintain a premium price but also to receive a 15 percent of the operator's revenues from each user. A similar arrangement was done with O_2 in the UK and Orange in France. At the same time, to overcome the control desired by the company, an illegal market of unlocked iPhones

that could work with any SIM was growing through non-official channels.

A second cause of gray market development was the product's international roll-out. A staggered launch due not only to the limited number of handsets initially available but also to the will to maximize the impact in each country created an unsatisfied demand that was targeted by gray marketers. But what especially made the gray markets flourish was Apple's strategy to extract different prices for different countries, a situation that was worsened by currency fluctuations when Asian gray-market entrepreneurs found it extremely attractive to buy iPhones in United States dollars and sell them in Chinese Yuan.

Sources: Ritson, M. (11 June 2008). iPhone strategy: No longer a grey area. *Marketing*, 21; Burrows, P. (12 February 2008). Inside the iPhone gray market: A global network is thriving by selling up to 1 million iPhones that bypass Apple's restrictions. *Bloomberg Businessweek*. Retrieved from www.businessweek.com/technology/content/feb2008/tc20080211_152894. htm; Kharif, O., & Burrows, P. (28 January 2008). Millions of iPhones go AWOL. *Bloomberg Businessweek*. Retrieved from www.businessweek.com/technology/content/jan2008/tc20080128_984623.htm.

- Increasing globalization requires standardized prices in the different markets, or there would be a risk of the development of parallel imports that are difficult to control. This is also true in the case of globalization of retailers, which can develop an opportunistic behavior of buying the product in another country where the price is lower.

- Internationalization of competition and homogenization of competitive structure requires globally coordinated competitive strategies.

- Price decisions are often closely related to production volume planning, production capacity, economies of scale, etc. Hence, centrally directed prices facilitate the forecast of worldwide annual revenues, and this activity is performed at the corporate level.

- Finally, price positioning is a relevant component of brand image. Global positioning requires price homogeneity, which is coordinated better centrally by the company headquarters.

Similarly, there are many reasons that can lead a company to prefer a decentralization strategy:[60]

- Local prices are a necessity if in different countries the company has to target different price segments or if the competitive structure is different. In some

---

60. See: Cavusgil, T. S. (1996, Winter). Pricing for global markets. *Columbia Journal of World Business, 31*, 67–78; Bertoli, G., & Valdani, E. (2010). *Mercati internazionali e marketing*. Egea, Milano; Hollensen, S. (2010). *Global marketing* (5th ed.). Essex, UK: Pearson Education Limited.

BOX 11-5   TECHNOLOGY IN FOCUS: GRAY MARKETING IN THE INTERNET ERA

Today the proliferation of global connectivity and the Internet is making this type of marketing easier than ever. Whether it is French champagne, Italian furniture, or American cigarettes, no consumer goods seem immune to the trend. Many manufacturers and retailers are unhappy about it but have little room for recourse. For example, several high-end Italian furniture makers recently attempted to prevent Europe by Net, an Internet company based in London, from selling their products at a 20 to 40 percent discount compared to their authorized retailers in the United States. The manufacturers threatened to pull their ads from *Elle Decoration*, a magazine which was distributing in Europe by Net's catalog along with its newsstand copies sold in Britain. In turn, the Internet company is asking the European Union's trade administration to investigate whether the furniture makers are illegally attempting to prevent Europe by Net from advertising and selling its products. At the same time, the reseller does not hide its gray market designation and is, in fact, proud of it. "Gray market is what we're doing, and we don't shy away from it," says Julie Edwards, the owner of the online business. She and most of the other gray marketers defend their business model as offering more choices and fairer prices to consumers.

Retailers don't see it this way, however. Cigarette vendors, especially those in border communities, are feeling the effect of the gray market more acutely. "It is cutting into business, but the only problem is that it's awfully hard to prove," says a wholesaler in Massachusetts. The merchant's sales are affected by the sale of cigarettes manufactured in the United States and intended for sale abroad. Massachusetts happens to be the only state in the United States that does not yet have a ban on gray market cigarette sales.

At a federal level, gray market goods are subject to a nearly 80-year-old law, the Tariff Act of 1930, which expressly forbids importation of goods of foreign manufacture without the permission of the trademark owner. There are, however, several exceptions spelled out in the act. The United States Customs Service, which implements the regulation, and the court system have considerable leeway in decisions regarding gray market goods, and in many instances the interpretations of the law between the two differ. With the many legal loopholes and the increased gray market activity, more and more consumers are finding themselves caught in the middle. They often find that the "bargain" they found online turned out to come with many of the standard accessories or warranties, or even instructions written in their language.

Some experts suggest that, because of problems with regulating gray markets, companies should develop proactive strategic responses to them. For example, improved market segmentation and product differentiation can make gray market products less attractive. Another strategy would be to aggressively identify and terminate distributors that are involved in selling to gray markets.

Sources: Tedeschi, B. (3 July 2006). A gray market in furniture spawns a feud in Europe. *The New York Times;* Deusser, R. (5 December 2005). State lawmakers consider imposing ban on gray-market cigarette sales. *The Berkshire Eagle;* Kessler, M. (11 December 2006). Some see red over gray-market goods. *USA Today,* B1.

cases, especially if the company is a price follower, the company has to set local prices to react to price changes of competitive leading products.

- Decentralization is necessary when there are significant differences in end-user characteristics (typically a lower income) and in price sensitivity, as well as consumer preferences.

- Flexibility in local price setting is often required when specific factors such as added taxes, product adaptation costs, differences in transportation costs, and local economic and financial conditions (e.g., interest rates and inflation) cause situations that induce a company to diverge from the standard corporate guidelines.

■ Decentralization in price setting can be also related to different retail power, which forces local managers to reduce selling prices. On the other hand, terms and conditions diverging across different countries can also impose price decentralization.

What clearly emerges is how some of these factors are strictly linked to the alternative choice between standardization and adaptation. Similarly, the final decision is a balanced approach between centralization and decentralization.

Taxonomy of Pricing Practices

Some researchers have suggested that companies' pricing strategies are influenced by the industry in which they operate and by the firms' own level of experience when selling internationally, and thus can be sorted into four general **pricing prototypes:**[61]

■ Local price follower
■ Global price follower
■ Multi-local price setter
■ Global price leader

As pointed out by the authors, a multi-domestic industry where the exporter shows low preparedness for internationalization identifies a "local price follower". The exporter has little knowledge of foreign market conditions. Information is received from local agents and distributors. This information, which can be sometimes altered to pursue personal interests, often lacks local insight and market knowledge. This induces the exporter to be local cost-oriented and competitor-based, which results in setting different prices for each of its foreign markets.

The "global price follower" has limited internationalization experience but operates in a more globalized industry characterized by standardized prices across different countries, mainly set by global price leaders. They are sometimes able to target special niches where they can set higher prices associated with better quality. Nevertheless, they are under constant pressure by local distributors and by pricing strategies of competitive global brands.

The third typology is the "multi-local price setter". International experience allows these firms to control and receive adequate feedback from their distributors, adapting price strategies to local requirements and to each country's market conditions. They are often price leaders and implement this multi-local approach by leaving pricing decision making to the autonomy of local subsidiary managers. Nevertheless, the latter are often induced to align their prices across different subsidiaries in order to avoid gray market imports.

The "global price leader" can be considered among the major "chess players" within its industry at a global level.[62] They often target and dominate a transnational segment where prices are rather homogeneous. Their price level tends to be higher, often resulting in a lower market penetration compared to multi-local competitors who are more adapted to the needs of domestic consumers and distributors.

61. Solberg, C. A., Stöttinger, B., & Yaprak, A. (2006). A taxonomy of the pricing practices of exporting firms: evidence from Austria, Norway, and the United States. *Journal of International Marketing, 14*(1), 23–48.

62. Solberg, C. A. (1997). A framework for analysis of strategy development in globalizing markets. *Journal of International Marketing, 5*(1), 9–30.

TRANSFER PRICING

Transfer pricing is the price set and paid for products shipped between units of the same organization. The unit can be a division, a foreign subsidiary, or a joint venture. Not only will these prices determine duties and taxes that are relevant for customs and tax authorities, but they will also affect the profitability of the divisions involved in intra-corporate exchange. The latter is particularly critical when the foreign unit is an intermediary, whose financial performance strongly depends on transfer price levels.

Different methods can be used to determine transfer price:

- Cost-plus pricing
- Market-based transfer price
- Negotiated transfer prices
- Arm's-length transfer pricing

The *cost-plus pricing method* uses product costs as a base for determining final price.

The *market-based transfer price* is based on the market price of goods, services or know-how internally transferred. Hence it would be the local market price minus the margin to be obtained by the subsidiary to cover its costs.[63]

The *negotiated transfer price* applies when market prices frequently change.[64] In these cases a constant internal price becomes a necessity between subsidiaries.

The *arm's-length price* is based on the results of a hypothetical negotiation with an independent business partner. The limitations of applying this method are numerous. Not only are data extremely hard to obtain, there can also be significant difficulties in identifying the right market price in the open market, since most of the time there are no substitutes or the quality of similar products and services is different. In addition, suppliers' cost structures can be significantly different, determining a non-comparability of the alternative offers.

Actually, for products flowing from the parent company to its foreign subsidiaries, transfer prices are determined at a higher level than arm's-length prices when the company finds it beneficial to maximize profit in the domestic market. Reasons can include the following:[65]

- Corporate income tax is higher in the foreign country than in the parent country
- A significant political risk of nationalization exists or expropriation of high-profit foreign firms
- The foreign country is characterized by political instability and/or a high inflation rate
- The desire of the parent company to mask foreign profitability, keeping competitors out of the market

TERMS AND METHODS OF PAYMENT

Payment methods regulate commercial relations between all parties directly or indirectly involved in the exchange of goods and services. Parties such as the exporter, the importer, and importer and exporter banks can be directly involved. On the other

63. Muhlbacher, H., Leihs, H., & Dahringer, L. (2006). *International marketing: A global perspective* (3rd ed.). London: Thomson Learning.

64. Keegan, W. J., & Green, M. C. (2008). *Global marketing* (5th ed.). Upper Saddle River, NJ: Pearson International Edition.

65. Bradley, F. (2002). *International marketing strategy* (4th ed.). Essex, UK: Pearson Education Limited.

hand, third parties such as other banks or professional traders involved in the financial arrangement can, at the same time, be indirectly involved in the transaction.

Payment methods are characterized by different risk levels. For this reason, it is always advisable to insure export orders against non-payment. Following are the available payment methods, starting from the most secure.[66]

Advance Payment—The payment, which can be done with a bank transfer, is cleared before the goods are shipped. This method is typical in the case of high-risk countries or low reliability of the customer. It is also preferred by small and medium enterprises which cannot be exposed for a long-term period. To avoid possible alterations in the communication of payment, it is usually preferable to create a direct link between the seller's and the buyer's banks.

Letters of Credit—This method can be considered a guarantee more than a method of payment. In fact, it is an undertaking by a bank to make a payment to the supplier (seller), against the presentation of documents that certify the transaction. Its main advantage is providing security to the exporter, because if the payment occurs regularly, the letter will not be activated. Vice versa, the exporter will send the documents to the bank, which will then proceed with the payment. Also, an importer may open a letter of credit in order to ensure that the exporter or seller has correctly performed the requirements of the sales contract. However, the main disadvantage of the letter of credit is related to the additional costs resulting from bank charges.

Documentary Collection—This is a process developed to facilitate import and export operations. After shipping the goods to the customer, the exporter sends the related shipping documents (necessary for the buyer to obtain the goods and clear them through customs) to its bank, which will conclude the payment and satisfy all the related requested payments of the exporter. The bank can send the shipping documents to the buyer after receiving the payment ("documents against payments") or after receiving the acceptance of a bill of exchange issued by the seller ("documents against acceptance").

Open Account—This method of payment is highly risky because the goods are shipped before payment; therefore, it is recommended only when none of the above methods are suitable or when there is a complete trust between the exporter and the importer. In an open account, the credit will be paid at a future date, and the terms can be 30 or 60 days or more. It is recommended to check the buyer's credit reliability because of the high risk level.

COUNTER TRADE

Counter trade is an umbrella term that encompasses the trading or exchange of goods or services without using currency. A variety of trading practices are included, from the simple exchange of goods for goods at an agreed value (barter) to more complex export transactions. The recent deal between DR Congo and the China Railway Engineering Corporation, a Chinese state-owned company, is an example of barter: the building of social infrastructures in Africa in exchange of natural resources for China. DR Congo will benefit from $6 billion of infrastructure (2,400 miles of road, 2,000 miles of railway, 32 hospitals, 145 health centers, and two universities). In return, China will receive natural resources (10 million tons of copper and 400,000 tons of cobalt) relevant for its industries. "It's a barter deal, what the Chinese side loves to call

66. Johnson, T. E., & Bade, D. L. (2010). *Export import procedures and documentations.* New York: Amacom; SITPRO Ltd. (2007). International trade guides: Getting started in international trade. Retrieved from www.sitpro.org.uk/trade/getstarted. html; Corradini, G. (2001). *L'impresa globale.* Milan, Italy: Giuffrè editore.

win-win. Not aid with strings attached, like Western powers have given DR Congo over the years, but pure business."[67]

According to the London Counter trade Roundtable (LCR), counter trade practices can vary according to local regulations and requirements, to the nature of the goods to be exported, and to the current priorities of the parties involved in the deal.[68]

From a marketing point of view, the main advantages given by counter trade are:

- The potential to capitalize excess capacity and transforming unproductive assets in profitable deals, helping domestic industries to find new foreign markets.
- The capacity to stimulate trade between markets that are unable to pay for imports; for example, because of lack of commercial credit or having a non-convertible currency

The most common forms of countertrade are described in Table 11-5. Nevertheless, as pointed out by the London Counter trade Roundtable, deals frequently involve several countertrade arrangements instead of fitting into only one specific category. For example, a company can undertake a long-term buyback plus counter purchase to finance initial down payments.

TABLE 11-5 Types of Counter trade
BARTER
Barter is based on the direct exchange of goods and services, and in the simplest case, no cash is involved. Whilst in a single contract, both flows from the import and the export market are covered, the exporter usually supplies the goods only after a relevant cash generation has been obtained from the sale of the bartered goods.
Barter was the first form of commerce and it is still today the main means of trading in many underdeveloped economies. It may also be used by companies or countries in more developed markets when they have commodities to offer.
COUNTER PURCHASE (OR PARALLEL TRADING / PARALLEL BARTER)
Due to its characteristics, this method is generally suggested when there is the objective of stimulating exports or to equilibrate an import/export deficit of the balance of payment.
In a counter purchase agreement (called also parallel trading or parallel barter), two separate contracts are signed. One is for the principal supply related to the import of goods, generally paid with normal cash or credit terms. The second is signed by the foreign supplier, which in exchange undertakes to purchase goods and services from the other party. If the exchange is not of equal value, some cash is involved. The agreement can vary from a general declaration of intent to a binding contract with specific details related to the goods and services to be supplied, the markets where they may be sold, and the penalties for nonperformance.
OFFSET
Offset has frequently been used by governments in the defense industry, both for purchasing high-priced items such as aircraft and for investing in manufacturing plants. Purchases of military goods face the necessity not only of promoting import substitution but also lowering the balance of payments deficit for military expenses promoting local production. Nevertheless, other sectors have also adopted this form of countertrade arrangement.
Offset can be direct or indirect. Direct offset is prevalent in the defense and aerospace industry, while indirect offset is also frequent in the civil industry. In direct offset, the purchaser requires the supplier to incorporate materials, components, or sub-assemblies provided by the purchasing country and, in some cases, to establish local production. In indirect offset, the purchaser generally requires suppliers to enter into long term industrial cooperation and investment, but these are not connected to the specific supply contract.

(Continued)

67. $9 billion barter deal. (19 April 2008). *Barter News*. Retrieved from www.barternews.com/9_billion_dollar_barter_deal.htm.

68. www.londoncountertrade.org/index.html.

BUYBACK (OR COMPENSATION AGREEMENT / COMPENSATION TRADING)

With a buyback agreement, a party supplies technology, equipment, capital plant, etc., all that is necessary to enable the other party to produce goods. In exchange it agrees to be repaid by the other party with part of the produced future output. While common with exports of process plants, mining equipment, and similar orders, this practice can also be found in other sectors and tends to be applied for larger amounts more commonly than counter purchase or barter deals.

CLEARING AGREEMENT

When two parties, typically two governments, are not able to make a trade simultaneously, it is possible to establish clearing accounts to hold deposits and effect withdrawals for trades. These trades (for example, coffee and salmon) are usually valued in a major currency (for example, the United States dollar), and the value of the account represents the purchasing power. In the contract, the parties can establish a plan to purchase goods or services at a specified value. On a transaction-by-transaction basis, the account can go out of balance, but in the long term the equilibrium is restored.

SWITCH TRADING

Switch trading is sometimes introduced to give flexibility to the clearing accounts, allowing a switch of the documentation and destination of goods. In fact, imbalances in long-term bilateral trading agreements sometimes lead to the accumulation of uncleared credit surpluses in one or the other countries or parties. Therefore a credit can be sold or transferred to another country or party. For example, if country A has a large credit surplus with country B, country A can finance imports from country C with the sale of country B goods to country C.

DEBT SWAPS

When debtors are unable to pay, debt holders can exchange the debt for something else. The exchange of a loan held by one creditor with a loan held by another creditor is a case of "debt for debt" swaps and is the most diffused. "Debt for equity" occurs when a debt is converted into foreign equity in a domestic firm, transforming the debt in a foreign direct investment. "Debt for product" is a swap converting the frequently high-risk debt into goods and services needed by creditor businesses. There are also "debt for social purposes" swaps when, for example, there is a conversion of foreign debts of developing countries to local currency set aside for specific social purposes such as preservation of nature or education.

TOLLING

In a tolling deal, a party (the supplier) provides a manufacturer with raw material necessary to process the production and obtain finished goods. Throughout the process the supplier retains ownership of the raw material and is paid back only when the manufacturer's products are bought by a final customer, who pays the supplier in cash. This agreement is favorable for those manufacturers who face the risk of limiting their production processes because they frequently lack the foreign exchange to buy raw materials.

Sources: Adapted from: London Countertrade Roundtable. (2007). Retrieved from www.londoncountertrade.org/countertradefaq.htm; Czinkota, M. R., Ronkainen, I. A., & Tarrant, J. J. (1995). *The global marketing imperative: positioning your company for the new world of business.* Lincolnwood, IL: NTC Business Books; Online Business Dictionary (www.businessdictionary.com).

SUMMARY

- Price is one of the more challenging decisions of a global marketing program. Defining a correct global pricing strategy is fundamental to long-term success.

- Price must reflect the value that the consumer is willing to pay for the company's product.

- Factors influencing international pricing decision can be categorized into competitive factors, consumer factors, country factors, product factors and distribution channels, and company factors.

- There are several strategic alternatives or approaches to be considered when setting international prices: cost- versus market-based approach; new product pricing; standardization versus adaptation; centralized versus decentralized approach; alternative pricing strategy prototypes.

• The price set and paid for products shipped between units of the same organization is defined as transfer pricing and can be determined using different methods.

• Countertrade refers to the trading or exchange of goods or services without using currency. Types of countertrade include barter, counter purchase, offset, buyback, clearing agreement, switch trading, debt swaps, and tolling.

DISCUSSION QUESTIONS

1. What are the factors influencing international pricing decisions? Take the example of a foreign brand that is marketed in your country: what local factors have to be taken into consideration when defining pricing decisions?

2. When you compare prices using the Internet, in what way do you use this information in your buying process?

3. Compare two similar products with a different price positioning (for example, two brands of jeans or motorcycles): what are the factors that affect value creation?

4. What are the advantages and disadvantages of using a cost- versus a market-based approach?

5. When a company launches a new product abroad, what are the opportunities and risks of a skimming versus a penetration pricing policy?

6. In which sectors is gray marketing more frequent? Why? Give some examples.

EXPERIENTIAL EXERCISES

1. How is Mattel managing Barbie's prices in a sensitive price market like China? Listen to the NPR story "Mattel hopes Shanghai is a Barbie World" (http://www.npr.org/templates/story/story.php?storyId=101479810) and describe the marketing strategies that support the upper-end price. In your opinion, how they can compete against cheap copies? After two years, the Barbie flagship store closed in March 2011 (http://www.bbc.co.uk/news/business-12670950). Can you point out the main mistakes of the company?

2. Select a product from your country and develop a pricing strategy in one emerging market of your choice. Point out which are the factors (competitive, consumer, country, product factors, and distribution channels) influencing your international pricing decisions.

KEY TERMS

Cost-based method, p. 315

Countertrade, p. 324

Currency, p. 310

Dumping, p. 317

Full-cost pricing, p. 315

Gray marketing, p. 318

CASE 11-1

Price Wars in the Chinese TV Manufacturing Industry: The Case of Hisense

Hisense (China)

Hisense, founded in 1969 as a Qingdao radio factory, has seen itself emerge as a multibillion-dollar conglomerate through a combination of effective management, a world-class staff, superior innovation and quality, and unique marketing strategies. Chairman Zhou Houjian joined Hisense in 1982 and directed the company to its record growth with total revenues reaching in 2008 of RMB 13.4bn and gross profit of RMB 2.3bn (Reuters Stock Quote, 2009). Twice named by China Central Television (CCTV) "Business Man of the Year," Zhou has led Hisense to an average year-to-year growth of over 30 percent and has seen the firm emerge as the flat televisions sales leader in China for the past six years. The company has about 10,800 employees and maintains 12.5 percent market share (see Appendix, Table 3A), a leading position in the LCD market among all Chinese firms (See Appendix, Tables 3A and 3B). As a result of such success, Hisense has been identified as China's twentieth most valuable brand in 2008, valued at RMB 8.45bn according to a study by World Brand Laboratory (Access Asia Limited, 2009).

Hisense (International)

In 1991, Zhou Houjian embarked on his mission to establish Hisense as an internationally renowned company by creating Hisense Export & Import Co. in Qingdao. Its sole task consisted of exploring potential overseas markets and introducing advanced foreign technologies to the company. As a result of intense barriers to the United States and European markets, Hisense initially shifted to emerging markets, as it entered South Africa (1996), Hong Kong (1997), and Brazil (1999). In the following years, Hisense launched a full-scale international expansion strategy, entering the markets of the United States (2000), Italy (2001), Indonesia (2001), Japan (2002), and Australia (2003), among others. Today, Hisense maintains 22 subsidiaries and sells its products in over 130 countries in regions as diverse as Southeast Asia, the Middle East, Europe, and South America. Throughout international markets, the firm distributes its products through large-volume retailers, such as Best Buy and Walmart in the United States, while relying on word of mouth and strategically placed billboards as its primary forms of advertising. These efforts have proven to be very successful, as Hisense's overseas revenues and televisions exports have increased significantly, and the brand name has even become commonplace in some regions.

Domestic Price Wars

Despite its dominant position in the domestic market and its successful internationalization strategy, in the mid-1990s, a variety of factors contributed to an industry-wide slump: overcapacity, increasing domestic competition, lack of technology standards,

Case prepared by Dr. Marc Fetscherin and Paul Beutenmueller, Rollins College. Reprinted with permission. The case authors would like to thank the Alexander von Humboldt Foundation for sponsoring parts of this research.

TABLE 1 Average Retail Prices of Television (RMB)							
Type of TV	**2002**	**2003**	**2004**	**2005**	**2006**	**2007**	**2008**
Cathode Ray Tube	2,020	1,960	1,970	1,870	1,660	2,050	1,770
Flat Panel	N/A	N/A	7,100	10,420	8,770	8,280	7,790
LCD	10,080	9,600	9,540	9,950	8,740	8,130	7,630
Plasma	38,330	35,340	26,690	18,170	11,560	10,430	9,620
PRTV	2,730	2,560	2,460	2,570	2,620	2,820	2,920

Source: Televisions in China 2009: A market analysis. (2009, January). *Access Asia Limited.*

TABLE 2 Comparative Starting Prices in USD in the Chinese Market				
Model	**Konka**	**Changhong**	**Hisense**	**US Price**
42 inch Plasma, wall mountable	1,500	1,300	1,250	2,000
LCDTV, 32-36 inch	600	700	600	1,000
32-inch-wide HDTV	415	430	450	800
Set-top decoder, SDTV	150	125	150	250
Set-top decoder, HDTV	220	200	200	550

Source: Compiled from company websites, 2009.

the spread of several small "no-name" manufacturers producing high-tech sets and selling them at knock-off prices, and an increasing grey market due to the smuggling of color sets into the country. The result was excess of supply and price wars. Hisense and the other leading TV manufacturers faced price pressure, as shown in Tables 1 and 2.

China's TV manufacturing industry is a two-tier market. Foreign brands controlled the high-end segment while enjoying a 20 percent price premium over local brands, permitting them to maintain a certain profitability. Consequently, local brands competed in the lower-end segment. This left Chinese domestic manufacturers at a distinct disadvantage, as they had little potential to increase profitability. As a result, the survivability of Chinese TV manufacturers was threatened. With no options remaining, China's largest domestic firm at the time, Changhong, launched a price war to put pressure on foreign competitors. These firms could either avoid slashing prices and allow domestic firms to gain market share at their expense, or they could lower prices and suffer from reduced profitability. The majority of the foreign brands elected to focus on functionality and increasing the value of the product rather than reducing the price. Their success declined as market share diminished.

Domestic manufacturers, on the other hand, responded in several different ways. The four biggest domestic players at the time elected to avoid entering a price war as a result of already thin profit margins and high costs per unit. However, when local brands such as Today China Lion (TCL) and Konka quickly announced price cuts, the rest of the industry had no choice but to lower prices. Small domestic manufacturers, already struggling to maintain profitability, suffered, and about 20 local brands went bankrupt. Within one year, those firms that had immediately responded to the price war saw their market share and revenue increase (see Appendix Table 4), whereas those that delayed it suffered. Furthermore, the dominance of foreign firms became less apparent, as eight out of the top 10 best-selling brands in China were local brands. However, while these price wars offered short-term payoffs, the long-term effect was not so clear. Record low profit margins, overcapacity, and a growing grey market are a few of the challenges China's domestic TV manufacturers are currently facing. With a penetration pricing strategy no longer feasible, companies such as Hisense and Changhong must turn to new competitive and pricing strategies that will provide them with long-term sustainability and profitability.

Hisense's Strategy for Survival and Amazing Turnaround

In response to the current domestic challenges, Zhou emphasized full-scale international expansion and exposure to reveal the Hisense brand. The company has attended nearly every main international tradeshow, displaying its high-tech televisions to consumers all over the world. However, the firm's primary method of survival is its sales of LED LCD TVs. In 2007, China's LCD TV shipments exceeded those of Japan, making China the world's third largest LCD exporter. Hisense, unlike its competitors, possesses its own LED blacklight module production line. Therefore, while other firms encounter additional costs of production in acquiring the resources necessary for developing such televisions, Hisense minimizes its costs, permitting the firm to produce in mass quantities and invest in future R&D. Finally, while competitors experienced substantial losses due to the global economic crisis, Hisense re-shifted its focus to developing markets like South Africa and Indonesia. Through its differentiation strategy and high-end products, Hisense has upgraded its product structure amid fierce competition. For the first half of 2009, net profits surged 87.9 percent and sales of LCD TVs were up 229 percent from the same period the previous year. In its key overseas market, Hisense witnessed increases in sales of 89 percent in South Africa and over 120 percent in Indonesia, for example.

Looking into the Future

With China entering the WTO in 2001, competition increased further as global brands or companies entered the Chinese TV manufacturing industry not only as a location for producing their products but also selling them. In fact, the world's top 10 manufacturers of consumer electronics all have production facilities in China and are investing heavily, as competition is now shifting toward the high-end market. Although Hisense has already distinguished itself as a top-selling brand in the Chinese domestic market, it has challenges to overcome domestically as well as to enter foreign markets in the current economical global crisis. It appears that Zhou has steered Hisense down the right path, having experienced some initial success in developing countries and invested in the high-end sector for the future. Through fulfilling its commitment to delivering innovative products and services, will Hisense be able to enhance its domestic and global presence in the television manufacturing industry?

Appendix

TABLE 3A LCD Market Share, First Half of 2008		
Ranking	**Brand**	**Share (%)**
1	Hisense	12.6
2	Samsung	8.7
3	Skyworth	7.8
4	Sony	7.7
5	Konka	7.6
6	Philips	7.4
7	Toshiba	7.3
8	Changhong	7.2
9	Sharp	7.0
10	TCL	6.5
NR	Others	20.2
	TOTAL	100.0

Note: NR: Not ranked

TABLE 3B Plasma TV Market Share, First Half of 2008		
Ranking	**Brand**	**Share (%)**
1	Panasonic	21.9
2	Hitachi	21.4
3	Hisense	17.6
4	Changhong	16.1
5	Haier	10.3
6	Skyworth	4.3
7	Konka	3.3
NR	Others	5.1
	TOTAL	100.0

Note: NR: Not ranked
Source: Televisions in China 2009: A market analysis. (2009, January). *Access Asia Limited.*

TABLE 4 Competitive Financial Analysis of Chinese TV Manufacturers, 2008				
Company	**Total Revenue mn RMB**	**Gross Profit mn RMB**	**Employees**	**Stock Market Code**
Changhong	27,930	4,787	30,000	SH 600839
TCL	22,731	3,622	50,000	HK 1070
Hisense	13,407	2,327	10,800	SH600060
Skyworth	12,294	2,631	5,200	HK 0751
Konka	12,205	2,361	17,000	SZ 200016

Source: Compiled from Reuters Financial Statements (2009). Retrieved from www.reuters.com/finance/stocks.

Questions for Discussion

1. How attractive is the domestic Chinese TV manufacturing Industry?

2. What is the source of Hisense's competitive advantage and how should the company compete?

3. What pricing strategy should Hisense follow, and is it sustainable and profitable?

References

Televisions in China 2009: A market analysis. (2009, January). *Access Asia Limited.* Retrieved from www.accessasia.co.uk/showreport.asp?RptId=12.

Sandra D. (2008), *International brand management of Chinese companies: case studies on the Chinese household appliances and consumer electronics industry entering US and Western European markets (Google eBook),* Springer, pp. 211–232/369.

Beyer von Morgenstern, I., & Shu, C. (2006). The great electronic wars. *McKinsey & Company.* Retrieved from www.mckinsey.com/locations/greaterchina/mckonchina/industries/high_tech/electronics_war.aspx.

Hisense Company Ltd. reports earnings results for the first quarter of 2009. (14 April 2009). *BusinessWeek.* Retrieved from http://investing.businessweek.com/research/stocks/private/snapshot.asp?privcapId=5491388.

Chen, Z. (2 May 1999). Changhong sparks new television price war. *Business Weekly*, 3–8.

Hisense Company Limited Website. (2009). Retrieved from http://www.hisense.com/en/.

Hoover's Company Records. Hisense Company Limited. Retrieved September 2009 from http://proquest.umi.com.ezproxy.rollins.edu:2048/pqdweb?index=1&did=1014562891&SrchMode=2&sid=1&Fmt=3&VInst=PROD&VType=PQD&RQT=309&VName=PQD&TS=1253903046&clientId=394.

Reuters Stock Quote. *Hisense Company Limited.* Retrieved September 2009 from http://www.reuters.com/finance/stocks/overview?symbol=600060.SS.

Yu, H. (9 January 2009). Hisense awarded CES 2009 "Global TV Brand Top 7. *PR Newswire*, *Asia.* Retrieved from www.reuters.com/article/pressRelease/idUS31723+10-Jan-2009+PRN20090110.

CASE 11-2

Can Long Haul Be Low Cost in the Traditional Airline Market?

Oasis Hong Kong Airlines Limited was established in February 2005 by Raymond Lee and his wife, Priscilla Lee. It was a low-cost airline based in Hong Kong and operated scheduled services to London, initially from Hong Kong. The chief executive, Steven Miller, was founder and first chief executive of another Hong Kong-based airline, Dragonair. The first flight to London commenced service on October 26, 2006. Originally, the airline scheduled to begin operations on October 25, but Russia revoked its fly-over rights just before the flight's scheduled departure.

Budget airlines operate within one country or within Europe, because the airline companies can turn their aircraft around quickly and are not subject to different regulations that govern in different countries. Also, seat dimensions could be smaller and no meals are provided in order to save costs. This may not affect the customer too much because of the short duration of flights. Oasis Hong Kong Airlines Limited was an exception. Its business model was to offer a premium class, long-haul product at an affordable price, which seemed impossible at first sight.

Oasis had direct competition in established airlines such as Cathay Pacific, British Airways, and Virgin Airlines. On June 28, 2007, Oasis announced that it was going to introduce scheduled services to Vancouver from Hong Kong, another hot long distance route. Other routes such as San Francisco, Chicago, and New York were planned at the same time.

Raymond Lee, Chairman of Oasis Hong Kong Airlines Limited, said that they were proud of their achievements. There was a demand for high-quality service at an affordable price for both Canadian and Chinese travelers. He believed that Oasis's business model had huge growth potential around the world as a value-focused, long-haul carrier. Oasis had an average load factor of 90 percent and on-time performance of 86 percent. Both were indicators of the high-quality, reliable service that passengers were experiencing on the new airline.

Oasis Hong Kong Airlines Limited was voted "World's Leading New Airline" and "Asia's Leading Budget/No Frills Airline" at the Annual World Travel Awards 2007. It was also named "New Airline of the Year" by the Centre for Asia Pacific Aviation of Australia, and was voted "Best New Service" and "Best Business Class Carrier" at the 2007 World Low Cost Airline Congress Awards held in London.

Oasis had planned to hedge a proportion of its fuel purchase to guard against future fuel price increases. On November 24, 2006, instead of leasing aircraft like other budget airlines, Oasis bought two aircraft initially in order to offer daily non-stop flights between Hong Kong and London. Later Oasis bought three aircraft from All Nippon Airways. Thus, the Oasis Hong Kong Airlines fleet consisted of three Boeing 747-481 and two Bowing 747-412 aircraft. The company hired 200 crew members. Total staff was 700.

Tickets were sold through the company's website and travel agents, similar to the other airlines. One-way fares between Hong Kong and London were initially available from U.S.$128 (excluding taxes and charges) for economy class. Two hot meals and

---

Case prepared by Tai Ming Wut, Senior Manager at Sigma Elevator, Hong Kong, Marketing and Advertising. Reprinted with permission.

soft drinks were served free on all routes in all classes. Free headphones, blankets, and pillows were also distributed. Each passenger had their own seat-back television, which had at least 16 channels and 12 audio music channels available. The seat width in economy class was thirty-two inches, which was the same as Cathay Pacific and Air Canada, and one more inch more than British Airways and Virgin Atlantic. The airline offered a business class as well, which it claimed was cheaper than economy on established airlines. Responses from customers were great and most Oasis flights were full. After a promotional period at the beginning, tickets normally cost only one-third or half of the other airlines. Oasis hoped that they could not only gain market share from existing airlines but also make the market segment bigger.

However, Edward Wong, an airline analyst for the Hong Kong financial services company Quam, pointed out that Hong Kong is not a good hub for budget airlines because landing fees are high there. This would not be the case in Europe, because those budget airlines could use second-tier airports to lower their airport fees. During 2007, fuel prices increased several times compared with 2006. It was a hard time to operate a long distance airline at a low cost. In the meantime, almost all the other airlines, including Cathay Pacific, offered discounts to their loyal customers.

Finally, on April 9, 2008, Oasis Hong Kong Airlines applied to the High Court of Hong Kong Special Administration Region to appoint provisional liquidators. The last flight, flight number O8901, departed from Vancouver at 10:15 A.M. and arrived in Hong Kong at 3:09 P.M. The court appointed KPMG as provisional liquidators, and KPMG assumed control of the airline at the same day. Oasis's CEO Stephen Miller announced at a press conference that the company would cease operations after suffering an accumulated loss of U.S.$128 million since beginning operations. "It is with great regret that Oasis Hong Kong announces that today the airline applied to the Hong Kong court to appoint a provisional liquidator. We have thus suspended all passenger services with immediate effect," he said. The Bank of China (Hong Kong) sued Oasis Hong Kong Airlines for U.S.$21.67 million, claiming the airline was unjustified in seeking a voluntary winding-up order. About 700 staff lost their jobs and 50,000 travelers who had booked flights were affected.

Global Placement and Distribution Channels

We are striving to achieve noticeable improvements for our customers and distribution systems. The various sales formats in all major markets will be adapted to new customer requirements. Every day is a chance to improve our service and make it more accessible.

MICHAEL DIEKMANN, CHAIRMAN OF THE BOARD OF MANAGEMENT, ALLIANZ GROUP[1]

LEARNING OBJECTIVES

After reading this chapter, you should be able to:

- Understand the role of distribution in the international marketing mix.
- Identify the main internal and external factors influencing distribution decisions.
- Understand how to manage global placement and international distribution channels.
- Evaluate different types of channel intermediaries.
- Recognize the existence of many differences in the retailing system of different countries.
- Elaborate a framework for selecting channel members.
- Understand the importance of managing and controlling channel members.
- Describe the main activities related to physical distribution.

The Power of Distribution

Few products lose their value as quickly as raw fish. And few products have gained as much value and popularity as quickly as blue-fin tuna, the preferred fish for making sushi, the traditional Japanese raw fish and vinegary rice delicacy that has been taking the world by storm. In his book, *The Sushi Economy,* Sasha Isenberg demonstrates how sushi's popularity around the world has not only become one of the best examples of the globalization of cultures and tastes, but also how technology and the modernization of distribution channels have made it all possible. Sushi's path to global fame started in the 1970s, when a Japan Airlines official was looking to find valuable cargo for his planes' return flight after delivering cameras, textiles, and electronics to North America. Thus, jet travel, with its speed and efficiency, opened a new

1. Quoted in the Annual Report 2007, Letter to the Shareholder, p. 3, retrieved from www.allianz.com/static-resources/en/ investor_relations/reports_and_financial_data/annual_report/archive/az_group_e_2007.pdf

distribution channel for tuna caught off Canada's Maritime Provinces to be sold in the Japanese market. Channel innovations did not stop there, however. Armed with satellite phones, fishermen soon could call in their catch ahead of time, fax machines made it possible for a boat owner to know what his haul would bring on Tokyo's fish market, and nitrogen-filled deep freezers have allowed the catch, frozen at minus 70 degrees, to find its way to your local restaurant from a farm off the coast of Spain or the North Pacific or from the shores of Cape Cod.

Sushi's globalization continued as the Japanese adopted the American fast-food restaurant model to market sushi as a quick snack food at *kaiten-zushi*, self-serve restaurants where a conveyor-belt circulates small plates of sushi around the bar. And now, a Seattle, Washington-based *kaiten-zushi* restaurant group has introduced yet another new method to improve on time utility by ensuring that only freshly made sushi is served to its customers. By tacking Radio Frequency Identification (RFID) tags to the bottom of the small plates on the conveyor belt, the restaurant can track which have circulated for 90 minutes—the self-imposed maximum time allowed. With this new system, the restaurant has succeeded in reaching its two goals: to achieve better inventory control and higher customer satisfaction. Meanwhile, the Taj hotel chain has also chosen sushi as a way to differentiate itself. It is launching sushi bars in India. Talking about the role of these new distribution channels, modern technology, and international marketing practices that have made sushi a symbol of globalization, Martin (2007) concluded in a recent interview: "the sushi economy is a quintessentially global industry that couldn't exist without the sort of revolutions of technology and finance of the last generation."[2]

The example of sushi shows how powerful distribution can be in the development of market penetration worldwide. In fact, after defining the appropriate entry mode for a company targeting a foreign market, the determining dimensions are, on the one hand, the definition of distribution channels with all its members: organizations, agents, wholesalers, retailers, etc., who move the product to the final consumer. On the other hand is the organization of physical distribution, which involves logistic activities such as transportation, packaging, inventory, and storage of the product to be exported to another country. Designing and managing efficient international distribution networks should concentrate on giving the final customers product information and accessibility, maintaining profitable distribution, partner relationships, and strengthening the company's global marketing strategy. But the challenging issues are: what kind of influencing factors such as differences in the macro environment, the competitive structure, or the distribution system have to be taken into consideration when designing a distribution network internationally? Which managerial factors are relevant in channel and logistic decisions? What is the involvement level of retailers in the internationalization process? All these issues will be presented and discussed in this chapter, and the importance of distribution decisions in the company's international marketing strategy will be emphasized.

FACTORS INFLUENCING INTERNATIONAL DISTRIBUTION DECISIONS

After defining the entry strategy into a foreign market, a company has to evaluate the most suitable channels in terms of structure, management, and control. Several internal and external factors have to be taken into account when a company is planning

2. Martin, D. B. (2007, June). Fishy expedition. *Fast Company*, 54; Ryssdal, K. (30 May 2007). Interview with Sasha Issenberg. *Marketplace, National Public Radio;* Malone, R. (23 May 2007). Tracking sushi. *Forbes.* Retrieved from www.forbes.com/logistics/2007/05/23/logistics-restaurants-biz-logistics-cx_rm_0523sushi.html; Issenberg, S. (24 May 2007). As the conveyor belt turns, *FC Experts Blog.* Retrieved from http://blog.fastcompany.com/experts/sissenberg/.

to build and develop its intended position in the global market. Among the internal factors are:

- The international marketing strategy of a company, with a given entry strategy and a degree of control that the company aims to reach
- The distribution strategy, mainly influenced by objectives of market penetration, by the competitive structure, and by the financial strength of the company
- The product complexity
- The size and development of the company's marketing and sales functions

On the other hand, external factors include:

- The characteristics of the distribution system
- Local regulations
- The stage of the product's life cycle
- Consumer shopping habits and market size
- The competitive climate

Internal Factors

One of the main elements to take into consideration when making distribution decisions in foreign markets is the company entry mode and the degree of control that the company aims to obtain in the foreign market. As a matter of fact, the choice of less risky modes of entry, which do not allow complete control of the foreign marketing strategy (for example, indirect export), often force the company to delegate its distribution choices to a foreign partner, who is autonomously responsible for the product distribution in the country. Intermediate entry modes, strategic alliances, franchising agreements, joint ventures, or greenfield investments allow the company to develop direct or short distribution channels that allow constant monitoring of sales activities abroad.[3]

Another important element is the determination of distribution strategy: Does the company want to develop an intensive, selective, or exclusive strategy? An **intensive distribution strategy** occurs when producers use as many outlets as possible. For example, the France-based Michelin Group decided on an intensive strategy when it entered Russia with its Michelin Truck Pro and Tyre Plus partnerships. Michelin already had 82 existing branches in 61 towns when it decided to extend its sales network in 2006 to every Russian town of 150,000 residents or more in order to provide proper coverage in this vast country.[4] Moreover, an intensive strategy is common when considering fast-moving goods manufactured by large multinational companies that aim to penetrate their brands to all segments of the population.

Companies such as the Armani Group, in the apparel sector, use a **selective distribution strategy.** A selective strategy is based on using fewer but selective intermediaries. Armani distributes its high quality products not only through its own stores (exclusive approach) but also penetrates some countries by selecting the finest apparel stores in the main cities. Finally, in the case of **exclusive distribution strategy,** the producer gives a limited number of retailers the right to sell its products in their specific territories. In exchange the retailer is generally requested not to sell competitive products. An example of a total exclusive strategy is Zara, the brand of the

---

3. See Chapter 8 for an analysis of entry modes.

4. Michelin Group 2006 Annual Report, "Highlights: Specialties", p. 10. Retrieved from www.michelin.com/corporate/finance/documents.

Spanish group Inditex. With a retail network of 1,361 stores worldwide, Zara usually penetrates foreign countries through store chains where only the company's brand is sold. These stores are managed directly by companies in which Inditex holds all or the majority of the share capital (88 percent of the stores), with the exception of certain countries, mainly in the Asia-Pacific area, where the retail selling activity is performed through franchises (12 percent of the stores).[5] These choices will depend on the company's market penetration objectives, the competitive structure, and its financial strength. For example, high penetration objectives necessarily require an intensive strategy that, as in the case of Michelin, cannot be pursued unless a strong financial investment is forthcoming.

Product complexity is another element that needs to be taken into consideration. Given different levels of product complexity, exporters should differentiate their relationship with intermediaries, because complex products require extensive information exchange and interaction in order to solve functional problems related, for example, to product delivery, installation, and/after-sale service.[6] In some cases, complexity is so high that it directly involves top management.

Finally, one last important element that influences companies' distribution choices is constituted by the characteristics of the export department's internal organization. Organization is defined by the number of managers employed in the department, their international professional background, marketing skills, and their operating budget. Companies that have a very simplified export department are not able to directly manage diverse foreign markets, and as a result, they will tend to opt for indirect distribution choices using local intermediaries and delegating to them all distribution activities despite lower control over the target market.

External Factors

Some external factors play a relevant role on international distribution decisions. A company must often come to terms with differences in the **distribution system,** logistics, and transportation infrastructure that will influence not only distribution decisions but also their own product and price decisions. For example, the inefficiency of logistics and of transport infrastructure makes it necessary for the company to use local intermediaries that are able to manage any problems that may occur. At the same time, using numerous intermediaries means lower control over the final market and may cause price escalation that can make the product unsellable.[7] Similarly, differences in distribution systems requires, for example, the use of alternative channels in which both the company and its sales network have no experience.

Take for example the OTC pharmaceutical industry. A global pharmaceutical company has to market its products in countries that are very different from a distributive point of view. For example, in France, pharmacies and drugstores distribute 65.7 percent of the total OTC national market value while supermarkets and hypermarkets account for only 8.3 percent. In markets such as the United States, supermarkets and hypermarkets account for up to 28.8 percent and pharmacies and drugstores distribute 49.1 percent of the OTC pharmaceuticals (Datamonitor, 2008).[8] The situation

5. Inditex 2007 Annual Report. Retrieved from www.inditex.com/en/shareholders_and_investors/investor_relations/annual_reports.

6. Solberg, C. A. (2008). Product complexity and cultural distance effects on managing international distributor relationships: A contingency approach. *Journal of International Marketing, 16*(3), 57–83.

7. For a description of the problem of price escalation, see Chapter 11.

8. Datamonitor. (2008). OTC pharmaceuticals in France. Retrieved from www.datamonitor.com; Datamonitor. (2008). OTC pharmaceuticals in United States. Retrieved from www.datamonitor.com.

TABLE 12-1 Beer Distribution Worldwide: Some Examples (% Share by Volume)						
Channels	**Brazil**	**India**	**Ireland**	**Singapore**	**Germany**	**Russia**
Specialist retailers	48.60	56.60	7.60	6.80	7.30	30.20
Supermarkets/hypermarkets	29.70	0.20	–	17.80	61.30	48.10
On-trade (restaurant, etc.)	14.90	43.10	78.70	63.80	22.90	8.80
Other	6.80	<0.1	13.80	11.60	8.50	12.90
	100.0	100.0	100.0	100.0	100.0	100.0

Source: Based on data provided by different reports: Datamonitor. (2008). Beer in Brazil; Beer in India; Beer in Ireland; Beer in Singapore; Beer in Germany; Beer in Russia. Retrieved from www.datamonitor.com.

in the United States requires the development of a sales network specialized in negotiating with a modern distribution system that in other countries has only a marginal role.

Another example is beer. In Table 12-1 it can be noted that in some countries such as Germany, distribution is dominated by the supermarket and hypermarket channel, while in countries such as Ireland and Singapore it is the on-trade channel[9] that prevails. India's case is striking; more than half of its sales are sold through specialist retailers.

The differences that we have just underlined can be determined by various factors. One of these is local regulations. In China, due to legislative changes, companies such as Mary Kay, Amway, and Avon were not permitted anymore to engage in the use of network marketing. After losing 50 percent of their sales, these companies had to adapt to new regulations which required their sales people to pass an exam administered by local authorities.[10]

Differences in distribution systems can also be linked to the stage of the product life cycle. In the introductory stage, market penetration and market coverage are very low; in the growth stage, selective distribution is recommended, while in the maturity stage, intensive distribution is usually required.

Other dimensions that need to be considered are consumer purchasing and **shopping habits** as well as outlet preferences. These represent behaviors that are deeply rooted in the country's culture and are difficult to change. A recent study by Maruyama and Trung (2007)[11] on retail formats in Vietnam reported that in 2005, one decade after the introduction of supermarkets, only 10 percent of all the products were distributed through modern distribution channels, while 90 percent continued to be sold through traditional channels such as organized bazaars, informal bazaars, and mom-and-pop stores. In Vietnam, a formal bazaar is an established market approved by the authorities; it is typically crowded, chaotic, and colorful, but also dirty and without product standards or trademarks. Informal bazaars (called *Cho Coc*) are not approved by the local Vietnamese government, which has tried (unsuccessfully) to eliminate them. Retailers are either stationary or mobile street vendors who typically sell vegetables, eggs, meat, and fish. Finally, traditional mom-and-pop stores are small family-owned shops selling food, drinks, toys, and personal care products. In some streets within a few hundred meters from each other, there can be 200–500 similar mom-and-pop stores. Why do consumers continue to do most of their shopping in these traditional outlets? There are many explanations, but most relate to the fact that long-established purchasing habits are difficult to change.

9. On-trade channel is known as the Horeca channel (Hotel/Restaurant/Café).

10. Ambler, T., & Witzel, M. (2004). Doing business in China (2nd ed.). New York: Routledge Curzon.

11. Maruyama, M., & Trung, L. V. (2007). Traditional bazaars or supermarkets: A probit analysis of affluent consumer perception in Hanoi. *International Review of Retail, Distribution and Consumer Research, 17*(3), 233–252.

BOX 12-1 COMPANY IN FOCUS: PROCTER & GAMBLE

In addition to key success factors such as afford-ability, lower costs, and product adaptation, Procter & Gamble (P&G) recognized early that it needed a robust and flexible distribution network to move into the fast-developing consumer products market of rural China. In addition to conducting thorough market research on consumer tastes and prefer-ences deep into China's interior, P&G is giving as much time and attention to building a large network of distributors that can reach even the most remote villages. Its current distributors cover half a million shops in most towns and cities, and many are now entering ever-smaller populated areas where mom-and-pop stores are the main retail centers. From vans branded with P&G's most popular lines, such as Tide, Safeguard, and Pantene shampoo, these dis-tributors deliver products as well as colorful posters, signage, and other sales props that help establish the company's identity and communication in the local market. But P&G is going a step further: it recently signed an agreement with China's Commerce Min-istry to update existing stores, build new ones, and teach the local workforce in nearly 10,000 villages how to sell consumer products. With a market share of 19 percent, China is the second largest market for P&G, following the United States. These actions will further boost P&G's presence in rural China, put the company in direct competition with regional and national Chinese enterprises often characterized by lower costs and better market knowledge, and also make it harder for rivals such as Unilever to com-pete. That Anglo-Dutch company, which lost mar-ket share to P&G due to a lack of clear distribution strategy, is now working to catch up. "We have made some errors and that has made us into a wiser com-pany," says Frank Braeken, Unilever's chairman for greater China.

Sources: Roberts, D. (2007, June 25). Scrambling to bring Crest to the masses in China. *Business Week.* Retrieved from www.businessweek.com/magazine/content/07_26/b4040058.htm; Penhirin, J. (2004). Understanding the Chinese consumer. *The McKinsey Quarterly* [Special Edition], 46–57. Retrieved from http://mkqpreview2.qdweb.net/PDFDownload.aspx?ar=1468; New President for P&G, (2010, March 25). *China Retail News.* Retrieved from www.chinaretailnews .com/2010/03/25/3467-new-president-for-pg-greater-china/.

Additional external factors that are worth considering are market size and the distribution of consumers across the country. The distribution strategy Procter & Gamble developed to target rural China demonstrates how the company's success in relation to competition has been determined by its ability to develop distribution strategies that target a huge market with a rural population spread over a vast area (Box 12-1).

Distribution strategies can also be influenced by choices made by competitors, which have paved the way for sales strategies in the country using specific channels. Moreover, competitors may have exclusive contracts with local retailers or wholesal-ers, creating entry barriers that tend to bar the company from some key channels. In other instances, competitors own their sales channels, allowing them to stay very close to the local market. Voluntary chain stores developed by Shiseido in Japan and, more recently, in China, represent a tool that provides high-quality counseling and services tailored to each consumer's requests, and constantly meet customer needs for skincare and makeup. Direct control of the distribution channel allows Shiseido to train its employees to fully acquire high service skills with high-level techniques and the spirit of *omotenashi* (hospitality; i.e., "enriching people's spirits through inter-actions between customers and products") in order to respond to customer needs (Illustration 12-1).[12]

12. www.shiseido.co.jp/e/ir/acc/ir_e0804acc/img/brf_08041.pdf; www.shiseido.co.jp/e/ir/annual/index.htm.

Illustration 12-1 Shiseido Stores in Japan

Source: Reprinted by permission from SHISEIDO© CO., LTD.

MANAGING INTERNATIONAL DISTRIBUTION CHANNELS

The distribution **channel structure** is strongly influenced by the country's economic development, which creates the need for more efficient channels.[13] In a growing economy it is expected that retail and wholesale institutions becomes larger and more specialized, while less efficient intermediaries exit the market.[14] A recent study focused on the Chinese market (Yi and Jaffe, 2007)[15] found that channel structure is determined by economic development and partially by government policy which can encourage this development. For example, in China the government promoted an "open policy", allowing market access by foreign firms and local ones; furthermore, the sale of goods by manufacturers directly to retailers was also permitted, making some state intermediaries redundant.

From a company's perspective, managing a distribution channel requires many decisions based on the evaluation of the advantages and disadvantages of different alternatives:

1. Direct versus indirect channels

2. Conventional distribution channels versus vertical marketing systems (VMS)

3. Selection among different types of intermediaries (agents, wholesalers, and retailers) identifying which ones are considered more suitable

13. Mallen, B. (1996). Marketing channels and economic development: A literature overview. *International Journal of Physical Distribution & Logistic Management, 26*(5), 42–57.

14. Olsen, J., & Grazin, K. (1990, Fall). Economic development and channel structure: A multinational study. *Journal of Marketing, 10*, 61–77.

15. Yi L., & Jaffe, E. (2007). Economic development and channel evolution in The People's Republic of China. *Asia Pacific Journal of Marketing, 19*(1), 22–39.

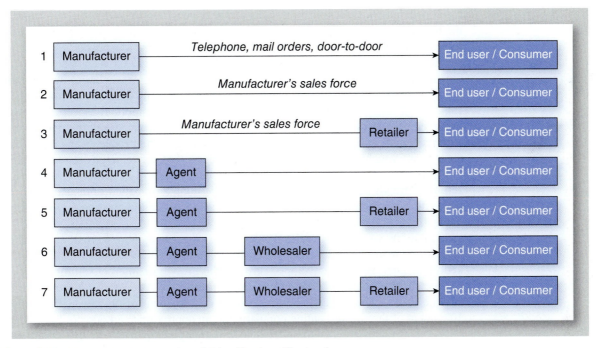

Figure 12-1 Alternative International Distribution Channels

Direct and Indirect Distribution Channels

In a direct distribution channel, the manufacturer sells directly to the final customer. A channel is indirect when one or more intermediaries (i.e., agent, wholesaler, retailer.) are involved in the transaction creating different levels of sales. While direct and indirect strategies are quite different, it is not unusual that both are used in a given country. Figure 12-1 describes the alternatives pointed out above. Alternatives 1 and 2 represent examples of **direct channels,** while alternatives 3 to 7 are examples of **indirect channels.**

The structure of the distribution channel can be described considering its length and its width. The length of a distribution channel is determined by the number of levels and types of intermediaries which perform some work to bring the product to the final user. For example, in Figure 12-1, channel number 7 is longer than channel number 3 because more types of intermediaries are involved in the transaction. In some long channels, there can be also different levels of the same type of intermediary; for example, there can be a principal wholesaler, an intermediate wholesaler, and an ultimate wholesaler. The width of the channel can be evaluated for each type of channel member, and it is defined by the number of intermediaries of the same typology operating in the channel. For example, the width of the channel is high when retailing is very fragmented (take the example of Coca-Cola, sold in an enormous number of retailers all over the world), and is low in the case of concentration (for example, Dolce & Gabbana collections are sold in a select number of stores).

DIRECT CHANNELS

If a company has a limited number of customers, it can serve the market directly through a specialized internal sales force or through a global key account organization that works in close contact with these clients. In general, a direct channel is recommended when technical products and services are provided to the consumer or the industrial target only by an internal qualified staff. A direct control by the company is typical for industrial goods, where the scenario is that of a business-to-business transaction between the manufacturer, through its sales force, and a company that uses the product in its production process. If the product is complex, it has to be presented and explained directly by the company to its clients. In some cases, with important clients, a high-level manager conducts the negotiation. An important aspect to consider is the required level of service; if it is high, the company has to work in direct contact with its clients, and must react directly and promptly to their requests and provide all the necessary technical skills to solve the problems that may emerge after the sale.

Similarly, if the company is a retailer, it tends to control backward its purchasing activity through agents that are internal to the company, called purchasing offices. International retailers usually localize purchasing offices in the main countries of interest.

Until a few years ago, besides the company sales force, there were direct channels only for door-to-door sales, mail orders, or telephone selling. Today, the direct marketing channel has been developed through the growth of Internet selling. A survey conducted by Nielsen in 48 countries from Europe to the Asia Pacific, North America, and the Middle East reveals the tremendous development of online shopping, from 10 percent of the world's online population to an approximate 84 percent from 2005–2010.[16] It is therefore easy to understand why many companies perceive the Internet not only as a communication tool but also as a sales generator. To confirm this, another global study of 27,000 Internet users[17] has pointed out that online purchases, which in the past used to be confined only to products like books and airline tickets, nowadays are expected to develop in other categories such as clothing and electronic equipment.

INDIRECT CHANNELS

In the case of indirect marketing channels, the relation between the manufacturer and the final consumer is filtered by intermediaries—agents, wholesalers, and retailers—who perform different functions such as holding inventories, financing, selling and promoting, and managing after-sales services.[18]

The channel can be short or long, depending on the number of intermediaries used by the company. When the company has many foreign clients, the role of these intermediaries is fundamental to reduce the number of exchanges, to overcome cultural barriers, and to simplify the selling process. On the other hand, using indirect channels carries the risk of losing control of the physical flow of products, the ability to determine pricing policy at every stage of the channel, inventory payment, and promotion policy.

Conventional versus Vertical Marketing Systems

Channel organization is another important issue that considers using **conventional distribution channels** versus **vertical marketing systems (VMS).** In a conventional channel, intermediaries are independent and act as if they are running a separate

16. The Nielsen Company. (2008). Trends in online shopping: A global Nielsen consumer report. Retrieved from http://th.nielsen.com/site/documents/GlobalOnlineShoppingReportFeb08.pdf; The Nielsen Company. (2010, June). Global trends in online shopping: A Nielsen global consumer report. Retrieved from http://at.nielsen.com/site/documents/Q12010GOS-OnlineShoppingTrendsJune2010.pdf.

17. The Nielsen Company. (2010, June). *Global trends in online shopping: A Nielsen global consumer report.* Retrieved from http://at.nielsen.com/site/documents/Q12010GOS-OnlineShoppingTrendsJune2010.pdf.

18. A description of the types of intermediary that international companies can use is provided on p.361–364.

Complete Vertical Integration				Partial Vertical Integration			
R	W	M	Manufacturer	M	W	M	M
R	W	M	Wholesaler	M	W	W	R
R	W	M	Retailer	R	R	W	R
1	2	3		4	5	6	7

Figure 12-2 Examples of Complete and Partial Vertical Integration

business. In a vertical system, intermediaries are linked in a unique integrated system that favors cooperation and synergies. As pointed out in Figure 12-2, a manufacturer (case 3) can control both the wholesaling (the process of sorting, assembling, and warehousing goods) and retailing activity (for example, managing direct stores). The same can be done by a wholesaler, which can manufacture its own goods and perform retail activities (case 2) or by a retailer (case 1). Integration can also be limited to only a few of the functions, as pointed out in cases 4–7. In all of these cases, the control can be developed as a corporate, contractual, or administrative VMS. In the corporate VMS, the control is determined through the ownership of the company (examples are DOS—directly owned stores). In the contractual VMS, control is realized through contracts with independent firms at different levels of production and distribution (this is the case in franchising, for example). Finally, when considering an administrative VMS, production and distribution can also be coordinated and controlled through the size and power of one of the parties.

A vertical system is usually required in situations where it is necessary to manage a complex product both in the sale and after-sale phases. There are also cases in which a company cannot find reliable distribution partners or in cases where the channel partners operate with very high mark-ups that make the manufacturer's final price uncompetitive. In both of these situations, a manufacturer can be interested in increasing the control of its sales process by integrating distribution activities. Consequently, if the size of the foreign market justifies the investment, many manufacturers often create sales branches and offices that perform the wholesale function, since they sell the parent manufacturer's products directly to retailers and industrial users.[19]

Furthermore, when the retailing format available in the foreign country is not suitable for its goods, a company can opt for forward integration through owned stores or franchising. It is a known fact that the owners of luxury brands open their own stores, especially in markets where they see the potential for growth and where they want to maintain a certain image of quality and exclusivity.

Multichannel Strategies

Depending on the characteristics of the foreign market, companies usually define multiple channels (direct and indirect, with different types of intermediaries) and choose the more suitable channel organization (conventional or vertical), often proposing

19. Sales branches set up by manufacturers in foreign countries are not considered wholesalers. However, since in practice they perform a wholesale activity, they are usually classified as wholesalers by national statistical offices. The difference between sales offices and sales branches is that sales offices do not carry inventory. See Chapter 8 for a discussion of entry strategies.

TABLE 12-2 Distribution Channels in L'Oréal	
Distribution Channels	**Brands**
Hairdressing salons	L'Oréal, Kérastase, Redken, Matrix, Mizani, Pureology
Mass market	L'Oréal, Garnier, Maybelline, Softsheen-Carson
Cosmetic boutiques and other specialist outlets and department stores	Lancôme, Biotherm, Helena Rubinstein, Diesel, Giorgio Armani, Kiehl's, Guy Laroche, Ralph Lauren, Cacharel, Shu Uemura, Victor Rolf, Paloma Picasso, Yue Sai
Pharmacies	Vichy, La Roche-Posay, SkinCeuticals, Sanoflore, Inneov
Owned Stores	The Body Shop
E-channel and catalogue selling	Lancôme e-shop, Le Club des Créateurs de Beauté

Sources: Adapted from: www.careernomics.com/Loreal0709/can/excelling.php; www.loreal.com/_en/_ww/index.aspx; http://www.ccbparis.fr/index.aspx; Dudson, D. (2008, March 7). L'Oréal has been on a spending spree in recent years to build up its ethical credentials, explore alternative distribution channels and lessen its dependence on Western Europe. *Cosmetics International*, 6(1).

differentiated offers or brands. L'Oréal, for example, the French cosmetic industry giant with 25 brands in 130 countries worldwide, is the only cosmetics group that uses a wide variety of distribution channels (Table 12-2): hairdressing salons with professional products, mass market (food, drug) with consumer products, cosmetic boutiques and other specialist outlets and department stores with luxury products, and pharmacies and dispensing doctors with active cosmetics.[20]

L'Oréal also uses a vertical marketing system exemplified by the acquisition of the ethical beauty retailer, The Body Shop, in 2006. The acquisition provided the company with an important platform for entrance into countries with underdeveloped retail markets. Finally, direct channels in L'Oréal are developed through initiatives of e-commerce and catalog sales such as the Lancôme e-shop and Le Club des Créateurs des Beauté.

One of the main issues in a multichannel strategy is the coordination necessary in order to convey the same message to the final consumer. The Allstate Corporation, operating in the United States and Canadian insurance industries with a distribution network of approximately 14,900 exclusive agencies and financial representatives, is an example of successful coordination that has also been achieved thanks to technology (Box 12-2).

Types of Channel Intermediaries

Basically, three groups of channel intermediaries can be identified: agents, wholesalers, and retailers. **Agents** operate in the name of the company but they do not take title to the goods they sell. **Wholesalers** take title to the goods and sell them to customers buying for reselling or for business use. **Retailers** manage the final link between the provider and the consumer. Each and every one of these intermediaries often has different characteristics, depending on the developed strategy; for example, some wholesalers are integrated forward, and they also manage retailing activities. Similarly, some retailers can be integrated backward and carry out activities that are typical of the wholesaler. Inside the single categories of agents, wholesalers, and retailers, different types of intermediaries can be identified and will be presented in the following paragraphs. From an operational point of view, these actors are generally highly reliant

20. Retrieved from www.careernomics.com/Loreal0709/can/excelling.php on March 3, 2009.

BOX 12-2   TECHNOLOGY IN FOCUS: MULTICHANNEL COORDINATION REQUIRES IT INVESTMENTS: THE ALLSTATE CORPORATION CASE

Being a multichannel company is not a guarantee of success if integration is not pursued. In order to reach integration, technology is the essential starting point. Allstate Corporation undoubtedly understands that investments in business process management and data management can be the key success factors for implementing multichannel projects characterized by a strong integration.

The Allstate Corporation is the largest publicly held personal lines insurer in the United States. Founded in 1931, it became a publicly traded company in 1993. Today the company has $133 billion in total assets. Its product portfolio is made up of 13 major lines of insurance, including auto, property, life, and commercial; it also sells retirement and investment products and banking services. All of these product lines are offered through a multichannel distribution network based on Allstate agencies, allstate.com, 1-800 Allstate, independent agencies, financial institutions, and broker–dealers.

The main consumer advantage is the possibility to benefit from a distribution network that is not only extremely varied but also strongly integrated. Allstate agents are connected with customer call centers and the Internet. This implies that a consumer can use an innovative channel such as Internet but also has the ability to conduct the transaction through traditional routes such as the agent or via phone. For example, a potential customer can obtain estimates on auto policies in about two minutes, and the company immediately displays on its website the name of an agent who can be contacted

at any time. Technology allows the customer to start the transaction on the Internet and to conclude it with an agent, but eliminates the need to redo the entire transaction; they simply continue where they previously stopped and then conclude the process.

Multichannel integration also represents an advantage for the agents, who can quickly and easily quote, follow up, and track new sales, pursuing their sales objectives more efficiently than in the past. Nevertheless, multichannel distribution also imposes integrated communication: in fact, it becomes crucial for the company to ensure that all channels are all emitting the same service and message, conveying brand and information consistently and enhancing a coherent positioning strategy.

Allstate Insurance Co. started this project of channel integration in 2000, and since then sales have significantly improved. Technology, integration, and continuous investments on enhancing distribution channels: these are the main ingredients of a successful relation between the company and the clients. As a manager of distribution, marketing, and process solutions at Northbrook, Ill.-based Allstate Insurance Co. says: "We want to provide a superior customer experience, and being multichannel is essential."

Sources: www.allstate.com/about.aspx; Burns, C. (2008, August). Channels work together toward the same goal. *Insurance Networking News: Executive Strategies for Technology Management, 12*(1), 1430; Viscusi, S. (2009, June 4). Allstate agents improve sales and marketing capabilities with Leads360 and Quote Burst. Tmcnet.com. Retrieved from http://outbound-call-center.tmcnet.com/topics/outbound-call-center/articles/57392-allstate-agents-improve-sales-marketing-capabilities-with-leads360.htm.

---

on the services offered and on the industry in which they operate, often resulting in a mixture of the types of intermediaries and contracts used by a company in different foreign markets.

Agents and Wholesalers

Agents sell supplier-owned products primarily to retailers and other wholesalers, but do not take title to goods or act in the name of the company they represent (called the "principal"). They offer a limited service and usually work for a commission or fee. Agents are generally used for products such as textiles, clothing, and footwear.

Wholesalers sell goods supplied by other firms to retailers or directly to industrial, commercial, and other end users serving a specific geographic area. They are distinguished from other types of intermediaries in that they take title to the goods they sell. Functions performed by wholesalers are numerous, from sorting, assembling, and warehousing goods to providing services such as packaging and labeling, contacting new clients, negotiating, and selling.

Analyzing the activity carried out by this type of intermediary, it is possible to distinguish "full service wholesalers," offering a full line of services to the company, and "limited service wholesalers," providing a limited number of services. Depending on their relation with supplier or customers or the distribution method employed, wholesalers assume different trade designations. The most important typologies of agents and wholesalers in an international context are described in the Appendix at the end of this chapter. It is important to understand that these are not always universal definitions but rather tend to vary depending on the sector.

Especially in underdeveloped country markets, wholesalers play a fundamental role in bridging the gap between demand and supply. Scattered markets throughout the countryside, where consumers have a limited income and local retailers can buy a very limited volume of many different products, can be reached by wholesalers who are able to handle a large variety of low-priced products.[21]

While the wholesaler role remains critical in providing value-added services, nevertheless, their structure can differ significantly country by country, mainly due to the economic development of the market. An important aspect to consider is the power concentration of wholesaling activities. In some countries, power is concentrated in the hands of few companies that operate on a nationwide basis and benefit from significant economies of scale in purchasing. An example is Japan, where more than 66 percent of total sales are generated by the largest wholesales outlets that account for only 10 percent of all outlets.

If wholesalers have a global presence, they can also distribute their products in global markets. Their strength influences foreign companies that wish to enter the country, since the possibility of distributing the product is almost all in their hands.

To have an idea of the power of wholesalers, we may consider the revenues of some of the world's largest distributors.

Table 12-3 shows the revenues of a select number of wholesalers, giving them significant channel power. However, power is not always this concentrated. Smaller distributors can be specialized in one product or brand, and they can even gain the exclusive right to distribute an imported product in the country.[22]

TABLE 12-3 The Leading Global Distributors			
Company	**Industry**	**Revenues (2010—US$ millions)**	**Country**
McKesson Corporation	Pharmaceutical	112,084	USA
Genuine Parts Company	Automotive	11,207	USA
China Resource Enterprise	Retail, beverage, food processing, etc.	11,188	Hong Kong
Inchcape	Automotive	9,570.1	UK

Source: Companies' annual reports (2010) retrieved from http://www.mckesson.com; http://www.genpt.com; http://www.cre.com.hk; http://www.inchcape.com/.

21. Samli, A. C., & El-Ansary, A. I. (2007). The role of wholesalers in developing countries. *International Review of Retail, Distribution and Consumer Research, 17*(4), 353–358.

22. Johansson, J. K. (2000). Global marketing: Foreign entry, local marketing and global marketing (2nd. ed.). New York: McGraw-Hill.

The degree of vertical integration also determines the power of a foreign distributor. Take for example the Chinese holding group China Resources Enterprise Limited. The group, primarily operating in Mainland China and Hong Kong, is both integrated backward into manufacturing and forward through distribution and retailing.

Retailers

Retailers are intermediaries that sell directly to the final consumer. Among the different activities carried out by retailers are ordering, storing, creating assortments, presenting goods in the most attractive way, packaging, financing, and providing after-sales services.

There can be wide differences in the retailing format between countries due to local shopping habits, lifestyle, economic progress, and local regulation. It is not a coincidence that Walmart, the world's largest retailer with more than 9,667 retail units under 60 different banners in 28 countries, operates retail stores in various formats including discount stores, supercenters, and Sam's Club.[23] However, even considering geographical areas such as the European market, it is impressive how the retailing formats for groceries are so differentiated. For example, in France, 54 percent of the retailing formats are represented by hypermarkets, followed by large and small supermarkets (respectively, 23 percent and 19 percent) and only 4 percent of other formats (such as specialty stores). A similar situation can be found in the UK, but not in other countries. Spain has 32 percent hypermarkets, 28 percent and 19 percent of large and small supermarkets, and 21 percent of other formats. The situation is even more differentiated in Italy, where hypermarkets are only 25 percent of total retail institutions while specialty or other stores cover 32 percent of the retailing formats for grocery goods.[24]

Sometimes differences in the retailing format have been determined by local legislation. For example, only 3 percent of Indian shoppers use Western-style supermarkets and hypermarkets, compared to 20 percent in China, 30 percent in Indonesia, and 40 percent in Thailand. Some of this disparity may be attributed to the fact that the Indian market has been closed to foreign food retailers in part to protect the millions of small, family-run grocery stores that are the livelihood of many Indian families. Nowadays the situation seems to be gradually changing; some 30,000 such small shops were closed in New Delhi alone in 2006, because they were operating illegally.[25]

Manufacturers have a number of alternatives to sell their products to the final consumer. First of all, they can consider the variety of independent retail intermediaries that can be used in a foreign market and choose those that are best for their products. In some cases, manufacturers have taken advantage of strong partnerships with some global retailers that heavily invest in their foreign development. For example, Unilever expands in international markets through the continuous internationalization process of global retailers like Carrefour, Walmart, Ahold, and Tesco, with whom it has developed strong partnerships. The choice of an independent retailer already present in the market doesn't eliminate the option of introducing innovations that can favor product sales, as happened for Beiersdorf, the German group selling brands such as Nivea, La Prairie, Juvena, and Eucerin. The company is trying to innovate, focusing on retail formats. In its traditional distribution outlets, supermarkets,

23. With nearly 600 locations and 47 millions members, Sam's Club is a membership warehouse club offering grocery and non-grocery products, serving both individuals and businesses. Retrieved from http://walmartstores.com/AboutUs/; http://www3.samsclub.com/NewsRoom/AboutUs/History.

24. The Nielsen Company. (2008). What in the world is happening: A global overview of economic and shopping trends. *Consumer Insights*. Retrieved from http://en-us.nielsen.com/content/dam/nielsen/en_us/documents/pdf/Consumer%20Insight/Consumer%20Insight%20Magazine%20Issue%208.pdf.

25. Giridharadas, A., & Rai, S. (28 November 2006). Wal-Mart's superstores gain entry into India. *The New York Times*, C3.

Illustration 12-2 Bulgari Stores in Rome and Paris

Source: Reprinted by permission from Bulgari SpA.

and drugstores, the company launched the Blue Wall, an area that features only Nivea products grouped together, all characterized by the common blue color of all Nivea packaging. The company is planning to roll out the Blue Wall concept not only in Germany, its main country (where after its initial success is planning to open about 100 shop-in-shops), but also internationally throughout the most mature Eastern and Western European markets.[26]

Nevertheless, in some cases manufacturers have to develop wholly owned stores or franchising networks that are more suitable to promote and sell their brands. For example, Bulgari's retail network consists of 293 exclusive Bulgari stores; 173 are DOS (directly owned stores), 54 are franchised, and 49 are travel retail and wholesale stores. Bulgari also distributes through independent watch retailers and through the finest select perfumeries and department stores (Illustration 12-2).[27]

INTERNATIONAL RETAILING

Internationalization of the retailing industry is a growing phenomenon that involves big retailers as well as small ones. The prerequisite to manage the development of an international network is the creation of a brand value recognized by foreign consumers. But the model of value creation is not the same for all retailers. Take the examples of Walmart, H&M, and Dior. Walmart is targeted to mass consumers and offers a wide assortment of "value for money" products of different brands in a store environment that conveys, with its design and atmosphere, the Walmart brand image around the world. H&M has a different approach, which is focused on its store brand built around the philosophy of bringing fashion and quality to consumers at the best price: the shopping experience enhances this philosophy, which is conveyed to consumers through more than 2,200 stores around the world, from Sweden to South Korea and China. In contrast to H&M, Dior is a producer first and a retailer second, and this characteristic determines a different approach to the retailing model. The brand is sold all over the world through independent retailers, franchisees, and directly owned stores. But the store was built around the manufacturing brand, not vice versa (Illustration 12-3).

One of the main decisions that international retailers must face is related to standardization / adaptation issues. On the one hand the growing globalization of consumer goods is seen as one of the variables that will gradually encourage standardization. On

26. Euromonitor International. (2007, June). Beiersdorf AG: Cosmetics and toiletries—World. *Global Company Profile.*

27. Retrieved from http://ir.bulgari.com/~/media/Files/B/Bulgari-IR-2010/presentations/2008/fy_result/fy_result.pdf; www.bulgari.com.

Illustration 12-3 A Dior Boutique in China

the other hand, there are still researchers who claim that format adaptation (i.e., the adaptation of the style, design, layout, and assortment of the store) is an almost necessary choice.[28] The need to adapt to national cultures is strongly perceived by global retailers who are far from standardizing not only their retailing format but also their local offer in terms of assortment, promotion, and selling techniques. Take for example Tesco. One of the reasons for its success internationally is attributed to its ability to adapt to local reality, to understand its needs and purchasing behaviors and adapt both format and assortment (Box 12-3).

Global retailers face a highly competitive environment in their internationalization process. Domestic competition is strong even in many emerging countries where local retailers are speeding their expansion plans improving their merchandising, products, and know-how, in order to strengthen their presence before the arrival of foreign retailers. This often requires global retailers to develop local strategic alliances. In India, for example, the United States-based Walmart has reached an agreement with the leading Indian cell phone provider, Bharti, to open hundreds of superstores across the country.[29]

In the global retailing industry, the Internet and catalog category, generating 6.9 percent of global value, has to be included in this discussion.[30] One of the companies that has undoubtedly paved the way for Internet selling is Amazon. As booksellers were stuck in the old model of selling books in brick-and-mortar stores, Amazon was busy building its market share by using the Internet for marketing and enlarging its customer base. The low-cost Internet operations allowed Amazon to offer substantial price discounts and larger selections. More importantly, Amazon's online model provided it with the ability to offer two differentiating services that became critical to its early success: customized recommendations based on tracking a customer's browsing and buying patterns, and product peer-reviews that gave it a sense of community.[31] Amazon has been successful in replicating this model in several international markets,

28. de Mooij, M., & Hofstede, G. (2002). Convergence and divergence in consumer behavior: Implications for international retailing. *Journal of Retailing, 78*(1), 61–69; Goldman, A. (2001). The transfer of the retail formats into developing countries: The example of China. *Journal of Retailing, 77,* 221–242; White, D. W., & Absher, K. (2007). Positioning of retail stores in Central and Eastern European accession states: Standardization versus adaptation. *European Journal of Marketing, 41*(3/4), 292–306.

29. Kearney, A. T. (2008). *Emerging opportunities for global retailers: The 2008 A. T. Kearney Global Retail Development Index*. Retrieved from www.atkearney.de/content/misc/wrapper.php/name/pdf_atkearney_bip_grdi_2008_1212762749d09c.pdf.

30. Datamonitor. (2008). *Global retailing: Industry profile*. Retrieved from www.datamonitor.com.

31. Flavián, C., & Guinalíu, M. (2005). The influence of virtual communities on distribution strategies in the Internet. *International Journal of Retail & Distribution Management, 33*(6), 405–425.

BOX 12-3   COMPANY IN FOCUS: TESCO

One of the reasons why the largest British mass retailer, Tesco, has been so successful overseas is its attention to local tastes and customs. Tesco store managers plan their promotional campaigns around country-specific events. Thus, Tesco stores in Poland have plenty of candles for November's All Saints' Day, Korean stores are packed with products promoting reading for October's Alphabet Day, and bathing suits are on display throughout much of Central Europe in July, while its domestic stores push the latest Harry Potter book.

Although it had entered numerous other overseas markets, Tesco was doing just that as it prepared to enter the United States market. CEO Terry Leahy conveyed the importance of planning for the company: "It's a format designed just for the American consumer, after a lot of research . . . We've been working hard on it." Tesco's American stores, to be called Fresh & Easy, are expected to incorporate some elements of the retailer's

European Tesco Express stores, which sell a few health and beauty products and offer a large selection of quick, easy meals, such as private-label entrées, side dishes, and desserts as well as wine, beer, and soft drinks. Tesco's new store formats in the United States have no cashiers at all: every transaction is self-managed. Such impactful innovation may have been difficult to accept in other markets, but not in the United States, where consumers show self-reliance on technology and the opportunity for resulting margin creation. It is expected that Tesco's stores will compete directly with German-owned Aldi, a discount retailer that currently operates Trader Joe's stores in several United States states.

Sources: Griffith, V. (2002, First Quarter). Welcome to Tesco: Your glocal superstore. *Strategy + Business*. Retrieved from www.scribd.com/doc/37855316/TESCO-Case-Study; Anonymous. (2007, February 12). No 'easy' United States entry for Tesco. *Retailing Today, 46*(2), F2; Interbrand. (2008). *Brands that have the power to change the world*. Retrieved from www.brandchannel.com/images/papers/382_European_Retail_Brands_final.pdf.

which accounted for 45 percent of sales in 2006.[32] At around the same time, online retailing began to emerge, and today it constitutes one of the largest marketplace shifts to which retailers need to adjust.[33]

Selection of Channel Members

When evaluating potential distribution partners, it is important to define contract and relationship development. The **partner selection** is a long process, and each phase, from partner assessment to final review, has to be carefully evaluated. A planning example is shown in Figure 12-3 with reference to a company facing the internationalization process.

In general, the most important attributes to be evaluated when selecting a distributor are its company's strengths, financial resources, marketing and sales skills, and commitment.

For example, when considering company characteristics and financial resources, it is important to verify the authenticity of the information provided by the potential partner using reliable sources (for example, companies such as Dun & Bradstreet provide specific products and services for all these information needs) and asking for references from some of its current clients. This is relevant not only from the financial point of view but also to verify the compatibility between the company and distributors in terms of image, positioning, and marketing strategies. Furthermore, the existence of facilitating factors such as experience with other exporters and a management

32. Bezos, J. P. (2006). Letter to Shareholders. *Amazon.com 2006 Annual Report*. Retrieved from http://media.corporate-ir.net/media_files/irol/97/97664/2006AnnualReport.pdf.

33. Hot topic: Web can pay off for traditional retailers. (23 December 2006). *The Wall Street Journal*, A7.

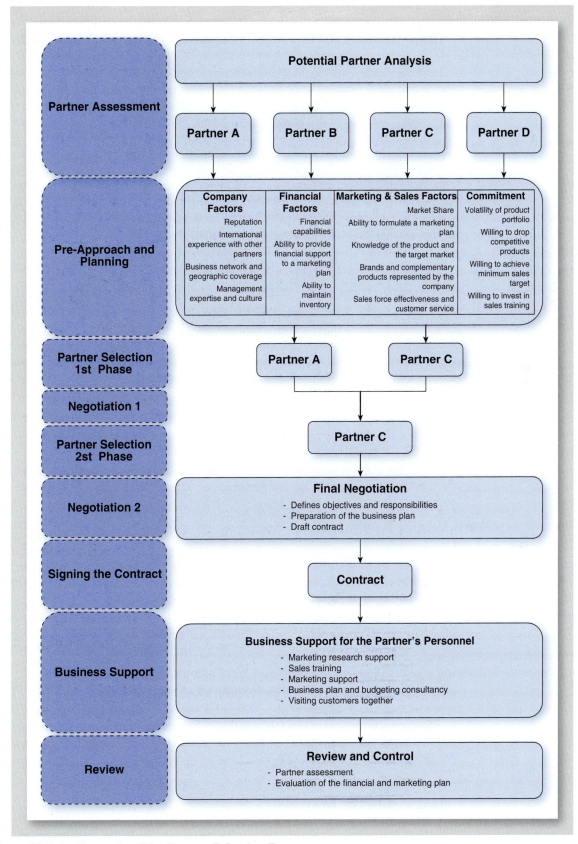

Figure 12-3 An Example of the Partner Selection Process

Sources: Varis, J., Kuivalainen, O., & Saarenketo, S. (2005). Partner selection for international marketing and distribution in corporate new ventures. *Journal of International Entrepreneurship 3,* 19–36; Cavusgil, S. T., Yeoh, P., & Mitri, M. (1995). Selecting foreign distributors: An expert systems approach. *Industrial Marketing Management, 24,* 297–304; Hollensen, S. (2010). *Marketing management: A relationship approach.* Harlow, Essex, England: Pearson Educated Limited.

culture open to international collaborations reveal the capacity to reduce the cultural, social, and geographic distance between the manufacturer and the foreign partner.

Marketing and sales factors are particularly relevant when the company must manage not only a product but a brand image abroad. This is the reason a manufacturer has to evaluate not only product knowledge and the complementary and competitive products already offered, but also the brands already represented by the foreign channel member. When considering marketing skills, it is very important to evaluate market coverage (both the geographical area and market segments) and power of the distributor within the marketing channel. Marketing skills can be evaluated by checking the distributor's business contacts, its capacity to develop promotional activities, selling support, and after-sales services in the local market.

Commitment is extremely relevant when a company wants to develop a long-lasting relationship with the foreign supplier. In fact, commissions and margins required by the intermediary are not always enough to maintain a profitable relationship.

It is true that selecting intermediaries is not an easy task, because often the company is faced with countries that are culturally very different. The choice process is difficult, and it is important to evaluate carefully the costs that the company will face. It is indeed not enough to consider the commissions and margins required by the intermediary, but also all the costs necessary for defining the distribution agreement, supporting the promotional expenses, and maintaining the business relation (for example, travel expenses to visit the distributor). Experience and method are useful in all of these evaluations in order to minimize the risk of failure.

CHANNEL MANAGEMENT AND CONTROL

Relationship management becomes especially crucial when it is necessary to control the product / brand positioning and performance in the foreign market. For this reason, companies are willing to **control** their distributors, trying to obtain maximum commitment from them by transferring all the knowledge necessary to sell their products. For this purpose, it is necessary to guarantee exclusivity whenever possible and to provide information technology and financial and marketing support. Strengthening the liaison with the intermediary brings positive results not only in terms of greater sales, but also in terms of higher levels of trust that are fundamental for a good relationship and for better distribution performance in the long term.[34]

The Michelin Group case is a representative example of such a relationship. When the Michelin Group decided to enter the United States agricultural business market for tires, it first held extensive training sessions for its distributors to teach them how to sell agriculture tires based on value, not price. Until then, the company's distributors felt that, to compete, they had to discount Michelin's tires, which cost 5 to 10 percent more than rival products. By teaching its distributors how to promote its new line of tires based on their superior performance, Michelin not only increased sales in that market by 35 percent, but was also able to strengthen the relationship with its dealer network.[35]

Successful channel management practices should be based on four dimensions:[36]

- Performance management
- Coverage management

34. Obadia, C. (2008). Cross-border interfirm cooperation: The influence of the performance context. *International Marketing Review, 25*(6), 634–650.

35. Huls, R. (2006, June). Michelin's value—Innovation strategy. *Corporate Event*. Retrieved from www.exhibitoronline.com/corpevent/article.asp?ID=1034.

36. Bellin, H. (2006). Best practice channel management: The channel management framework. *Journal of Marketing Channels, 14*(1–2), 117–127.

■ Capability-building programs

■ Motivational programs

Performance management identifies those activities that are finalized to improve operating performances through the definition of roles, responsibilities, and measurable performance goals. Coverage management focuses on channel structure efficiency and its coordination with the target market. Capability building includes all those activities that facilitate the operations of the channel members. For example, the manufacturer provides marketing and sales support, such as promotional material written in the local language. The manufacturer can also train the partner's sales personnel, visit clients together, develop business planning, and offer technology support to enhance the efficiency and efficacy of partner's activities. Finally, partners' motivation can be increased not only through monetary benefits (for example, higher commissions) but also with transparent relations, providing frequent updates on products, market, and company developments, regularly inviting partners to visit the company headquarters, and implementing other programs that can strengthen the relationship.[37]

It is important to underline how the implementation of these channel management programs requires first of all an efficient organizational structure. When managing a relationship with a middleman, not only the employees in the company's sales department are involved, but also employees in the production, logistics, information technology, and service departments. Their actions must be coordinated and coherent to assure the good functioning of the channel relationship. In order to monitor the functioning of the relationship when the company manages global clients, the role of centralized key account managers is necessary to provide homogeneous treatment in different countries. They are fundamental, especially in order not to have a nonstandardized treatment of international clients. The relationship's success and therefore its duration are mainly linked to the ability of intermediaries to satisfy the manufacturer's expectations in terms of performance and the achievement of the goals defined in the contract.

One of the difficult issues in a relationship with an international agent or distributor is performance evaluation. One of the reasons it is hard to properly evaluate a foreign distributor stems from the necessary vagueness of the distributorship contract itself. In a dynamic relationship such as one between manufacturer and distributor, it is impossible to craft an all-encompassing contract that takes into account all possible situations that may arise in the course of the relationship. Therefore, it is hard to ascertain when the conditions of the contract have not been followed (indicating poor performance). The physical distance separating manufacturer and agent, and cross-cultural communications that often characterize such relationships, complicate the evaluation process even further. Thus, two specific methods for controlling distributor relationships have emerged. The first gives precedence to costs; it is control-based and exercised by influencing decisions of foreign distributors in order to avoid opportunistic behaviors and obtaining information about their actions. The second emphasizes the establishment of common values, such as trust, commitment, and flexibility, and is norm-based. Both of these governance methods were found to influence the performance of foreign-market agents and distributors. Nevertheless, norm-based governance, where manufacturers showed support and involvement with their distributors, had double the impact, raising both the agents' market performance and manufacturers' satisfaction of the relationship. The positive effect of norms-based governance was even more pronounced in unstable markets with high levels of uncertainty.[38]

In fact, no matter how much the manufacturer and intermediary make efforts to successfully manage the relationship, such agreements are often terminated. A recent study of the relationship process identified two main triggers for the initiation of legal termination proceedings: proactive and reactive. Proactive terminations occur when internal decisions prompt the manufacturer to want out of the distribution agreement. Examples of such changes include change of ownership, the need to integrate channels establishing sales subsidiaries in the foreign country, or the decision to form relationships with more appropriate distributors. Reactive termination is initiated when either party finds the other to be uncooperative or opportunistic. Recent legal cases involving distribution agreement termination include, among the others, examples of distributors caught selling counterfeit products or giving other dealers more favorable price concessions.[39]

PHYSICAL DISTRIBUTION

The prime objective of **physical distribution** is to manage the movement of finished products from the company to its customers. Efficiency and service quality are guaranteed by an effective coordination of **logistic activities** that include handling, transport, inventory, labeling, and storage. All of these activities are mainly formalized by export documents such as the commercial invoice, the consular invoice, the certificate of origin, transport and bank's documents, government documents, and many others.

It is not uncommon that in some countries, companies encounter a lot of difficulty in obtaining the requested documents from the government; in some cases bureaucratic obstacles become strong entry barriers that foreign companies can overcome only with alliances with local partners that support physical distribution activities.

Transport decisions are also a big issue. Where there are poor transportation and logistics standards, foreign companies have to face inefficiencies that can significantly affect their costs (Illustration 12-4).

As an example, Box 12-4 shows the case of China and India, countries where transportation and logistics remain difficult not only in the countryside but also in fast-growing cities. A recent analysis of the Chinese logistics and distribution industry estimates that total company spending (including rail, road, inland water, air, and warehousing storage) amounts to nearly $490 billion, representing 20 percent of China's GDP. Compare that figure to the United States, where logistics spending makes up only 9 percent of GDP.[40] It is important to underline how the growing presence of foreign companies can bring improvement of physical distribution management. For example, fast-food chains like McDonald's and KFC have set up cold chain systems that service nearly 200 outlets throughout China.[41]

The need to improve physical distribution efficiency is strongly felt in most of the companies that operate on an international level. On the one hand, cost control has

38. Gencturk, E. F., & Aulakh, P. S. (2007). Norms- and control-based governance of international manufacturer-distributor relational exchanges. *Journal of International Marketing, 15*(1), 92–126; Zhang, C., Griffith, D. A., & Cavusgil, S. T. (2006). The litigated dissolution of international distribution relationships: A process framework and propositions. *Journal of International Marketing, 14*(2), 85–115.

39. Zhang, C., Griffith, D. A., & Cavusgil, S. T. (2006). The litigated dissolution of international distribution relationships: A process framework and propositions. *Journal of International Marketing, 14*(2), 85–115.

40. Feuling, B. A. (2008, September/October). China supply chain development. Retrieved from http://chinabusinessreview.com.

41. Gain Report. (2005). China, Peoples Republic of. Food processing ingredients. Sector food processing. *GAIN Report Number: CH5607,* USDA Foreign Agricultural Service.

Illustration 12-4 Transportation of Goods in Beijing

Source: Photo courtesy of Francesco Venier. Reprinted with permission.

BOX 12-4   COUNTRY IN FOCUS: CHINA AND INDIA

Logistics management, with more than 730,000 logistic operators, is highly fragmented in China, and a lot could be done to improve the efficiency and the quality of the physical distribution system. Today, for example, once shippers have delivered a load to a retailer, trucks are often empty on the return trip. In addition, current regulations influence long-haul freight, causing delays and increasing costs. For instance, some drivers avoid toll roads to cut expenses. Consequently the use of non-toll roads, poorly maintained and indirectly routed, lengthens transportation time and increases indirect costs and the likelihood of delays. Also, the lack of nationwide connectivity in transportation significantly affects material movement flows, costs, and throughput capacity. When a truck reaches provincial borders, it must often unload and reload its cargo into a new truck with the appropriate provincial license plates. This can determine an increase of material handling costs and may lead to product

damage. City restrictions to alleviate traffic jams can also complicate distribution. During certain times of day, distribution companies have to choose between the use of smaller cars and vans or, vice versa, pay high taxes for truck circulation.

The situation is not so different in India, where a lot has to be done to improve infrastructure; for example, with no warehousing or refrigerated trucking from the farm to the shelf, today 40 percent of the farmer's fruits and vegetables go to waste. India's cold chain logistics cannot be fixed unless large-scale investments are made, and the decision the government must make is about the need of foreign direct investment in the retail industry, which is strongly opposed by millions of middlemen.

Sources: Feuling, B. A. (2008, September/October). China supply chain development. Retrieved from http://chinabusinessreview.com; Schept, K. (2008, July). Retailing in India: Challenges and opportunities. *Chain Store Age,* 23–25; Kazmin, A., & Leahy, J. (5 July 2010). Grocery debate. *Financial Times,* p. 19; Feuling, B. A. (2010, July–August). Developing China sales and distribution capabilities. Retrieved from http://chinabusiness.com.

become more critical; on the other hand, there is an increasing need to distribute products quickly to customers and to guarantee high quality service. For example, Unilever in Russia established twelve regional distribution centers in order to implement a flexible and responsive supply chain which guarantees product availability in "one day's reach".[42]

There are companies that have turned logistics into a corporate philosophy. One of these is undoubtedly the Spanish Group Inditex, whose most famous brand is Zara, which believes that "logistics is at the service of the store," and has always considered the efficiency of physical distribution as one of the key factors for success. Together with investment in opening and renovation of stores, investment in logistics and information technologies is one of the most significant of the group, as it is considered a key aspect to ensure business growth. In fact, logistical facilities exceed one million square meters and have more than 4,000 employees. In Inditex, a computerized logistics system manages the process, starting from order receipt in the distribution center up to goods delivery to the store. The system enables an average deadline of 24 hours for European establishments and up to a maximum of 40 hours for stores in America or Asia. Inditex's logistics is carried out from eight distribution centers located in Spain, from which the product is regularly sent to all the group's stores all over the world. A constant improvement in the logistics system is an essential requirement in order to reach the necessary speed to respond to customer requests and to reach the capacity necessary to absorb the international growth of the company.[43]

SUMMARY

- When a company is planning to build and develop its intended position in the global market, the most suitable distribution channels in terms of structure, management, and control have to be defined.

- Several internal and external factors have to be taken into account when defining distribution in the foreign markets. Among the internal factors are the international marketing strategy of a specific company, the size and development of its marketing and sales functions, the financial strength, and the complexity of its products. On the other hand, external factors include the characteristics of the distribution system, local regulations, the phase of the product's life cycle, consumer shopping habits, and the competitive climate.

- The distribution channel structure is strongly influenced by the country's economic development, which creates a need for more efficient channels.

- Managing a distribution channel requires many decisions based on the evaluation of the advantages and disadvantages of different alternatives: direct versus indirect channels; conventional distribution channels versus vertical marketing systems (VMS).

- When entering foreign markets, a company has to choose among different types of intermediaries (agents, wholesalers, and retailers), identifying which are considered more suitable. Different typologies of agents and wholesalers can be identified in an international context.

- There can be wide differences in the retailing format between countries due to local shopping habits, lifestyle, economic progress, and local regulation. A growing phenomenon is the internationalization of the retailing industry.

- When evaluating potential distribution partners, it is important to

42. Unilever in Russia. (16 May 2008). JP Morgan Investor Conference, Moscow. Retrieved from www.unilever.com/images/ir_Unilever-in-Russia-Field-Trip-Presentation_tcm13-125538.pdf.

43. Inditex 2007 Annual Report. Retrieved from www.inditex.es/en/downloads/Annual_Report_INDITEX_07.pdf.

define contractual and relationship development. In general, the most important attributes to be evaluated when selecting distributor are financial resources, company strengths, product factors, marketing skills, and commitment.

- Successful channel management practices should be based on four dimensions: performance management, coverage management, capability-building programs, and motivational programs.

- Decisions related to physical distribution are also a big issue: where there are poor transportation and logistic standards, foreign companies have to face inefficiencies that can significantly affect their costs.

DISCUSSION QUESTIONS

1. What are the external factors influencing international distribution decisions? Take the example of a foreign brand that is marketed in your country: compared to other countries, which local factors have to be taken into consideration when defining distribution decisions?

2. What are the advantages and disadvantages of direct versus indirect distribution channels? Discuss and give some examples of brands using one of the two channels or both.

3. How can companies be successful developing a vertical marketing system (VMS)? What are the main risks? Discuss some examples of global companies successfully implementing VMS (for example, Inditex Group–Zara, or McDonald's).

4. Discuss the problem of coordination of brand image in multichannel strategies.

5. Discuss advantages and disadvantages of using an agent to enter foreign markets.

6. Discuss advantages and disadvantages of using a wholesaler to enter foreign markets.

7. Compare two different global retailers operating in your country and describe their competitive advantages.

8. When evaluating potential distribution partners, what are the most important attributes to evaluate? Discuss their relevance for different product categories.

EXPERIENTIAL EXERCISES

1. As a marketer for a large United States-based clothing company targeting the young segment, you have the task of developing the online channel marketing strategy for the firm's entry into the European Union market. Your main competitors are Zara, H&M, and Mango, which have already developed online stores. In the course of your research, you have also found the following information:

   ■ 78 percent of Europeans shop online and buy an average of 10 items with a total value of 750 € in a six-month period.

   ■ The product categories with the highest conversion rates (consumers who research a product online and go on to buy it online) in Europe are event tickets (75 percent), travel tickets (72 percent), books (71 percent), and clothes (70 percent).

■ Online shoppers in the United Kingdom and Scandinavian countries are the most active.

■ Shoppers from the Netherlands, Germany, and France use the Internet to do the most comparison shopping.

■ Auction sites are most popular in Germany and the UK.[44]

Given these considerations, make a competitive analysis and propose a channel strategy that includes product, pricing, promotion, and distribution suggestions that will make your brand relevant and attractive to European consumers.

KEY TERMS

Agents, p. 346

Channel structure, p. 342

Control, p. 354

Conventional distribution channels, p. 344

Direct channels, p. 343

Distribution system, p. 339

Exclusive distribution strategy, p. 338

Indirect channels, p. 343

Intensive distribution strategy, p. 338

Logistic activities, p. 356

Partner selection, p. 352

Physical distribution, p. 356

Retailers, p. 346

Selective distribution strategy, p. 338

Shopping habits, p. 340

Vertical marketing systems (VMS), p. 344

Wholesalers, p. 346

44. Harwood, S. (2007, March). Brits and Scandinavians top web shoppers. *Revolution,* 27.

A P P E N D I X

Agents and Wholesalers in an International Context

TYPOLOGIES OF AGENTS IN AN INTERNATIONAL CONTEXT

Representatives

Representatives operate in a specific geographic area on behalf of the principal, without taking physical possession of the product. They develop relationships with new customers or maintain contacts with old ones. In exchange for a commission, they arrange sales but cannot sign contracts and must pass all legal documents to the principal that will take the credit, market, or exchange risk. If the contract is approved, the principal will arrange for shipping and handling. Representatives represent either buyers or sellers on a more permanent basis than brokers do.

Manufacturers' Agents

Manufacturers' agents are hired by small manufacturers who cannot afford the cost of developing their own sales network, but they are also used by large manufacturers to enter new countries where the limited market potential and high risk do not suggest the use of full-time salespeople. They are located in the clothing, furniture, and electrical goods industries and usually represent two or more manufacturers of complimentary lines. The written agreement that regulates the relationship usually covers pricing, territories, order handling, delivery services, warranties, and commission rates.

Selling Agents

Selling agents are hired by manufacturers that are not interested in the selling function or that feel unqualified. They serve as a sales department and have the contractual authority to sell a manufacturer's entire output. As a consequence, even if they do not take title to goods, they have a key role in setting prices and general terms and conditions of sales.

Purchasing Agents

Purchasing agents make purchases for buyers. They usually establish a long-term relationship, offering numerous services such as receiving, inspecting, storing, and delivering the merchandise to buyers. Purchasing agents also represent for the buyers a precious information source in relation to the best goods and prices available in the market.

Brokers and Factors

Brokers and factors are independent individuals or organizations that facilitate buying and selling, assisting in negotiation and legally binding the principal to a sale contract without taking any risk themselves. In exchange for the service offered, they receive a commission on the selling price. Both brokers and factors usually do not develop a long-term relationship, and the contract is not expected to be exclusive. They are usually specialized by product line or customer type (food brokers, insurance brokers, etc.). Factors perform all normal brokerage functions plus financing. This is the reason why factors are frequently banks that may finance goods and cover the credit risk.

TYPOLOGIES OF WHOLESALERS IN AN INTERNATIONAL CONTEXT

Wholesale Merchants

Wholesale merchants can be classified by the number of product lines they carry. *General merchandise wholesalers* carry several merchandise lines; i.e., a wide variety of nonperishable items such as hardware, electrical supplies, and furniture. *Single-line* (or *general-line*) *wholesalers* carry only one or two lines (only food, or only a specific type of industrial tools, for example) but in greater depth than general merchandise wholesalers. As a consequence, they generally serve single-line and limited-line stores. When they sell industrial products, they usually cover a wide geographic area and offer more specialized service. *Specialty wholesalers* carry a very narrow range of products and in only one part of the line (for example, biological food or children's food). For this reason they are able to offer more information on their target market and more specialized services than other wholesalers.

Distributors

Distributors sell primarily to wholesalers, retailers, or final consumers. They usually stock the products up to one year or more. They have a formalized and long-lasting relationship with the manufacturer, with exclusive selling rights for a specified geographic area. This close collaboration allows the manufacturer to exercise higher control over the final price, promotional activities, inventory, and service policies than when it sells its products through a merchant wholesaler.

In the business-to-consumer market, distributors sell large volumes of goods to retailers such as supermarkets or hypermarkets. They can also sell to merchant wholesalers that serve a specific retail channel. In the business-to-business sector, industrial distributors handle large quantities of standardized items such as standard industrial components, or building materials, to be sold to manufacturers.

Distributors negotiate their margin with the supplier, represented by the difference between the buying and selling prices of the products they carry, minus their costs. Margins can vary significantly country by country, and they mainly depend on different factors such as the level of service offered by the distributor, the intensity of competition, sales volume, and purchasing power.

Commission Merchants

Commission merchants are wholesalers that are mostly used in agriculture. For farmers who do not want to perform sales activity and do not belong to producers' cooperatives, commission merchants take commodities to a central market, sell it for the best price, and remit the revenues to farmers after deducting commission and expenses.

Dealers

Dealers execute trades for their company's own account and provide the manufacturer (the principal) with a great deal of market information. Furthermore, besides having the same type of continuing relationship with suppliers that distributors have, they also carry out the same functions as retailers, since they sell the principal's products directly to final customers. Dealers frequently have exclusive selling rights for the manufacturer's products in a specified area. Sometimes the control of the manufacturer over the relationship is strengthened by holding an equity share in the dealer's business.

Importers

Importers provide the same services as distributors but they may be either wholesalers or retailers and, generally, they do not have exclusive territorial rights. The principal has limited control over them, because they may sell the products of many suppliers, sometimes even for competing product lines. Similar to distributors, they negotiate their margin with the supplier, with significant differences between countries depending on the level of service and local competition.

Cash-and-Carry Wholesalers

Cash-and-carry wholesalers are limited service wholesalers. They supply those retailers that are too small to be served profitably by merchant wholesalers. In recent years their target has been significantly extended to the *horeca* segment (hotels, restaurants, etc). Customers must pay cash, but they can benefit from lower prices; in fact, these wholesalers can operate at lower cost because retailers or customers take over many wholesaling functions. For these reasons, cash-and-carry operators are especially common in less-developed nations.

Truck Jobbers

Truck jobbers provide almost the same functions as full-service wholesalers; their characteristic is that they stock perishable products in their own trucks and may be able to deliver an order door to door within hours, operating 24 hours a day every day.

Drop Shippers

Drop shippers are limited service wholesalers because they sell goods, but they do not actually handle, stock, or deliver them, so their operating costs are lower. More specifically, they get orders from buyers that can be other wholesalers, retailers, or business users in general. They take title to the products they sell, but they ask the producer to ship the order directly to the customers. This system can be advantageous to avoid handling bulky products, reducing costs and the risk of damage.

Producers' Cooperatives

Producers' cooperatives are diffused in agricultural markets where many small producers join together creating a cooperative which operates like a full-service wholesaler. Profits are shared between the members who are at the same time members and customers of the cooperative. Some of these cooperatives are successful in creating well known brands, affording marketing costs that they wouldn't have been able to afford had they acted alone.

Rack Jobber

Rack jobbers are wholesalers specialized in nonfood products such as stationery, books, and magazines. They sell through grocery stores and supermarkets, displaying their products on their own wire racks, fixing prices, and so forth. This allows retailers the freedom of not having to reorder and guarantees the maintenance of displays of small quantities of many different kinds of nonfood items. For their service, rack jobbers are usually paid cash for what is sold or delivered.

Mail-Order Wholesalers

Mail-order wholesalers sell their products to small industrial customers or retailers through catalogs that include complete lines of specific products. Items such as jewelry, computer accessories and supplies, sporting goods, and general merchandise lines are the most diffused for this type of wholesaling. For example, LTD Commodities is a business-to-business supplier of apparel, home and garden accessories, jewelry, electronics, luggage, toys, etc., selling its products through catalogs and the Internet and shipping only to business addresses.

Sources: Sciarelli, S., & Vona, R. (2009). *Management della distribuzione*. Milan: McGraw-Hill Companies; Mühlbacher, H., Leihs, H., & Dahringer, L. (2006). *International marketing: A global perspective*. London: Cengage Learning; Kotler, P., Wong, V., Saunders, J., & Armstrong, G. (2005). *Principles of marketing* (4th European ed.). Essex, England: Pearson Education Ltd.

CASE 12-1

The Chinese Online B2C Market

Introduction

China's retail sales of consumer goods have grown by about 200 percent to reach 6.7 trillion RMB in a 10-year period ending 2005.[1] Goldman Sachs has projected that China will overtake America by 2039 and become the world's largest retail market.[2] However, the size of its e-retailing (B2C) market is still very tiny. In 2008, the Internet research organization iResearch indicated that China's online shopping market recorded a turnover of 120 billion Yuan, up 128.5 percent year-on–year.[3] In fact, China is the world's largest Internet market, with 210 million online users but only 22.1 percent or 46.41 million of them performing transactions on the Internet. Most online transactions are in the customer-to-customer (C2C) area. According to the China Internet Research Center in Beijing, 80 percent of the 43.3 billion Yuan online sales in 2007 were transacted through the C2C website Taobao.com, a subsidiary of online portal Alibaba.com, on which online users auction their own products.[4] As a result, China's B2C market scale remained small and reached 12.5 billion RMB in 2008.[5]

On one hand, the Chinese Internet market is promising thanks to its huge market potential. On the other hand, it is also challenging, because e-retailers have to face many difficulties when they plan their online marketing activities. These difficulties are related to quality of the market data, consumer confidence, market infrastructure, and culture.

Data Quality

A problematic issue for e-retailers to consider is the estimation of the actual market size in China. China had 210 million Internet users in 2008. However, this number must be interpreted with extreme caution.[6] It is not surprising to find that most families have access to the Internet through their own computers at homes in major Chinese cities like Beijing and Shanghai. However, going online in smaller cities and rural areas is relatively difficult, and millions of Chinese depend on Internet cafés to go online because they don't have their own Internet access at home. It was estimated that there were 185,000 Internet cafés in China at the beginning of 2009.[7] Some Internet cafés are enormous; they have 300 to 400 computers inside! Internet café users are mainly young people who play online games and chat with their friends rather than buying goods and services from Internet stores. It is difficult to convert this huge number of Internet users, who are actually Internet gamers and chatters, into Internet shoppers. In fact, Internet cafés in China play a far more important role than their counterparts in the United States and other Western countries. E-retailers may have to adjust the official numbers when they do their Internet market projections.

Case prepared by Dr. Thomas K. P. Leung of the Department of Management & Marketing, The Hong Kong Polytechnic University, Hung Hom, Kowloon, Hong Kong. Reprinted with permission. No part of this case can be reproduced without the written permission of the author. Dr. Leung can be contacted at msthomas@polyu.edu.hk.

Consumer Confidence

How to motivate Chinese shoppers to buy products and services online is trouble-some. In general, Asian consumers feel less secure when shopping online,[8] and personal interaction in purchasing behavior is prevalent in a high-context, Confucian-based Chinese society.[9] They feel unsafe buying a product online without any physical contact. They prefer to deal with someone who either possess the knowledge about the product or who is a member of their social network whom they can trust.[10] Face-to-face transactions with reputable brick and mortar stores dominate the Chinese retailing scene because consumers, in general, want to touch the physical product to help make their purchasing decisions. As such, how to build a good relationship with Chinese consumers so that they can buy products confidently from an online store remains a challenge for any e-retailer to consider.

Market Infrastructure

The first issue here for e-retailers to embark upon is that only a small percentage of online users have credit cards. Up until 2007, only 75 million credit cards were in circulation.[11] Those who do have them are often reluctant to use them for fear of fraud. Most Chinese online shoppers, in fact, pay for online purchases with cash on delivery.[12] The small percentage of online users and online shoppers when compared to China's population of 1.3 billion and its huge retail market size shows that the Internet, and the e-retailing market in particular, are both at the introductory stage of their product lifecycle.[13] If payment security can be improved and become trusted by Chinese online shoppers, its e-retailing market size could be enormous. Recent evidence shows that Chinese banks have started developing some reputable and innovative online payment options similar to the popular United States service PayPal, and that online Chinese shoppers are becoming more adapted to them.

The second issue for e-retailers to tackle is that consumers feel very unsafe buying goods and services on the Internet. Online shops are spread all over the country and most of them do not have industrial and commercial registration. This poses certain threats for supervision. Coupled with exaggerated advertising, passing of inferior goods as high-grade ones, and harsh conditions for product returns or replacement, technically there is not much online consumers can do if they receive fake goods. Recent service merchants such as Taobao.com have established their own grading and complaint-lodging systems, but consumers still have doubts about their effectiveness.

In 2008, Beijing Administration for Industry and Commerce became the first in China to require all profit-generating online stores to apply for operation licenses. This approach provides a basis for law enforcement in terms of management and guides individual online business operators to adapt standardized operations. Most online shopping websites now adopt the third-party guaranteed payment system, such as Alipay, used by Taobao.com, and Anfutong, used by Eachnet.com. When using these payment tools, cash is paid on delivery, and therefore the system is safer. But if buyers need to return purchases for reasons other than a quality-related problem, sellers often find it hard to agree, and hence a dispute typically emerges. An industry insider said that dispute settlement mechanisms must be established and improved, and that consumers are better off choosing large-scale service institutions and sellers with sound credibility in order to strengthen safety.[14]

The final issue is that online shopping in China faces the unreliable and highly regulated distribution system dominated by state-owned China Post. As sales to rural regions rise, officials in some areas are known to occasionally, and illegally, levy taxes on goods arriving from another province. In fact, "(China Post's) customer service is considered poor and its costs for transferring money are unreasonably high," Eric Wen of Morgan Stanley wrote in a research report.[15] Online retailers such as Dangdang.com and Joyo.com, bought by Amazon in August 2004 for U.S.$75 million, have opted to strike out on their own, starting delivery fleets staffed by young men on bicycles who accept payment and wire back the money.[16] This inefficient distribution system may be alleviated when the Chinese government opens up its courier sector to foreign competitors such as United Parcel Service, FedEx, and DHL.

Cultural Adaptation

Many may think the World Wide Web (www) is a communication media without any boundaries and that the same message can quickly be made available to people around the world. However, evidence shows that this may not be the case in China. Besides language, research shows that cultural adaptations should be implemented whenever foreign e-retailers want to use a website as a channel to sell their products to Chinese consumers.[17] In fact, a website is full of country-specific cultural markers. For instance, the Chinese websites are "pregnant" with Chinese cultural symbols such as the Great Wall, Chinese festivals, the Chinese Flag, and other Chinese landmarks.[18] Another important distinction between a Western and a Chinese e-retailing website is the tone of communication. For instance, American-style promotional messages like to use superlatives such as "the world's greatest" or "the world's number one," but this kind of message may need proof on a Chinese website.

Conclusion

The Chinese online market is attractive, but it also presents remarkable challenges for an e-retailer to consider. In saying that, an e-retailer must be aware of the deficiency of Chinese official statistics, and research must be carefully conducted before it incorporates the statistics on its e-retailing plan. Also, it needs to determine a unique product policy to ensure online customers can obtain its products and services in a satisfactory manner. In addition, the problems related to infrastructure have to be addressed. Specifically, the options of whether to use its own delivery or outsource it to couriers like UPS need to be considered together with payment method. Finally, an e-retailer must realize the Internet has cultural boundaries. It has to admit that the Chinese online market is unique and ethnocentric. As such, an e-retailer must have a Chinese-specific cultural strategy.

References

1. National Bureau of Statistics of China. (2006). *China Statistical Year Book 2006* (Table 17-3). Retrieved from www.stats.gov.cn/tjsj/2006/indexeh.htm.

2. Chandler, C. (2004, October). Inside the new China. *Fortune* (Special Issue), *150*(6): 28–46.

3. Anonymous. (2008). Youngsters in search of sound of music online. *China Daily*. Retrieved from www.english.people.com.cn/900001/90776/6340557.htm.

4. Anonymous. (17 March 2008). E-commerce gaining a new foothold in booming market. Retrieved from www.chinapost.com.tw/print/147480.htm.

5. Anonymous. (5 March 2009). The research report of online shopping market in China 2008. *Business Wire*. Retrieved from http://proquest.umi.com.ezproxy.lb.polyu,edu,hk/pqdweb?index.htm.

6. This comment is based on the author's telephone interview with an independent consultant, Paul Leung, who has extensive experience in the Chinese Internet market.

7. Anonymous. (2009). Research and markets: Analysis of China's U.S.$20 billion internet café industry, with an estimated 185,000 cafés. *Reuters*. Retrieved from www.reuters.com/article/pressRelease/idUS22125+12-Jan-2009+BW20090112.

8. Lynch, P. D., & Beck, J. C. (2001). Profiles of Internet buyers in 20 countries: Evidence for region-specific strategies. *Journal of International Business Studies, 32*(4), 725–748.

9. Hofstede, G. (1991). *Cultures and organizations: Software of the mind*. Berkshire, UK: McGraw-Hill.

10. Yu, J. (2006). Marketing to Chinese consumers on the Internet. *Marketing Intelligence & Planning, 24*(4), 380–392.

11. Anonymous. (17 March 2008). E-commerce gaining a new foothold in booming market. Retrieved from www.chinapost.com.tw/print/147480.htm.

12. Einhorn, B., & Tschange, C. (8 November 2007). China e-tail awakening: New online-payment systems are drawing wary consumers into the world of web commerce. *Business Week*. Retrieved from http://blog.udn.com/clcs1386680.

13. Anonymous. (2008). Online shopping requires effective supervision. *People's Daily Online*. Retrieved from www.english.people.com.cn/900001/90776/6340557.htm.

14. Anonymous. (8 June 2009). Online shopping requires effective supervision. *People's Daily Online*. Retrieved from http://paper.people.com.cn/mrb/html/2009-06/08/content_269944.html.

15. Anonymous. (23 September 2004). China's online shopping in web of problems. Retrieved from www.travellodge.info/china_travel/0408/shopping.htm.

16. Ibid.

17. Singh, N., Zhao, H., & Hu, X. (2003). Cultural adaptation on the web: A study of American companies' domestic and Chinese websites. *Journal of Global Information Management, 11*(3), 63–80.

18. Ibid.

CHAPTER 13

Launching Global Communication and Advertising

If communication is to change behavior it must be grounded in the desire and interests of the receivers.

ARISTOTLE

LEARNING OBJECTIVES

After reading this chapter, you should be able to:

- Explain what constitutes a global promotional strategy and what marketing activities are included in it.
- Discuss some of the challenges and opportunities marketers face on a global scale since the advent of digital marketing channels.
- Define the differences between global and localized brands and marketing communications.
- Understand how culture influences advertising preferences.
- Provide examples of regulatory issues that advertising executives may encounter around the world and explain why they are needed.

Founded in 1847 in Copenhagen, Carlsberg Breweries has been a major player in the European beer industry for well over a century. In the last decades, it has made a concerted effort to enter emerging markets from Eastern Europe to Russia and China. Meanwhile, in addition to the typical challenges of entering new markets, Carlsberg has been dealing with several industry shifts that have made the task of keeping its market share in existing markets and winning new ones on a global scale that much harder. Trends such as aging populations, antismoking laws, and healthy living, as well as new competition from wine and fizzy drinks have chipped away at Carlsberg's core market, prompting it to restructure its operations and rethink and reinforce its marketing and advertising.

Alex Myers, Carlsberg's senior vice president for Western Europe and former senior vice president for group sales and marketing, described the company's marketing communications strategy: "When we want to build awareness—in Asia and Eastern Europe at the moment, for example—we use sponsorships, festivals and that type of activity. When we're consolidating and seeking greater loyalty, we shift our resources to media like television, where the message can be communicated more effectively. After that, it's about activating the brands in stores and winning greater visibility in restaurants and pubs. This evolution has been very difficult to measure, which is the main reason we launched a commercial-excellence program to evaluate the different elements of the marketing and sales mix and are trying to develop a best-practice approach for the group."[1]

Brands must remain in continuous communication with their markets in order to acquire and maintain "top of mind" status and market share. And the more global the brand, the more complex communications become. From language and cultural barriers to advertising channel selection and organizational structure, the communication strategy for global brands is often difficult to reconcile because it depends on a myriad of external and internal factors.

GLOBAL PROMOTIONAL STRATEGY

By far the largest part of all marketing communications takes place under the fourth "P" of the marketing mix—promotion. **Promotional activities** fall roughly into four main categories: advertising, sales promotion, public relations, and personal selling. Some other activities are also part of the promotional mix but are harder to categorize, such as sponsorships, product placement, events, certain forms of direct marketing, and others.

With the advent of social media marketing and "two-way" communications between brands and customers, the lines between "communications" and "promotional communications" continue to blur. For most of its existence, marketing communications simply meant marketers repeating their brand's message through advertisements, jingles, billboards, and other "one-way" mass communications. With the arrival of the Internet, and Web 2.0 in particular, customers built their own media platforms to communicate their opinions about brands. Through blogs, forums, message boards, wikis, videos, websites, etc., they share their views and their brand experiences with other consumers and with the brands themselves. Marketers are learning the importance of these one-on-one, personalized communications and are incorporating them into their communication plans more and more often.

What does all of this mean for global marketers? Communicating the essence of a brand on a global scale has never been easy. Creating a coherent, effective, and efficient global campaign in today's increasingly connected and digital world presents a new set of challenges, some of which are listed below:

- A number of new channels with global reach have opened up for marketers with satellite and Internet networks, multimedia mobile phones, and popular social networking tools such as Facebook, YouTube, MySpace, Flickr, blogs, and others. This has not meant that traditional channels such as TV or print ads are no longer viable in certain markets, however, only that global promotional campaigns would have to incorporate all of the above and be planned accordingly.

- Digital technologies have nearly erased the distinctions between global and local communications. Today, a promotional video posted on YouTube can "go viral" and be accessible to 20 million viewers in more than 20 countries every month, regardless of what audience it was intended for originally. This certainly offers more reach for each marketing dollar, but it also increases the chances for misinterpretation across cultures and languages.

- Communications about a brand can be started by consumers as well as by companies. This is forcing marketers to relinquish some of the control over

1. Knudsen, T. R. (2007, May). Confronting proliferation . . . in beer: An interview with Carlsberg's Alex Myers. *McKinsey Quarterly* [web exclusive].

their campaigns, pick up new skills such as reputation management, and aim for the type of authentic and open communications that are valued by today's consumers.

■ Audience tracking, sales conversion rates, and other measurements available through digital marketing campaigns have raised the bar of accountability for marketers, who are required now more than ever to provide clear Return on Investment (ROI) metrics for their campaigns.

To deal with these challenges, many global marketers rely on an **integrated marketing communications (IMC)** strategy. The latest thinking on the IMC approach recognizes that the various elements of a company's communication strategy must be not only carefully coordinated, but that their impact as a whole on the market should also be considered. Currently, marketing mix modeling is used to identify the results of the separate communication and promotional elements without consideration for the interactions among them or for their overall effect and that of the rest of the marketing programs.[2] The "whole impact" approach to IMC management advocates for a cross-functional view of marketing communications, which is particularly relevant to a company's global promotional strategy.

At IBM, the IMC strategy has been an established practice for years. The global information technology giant even has a separate IMC organization dedicated to measuring and communicating the performance of the company's communication campaigns around the world to ensure that the hundreds of millions of dollars invested in them pay off. The IMC division tracks all types of communications—from advertising and sales promotions to events and sponsorships. Over the years, the IMC team has developed a highly sophisticated and effective measurements and research methodologies that provide actionable insights into IBM's global marketing communications.[3]

Levi Strauss has been one of the companies that have struggled with global marketing in this brave new world. It marketed its brand and products in separate, often locally conceived and produced campaigns that took into consideration the different positioning used for Levi's jeans in various regions of the world. For example, Levi's are considered premium jeans in Europe and are priced accordingly, while in the United States they are marketed as casual clothes that represent traditional American values.[4]

In 2008, the company took a bold step forward with a truly global product launch and a global promotional campaign to match. Built around the newly redesigned Levi's 501 jeans model that will be sold in the same fit across the world, the campaign's "Live Unbuttoned" theme is meant to communicate the freedom that "personal expression and revelation" can bring. The global campaign incorporates a number of promotional and advertising activities, including viral videos, print ads, TV ads, limited edition button covers, and digital campaigns featuring emerging talent from around the world, as well as outdoor advertising in select United States markets.[5] Given its edgy message, sexy images, and daring acts featured in the ads, some analysts concluded that the campaign's strong emphasis on individualism have not resonated well with some international audiences, even when the ads used

2. Shultz, D. E. (15 February 2006). Measure IMC's whole—not just each part. *Marketing News,* 8.

3. Powers, T. M., & Menon, A. (2008). Practical measurement of advertising impact: The IBM experience. In Roger A. Kerin and Rob O'Regan (Eds.), *Marketing mix decisions: New perspectives and practices* (pp. 77–109). Chicago: AMA.

4. Smith, R. A. (18 July 2008). Levi's marketers hope one size fits all. *Wall Street Journal Online.*

5. "Live unbuttoned" with global launch of new, innovative Levi's 501 marketing campaign. (21 July 2008). *PR Newswire* [press release].

characters that looked like the local population.[6] But Levi's is betting that global youth—the segment targeted for the "Live Unbuttoned" campaign will eventually to embrace the uniform message and the global product in the same way that they have embraced music stars and pop culture in general.[7] "This is about stepping up and being a global leader," says John Anderson, president and CEO of Levi Strauss & Co. "With our Levi's brand sold in more than 110 countries, we are the No. 1 jeans company in the world. This campaign gave us a unique opportunity to let a new generation of jeans consumers around the world know that the original, quintessential 501 jeans is contemporary and relevant to their lifestyle. No other jeans brand can do this."[8]

The financial performance of the company seems to support Mr. Anderson's statement, with global sales and net revenue and income rising for the quarter following the launch of the campaign.[9] Some critics remain skeptical of the effectiveness of the campaign, however. Neil Parker, of the branding agency Wolff Olins, maintains that branding needs to "be flexible to accommodate regional differences" today, while preserving its identity. In addition, promoting a single style jeans in a world where an individualized fashion styles is a matter of pride could be a tough sell, he says.[10]

Globalized vs. Localized Communication

In "Managing Brands in Global Markets," Day and Reibstein (2004) suggest that, despite all the talk about globalization of companies and brands, there are still very few companies that are truly global in their brand strategies. Instead, the authors believe that most brands lie somewhere between the extremes of having a "common global position" and a "collection of local identities" (see Figure 13-1).

The five most important attributes[11] that constitute a truly global brand, according to the authors, are:

1. Consistent, easy-to-pronounce name in all markets
2. Evenly dispersed sales across the world without one dominant market
3. Preserving the true nature and positioning of the brand in all markets and cultures
4. Offering solutions to the same customer needs or serving the same target markets everywhere
5. Consistently presenting the brand through packaging, pricing, advertising, etc., in all markets

At least three out of the five requirements above are directly related to how companies communicate with their global audiences. Clearly, crafting a solid and effective global communication strategy is one of the most important tasks that global marketing leaders face.

6. Smith, R. A. (18 July 2008). Levi's marketers hope one size fits all. *Wall Street Journal Online*.

7. Morrissey, B. (11 August 2008). EVB 'unbuttons' bunch of Levi's next-gen celebs. *AdWeek.com*.

8. "Live unbuttoned" with global launch of new, innovative Levi's 501 marketing campaign. (21 July 2008). *PR Newswire* [press release].

9. Levi Strauss & Co. announces third-quarter 2008 financial results. (2 October 2008). *Business Wire* [press release].

10. Smith, R. A. (18 July 2008). Levi's marketers hope one size fits all. *Wall Street Journal Online*.

11. Day, G. S., & Reibstein, D. J. (2004). Managing brands in global markets. *The INSEAD-Wharton Alliance on Globalizing: Strategies for Building Successful Global Businesses* (p. 192). New York: Cambridge Press.

Brand type	Prestige	Master	Super	Glocal
Nature of the category	Luxury Examples: Rolex Ferrari Louis Vuitton Mercedes Gucci	Fashion Examples: Pierre Cardin Benetton Donna Karan LaCoste	Household Services Personal Care Examples: Colgate-Palmolive Unilever household care Procter & Gamble beauty products	Food Retail Nestlé Danone McDonald's Jollibee (Philippines) Kentucky Fried Chicken
Level of aspiration	High	High-Medium	Medium-Low	Low
Nature of the local culture	Global	Global	Local	Local
——————— Extent of localization required ————————→				

Figure 13-1 Localization Road Map

Research conducted by Research International Observer (RIO) suggests that it makes sense to globalize some brands and localize others, depending on these four key factors:[12]

1. *Type of brand.* The RIO study discovered four types of global brands that display specific characteristics.

    Prestige brands (Chanel, BMW, Gucci, Mercedes) also possess a powerful attraction based, however, on much more specific myths associated with the country-of-origin, company founder, or the emblematic technology developed by the particular company. Think of Swiss precision embodied in a watch and Italian design defined by a Ferrari car. Prestige brands represent the desire for status and high aspirations and they, too, actively refuse to localize in order to maintain their inherent exclusivity.

    Master brands (Nike, Sony, Coca-Cola, Nokia) have come to be associated with universal ideals and narratives, such as independence, connection, friendship, quality, individualism, etc. Thus, these brands have built a powerful appeal that often transcends their national origins to become truly global. They must remain so and resist localization for strategic reasons.

    Super brands (Procter & Gamble, Colgae-Palmolive, Dove, Philips) are category-specific and are more known for their dependability than for their mythology, as master brands are. They often localize their offerings and constantly innovate to remain relevant in their markets.

    Glocal brands (Nestlé, Danone, Jollibee) are distributed worldwide but "hide" their origin to blend in the local culture and market. They rely on building a

12. Baker, M., Sterenberg, G., & Taylor, E. (2003). Managing global brands to meet consumer expectations. *ESOMAR Global Cross-Industry Forum, Miami.* Retrieved from www.warc.com.

familiarity and comfort level with their consumers and aim for the greatest degree of localization. Often found in categories such as food products, these brands may become aspirational in developing countries, as consumer societies begin to emerge there.

2. *Nature of the category.* The higher the display value of a category, or the aspirational positioning of a brand within it, the less likely it is for that brand to localize. As mentioned above, food, household, cleaning, and personal care products, which have low display value, are the most localized.

3. *Level of aspiration.* Although Toyota is a brand in a high display value category, it intentionally positions itself in the low end of the spectrum to blend in with the local culture and values. Conversely, Nike is known for sponsoring local events, such as a marathon in Budapest, Hungary, but it signals the high aspirational value it carries with the high profile spokespeople it associates with, like Michael Jordan and Tiger Woods.

4. *Nature of the local culture.* A culture's orientation toward brands may be defined by degrees of individualism or collectivism and of local or global focus, but those values may not always correspond to the traditional definitions assigned to these terms in Chapters 3 and 4. For example, Japan, which is defined as a highly collectivistic society in Hofstede's framework, rates as highly individualistic when it comes to brands. Japan, together with Germany, Belgium, Italy, and Sweden, among others, represents the Global Individualists category. The Cultural Individualists countries, including France, the United States, the UK, Austria, Russia, and Spain, among others, require more localized products that still reflect their individual tastes and values. The global-local axis also divides Cultural Sensitives from the Global Sensitives. Both of these categories are represented by collectivist markets, but the former (China, Turkey, India, Indonesia, Hungary) expect global brands to respect and adjust to local culture, while the latter (Brazil, Korea, Kenya, Chile, Colombia) are more open to global brands and require only some degree of localization. However, Global Sensitives are conscious of a brand's origin, as well as the country in which individual products are manufactured.

Based on these four key factors, the authors of the study have designed a road map (Figure 13-1) that guides marketing managers in their decision process of whether to pursue a local or a more standardized strategy in their global communications plans. It is important to note that, since brands do not remain static in their perceived stature or character, marketers need to periodically adjust their approach to achieve the desired positioning in a particular market.

Advertising is the most prominent part of just about any global communication strategy. Therefore, the rest of this chapter will focus on global advertising and the issues relevant to it in the context of global communications.

STANDARDIZED ADVERTISING

The classic definition of **standardized advertising** has meant that nothing changes in a given advertisement except the language translation. Over the years, these strict parameters have relaxed somewhat, to where many today consider an advertisement standardized as long as it maintains the same theme across the world.[13]

The appeal of standardized marketing and advertising on a global scale is by now well understood: it offers savings, consistency, control, stronger brand recognition,

---

13. Onkvisit, S., & Shaw, J. J. (2004). *International marketing: Analysis and strategy* (p. 455). New York: Routledge.

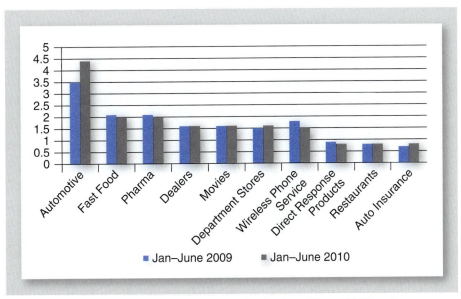

Figure 13-2 Top Global Advertising Categories by Spending ($Billions)

Source: Adapted from: AdAge.com; The Nielsen Company.

and the ability to leverage products and know-how across multiple markets. However, there are only a few brands that have been able to fully benefit from these advantages. Day and Reibstein list brands such as British Airways, GE, Heineken, IBM, Intel, Marlboro, Prozac, Siemens, Starbucks, Tagamet, and Viagra as some of the most globalized brands.[14]

Products Suitable for Standardized Advertising. "It's much easier for a company like Intel to establish a global brand," says Day. "Intel has a smaller number of buyers [than many other global companies] and all of those buyers are using computer chips for the same purpose. And all of Intel's competitors are global. Intel is a global brand without significant local adaptation."[15]

Advertising campaigns for industrial brands such as Intel, as well as for the prestige and master brands in the luxury, high tech, fashion, and automotive categories (as shown in Figure 13-2) are more easily standardized than campaigns for food or personal care products, for example. The former aim to appeal to their customers' ambitions and desire for exclusivity—more universal feelings—while the latter have the goal of becoming part of the cultural landscape in every market and the personal routine of consumers.

Life Fitness, a maker of high-performance fitness equipment, has been rather successful in launching a new standardized global campaign that aims to broaden the appeal of its products to include not only their traditional hard-core fitness enthusiasts, but also regular gym-goers and practitioners of healthy lifestyles (see Figure 13-3). The company, which derives 45 percent of its sales internationally, recognized the growing interest among consumers worldwide in achieving overall health and well-being and designed its new ads with a focus on the everyday benefits of fitness for all people. Its earlier ad campaigns had emphasized the machines' technical features and

14. Day, G. S., & Reibstein, D. J. (2004). Managing brands in global markets. *The INSEAD-Wharton Alliance on Globalizing: Strategies for building successful global businesses* (p. 194). New York: Cambridge Press.

15. Managing brands in global markets: One size doesn't fit all. (1 June 2005). *Knowledge@Wharton.* Retrieved from http://knowledge.wharton.upenn.edu/article.cfm?articleid=1206.

Figure 13-3 Images from the New Marketing Campaign for Life Fitness

Source: Images supplied by Life Fitness. Reprinted with permission.

performance by showing muscular, body-builder types. Now the new tag line, "What We Live For," is reinforced with images and messaging that show healthy, fit people enjoying activities such as mountain biking, hiking, surfing, and other common pastimes. Ninety percent of the new marketing campaign is distributed to the gyms and other fitness facilities around the world which comprise the vast majority of Life Fitness's clients. The company still needed to tweak its globally standardized message and imagery, however, to take into consideration local cultural mores. Thus, its ad featuring a bikini-clad snorkeler was removed from the lineup for Dubai, whereas its ads for Italy and Spain required an extra helping of sex appeal to match local tastes.[16]

Despite the perceived advantages of standardized advertising, many challenges to its successful implementation remain. Besides the different cultural tastes for images, another of those challenges is the effectiveness of the message. As Marieke de Mooj (2005) notes, people across the world may be willing to buy standardized products, but they're likely buying them for completely different reasons—for some that pair of Levi's jeans may symbolize status or American lifestyle affiliation, while for others it is simply everyday clothing. "If buying motives for standardized products vary by country or area, how can a standardized advertising campaign be equally effective in all countries?"[17]

ADAPTED ADVERTISING

As the name suggests, **adapted** (or **localized**) **advertising** communications reflect each market's cultural and social conditions. The goal of adapted advertising is to increase recognition and acceptance of the advertised brand and product. The theory is that presenting a brand in the context of local cultural values and tastes will allow more people to identify with the brand, creating higher affinity for that brand and, ultimately, more sales.

16. Borden, J. (15 September 2008). Fitness for the everyday consumer. *Marketing News,* 17–19.

17. de Mooij, M. (2005). *Global marketing and advertising* (2nd ed.) (p. 8). London: Sage.

BOX 13-1   COMPANY IN FOCUS: FORRESTER RESEARCH

Social Computing Offers a New Way to Connect with Consumers

Forrester Research, Inc., studied the new world of social computing, a new development that is reshaping the way companies interact with their customer base. Forrester Research defines social computing as "a social structure in which technology puts power in communities, not institutions."

According to Forrester, social computing will transform almost all areas of business, not just marketing, through peer-to-peer activities such as blogging, file sharing, podcasting, and search engines. Rather than solely rely on traditional marketing practices, the firm suggests that marketers listen more to their customers through cyber communities like eBay and Craigslist, or to develop their own cyber platforms where customers can directly contact the firm. A number of companies (e.g., P&G and Heineken), have already done this successfully. Such a strategy can create customer loyalty if they view themselves as an equal partner in the dialogue, rather than perceiving the platform as only a commercial tool.

A New Marketing Tool Kit for Social Computing

THE MARKETING TOOL KIT TODAY		THE MARKETING TOOL KIT IN THE AGE OF SOCIAL COMPUTING	
		Today's Marketing Tool Kit, PLUS	
Channels:	Tactics:	New Channels:	Technology:
■ TV/cable	■ Coupons	■ Website	■ Personalization
■ Radio	■ Customer	■ Online ads	■ Search
■ Magazine	promos	■ E-mail	■ Site merchandising
■ Newspaper	■ Trade promos	■ Blogs	■ Customer database
■ Outdoor	■ Sales force	■ Interactive TV	■ Web analytics
■ Direct mail	Metrics:	■ Podcasting	■ Brand monitoring
	■ Reach	■ Kiosks	■ Content syndication
	■ Frequency	■ Mobile ads	Metrics:
		■ Viral/WOM	■ Conversion rates
			■ Cost per sale

Source: Charron, C., Favier, C., & Li, C. (13 February 2006). Social computing [white paper]. *Forrester Research.* Presented by Brian Kardon, MPlanet conference, November 29–December 1, 2006, Orlando, Florida.

In Pakistan, for example, P&G has achieved great success with a local campaign featuring "Commander Safeguard," a superhero action figure. By celebrating the tradition of storytelling in that part of the world, and appealing to children through a variety of channels—Commander Safeguard has a TV show, radio show, website, DVDs, and music videos—P&G was able to not only change hygiene habits but also increase its brand recognition and sales in a very significant way. According to the agency that created the campaign for P&G, Saatchi & Saatchi, Safeguard soap is the most expensive brand of soap in the country, but it is also purchased the most by families in Pakistan.[18]

Not coincidentally, the soap advertised by P&G in this successful campaign falls in the Super category of personal care: household products that are most likely to be localized, according to the RIO study.

18. Lindstrom, M. (21 May 2007). P&G cleans up in Pakistan. *AdAge.com* [*BrandFlash: Martin Lindstrom's Weekly Reports*]. Retrieved from http://adage.com/article?article_id=115637.

BOX 13-2 TECHNOLOGY IN FOCUS: ADAPTING B2B SALES PROMOTIONS TO LOCAL DIGITAL TASTES

Sales promotions and communications are an important part of the global promotional mix and as such they require their own set of considerations, especially when it comes to online business-to-business marketing. In a recent report, Forrester Research analysts discussed the importance of localizing promotional sales communications, particularly for technology B2B buyers. They identified the following three important considerations for designing B2B communications for the global markets:

- Find out who the key decision makers are in each market and what the main business concerns are for them. It is likely that each participant in the decision-making process will have different priorities. It is important to address as many of these top issues as possible in your localized sales communications.

- Familiarize yourself with the preferred ways in which business executives collect information during the decision-making process and make your sales communications available through those channels. For example, Forrester's research found that 73 percent of American executives rely on information from industry, vendor, or trade websites during their decision-making process, while only 52 percent of French executives do.

- Ensure that localized online access is available not only for information, but also for features such as free trials and demonstrations, payment options, etc.

Source: Adapted from: Jennifer Bélissent, "Expanding Globally, Marketing Locally," teleconference presentation slides 15–17, Forrester Research, March 25, 2009.

Besides product type, other factors have been found to influence the decision to localize advertising. For example, one study has found that the level of familiarity with a global brand affects local consumers' perception of that brand's advertisements. When consumers know a global brand, they are more likely to accept its standardized advertising message. On the other hand, the less familiar they are with the brand, the more they are likely to respond favorably if its advertising is localized.[19]

Marketing consumer services, as opposed to marketing products globally, also tends to be more effective when advertising is localized. Because services are experienced personally by the client, it is easy to see why conforming to local cultural considerations, language, and social norms would be more important to service providers. Another obstacle to using standardized advertising for service is the fact that services are highly regulated by the government in most countries, further preventing a direct transfer of advertisements from one national market to another.[20]

Cultural taboos and perceptions can also present challenges to marketers who localize their messages. For example, many global cosmetic companies such as L'Oréal, Avon, Ponds, and others are heavily marketing and selling skin-lightening creams to women in India, China, Korea, and Japan, much to the consternation of Western public opinion, which sees the practice as reinforcing bad stereotypes and prejudices. Ashok Venkatramani, the head of the skin care category at Hindustan Lever, counters this view: opposing certain products on ideological grounds is "a very Western way

19. Pae, J. H., Samiee, S., & Tai, S. (2002). Global advertising strategy: The moderating role of brand familiarity and execution style. *International Marketing Review, 19*(2/3), 176.

20. Kanso, A., & Kitchen, P. J. (2004). Marketing consumer services internationally: Localisation and standardisation revisited. *Marketing Intelligence & Planning, 22*(2/3), 201.

of looking at the world," according to him. "The definition of beauty in the Western world is linked to anti-aging," he continues. "In Asia, it's all about being two shades lighter." In India, skin-lightening products have been the most popular category in already fast-growing cosmetics markets.[21]

The trade-off in choosing a localization strategy in marketing communications is often between higher efficiency of the campaigns and increased costs and complexity. The constantly evolving marketing landscape, especially when it comes to technology, adds to that complexity. Mary Dillon, the global CMO of McDonald's, recently mentioned that "[a]s technology continues to erase borders, a growing challenge for global brands is trying to create intimate bonds and universal connections all at the same time." Her advice to marketers to get to know "how your customers live and how your brand adds value to their lives" speaks to the power of localized communications that are nevertheless centered on common needs and desires.[22]

In fact, over the years, the advertising campaigns that have qualified and won a Global Effie—the industry's top honor for global campaigns—have all demonstrated that a universal idea or ideal made perfectly "local" with the use of realistic and relevant language and imagery is the winning recipe for global marketers. Some of the judges expressed their definitions of "great" global campaigns after the 2007 Global Effie Awards this way: "A big idea, a clear focus and breakthrough communication that builds off of real consumer insights"; "An idea large and iconic enough to travel broadly yet still touch local consumers emotionally"; "A big, broad, flexible and holistic idea that leaves room for local differences and cultures"; and "creative quality, consumer insights, a unique single-minded idea based on a global human truth."[23]

GLOBAL ADVERTISING STRATEGY

Overall, global advertising spending was estimated at US$665 billion in 2008, with global markets growing slightly faster than the United States advertising market.[24] How that money is distributed, however, varies greatly from industry to industry. A recent survey[25] of senior marketing executives from around the world revealed that over a third of them believe that marketing strategy is best set up on a national level, a quarter preferred the regional level, and only 19 percent deploy a global marketing strategy. IT industry marketing executives are most likely to prefer a worldwide marketing strategy, consistent with earlier findings that high tech B2B sectors tend to be most globalized.

Media and advertising were listed as top priorities for all marketers in the study, particularly those in the IT, finance/insurance, and telecommunications industries, who are said to be looking to communicate to their customers a new positioning for their company or the launch of new products in the next year.

Such strong and focused advertising campaigns with a repositioned message worked for Kraft's Philadelphia cream cheese brand. Kraft's long-running global campaign, "Philadelphia—A Little Taste of Heaven," covers (with customizations) over 35 countries, with the concept of the Philly angel in heaven eating light yet indulgent

21. Timmons, H. (30 May 2007). Telling India's modern women they have power, even over their skin tone. *The New York Times,* C5.

22. McDonald's CMO: Erase borders and create bonds. (15 October 2008). *Marketing News,* 20.

23. Langton, C. (4 June 2007). What wins Effies? Simple ideas. *Advertising Age, 78*(23), 32.

24. Interpublic unit sees '08 global ad spending up. (26 June 2007). *Reuters.* Retrieved from http://today.reuters.com/news/articleinvesting.aspx?type=comktNews&rpc=33&storyid=2007-06-26T134448Z_01_WEN8979_RTRIDST_0_UNIVERSALMCCANN-FORECAST-URGENT.XML.

25. Gritten, A. (2008, July). Inside the marketing department. *Research,* 29.

cream cheese. In 2000, rival Parmalat launched its own brand of cream cheese in Canada and, through aggressive pricing, advertising, and in-store merchandising, quickly gained significant market share over the Philadelphia brand, especially in the francophone Quebec province. Kraft quickly reacted, refreshing its campaign with an additional character and a broader product appeal. But in Quebec, it went a step further—it replaced the face of the angel to give the character a more empathetic appeal. The plan worked: Philadelphia cream cheese sales reversed course to gain 8.5 percent in the first year of the new advertising campaign, with especially strong results in Quebec. With a little extra attention to a particular local market, Kraft was able to invigorate its advertising campaign and sales and protect its market share from a serious threat.[26]

It is important to remember that global advertising strategy should not be designed or executed in isolation. It should be an integral part of a coherent promotional strategy and the overall marketing mix. Unfortunately, given the complexity of marketing mix decisions in the global context, very little research has been done to establish best practices for resource allocation across markets and countries. Some studies propose that marketers should base their decisions on local market conditions but also consider how global competition, market learning, and diffusion can influence response. Others suggest that a staggered market entry, where more marketing dollars are spent in the countries entered later on in the campaign, improves marketing effectiveness.[27]

In recent years, Samsung Electronics has proved that a disciplined, well-integrated, and well-researched strategy can improve a firm's global marketing performance substantially. After a thorough evaluation of how it was spending its $1 billion marketing budget across 14 product categories and 200 countries, Samsung realized that, by decreasing its advertising budgets in Russia and North America by 10 percent and increasing them by 11 percent in Europe and China, it could improve the effectiveness of its marketing dollars. As a result, Samsung gained significant market shares and sales in several product categories and increased its global brand value by 30 percent.[28]

Global Campaigns and Their Media Mix

Companies in certain product categories, such as personal care products and automotive, spend much more on advertising than others (see Table 13-1). But with the proliferation of new advertising channels, the marketers' job of deciding where to spend their often limited advertising budget is becoming even harder. The main culprits in this development have a digital dimension. Technologies, such as blogs, podcasts, online videos, and viral e-mails have created unprecedented opportunities for marketers to go beyond the local/global debate and create advertising messages that are customized for very specific yet global groups of consumers whose common interests connect them online. There, marketers can target these groups with precision and messages that generate immediate consumer response, if done right. Doing it right, however, means engaging consumers with an effective, compelling, and relevant message that is not lost in the ocean of advertising noise that surrounds them.

These new and higher standards are forcing many marketers to rethink their role and strategy. "We've got RSS, wikis, podcasts, videocasts. It can have an immobilizing effect on marketers. If what was working isn't, and what is being talked about is unproven, where do you go?" says Paul Rand, president and CEO of Zócalo Group.

---

26. Anonymous. (18 November 2002). Philadelphia cream cheese. *Marketing Magazine, 107*(46), C14. Accessed in ProQuest.

27. Shankar, V. (2008). Strategic allocation of marketing resources: Methods and insights. In Roger A. Kerin and Rob O'Regan (Eds.), *Marketing Mix Decisions: New Perspectives and Practices* (pp. 154–183). Chicago: AMA.

28. Ibid.

TABLE 13-1 Top Global Advertisers

Rank			Worldwide Advertising Spending
2007	Advertiser	Headquarters	2006
1	Procter & Gamble	Cincinnati	$9,358
2	Unilever	London/Rotterdam	5,295
3	L'Oreal	Detroit	3,345
4	General Motors Corp.	Clichy, France	3,426
5	Toyota Motor Corp.	Toyota City, Japan	3,202
6	Ford Motor Co.	Dearborn, Mich.	2,902
7	Johnson & Johnson	New Brunswick, N. J.	2,361
8	Nestlé	Vevey, Switzerland	2,181
9	Coca-Cola Co.	Atlanta, Georgia	2,177
10	Honda Motor Co.	Tokyo	2,047

Source: Data from: Top 100 global marketers by media spending. (19 November 2007). Adapted from: *Global Marketers, Advertising Age.*

BOX 13-3   COMPANY IN FOCUS: AXE'S GLOBAL CAMPAIGN

The demographic group comprising young people around the globe who are tech savvy, have disposable income, and are in regular communication with "virtual friends" across the globe is known as Generation Y, or the Millennials. They are the first generation to have come of age in a connected, digital world. They present both a challenge to the old ways of doing business and an opportunity for companies to gain leverage with this audience by communicating with them in a meaningful way. Companies can do that with new forms of viral marketing that target this demographic, which is likely to share what it considers to be edgy and interesting advertisements. Here's how one company did it:

From the beginning, Unilever had ambitious plans for the global launch of its Axe spray deodorant for men: make one marketing message work in 75 countries. The answer? "Bom Chicka Wah Wah." The phrase, pitched by Axe's advertising agency BBH in London and dreamed up by its creative team in New York, was soon a hit around the world. Through ads, YouTube videos, live band performances, and online games, the company unleashed a viral campaign that spread far beyond its markets thanks to a simple, universal idea of attraction between the sexes and the edgy humor with which it was conveyed. People all over the world forwarded the funny videos and played the online game that recommended the right Axe fragrance depending on the player's professed preferences in women. Sales of Axe in the United States jumped 0 to $500 million in just over five years.

But Axe did not stop there. It followed up with a new bottle design and a line of new scents that were specifically designed by a renowned expert to appeal to young males the world over. The concept stayed the same, however: Bom Chicka Wah Wah from New York to Tokyo and beyond. The campaign has been so successful that scented Axe now enjoys a 12 percent market share in Japan, where men's deodorants are usually unscented. "The strategy is to take the best of global practices and adapt them locally," says Dan Burdett, Axe executive for Northeast Asia. David Rubin, his North American counterpart, adds: "The idea isn't done somewhere in particular. It's just done. And it suddenly just happens. There are no borders. You can't control who sees it and comes to it." But can it work for all products?

See www.theaxeeffect.com.

Adapted from: Hamm, S. (2 July 2007). Children of the Web. *Business Week.* Retrieved from www.businessweek.com/magazine/content/07_27/b4041401.htm.

TABLE 13-2 Country-Specific Advertising Styles	
Country	**Advertising Styles**
China	Educational, emphasis on quality, tradition, status, respect.
France	Symbolism, sensuality, humor.
Germany	Logic, testimonials, tradition, value for money, authority.
Italy	Emotional, lifestyle, use of celebrities, theatrical.
Japan	Indirect appeals, soft-sell, entertaining, mood, symbolism.
Spain	Indirect appeals, idealistic, pleasant.
The Netherlands	Entertaining, realistic, modesty.
United Kingdom	Presentational, humor, subtle, testimonials, shows class differences.
United States	Lecture, direct appeals, hard-sell, argumentative.

Source: Adapted from: de Mooij, M. (1997). *Global marketing and advertising: Understanding cultural paradoxes* (pp. 272–283). Thousand Oaks, CA: Sage.

"The rules are being redefined by the day. It's creating a whole new set of winners, losers and has-beens among marketers. I think that's stimulating."[29]

Media channels and technologies such as social computing that empower consumers are just a few of the new tools that enable any consumer to broadcast his or her own opinions about a product or a brand and possibly generate as much interest as any official campaign by the company. In the process, consumers can quickly build up or damage a brand's reputation on a global scale (see Box 13-1).

Culture plays a central role in how people perceive and react to advertising. Much research over the years has confirmed that the more likable advertising is, the more likely it is to be effective. One recent study was designed to see what attributes exactly make commercials likable in Asian countries and how they differ from the attributes in American and European markets, particularly for Generation X consumers. The study found that Asians most liked ads that evoked "Entertaining" qualities most, followed by "Warmth," "Soft Sell," "Strong/Distinctive/Sexy," "Relevant to Me," "Trendy/ Modernity/Stylish," and "Status Appeal." The results were remarkably close to the findings in the other two world regions, where "Entertaining," "Warmth," and "Relevant to Me" were also considered most likeable qualities for ads. However, several other attributes were deemed distinctly Asian, including "Soft Sell," "Strong/Distinctive/Sexy," "Trendy/Modernity/Stylish," and "Status Appeal."[30]

The role of cultural differences in advertising styles have long been the topic of research for Marieke de Mooij, whose summary of country-specific advertising styles is shown in Table 13-2.

GLOBAL ADVERTISING REGULATIONS

When planning a global marketing strategy, marketers have to consider the myriad standards, regulations, and laws that govern the advertising industry in the different countries and regional jurisdictions. The regulatory bodies that monitor and control advertising have been established, among other things, to respond to public complaints, to ensure that claims made by advertisers are accurate, and to ensure that the products advertised are legal. This oversight is particularly pertinent for certain categories of products such as pharmaceuticals, alcohol, tobacco, and gambling, where consumer protection is important.

29. Fielding, M. (15 March 2007). Eliminate waste: Determine which media channels truly engage customers. *Marketing News,* 10–12.

30. Fam, K. (2008, September). Attributes of likeable television commercials in Asia. *Journal of Advertising Research, 48*(3), 418–432.

Illustration 13-1 Innovative Outdoor Advertising
This advertising prop is for a dating service in Vancouver, Canada.

Source: Executive Search Dating Trap. Reprinted by permission of Rethink Canada.

The landscape for advertising regulations is broken up not only by national and local authorities, but sometimes even by advertising medium. For example, in the United Kingdom, the Committee of Advertising Practice (CAP) regulates print, new media, and cinema advertising, as well as sales promotions, direct marketing, and the delivery of mail order goods. The Broadcast Committee of Practice (BCAP), on the other hand, is responsible for TV and radio commercials, interactive TV services, TV, shopping, and teletext services. Both independent committees are under the administration of the British Advertising Standards Authority (ASA).

In Beijing, for example, a massive "urban reorganization exercise" dismantled all billboards in the heart of the city, leaving advertisers and advertising agencies reeling. "Outdoor advertising is part of our marketing mix in China for Mercedes-Benz, Chrysler, Jeep and Dodge," lamented one spokesman for Daimler-Chrysler. After the ban on billboard advertising in Beijing, many companies flocked to outdoor video screen advertising, available in the city's business centers. One company with 100,000 such screens saw its quarterly revenue jump by 75 percent as a result.[31] Other cities that are considering such bans on advertising have been São Paulo and Moscow.[32] See another clever example of outdoor advertising that goes beyond billboards in Illustration 13-1.

THE GLOBAL ADVERTISING AGENCY

In the challenging global market, many companies rely on the help of global advertising agencies to find a competitive edge in marketing. The degree to which an agency is integrated into the marketing function of a company can vary, depending on the size of the company, its strategic marketing focus and leadership, its industry or its markets, to name a few factors. For most MNCs, however, relationships with one or more advertising agencies or networks are an important and often scrutinized aspect of their global marketing strategy.

31. Leow, J. (25 June 2007). Beijing mystery: What's happening to the billboards? *The Wall Street Journal*, A1.
32. Ibid.

TABLE 13-3 Omnicom Group			
	BBDO	**DDB Worldwide**	**TBWA/Worldwide**
Number of employees	15,000	–	11,000
Number of offices	287	200	267
Number of countries	79	90	77

Some large global advertisers prefer to hire local ad agencies for each market they enter, others may opt to retain their home market agency, and yet others may hire a large agency with offices around the world or align themselves with one of the worldwide networks such as Leo Burnett Worldwide, Y&R, or McCann Erickson. Many of these agencies form the WPP Group, the largest multinational ad agency, headquartered in Ireland with approximately £6 billion sales as of 2010. WPP has 146,000 employees in 2,400 offices operating in 107 countries. Next in size is the Omnicom Group (Table 13-3). As mentioned earlier, many MNCs maintain relationships with different agencies to match the goals and objectives for specific campaigns. For example, Visa selected the independent, London-based Wieden & Kennedy agency for its World Cup soccer sponsorship, while maintaining California-based TBWA/Chiat/Day as its agency on record for the Visa brand.[33]

There are many reasons why companies choose advertising agencies for their global marketing needs. Some of them are:

- *Cost-effectiveness.* As companies expand internationally, it may become financially unproductive to enlarge the internal marketing and creative services units to meet all international marketing needs. By selecting an agency with the right market reach, a company can save resources and centralize decision making at the same time. Additionally, agencies can deliver media-buying savings based on preferred relationships with media outlets.

- *Market knowledge.* In choosing a global agency with offices around the world or a number of local agencies in their target markets, a company is presumably buying the expertise that will make its advertising campaigns effective for local audiences.

- *Superior creative work.* Ad agencies specialize in the development of original, polished creative materials designed by talented and experienced professionals. Such creative focus and expertise is hard to build up or maintain internally for most companies.

- *Specialized services.* Some agencies develop signature competencies like media planning and buying or digital marketing. In addition, they usually offer a number of other specialized services such as crisis communications, market research, or other support services that are often sought by companies with limited internal resources.

Most companies consider additional factors, such as strategic marketing alignment, agency reputation and size, or industry specialization as they review their agency relationships. Often, changes within the company, at the agency, or both could prompt a change in direction. Coca-Cola had its own agency, Edge Creative, for most of the 1990s, but switched strategies in 2000, appointing Interpublic as its global ad agency while still using the services of outside agencies such as WPP's Red Cell Berlin Cameron and UK's Mother. More changes came in 2005, when the company handed its

33. Cuneo, A. Z. (28 June 2007). Visa teams with Wieden for soccer sponsorship. *Advertising Age.* Retrieved from http://adage.com/abstract.php?article_id=118886.

TABLE 13-4 Factors Determining Advertising Agency Selection and Termination					
Factors for Selecting Advertising Agencies from Client's Perspective	Rank	Factors for Switching Advertising Agencies from Client's Perspective	Rank	Factors for Losing Clients from Agency's Perspectives	Rank
Qualifications of personnel	1	Dissatisfaction	1	Change in client firm's size	1
Fits the client's advertising strategy	2	Disagreement over objectives	2	Poor communication, performance	2
Part of an international consortium	3	Insufficient attention by senior staff	3	Personnel changes	3
Agency size	4	Time for a change	4	Change in client's strategy	4
Past record	5	Decrease in sales, profits	5	Policy change	5
Agency facilities	6	Not sure that ads were effective	6	Declining sales	6
Recommendations	7	Key personnel left the agency	7	Unrealistic demands by client	7
Advertising awards	8		8	Conflict in remuneration	8
Reputation	9		9	Conflict of interest	9
	10				

Source: Adapted from: Yuksel, U., & Sutton-Brady, C. (2007, January). From selection to termination: An investigation of advertising agency/client relationships. *Journal of Business & Economic Research, 5*(1), 31–39.

Classic Coke account for North America to yet another agency, Wieden & Kennedy.[34] Similarly, as Toyota prepared to introduce Lexus, its luxury brand, in Japan (the company's home country) in 2005, it selected Dentsu, Japan's advertising giant, and several other Japanese agencies to handle the advertising for the launch, in addition to its own in-house ad firm.[35] For a list of the most common reasons why companies select and switch agencies, and for the agencies' perspective on the same issue, see Table 13-4.

It is indisputable that the relationship between an agency and its client is important to the firm's business. It can impact changes in its strategic marketing direction, deliver a successful image makeover, and have a direct effect on sales, for example. When the Korean conglomerate LG Electronics decided to appoint the London-based Bartle, Bogle, Hegarty (BBH) for the strategic and creative development of its worldwide marketing communications, its global brand marketing executive cited the company's desire to develop "one single powerful LG brand."[36] IKEA's agency, Mediaedge:cia, noticed that the furniture retailer's image was suffering in Poland and that growth was stagnating. The agency designed an unconventional campaign that prompted the Polish market to jump 22 percent in visitor growth, becoming the leader for all of Ikea's worldwide stores in that category. The campaign also increased traffic to the IKEA Poland website by 45 percent.[37]

As evident from these examples, client-agency partnerships can take on many forms and dynamics. But few basic factors remain at the core of any successful partnership between a client and its agency: trust, confidence, effective communications, and strategic alignment in the overall marketing vision and goals, paired with the internal skill set and the external reach to match.

34. Coca-Cola: Brand Profile. (2007, March). Retrieved from http://WARC.com.

35. Madden, N. (15 August 2005). Home-field advantage? Toyota readies Lexus for its debut in Japan. *Advertising Age.*

36. Anonymous. (3 December 2007). LG appoints new global advertising agency. *Cellular-news.com.* Retrieved from www.cellular-news.com/story/27823.php.

37. Hall, E. (3 March 2008). Global media agency network of the year: Mediaedge:cia. Advertising Age.

SUMMARY

- Social media has gained importance in the global advertising and communications mix.

- Digital technologies have closed the gap between global and local advertising. They enable advertisers to obtain a global reach for their messages instead of communicating on a country by country basis.

- Integrated marketing communication strategies have gained importance among multinational firms. Such a strategy enables the firm to not only plan communications on a regional or global basis, but also to immediately track performance.

- While advertising messages are localized, there is increased use of global media.

- It is important to identify those products that are suitable to a globalized advertising campaign.

- Global advertising agencies play an increasing role in coordinating campaigns across countries.

DISCUSSION QUESTIONS

1. How does an integrated marketing communications strategy differ from traditional marketing communications?

2. How has social media impacted global promotional communications? Provide specific examples.

3. What are some of the attributes of global brands, according to Day and Reibstein? Do you agree with their conclusion that only a few truly global brands exist?

4. What trade-offs do marketers have to make when deciding whether to standardize or localize their global advertising and communications?

5. Keeping in mind that culture influences advertising preferences, can you think of a commercial or an advertisement that you have seen recently that did not match your own cultural expectations?

6. What are some of the advantages that global advertising agencies offer to global companies?

EXPERIENTIAL EXERCISES

1. Create an outline of a digital advertising campaign for your consumer product of choice that can be targeted to the global segment of 18–34 year olds. Include:

   - Your selected geographic markets and the reasons you picked these countries or regions

   - Proposed websites for each of these countries or regions and justifications for them

- Proposed advertising methods and why
- Proposed frequency and why
- Proposed ROI metrics

KEY TERMS

Adapted (or localized) advertising,
   p. 376

Integrated marketing communications
   (IMC), p. 371

Promotional activities, p. 370

Standardized advertising, p. 374

CASE 13-1

Entrepreneurship in Jordan: Founding an Advertising Business

Amman, Jordan

"This is what I want to do! I know it's going to work. The only question is how do I get the money I need to turn my idea into a business?" So concluded Nahla when she presented her proposal for a business venture to her father over 10 years ago. The presentation was the final step in her efforts to plan a new advertising agency. For several months she had been consumed with detailed deliberations and preparations to nurture the idea along. She wanted to start an advertising business that would help clients sell their products and services using a variety of media. She passionately argued that she had the necessary qualifications and qualities to launch such a business and that now was the time to act.

Nahla was too strong-minded, creative, and energetic to spend the rest of her life bound by the conservative hierarchy and rigid management style typical of Arab-world enterprises. She was convinced that an advertising business would be a good outlet for her skills and creativity in design and innovation. Advertising was a growing field in her country and she wanted to establish her own shop. Before approaching her father with the idea, she tested it with some friends and family. She found immediate support for the idea and her family had clear confidence in her abilities. Some friends were so enthusiastic they asked to become her business partners. She had no background managing a business, so she approached Karim to join her as general manager; together they asked Khalid to be their designer and Waseem to be their marketing director. Nahla would be the "creative" manager. They hoped Nahla's father, a prominent businessman, would agree to join them, as his reputation and family name would lend instant credibility to the new business.

The idea of the advertising business appealed to Nahla's father, and he reacted positively to her presentation. He recommended that she "bootstrap" the business; i.e., get startup capital from the family's personal savings and build the business from there. That said, her business The Media Group was started. It began with a computer, scanner, printer, software, and some supplies, operating out of the conference room in Nahla's father's office.

Entrepreneurship in Jordan

Nahla's initiative was representative of changes underway in Jordanian society, where non-traditional policies were encouraged to foster economic growth. But looking at women's economic activities as a whole, Nahla's case was truly exceptional. In 1999, 12.5 percent of Jordanian women worked, only 12 percent of those had their own

This case was written by Susanna Aulbach of George Mason University and Professor Richard Linowes of the Kogod School of Business of the American University in Washington, D.C. It was produced under the auspices of the Emerging Market Development Advisors Program (EMDAP) of the United States Agency of International Development (USAID) and administered by the Institute of International Education (IIE). Reprinted with permission.

business, and three-quarters of those were home-based, so only 0.375 percent or 1 out of 266 women owned a formal business.

Being a woman in a top position was at times difficult. Both clients and employees were not always sure how to deal with Nahla. Initially, clients were uncertain of her expertise and capabilities and male employees were confused about taking orders from a woman. As her reputation grew, however, she overcame these doubts, but that required much self-confidence and personal stamina.

Nahla, a Muslim, went against established norms in her country and accepted a Christian as her business partner. This was considered a most unusual step that drove away some potential clients, but her willingness to work with people from different backgrounds made her firm distinctive and bore fruit in the future. She was able to work successfully with people from vastly different cultural backgrounds, including Koreans and Japanese, when they came to sell their goods in the Jordanian market.

Nahla's advertising business survived the next decade, as advertising became a much more accepted part of the Jordanian business world. Many new competitors entered the field; from 25 agencies when she started to 150 now. Not everyone was a qualified professional; some were simply solo practitioners with a personal computer and enough software to sell their services. But the new competition forced a significant drop in prices. Years ago she charged JD200 to design a logo, but now that work seldom earned more than JD75.

The turning point for Nahla's business was the contract with the Korean firm LG. It allowed her to hire needed staff. Now she has four large clients, 12 stable client accounts, and about 10 to 20 "walk-ins" per year. Clients include shipping lines, business development services, beauty industry companies (cosmetics, etc.), confectionary companies (pastry and chocolates), embassies, and magazines. Most of her clients were from Jordan, but a growing number came from the United Arab Emirates.

In the Arab world in general, there has been a discreet but dramatic shift in attitudes toward women in business. Women's business networks have mushroomed across the Middle East, often with the blessing of Arab first ladies, such as Suzanne Mubarak of Egypt and Queen Rania of Jordan. Some note a competition between Arab governments to encourage women to enter business and the political process. There is now the Arab Women Organization (AWO), under the auspices of the Arab League, that aims to harmonize laws across the region.

There is still plenty to be done. About half of Arab women remain illiterate, and segregation of the sexes in some countries presents obstacles. In Bahrain, the number of women in the labor force has increased from 5 percent in 1971 to 40 percent in 2005. But in Saudi Arabia, women comprise 50 percent of the population while contributing only 3 percent to the economy. There are few jobs available to women, so they are creating their own opportunities—creating their own businesses. "We acknowledge there is more work to be done, but what we have achieved is phenomenal," said Haifa Fahoum Al Kaylani, chair of the Arab International Women's Forum.

Nahla strongly encouraged women, particularly young Arab women, to consider starting a business. Before launching the venture, she advised that they study the market well, do a SWOT analysis, have at least five years' experience in the field, and know the competition. She also recommended they begin with sufficient startup capital. Then . . . *be strong and bold*. "Success has nothing to do with being a woman or a man," Nahla affirmed. "As long as you are ambitious and know what you want, go for it!"

Questions for Discussion

1. What entrepreneurial characteristics did Nahla display? Do you think the qualities required of entrepreneurs in Jordan vary from those required in the United States?

2. Given her business' rocky start over its first few years, what should Nahla have done differently in assessing the feasibility of her idea?

PART 4

New Trends in Global Marketing

Using Social Media for Global Marketing

Right now, a conversation is going on . . . That conversation has your old customers talking to your former employees, while investors and prospective new customers review the conversation to help them make "informed" decisions about what to do next. Are you engaged in that conversation?

DAS GLOBAL MEDIA

LEARNING OBJECTIVES

After reading this chapter, you should be able to:

- Understand what social marketing is and its use globally.
- Identify the major global social media networks.
- Understand how global marketing networks can be used as a promotional tool.
- Discuss how global social networks can be localized.
- Relate the difference between advertising on social media and traditional advertising.
- Discuss some of the privacy problems inherent in the use of social networks.

Elaine and Roz, two homemakers and friends, are connected to Facebook, discussing a new refrigerator model that Elaine saw on Best Buy. They particularly like the idea of the three-door configuration and a number of other features. Two days later, they are joined in their Facebook conversation by 20 people who had either purchased the refrigerator or heard comments about it. One person in particular was a good friend whose opinion was highly regarded. As a result of the discussion, Elaine decided that she should take another look at the refrigerator, pretty much convinced to make the purchase either on the Internet or in a retail store.

This scenario describes a trend that is occurring globally. **Social media** like Facebook, Twitter, and LinkedIn connect people with similar interests or likes. Through these media, a marketer's message can be communicated to potential consumers, while in the other direction, marketers can learn how their product or service is evaluated in the eyes of the consumer. This two-way communication is the essence and importance of social media.

AN INTRODUCTION TO SOCIAL MARKETING

Kotler and Zaltman (1971, 5) were the first to define social marketing as "the design, implementation and control of programs calculated to influence the acceptability of social ideas and involving considerations of product planning, pricing, communication, distribution, and marketing research."[1] Kotler later defined **social marketing** as "[determining] the needs, wants, and interests of target markets and to deliver the desired satisfactions more effectively and efficiently than competitors, in a way that preserves or enhances the consumer's and the society's well-being."[2] A similar definition has been proposed by the Social Marketing Institute, as the planning and implementation of programs designed to bring about social change using concepts from commercial marketing.[3] Nonprofit institutions, such as government agencies, charities, educational bodies (universities, schools), and ecology groups adapt modern marketing techniques to advance social marketing objectives.

Social marketing later developed into what is called cause-related marketing (CRM), which combines a cause (e.g., a charitable agency such as the London Children's Museum) with a for-profit company (3M). The idea is to provide a synergy between the two that will result in raising money for the cause while promoting the sale of the company's products. One of the most noteworthy campaigns was the linking of American Express credit cards with the restoration of the Statue of Liberty in New York during 1983. For each purchase made with an American Express card, AMEX contributed one penny, and $1 for each new card issued. Within three months of the campaign, $1.7 million was raised for the restoration while the sale of AMEX cards rose by 27 percent. However, the major difference between social and cause related marketing is the absence of a continuing relationship between the two. CRM campaigns are limited to a given time cycle, while social marketing networks are long lasting. A definition of social marketing networks is proposed by Kaplan and Haenlein[4] (2010) as a "group of Internet-based applications that build on the ideological and technological foundations of Web 2.0, which allows the creation and exchange of user-generated content."

Social Marketing Networks

Social marketing networks are synonymous with Internet marketing. Marketing on the Internet is accomplished through such methods as blogging, press releases, and social network websites. Social networks in particular have revolutionized the use of the Internet. Instead of just using the Internet to search for information, people are now connecting with others who have similar interests and habits. The connection is made via social network media such as Facebook, Twitter, My Space, and LinkedIn. People can be connected not only locally but also regionally and globally. For example, Google's Orkut and Facebook are utilized by those who are looking for friendships; LinkedIn (United States) is a professional network; while WELCOM: The World Economic Leaders Community, was designed for world political and economic leaders to discuss global, regional, and industry agendas and are used for professional or business contacts. While Facebook, Orkut, and LinkedIn are used to find people you know, Twitter is used to find people you don't know yet but who have similar interests. Orkut is truly global; it is headquartered in Brazil, and 48 percent of its users are from Brazil, followed by India with 39.2 percent, and the United States with 2.2 percent. It is also popular in the Baltic States, especially Estonia. Facebook is the largest social global network, with over 500 million active users, 70 percent of whom are outside the United States.

Of the countries shown in Table 14-1, Facebook is the number one social network in all but one, and Twitter is number two in six countries. Two-thirds of the world's

1. Kotler, P., & Zaltman, G. (1971). Social marketing: An approach to planned social change. *Journal of Marketing, 35*, 3–12.

2. Kotler, P., Roberto, N., & Lee, N. (2002). *Social Marketing* (2nd ed.). Thousand Oaks, CA: Sage.

3. The Social Marketing Institute is located at 1825 Connecticut Avenue NW, Suite S-852 Washington, DC 20009.

4. Kaplan, A., & Haenlein, M. (2010). Users of the world unite! The challenges and opportunities of social media. *Business Horizons, 53*(1), 59–68.

TABLE 14-1	Top Social Networking Website Rankings			
	Facebook	**Twitter**	**LinkedIn**	**Other**
Australia	1	2	3	
Canada	1	2	3	
France	1	2		3
Germany	1	2		3
Italy	1	3		2
Russia				1, 2, 3
Spain	1			2, 3
United Kingdom	1	2	3	
United States	1	2	3	

Source: Data from: World map of social networks. (2011, June). http://Vincosblog.com.

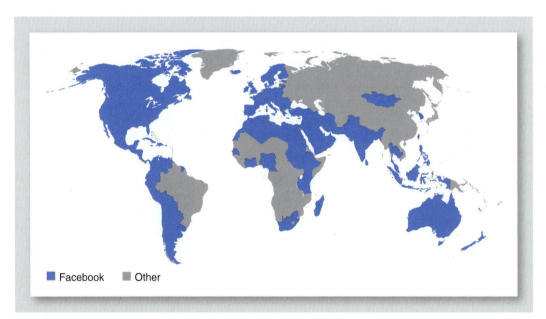

Figure 14-1 Social Networks Across the Globe, June 2011

Source: Data from: World map of social networks. (2011, June). http://Vincosblog.com.

Internet population connects to a social network or blogging site, and the sector now accounts for almost 10 percent of all Internet time. Smith (2010)[5] found that digital communication via social networks has outpaced face-to-face communication. He reports that the average United States face-to-face network is 21.4 people, compared to 49.3 people on social online networks.

Figure 14-1 shows the global dispersion of these and other popular social networks. Facebook covers all of North America, Europe, and a good part of South America.

Behavioral Implications of Networks

Network analysis (social network theory) is the study of how the social structure of relationships around a person, group, or organization affects beliefs or behaviors.

5. Tom Smith, http://globalwebindex.net/thinking.

BOX 14-1   PEOPLE IN FOCUS: ORKUT BÜYÜKKÖKTEN

While many people are familiar with the name Mark Zuckerberg, the founder of Facebook, not many are familiar with the name Orkut Büyükkökten, the founder of the social network, Orkut, named after him. Founded in 2004, as of 2010, Orkut had about 100 million users, about half located in Brazil and 39 percent in India. It became the third largest social network in the world.

Orkut Büyükkökten, originally from Turkey, came to the United States to study for a PhD degree in engineering and information science from Stanford University in California. He developed the concept for Orkut as a 20 percent independent project while working for Facebook. At the time, he was only in his mid-twenties. His goal was to "experience all the wildest things in life and never look back or regret about anything." He has achieved it.

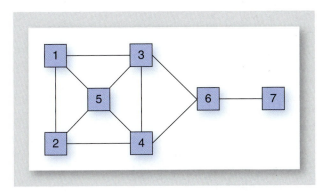

Figure 14-2 A Social Network

Network analysts believe that how an individual lives depends in large part on how that individual is tied into the larger web of social connections. Social networking often involves grouping specific individuals or organizations together. Social networking, of course, can be accomplished by face-to-face communication at a place of business, club, or place of worship, to name a few. However, face-to-face interactions are limited to a specific group and the network is largely static. The Internet has provided the opportunity to communicate with a much larger group that can be widened over time. While there are a number of social networking websites that focus on particular interests, there are others that do not. For example, LinkedIn mainly attracts professional and business people. A more exclusive network was founded for delegates of the World Economic Forum, mentioned above.

A network is composed of actors, represented as nodes in Figure 14-2, and the relations among them are represented as edges, or paths, while the links show relationships or flows between the nodes. Based on the six degrees of separation concept (the idea that any two people on the planet could make contact through a chain of no more than five intermediaries), social networking establishes interconnected Internet communities. Assume that each node is a person. From the figure, we can tell which two persons interact with each other and which person or persons is a leader (connects with more than one person). The leader in this case is person number 5, who is the central point in the network. Person 5 has the most influence on the behavior of the other nodes. Person number 6 has fewer connections than

---

BOX 14-2 COMPANY IN FOCUS: CHILEAN WINES IN CHINA

Even though Facebook, Twitter, and YouTube are blocked in China, the Chinese constitute the largest Internet population in the world. There are also several local social media networks in China that are permitted.

Chilean wine producers mounted a campaign to introduce their products to Chinese consumers. Social media were chosen to help establish a community where consumers would be able to discuss wine. Specifically:

■ **Kaixin**—A social network site where wine fans could come together and share wine drinking tips.

■ **Youku**—A video sharing site (like YouTube) where content was produced specifically about Chilean wine and was uploaded for all to view.

■ **Flickr**—Furnished numerous photos of Chilean wine, landscapes, and other activities by ProChile in China.

As a result of the campaign, Chilean wine became the fourth best-selling wine in China.

Source: Information culled by Michael Darragh, "Discovering Social Media in China," http://blog.ogilvy.pr.com/2009/11/discovering-social-media-in-china. Retrieved January 13, 2011.

---

number 5, but plays an intermediary role with connections 3 and 4, who are connected with persons 1, 2, and 5.

One of the implications of social networks is that people learn about and choose among behavioral options not only based on directly observing how others in their social circle engage in behaviors, but they also learn with whom their friends and associates connect with outside the network and then bring that information or those practices back to the immediate network.

What are the implications of social networks for marketers? Christakis and Fowler (2009) suggest that the world is governed by what they call "three degrees of influence"—that is, your friend's friend's friend, most likely someone you don't even know—who indirectly influences your actions and emotions.[6] Discussions among network participants about what products to buy, what restaurants to frequent, what places of entertainment to visit, and what electronic and print media to watch and read are highly influenced by Internet networks.

MOTIVATIONS TO USE SOCIAL NETWORKS

What motivates people to use social networks? A partial answer to this question is afforded by the Global Web Index.[7] This index is based on a survey of some 29,000 global social media users in Asia, Europe, South America, and the United States. Users can be segmented by age group, behavior (e.g., risk taker, thrill seeker, internationals) and an overall country index. Table 14-2 is based on the overall index for selected motivations and for the BRIC countries for illustration. The most important motivation to use social media in Brazil (69 percent of all respondents) and Russia (53 percent) was to "Stay up to date on news/events." In India, the most important motivation was "Searching for work" (61 percent of all respondents), and in China, "staying in touch with friends" (51 percent of all respondents). Many people use social

6. Christakis, N., & Fowler, J. (2009). *Connected: The Surprising Power of Our Social Networks and How They Shape Our Lives.* New York: Little, Brown.

7. http://GlobalWebIndex.net.

TABLE 14-2 Motivation to Use Social Media

(Percent Motivated)

Motivations	Brazil	Russia	India	China
Research to find products to buy	61	46	50	40
Promote something	27	11	32	16
Find music	48	33	38	36
Stay up to date on news and events	69	53	58	40
To get inspired/new ideas	50	30	50	32
Express myself	28	15	37	27

Source: Data from GlobalWebIndex.net. Global State of Social Media in 2010.

media to search for products to buy. Sixty-one percent do so in Brazil, 50 percent in India, followed by 46 percent in Russia and 40 percent in China. From these results and those shown in Table 14-2, we learn that social media usage differs by country. Both the relative importance of social networks as a source of information and influence and the differences between countries must be taken into account when planning global advertising on social networks.

In relation to the above motivations, R. Craig Lefebvre[8] (2009) suggests the following social marketing strategies:

1. **Focusing on people with large numbers of connections** within a network (connectors, influentials, or opinion leaders)

2. **Reducing the density of a network** in which risk behaviors are concentrated by introducing more boundary spanners or increasing social connections of members of the group outside of their immediate network

3. **Understanding the members of a network who are most attentive and responsive to the behaviors of others** (or more easily influenced or persuadable) and providing them with protective or alternative behaviors to prevent adoption

4. **Enhancing the salience and attractiveness of the "out group"** [positive deviants] by positioning these practitioners of desired behaviors in a way that attracts imitation or modeling

THE NETWORKED ENTERPRISE—BUSINESS USE OF SOCIAL NETWORKS

While it is generally assumed that social networks are used mainly by household consumers, there is growing use by business firms. A survey[9] by McKinsey & Company found that businesses gained benefits from utilizing social networking applications. These benefits are grouped into three categories: Internal, Customer-Related, and Working with External Suppliers and Partners. In both internal and external categories, the benefits include increasing speed of access to knowledge, reducing communication costs, increasing employee satisfaction, and increasing satisfaction of suppliers, partners, and external experts. Some of these applications allow management to see which employees are in contact with each other and what subjects they are discussing.

8. Retrieved from http://lefebvres_social2009/10/social_models_for_marketing_social_networks.html on November 28, 2010.

9. Retrieved from www.mckinseyquarterly.com/article_print.aspx?L2=18&L3 on December 16, 2010.

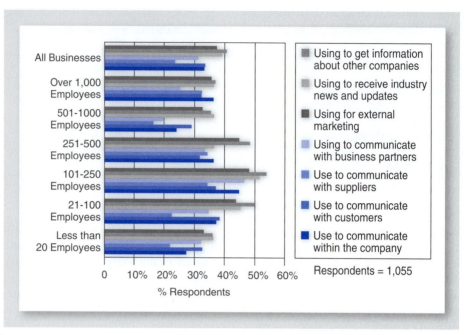

Figure 14-3 Business Use of Social Networking

Source: Top business uses of social networking: Information gathering and marketing ranked above collaboration. (14 May 2009). *TMC.net News.*

Customer-related benefits include increasing the effectiveness of marketing, increasing customer satisfaction, and reducing marketing costs. Some firms emphasize one of three applications, while about 3 percent of the firm's surveyed are fully networked, utilizing all three applications. Most commercial firms are networked to Web 2.0, which is designed for them. They are similar in scope to Facebook but are not connected to the public domain and are protected behind a corporate firewall. Security is a main feature of these networks. Since both consumer and business-based networks are used for collecting internal and external intelligence, there are privacy issues that have to be considered. We will consider these in a separate section below.

A global survey of 1,000 executives by TMC.net Communications and Technology Industry Research found that the most prevalent use of social networks among all firms is to obtain information about other companies' industry updates (see Figure 14-3). External marketing is the third most frequently mentioned use of networks. Following marketing, external and internal communications were used as a means to reach both customers and employees. A number of polls such as Online Social Networking and TopRank found that Facebook, LinkedIn, and Twitter, in that order, are the most used social networks by business firms.

An example of social network external marketing communication is illustrated by Regus, a global provider of virtual offices and meeting rooms. The company used a combination of social media such as Facebook and Twitter to enlarge their sales in New York. The campaign resulted in increased revenue of 114 percent compared to the same period the year before.[10] The campaign manager concluded that:

> Social media enables companies to engage directly with their target audiences . . . these audiences self-identify online as interested in specific topics, themes, products and/or

10. www.mashable.com/2010/11/04/b2b-social-marketing-strategies/.

services . . . This type of focus is fertile ground for lead generation and driving revenue for business-to-business marketing.[11]

Using social media to reach consumers is by no means an easy task. It is similar to relationship marketing, where the marketer responds to consumer dialog on the media. This requires manpower dedicated to monitoring social media in order to determine what consumers have experienced with the company's products or services. The dialogue between consumer and marketer is two-way: experiences with a brand are related by consumers and the marketer responds via the same social media. This two-way communication between consumer and marketer requires a shift in traditional advertising strategy. If done successfully, the return can be substantial. P&G, the largest advertiser in the United States, decided at the end of 2010 to discontinue advertising on day-time television programs (so-called soap operas) after its success with a campaign for its brand Old Spice was posted on YouTube. The campaign generated over a million Facebook fans.

The Growth of Global Social Marketing Advertising

Advertising and promotion are other major uses of social networks by business. The amount spent on global social advertising has been estimated at $3.3 billion in 2010 and is expected to grow to $4.3 billion in 2011 (Figure 14-4). Advertising expenditures on global media have increased annually at an average of 30 percent. The United States has accounted for about half of worldwide spending in social media, but other regions of the world, such as Europe and Asia, are expected to increase their share of world spending.

Even in some of the BRIC countries, advertising in social media is extensive. For example, the social network/blog category reached 86 percent of active Internet users in Brazil in 2010, while the number of social network users in China reached 245 million in 2009, up 34 percent over 2008. PricewaterhouseCoopers predicted

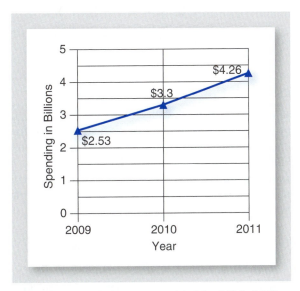

Figure 14-4 Social Network Ad Spending Worldwide, 2009–2011

Source: Data from eMarketer, July 2010.

11. Ibid.

TABLE 14-3 Facebook Growth in their Global Audience (2007–2008)		
Increase in Millions of Users		
Age Group	**Male**	**Females**
2-17	3.7	3.6
18-34	10.9	11.9
35-49	12.4	11.7
50-64	6.0	7.6
65+	1.9	1.3

Source: Adapted from: Nielsen Online Global Index.

that by 2013, 36 percent of all cash spent on advertising will go toward Internet-based campaigns.

Social marketing is truly global. By the end of 2009, there were nearly 250 million monthly users on the top nine social networks, such as Facebook, YouTube, and Twitter. Facebook is growing rapidly outside the United States. In New Zealand, Hong Kong, Canada, and Singapore (as well as in the United States), Facebook was the No. 1 website based on market share of visits in June 2010, according to Experian Hitwise.[12] Its fastest growth rates have been among the 18 to 49 age group (Table 14-3). Between the age group of 16 to 54, Denmark has the highest penetration of social media followed by Malaysia, Norway, and Sweden. According to The Nielsen Company, the social network/blog category reached 86 percent of active Internet users in Brazil in 2010, and 78 percent of active users in Italy. By comparison, the percent of active Internet users in the United States during the same year was 74 percent.

Social networks are also on the increase in China. According to the Chinese Data Center, the number of social network users in 2009 was 245 million, an increase of 34 percent over the preceding year. Although Internet users in China number approximately 500 million, there were almost 600,000 social network accounts by 2010.

CASE STUDIES OF SOCIAL MARKETING CAMPAIGNS

The Starbucks Fan Page

Starbucks has created a social network called Starbucks Fan Page on Facebook that is aimed mainly at people in the United States but is also localized for foreign markets. As a result, Starbucks' Fan Page has become the largest on Facebook, with six million fans in the United States and additional but smaller numbers of fans in other countries. Promotions and messages are localized for individual markets. A major advantage of such an approach allows Starbucks to not only aim its advertising globally where possible, but also to measure its effectiveness across target markets.

Bringing the "Like" Button into the Real World: Coca-Cola (Israel)

The Coca-Cola Village is a special summer experiential event in Israel. Every year Coca-Cola (Israel) invites 10,000 teenagers to the village, which is run on Facebook.

12. Hitwise Rankings are updated daily and provide a comprehensive overview of top performing websites across more than 160 industries. See www.hitwise.com.

BOX 14-3   COUNTRY IN FOCUS: EGYPT

Egypt has a population of 80 million, but only 13 million Internet users. Nevertheless, when regulatory and social barriers (e.g., literacy, religious) are taken into consideration, the number of users becomes significant. Facebook, for instance, continues to gain ground in the social media arena in Egypt. There are three million Facebook users in Egypt, which is a little under 4 percent of the total population. Relative to 24 percent total online penetration, this is a relatively low percentage; however, user growth is measured at 7.63 percent. Sixty-two percent of Facebook users are men and 38 percent are women, and growth still favors the male element. The majority of users are young, with 48 percent between the ages of 18 and 24, and 28 percent between the ages of 25 and 34.

In late 2008, Nokia created a campaign that was built on the use of social media and user-generated content. The campaign utilized traditional and non-traditional mediums (TV, radio, print, social media) to encourage users to participate in a competition on Facebook. The campaign utilized a popular Egyptian actor and rapper (Ahmed Mekky) who had a leading role in several popular Egyptian youth films.

A music video with a catchy tune and colorful incidents that are locally insightful ("only-in-Egypt-type" scenarios) encouraged viewers to use their Nokia phones to create their own videos and upload them to the Nokia N96 Facebook group and enter the competition. Competition winners were listed on the website and their videos were posted to the group. Today, the group has more than 24,000 members and continues to be an active forum for users to share their content.

Sources: Adapted from: Facebakers. (2010, April). Retrieved from www.facebakers.com; Egyptian Information Bureau. (2010). Retrieved from http://Eccosocialmedia.files.wordpress.com/2010/04/Egypt/pdf.

Teenagers have to collect 10 Coca-Cola caps each, gather eight friends who did the same, and then register online through Facebook to gain exclusive entry. Arriving at the Coca-Cola Village, they are asked to wear a special wristband that would securely hold their Facebook login and password to swipe across a radio-frequency identification device (RFID) when starting each activity. The devices were installed in strategic places (swimming pools, dining rooms). Teenagers were then asked to place the bracelet alongside the RFID device signifying that the person "liked" the facility. This action would automatically post a Facebook message, keeping friends updated about the person's activities. Snapshots were taken by a photographer and these were also posted to the Facebook page. The village hosted some 650 participants daily, with 35,000 postings or over 100,000 during the three days of the event. Thus, the Coca-Cola Village Facebook page became the most "liked" in Israel, and of course generated hundreds of thousands of social media interactions.

Kraft Foods' Aladdin Chocolate Box

Aladdin chocolates have been sold in Sweden for 70 years and are a popular gift for Christmas. For Christmas 2009, Kraft planned to introduce a new type of praline chocolate to the box. Instead of advertising the new product, Aladdin arranged a community-voted competition wherein people would decide which praline would be eliminated to make room for the new entry (see Figure 14-5).

Aladdin established a digital polling station four weeks before Christmas where consumers could cast their vote for their favorite chocolate. The largest newspaper in Sweden, *Aftonbladet*, reported extensively on the campaign. Organizers of the campaign designed a "personality test" on Facebook so that people could determine their

Figure 14-5 Aladdin Chocolates Voting Advertisement

personality based on their favorite chocolate praline. About 14,000 people took the test. The campaign generated more than 400,000 votes, which was more than the most-voted-for politician in the 2009 Swedish elections for representatives in the European parliament. The campaign resulted in an increase of both sales (26.5 percent) and market share (2.8 percent).

Legal Aspects of Social Marketing: The Privacy Question

Unwarranted access to private information is a concern to anyone who uses the web. It is especially an issue when third parties gain access to information stored on social network platforms. In addition, most employees view their personal social media site pages as private. Employees are often unaware that personal information posted on these sites may be accessible by their employers and co-workers. If an organization monitors its employees' use of social media, it must inform them of the practice.

Examples of the information that is a privacy concern includes a customer's browsing and buying patterns, negative comments about brands or specific companies and products, and personal experiences. Are social network users aware of the privacy issue? While we cannot generalize, there are some indications from around the world that many users are not fully aware of this issue. For example, a survey by the Norwegian Consumer Council found that 66 percent of Norwegian Internet users are using social networks and that almost all (94 percent) said it is important to have control over the personal information they provide online. In spite of this, users rarely read the terms and conditions governing their privacy and the content they share on social networking sites.[13]

A Canadian study reported that most of the 86 percent of respondents who said they use social networking sites "fail to perform the following basic security measures on a regular basis," including changing passwords, while 65 percent said they infrequently or never adjust privacy settings, and 57 percent infrequently or never "inform their social network administrator on security issues."[14] On the other hand, a Pew Research Center study of American's use of social marketing networks found that two-thirds of all users claimed that they have changed the privacy settings for their profile to limit what they share with others online. Among users who worry about the availability of their online information, 77 percent have changed their privacy settings.

13. Retrieved from http://forbrukerportaler.no./Artikler/2009/social_network-sites-grossly-undermines-users-privacy.

14. Bhandari, B. (2009). Internet users: Be aware of the dangers of social networking and community sites. Retrieved from http://gosecure.wordpress.com.

However, even those who don't worry about such information are relatively active in this regard—59 percent of these less-concerned users have adjusted their privacy settings in this way.[15]

Balancing privacy concerns with the benefits of social networking is not an easy task to achieve. Much of the adoption value in social networking sites flows from social browsing, being able to see the "publicly articulated social networks" of others. The more private the profiles, the less valuable the social network site is to its users. Orkut users in Brazil, for example, have been nearly unanimous in saying that, since profiles have become more private, it is "less fun" to use the site and people spend less time doing so. Yet most users also want Orkut to give them more privacy options. In other words: They want to be able to see others' data, but they don't necessarily want others to be able to see theirs.[16]

SUMMARY

- Social media has a global reach penetrating both developed and emerging markets. Two-thirds of the world's Internet population visit social networking or blogging sites, accounting for almost 10 percent of all Internet time.

- Social media networks are aimed at both consumer and B2B markets. Companies that will succeed in the twenty-first century will be social businesses, committed to forging deep and meaningful relationships with their customers. Its use is challenging traditional marketing media such as television advertising.

- Seventy-nine percent of the largest 100 companies in the Fortune Global

500 index are using at least one of the most popular social media platforms: Twitter, Facebook, YouTube, or corporate blogs.

- Companies based in the United States and Europe are more likely to use Twitter or Facebook than they are to have corporate blogs, while companies from Asia Pacific are more likely to utilize corporate blogs than other forms of social media.

- Privacy has become an important issue regarding the protection that social media users have concerning the information they place on the web. Users of social networks are taking more precautions by upgrading their privacy settings.

DISCUSSION QUESTIONS

1. How can a manufacturer of kitchen utensils best use social media?

2. What is the difference between social media marketing and cause-related marketing?

3. Comment on the statement that social media is driven by people's need to create, share, discover, and participate.

4. While Facebook is the most popular social networking website in the United States and the UK, most people in India use Orkut. Why so you think this is so? Is it because of cultural differences? Other reasons?

15. Retrieved from www.PewInternet.org/Reports/2020/Reputation-Management/Methodology/About.aspx on January 8, 2011.

16. Recuero, R. (2010). Privacy and social media sites: A growing global concern. Retrieved from www.dmlcentral.net/blog/raquel-recuero/privacy-and-social-media-sites-growing-concern.

EXPERIENTIAL EXERCISES

1. Now that the importance of social media has been reported, how can its effectiveness be measured? Use any available source and determine what measurement tools are available.

2. Compare two company fan pages on Facebook. Analyze the strategies used by both. What are the similarities and differences in their approaches?

KEY TERMS

Social marketing, p. 393

Social media, p. 392

CASE 14-1

In Search of Book Sales

Social Media Marketing as a Tool for Search Engine Optimization

> *"Social media is like teen sex.*
> *Everyone wants to do it. Nobody knows how.*
> *When it is finally done, there is surprise it's not better."*
>
> —AVINASH KAUSHIK, GOOGLE ANALYTICS

In October 2008, Allen H. Kupetz was standing on a stage in the massive downtown Orlando, Florida, public library for the official launch of his book, *The Future of Less—What the WireLESS, PaperLESS, and CashLESS Revolutions Mean to You.* In front of about 200 people, Kupetz joked about the irony of being in a library selling a book about going paperless. Most people there that night bought a copy of the book, but Kupetz knew he didn't have the time to do enough of these kinds of events to sell a lot of books. He needed direct and indirect distribution channels, and in the world of books, this meant a relationship with Amazon.com. But how could he get people to Amazon.com to buy his book from it or directly from him, where he made more money? The answer seemed to be in using social media to increase his presence on the results pages of the various searches engines. This was not a get-rich scheme for authors, but it needed to be part of an overall marketing campaign that also included additional public events.

First Things First

> "Searching is easy. *Finding* is hard.
> A needle in a haystack is hard to find.
> But try finding a needle in a needle stack."
>
> —Anonymous

According to Worldometer (http://www.worldometers.info/books/), as many as 172,000 new book titles were published in the United States in 2005, second only to the United Kingdom. So three years before *The Future of Less* was published or the revolutions in self-publishing, e-books, and e-book readers like the Kindle, there was already a tremendous amount of new English-language content constantly coming on the market. The challenge for Kupetz was how not to be just another needle in the needle stack.

Prior to the book launch, Kupetz bought the domains futureofless.com and thefutureofless.com, which he forwarded to futureofless.com to avoid having to build and maintain two sites. Although Google and other search engines have never confirmed that some sites must wait up to six months before appearing in search engine results, referred to as the Sandbox Effect, Kupetz wanted to get the sandbox clock ticking just in case. He knew it was not enough just to buy the domain and have an automated "Under Construction" page appear, so he put up some relevant text about the upcoming book launch. Then Kupetz downloaded the Google toolbar for his Internet browser

Case prepared by Allen H. Kupetz, Rollins College. Reprinted with permission.

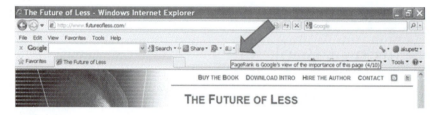

and installed the Page Rank button. He could then visit www.futureofless.com regularly and see when Google "had found it."

Kupetz also staked out his territory on the two most popular blog sites, blogger.com and WordPress. At no cost, he obtained futureofless.blogspot.com and futureofless. wordpress.com. He also went to Twitter, a micro-blogging site, and reserved twitter. com/future_of_less rather than twitter.com/futureofless or twitter.com/ofless, which was actually a mistake. Since Twitter limits users to 140 characters, at that time longer names limited the ability of others to retweet long messages to others.

Blogs and Twitter were critical to Kupetz's search engine optimization (SEO) strategy, since search engines prefer sites that are text-based (it is difficult for search engines to evaluate photos or videos) and sites where the content is updated regularly. Blogs and Twitter fulfilled both of these requirements nicely.

The final step to tie all these seemingly disparate pieces together was to point all of them to the website www.futureofless.com. Kupetz knew that as his blog and Twitter sites grew in popularity and increased their own Page Rank, this would increase the Page Rank of www.futureofless.com. Kupetz also added his website, blog, and Twitter sites to his LinkedIn profile. And when he spoke before different organizations, he asked that they also include a link in the speaker's bio section that pointed to www .futureofless.com. The strategy was to point everything to that site and the tactics were to use all forms of social media as pointers. Since Kupetz could not optimize Amazon .com, he optimized his site, which had a link to Amazon.com, as well as to his blog and Twitter accounts. Social media is about having a conversation, so Kupetz wanted people following his blog and Twitter to buy his book and for those who bought the book to comment about it on his blog and Twitter account. The goal was to create a buzz around the ideas of wireless, paperless, and cashless—interest in any of the three might motivate someone to buy the book.

Looking for an International Market

When *The Future of Less* was published, Kupetz retained the international publication rights, meaning he could sell the right to translate, publish, and distribute his book in any country outside the United States. Given how far ahead most of Asia and Europe were in terms of wireless networks compared to the United States, he didn't find a lot of interest in these markets. But Kupetz used South Korea as an example in the book of successful private-public partnerships and found a South Korean publisher who wanted to translate the book into Korean and sell it. Although that publisher had an extensive and mature distribution network, Kupetz again chose to augment that with social media marketing (SMM).

Kupetz had an award-winning blog, www.koreality.com, which had a Page Rank of 2. Kupetz thought that was pretty good for a narrowly focused blog on a country that didn't get as much press as China or India. He had the publisher buy www.koreality.co.kr and point it at his own blog. Then he created his own ads on the right side of the blog to buy the Korean-version of his book from Amazon.com and the four leading Korean online book publishers, Aladin, Interpark, Kyobo, and Yes24.

The Korean-language version of the book sold over 1,500 in the first seven months it was available, May–December 2009.

Measuring Success

With many SMM tools, it can be difficult to measure the impact of a campaign on revenue or even less tangible things such as brand awareness and brand equity. The good thing about selling a product is that it is easier to discern the correlation and causation of SMM to sales because one can track the rate of book sales immediately after a social media tactic is used.

There are also several suites of tools to measure how many people are visiting your website, what site they were on immediately before arriving at yours, how long they stayed on your site, how many pages they clicked on, and from what country they originated. Kupetz used Google Analytics (http://www.google.com/analytics/). In a corporate environment, this allows a chief marketing officer to tell his boss specifically what is working and what is not, and to start to calculate the return on investment of various SMM campaigns.

Definitions

Page Rank—An algorithm, named after Google co-founder Larry Page, that is used by the Google search engine to measure the value of a site based largely on which sites link to it.

Sandbox Effect—"According to the sandbox effect, Google temporarily reduces the page rank of new domains, placing them into what is referred to as its sandbox in an effort to counter the ways that search engine optimizers attempt to manipulate Google's page ranking by creating lots of inbound links to a new web site from other web sites that they own."

(Retrieved from http://en.wikipedia.org/wiki/Sandbox_effect)

Search Engine Optimization—The process of improving the volume of traffic to a web site from search engines via organic (i.e., unpaid) search results.

Social Media—"A social trend in which people use technologies to get the things they need from each other, rather than from traditional institutions like corporations." (Li, Charlene and Bernoff, Josh. *Groundswell.*)

Social Media Marketing—The process of using social media as one aspect of a broader marketing plan.

Questions for Discussion

1. Kupetz started his SMM and SEO strategies in 2008. What changes have occurred in social media since then that could be used today instead of—or in addition to—what Kupetz did in 2008?

2. As *The Future of Less* continues to mature—two years on the market is a long time for a book about technology with *future* in the title—what can Kupetz do to continue to sell books and keep his Page Rank and search results at current levels?

3. What sites do you visit the most often and what are the Page Ranks? Do you see a difference between domestic and more global sites; i.e., does yahoo.com have a higher Page Rank than yahoo.cn or br.yahoo.com? What are some of the variables that Google and other search engines use to rank a site or to have a site appear on the first page of a search?

Designing and Controlling Global Marketing Systems

The way you will thrive in a business environment is by innovating—innovating in technologies, innovating in strategies, innovating in business models.
SAMUEL PALMISANO, CEO, IBM

LEARNING OBJECTIVES

After reading this chapter, you should be able to:

- Understand the importance of selecting the optimum organization structure for a global business.
- Identify the differences between alternative organization structures.
- Discuss how a company's organization structure may have to be adapted to its internationalization process.
- Distinguish between a company's domestic and international organizational needs.
- Understand how globalization affects a company's organizational structure.
- Explain the difference between formal and informal control mechanisms.

Nortel Hires a Turnaround CMO

Lauren Flaherty worked at IBM for 25 years after she graduated from college. She was credited with working with a team that revitalized the IBM brand. This is what Nortel was looking for when it lured her to become its Chief Marketing Officer (CMO). In May 2006, the Toronto-based global telecommunications giant was in trouble. Its challenges began with the bursting of the dotcom bubble and the subsequent telecom industry slump, accelerated with a shocking accounting scandal, and ended with a $2.5 billion settlement agreement between Nortel and its shareholders. Meanwhile, the company's competitors, including Cisco and Lucent, had continued to aggressively pursue market share at Nortel's expense.

The first thing Lauren did at her new job was to set up a global brand audit. Similar to a SWOT analysis, the idea was to learn about the company's strengths and weaknesses and perform an in-depth segmentation analysis. Her major objective was to improve Nortel's brand value and increase revenue. Given her major role in this process, combined with her 25-year marketing career at one of the most metrics-driven companies in the world (IBM), Flaherty combined traditional segmentation methods with algorithms designed to identify the odds of winning customers in various segment designations. It took her a couple of years to learn the implications derived from the audit.

One of most important steps Flaherty took was sharing the lessons with the global organization's local marketing and sales teams: "We have to enlist the support of everyone who will be required to execute it." Nortel had decided to test the new strategy in four key markets: London, Singapore, Chicago, and Mexico City, determining specific targets and objectives in each area.

The new strategy initially resulted in two successful marketing campaigns for Nortel's networking business. Using a number of media such as TV, print, and online ads, as well as blogs and other social media channels, the campaigns seized on the timely issue of energy conservation and proved to business executives how Nortel's products could save them up to 50 percent in energy costs compared to the company's biggest competitor in that space, Cisco. The campaign resulted in a fourfold increase in qualified leads, three to five times higher conversion rates and a 20 percent increase in sales in the pipeline. The Nortel brand also got a helping hand with the announcement in July 2008 that the company would be the official network infrastructure partner for the 2012 London Olympics. And Lauren Flaherty deservedly won a spot on *BtoB* magazine's 2008 list of Top Marketers for Nortel's remarkable turnaround.[1]

Successful leaders of global marketing organizations, such as Ms. Flaherty at Nortel, are often distinguished by their ability to deftly navigate the three functions we review in this chapter: organization, control, and leadership. These CMOs shape the marketing organization within the context of the larger company and position it for success; they develop control mechanisms and methodically track performance; and they exude the leadership qualities that allow them to develop and implement their strategic vision, motivate their staff, and contribute to the overall success of the global organization by being champions for its customers. According to Steve Noble, senior analyst with Forrester Research, CMOs are entering a new period of organizational change as they restructure to minimize costs, maximize flexibility, and place digital and social media at the heart of their global strategies. In fact, 75 percent of chief marketers are either restructuring their marketing organizations now or will do so by the end of 2011, according to a new Forrester Research survey.[2]

In many companies, the global marketing function develops organically, as the organization expands into more and more international markets. In the beginning, international marketing may be a function of the export department or, in bigger organizations, of the international division. As companies and their global marketing organizations (GMOs) evolve and grow, however, it is important that executives take the time to formulate and establish solid strategy, leadership, and cultural drivers. Recent research confirms that having these three building blocks not only leads to a more natural and efficient organizational structure, but also positively influences marketing and financial performance. As the authors point out, "[It] would be prudent for the senior leadership of a GMO to formulate a global strategy and to build an organizational culture, which should then pave the way for tackling structural issues and organizational routines."[3]

Traditionally, marketing organizations take one of the several established organizational formats: regional, functional, product-centric, or matrix. In the following sections, we'll review each of these formats and present new and emerging ones that may completely change the future of the global marketing organization.

1. *BtoB* magazine, Nortel Corporate website (www.nortel.com/corporate/exec/flaherty.html); www.b2bmarketing.net/node/1225; Carter, S. (2009). *The new language of marketing 2.0: How to use ANGELS to energize your market.* Cambridge, UK: IBM Press.

2. How to create an adaptive global marketing organization. (26 November 2010). *Advertising Age.*

3. Hult, G., Cavusgil, S., Kiyak, T., Deligonul, S., & Lagerstrom, K. (2007). What drives performance in globally focused marketing organizations? A three-country study. *Journal of International Marketing, 15*(2), 58–85.

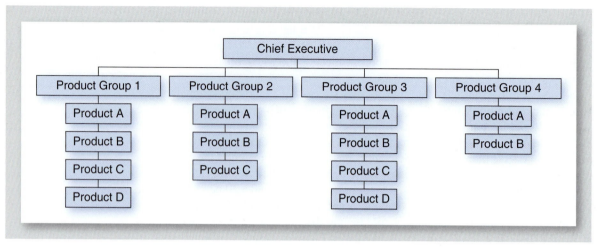

Figure 15-1 Global Product Lines Structure

PRODUCT-BASED ORGANIZATIONAL FORMAT

MNCs, especially those marketing consumer products and those with very diverse end-user markets, commonly organize their global strategic business units based on products (see Figure 15-1). Since each unit is responsible for the worldwide marketing of a specific product line, it is able to focus on continuous innovation and improvement of the products to keep them competitive on a global scale. When combined with an efficient and globally positioned manufacturing and distribution operations, the **product-based organizational structure** provides companies with the flexibility to quickly respond to changing market needs and competitive pressures.

An organization based on product lines has certain drawbacks, however. It often results in duplication of resources and efforts among the different product teams. It may also prevent the organization from accumulating a common body of knowledge about shared markets, product design issues, or other areas where cooperation and coordination can produce long term benefits for the organization as a whole. Marketing, in particular, is very positively affected by shared know-how. Research findings confirm that there are significant benefits to integrating the marketing function by sharing market and industry information across units and, to a lesser degree, by centralizing the decision-making process but not integrating staff.[4]

REGIONAL ORGANIZATIONAL FORMAT

A recent survey of CMOs conducted by the Economist Intelligence Unit indicated that nearly a third of them believe that marketing organizations are likely to become more centralized than localized. The report's authors speculated that the trend most likely represented the empowerment felt by global marketing executives who, thanks to the Internet and powerful business intelligence and analytics tools, can now better track regional and global trends and develop marketing strategies accordingly.[5]

In firms that base their organizational structure on the geographic areas which they serve, corporate headquarters usually becomes the hub for strategic planning, control,

4. Kim, K., Park, J. H., & Prescott, J. E. (2003). The global integration of business functions: A study of multinational businesses in integrated global industries. *Journal of International Business Studies, 34*, 327–344.

5. Economist Intelligence Unit. (2008, September). *Future Tense: The Global CMO.*

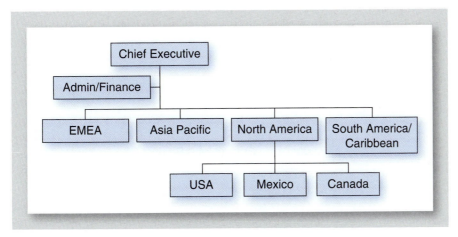

Figure 15-2 Global Regional Structure

and coordination (see Figure 15-2). The regions most often included are North America, South and Central America, Europe, Middle East and Africa (EMEA), and Asia Pacific. However, regions may also be organized by other criteria, such as a common language or belonging to the same trade bloc such as the European Union or NAFTA.

The focus on specific geographies works to marketing's advantage, where knowledge of regional market conditions and cultural preferences helps with uncovering potential standardization opportunities in product design and promotion and can lead to economies of scale. Conversely, if individual markets within the region experience changing conditions or user needs, they can receive timely special attention.

Regional organizational formats work best for companies with a limited number of products and similar market segments throughout the world. This structure naturally requires a greater emphasis on marketing, price, and product design as the differentiating factors.

One disadvantage of regional organizations is that they don't scale well. Should the organization decide to expand and diversify its products, the coordination of its product lines and regional and country units may become cumbersome and expensive. Also, regional divisions often become too focused on their own operations, hindering inter-divisional cooperation and transfer of knowledge and spurring unnecessary rivalry and duplication of efforts.

FUNCTIONAL ORGANIZATIONAL FORMAT

One of the classic organizational structures is the functional one. It is based on the processes performed by an organization, such as operations, finance, marketing, human resources, etc., and it involves building highly specialized teams that report to the respective division head—VP of Finance, VP of Marketing, and so on (see Figure 15-3). This simple and easy to grasp and navigate structure provides clear lines of communication and task management, which facilitate project coordination within the divisions.

On the other hand, functional organizations are prone to develop "divisional silos" that interfere with cross-departmental communications and encourage an "us vs. them" mentality within the departments. Such developments can slow down decision making and impede problem solving in today's fast-paced, competitive environment, where cross-functional solutions are often needed. Because of its limitations, the functional

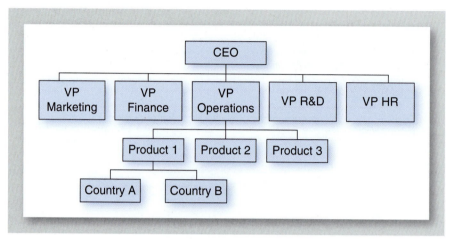

Figure 15-3 Global Functional Structure

organizational format is often abandoned once companies reach a critical mass of diverse products and customers.

MATRIX ORGANIZATIONAL FORMAT

Some organizations have turned to the matrix structure (see Figure 15-4) to avoid some of the drawbacks of the formats described earlier. **Matrix organizations** may include aspects of two or more of the product, geographic, or functional structures. They combine a product-based structure with key geographic regions, for example,

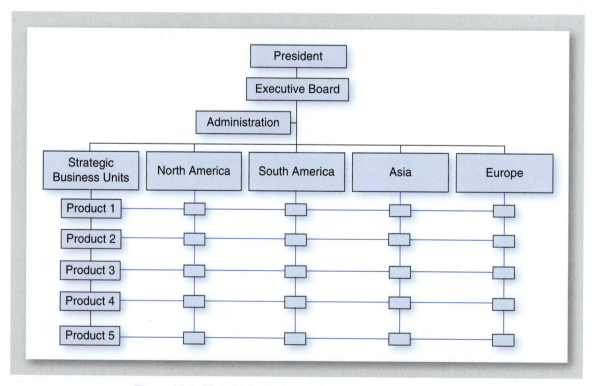

Figure 15-4 Global Matrix Structure

or functional and geographic divisions. The advantages gained in such hybrid structures may include improved communication and teamwork and better market coverage where both global and local perspectives are, presumably, integrated. Matrix organizations attempt to adapt to the multi-dimensional global business environment.

The inherent duality of the structure may also causes problems, however. Many managers find it difficult reporting to two separate channels, and conflicts or confusion may become common. Decision making also may become slower, as disparate objectives and priorities compete for attention and divisional overlaps often turn into turf battles. These issues have resulted in the gradual departure from the matrix organization among MNCs.

NEW ORGANIZATIONAL DIRECTIONS

The job of implementing a global marketing strategy within the context of the described organizational structures and their variations is not an easy one. The degrees of integration among the worldwide business units and headquarters or among various local and regional subsidiaries play a critical role in the success or failure of global marketing campaigns.

One recent study has attempted to classify the relationship between some common marketing strategies and the organizational structures within which they may play out. It contends that "global marketers"—MNCs that rely on a standardized marketing strategy—fit better in an organizational structure that favors globally dispersed but functionally limited subsidiaries dependent on the central office, as well as dependent upon each other for support. Another type of marketer, what the authors call "infrastructural minimalists," are companies that mix standardized elements, such as brand names and channels, with localized ones, such as adapted advertising and sales campaigns. Their strategy would be more at home in organizations that rely highly on headquarters and each other but have a rather limited geographic scope. Lastly, those marketers dubbed "tactical coordinators" are most likely to localize their strategy and thus fit best in organizations where individual subsidiaries are granted wide geographic coverage and autonomy and experience limited control by headquarters.[6] Another study also suggests that the strength of the relationship between headquarters and subsidiaries plays an important role in the formulation of a marketing strategy.[7]

In addition to their concern for strategic fit within the organization as a whole, marketing leaders are continuously challenged by the evolving nature of the marketing organization itself. Two significant developments accelerating this evolution have been the increasing power of the customer and the relentlessly growing global competition.

CUSTOMER-CENTERED ORGANIZATIONS

Marketing has been one of the first organizational functions to be affected by and to respond to the changing balance of power in favor of customers by advocating a fundamental shift to a more customer-centered organizational design. Such design is hailed as a way to avoid many of the limitations of the traditional organizational structures and to increase a firm's competitiveness by bringing better understanding of the markets' needs. As research indicates, the long and complex transition process may

---

6. Lim, L. K. S., Acito, F., & Rusetski, A. (2006). Development of archetypes of international marketing strategy. *Journal of International Business Studies*, *37*, 499–524.

7. Hewett, K., Roth, M. S., & Roth, K. (2003). Conditions influencing headquarters and foreign subsidiary roles in marketing activities and their effects on performance. *Journal of International Business Studies*, *34*, 567–585.

BOX 15-1 COMPANY IN FOCUS: STARBUCKS

An Announcement of an Organizational Restructure at Starbucks from CEO Howard Schultz

Dear Partners,
Since I returned as CEO six weeks ago, we have experienced a lot of change in
a very short period [. . .]

Schultz's goals were to fix troubled stores, rekindle an emotional attachment with customers, and make longer-term changes such as reorganizing executives and revamping the supply chain. The first step was to conduct a thorough organizational analysis that eventually led to the decision that the company had to be restructured in order to strengthen its focus on the customer in United States field operations, and to centralize or consolidate many of the support functions to drive functional excellence and reduce redundancies

United States Field Operations

Effective Monday, February 25, 2008, the United States field organization began reorganizing from two divisions to four, with full implementation completed by March 24. The new divisions are: Western/Pacific, Northwest/Mountain, Southeast/ Plains, and Northeast/Atlantic. The restructuring was designed to accomplish:

- A re-designed cost structure to allow for long-term operating margin expansion
- A healthier store portfolio achieved through closure of underperforming stores
- A stronger value and rewards platform— consistent with the Starbucks premium brand

- A renewed emphasis and investment around coffee leadership
- A galvanized company with a common purpose

The new organizational structure enabled the company to position key executives closer to customers and partners. This ensured a stronger level of support in partner development, coaching, and accountability in the field. Establishing a customer-centric field support structure in the United States enabled field teams to focus on partners, customers, and the product: coffee.

By April 2009, same-store sales, though still down from a year earlier, were finally rising. By the holidays, they had turned positive. In January 2009, a new instant coffee product, Via, was scheduled for a full-scale introduction, although some executives were not sure it would succeed. However, Schultz decided to go ahead with its introduction and in 2010, sales of Via were more than $200 million. The instant coffee is now also sold in grocery stores and in Britain, Canada, Japan, and the Philippines. The company also plans to sell a wider variety of drinks and foods in grocery stores and its own shops, like Kind fruit and nut bars.

Did the reorganization succeed? First quarter returns in 2011 showed an increase of 7 percent in global comparable store sales and record operating margins of 21.9 percent in the United States and a 16.3 percent increase of margins in international operations. It was also the strongest holiday season in company history.

Source: Adapted from: Starbucks makes organizational changes to enhance customer experience. (21 February 2008). Starbucks press release, company records.

involve changes to specific management roles, such as those of the account, country, and product managers, as well as changes to the marketing function as whole, with marketing activities becoming more and more dispersed within the organization as it attempts to adapt itself to a more cross-functional, customer-centric perspective.[8]

Dell's B-to-B division recently underwent a major reorganization prompted by the desire to be more focused on its different customer segments rather than on its

8. Homburg, C., Workman, J. P., & Jensen, O. (2000, Fall). Fundamental changes in marketing organization: The movement toward a customer-focused organizational structure. *Journal of the Academy of Marketing Science*, 459–478.

geographic coverage. It is now structured around Dell's three major segments of business clients: large enterprise clients, public clients (government, education, health care, and environment), and small and medium business clients. Such customer-based segmentation was first introduced in Dell's Global Consumer group, where it "has proved that an integrated business unit can move with greater agility to unleash innovation to respond to the changing needs of customers," according to the company's CEO, Michael Dell. Interestingly, Dell announced a change in marketing leadership at the same time. The outgoing CMO, Mark Jarvis, is retiring after completing the transformation of the company's brand and marketing organization with "new levels of marketing effectiveness and efficiency." The incoming CMO, Erin Nelson, will assume her new role after serving as VP of marketing for Dell's EMEA region.[9]

GLOBAL MARKETING TEAMS

Cross-functionality and customer-centricity are seen also as a response to mounting global competition. Some researchers contend that multinational firms are adapting to the new reality by increasingly forming global task teams and, specifically, global marketing teams (GMTs), which "are taking on a strategic dimension that has traditionally been reserved for top management teams. [These GMTs] are acting as the key decision makers and are identifying and implementing the means to build competitive advantage in multiple markets."[10]

BORN-GLOBAL FIRMS

In recent years, a whole new breed of global businesses has emerged, however, that challenges the assumption that large MNCs with multitudes of international divisions and staff are the main players in the global marketplace. **Born global firms,** a dynamic and fast-growing type of international organization are characterized by their youth, small size, limited resources, and entrepreneurial orientation. They lack the hierarchical structures found in larger organizations, giving them the flexibility to adapt easily to changes. This adaptability explains why they are usually successful at expanding globally within the first three years of their existence. To do so, they depend strongly on technology, their innovative strategies and products, and their network of foreign distributors. Most importantly for marketers, these firms possess a strong international marketing orientation and competency that allows them to focus intensely on the needs of customers in each new market and deliver high-quality, unique products.

The rapid growth of such born global firms all over the world is a testament to a new, evolutionary trend in the global business arena where company size, age, and national origin are no longer the determinants of success internationally. Rather, flat organizational structure, innovation, strong relationships, and deep market knowledge are predictors of success in global markets.

In summary, a global company's marketing structure needs to balance four major considerations:[11]

1. **Local customization vs. global consistency:** Vesting decision-making power with regional marketing teams through a decentralized organization structure allows for greater customization and responsiveness to local conditions.

9. Dell Globalizes Business Groups Around Major Customer Segments. (31 December 2008). Press release.

10. Kiessling, T. S., Marino, L. D., & Richey, R. G. (2006). Global marketing teams: A strategic option for multinationals. *Organizational Dynamics, 35*(3), 237–250.

11. Lynch-Klarup, E. (2010). Striking a balance in global marketing structure. *Marketing Leadership Council.* Retrieved from www.mlcwideangleexbdblogs.com/tag/organizational management/.

However, this structure can lead to inconsistent branding and variable marketing quality across regions, as well as unnecessary rework.

2. **Budgeting-global prioritization vs. local accountability:** Central budgeting has the benefit of enabling concentration on the best market opportunities. Alternatively, budgeting regionally allows for profit and loss accountability at the regional level.

3. **Flexibility vs. continuity and expertise:** Most organizations need some amount of flexibility to respond to new priorities and changing strategies. At the extreme, a project-based organization is structured around teams that form and dissolve according to shifting priorities. However, structures with continuity of roles and responsibilities allow for in-depth organization knowledge and expertise.

4. **Collaborative decision making vs. organizational simplicity:** A matrix structure keeps multiple stakeholders involved in decisions—for better or for worse. Organizations need to be sure that the benefits of each additional reporting line are not outweighed by the loss of flexibility and costs of coordination.

BOX 15-2 TECHNOLOGY IN FOCUS: BORN GLOBAL FIRMS CHANGE THE RULES

eSys Technologies, a firm distributing computer components, was founded in Singapore in 2000, at a time of crisis in the information technology industry. In addition to its founder, Vikas Goel, it had one employee and operated out of a one-room office. Four years later, it boasted 112 offices and four manufacturing facilities in 33 countries, and sales close to US$2 billion. Most amazingly, it had been able to expand this fast while being profitable despite its razor-thin margin—3 percent—and remaining debt-free from the beginning.

Goel's knack for innovation, and the technologies that enabled him to implement his ideas, have made it possible for eSys to become one of the most successful examples of the new breed of young, aggressive, and technology-driven firms that define the term "born global." For example, eSys has perfected a process it calls Total Business Outsourcing, which centralizes core business functions, such as sales, marketing, finance, and human resources in one high-skill but low-cost country such as India. From there, employees are able to operate or monitor eSys offices around the world using cutting-edge technologies. Thus, visitors to the Chino, California, office are greeted in real time by a receptionist in India via a plasma screen and an Internet-enabled phone connection (VoIP), while managers oversee

the company's worldwide plant operations online which are also fully automated. Lastly, a state-of-the-art distribution system is responsible for linking these manufacturing facilities with the regional distribution hubs, giving the company some of the lowest inventory holding costs and sending its products to market at a fraction of the time needed by its competitors. But Goel's innovative ideas extend beyond technology. The reason eSys has been able to stay debt-free has to do with another unique process that Goel has implemented in the area of business financing.

Location is another important factor in eSys's strategy. The company seeks to base every aspect of its business where it can get the greatest savings. Accordingly, distribution hubs are found in Singapore, New Delhi, Dubai, Amsterdam, and Los Angeles; credit insurance is issued in Switzerland and Germany, where the rates are lowest; back office and IT operations are based in India; and the company's financial operations are in Singapore, which has the lowest corporate tax rates in the world.

Sources: Stack, J., & Burlingham, B. (2007, April). My awakening: How an entrepreneur from Singapore opened my eyes to what I have to do remain competitive in Springfield. *Inc.*, 93–97; Singapore ICT sector to grow exponentially. Retrieved from AsiaMarketingResearch.com; eSysglobal.com website.

CONTROL MECHANISMS

Companies today are scrutinized on many different levels. Shareholders, regulators, customers, analysts, suppliers and the general public can quickly form an opinion about a firm just by performing a quick Internet search or accessing specialized information databases—all tools that are practically at their fingertips. In response to the need for increased transparency, many companies have implemented strong control practices for all of their business units and levels of management. In marketing, this trend has been met with even greater emphasis on planning and on establishing specific objectives, processes, metrics and accountability measures that can prove marketing's impact on the overall profitability of the firm.

In the context of a global marketing organization, **control mechanisms** become doubly important. As one author notes, "[W]ith more countries, more customer segments, more media, and more distribution channels, companies and their CMOs are waging battle with complexity." As an example, he points to large consumer companies which may have to make decisions for as many as 20 million single price points in a year, if they operate in multiple channels, markets, and segments. With such amounts of data, it is clear that marketing executives have to delegate certain decisions to the local and regional levels of management, while retaining control over the consistency of the company brand across geographies, segments, and distribution channels.[12] Achieving this balance between central control and local initiative is one of the main challenges for any global marketing executive.

FORMAL CONTROL MECHANISMS

By setting some specific long- and short-term plans, performance standards, and reporting structures, leaders can begin to align the global marketing organization for consistent, measurable operations. These mechanisms are planning, budgeting, and reporting.

Planning

At their best, strategic and operational plans are the roadmaps that explain why, how, when, and who will accomplish the tasks necessary to achieve marketing success. To be effective, the planning process should take into account the overall company goals and objectives, as well as the local and regional perspectives. Communications among all levels of the marketing organization are also very important to ensure that all those responsible for the realization of the plans are on board with the final goals and objectives, performance measures, and deadlines.

At Tektronix, a global manufacturer of test, measurement, and monitoring devices, the incoming CMO faced the challenge of a marketing organization in disarray, where marketing initiatives—some 4,000 of them—were being executed with no connection to the company's (also numerous) strategic objectives, no performance metrics, and no relevance to the sales division. His "get well plan" entailed massive streamlining of all strategic objectives, realignment of the marketing activities to match both corporate and sales objectives, and a radical simplification of the marketing organization from 10 to only three or four job levels. The CMO, Martyn Etherington, credits these "painful steps" as some of the reasons for Tektronix's continuous revenue growth and solid culture of accountability.[13]

---

12. Court, D. (2007, August). The evolving role of the CMO. *The McKinsey Quarterly*.

13. Economist Intelligence Unit. (2008, September). *Future Tense: The Global CMO*.

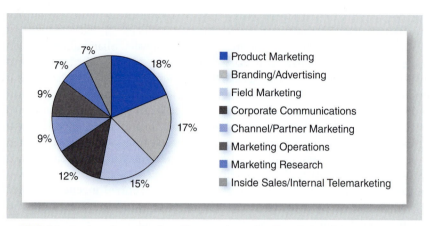

Figure 15-5 Marketing Area Budget Proportions for B-to-B Marketers in 2008

Source: Data from *B-to-B Marketing in 2008: Trends in Strategies and Spending.* MarketingProfs.com in conjunction with Forrester Research.

Budgeting

Budgets are more specific answers to the "how" and "when" questions outlined in the planning stage. Usually established on a yearly basis, budgets are used to allocate funds across the marketing organization—from how much is allotted to regional offices and service providers such as PR agencies, to how much is spent on specific campaigns, sponsorships, and other marketing initiatives. Budgets are also one of the tools used to determine the performance of the marketing organization and its units. A recent EIU report found that nearly 60 percent of CMOs operate with a centralized marketing/advertising budget, but allow for decentralized spending and allocation.[14] For an example of how B-to-B marketers worldwide spend their budgets, see Figure 15-5.

Reporting

Proving marketing's value to the organization has been a historically contentious issue. Therefore, establishing metrics that show its impact and regularly reporting their performance has become one of the most critical issues for today's marketing leaders.

The questions of how and what to measure in order to quantify return on marketing investment (ROMI) has plagued marketers since the dawn of the profession. As the ways of spending marketing budgets continue to increase (with the advent of Web 2.0, mobile marketing, etc.), new marketing mix models and other analytical tools to measure performance have emerged. It has become clear that using traditional metrics, such as market share or mass awareness is not enough; so much so that Jim Stengel, the now retired global marketing officer of P&G, has declared, "I believe today's marketing model is broken. We're applying antiquated thinking and work systems to a new world of possibilities."[15]

Current marketing thought is focusing on the customer instead of on the brand—the customer lifetime value (CLV) concept, quantified in the customer equity measure, is what should drive marketing strategy and budgets, argue many contemporary academics and practitioners. CLV is a metric that allows marketers to measure the overall effect of their marketing investment (see Figure 15-6). As the authors of one of the most popular CLV and customer equity frameworks summarize it, "[C]ustomer equity

14. Ibid.

15. Auletta, K. (28 March 2005). The new pitch. *New Yorker.*

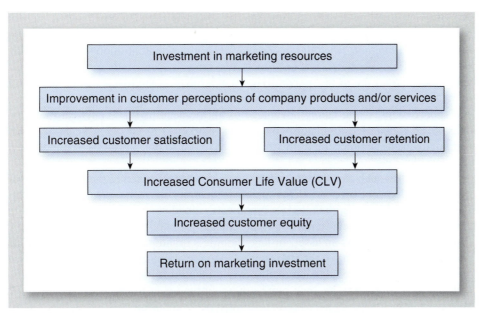

Figure 15-6 Customer Lifetime Value as a Measure for ROMI

TABLE 15-1 Majority of Marketers Base Budget Decisions on Performance	
Performance Measures	**Percent**
Comparison of increased marketing expenditures to business outcomes like revenue, customer growth, and market share	81
Budgeting decisions are based on program track records and prior spending	78
Marketing mix models facilitate planning budgets effectively	75
Budgeting decisions are based on data gathered about the effectiveness of marketing tactics	74
Established marketing budgets can be changed quickly and easily if ROI reports show tactics are not achieving expected goals.	71
Budgets can be planned effectively because we track campaign/program spending	70

Source: Data from *B-to-B Marketing in 2008: Trends in Strategies and Spending* at MarketingProfs.com in conjunction with Forrester Research.

provides an information-based, customer-driven, competitor-cognizant, and financially accountable strategic approach to maximizing the firm's long-term profitability."[16]

Many new tools are addressing the issue by providing better and easier ways to analyze marketing program performance. Powerful statistical software programs have made it possible to create so-called "marketing dashboards" where data can be tracked in real time, giving marketers unprecedented powers to adjust campaigns as they unfold (particularly in the digital domain). Such data availability and control options are very attractive to marketers who have to report bottom-line results. Not surprisingly, a survey by Forrester Research discovered that investment in marketing technology will continue to grow.[17] Indeed, in a recent survey of marketing executives, over 70 percent claim to track marketing's performance to the overall business objectives of the firm (see Table 15-1).

16. Rust, R. T., Lemon, K. N., & Zeithaml, V. A. (2004, January). Return on marketing: Using customer equity to focus marketing strategy. *Journal of Marketing, 68*, 109–127.

17. Enright, A. (October 1 2006). Real-time analytics boost ROI, accountability. *Marketing News*, 20.

However, some marketers caution against complete reliance on financial metrics for evaluating marketing performance. Rob Duboff, the author of *ROI for Marketing: Balancing Accountability with Long-Term Needs*, argues that intuition should still play a role in the field. Marketers can be "precisely wrong" by using only quantitative tools, when they should try to be "generally correct." Such an approach would still leave room for marketing tools that employ intuition, such as advertising, public relations, and sponsorships, while taking advantage of all the benefits that analytical tools can offer. Such a balanced approach would allow marketers to be " . . . generally right and not oversell the precision of the tools we have. I also don't want us to blindly say, 'Believe me.' "[18]

For activities such as branding, advertising, or market research, the current corporate toolset does not offer adequate means to quantify the value created by marketing. For example, although Google's brand was valued at an estimated $66 billion in 2007, the current financial reporting requirements for public companies do not allow the company to list it as an asset. In fact, Google's brand value was mentioned in its annual report only as one of the risk factors that may affect the company's stock price should it suffer damages. Paradoxically, while intangible assets such as brand value and intellectual property become more important than ever in the global competitive landscape, they are rarely measured and almost never reported.[19]

INFORMAL CONTROL MECHANISMS

By establishing a distinctive corporate culture and hiring and promoting managers with certain qualities, companies utilize some of the informal methods of exerting control on the organization. For global firms, these types of "soft" controls are often more important than formal ones, especially if they operate in many cultures where the data-driven management style favored in many Western cultures clashes with local social values that emphasize relationship-building, hierarchy, and social networks.

Corporate Culture

Certain corporations are known for their strong corporate culture. Johnson & Johnson, Walmart, Sony, and many others have spent years instilling certain values and work ethic in their employees around the world in an effort to build cohesive, productive units that can perform to the company's standards regardless of their size, location, or national culture. Lenovo, the Chinese computer giant, has addressed the corporate culture issue head on, working hard to establish a truly global, inclusive culture. It has refused to establish an official central office. Its executives are stationed across Lenovo's worldwide offices on a temporary, rotating basis and even its chairman relocated his family to the United States in order to learn more about American culture and to perfect his English language skills. Development teams based in different countries often collaborate virtually; the marketing department is based in Bangalore. Company-issued tip sheets are used to foster cross-cultural understanding and cooperative spirit among employees. "In all situations: assume good intentions; be intentional about understanding others and being understood; respect cultural differences," reads one of them.[20]

18. Krauss, M. (1 June 2007). Balance attention metrics with intuition. *Marketing News*.

19. Caruso, D. (26 August 2008). The real value of intangibles. *strategy + business*.

20. A bigger world. (18 September 2008). *The Economist* [special report].

Management Selection and Training

Lenovo has been very smart in addressing another key issue that often handicaps many fast-growing companies, especially those in developing countries. It has made a point of hiring a number of respected and experienced senior managers with substantial international experience.[21]

Management selection and promotion practices represent another informal control measure. Managers are the primary conduit for the dissemination and maintenance of a company's mission, vision, and culture. By training and promoting managers who best represent its core values, a firm can do a lot to ensure that the desired corporate culture "lives" throughout the organization. This practice also facilitates collaboration and knowledge transfer among all business units around the world.

Consider the recent transformation of the Italian carmaker Fiat. The first major initiative that Sergio Marchionne, the CEO responsible for the turnaround, embarked on was to identify and promote to positions of leadership a new crop of managers. He found most of them at Fiat's far-flung subsidiaries, where they have shown initiative and independence, unlike the senior managers at headquarters. Once he had the right people, Marchionne spent several months evaluating them on whether they had the right qualities needed to lead radical organizational change, such as the ability to handle more responsibilities and accountability. He also built a strong personal connection with each one. "If the organization can feel that kind of connection with its leadership, you're going to get a pretty sound culture aligned around strongly held common values," says Marchionne.[22]

Leadership

A recent article in the *McKinsey Quarterly* declared that "[F]ew senior-executive positions will be subject to as much change over the next few years as that of the chief marketing officer."[23] In this and other research[24] on the challenges of global CMOs, the authors found that the few key issues that will define marketing leadership in the near future include:

- Balancing a global reach with a local touch
- Finding effective ways to reach the new, informed, and vocal consumer
- Learning to market effectively in the rapidly changing technology and media environment
- Redefining marketing's position as a strategic function that can shape a company's course with its knowledge of global markets and customers and stand accountable for the results

There has never been a better chance for marketing to establish its central role, given the newly discovered importance of customer insight to the organization. To be successful, however, marketing leaders need the strength and skills to prove that marketing can be more than marketing services such as advertising, branding, or market research. They need to become change agents for the organization as a whole, "driving innovation through the business and becoming evangelists of customer engagement."[25]

21. Ibid.

22. Marchionne, S. (2008, December). Fiat's extreme makeover. *Harvard Business Review*, 45–48.

23. Court, D. (2007, August). The evolving role of the CMO. *The McKinsey Quarterly*.

24. For example, see Economist Intelligence Unit, *Future Tense: The Global CMO*, September 2008, and ISBM "2010 B-to-B Marketing Trends 2010 Study."

25. Economist Intelligence Unit. (2008, September). *Future Tense: The Global CMO*.

TABLE 15-2 Successful Corporate Marketing Organizations Serve as Centers of Excellence

Primary Role of Corporate Marketing (Percent of Respondents)		
	High Performing Firms	**Other Firms**
Act as center of excellence to disseminate information and best-practices to line marketers	50	17
Manage global brands	0	42
Provide marketing services for the company	25	33

Source: Adapted from: Court, D. (2007, August). The evolving role of the CMO [Exhibit B]. *McKinsey Quarterly.* Retrieved from www.mckinseyquarterly.com/The_evolving_role_of_the_CMO_2031.

Top marketers can meet these higher standards for leadership by taking specific actions, according to researchers. For example, Forester Research emphasizes the importance of coming up with a specific definition and responsibilities for marketing and then educating, communicating, and collaborating with other members of the organization to achieve the agreed-upon goals while building a strong marketing team and proactively seeking accountability.[26] The management consulting firm McKinsey contends that divisional and corporate organizations also play an important role in the success of consumer goods marketers. The firm's findings reveal that companies with high-performing brand portfolios tend to be the ones that allow divisional marketing heads to exert more control over marketing strategy and execution—a finding particularly relevant to global marketing organizations. At these companies, corporate marketing plays more the role of a disseminator of information and best practices to line marketers than a provider of marketing services or a manager of global branding campaigns (see Table 15-2).[27]

David Aaker, the widely published branding expert and author of *Spanning Silos: The New CMO Imperative*, cautions against two common mistakes for marketers embarking on this transformational mission: underestimating the power of organizational silos and taking on too much too soon. Silos, be they country, product, or functional ones, are a fact of business today (as we saw in the Organization section), and marketers need to learn to gain access and credibility within them in order to succeed. In addition, marketing leaders must be careful not to over-promise the scope or speed of positive results that they can accomplish. To avoid these pitfalls, Aaker recommends cautious and well thought-out steps that include:

- Finding the right role and scope
- Gaining credibility and buy-in
- Using teams to link silos
- Developing common planning processes and information systems
- Adapting master brands to silo markets
- Prioritizing brands in the portfolio
- Developing winning silo-spanning marketing programs

26. Commander, C. (2006). *The Marketing of Marketing.* Forrester Research report brief for The CMO Group. Retrieved from www.forrester.com/role_based/pdfs/Marketing_Of_Marketing_ReportBrief.pdf.

27. Crawford, B., Mulder, S., & Gordon, J. (2007, May). How consumer goods companies are coping with complexity [web exclusive]. *McKinsey Quarterly.* Retrieved from www.mckinseyquarterly.com/article_page.aspx?ar=2004&pagenum=8.

TABLE 15-3 CMO and CELO Tenure by Industry (Data in Months—Rounded)		
Industry	**CMO**	**CEO**
Aviation	22	10
Media	29	17
Retail—other	26	33
Life sciences	24	34
Telecommunications	15	37
Restaurant	23	37
Health/Beauty	18	38
Hotels	19	40
Financial services	35	45
Automotive	26	46
Food	12	48
Beverage	26	48
Retail—apparel	19	52
Retail—department	26	61
Retail—home improvement	9	65
Technology	30	75
Apparel	10	229
Average	**23**	**54**

Source: Data from Welch, G. (2004). CMO tenure: Slowing down the revolving door [blue paper]. *Spencer Stuart.*

By following these steps, CMOs can gradually but credibly assume the leadership role they aspire to in the organization. "The ultimate source of influence is customer knowledge," claims Aaker. When CMOs and their teams become the go-to source for that knowledge, instead of the local, regional, or product teams, they will have earned their place as strategy leaders at the executive table.[28]

The global executive search firm Spencer Stuart recently underscored how difficult it is to achieve the position of a true marketing leader today. It conducted a study that revealed that CMOs have some of the shortest tenures in the "C" level suites of large organizations, with an average time spent at a company of less than two years (see Table 15-3). Spencer Stuart attributes some of this trend to the heightened visibility of the CMO and thus to the heightened expectations and accountability: "Over the last decade, the overall complexity and sophistication of the marketing function has grown by leaps and bounds. The top marketing executive, once only responsible for launching new advertising campaigns and crafting the annual promotional calendar, now oversees a wide array of integrated marketing and communication activities. Today's CMO is no longer buried deep within the hierarchal layers of an organization; rather, they are front and center in driving corporate strategy."[29]

Clearly, more is expected today from marketing leaders than ever before. They not only have to manage increased internal and external expectations but also become better at their main mission as staunch advocates for the customer. Chris Edgelow, founder and president of Sundance Consulting Inc., a Canada-based company that specializes in helping organizations change through leadership and management development, sums it up: "Marketers (represent) that conduit to the outside world; they must

28. Aaker, D. (2008). *Spanning silos: The new CMO imperative.* Cambridge, MA: Harvard Business School Press.

29. Welch, G. (2004). CMO tenure: Slowing down the revolving door [blue paper]. *Spencer Stuart.*

BOX 15-3   PERSON IN FOCUS: PERSPECTIVE FROM THE FIELD-WHAT MARKETERS SEE AS THEIR BIGGEST CHALLENGES TODAY

In a gathering of top marketers, Dennis Dunlap, the CEO of the American Marketing Association (AMA), delineated some of the main forces and trends shaping marketing today:

1. **The empowered consumer**—customers who have information, choices, control, and clout expect more from marketing communications.

2. **New media ubiquity**—the customer buying process has changed owing to the availability of networks and technologies that directly or indirectly influence customers' decisions.

3. **Audience fragmentation**—the increase in new (social and digital) media and channels has splintered audiences into ever smaller groups, making it harder for marketers to reach customers.

4. **Mass customization**—consumers demand it and technologies make it possible, so

marketers must adopt it if they want to stay competitive.

5. **Channel power**—the dynamics of channel partnerships are shifting, with retailers gaining more power and manufacturers losing some.

6. **More commoditization**—new product development and company-wide innovation are becoming more and more important as quality and price points become more and more alike.

7. **Globalization**—the stakes keep getting higher as the world gets flatter.

8. **Profitable growth quest**—increasingly, marketing is held to the same stringent standards for results and profitability traditionally reserved for operations.

Source: Adapted from: Dunlap, D. (1 March 2007). AMA CEO unveils five winning strategies for marketers today. *Marketing News,* 12–17.

bring the outside truth into the system," he says. "(Marketers) have to clearly tell the company what the customer thinks of us, what customers want from us, how competitors are beating the pants off (other companies). They can bring those reality statements back into the organization."[30]

SUMMARY

- There is no standard organizational control structure for global firms. An ideal structure depends upon the extent to which the firm has internationalized. Another factor that determines organizational structure is the extent to which the firm has integrated and coordinated its international operations.

- Most global organizational structures are either based on functional, product, or regional-area configurations. However, many advanced global firms have chosen a global-matrix structure.

- While many firms internationalize over several stages (e.g., from exporting to manufacturing abroad), there

30. Vence, D. L. (1 April 2007). Take the lead: marketers discuss ways to drive organizational change. *Marketing News,* 13–14.

are some that internationalize within a few years of their existence. These are the so-called born global firms.

• Global firms must establish both formal and informal control systems.

These systems take on greater importance as firms internationalize as the number of countries, consumer segments, distribution channels, and communication possibilities increase.

DISCUSSION QUESTIONS

1. Discuss how the organizational structure of a company has to be adapted as it progresses from a solely domestic to a global firm.

2. Why is the matrix form of organization difficult to implement for a global firm? Would such an organizational form be applicable to a domestic firm? Why or why not?

3. How does a corporate culture affect the choice of an organizational format?

4. Note the quotation above on page 421: "[F]ew senior-executive positions will be subject to as much change over the next few years as that of the chief marketing officer." Do you agree?

EXPERIENTIAL EXERCISES

1. Visit the Marketing Profiler site (http://marketingprofiler.com) and complete the questionnaire, basing your answers on your current marketing organization experience, if applicable, or on your knowledge of the marketing operations at any company. Write a short evaluation of the given profile and give your opinion on the strategic direction in which you believe the marketing department should move in order to achieve optimum results.

2. Select a company that you think can be better at marketing its products globally. Recommend an organizational structure that would be more suitable to improving marketing results. Provide the reasoning behind your recommendation: why do you think the new structure would yield better results? What are some of the potential pitfalls of this format? What are the advantages? Summarize your findings and recommendations in a PowerPoint presentation.

KEY TERMS

Born global firms, p. 415

Control mechanisms, p. 417

Functional organizational format, p. 411

Matrix organizational format, p. 412

Product-based organizational format, p. 410

Regional organizational format, p.410

CASE 15-1

Developing Shanghai into a World Fashion Center

In early 2003, SGTA's Chief Secretary, Madam Xu Xiu Qing, came home to Shanghai after a whirlwind tour to gather support and promote her idea for a new global fashion association in major fashion cities around the world. Although she was still tired from the month-long travel, Ms. Xu was also full of enthusiasm and hope that her efforts would position Shanghai as the new rising star in the competitive world of fashion. In the next weeks, she developed the first draft of Shanghai International City Fashion Federation's (SICFF) bylaws, tailoring them after what she had learned from her discussions with other trade professionals and from her visits to similar fashion organizations. She knew though, that she needed more than bylaws to turn her vision into reality. She needed to launch a strong and disciplined campaign to capture the attention of the fast-moving and fickle fashion world. That would require an aggressive and knowledgeable staff with skills in marketing, public relations, organizational design, publicity, fundraising, and a multitude of other skills that were new and rare in the developing economy and labor market of China. With her typical ingenuity and practical mind, Madam Xu soon found what she thought was an optimum solution: hire consultants from the United States, the country where nine out of 10 adults belong to at least one association, and the cradle of marketing and public relations.

The Shanghai Garment Trade Association

The mission of the Shanghai Garment Trade Association (SGTA) is to promote the interests and growth of its members and partners, which include over 1,000 members ranging from textile and garment manufacturers, to fashion schools, fashion designers, economic development organizations, and other groups interested in promoting Shanghai as a major fashion center. The SGTA is working hard to bring visibility to the Chinese fashion industry by organizing various fashion shows, competitions, and fairs, communicating with other international fashion organizations, promoting industry standards and training, and lobbying the government on behalf of the Shanghai fashion and garment sectors.

Key Issue: Turning Shanghai into a Global Fashion City

With its cosmopolitan look and glitzy shopping districts, as well as a continuously growing and fashion-conscious middle class, Shanghai was well on its way to becoming China's fashion center. Many domestic and international companies and fashion labels have placed their Asian headquarters there, and even more have begun producing the bulk of their merchandise in the region's enormous industrial zones.

Although fashion makers have long regarded the Far East and China in particular as an exotic source of inspiration and, more recently, as a source of cheap and quality labor, they have not yet accepted it as a serious fashion center, capable of offering trendsetting innovations or talented designers on a global scale. The SGTA wanted

Case prepared by Nadia Ballard & Ilan Alon, Rollins College. Reprinted with permission.

to change all that. To step up the Shanghai fashion industry's international exposure, it had started organizing annual fashion shows and festivals, inviting many industry luminaries and highlighting its accomplishments in the media. Now, with the organization's chairwoman as its champion, the SGTA was embarking on its most ambitious plan yet—the creation of a new global fashion federation with a seat in Shanghai that would bring instant cachet to the city. The purpose of this Federation would be to stimulate communication and cooperation among the leading fashion centers in the world by providing a common platform and base in Shanghai to all local, national, and international fashion organizations and, by association, establishing Shanghai as one of the world's leading fashion hubs.

Consultation Process and Research Findings

Global Garment Industry Analysis

Several trends exist in the industry:

Consistent Move Toward Cheapest Production Markets. In the last 20 years, garment and textile manufacturing has continued to move to the regions of the world that offer the lowest production costs and cheapest labor. Thus, while China still attracts investors with its relatively cheap but skilled labor and compliance with world standards for quality and workforce management, countries like Pakistan, India, and most recently, many countries in southern Africa, have been luring manufacturers with the cheapest labor costs in the world despite bad economic, industrial, and legal infrastructures (India Mart, 2003; Clean Clothes, 2003). Similar transitions are occurring on a more "regional" level as well: garment factories in Thailand and Taiwan are closing only to open in cheaper markets such as Vietnam (Global Sources, 2003). Chinese and Indonesian manufacturers own the majority of garment factories in the United Arab Emirates and employ almost exclusively Indian and Pakistani workers (UAE, 2001). United States textile and apparel production continues to move south from Mexico to Guatemala, Costa Rica, and the Caribbean (Rosen, 2002). Western European textiles and clothes are increasingly produced in Eastern European countries (Enterprise, 2000).

Despite the competitive advantages of cheap labor, several factors provide enough incentives for some industry players to stay in China and other Asian countries, namely: high productivity, quality standards, skilled labor force, and continuously increasing investment in R&D and equipment modernization.

Product Diversification. "Diversity" is the hot topic for the garment industry in Asia and on a global scale (Woolmark, 2003). Fabrics, lining, accessories, design, style, and techniques push to seek new breakthroughs. The key to success involves introducing *new* products or new uses. For instance, there is an upsweep of microfiber usage: "The latest releases of microfiber fabrics have a range of applications and appearances. Products have gold-pressed, printed, embossed, embroidered, coated, and waterproof finishes." (Global Sources, 2003). Microfiber makers are also marketing their fabric as functional. The latest models from Mainland China and Taiwan companies have breathable, "moisture wicking, anti-bacterial, and sweat-eliminating characteristics," among other special traits, making them ideal for sportswear and outdoor clothing (Global Sources, 2003). Production is mainly according to buyer specifications: most design changes throughout the entire industry are driven by buyer requests.

High-Tech Invasion. The increasing competitiveness in the industry is further stoked by the recent introduction of many technological advances in textile and apparel manufacturing. For example, India keeps an watchful eye on Italy, where clusters of small, specialized textile firms are competing on end products. Germans weave for 24 hours under "lights out" arrangements. Total quality management is ensured in Japanese and American plants that have installed "looming robots." Firms in the southern United States are reported to be researching the use of "genetic engineering, cellular biology, and tissue culture" to grow colored cotton. Additionally, mass customization is made available through "three dimensional, non-contact body measurement and 'digital printing,'" making it easier to meet unpredictable demand levels and luxury goods customization (India Mart, 2003).

New Criteria. While price still dictates the purchasing habits of many consumers, the majority of European and United States customers see comfort as the most important factor in their purchasing decision. As a result, many garment manufacturers are focusing on innovative designs that offer optimum comfort.

In addition to the ones outlined above, there are always trends in the garment industry directly related to the evolution of consumer preferences and product design. Those were not subject of this study.

Trade Associations Analysis

While many national and regional differences were encountered, the main characteristics of all organizations seem consistent across borders.

Structure. The role of most garment associations is to unite the apparel industry and to promote its growth and technological development. Some organizations do it by being closely integrated with their national governments, while others rely on independent industry leadership and not-for-profit status. A third kind of organization, such as those in the European Union, are merging or transforming in other ways to better serve their members in Europe's common marketplace. Such multinational organizations serve a much broader role and attempt to promote innovation, market research, and brand development among its members.

Membership. In order to promote relationships and growth, the trade associations have made becoming a member a very easy process with few requirements. In general, a prospective member must be an individual or a legal entity, national or international, that is active in the design, manufacturing, transportation, trade, or other services for textiles, garments, or fashion accessories; must complete an application form and provide a copy of the business license or license of incorporation; and must pay an initial fee and subsequent regular dues. Many industry organizations allow several tiers of membership depending on how directly the prospective member is involved in the textile or apparel industries. Full, associate, and affiliate membership levels are the most common and delineate varying levels of fees, benefits, and access to the services of the organization.

There are two prevalent structures for membership dues. One involves the application of annual membership dues; the other is based on sales. The pricing in an annual dues structure is based on the perceived value of the benefits provided by the association. This structure assures a fixed level of financial stability and fairness as each member is charged the same amount. The sales based structure provides for the collection of dues on a monthly, quarterly, or annual basis determined by sales levels. The more prosperous the member becomes, the more income for the association. This structure allows the association to reap financial benefits as the member becomes more prosperous. However, if the member loses business or demand drops, so will the dues paid to the association. This structure allows for variable income, which involves added risks. Additionally, each member receives the same association benefits but at different costs—making fairness a potential issue.

Services. The services provided by the associations focus either on the members of the associations or on the potential customers for the members. The associations that focus more on the customers tend to have primarily a marketing role and do not provide much in the way of other support and services to their members. The more sophisticated associations are those that focus on the members and the benefits that the affiliation can provide them. The primary services that almost all associations provide include governmental relations, research and information systems and databases, training and development, legal assistance and consulting, networking opportunities, and foreign and national representation. Some associations also offer marketing and trade promotion, transportation support, credit reporting, and facilities for meetings, exhibitions, and conventions. The more developed the country, the more of these services are offered online, through well-designed and marketed websites.

Best Practices of Other Trade Associations

Several diverse trade and professional organizations similar to SGTA were analyzed, including Working Group on Trade Promotion Canada–APEC (www.dfait-maeci. gc.ca/canada-apec/tp-en.asp), Orlando Economic Development Commission (www .orlandoedc.com), American Marketing Association (www.marketingpower.com), Office Furniture Dealers Alliance (www.ofdanet.org/), Industrial Designers Society of America (www.idsa.org/), Society for Marketing Professional Services (www.smps. org/), and the Society for Technical Communication (www.stc.org/). All information provided below was extracted from these organizations' websites, visited intermittently during February 2003.

Most of these organizations have nonprofit status and are supported by their individual and business members. The common mission of these organizations is to facilitate and promote their specific trade activity or profession; share knowledge of business and industry developments, initiatives, and techniques with their members; increase the networking, information exchange, and cooperation between their members; and promote the thought, application, and ethical practice of their profession or trade.

Most organizations have national headquarters with administrative and executive staff and a Board of Directors. They also have numerous regional chapters, usually in major cities or regions where the certain trade or profession is practiced. The leadership of the regional chapters usually consists of a president, a secretary, a treasurer, and vice-presidents for membership, events, education and other functions, depending on the organization. Some of these organizations also have international offices located in countries and cities where the organization has strategic interests to develop or maintain membership base and external partners. Some organizations have separate special interest groups (SIGs) or committees that focus on specialized areas within the profession or trade activity. For example, the Society for Technical Communication has SIGs for education and research, illustrators and visual designers, indexing, management and others. The Industrial Designers Society of America has "professional interest sections" for automotive design, medical design, and furniture design.

Most organizations elect their leadership during their annual global conferences, which are open to all of their members. The individual chapters also elect their executives on an annual basis, during the last monthly or quarterly meeting of the year.

Besides the annual conference, many of the organizations hold separate seminars, lecture series or forums throughout their countries. Each of these events usually has a common theme around which the presentations and/or exhibits are organized. The local chapters of professional organizations hold special events where their members can network with each other, learn the latest developments in their profession, meet with important community or national leaders, and celebrate special occasions. Examples of such events include lectures, presentations, panel discussions, fundraising events, silent auctions, holiday dinners, and visits to specific sites of interest, such as trade missions to other countries or regions.

In addition to the educational and networking opportunities, many organizations include additional benefits such as subscriptions to professional publications (magazines and newsletters), access to directories of their members, award programs, industry research, book reviews, job listings, and other similar information or activities that can be useful to their members.

Some of the more unusual benefits found included directories of industry-specialized suppliers; mentor directories; local job fairs; member discounts for financial services, shipping, and other goods or services; group and/or liability insurance; scholarship funds; certification programs; travel services; student competitions; best practices collections; benchmarking studies; and others.

Global Fashion Cities Analysis

An examination of the epitomes of global fashion—the cities that are famous for starting trends and attracting talent—revealed the basic ingredients needed for fashion to become an indelible part of each city's image in the world. To truly harvest a fashionable city into the status of fashion "capital," a fertile ground for style, sophistication, image, and exclusivity must be present. More than just a history of famous designers and changing styles, fashion is a cultural idea and social "phenomenon" due to the assembly of the key characteristics listed in this section; an unexplainable event that occurs due to the collective synergy of all these parts working in harmony.

The Arts

Support for culture and the arts exists in every fashion capital that fosters an encouraging, inspirational environment for fashion. Milan, for instance, has a vibrant art and entertainment scene that provides inspiration for the local designers, artists and fashion students. London has the renowned ability to attract global buyers, media, advertisers, and world-class models. New York gained its credibility in fashion by cultivating a creative environment—an atmosphere that encourages innovation and freedom of expression via population diversity and a well-developed cultural life through the fine and popular arts. Without a network of established theater, art and entertainment "scenes," fashion will have a hard time creating this flourishing environment on its own.

Terminology

To create a fashion capital, everything must be aligned to develop an image, lifestyle, and fashion "reality." Proper terminology must be implemented in all marketing and promotional efforts, changing the names of places and concepts to fit a mode of fashion and style. For example:

A Famous Fashion "Avenue" or "Triangle." In Paris, the ritzy, upscale, established designers—Chanel, Dior, and Yves Saint Laurent—showcase their talent in "fashion houses" in an area called "the golden triangle," formed by the perimeters of the Champs-Elysees, Avenue Marceau, and Avenue Montaigne (ParisBreak, 2003).

New York has a clearly defined garment district with its own identity, yet it also has a clearly defined fashion (i.e., Fifth Avenue) and shopping (i.e., Soho) district, not necessarily in the same location as the garment district.

Milan's "Golden Triangle" area of Via Montenapoleone, Via della Spiga, and Via Sant'Andrea is also known around the world for its exclusive fashion houses and upscale shopping (The Great Outdoors, 2003).

Tokyo currently has a "fashion center." However, this fashion center is more of a fashion mall. There is a lack of "fashion houses" for the top designers of the city. One of the reasons Tokyo fails to achieve similar fashion status as Paris or Milan is because it lacks the sophistication and upscale environment often associated with a "fashion triangle" (Japan Today, 2003).

Fashion Tiers. Fashion has a clearly defined and respected hierarchy. Three categories are most commonly described: high fashion (*haute couture* or runway), ready-to-wear (*prêt-a-porter*), and low fashion (mass production, basic). The fashion capitals are responsible for creating and designing high fashion, which is regarded as an exalted art. These are not "fashions" you typically buy on the street; rather, you find them in the magazines *(Vogue, Harper's Bazaar, W)* and on the runways and they are regarded more as works of art than actual clothes. Successful fashion capitals have done a careful job of not intertwining the three tiers, keeping them physically and mentally separate.

Seasons

Every fashion capital ensures adequate hype and buzz during the popular and acclaimed "fashion seasons" and their respective trends. Hype is created by stylish and strategic visual merchandising efforts in all retailing establishments, as well as promotional efforts. Seasons differ in scope depending on the region—climate, culture, and society influence trends. For example, in Paris, shopping is conducted much like hunting and fishing—creating short, allotted seasons, like a three-week "handbag season" to create ultimate exclusivity and unmatched hype (Fashion Windows, 2003).

Designers

Fashion capitals provide good general education with significant fashion-specific schools. To gain recognition as a fashion capital, the design talent must exceed all expectations, create and adhere to trends, and establish strong "houses" that invite new, up-and-coming designers to work collaboratively on projects (i.e., "David Chu for Nautica"). Name recognition is a must, and truly famous designers use their name on all labeling to ensure maximum brand strength and to provide cultural identity. Consumers who know fashion know that Chanel and Dior are French, thus forming a favorable notion of France and fashion.

England's Burberry shows off its heritage through its unmistakably prim and proper British name. Versace and Armani are bold Italian names, and "Tommy" automatically conjures an image of red, white, and blue. Milan makes a concerted effort to attract native and foreign fashion designers to open ateliers, stores, and exhibits in the city and provides incentives for them to do so (United States Commercial Service, 2003).

To preserve a strong identity yet maintain the status of promoting innovative fashion, many famous designers attract talent from all over the globe and provide them with the opportunity to design for their "house" (i.e., Tom Ford for Gucci). This is good and bad for the up-and-coming designer and his or her respective country of origin. As a positive, the designer gets the privilege of designing for a fashion legend, thus elevating his or her career by building recognition and creating a solid following. As a negative, often the new designer loses his/her individual "edge," masked by the house's master label. For instance, the consumer will not recognize Chu as Chinese as evidently as if the name stood alone instead of under the Nautica label. Sometimes designers even lose their cultural touch—Japanese designer Kenji Ito, for example, released a collection that had heavy British influence (Tokyo, 2000).

It is important for the fashion capital to cultivate fashion talent and keep it local. London produces a lot of talented designers that flee to New York, Paris, and Milan. A growing number of top design students also leave Tokyo to develop their talents in Milan and Paris. However, these students are deciding to stay in Milan and Paris to work rather than return to Tokyo where the economic conditions are currently undesirable. For these reasons, Tokyo's recognition as a fashion capital is being restricted and limited. The major players in fashion design need to be "global" players in the industry by bringing light to their locality. Tokyo has become known for not cooperating with the other global players like New York, Paris, and Milan designers. Tokyo designers tend to accommodate the local fashion industry instead of the global market. Additionally, the fashion industry in Tokyo continues to play by its own rules and expect the global players to change (Council, 2003).

The power of these designer "brands"—if positioned correctly—is truly phenomenal, often leading to consumer behavior that is quite illogical. For example, disregarding Communism's efforts to eradicate fashion, Chinese youth of today have shunned domestic apparel lines only to pursue Western brands like Ralph Lauren and Calvin Klein, which are actually manufactured in China (Fashion Windows, 2003).

Models

Models often achieve a similar international status to the designers they promote, sometimes elevating the designer to fame and sometimes having their careers bloom as a result of modeling the "art" of a particular well-known designer. Today's definition of a model is blurring, however, as more and more designers rely on celebrities to bring instant mass appeal to their lines while the celebrities aspire to elevate their appeal by being associated with style and high fashion. Whether it is the singer Christina Aguilera posing for Versace or the Oscar winner Adrien Brody hawking Ermenegildo Zegna suits, the "buzz" created usually benefits both the designer and the celebrity and, by association, the locale (*USA Today,* 2003).

Schools of Design

Top-tier prestigious schools of art and design are a must for any city to succeed as a fashion capital. The Fashion Institute of Technology (FIT) in New York City boasts renowned alumni such as Calvin Klein and Norma Kamali. Paris is full of opportunities for design students; however, it is the most competitive city in the fashion world. One of the reasons may be that the Paris Fashion Institute is the only school offering both fashion design and marketing/merchandising disciplines as a joint entity.

The existence of top design schools has prevented London from disappearing from the fashion scene. While many of its graduates leave for Paris, New York, and Milan, some designers do remain—at least initially—and the innovative designs that come out of London's design schools keep the city on the fashion map (*The Guardian,* 2003). Tokyo's lack of success in the fashion world further emphasizes the importance of a strong network of design schools. As economic conditions declined in Japan, most schools had to be closed. Tokyo now has only three design schools left, and the lack of quality educational facilities has led to the demise of innovative fashion design in Tokyo (Japan Today, 2003).

Fashion Associations/Organizations

Fashion capitals cannot grow without well-managed and focused fashion associations that direct the industry and support its many players. A federation of "ready-to-wear" couture firms and designers leads Paris fashion: the influential Chambre Syndicale decides who qualifies as a "couturier" and organizes the major fashion shows. New-comers are either accepted upon submitting designs or allowed to "slot" into the diary of shows as "fringe" or "off" participants (Europe, 2000).

The National Association for the Development of the Fashion Arts was founded in 1989 for the purpose of aiding and promoting fashion creation in France. Each year a nationwide competition is held to award fellowships to young designers. The money is used to help them mount a collection of haute couture, ready-to-wear, or accessories, thus giving them a decisive boost for the launch of their own labels.

There are two fashion associations in Tokyo, and many designers belong to both. The associations continue their struggle to define Tokyo as the next fashion hub. However, the lack of infrastructure as well as the support from the citizens and government of Tokyo has been detrimental to the success of the associations.

Milan has active professional organizations for the fashion industry that are committed to cooperating by promoting the city with an organized, focused strategy that covers all aspects of the fashion industry, from fashion show events to textile fairs, to traveling show exhibits, to contests featuring young or established local fashion designers (Merlo, 2001).

Government Support

Support from both local citizens and the government are an absolute necessity in cultivating a welcoming and enriching environment for fashion to grow. Milan has the support of the local and national government bodies to promote and develop the city as a fashion industry hub. Milan is promoted as a "fashion capital" to important public figures and media representatives in order to generate international interest via publicity and press.

London has slipped from the public eye recently in terms of trendsetting, due to many factors; one stemming from a lack of government support (*Evening Standard,* 1999). Many designers have to turn to support from big businesses to sustain their shows. This makes the shows less about fashion and more about the sponsor's products. New York maintains enviable governmental support on all levels—federal, regional, and local—to fully harvest the growth of the industry and reap potential benefits.

Business Support

Milan solicits approval and support for its activities from local businesses that can provide additional funding and publicity for fashion activities. New York is a great example of a city with strongly related or supporting industries—modeling, photography, advertising, public relations, and publishing, to name a few.

Infrastructure

Building a strong network is essential to a fashion capital but can only be achieved through complimentary infrastructure. Milan and Paris have infrastructure (transportation hubs, communication facilities, and exhibition facilities) and resources (fashion design schools, advertising and public relations agencies, photographers, and publications) to support an active fashion scene. New York, too, possesses excellent infrastructure—harbors, airports, roads, railways, and communication.

Production/Manufacturing

London offers close proximity to production facilities, which helps provide the raw materials needed for the new designs coming out of the design schools; however, the disappearance of garment manufacturing has made London more detached from the industry. New York succeeds at maintaining a comprehensive garment industry—not just design, but also manufacturing, wholesalers, retailers, and marketers.

Global Focus

Each fashion city makes a commitment to preserve a global focus in respects to growth, diversity, innovation, and collaboration. The best and most respected fashion cities (Paris and Milan) remain timeless due to their ability to serve as the "fashion headquarters" of the world, yet never lose their cultural identity. Paris, for example, never becomes too diluted with diversity as to lose its French "touch."

Paris has advanced strategic partnerships and networks in order to present a unified appearance for the French fashion industry. All partners must be involved with the industry or present a comparable image to that of French fashion culture. All brands associated with the industry enhance the fashion event (Paris Break, 2003).

Milan succeeds at these partnerships, too: Milan associates with other similar domestic and international cities to jointly promote fashion on a global scale, and it cooperates on worldwide fashion initiatives and campaigns that are beneficial to all regions involved (Foundation, 2003).

The analysis of the five most distinguished world fashion centers underscores that a fashion city is larger than any individual association or federation. It is a cultural way of thinking, that is weaved within the fabric of the city itself. It is the ability to incorporate the historical values of yesterday with those of today's society, and blend them with the artistic talents of individuals to develop the next globally recognized style. To be successful, an inspirational environment is necessary—not just an office or a space. The whole city needs to live, eat, breathe, and nurture such things as art, innovation, and creativity.

Discussion Questions

1. What are the possible recommendations for Madam Xu as she tries to position Shanghai as a global fashion capital?
2. What should be the structure and role of the Shanghai Garment Trade Association in developing Shanghai's global expansion as a fashion center?
3. How can Madam Xu position her association for the expansion of China in the field of textile and garment manufacturing and distribution?

References

American Society of Association Executives. (2004). *Associations in a nutshell: Why are associations so important?* Retrieved from www.asaenet.org/asae/cda/index/1,,ETI10471,00.html.

Clean clothes campaign. (2003). Retrieved from www.cleanclothes.org.

Council of Fashion Designers Tokyo. (2003). Retrieved from www.cfd.or.jp.

Enterprise Directorate General of the European Commission. (2000, October). *The Textile and Clothing Industry in the EU: A Survey*. Retrieved from http://ec.europa.eu/enterprise/newsroom/cf/itemlongdetail.cfm?displayType=library&tpa_id=203&item_id=2449. The direct link to the PDF is: http://ec.europa.eu/enterprise/newsroom/cf/_getdocument.cfm?doc_id=1856.

Europe: The haute and mighty. (2000, November). *ProQuest Direct.* Retrieved from http://proquest.umi.com.

My fears for the fizz in London fashion. (26 February 1999). *Evening Standard.* Retrieved via ProQuest Direct at http://proquest.umi.com.

Fashion windows. (2003). Retrieved from www.fashionwindows.com.

Foundation Nicola Trussardi. (2003). *City of Fashion Project.* Retrieved from www.fondazionenicolatrussardi.com/fondazione/EnCittadellamoda.htm.

Global sources: fashion accessories and supplies. (2003). Retrieved from www.fashion.globalsources.com.

Milan fashion. (2003). *The Great Outdoors.* Retrieved from http://thegreatoutdoors.com.au/display.php?ID=2722.

Fashion victims: London fashion week starts tomorrow—but why does a country that produces so many first-class talents have such a second-class industry? [Comment and analysis]. (14 February 2003). *The Guardian.* Retrieved via ProQuest Direct at http://proquest.umi.com.

India Mart. (2003). Retrieved from www.apparel.indiamart.com.

In and out of fashion [Metropolis section]. (2003). *Japan Today.* Retrieved from http://metropolis.japantoday.com.

Merlo, E. (2001, June). Knowledge as a basis for collective action: the case of the Italian fashion industry. *EBHA Conference 2001: Business and Knowledge* [Presentation].

Paris Break. (2003). Retrieved from www.parisbreak.com.

Rosen, E. I. (2002). *Making sweatshops: The globalization of the United States apparel industry.* Los Angeles, CA: University of California Press.

Tokyo International Forum. (2000). Retrieved from www.tif.or.jp.

UAE urges revamp of garment industry run by Asians. (June 16 2001). *Middle East News Online.* Retrieved via ProQuest Direct at http://proquest.umi.com.

Celebrities are stylin' as high fashion models. (May 11 2003). *USA Today.* Retrieved from http://www.usatoday.com/life/2003-05-11-celebs_x.htm.

The organizers of "Milano Vende Moda" are offering a unique opportunity to emerging and trendy women fashion designers. (April 3 2003). United States Commercial Service. Retrieved from www.buyusainfo.net/info.cfm?id=113378anddbf=imi1andloadnav=noandarchived=noandaddid=.

The Woolmark Company. (2003). Retrieved from www.woolmark.com.

Defining Ethics and Corporate Social Responsibility in the International Marketplace

We need to address transparency, accountability, and institutional capacity. And let's not mince words: we need to deal with the cancer of corruption.

JAMES WOLFENSOHN, PRESIDENT OF THE WORLD BANK, ANNUAL MEETING, 1996

LEARNING OBJECTIVES

After reading this chapter, you should be able to:

- Understand the ethics of doing business abroad.
- Differentiate between the law and ethics.
- Determine whether there are universal ethical standards.
- Argue whether an MNC can be an ethical citizen.
- Determine the social responsibility of an MNC.
- Argue whether a company can afford not to be ethical.

You are the newly appointed manager of ABC (Ltd.) Company's subsidiary in Manila, the Philippines. Your company manufactures and distributes educational equipment for high schools, including audiovisual teaching materials. A large shipment worth about €50,000 has just arrived and is waiting to be released at customs. The customs authorities have informed you that there are "administrative delays" preventing the release of the equipment. After a week, you are told that "delays" are still in force. When you ask the customs official in charge when the equipment will be released, he replies that it is hard to say but, if you would make a small donation to the union vacation fund, it would be possible to secure a prompt release. You know that the shipment is being stored in an unsecure place and theft is certainly a possibility. Also, many schoolchildren are in need of the educational equipment. Payments to government officials are frequent in this country in order to "prioritize" decision making. They are not illegal here. However, you are also aware that your home government has anti-bribery legislation that could apply to this situation and possibly result in a fine for your company. What are the alternatives to this dilemma? What should you do?

Cases like the above occur only too frequently in international commerce. The solutions to such dilemmas are all the more difficult when both parties come from different ethical cultures. This chapter deals with providing a framework that will help dealing with dilemmas in a global environment and provide a response that is acceptable to both sides. First, let us review some of the costs that accrue from unethical practices such as bribery and corruption.

THE COST OF DOING BAD BUSINESS

Taking the path of least resistance to requests for bribes, companies and individuals risk the chance of being caught and subjected to investigation, bad public relations, and if convicted, fines and even imprisonment. While there are many examples of firms and individuals being fined for illegal payments (Example 1), there are examples of fines being levied for lacking proper safeguards against such practices (Example 2).

Example 1: An employee of CBRN Team, a UK consulting firm and an official of the Uganda government, pleaded guilty to bribery charges stemming from a payment by the British firm in order to secure a contract to advise the Presidential Guard of Uganda. The UK Serious Fraud Office gave the CBRN employee a suspended sentence, while the Ugandan official was sentenced to serve a year in prison.

Source: Adapted from: www.badfaithinsurance.org. Retrieved May 10, 2009.

Example 2: A subsidiary of Aon Corp (UK), the world's largest insurance broker, was fined 5.25 million pounds ($7.9 million) by Britain's Financial Services Authority for not having sufficient anti-bribery controls. Aon Ltd. made allegedly "suspicious payments" totaling approximately $7 million to overseas companies in countries such as Indonesia, Vietnam, Bahrain, and Burma from 2005 through 2007.

Source: Adapted from: "The Global Bribery Crackdown," growthbusiness.co.uk. Accessed June 22, 2011.

These two examples show that there are regulatory agencies at the country level that monitor bribery and corruption behavior on the part of companies and individuals. As we will learn below, governments and multinational organizations such as the United Nations and the International Monetary Fund (IMF) monitor such activities. However, monitoring illegal and unethical activities starts at home. Companies have to monitor themselves, and many do. Bribery and corruption on a global scale are activities that cannot be ignored. According to the United States Department of Commerce, bribery affected the outcome of 294 international contracts amounting to $145 billion over a five-year period from 1994 to 1999. In another area of the world, the Asian Development Bank estimated that the "corruption task" in Asia costs governments approximately 50 percent of their tax revenues.[1]

According to a survey by **Transparency International,**[2] global bribery amounts to $1 trillion annually, and as shown in Table 16-1, the incidence of payments is greater in developing countries. Bribery and corruption hurt the poor disproportionately—by diverting funds intended for development, undermining a government's ability to provide basic services, feeding inequality and injustice, and discouraging foreign investment and aid. Bribery and corruption are not the only problems that managers face in a global world. Dishonesty, fraud, occupational health, safety, environmental concerns, and industrial espionage are also prevalent. Employee fraud alone costs firms $600 billion annually in the United States, which amounts to approximately six percent of GDP.[3] While many of these practices are monitored by laws and regulations, they are

1. "The Global Fight against Bribery and Corruption: United States Law and Policy," speech by Ambassador Schneider "Transparency Unveiling Corruption," Deloitte & Touche, Amsterdam, October 1, 1999.

2. Transparency International is an NGO based in Germany that monitors the incidence and content of global bribery and corruption. See a full discussion of this agency on page 447.

3. www.josephsoninstitute/org/pdfworkplace-flier_0604.pdf

TABLE 16-1 Prevalence of Bribery in Selected Countries

Countries	% Reporting a Bribe Paid in Last 12 Months*
Austria, Canada, Costa Rica, Denmark, Spain, Finland, France, Germany, Hong Kong, Iceland, Ireland, Israel, Japan, South Korea, Netherlands, Norway, Portugal, Singapore, Switzerland, Taiwan, UK, Uruguay, United States	Less than 5%
Argentina, Bulgaria, Bosnia and Herzegovina, Columbia, Croatia, Kosovo, Luxembourg, Macedonia, Malaysia, Nicaragua, Panama, Philippines, Poland, South Africa, Thailand, Turkey, Venezuela	5–10%
Ethiopia, Ghana, Guatemala, Lithuania, Nigeria, Romania, Togo, Bolivia, Czech Republic, Dominion Republic, Ecuador, Greece, Indonesia, India, Kenya, Pakistan, Peru, Russia, Senegal, Serbia, Ukraine	11–30%
Cameroon, Paraguay, Cambodia, Mexico	31–45%

*Question: "In the past 12 months, have you or anyone living in your household paid a bribe in any form?"

Source: Adapted from: Transparency Global Corruption Barometer. (2005).

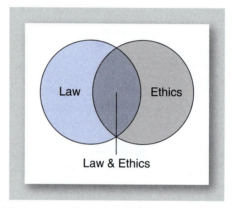

Figure 16-1 Relationship between Law and Ethics

not uniformly enforced around the world. Therefore, managers of global corporations must have answers to questions like these:

- If ethical mores differ from society to society, whose rules do you follow?

- How do we do business with integrity in countries where bribery and corruption are widespread?

- How can we develop ethical norms that can guide global marketers and business people to act with integrity and accountability?

ETHICS AND THE LAW

Ethics are behavioral standards determined by society that stipulate how its members should act in a moral manner. Ethical standards vary from society to society, but individuals within the society are expected to maintain these standards. Laws are codes of conduct stipulating how members of a society are *required* to act and are enforced by relevant governance agencies such as the police and courts. Breaking the law carries penalties (fines, prison terms), while disregarding an ethical code may result in sanctions (losing one's job) that are short of criminal proceedings. Law and ethics overlap (Figure 16-1), and what is perceived as unethical may also be illegal (e.g., bribery). In other cases, they do not overlap. In some situations, what is perceived as unethical is

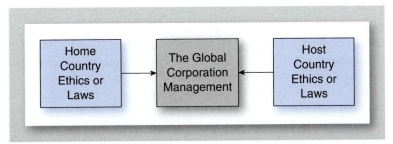

Figure 16-2 Companies in the Global Environment are Affected by both Home and Host Country Ethics and Laws

TABLE 16-2 Three Ethical Philosophies		
Ethical Relativism	**Ethical Absolutism**	**Ethical Universalism**
No universal set of ethical standards The ethical nature of an action can only be determined relative to the moral norms of the particular culture where the action takes place. "When in Rome, do as the Romans do."	Giving preference to one's own ethical values "When in Rome, do what one would do at home."	A set of universally accepted and valid ethical standards The ethical nature of an action is independent of cultural settings.

still legal (polluting the environment, paying substandard wages), and in others, what is illegal may be perceived as ethical (using company equipment for personal use). In sum, a legal system may not cover all dilemmas concerning "right" and "wrong" (the left side of Figure 16-1). Therefore, the problem of how to behave in such situations falls on ethical codes (the right side of Figure 16-1).

There are those who argue that right is synonymous with legal; i.e., whether an action is ethical is not important as long as one does not break the law. In this case, it is the legal system alone that governs behavior: "If it is legal, it is ethical." However, when doing business globally, the question is, whose law or whose ethics? Is it the law that is in force where a transaction takes place, or is it the law of the home country? Is it the ethical standard of the home or host country that should be followed, especially in those cases when they differ from one another? (See Figure 16-2.)

What happens when cultures collide? Whose standards do you follow: your home standards or those of the host country? There are three broad ethical philosophies or alternatives to choose from when doing business outside of one's home country (see Table 16-2).

Ethical relativists may plan globally, but they act locally when it comes to ethics. They try to adapt the "When in Rome, do as the Romans do" adage. **Ethical absolutists** (some call this "ethical imperialism") "import" their ethical norms to the countries in which they operate. Generally, they believe that their norms are superior and therefore should be adopted by the host country. **Ethical universalists** believe that there are enough universal standards that are found in cultures that vary from one another. These three frameworks suggest that there is no simple answer to the question of what is right and wrong when doing business across different national cultures. This debate leads to questions pertinent to the global community in which MNCs operate: are standards of good and bad relative to the culture and place in which they exist? Are values absolute or could they change over time with each new generation or management structure, for instance? If they vary, whose ethics should prevail? Should social responsibility practices presuppose the existence of a universal set of values?

"Companies must help managers distinguish between practices that are merely different and those that are wrong. For relativists, nothing is sacred and nothing is wrong. For absolutists, many things that are different are wrong. Neither extreme illuminates the real world of business decision making. The answer lies somewhere in between."[4] A typical dilemma of what to do in a seemingly ethical situation is exemplified by the example of gift giving, a normal tradition in many non-Western societies. Sharing small gifts in the Japanese culture, for instance, is an intrinsic part of business interaction, symbolizing reciprocity and relationship building, although it is commonly misconstrued as bribery by Western corporations and misinterpreted as wrong rather than culturally relative. This sort of dilemma illustrates the importance of context when evaluating different practices, while ensuring that they do not violate universal norms. The solution of a dilemma of this sort would depend on the material value of the gift. One should be able to differentiate between what is clearly a bribe and what is an acceptable gift.

THE MULTINATIONAL CORPORATION AS A GOOD CORPORATE CITIZEN

The ethical and social responsibility of the multinational corporation (MNC) is of concern to both host and home country. Because of their large size and economic power, the expectation is that the ethical and social behavior of MNCs should go beyond what is required by law. Social responsibility is a concept of ethics that businesses should act in the interests of society at large, taking into consideration all of its stakeholders and not only stockholders. Thus, the MNC has economic, ethical, legal, and social responsibility to its stakeholders. Therefore, the MNC should integrate core ethical and social responsibility values and goals into its strategic management process.

What is **corporate social responsibility (CSR)?** The European Union Commission defines it as a concept "whereby companies integrate social and environmental concerns in their business operations and their interactions with their stakeholders on a voluntary basis."[5] Likewise, the World Bank views CSR as a contribution by business to "sustainable economic development working with employees, their families, the local community, and society at large to improve their quality of life, in ways that are both good for business and good for development."[6] The International Labor Organization sees CSR as a way in which enterprises give consideration to the impact of their operations on society and affirm their principles and values both in their own internal methods and processes and in their interaction with other actors.[7] In summary, these definitions imply that CSR goes beyond just being ethical and obeying the law in business practice. It assumes that a business should contribute to the welfare of all its stakeholders beyond the goal of providing employment and making a profit (some of which should be shared by the community in which the firm operates).

4. Donaldson, T. (1996, September/October). Values in tension: Ethics away from home. *Harvard Business Review*, 47–62. Reprinted with permission.

5. European Commission. (2001). Retrieved from http://eurlex.europa.eu?lexuriserv/site/en/com/2001/com2001_0366en01.pdf.

6. World Bank. (2003). *Corporate Social Responsibility Practice: Strengthening Implementation of Corporate Social Responsibility in Global Supply Chains*. Washington, D.C.: World Bank.

7. Retrieved from www.ilo.org/public/english/support/lib/resource/subject/csr.htm.

What are the views of business management around the world? While CSR activities and reporting are extensive in developed countries, they are less so in developing and emerging countries. Some of the adoption of CSR activities in non-developed countries is attributed to NGO organizations such as the Global Reporting Initiative and the International Labor Organization. The Global Reporting Initiative (GRI) is a large NGO multi-stakeholder network of thousands of experts, in dozens of countries worldwide, who participate in GRI's working groups and governance bodies, use the GRI Guidelines to report, to access information in GRI-based reports, or to contribute to developing the Reporting Framework in other ways—both formally and informally.[8] Based in Amsterdam, the organization has developed a widely used sustainability reporting framework that has been adopted by 1,500 companies worldwide.

CSR IN THE BRIC COUNTRIES

A study by the Brazilian Institute of Applied Economics showed that about two-thirds of the 445,000 firms surveyed had invested in social programs, while half had intentions to increase their involvement.[9] The adoption of CSR programs in Brazil has been attributed to the increase of NGOs operating in the country, a desire by companies to gain more legitimacy and increase customer loyalty, and the rise of global codes. Some 950 Brazilian companies that account for annual revenues of approximately 30 percent of the Brazilian GDP and employ roughly 1.2 million people are members of a local organization, *Instituo Ethos*, a network of businesses dedicated to social responsibility. About 150 companies have signed the United Nations global compact, agreeing to adhere to fundamental principles in the areas of Human Rights, Labor Relations, Protection of the Environment, and the Combat of Corruption. Box 16-1 is an example of the application of CSR in Brazil.

CSR IN RUSSIA

During the era of the Soviet Socialist Republics, all industry was state-owned. The Soviet economy was based on large industrial plants that encompassed large areas that included housing, schooling, and health and recreation facilities for employees and their families. Thus the industrial complex was socially responsible for its employees. The breakup of the Soviet Union resulted in the privatization of many of these

---

BOX 16-1   COUNTRY IN FOCUS: BRAZIL

Project Plasma, a partnership between Klabin (paper), Tetra Pak (long-life packaging), Alcoa (aluminum), and TSL Ambiental (residue treatment) joined forces to solve a serious environmental problem in a creative and profitable manner. All three had an interest in recycling the three materials that make up long-life packaging (aluminum, paper, and plastic), used mainly for juices, milk, and other beverages.

---

8. Retrieved from www.globalreporting.org/AboutGRI/WhoWeAre/.

9. Nascimento, A. (2004). *Corporate Social Responsibility in Brazil: A Comparative Analysis of Two Paper Companies.* Cambridge, Mass.: Massachusetts Institute of Technology.

industries, while others remained state-owned. Thus the industrial complex did not automatically take over the social welfare of employees; this task was now the responsibility of government which, because of budgetary constraints, found it difficult to provide aid for recreation, the environment, contributions to charity organizations, and the like.

To what extent did private business take over the social role of the government? While Russian businesses have come to realize that CSR is crucial to their sustainability, most efforts in this direction are made by large companies such as Norlisk Nickel, Lukoil, Novolipstek Steel, and Yukos (before its takeover by the government), as well as companies that serve Western markets. Two main factors that constrain the adoption of CSR practices in Russia are the lack of transparency of Russian business and a faulty definition of what CSR is all about. According to one observer, CSR is "thought by Russian top managers to be mainly a tool to managing non financial risks and improve capitalization via better public image."[10] According to the Center for Political Technologies in Russia, the issue of corporate social responsibility can only be solved through the modernization of state institutions and the creation of civil institutions to monitor the interaction between businesses and the state.

CSR IN CHINA

CSR is a relatively new phenomenon in China, and the government thus far has not actively promoted it. The large Chinese government bureaucracy hampers the realization of CSR programs.[11] There are more issues related to safety and intellectual property rights violations for Chinese products (81 percent) than for Indian products (6 percent).[12] China accounts for the largest percentage of all illegal products seized by the United States Customs and Border Protection, while India is a distant second. However, the government has recently made efforts to improve the relevant laws and market regulations and to expand supervisory practices to decrease irresponsible corporate behavior. The Chinese Federation for Corporate Social Responsibility was launched in Shanghai during 2007 by 13 foreign and domestic companies. China is only at the beginning of forming a viable CSR philosophy and governance. Examples of initiatives and guidelines include the Recommended CSR Standards for Chinese Corporations and the Compilation of Best Practices published by the Chinese Business Council for Sustainable Development, as well as the Ministry of Commerce guidelines for the preparation of CSR reports.

However, CSR guidelines that require companies to address social and environmental considerations alongside the drive for profits remain unfamiliar to most Chinese businesses. The main cause of the Jilin City chemical explosion in 2005, which killed six and wounded others, was caused by improper handling of equipment by workers. In the same year, another tragedy struck. This time it was the Dongfeng coal mine explosion that resulted in more than 100 worker deaths. In this case, mine managers did not know about the central government's emergency instructions on mining safety and could not tell how many workers they had dismissed immediately following the blast. Such ignorance of work safety, pollution, and educational needs—the underlying

10. Dayman, S. (2008). Russia in 2008: Corporate social responsibility in a post-socialist state. Retrieved from www.ecologia .org/isosr/sergey.html.

11. Lattemann, M., Fetscherin, M., Alon, I., Li, S., & Schneider, A. (2009). CSR communication intensity in Chinese and Indian multinational corporations. *Corporate Governance: An International Review (17)*4, 426–442.

12. Ibid.

BOX 16-2   COMPANY IN FOCUS: LENOVO

Lenovo China has been working with Lenovo International to launch its Environmentally Conscious Products program, which integrates environmental management systems with product specifications. Lenovo uses ISO 14001 as an environmental management system, which includes end-of-life management, supplier environmental performance, and greenhouse gas emission factors.

Yantai in Shandong Province aims to increase the number of green tourist hotels and economy hotels to promote energy saving and emission reductions. The term "green tourist hotel" refers to a hotel that can adhere to clean production, advocate green consumption, protect the ecological environment, and use resources in a rational way.

---

cause of thousands of tragedies—exists widely in Chinese industries.[13] Some people argue that it is too early for Chinese companies to embrace the CSR concept, since most businesses are still at the early stages of developing technological know-how and are struggling for their survival. However, as Gary Dirks, president of BP China, has noted, CSR goes beyond simply "charitable efforts" and addresses more fundamental questions of profit-making; therefore, it should be mainstreamed into a company's business model from the start, not considered a luxury to add later on. There are optimistic signs, however. The Chinese government and economic organizations are establishing Chinese standards and accreditation criteria of CSR reports and health and safety standards. Western companies operating in China should be aware of and promote CSR standards.

CSR IN INDIA

Spirituality and CSR are deeply rooted in the Indian tradition. Therefore, CSR is not a new phenomenon, but rather is linked to Indian culture and religion. Social duties and engagement in charity by Indian corporations were often implicit, but over time, CSR has become more dominant and broader in scope. Corporate philanthropy is now part of normal business operations and is embedded in corporate activities.[14]

India also has a long tradition of paternalistic philanthropy. Big family-owned firms such as Tata are particularly active in providing basic services, such as schools and healthcare, for local communities. For example, organizations like Bharath Petroleum Corporation Limited, Maruti Suzuki India Limited, and Hindustan Unilever Limited, adopt villages where they focus on holistic development. They provide better medical and sanitation facilities, build schools and houses, and help the villagers become self-reliant by teaching vocational and business skills. Some examples where CSR has paid dividends to Indian companies appear in Table 16-3.[15] Nevertheless, it has been reported that few Indian companies publish a Corporate Sustainability Report or state how much they spend on CSR activities.[16]

13. Zinjung, L. (2005). Lack of corporate social responsibility behind recent China accidents. *World Watch Institute*. Retrieved from http://www.worldwatch.org/node/3859.

14. Lattemann, M., Fetscherin, M., Alon, I., Li, S., & Schneider, A. (2009). CSR communication intensity in Chinese and Indian multinational corporations. *Corporate Governance: An International Review (17)*4, 426–442.

15. The state of CSR in India 2004, acknowledging progress, prioritizing action. (2004, November 10). National Seminar on Corporate Responsibility, New Delhi.

16. Retrieved from www.karmayog.org/redirect/strred.asp?docId=13270.

TABLE 16-3 Corporate Social Responsibility Pays Off	
Boosting Profits	Gujarat Ambuja, one of the country's leading cement manufacturers, reports that "our efforts to achieve world standards in environment protection had the outcome of substantially improving efficiency and profitability."
Cutting Costs	Reliance Industries' energy conservation measures have saved the company 1,150 million rupees per annum.
Increasing Revenues	HLL's Project Shakti creates income-generating opportunities for underprivileged rural women, while giving the company enhanced access to hitherto unexplored rural areas.
Strengthening Brand Value	Infosys was among seven international companies to be chosen in the first annual list of "Top Brands with a Conscience."
Enhancing Reputation	The Oil and Natural Gas Corporation has found that its community development program has "generated goodwill and earned the company the reputation of being a company that cares."
Improving Morale	Tata Steel believes that helping the community also provides a new perspective to its employees, thereby strengthening employee morale.

BOX 16-3   COMPANY IN FOCUS: INDIAN INSTITUTE OF MANAGEMENT

The post-graduate programs at the Indian Institutes of Management have initiated an ethics program in the schools. One of their educators was quoted as saying: "Our social conditioning by and large makes us unethical vis-à-vis a lack of civic sense and concern for the environment. Management students are at an age when they are less vulnerable and can differentiate the right from the wrong. The subject has been introduced to sensitize students about ethical issues as and when they take up responsibilities later in their career."

The ethics course is compulsory for all students, and it is joined by a course on social transformation in India, which focuses on the societal issues across the country. Such courses should help the students take sustainable decisions for society when they graduate.

CAN A COMPANY AFFORD NOT TO BE ETHICAL?

Maintaining an ethical stance in all situations may be difficult. As an anonymous reader of a business magazine commented in an article supporting ethics in a global organization:

> *Ethics do differ around the world. [In] some countries a bribe is required to do business and in others it is illegal. The only thing to do is follow your own country practices and live with the results.*

A study of 127 companies in the UK, taken from the FTSE 350 for which full and comparable company data was available for the years 1997–2001, was divided into two cohorts: those who have had codes of ethics/conduct/principles for five years or more and those who explicitly said they did not. The results showed that:

- Regarding financial performance, from three of the four measures of corporate value used in this study (EVA, MVA, and P/E ratio), it was found that those companies in the sample with a code of ethics had, over the period 1997–2001, outperformed a similar-sized group who said they did not have a code.

- Companies with a code of ethics generated significantly more economic added value (EVA) and market added value (MVA) in the years 1997–2000 than those without a code.

- Companies with a code of ethics experienced far less P/E volatility over a four-year period than those without them. This suggests that they may be a more secure investment in the longer term. Other research has suggested that a stable P/E ratio tends to attract capital at below average cost; having a code may be said to be a significant indicator of consistent management.

- The indicator that showed a different result pattern to the others was Return on Capital Employed. No discernable difference was found in ROCE between those with or without a code for 1997–1998. However, from 1999 to 2001, there was a clear (approximately 50 percent) increase in the average return of those with codes, while those without codes fell during this period.

Some academic work has been done in the United States comparing the long-term added value of corporations with business ethics policies (e.g., codes of ethics) with those who do not have them. It indicated that there is a correlation between those with a reputation for integrity and the growth of long-term shareholder value. A 2006 study of nearly 100 research studies that investigated the relationship between corporate performance and ethics found:[17]

- In the 80 studies evaluating whether corporate social performance contributes to corporate financial performance, 53 percent of them point to a positive relationship. No relationship is identified in 24 percent of the studies, 4 percent find a negative relationship, and the remaining 19 percent of the studies yield mixed results.

- Of the 19 studies evaluating corporate social performance as an outcome of financial performance, 68 percent identify a positive relationship, with 16 percent showing no relationship and 16 percent providing mixed results.

Some studies have found that ethical behavior has less impact on corporate performance in the short run than in the long run. In an informal survey of a group of 51 employees of Hungarian companies from the fields of advertising, logistics, packaging, travel, recruitment, and a few others, 67 percent found that companies in Hungary that do business legally and ethically are more successful than other companies in the long term, but may be less successful in the short term.[18]

Are socially responsible companies sustainable? Table 16-4 lists some sustainable companies by their corporate social action. Most of them are well known and successful in what they do. The table lists a few representative companies in several industrial categories.

17. Margolis, J., Walsh, J., & Krehmeyer, D. (2006). *Building the Business Case for Ethics*. Business Roundtable Institute for Corporate Ethics.

18. Retrieved from www.ethicalleadershipgroup.com/blog/2006/04/budapest_hungary_does_ethics_p_1.html.

TABLE 16-4 Socially Responsible and Successful Companies	
Company	**Action**
Toyota	Developer of hybrid gas-electric vehicles
Renault	Fuel-efficient cars
Volkswagen	Clean diesel technologies
Hewlett Packard	Ecological standards
Toshiba	Developer of eco-efficient products
Dell	Recycling of used computer hardware
Royal Dutch Shell	Invests in wind and solar energy
Norsk Hydbro	Assesses social and environmental impact of its operations
Suncor Energy	Helps solve ecological and social issues in Northern Canada
Nokia	Leads in phasing out toxic materials
Ericsson	Wind- and fuel-cell-powered telecom systems in Nigerian villages
Motorola	Disclosure of environmental impact of operations
Philips Electronics	Innovator of energy-saving appliances
Sony	Considerate of green issues and monitors safety and labor standards of its suppliers
Matsushita Electric	Produces state-of-the-art green products
Roche	Invests in drug research for third world use
Novo Nordisk	Sells diabetes drugs in poor nations at a substantial discount
GlaxoSmithKline	First to offer AIDS drugs at cost

A study of firms in the UK examined the impact of ethical identity on their financial performance by comparing two dimensions of a firm's ethical identity: corporate applied ethics (CAE) and corporate revealed ethics (CRE). Since most companies have a revealed code of ethics, those companies that specifically provided training on their code of ethics to their employees were categorized as those with corporate applied ethics. It also tested whether business ethics has a stronger influence on accounting measures than on market measures. Corporate financial performance was measured using both accounting-based and market-based indicators over a five-year period (2001–2005). It was found that in the short run, there was no significant difference between the financial performances of the companies in both categories, while in the long run, companies with CAE significantly outperformed those with CRE. Also, this study found an indication that accounting measures are more influenced by business ethics than market measures.[19] In effect, the ethics code is a policy statement that employees are expected to follow. However, a code in itself is not sufficient; it has to have monitoring features and someone who is responsible for overseeing that the code is implemented. The *Sarbanes-Oxley Act* requires a company to publicly disclose their code of ethics if their stock is traded under the auspices of the Securities Exchange Act of 1934.

THE FIGHT AGAINST CORRUPTION AND BRIBERY

There are two major factors that motivate corruption and bribery: monetary gain and weak governance. While the monetary motive is difficult to remove, there is much that can be done to improve governance. There are three main organizations that have the resources to monitor and prevent corruption and bribery: governments, non-governmental organizations, and business firms. Before the 1990s, there were few non-governmental

19. Ugoji, K. (2006). *Does Business Ethics Pay? Ethics and Financial Performance* [MSc thesis]. Cranfield School of Management.

TABLE 16-5 A Chronological Listing of Anti-Corruption Organizations	
1993	Transparency International
1995	Transparency International Corruption Perception Index
1997	OECD Anti-Bribery Convention
1999	Transparency International Bribe Payers Index
2001	Transparency International Global Corruption Barometer
2003	UN Convention Against Corruption

agencies that dealt with these problems; since then, some non-governmental organizations have been formed, like Transparency International, and conventions have been enacted by existing bodies such as the OECD and the UN. Table 16-5 shows some of these developments chronologically.

One major non-governmental organization is *Transparency International* (TI), a global network headquartered in Germany with more than 90 national chapters and chapters-in-formation around the world. These chapters bring together relevant stakeholders from government, civil society, business, and the media to promote transparency in elections, in public administration, in procurement, and in business. TI's global network of chapters and contacts also use advocacy campaigns to lobby governments to implement anti-corruption reforms. TI publishes a number of surveys that measure the extent of corruption and bribery including the Corruption Perception Index, Bribe Payers Index, and Global Corruption Barometer. The 2008 CPI ranks 180 countries in terms of perceived levels of corruption, as determined by expert assessments and opinion surveys; the TI Bribe Payers Index evaluates the supply side of corruption—the likelihood of firms from the world's industrialized countries to offer or pay bribes abroad—while the Global Corruption Barometer is a survey that assesses general public attitudes toward and experience with corruption in dozens of countries around the world.

Figure 16-3 shows the 2008 CPI rankings. The three least corrupt countries are Denmark, New Zealand, and Sweden, while the most corrupt are Somalia, Myanmar, and Iraq. In the Bribe Payers Index, of the 22 countries surveyed, the firms least likely to bribe when operating abroad are headquartered in Belgium, Canada, the Netherlands, and Switzerland, in that order, while firms headquartered in Russia, China, Mexico, and India are the most likely to bribe when operating abroad. Note that companies operating in these countries are not necessarily owned by nationals but could also be affiliates of multinationals.

THE OECD BRIBERY CONVENTION

The **OECD Anti-Bribery Convention** establishes legally binding standards to make bribery of foreign public officials in international business transactions a criminal offense and provides for a host of related measures that make this effective. The 30 OECD member countries and eight non-member countries—Argentina, Brazil, Bulgaria, Chile, Estonia, Israel, the Slovak Republic, and South Africa—have adopted this convention. The convention forbids payments to public officials, elected or appointed, in order to obtain business favors. Such payment is a criminal offense under the convention. Enforcement of the convention is the responsibility of the signatory countries who are expected to enact legislation dealing with such activities. While the OECD does not have the authority to implement the convention, it does monitor the effectiveness of legislation in force by member countries. This monitoring

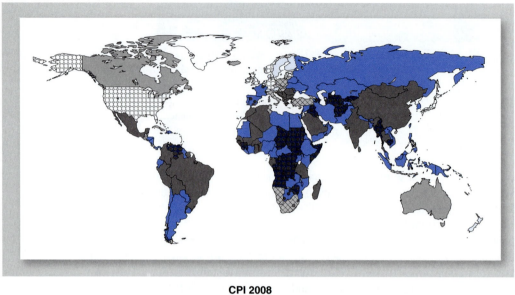

CPI 2008

9.0 – 10.0	8.0 – 8.9	7.0 – 7.9	6.0 – 6.9	5.0 – 5.9
4.0 – 4.9	3.0 – 3.9	2.0 – 2.9	1.0 – 1.9	no data

Figure 16-3 Map of Countries Rated by the Corruption Perception Index

Source: Data from Transparency International. Retrieved from www.transparency.org/policy-research/surveys-indices/cp/2010.

does have weight, as exemplified by the United Kingdom's Serious Fraud Office. The UK Serious Fraud Office's decision to drop an investigation into BAE Systems over bribery allegations relating to a £43bn arms deal with Saudi Arabia, and other alleged corruption cases, led to an investigation by the OECD that concluded that reform was urgently needed in the UK to address "systemic deficiencies" in the legal system.

The report sharply criticized the UK for failing to bring its anti-bribery laws into line with its international obligations under the OECD Anti-Bribery Convention and urged the rapid introduction of new legislation. Existing UK laws made it very difficult for prosecutors to bring an effective case against a company for alleged bribery offences, the OECD said. The criticism was a major factor in the enactment of the UK Bribery Bill, making it a criminal offense to offer a bribe at home or abroad.

UN CONVENTION AGAINST CORRUPTION

The **UN Convention Against Corruption** prohibits corruption in both the public and private sectors, although the prohibition concerning the private sector is not mandatory. The convention covers four areas: prevention, criminalization, anti-corruption policies, and coordination for implementation. Corruption also includes money laundering and embezzlement. Embezzlement is a sensitive issue because it raises questions about public officials who live beyond their means in expensive housing and lead egregious lifestyles. However, the convention calls for an investigation whenever such asymmetries arise. International cooperation also calls for repatriation of assets that have been transferred illicitly to another country. The UN Convention has limitations. It does not cover bribery in the private sector, nor political corruption. Moreover, the UN does not have authority to enforce state compliance with the rules of the convention; it only serves as a watchdog agency that leaves enforcement to the countries involved.

GOVERNMENT ANTI-CORRUPTION AND BRIBERY ENFORCEMENT

Governments have a key role to play in ensuring that foreign bribery is stopped at the source—and by making good on commitments to prevent and prosecute such practices. Some governments have enacted anti-corruption and bribery legislation in accordance with the OECD and UN conventions. Some examples follow.

UNITED STATES FOREIGN CORRUPT PRACTICES ACT OF 1977

The United States was the first country to enact ant-corruption legislation. The **United States Foreign Corrupt Practices Act of 1977 (FCPA)** contains two major provisions. First, its anti-bribery provision makes it illegal to bribe foreign officials to retain or obtain business. Its second provision requires companies to make and keep books, records, and accounts that accurately and fairly reflect their transactions. Companies are also required to maintain a system of controls that can provide reasonable assurances of the propriety and legality of those transactions.

The FCPA began to take on a higher profile in the early 2000s. One key factor of this was the passage of the **Sarbanes-Oxley Act of 2002,** which emphasized greater corporate transparency, senior management accountability, enhanced control systems, and whistle-blower protections. The increased focus on Sarbanes-Oxley requirements and the additional resources dedicated to implementing them in many instances led to the discovery of improper payments and of control and compliance weaknesses that enabled such payments to go undetected. Moreover, companies sought to reduce their potential liability for violations found by voluntarily disclosing such conduct to the authorities and pledging to conduct thorough investigations, report the results of such investigations to the government, and remediate the gaps in their control structures.[20]

The number of FCPA investigations and cases brought by the Department of Justice and the Securities and Exchange Commission grew from nine in 2003 to 29 in 2007, and, on a cumulative basis, investigations involving 82 corporations remained open at the beginning of 2008. Similarly, corporate FCPA anti-bribery prosecutions and enforcement actions rose from five in 2004 to 38 in 2007. At mid-year 2008, 16 new prosecutions were underway—more than in any full year prior to 2007.[21]

UK BRIBERY BILL

The UK Bribery Bill:

- Makes it a criminal offense to give, promise, or offer a bribe and to request, agree to receive, or accept a bribe either at home or abroad. The measures cover bribery of a foreign public official.

- Increases the maximum penalty for bribery from seven to 10 years' imprisonment, with an unlimited fine.

- Introduces a corporate offense of negligent failure to prevent bribery by persons working on behalf of a business. A business can avoid conviction if it can show that it generally has good systems in place to prevent bribery.

20. Rial, E. (17 April 2009). Beyond reproach, why compliance with anti-corruption laws is increasingly critical for multinational businesses. *Deloitte Review.*

21. 2008 Mid-year FCPA update. (2008, July). Gibson, Dunn & Crutcher LLP.

■ Ensures that evidence from proceedings in Parliament can be considered by the courts in bribery cases by removing Parliamentary Privilege in the prosecution of an MP or Peer.

Emerging countries have also passed anti-corruption and bribery legislation. Take Lithuania, for example. Article 282 of the criminal code defines the *acceptance of a bribe* as accepting, promising to accept, or demanding a bribe by a public official or a civil servant, for himself or herself or for anyone else, for him or her to act or refrain from acting, to make a decision, vote, or express an opinion in favor of a bribe-giver, or the promise to do so. The criminal code also stipulates other corruption-related crimes. These include abuse of office, refraining from official duties (non-feasance), fraud (related to document handling) in office (malfeasance), exceeding one's authority, commercial bribery, and acceptance of undue remuneration.

ANTI-CORRUPTION AND ETHICS POLICY BY BUSINESS FIRMS

One of the options available to business firms is to compile a code of ethics. An **ethics code** is a set of guidelines that stipulates a set of acceptable behaviors. However, a written code is not sufficient unless it includes a mechanism for its enforcement, such as penalties for not adhering to the code and, in some cases, rewards for following it. An ethics code needs the support of all top executives of the firm. A survey by Deloitte & Touche among 4,000 of the top publicly traded firms in the United States found that 83 percent of respondents had codes of conduct but that one-fourth were not enforcing them.[22] About one-half of the firms reported that ethics issues are taken up by the board of directors only when failure occurs.

In order to implement an ethics code, it is necessary to appoint an ombudsman, a manager who has the responsibility for coordinating ethical policy throughout the organization and who serves as an advocate for employees and board members who report, or are involved in, an ethical dilemma. If employees are expected to report what they observe as unethical behavior by their peers (whistle-blowing), they must be protected by the organization (and perhaps rewarded for their actions).

Attempts have also been made to motivate ethical behavior in a company's supply chain. An example of this is the Sedex nonprofit organization based in London, UK, which is open for membership to any company anywhere in the world. Sedex is a knowledge management provider for measuring and improving ethical and responsible business practices in global supply chains. The organization enables member companies to manage efficiently the ethical and responsible practices of their global supply chains, generating transparency through the provision of a secure and user-friendly data exchange.

GLOBAL CORPORATE CITIZENSHIP

Nations are interdependent in a world of globalization. Corporations operating in this world have the opportunity to build an international community of virtue and protection of basic human rights.[23] This task can be performed by adhering to universal

22. Retrieved from www.deloitte.com/us/ethicssurvey.

23. Rendtorff, D. *Toward ethical guidelines for international business corporations: Aspects of global corporate citizenship.* Proceedings of the Fourth ISBEE World Congress, Cape Town, South Africa, 15–18 July 2008. International Society of Business, Economics and Ethics.

codes of behavior such as those promulgated by the United Nations, OECD, and relevant NGOs such as Transparency International. Firms can promote basic, universal human principles, such as physical security, education, decent working conditions, and wages by practicing them in the workplace.

In addition to the Sedex organization, a group of business leaders from Europe, Japan, and the United States met in Caux, Switzerland, to develop "a shared perspective on business behavior acceptable to and honored by all."[24] The deliberations of the group led to the publication of seven general principles of behavior:

1. The responsibilities of businesses: Beyond shareholders toward stakeholders
2. The economic and social impact of business: Toward innovation, justice, and world community
3. Business behavior: Beyond the letter of the law toward a spirit of trust
4. Respect for rules
5. Support for multilateral trade
6. Respect for the environment
7. Avoidance of illicit operations

These suggested modes of behavior contain both ethical (e.g., avoidance of illicit operations) and social responsibility (e.g., respect for the environment) principles that may be applied across nations.

A number of ethicists such as Richard De George,[25] Thomas Donaldson,[26] and Thomas Dunfee[27] have written broadly on the subject of moral values that corporations should follow when doing business abroad (see Table 16-6 for some examples). All three educators have grappled with the problems that arise when home and host cultures differ, especially with respect to moral values. Business practices that may be considered unethical in one culture may be acceptable in another. The dilemma is how to act in a situation where what you consider unethical at home is acceptable elsewhere. This situation is what Donaldson and Dunfee call **moral free space.**[28] In this space there are no right answers, so managers must chart their own course of action, as long as they do not violate **core moral values.** Generally, these core values stem from a company's code of ethics. In the absence of such a code, or if the code does not fit the situation, then the manager must use his or her judgment. Donaldson suggests that most dilemmas occur because of differences between two cultures are of two kinds: **conflict of relative development** and **conflict of tradition.** In the first conflict, a dilemma occurs because of a difference between stages of economic development. In this situation, it is suggested that managers ask whether the practice in question would be acceptable if his or her country was in the same stage of development. If so, then the practice would be ethical. The second case is one of traditional differences. The most prevalent situation is gift giving. In Asian and Middle Eastern countries, it is customary to give business gifts. Here the problem is one of intent and magnitude. If the intention is to fulfill a cultural norm, then the gift may be considered ethical if its magnitude cannot be construed as being beyond the normal value of a gift in the context in which it is given.

24. *Caux Round Table Principles for Business.* (1994). The Hague, Switzerland.

25. De George, R. (1993). *Competing with integrity in international business.* New York: Oxford University Press.

26. Donaldson, T. (1989). *The ethics of international business.* New York: Oxford University Press.

27. Dunfee, T. (2003). Taking responsibility for bribery: The multinational corporation's role in combating bribery. In Rory Sullivan [Ed.], *Business and Human Rights: Dilemmas and Solutions.* Sheffield, UK: Greenleaf Publishing.

28. Donaldson, T. (1996, September/October). Values in tension: Ethics away from home. *Harvard Business Review*, 44–52.

TABLE 16-6 Moral Values and Principles of Selected Firms

Bell Canada Enterprises	Bank of Montreal	General Electric	Nortel
Comply with applicable laws.	Do what is fair and honest.	Obey applicable laws and regulations.	Compete vigorously and fairly in the marketplace.
Work with integrity, honesty, fairness.	Respect the rights of others.	Be honest, fair, and trustworthy.	Treat others with dignity and respect.
Foster environment of trust, respect, and open communication.	Work to the letter and spirit of the law.	Avoid conflicts of interest.	Do what we say we will do.
Maintain a safe and secure workplace and protect the environment.	Maintain the confidentiality of information.	Foster an equal opportunity atmosphere.	Be honest and obey all applicable laws.
Sustain a culture where ethical conduct is recognized, valued, and exemplified by all employees.	Avoid conflicts of interest.	Strive to create a safe workplace and protect the environment.	Committed to live out our values.
	Conduct ourselves appropriately at all times.	Through leadership, sustain culture where ethical conduct is recognized, valued, and exemplified by all employees.	

Source: Adapted from: Schwartz, M. (2005). Universal moral values for corporate codes of ethics. *Journal of Business Ethics*, 59, 33.

SUMMARY

- As multinational companies expand globally and enter foreign markets, ethical conduct of officers and employees assume added importance, since the very cultural diversity associated with such expansion may undermine the much-shared cultural and ethical values observable in more homogeneous organizations.

- Unethical practices such as bribery and poor working conditions can have negative effects on the firm in the long run in terms of lower profits and tarnished image.

- According to ethical absolutism, global firms need to develop and enforce their own codes of ethics wherever they operate, specifically directed at the issues related to a multicultural, multinational business environment. However, there are those who believe that one should follow the ethical codes that prevail in the host country.

- Corporate social responsibility (CSR) in the international business environment is more challenging because there are many more and diverse stakeholders of international business firms. MNCs face wider CSR expectations and are under increasing pressure to exhibit socially responsible behavior in their global operations.

- International monitoring of bribery and corruption is more widespread thanks to organizations such as Transparency International, the OECD, and the European Commission. Organizations such as these have led to the strengthening of anti-corruption domestic legislation in many countries, as well as multilateral agreements to curb these practices.

- CSR in the BRIC countries ranges from moderate, in the case of Brazil and India, to rather weak in China and Russia.

DISCUSSION QUESTIONS

1. In doing business in a foreign country, whose ethics should you follow, the norms of the foreign country or those of your home country? Discuss.

2. Give three examples of corporate social responsibility in your state or city.

3. What can multinational corporations do to encourage corporate social responsibility among the companies with which they do business abroad?

4. Does a potential whistle-blower have a greater responsibility to the public, to the organization, or to him or herself?

EXPERIENTIAL EXERCISES

1. Obtain via the Internet the ethical codes of two American multinational corporations. Try to compare their codes to those of a French or British MNC (also obtained via the Internet). What similarities have you found in the company codes? Are there any differences?

2. Compare the anti-bribery legislation of the UK and the United States. Which legislation, in your opinion, will do the best job of preventing bribery?

KEY TERMS

Conflict of relative development, p. 451

Conflict of tradition, p. 451

Core moral values, p. 451

Corporate social responsibility (CSR), p. 440

Ethical absolutists, p. 439

Ethical relativists, p. 439

Ethical universalists, p. 439

Ethics code, p. 450

Ethics, p. 438

Moral free space, p. 451

OECD Anti-Bribery Convention, p. 447

Sarbanes-Oxley Act of 2002, p. 449

Transparency International, p. 437

UK Bribery Bill, p. 449

UN Convention Against Corruption, p. 448

United States Foreign Corrupt Practices Act of 1977 (FCPA), p. 449

CASE 16-1

The Sanlu Case

"To our knowledge there isn't a dairy company in the world that tests for melamine."

With those words, CEO Andrew Ferrier tried to explain how New Zealand's Fonterra Company never knew about the chemical contamination of a baby formula product developed in Fonterra's joint venture with Chinese company Sanlu . . . a contamination that ultimately claimed the lives of at least four children, left 104 in serious condition, sent 12,892 to the hospital, and affected nearly 40,000 others.

Background

New Zealand company Fonterra Co-operative Group Ltd. is the world's largest milk producer. It has built an international reputation for excellence in the production, processing, and sale of dairy products. Selling to 120 countries, Fonterra's 2005 revenue was US $8.5 billion. The company's website states corporate principles:

> Dairy is our life's work. It's our passion and it's what we do best.
>
> We have always marveled at the simple nutrition of dairy. In an age when you need a chemistry degree to understand food labels, milk is pure milk, providing the building blocks for a healthy life.

Shijiazhuang Sanlu Group Co. Ltd. was China's biggest producer of milk powder. In addition to powdered milk, it also produced product lines in liquid milk and other fresh dairy. As Sanlu had been the number one dairy company in China for blended milk products for 12 years prior to its joint venture with Fonterra, the 2005 JV represented a marriage of equals.

On December 1, 2005, Fonterra entered into a joint venture agreement in which Fonterra took a 43% stake in Shijiazhuang Sanlu Group Co. Ltd. This investment was one of the largest ever by a foreign company into a Chinese dairy company. The JV was to remain focused on the strong competencies of each of the organizations; the manufacture, marketing, and distribution of consumer dairy products. After 20 years of being the top exporter of dairy ingredients to China, the JV made sense for Fonterra. "We will complement our existing importing and consumer businesses in China by partnering with a successful local company that has access to local fresh milk supplies," said Fonterra Brands Managing Director Sanjay Khosla.

The hope of this strategy was for the JV to be competitive and profitable with an eye toward the eventual issuing of shares to financial markets. Working together toward this goal, the seven-member board of the JV included three Fonterra representatives. In addition, a senior Fonterra representative joined Shijiazhuang Sanlu Group's senior executive team. The potential for the JV was huge. Not only were Chinese consumers increasingly becoming open to more regular consumption of dairy products, but also of non-dairy foods, including cookies and candy, which can contain dairy products in the ingredients. Most of China's dairy exports go to other nations in Asia but, as world

Case prepared by Dr. Valerie Manna, Lincoln University, New Zealand. Reprinted with permission.

markets become increasingly integrated, they may end up on retailer's shelves or in products sold across the globe. Even in geographic areas like the European Union's 27 member states, which do not import any liquid dairy products from China, non-dairy products containing dairy from China are imported.

The Problem

Melamine is an industrial chemical used in making plastics, fire-retardants, counter-tops, glues, fertilizers, and cleaning products. Ingestion of melamine can lead to the binding of the chemical to components of urine, causing health problems. These problems can range from kidney stones, which block the ducts that bring urine out of the body, to kidney failure, reproductive damage, and bladder cancer.

When added to a food product such as milk powder, melamine allows for the product to be increased in volume by having water or other "fillers" added without this dilution being detected by standard quality tests. Melamine releases nitrogen into the food product. Typical standard food tests check for the amount of nitrogen (a proxy measure for protein) in the milk product; so, when melamine is added, expectations for the amount of protein in a product are erroneously met. As long as the price of melamine is less than the price of the comparable amount of milk powder, it becomes profitable to add melamine to the milk powder while appearing to meet food standards. Doing so can help producers undercut competition on price.

The Fonterra/Sanlu tragedy involving the contamination of infants' milk powder with melamine started well before the product was eventually taken off the shelves on September 11, 2008 (Appendix A contains a timeline of events). It is likely that the place in the supply chain in which the adulteration happened was at the stations that collect milk from individual farmers. Supervision of these stations was inconsistent, as dairy production and the overall huge growth in the industry was a relatively recent phenomenon.

Not an Isolated Case

Although much media attention centered on Sanlu, on September 22, a Fonterra spokesperson deflected this focus by saying that the problem "has been endemic in the Chinese milk market for some time." Unfortunately, there is some truth to this statement.

Outside of the dairy industry, in both 2007 and 2008, China has been in the middle of pet food scandals in which melamine was intentionally added to products in the efforts to falsely boost protein readings. Thousands of animals were sickened and hundreds died.

In 2004, more than 200 Chinese babies suffered malnutrition and at least 12 died after being fed formula that contained no nutrients. This formula was misrepresented as being manufactured by Sanlu when, in fact, it was not. One can only wonder if it was this incident or some other knowledge which motivated a Chinese television station to strongly suspect Sanlu's role in early reported infant health incidents linked with bad formula. In a television report on the issue, graphics of Sanlu's products were used as a background image while the report aired (and this occurred prior to the recall announcement).

Yet not all of the controversy centered on China. Three companies (Abbott Laboratories, Mead Johnson, and Nestlé) make more than 90 percent of all infant formula produced in the United States. The United States Food & Drug Administration detected trace levels of melamine in one formula (Nestlé's Good Start Supreme Infant Formula with Iron), and cyanuric acid (a chemical akin to melamine) in the product of another (Mead Johnson's Enfamil LIPIL with Iron), in addition to finding trace amounts in nutritional supplements for sick children. The agency explained that these contaminates resulted from the manufacturing process rather than being intentionally added to the products. Melamine can leach onto food products as a result of its use in plastic food packaging and cleaning solutions used on processing equipment.

On the first of October 2008, New Zealand's Tatua Dairy Company stopped exports of its lactoferrin product after melamine was found in products sold to China. Although the contamination was at what was considered a "safe" level, lactoferrin is used in baby formula so caution was justifiable. Efforts were made to see where in the manufacturing process the melamine was being introduced; the contamination could have resulted from insecticides used in food production breaking down into melamine or through stock feed imported into New Zealand.

Internal and External Stakeholders

Early on in the scandal, New Zealand Prime Minister Helen Clark defended Fonterra as having "behaved responsibly at all times." She explained the company had tried to recall formula at the earliest possible time but faced resistance from local Chinese officials. She blamed officials local to Sanlu as being likely to "try and put a towel over it (the scandal) . . . that is never what we would do in New Zealand." In short, Clark provided international milk giant Fonterra with the foundation to claim that they may have been "naïve" in dealings with their foreign partner, that they did not know what was being done in the JV and that, if they had known, they never would have condoned the purchase of adulterated milk for processing.

China's health minister, on the other hand, blamed Fonterra for not having warned the public earlier about the risks Fonterra knew were associated with the product. CEO Ferrier said Fonterra thought it would be more effective if it worked within the Chinese system to recall the contaminated product rather than reaching out to the Chinese public and recalling the products on its own. He is quoted as saying, "We'll never know if we had gone public at the beginning whether it would have made a difference at that time . . . We did the thing that in our judgment was going to get the product off the shelves as quickly as we possibly could."

No claim of naïveté could be made for Sanlu, though. At the time that Sanlu was beginning to fully recognize the scope of the problem, its PR department wrote a memo suggesting paying parents off to encourage them to stay quiet about the negative affects their child suffered from using the product. Sanlu management subsequently agreed to spend hundreds of thousands of dollars in such an effort and agreed to do this on August 11, *after* its New Zealand partner Fonterra learned about the poisonings.

As a further way to keep the story quiet, the PR department suggested that Sanlu work with Chinese Internet provider Baidu to block the transmission of information regarding the situation. In the transaction, Baidu would get nearly half a million dollars in advertising from Sanlu. The fact that this event happened after Fonterra learned about the contamination calls into question the New Zealand company's claim that it fought for a public recall of the formula as soon as it knew that the product was basically poison. Although Fonterra representative Graeme McMilan said that the plan "was never discussed at the Sanlu board or with any of the Fonterra-related staff," it is questionable how these payments to both the parents and the media could have been authorized without Sanlu's board of directors (on which Fonterra has representation) being aware of the actions.

In the end, Ferrier said that his company was trying to help make right a situation it did not cause and was leaving responsibility for responding to the public health crisis in the hands of the Chinese government: "We're not sitting here counting money; we're sitting here just making sure we do the right thing . . . Right now, we understand the Chinese government has stepped in and is looking after the health of the children. We will see . . . if there's something else we can do."

What should Fonterra have done?

1. Recalled the products in China as soon as it learned about the problem.
2. Informed the media in China as soon as it learned about the problem.
3. Informed the media in New Zealand about the product in the knowledge that the story would soon break in China. This may have "forced" local Chinese officials to act earlier (under the assumption that these officials were responsible for the delay in informing the public).
4. Fonterra did exactly what it should have: waited until it had better information while consulting with government officials.

Appendix A: TIMELINE

December 1, 2005	■ Fonterra and Sanlu enter into a joint venture agreement
March 2008	■ Sanlu begins to receive reports of ill health of children being fed its formula (other sources suggest reports began in December of 2007)
June 2008	■ Fonterra CEO says tests performed on milk product in question showed no quality problems
August 2, 2008	■ Fonterra directors on Sanlu board informed that tests of milk powder indicated melamine contamination
August 6, 2008	■ Trade recall initiated
August 14, 2008	■ Fonterra "informally" informed New Zealand embassy in Beijing of the problem; this was done by making a comment to an official while at a social function
August 19, 2008	■ Fonterra calls the New Zealand embassy for advice
August 22, 2008	■ Fonterra meets with embassy personnel
August 31, 2008	■ New Zealand ambassador sends report on problem to Foreign Affairs and Trade Ministry
September 2, 2008	■ Foreign Affairs Minister Winston Peters informed of problem
September 5, 2008	■ Prime Minister Helen Clark is issued a formal report about the situation
September 8, 2008	■ New Zealand officials given directive by Clark to notify Chinese officials in Beijing
September 9, 2008	■ Chinese government officials notified
September 11, 2008	■ Public recall of milk powder begins in China ■ Sanlu ordered to stop production ■ 2,176 tons of milk powder seized from a Sanlu warehouse while 8,218 tons recalled
September 15, 2008	■ PM Clark defends Fonterra in public media ■ China arrests 19 and interrogates 78 ■ One baby reported as dead while another 432 are cited as being sick with kidney damage ■ Estimates quickly raised to two infants dead and 1,253 being made ill by the product
September 16, 2008	■ Li Changjiang, head of the General Administration for Quality Supervision, sends officials to three different provinces to inspect other dairies and baby milk food factories. It is promised that the results of these inspections will be released in two days. ■ Sanlu vice president issues a public apology. Blames suppliers for providing tainted milk.

(*continued*)

September 17, 2008	■ Melamine is found in the infant milk powder made at 22 separate Chinese dairy companies. Sales halted. ■ More dairies slated for inspection ■ Problem also found in frozen yogurt made by Inner Mongolia Yili Industrial Group ■ Looking for answers, parents go to Sanlu's headquarters in Shijiazhuang ■ Sanlu's chairwoman, Tian Wenhua, resigns ■ Two more arrested ■ China's biggest milk producer, the Mengniu Dairy Group, issues a recall of its baby formula
September 18, 2008	■ China's health minister announces that a third baby has died ■ 6,244 infants sickened; 154 have acute kidney failure
September 19, 2008	■ Arrests total 18. Six of those arrested were suspected of selling melamine while others were suspected of adding the contaminant to the milk
September 21, 2008	■ In Hong Kong, a small amount of melamine is found in Nestlé's Dairy Farm brand milk, a Chinese-made product. Nestlé is forced by Hong Kong's food-safety governmental department to recall the product. ■ A three-year-old Hong Kong toddler is the first child outside of China to be documented as suffering as a result of ingesting melamine-contaminated milk powder
September 22, 2008	■ Government announces 53,000 infants and children sickened by contaminated milk ■ Li Changjiang, minister of China's General Administration of Quality Supervision, Inspection, and Quarantine, is encouraged to resign, as is Wu Xianguo, the top official of Shijiazhuang city, head-quarters locality for Sanlu. Both do so. ■ A fourth child is reported to have died as a result of the tainted formula, but is not added to the official figure ■ Other countries start to ban all Chinese milk products ■ Melamine discovered in non-dairy products motivates other countries to broaden the scope of Chinese food product bans
September 23, 2008	■ PM Clark now criticizing Fonterra for the delay they allowed to pass before acting on the knowledge they had. Yet it wasn't a criticism directed at the lack of communication between Fonterra and the Chinese public; instead she is quoted as saying "There was no sign of a proper communications strategy to the New Zealand public." ■ Four children dead, 104 in serious conditions, 12,892 admitted to the hospital, 39,965 treated without being admitted, and 1,579 discharged from the hospital
September 30, 2008	■ Cadbury PLC, one of the world's largest confectioners, recalls 11 different chocolate candies made in its Beijing factory after they are found to contain melamine ■ Police raid more than 40 dairy farms in northern China (the biggest dairy production area), arrest 22 managers of pastures and other establishments involved in the production of milk and seize 485 pounds of melamine ■ Government announces that two suspects admitted producing or selling to milking stations a "protein powder" made from melamine
October 7, 2008	■ Six more people detained, bring the total to 32 ■ Government tests show recently produced batches of milk to be melamine-free

CASE 16-2

Empowering the People: Lessons from a New Trend in Political Marketing

"Traaaaaa . . . " is the noise that suddenly wakes up Mrs. Maria Jose. Today she can breathe, though. The sound that now belongs to a crusher-machine, a tool that builds the sewer system and paves her street, is similar to the one emitted by machine guns that so often woke her and her children up in this needy neighborhood of a Brazilian city. It is not that the violence disappeared, but it was at least pushed away to more remote places. Good asphalt allows the police to reach her area, frightening the drug dealers. It also provides accessibility to ambulances, the mailmen, the delivery of foods and goods and, most important, the bus that takes her to her job on days of heavy rain that transforms streets into an inaccessible mud. Fortunately, this is all history now. That kind of story started 20 years ago in another location, a city called Porto Alegre. The Porto Alegre case is, according to some, an example of a new trend in political marketing, in the sense that a political party used a participative process, which claimed to "democratize democracy," in order to augment their local bases or the amount of votes in that area.[1] It is currently one of the most internationally publicized and positive experiences of participatory democracy and citizenship development,[2] and has now spread out to hundreds of municipalities including the city of Mrs. Maria Jose.

After the end of the dictatorship in 1985, people from social movements formed the Workers Party (PT) to seriously take up the agenda of deepening democracy through a "popular administration" of government. Having won several municipal elections in 1989 or, in other words, assuming political power, the PT began a creative experiment of engaging a wide spectrum of people to formulate city's budgets.[3] Such experiments acquire special relevance because of their capacity to offer the basic conditions for the population to debate about the priorities of the public investment in the local level. The popular participation, therefore, is a result of the recognition of the limits of the representative democracy, at least in Brazil. The objective is to provide solutions to the emergent incapacity of dealing with social differences and inequalities in a world that promotes war and exclusion and in which racism and discrimination still exist.[4] This recognition redefines the concepts of democracy and, consequently, the roles performed by policymakers, public servants, and citizens, as well as the objectives of political marketing.

The Porto Alegre's participatory budget process began its efforts in poor barrios, or slums, at Porto Alegre city in Brazil. It had been nominated by the 1996 United Nations Summit on Human Settlements as an exemplary "urban innovation," among the best 40 practices around the world, standing out for demonstrating an efficient practice of democratic resource management. Later on, the World Bank considered the process a successful example of the partnership between government and civil society. The cultural context of Porto Alegre City known for hosting a progressive civil society led by intellectuals and labor unions and for mobilizing people to participate in public

Case prepared by Evandro Bocatto, Assistant Professor, Grant MacEwan University (School of Business), bocattoe@macewan .ca, and Eloisa Perez-de-Toledo, Assistant Professor, Grant MacEwan University (School of Business), pereze2@macewan.ca. Reprinted with permission.

459

life, including opposing authoritarianism,[5] set the basis to implement the experiment. In 2009, the trend finally arrived in the United States. An experiment in democracy was brewing in Chicago's 49th Ward. The neighborhood was vying to become the first community in the United States to use participatory budget, in which residents directly decide how to spend public money or to allocate municipal funds.

In short, participatory democracy is made real through the democratic decisions citizens make regarding part of the municipal budget. The participatory budget is thus an instrument for social justice, promotes the amplification of the public space, encourages citizenship participation, and is a guarantee of more transparency in the public administration. It makes true the old demands of the people historically represented in social movements. The lack of resources forces the prioritization of some demands instead of others. The decision about the demands to be prioritized is taken in ideal-speech situations (i.e., respectful, face-to-face dialogues).

The participatory budget process is quite simple. The city hall has an annual budget. The majority of it is dedicated to the payroll of public servants, teachers, nurses, physicians, and so on. Another part goes to the maintenance of the facilities like official buildings, schools, and hospitals. Then, what remains (several millions of dollars depending on the size of the city) will be allocated as prioritized by the citizens.

The participation cycle represents how the process is organized, the format of the decision-making, and the opportunities for popular mobilization and participation.[6] The initial phase is the election of neighborhood delegates like Mrs. Maria Jose. The city hall explains the process and announces the election date through different media vehicles like radio and TV; outdoor advertisements such as posters, banners, and bus billboards; and "sound cars" that travel all over the city. It also created the "Participatory Budget Newsletter" to communicate to citizens the schedules and status of the processes (demand analysis, visits to sites, decision-making behind the priorities and resultant deliberations), as well the stage of each construction project per neighborhood (i.e., planning, initial stage, close to conclusion, finished), and, of course, photos of inaugurations and celebrations. More recently, some cities included in their websites updated information about the participatory process and also the possibility of voting online. In case citizens do not have access to the Internet at home, they can just go to the nearest public school, access the city's webpage and vote.

Thousands of people vote for representatives for their own neighborhood. Then, these delegates proceed through the process, bearing in mind the first objective: to define the needs that must be prioritized due to restricted resources. At first they are divided by region, and meet to discuss the specific need of different neighborhoods within their region. The other part of the demand is related to specific themes. The thematic meetings of Mrs. Maria Jose's city regards the Municipal Council of Rural Development, Urban Development, Cultural Patrimony, Culture, Environment, Social Assistance, Child and Adolescent Rights, Handicapped and Persons with Special Needs, Defense of Women's Rights, Elder People, Narcotics, Education, Municipal Schools, Schools' Cooking, Social Control, Housing Funding, Support for the Urban Sub-habitation, Public Security, Energy, Development and Participation of the Black Community, and Students' Parents Associations. These councils represent some of the historical demands proposed by social movements. Delegates listen to the arguments but also visit the places where the work is being demanded. With the information gathered, the participatory budget's delegates get together in several meetings in which they decide the priorities and justify the rejected demands. The typical type of projects approved are related to infrastructure (e.g., paving; construction of homes, parks, sewer systems, hospitals, schools, and so on); social issues (e.g., educational and health equipment, housing, social assistance, culture); and, government management (e.g., training of public servants). The whole sequence restarts every year.

The institution legally responsible for presiding over the allocation of the municipal budget is the Municipal Council. The municipal councilors were in fact elected to perform this duty. However, the way that history evolved proved that in many cases they become self-interested, or, in other words, they were interested mainly in attending the demands of the lobbyists who represent powerful groups of interest. Corruption and influence peddling are byproducts of such interests. The same corruption has been demolishing the morality of this institution, leading a quasi-character-assassinated council to have no choice but to support the democratic experiment.

Yet if the process is so simple, why have only a few hundred cities, among thousands, implemented it? The answer to that is hidden in the underlines. The participatory process is possible only through a complete conceptual change from a representative to a participative and deliberative kind of democratic system. In the former, the citizen votes and "rests," expecting that his or her representative will act in accordance with his or her will, but, in the latter case, the neighborhood delegate lives in the area, is empowered by the neighbors, focuses on both the neighborhood and the social movements' wishes, and, due to the transparency of the process, he or she becomes corruption-free.

The re-conceptualization opens new possibilities for political marketing; what once was a matter of researching local demands and adapting, accordingly, the political discourse in order to increase the amount of votes, has become a complex and integrated process in which interested people discuss a huge amount of different demands from the beginning of the political campaign to the prioritization, implementation, and audit of their implementation. The political marketing and communication must be accurate, transparent, and reliable as the truth. As some experts point out, "This seems to reveal a circular sequence of ideals, acts and outcomes in which stories about the future became realities and realities became new stories."[7] The Porto Alegre's case "stands apart from many other similar attempts to institutionalize public governance in Brazil and Latin America. Its breadth and scope distinguish it from other efforts, past and present, that simply do not involve as many persons or, more commonly, do not devolve as much decision-making power to popular mandate. Its central institutional feature of utilizing neighborhood-based deliberation also sets it apart from participatory governance schemes that rely on organized civil society through sectorial interfaces, for example by calling upon teachers to consult on education policy."[8]

Participation and deliberation is also different from the traditional "consultation." In fact, the consultative model[9] of asking for opinions and ideas but still making the final decision seems to be one of the main reasons why participative processes fail. If the process of participation becomes indirect, it lacks representativeness because the population's and social movements' interests have an indirect access to the budget division through the different City Hall's departments according to bonds established in advance.[10] After finding out that policymakers only "consult" or that "bonds" are necessary, citizens lose confidence and drop the process.

Changes to the citizens' approach to democracy are remarkable. A delegate said: "The participatory budget is a good thing because it gives us this advantage. It is the voice of the people that is there, people feel respected. It is sensational! . . . We have attained it (sewer system and asphalt) because we were able to take many people to the assemblies, taking them on busses to vote, leading, talking to the people, persuading them to give an opportunity to look after our own." As a consequence, a change in the traditional leadership style of politicians is needed. A municipal council argued that: "The distinction between us and other types, the old type of policymakers, is that we are not afraid to talk to the people. Like I said, when the processes are open and participants are allowed to discuss, they confront us and we learn from their different opinions and perspectives. In a representative democracy, policymakers are elected and after that they disappear." The public servants react well to these changes, find new motivations, and develop other professional skills, as the following discourse of a city's technician reveals: "I had no previous knowledge about the process, but when we start to know and to live the process, the feedback is great. You engage [in] a 'body-to-body' relationship. The citizens are thankful to us. They do not see you as a technician or a public servant but as a friend, as someone who will clarify things. This is very good; it is day-by-day feedback of thankfulness . . . We work along with the community. There is our role as public servants but we are also members of the community. I expect to stay on this department because this is what I like to do. Everyday I learn more and in the next ten years I want to have all [these] capacities developed because I am only starting to learn." (She laughs.)

In summary, political marketing and communication publicize, support the process, and make known that "face-to-face discussions of conflicting perceptions permitted policymakers and public servants to reinterpret their definitions of efficiency and duty, local communities embraced a participant and collaborative attitude dignifying their role as citizens, and companies optimized costs and quality of the services provided."[11]

On this lovely and noisy morning, Mrs. Maria Jose smells two delicious things in the air: a sense of accomplishment along with the flavor of freshly brewed Brazilian coffee.

Discussion Questions

1. What is the general marketing role in the case of democratic participation?
2. Demonstrate the marketing mix (the Four 'P's: product, price, promotion and place) in the situation of the participatory budget.
3. Is the marketing oriented to shareholders or stakeholders?
4. If the publicity is in accordance to the practice, what should the slogans or news look like? Develop some communication slogans and briefings based on the case.
5. Marketing and ethics are sometimes controversial. How do you see the coherence between what is communicated and what is actually practiced?

Visit the Website

Porto Alegre city: http://en.wikipedia.org/wiki/Porto_Alegre

Chicago experiment: http://today.brown.edu/articles/2009/05/baiocchi

World Bank comments on the participatory budget: http://siteresources.worldbank .org/INTEMPOWERMENT/Resources/14657_Partic-Budg-Brazil-web.pdf

Participatory Budget in Canada: www.chs.ubc.ca/participatory/

Sources

1. Wagle, S., & Shah, P. (2003). Participatory approaches in budgeting and public expenditure management. *World Bank's Case Study of the Participation and Civic Engagement Group for the Action Learning Program on "Participatory Approaches at the Macro Level."* Retrieved from http://info.worldbank.org/etools/docs/library/205481/Porto%20Alegre_English.pdf.

2. Abers, R. N. (2000). *Inventing local democracy: Grassroots politics in Brazil.* Boulder (Colorado): Lynne Rienner Publishers, Inc.

3. *Ibid.* 1.

4. Ruiz-Sánchez, F. (2002). *Orçamento participativo: teoria e prática.* São Paulo: Cortez, p. 12.

5. Genro, T. and Souza, U. de (1999). *Orçamento participativo: A experiência de Porto Alegre.* São Paulo: Editora Fundação Perseu Abramo.

6. Ribeiro, A. C. T., & de Grazia, G. (2003). *Experiências de orçamento participativo no Brasil.* Petrópolis: Vozes, p. 43.

7. Bocatto, E. and Perez-de-Toledo, E. (2008). A Democratic Story: Collaboration in the Use of Public Budget. *International Journal of Sociology and Social Policy, 28*(1&2), p. 30.

8. Baiocchi, G. (2003). Participation, activism, and politics: The Porto Alegre experiment. In Archon Fung and Erik Olin Wright (Eds.), *Deepening Democracy: Institutional Innovations in Empowered Participatory Governance* (pp. 45–76). London: Verso.

9. Likert, R. (1967). *The human organization.* New York: McGraw-Hill.

10. Singer, P. (1996). *Um governo de esquerda para todos: Luiza Erundina na Prefeitura de São Paulo.* São Paulo: Brasiliense.

11. *Ibid.* 7, p. 29.

PART 5

Comprehensive Global Marketing Cases

CASE P1-1

International Marketing at Marks & Spencer: A UK Retailer

For years, M&S had used a simple marketing philosophy: produce high-quality products under a recognized brand name at affordable (but not low) prices and advertise through word-of-mouth. In the past several years, however, this marketing philosophy has come under attack as the company's competitive edge has eroded. The move to develop a marketing department was a departure from a long tradition of ignoring marketing in favor of a product-oriented corporate culture. The problem facing James Benfield: how to help M&S emerge from the slump and reposition itself as a fierce global competitor in the international marketplace?

Brief Company Background

Marks & Spencer of Britain (often referred to as Marks & Sparks by locals) is a general retailer that sells clothes, gifts, home furnishings, and foods under the St. Michael trademark in the UK, Europe, the Americas, and the Far East. The company also operates a financial services segment, which accounted for some 3 percent of the company's 1998 profits (Dow Jones Industrial, 1999).

Marks & Spencer (M&S) started as a stall in 1884 by Michael Marks in the Leads market using a L5 loan from a wholesaler. The company stressed value and low prices as a hallmark for development. By 1901, the company had acquired 35 outlets as well as a new partner, Tom Spencer. By 1949, all the company's stores carried mostly private label (St. Michael) products produced by British suppliers (De Nardi-Cole, 1998).

For many years the company's mission has been to offer consumers quality, value, and service. The company relied on five operating principles to achieve its mission:

1. Developing long-term relationships with suppliers
2. Providing value through a narrow merchandise selection at affordable prices
3. Supporting local (British) industry (De Nardi-Cole, 1998)
4. Promoting from within (*The Economist,* 1998)
5. Using a single brand name—St. Michael—for most of its products (*Financial Times,* 1999).

These operating tenets have gained M&S the support of British producers, consumers, and workers. The sixth-largest employer in British manufacturing, the textile industry, with over 354,000 workers, owes a large part of its existence to M&S (*The Economist,* 1999c). M&S has encouraged British textile manufacturers to keep factories at home, leading to tighter quality control and more flexibility in manufacturing and distribution (*The Economist,* 1999c). The British have responded with affection. A British writer described M&S as a "quintessential British institution, woven into the fabric of our national life, as firmly lodged in our psyches as furniture in the front room" (*Financial Times,* 1999, p. 10)

Current Business Situation

Using the business model described above, M&S had achieved impressive growth rates and market shares in many of its business segments. By 1994, the firm had

18 percent of the UK retail market, 33 percent of the women's undergarment market, and 20 percent of the men's suit market (De Nardi-Cole, 1998). The company has 40 percent of the nation's underwear market and 14 percent of the clothing market—the only retailer in Europe to have double-digit market share (*Financial Times,* 1999). M&S's food market share has been around 4.3 percent (M&S Press Releasesm, 1999). These impressive market shares have gained M&S its reputation as a leading retailer in the United Kingdom.

The euphoria, however, did not last, as M&S caught investors and business spectators off guard. In 1998, the company's stock price slipped 34 percent (*Business Week,* 1998). Pretax profits fell by as much as 41 percent (to $1.09 billion) and market share declined, for the first time in years, by almost 1 percent (*The Economist,* 1999a). In May 1999, the company reported full-year profits of L630 million, a 50 percent fall from 1997–1998 (*Financial Times,* 1999). Warburg Dillon Read, an investment bank, reduced its profit expectations for M&S by 10 percent for 1999–2000 (Dow Jones Industrial, 1999).

Overseas profits have declined from their 1996–1997 high of L100 million (*Financial Times,* 1999) to a loss of L15 million, before exceptional items, for fiscal year 1998. Sales measured in local currencies were down by 3 percent (M&S Press Releases, 1999).

Table 1 represents a financial snapshot of the company. It also compares key financial measures of M&S (Britain's leading retailer) with those of Walmart (the leading retailer in the United States).

The company blamed consumer confidence and a strong pound for the decline in sales and company value. A recent M&S Press Release (1999) states that the deterioration in 1998–1999 profits has been the result of (1) a shortfall in expected sales, (2) a slowdown in overseas markets, and (3) the purchase of Littlewoods stores for L90 million. A recessionary business environment in Europe and the Asian crisis has put a great strain on global profitability. At the same time, domestic and international competition has intensified both from specialty retailers and mega-merchandisers, such as Walmart.

But stockholders and business analysts have not been convinced that the company's problems were merely external. M&S stock has underperformed other British retailers by more than 25 percent. Some have blamed M&S management for dull merchandising, poor inventory control, and slow responses to competitive environmental conditions (*Business Week,* 1998). Industry commentators have criticized the color, size, and shape of their clothes, the poor retailing climate, the unglamorous stores, the overpriced products, and the lack of personal service (*Financial Times,* 1999).

TABLE 1 Financial Snapshot of Marks & Spencer		
	Marks & Spencer	**Walmart**
Market Capitalization	$18 billion	$204 billion
Revenue	$14 billion	$144 billion
Return on Assets	13 percent	10 percent
Return on Equity	18 percent	23 percent
Current Ratio	0.98	1.30
Price-Earnings Ratio	31	44
52 Week Price Trend	−31 percent	63 percent

* Compiled by the author from Dow Jones Industrial (1999) and Market Guide (1999). Retrieved June 1999.

Competition

The core values of M&S—quality, affordability, and service—came under the greatest attack not from critics, but from competitors. Retailers such as Top Shop, Kookai, Miss Selfridge, Jigsaw, Oasis, Warehouse, and Gap offer more fashionable designs and trendier labels. Other retailers, such as Next, Debenhams, and BhS, offer better values. Food chains, such as Tesco, Waitrose, and Sainsbury's, have moved more fully into prepared foods (*Financial Times,* 1999). M&S is being challenged in every single business segment. By its own admission, M&S has not changed quickly enough to react to accelerating competition, which has resulted in an unacceptable fall in profitability and market share (M&S Press Releases, 1999).

Marketing at Marks & Spencer

Products

M&S products can be divided into three lines of business: (1) general merchandise, (2) foods, and (3) financial services. General merchandise includes clothing, undergarments, handbags, footwear, goods for the home, children's toys, books, and cosmetics.

The food business carries a wide range of prepared foods, perishables, ethnic foods, meats, and beverages, both alcoholic and not. Among the eclectic selection of foods are chocolate-covered ginger biscuits, salmon *en croute*, chicken tikka sandwiches, and mushroom risotto (*Financial Times,* 1999). Perhaps an example of the bridge M&S is building from its traditional image of itself as retailer to the upper middle classes, the food segment's upscale offerings will soon extend even further. The company is currently changing its food offerings with new bistro style meals and introducing juice and coffee bars in some stores (*Marketing,* 1999).

Finally, the company also sells financial services including secured store credit cards, personal loans, personal equity plans, unit trusts, and life insurance. M&S created a core of business for its own credit cards by refusing to honor other widely held cards, such as MasterCard, Visa, Discover, or American Express. As an inducement, and to offset any negative effects of this policy, customers who deposit money into their M&S credit card accounts receive up to 20 times the purchasing power of their deposits. For example, with a deposit of $100, the customer gets a line of credit of $2,000 (De Nardi-Cole, 1998). The company has also diversified into life assurances and group pension contracts (M&S Press Releases, 1999). While the financial services segment is relatively small (about 3 percent of profits), it is the fastest-growing segment of M&S's operations. Profits over 1998 have increased 24 percent to £111 million, while the number of card accounts has increased to 5.2 million (M&S Press Release, 1999).

Throughout its history, M&S has increasingly relied upon the St. Michael brand name to deliver its image to consumers. Since M&S's expertise has traditionally been its ability to consistently deliver high quality products, the St. Michael tag has become synonymous with that expertise, and has allowed M&S to target all sectors of the demographic market—from children to middle-class housewives. This overreliance upon one (house) brand, however, has not gone unchallenged in the wake of the plunge in value after 1997. A commentator in *The Financial Times* (1999) suggested that the company follow the example of Debenhams (a competing retailer) and use sub-brands to target specific segments of its market.

Price

Marks & Spencer has followed a value-price strategy from its inception, starting with Michael Marks, who put all his products for a penny on one side of the store with a sign saying "Don't ask the price, it's a penny." Since M&S has historically concentrated on middle-class customers, it has never reevaluated its value-pricing strategy. Although most of its suppliers have been from Britain, which has higher textile manufacturing costs than some developing nations, M&S was able to maintain its value by developing strong economic bonds with suppliers. Through its economies of scale in buying, M&S has been able to require manufacturers to adhere to strict quality standards and to bargain lower prices for its customers (De Nardi-Cole, 1998).

Due to the recent strength of the pound sterling, this high proportion of homegrown products has led to a substantially lower profit margin over the last several years. Still, M&S has held the line on prices even while its margins have decreased, remaining moderately priced relative to its European competitors.

In anticipation of the Euro conversion, the company features prices both in local currency and Euros in its European stores. It also has limited conversion tables by the cashiers. As it looks to the future, the conceptual change evident in Euro-Pound unit pricing may well herald an increasingly willingness to become international in its suppliers as well as its clientele.

Place

M&S stores come in two basic formats: a general merchandise store, with its basement dedicated to food, or a store that offers food only. The average size of the store ranges from 35,000 to 40,000 square feet (3,252 to 3,716 square meters), with a minimum of 100,000 square feet (9,290 square meters) for remote locations. In recent years the firm has been aggressively increasing the square-footage of its stores (M&S Annual Report, 1998).

M&S tries to locate its stores on the main streets of major cities, claiming that it seeks "to build critical mass around capital cities or across important conurbation, such as the Rhine-Ruhr area in Germany" (M&S Annual Report, 1998, p. 1). Paris, the most significant market in Europe, for example, hosts 20 percent of the country's population and 10 out of the 20 M&S stores in the country (M&S Annual Report, 1998). The company owns a very valuable global portfolio of property, with footholds in prime cities and districts across the world (*The Financial Times,* 1999). Competition for prime space, however, has made it necessary to locate in more remote locations.

In 1994, M&S started to aggressively focus on building distribution networks to supply its growing global operations (De Nardi-Cole, 1998). The focal point of this network, however, has remained in the United Kingdom.

Promotion

M&S has tended to avoid media advertising in favor of the powerful, cost-effective traditional tendencies of word-of-mouth and social cachet. As we observed when looking at product diversity, the ubiquity of the St. Michael's label has allowed M&S to connect to its customer base over a broad segment of products. The implied quality of the brand has served the firm well, promoting consumption while spurring the cycles of word-of-mouth and copycat purchasing. Yet the success of the St. Michael brand has led to a blinkered vision of the benefits to be gained from the marketing support popular brand names generate. As in the case of its supply chain, an overreliance on one aspect has tended to create a *cul de sac* for the firm.

In the past, the company used advertising only in rare cases, such as when M&S was introducing a new product or retail format or when brand name recognition was low, as in the case of its store introduction in Paris (De Nardi-Cole, 1998). The media budget was L4.7 million, compared to the L18.8 million of 10 other leading retailers (Jardin, 1999b). After a succession of disappointing financial statements, the company has significantly increased its advertising budget to approximately L20 million (Jardin, 1999a). The company has already invited advertising agencies to pitch and is planning its second-ever television campaign, geared toward a focus on M&S products (*Marketing, 1999*).

Internationalization of Marks & Spencer

M&S experimental involvement with internationalization began in the 1940s. Unlike most service firms, however, the company began exporting its St. Michael brands overseas as a way to test the waters (the company did not and does not own manufacturers; it merely brands their merchandise using the St. Michael private label). Briggs (1992) estimated that in 1955 the company was exporting about $1,146,000 worth of merchandise.

The early internationalization of the company was mostly due to domestic factors. Internally, the company felt that it had saturated the domestic market and that expansion would have to come from overseas. Externally, some Labour Party members were suggesting nationalizing the leading domestic retailers (De Nardi-Cole, 1998). Internationalization was seen as a tool of diversification.

Out of the export business, some international franchising relationships were formed. Importers of the St. Michael brand, familiar with the success of the brand in their countries, also bought the business format (including store layout and operating style) from M&S. By the early 1990s, St. Michael franchises were operating in 14 economies including those with ties to the Commonwealth, such as Gibraltar, Bermuda, Israel, and Philippines (Whitehead, 1991). Franchising allowed the company to achieve a global presence with minimal economic and political risks. As M&S' familiarity with internationalization grew, more direct modes of entry, such as acquisitions and joint ventures, were being used. By 1996, the company had 645 outlets worldwide, most of which (58 percent) were in the UK, Europe, and Canada (De Nardi-Cole, 1998).

Modes of Entry

The internationalization of M&S resembles the theoretical explanations of service firm internationalization (Alon, 1999; McIntyre & Huszagh, 1995). These theories suggest that service firms look to international expansion as they gain experience, and experience a subsequent willingness to commit more company resources and take additional risks. Retailers will tend to use relatively less risky modes of entry, such as exporting and franchising, in markets where market and political risk are high. Retailers will tend to share ownership where sole ownership is prohibited or restricted. In markets with significant per capita purchasing power, large populations and developed infrastructures—such as in the United States and European—retailers are more willing to enter through high-control, high-risk modes of entry, such as sole ownership and acquisition.

M&S utilizes various modes of entry around the world. The company believes in opening its own stores and expanding through acquisitions in major economies. On the other hand, M&S has expanded through franchise agreements into countries where a partner's local expertise is viewed as beneficial (M&S Annual Report, 1998). The company owns stores in Belgium, Canada, France, Germany, Hong Kong, Ireland, Spain, and Netherlands; there are franchises in countries such as the Bahamas, Bermuda, Canary Islands, Cyprus, the Czech Republic, Gibraltar, and Israel (De Nardi-Cole, 1998). Whitehead (1991) proposed that the company used franchising in countries that had relatively small population sizes or low per capita incomes, but were sufficiently promising as markets to warrant a small number of stores.

When forming international alliances, M&S has often preferred an experienced retailer with significant market share. In 1990, M&S went into its first joint venture with Cortefiel, one of Spain's leading retailers. A joint venture was initially used in Spain because it was felt that the market knowledge and power of an existing retailer would help mitigate the problems of cultural distance and of the sometimes adverse political climate (De Nardi-Cole, 1998). In Australia, M&S chose a partner who was an experienced local clothing retailer. In China, the company is looking for a likely candidate as the industrial structure of the economy develops (M&S Annual Report, 1998).

Maureen Whitehead (1991) was one of the first researchers to examine international franchising at M&S. Whitehead's research revealed that M&S used a franchise format that was a hybrid between first-trademark franchising and business-format franchising. Trade name franchising is based on the supply of merchandise and trade marks, such as gas service stations and automobile dealerships, while business format franchising relies on the transfer of a formalized operating style. M&S's franchisees need to show short and medium-horizon business plans and demonstrate a minimum level of turnover. The franchisee pays through merchandise purchases and a percentage of inventory turnover. Franchisees can pick selectively from the M&S inventory, instead of being forced to carry the full range of products available through the British-owned stores.

Regional Analysis of M&S Internationalization

A truly global firm should have operations in all three regional economic blocks. Since 1975, M&S has increasingly become a global retailer, with a presence in each of the major trading blocks: the Americas, Europe, and the Far East. Table 2 shows current operating results and comparisons of the three regions.

The Americas The first major round of acquisitions for M&S occurred in 1973 with the purchases of Canadian People's Department Stores (a budget retailer), DiAllaird's (an older women's store), and Walker's store (modeled after British M&S's own format). Canada was seen by M&S's executives to be a low-risk investment because of its high per capita incomes, solid infrastructure, large middle class, low political risk, and the predominance of English as both linguistic and cultural currency. Since they perceived little cultural distance, they transferred their business formula almost unchanged from the United Kingdom to Canada. They quickly found that even Canada required some modifications. The presumption that M&S would flourish without modifying itself to fit the cultural environment was one that would plague the firm.

After initially disappointing sales after entrance into the market, the Canadian stores were customized to suit local needs by increasing the amount of Canadian

TABLE 2 Operating Results and Regional Comparisons			
	The Americas	**Europe***	**Far East**
Turnover	606	538	128
Operating Profits	17	33	18
Number of Stores	43	53	10
(Franchised)	(5)**	(15)	(33)

Source: M&S Annual Report 1998.

* Includes some Middle Eastern states.

** Not including Brooks Brothers (119) or Kings Supermarkets (22).

merchandise, enlarging food departments, restructuring inner city stores, and opening suburban stores—re-jigging that was generally new to the M&S experience. The changes were made too slowly and, by 1988, the stores had lost about $7 million. Thereafter, the D'Allaird's stores were closed to cut costs and to focus the corporate gaze on more profitable operations (De Nardi-Cole, 1998). In May 1999, M&S announced that it would be closing all 38 M&S stores in Canada by September 1999 (Dow Jones Industrial, 1999). The company has decided that Canada no longer fits the strategic future, several attempts to return it to profit having failed. The cost of withdrawal is estimated at L25 million (M&S Press Releases, 1999).

M&S entered the United States in 1988 using a similar strategy to the Canadian one, through acquisitions. It bought Brooks Brothers (a department store, nicknamed Brooks Bros.) to market its clothes and Kings Supermarkets to sell its food line. Unlike M&S, which bought its supplies, these companies owned manufacturing facilities. Brooks Brothers and Kings Supermarkets are similar in format to M&S two-store formats.

After the acquisition, Brooks Brothers (M&S's largest operation in the Americas) expanded its sports selection, widened its product base, and enlarged its customer base. It opened a few locations in malls targeting a younger market. The company used some products from the Brooks Brothers clothing line to sell in its UK and European stores. M&S did not change the names of the United States chains, probably unwilling to toy with their loyal customer bases, nor did it significantly change the product offerings.

The purchase of Brooks Brothers contributed to continuing innovation in the merchandise mix, offered M&S an opportunity to compete in the largest economy in the world, and gave M&S a foothold in the Far East. While some believed that the purchase of Brooks Brothers was overpriced (30 times 1987 profits), it provided M&S with 21 joint venture stores with Daido Worsted Mills in Japan, three United States-based factories, a charge card business, and a direct marketing operation (De Nardi-Cole, 1998).

For the year ending 1998, Brooks Brothers increased its number of stores by 7 (to 119), increased its market share of the United States men's clothing market, improved direct marketing, and invested in a new warehouse management system to increase service efficiency. The chain expects to become more contemporary, broaden its market appeal (particularly to working women), and modernize its brand image (M&S Annual Report, 1998).

Kings Supermarkets have also shown satisfactory results; two new stores were added in New Jersey, and new stores are being pioneered in Florham Park, located in one of New York City's outer boroughs. Five new Kings Supermarkets are expected to open in 1999 (M&S Annual Report, 1998).

Europe

M&S entered the European market in 1975, less than two years after the soon-to-be disastrous Canadian acquisitions. France was chosen as the gateway country, and Paris the gateway city, to the rest of Europe (M&S Annual Report, 1998). Unlike Canada, it was understood that a great deal of market research would be needed if they were to thrive in the contentious Gallic market. The company decided to adapt the store to French reality by offering snugger fits to its clothing, a wide selection of French wines, and fewer British imports. Due to a lack of brand name recognition, the company also relied on advertising to spark interest in the stores (De Nardi-Cole, 1998). From there, M&S expanded to Belgium (1975), Spain (1990), Germany (1996), and recently to smaller economies, including Greece, Hungary, Portugal, and the Czech Republic.

The European report of M&S includes Eastern and Western Europe and some states in the Middle East. In Europe, the company owns 37 stores (in France, Belgium, Holland, Spain, Germany, and Ireland) and franchises 53 stores across the rest of Europe and the Middle East. M&S plans to open new stores in Spain, Belgium, Holland, and Ireland, develop new franchises in Turkey, Dubai, and Poland, and increase square footage in the Czech Republic, Greece, and Cyprus. The company hopes to have 60 stores in Continental Europe by year 2000 (*Business Week,* 1998). It is seeking to increase customization to local national tastes by adding brand names to the already successful St. Michael brand (M&S Annual Report, 1998). Still, about 80 percent of the stock sold in continental Europe is the same as the UK home market, while the other 20 percent reflects differences in culture, size, climate, and local preferences (Glew, 1994).

In Europe, sales from core stores and recently expanded stores were below expectations for 1998–1999, particularly in the major economies of France, Germany, and Spain. Profit margins have deteriorated as the company attempted to maintain good value (M&S Press Releases, 1999). Sales in the Middle East, on the other hand, were particularly strong, especially in a new operation in Kuwait (M&S Press Releases, 1999). To increase the profitability of European operations, the company (1) closed unprofitable stores (in Zaragosa and Parinor), (2) acquired full control of the Spanish business, (3) gave more control to local managers, and (4) developed a European buying department to meet local demand (M&S Press Releases, 1999).

Far East

The entry into the Far East was twofold. M&S's first exposure to business in the Far East occurred indirectly through the purchase of Brooks Brothers (1988), which co-owned affiliates in Japan. Building upon Brooks Brothers' 19+ years of brand-exposure trading experience with Japan, M&S opened two new franchises in the Hong Kong market in 1998. M&S believes that Asia will be a major market for Brooks Brothers because of the region's receptiveness to United States culture and because so much of the foreign value system (in terms of one's attempt to buy the culture by buying the clothing, for example) is bound up in the prestige factor of the commodities presented (M&S Annual Report, 1998). However, Brooks Brothers Japan has been adversely affected by recent recessionary conditions in the economy (M&S Press Releases, 1999).

Using the M&S brand name has allowed the firm its second market penetration. By keying on the brand name perception of its high(er) quality Western-style items, those customers prone to buying European styles have created the potential future base for internationalization at the store level. The stores that M&S opened in Hong Kong, which were supplied through the British home base, are the result of this strategy. All of the wholly owned stores in the Far East are in Hong Kong; the 33 other outlets are franchised across six other nations in the region. In recent years, the company has expanded to suburban areas of Hong Kong, a move it believes will help it penetrate the Chinese market (M&S Annual Report, 1998). The company already has a resident office in Shanghai whose purpose is to evaluate the market and to spark interest in a joint venture there (De Nardi-Cole, 1998). During the last couple of years, the company has expanded its presence in Thailand, the Philippines, Indonesia, Korea, and Australia (M&S Annual Report, 1998).

The 1997 Asian crisis had a dramatic effect on all retail sales in the region, and M&S stores were not exempt. Both franchised and non-franchised outlets were adversely affected by the crisis. Despite the slowdown, the company was able to increase the number of owned and franchised stores by nine to 43. The company's expansion and the adverse conditions created by the Asian crisis have hampered sales and profitability in Asia (M&S Annual Report, 1998). Therefore, no new development is planned in the near future (M&S Press Releases, 1999). The company plans to source locally and buy temporarily depressed properties. Hong Kong will remain a strategic base, despite sales being L20 million below expectations for 1998–1999 (M&S Press Releases, 1999).

Problems Identified by Industry Observers

According to popular magazines such as *Business Week* and *The Economist*, M&S's international marketing challenges fall into three broad categories: (1) overreliance on the British market, (2) top management's internal orientation, and (3) corporate culture.

Overreliance on British Market

M&S has relied too much on the British market both for its customers and its suppliers. This overreliance on the domestic market exposed the company to unsystematic risk. The British market constitutes 85 percent of sales and 94 percent of profits. The reduction in profits of 23 percent in 289 stores in Britain is largely what led to the depressed stock prices (*Business Week,* 1998).

M&S's insistence on buying its clothes from domestic manufacturers—a policy that gained it support from its citizenry, but not necessarily its customers—has been problematic. Approximately 65 percent of all products sold in M&S stores were manufactured in the UK (M&S Press Releases, 1999). This dependence on British suppliers has limited the scope of its product offerings and innovations, led to deterioration in its competitive position vis-à-vis retailers that import cheaper garments from abroad, and made its exported products expensive in relation to world markets (*The Economist,* 1998).

The insistence on buying British produced goods has also been unhealthy to M&S's suppliers. In response to the M&S slowdown of the late 1990s, suppliers had to cut almost 2,300 jobs. The company recently broke with tradition and has started to encourage suppliers to manufacture overseas (*The Economist,* 1999c). The need to lower global production and distribution costs is a key problem the company requiring attention.

Ironically, given the difficulties it has occasionally encountered overseas, M&S needs to internationalize even more than it has to further diversify the risk of a downturn in any one economy. *Business Week* (1998) recently suggested that M&S reduce its dependence on the local British market and continue its international expansion. However, additional international expansion would require a great resource commitment, a difficult task during hard economic times. Furthermore, as developed countries become saturated and highly competitive, retailers will need to expand to increasingly risky markets, including countries where substantial cultural, economic and political differences exist. Two core obstacles, requiring much forethought but crucial to success in internationalization, are the choice of a host country and the mode of entry decision.

Top Management's Internal Orientation

The top management and board of governors have been inward looking for too long (*The Economist,* 1998). The board is made up of no fewer than 16 executives—most of whom are career M&S employees—and six non-executives, including one each from the two co-founding families. A recent article in *The Economist* (1998, p. 68) argued, "With M&S now selling financial services and going overseas, the narrowness of experience of M&S's senior managers and board directors is a weakness."

The narrowness of top management is also reflected in the recent choice of a chief executive to replace Richard Greenbury. Keith Oates, who joined M&S in 1984 as finance director, having built a career with blue-chip companies, lost the top job to Salsbury, who joined the company in 1970 fresh out of London School of Economics (Gwyther, 1999).

The new marketing director, James Benfield, himself a 28-year M&S veteran, originally joined M&S as a graduate trainee (Jardin, 1999a). Despite his stated desire for new marketing input, his four newly appointed managers for each store type are also M&S employees (Buxton, 1999). M&S resembles Sears in that it has been inward looking for too long. It is not unreasonable to see a connection between corporate culture and the depressed stock prices of both companies (Pitcher, 1999).

The international orientation of top management at any given firm will tend to be function of four variables: cultural distance, levels of education, proficiency in foreign languages, and international experiences. These factors will inevitably influence the decision-making matrices of management, and an awareness of these variables has been shown to be an important internal factor of internationalization (Eroglu, 1992). M&S's top management personnel and board of directors are mostly white, British-born, British-educated males who have spent the majority of their careers at M&S, surrounded by the like-minded.

Corporate Culture

M&S corporate culture has always been of the top-down type. Decision making was (and is) centralized, and the company ruled from the top through command and control. Prices, products, colors, and even designs had to be approved at the top. "Those who were close to the customer weren't listened to or encouraged to be bold and take risks" (*Financial Times,* 1999, p. 8). While the company used famous designers, such as Paul Smith, Betty Jackson, and Ghost, it never used their names in promotions nor did it give them much latitude in designing new fashions (*Financial Times,* 1999).

Perhaps the biggest pitfall of M&S has been its attitude that "we know best" (*Financial Times,* 1999). This attitude has prevailed in many of its business practices. For example, the company accepted only M&S credit cards in its British stores, used very limited advertising, and insisted on buying British textiles. M&S's old business model does not fit the new realities of global marketplace. Competitors struggle for market share by offering increasingly better quality, nicer service, lower prices, and more pleasant shopping experiences. The result is a stepladder of increasing customer expectations that are more difficult to satisfy. Companies that cannot keep up with the pace of change will eventually perish. M&S's famous quality and service have not kept pace with the modern notions of these terms (*Financial Times,* 1999).

References

Alon, Ilan. (1999). International franchising modes of entry. In John Stanworth and David Purdy (Eds.), *Franchising beyond the millennium: Learning lessons from the past*. Society of Franchising 13th Annual Conference.

Angst in their pants [Weekend Financial Times]. (1999, June). *Financial Times* (37), 7–10.

Briggs, A. (1992). St. Michael Marks & Spencer PLC. In A. Hast (Ed.), *International directory of company histories* (pp. 124–126). St. James Press.

Business: Unraveling. (1999c, January 2). *The Economist,* 57–58.

Buxton, P. (1999). M&S chief rejigs retail operation. *Marketing Week, 22*(12), 6.

De Nardi-Cole, S. M. (1998). Marks & Spencer. In Brenda Sternquist (Ed.), *International retailing* (pp. 159–166). New York: Fairchild Publications.

Dress sense. (1999a, May 22). *The Economist,* 7.

Executive Report, Marks & Spencer PLC. (1999). *Dow Jones Industrial.* Retrieved from http:mrstg1s.djnr.com/cgi-bin/DJIntera..._binding=&get_name=null&searchText=U.MAR.

Eroglu, S. (1992). The internationalization process of franchise systems: A conceptual model. *International Marketing Review, 9*(5), 19–30.

Glew J. (1994, Spring). Meeting the European challenge (Marks & Spencer). *European Superstore Decisions*, 46–49.

Gwyther, M. (1999, April). King Richard: A tragedy in three acts. *Management Today*, 78–85.

Heller, R. (1999, February). No excuse for room at the top. *Management Today*, 23.

Jardin, A. (1999a, April 22). St. Michael's evangelist. *Marketing*, 25–28.

Jardin, A. (1999b, January 28). Time for M&S to follow Tesco. *Marketing*, 17–21.

Marks & Sparks isn't throwing off any. (1998, November 16). *Business Week,* 64.

M&S doubles ad budget in L20m branding review. (1999, March 25). *Marketing*, 9.

M&S (Marks & Spencer) Press Releases. (1999). Retrieved from www.marks-and-spencer.co.uk/corporate/press-releases/19990518.002.html.

M&S (Marks & Spencer) Annual Report. (1998). Retrieved from www.marks-and-spencer.co.uk...ate/annual-report/Europe(Far-East or America)/main.html.

McIntyre, F. S., & Huszagh, S. M. (1995). Internationalization of franchising systems. *Journal of International Marketing, 3*(4), 39–56.

Pitcher, G. (1999, January 21). Reality forces UK retail giants to check out their strategic options. *Marketing Week*, 21–24.

Poor Marks. (1998, November 21). *The Economist,* 68.

Taking over. (1999b, May 15). *The Economist,* 5.

Wal-Mart Stores, Inc. (1999, June 5). *Market Guide*, 1–15.

Whitehead, M. (1991). International franchising—Marks & Spencer: A case study. *International Journal of Retail & Distribution Management, 19*(2), 10–12.

CASE P1-2

MacEwan Goes Global: Internationalization at a Canadian School of Business

Richard Ivey School of Business
The University of Western Ontario

Gazing out of the window one cold December afternoon in 2008, Elsie Elford, LLB, the dean of the School of Business at Grant MacEwan College in Alberta, Canada, thought about the progress the college had made and how it had moved from being a community college to becoming a full-fledged comprehensive college with two-year programming and four-year baccalaureate degrees. The School of Business needed to support the needs of the business community, which were increasingly global. The school's mission and programs had also become increasingly international. What business students needed, she thought, was a global education, particularly one that focused on the emerging markets of Asia with which Canada enjoyed a growth in trade and investment.

Elford had been teaching at MacEwan for 17 years and knew firsthand the strength of the school's offerings and its people. During her tenure at MacEwan School of Business, Elford had focused on providing real world experiences for students, upgrading faculty expertise and experience through professional development, and working with industry leaders and professional associations to develop curricula to meet students' needs.

But how could a school of business already burdened by the growing needs of transitioning to degree-granting also satisfy the need for more globalized education? The secret, she thought, might be to leverage the diverse faculty and student body to provide new experiences for all students, particularly in larger emerging markets such as China, India or Brazil. Globalization for a school of business is not easy because of the many stakeholders involved: government ministries, students, parents, faculty, community and businesses to mention a few.

From a leadership point of view, Elford considered how to measure globalization; how to find the appropriate level of globalization; how to determine what competencies the School of Business should develop that would differentiate it from others in its category; and how to equip students with a global perspective, and an international, intercultural mindset.

Additionally, should the School of Business target a certain part of the world in developing international competencies in its graduates? If so, which parts and in what ways?

Ilan Alon, Mike Henry and Kimberley Howard wrote this case solely to provide material for class discussion. The authors do not intend to illustrate either effective or ineffective handling of a managerial situation. The authors may have disguised certain names and other identifying information to protect confidentiality.

Geographical Context: Alberta, Canada

Canada had the world's second-largest proven crude oil reserves (176 billion barrels), after Saudi Arabia, but less than three per cent of its established reserves had been developed. Alberta produced 70 per cent of Canada's crude oil and 80 per cent of its natural gas. Crude petroleum, gas and gas liquids, and petrochemicals made up most of Alberta's export value (about $62 billion of the total $89 billion).[1]

Alberta had approximately 3.5 million inhabitants and its landmass covered an area of about 660,000 square kilometers (an area about 1.75 times larger than the size of Japan). Alberta's population was among the youngest in Canada, with a median age of 35.5. Alberta's population density was comparatively low. In comparison, Taiwan was one-twentieth the size of Alberta, but had seven times the population.

Alberta was international. In 2007, one in seven Albertans was born outside Canada and one in 10 was from a visible minority.[2] Ethnic Canadians (2007) made up only 28 per cent of the population, followed by English, German, Scottish, Irish and French. Ukrainians accounted for almost 10 per cent of the population, followed by Dutch, Aboriginal, Polish and Norwegian. Chinese made up almost four per cent of the population. Most self-identifying Chinese in 2007 had emigrated from Hong Kong and the Guangzhou region of China. There were more Russians than Americans, with Russians accounting for about two per cent of the population. When coupled with the Ukrainian population, the Russian-speaking population exceeded 12 per cent.[3]

China (including Hong Kong) was Alberta's number two trading partner. In 2007, Albertan exports to Hong Kong alone accounted for more than C$1,090 million. In that same year, Japan was Alberta's number three trading partner, receiving about 14 per cent of Alberta's exports. South Korea was Alberta's number four export market, with demand for chemical wood pulp, ethylene glycol and wheat as the top export commodities. Alberta also had strong relations with Taiwan, with more than $160 million in exports and more than 32,000 tourists per year from Taiwan.[4]

In sum, Alberta was a high-growth province and Edmonton, the capital, where Grant MacEwan College was located, was a boom town. Unemployment was low; economic growth was high. The strong economy was a mixed blessing: on the one hand, a strong job market provided opportunities for graduates to plug into the business community and fill a void for talent, but, on the other hand, inflation was creeping in and colleges were competing with businesses for young talent. Put another way, the opportunity cost of going to college was high.

Education in Edmonton, Alberta

Alberta was a resource-rich province of Canada. The province was known for its wealth of oil and gas reserves and had a budget surplus and a provincial sovereign wealth fund. Education was one of Alberta's priorities. In its 2008–2009 budget, the government dedicated more than $6 billion to its K-12 education system. Fifteen per cent of total government revenue was allocated for primary and secondary education, making it the second largest government investment.[5]

Education was a provincial responsibility in Canada. Each province and territory funded and operated its own educational system as well as administered the educational framework for the region. A pan-Canadian forum established in 1967

1. Business Ambassador's Guide to Alberta, Canada, International Office and Trade, 2007.

2. Ibid.

3. Ibid.

4. Ibid.

5. Alberta Education Fact Sheet, www.education.alberta.ca/students/internationaleducation.apx, accessed Nov. 1, 2008.

coordinated educational initiatives at the national level through the Council of Ministers of Education Canada (CMEC).[6] The national (federal) government was the largest provider of research funds to the post-secondary system.

Canadian education was strong in comparison to OECD members: Canada was a net host of international students and the Albertan system, in particular, was among the best-performing. According to the 2004 students' achievement indicators program results, Albertan students aged 13 to 16 ranked highest in science. Albertan 15-year-olds ranked highest in 2003 in reading (tied with Finland), second in mathematics (behind Hong Kong) and fourth in science and problem-solving.[7]

The strengths of the Canadian school system stemmed from adequate funding for educational improvement, and choice for parents from a plethora of subsidized schools available to them: religious schools, Francophone schools, charter schools, private schools, virtual schools, alternative programs, distance learning and blended programs. Parents could choose from schools which specialized in music or hockey. Examples of multilingual schools included Chinese, Russian, Ukrainian, Spanish, French and Hebrew.

The Albertan primary education system focused on health, math, science, technology and, of course, resource-seeking industry studies. The development of a career-based workforce was stressed.

The Ministry of Advanced Education and Technology was the governing body responsible for monitoring approved degree programs through a process of peer reviews, accreditation and reaccreditation.[8] It ensured, among other things, that degree programs had proper faculty and staff, academic policies, resource capacity, credential recognition, program delivery, program content, program structure, program evaluation, and regulation and accreditation.

Grant MacEwan College

Established in 1971, Grant MacEwan College[9] was the largest college in Alberta and the fastest growing college in western Canada emphasizing liberal arts, health and nursing, fine arts and business programs in Edmonton. MacEwan served approximately 40,000 credit and non-credit students per year. Full load equivalent (FLE) students in academic year 2001–2002 totaled 8,740 for the College and 2,204 for the School of Business. The full load equivalent projections were 10,968 for the College and 2,621 for the School of Business for 2009–2010. The mission of Grant MacEwan College was to "inspire and enable individuals to succeed in life through career and university studies."

The College offered:

1. 5 Bachelor Degrees
2. 10 University Transfer Programs
3. 3 Applied Bachelor Degrees
4. More than 60 Diploma and Certificate Programs
5. Preparation for University and College
6. Professional and Personal Development Courses and Workshops

6. See: www.cmec.ca/index.en.html.

7. Alberta Education Fact Sheet, www.education.alberta.ca/students/internationaleducation.apx, Nov. 1, 2008.

8. See: www.caqc.gov.ab.ca.

9. Grant MacEwan College was named after Dr. J. W. Grant MacEwan, former lieutenant governor of Alberta, MLA for Alberta, mayor of Calgary, author, historian, environmentalist and educator.

7. Corporate Training
8. Alberta College Conservatory of Music

The College provided more than 70 full-time programs across its four campuses:

1. Centre for the Arts and Communications
2. Faculty of Arts and Science
3. Faculty of Health and Community Studies
4. School of Business

In 2005, Grant MacEwan College became the first college in Alberta to grant baccalaureate degrees. The move toward four-year baccalaureate degrees enabled the College to recruit a more diversified portfolio of Ph.Ds,[10] increase the resources available for scholarly activity and research, and provide more degree completion opportunities for students.

Alberta was geographically large, with its two main urban centers (Edmonton and Calgary) housing more than two-thirds of the population, leaving the remaining third spread over the rest of the province. In response to this reality, MacEwan had cooperated with other colleges on some select courses and programs it had developed for the online market. In 2002, the province of Alberta created a consortium of 15 colleges and technical institutes to develop and offer online learning opportunities for students. This consortium was called ECampus Alberta. If a member of the consortium developed a course, other members agreed to refrain from developing the same course. Course transfer credit between these institutions was well-articulated. ECampus "enables students from across the province to choose from more than 30 provincially accredited online certificate, online diploma and applied degree programs and 400 online courses offered by 15 Alberta colleges and technical institutes."[11]

Online course partners included Bow Valley College, Lakeland College, Medicine Hat College, Northern Alberta Institute of Technology, Northern Lakes College, Portage College and Southern Alberta Institute of Technology. Of the 7,128 students enrolled online, Grant MacEwan had about 1,364 in 2007–2008.

Internationalization at Grant MacEwan College

MacEwan School of Business was committed to internationalization through the development of knowledge, skills and attitudes for a global citizenry living and working effectively in an interconnected world. At the core of the College's internationalization efforts was the curriculum, around which professional development, international students, study abroad, exchange programs, community linkages, international development education, offshore education and institutional linkages existed. (See Exhibit 1.)

Though not all current international programs at the College were equally active, a few partnerships had already taken root by 2007, with arrangements in countries including Australia, China, Ecuador, Germany, Ireland, Japan, Mexico, the Netherlands, Russia, St. Lucia, Switzerland, Britain, Ukraine and the United States. International exchange agreements ranged from traditional exchange agreements to research collaborations, receiving students, delivering programs, and 2+2 joint academic degrees. However, few of these programs were administered by the School of Business; this

---

10. Provincial quality assurance required baccalaureate degree programs to have a minimum of 40 per cent of the faculty with Ph.D.s (Howard and Emberg, "MacEwan Welcomes Internationally Recruited PhDs to the School of Business," *Leadership,* 14:1, 2007, pp. 26–32).

11. ECampus Alberta web site, www.ecampusalberta.ca, accessed Jan. 21, 2009.

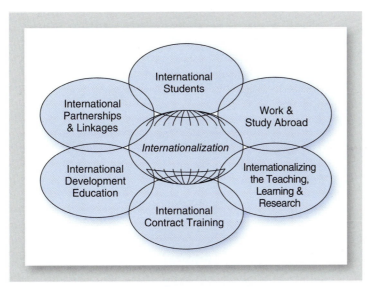

Exhibit 1 Internationalization Envisioned at Grant MacEwan College

Institution	Location	Description
Edith Cowan University	Australia	Accepts BCom grads into MBA programs
Griffith University	Australia	Accepts BCom grads into MBA programs
Zhong Guan Cun (Beijing Haidian Adults' University)	China	Developing 1.5 + 1.5 program
Education Forum for Asia	China	Memorandum of Understanding signed
Ludong University	China	Developing 2 + 2 program
Asia Pacific Institute of Management	India	Memorandum of Understanding signed
Athlone Institute of Technology	Ireland	Student exchange
Hogeschool van Arnhem en Nijmegen	Netherlands	Student exchange
Lucerne University of Applied Sciences and Arts	Switzerland	Student exchange
International Institute of Business	Ukraine	Offers MacEwan's Management Studies diploma
The Washington Center	United States	Student internships

Exhibit 2 List of School of Business International Relationships

was a situation that needed to change. (See Exhibit 2 for a list of School of Business international relationships.)

The School of Business had begun negotiations with a Beijing-based school and a Yantai-based school for joint programs. In Ukraine, the School of Business offered 2-year diplomas to students at a business school in Kiev. Edmonton had a large and active Ukrainian population who wanted to maintain links with the motherland, and the College wanted to capitalize on those ties.

Internationalization at MacEwan was a strategic priority. The 2007–2010 strategic plan highlighted a vision for globalization and a mission to sustain and support international initiatives. Elements of globalization were recognized in educational delivery, basic philosophy, work/study abroad, international student recruitment, local job creation for graduates, contract training, research, partnerships and reputation.

International student recruitment was particularly important for creating an international environment in MacEwan classrooms that mirrored conditions in the "real world." International student recruitment targets were established for segments of the globe that could maximize student yields for MacEwan. Of 830 expected international

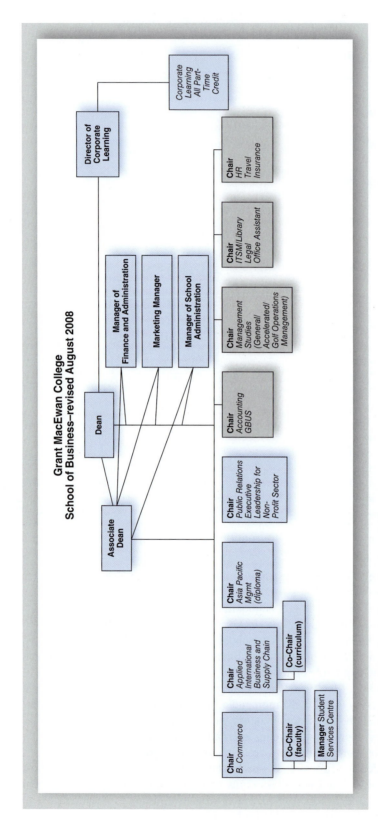

Grant MacEwan College
School of Business—revised August 2008

Exhibit 3 The School of Business Organizational Chart

students in 2008–2009, 409 came from China, 98 from Ukraine and Russia, 98 from Korea, 47 from Hong Kong, 43 from India and 31 from Japan. The remainder of the students came from places that included Vietnam, Taiwan, Mexico, Central America, Ecuador and Africa.

MacEwan also planned to team up with high schools in China, India and Vietnam, lending support to the internationalization strategy and to the commitment for global education in emerging markets.

The School of Business

The vision of the MacEwan School of Business was enunciated in its mission statement: "The School of Business is nationally recognized for the quality of its programs, the strength of its industry support, and the employment success of its graduates." (See Exhibit 3 for the School's organizational chart. The vision statement for the new Bachelor of Commerce degree is articulated in Exhibit 4.)

The School of Business offered the following new majors in its approved Bachelor of Commerce (B. Commerce) degree: International Business, Supply Chain Management and Management. (See Exhibit 5 for details on the Management major program of study.)

The B. Commerce majors were disciplinary and applied, integrating seven professional skills: (1) ethical business practice, (2) presentation skills, (3) writing skills, (4) research skills, (5) group-work skills, (6) case study/analytical skills and (7) technological fluency. The model for integrating professional skills was integrative in that instead of taking standalone courses in each skill, students were given learning opportunities and assessed on their progress and development in their professional skills in each course.

The International Business major, in particular, was designed to provide cultural literacy, introduce language study and provide the opportunity of international

---

The MacEwan Bachelor of Commerce is internationally recognized as a dynamic, innovative program providing a high quality, accessible business education in a personalized environment. It is known for its carefully articulated curriculum, committed faculty, and close relationships with business and industry. Bachelor of Commerce graduates are well-prepared for local or international employment in areas such as management, international business, supply chain management, human resource management and accounting.

The Bachelor of Commerce program at MacEwan is a destination of choice for business students. It encourages them to take their learning beyond the classroom, to value diversity in ideas and experiences, and to work toward social and environmental responsibility. Students are able to maximize their educational experience by choosing from a variety of delivery modes, taking advantage of multiple entry and exit options, and participating in cooperative work experiences. Their efforts are supported by a comprehensive range of student services.

Collegial relationships unite students, graduates, staff and faculty in the Bachelor of Commerce program. Faculty members' active involvement in research and scholarly activity promotes an ethic of inquiry and complements a strong curricular focus on research skills. The program strives to exemplify the values of teamwork and ethical practice.

Exhibit 4 Bachelor of Commerce Vision

Year 1	**Year 2**
❑ **ECON 101** Introduction to Microeconomics	❑ **ACCT 311** Introductory Accounting
❑ **ECON 102** Introduction to Macroeconomics	❑ **ACCT 322** Managerial Information and Control Systems
❑ **ENGL 101** Critical Reading and Writing	❑ **BUSN 201** Introduction to Canadian Business
❑ **LEGL 210** Business Law I	❑ **FNCE 301** Introductory Finance
❑ **MATH 112** Calculus with Business Applications **OR MATH 113/114** Elementary Calculus I **OR MATH 120** Basic Linear Algebra I	❑ **MARK 301** Fundamentals of Marketing
❑ **MGTS 103** Probability and Statistics I	❑ **MGTS 312** Probability and Statistics II
	❑ **ORGA 201** Introduction to Management
Three Non-Business Electives	Three Non-Business Electives
_____	_____
_____	_____
_____	_____
(CMPT 157 recommended)	

Year 3	**Year 4**
❑ **MGTS 352** Operations Management	❑ **BUSN 450** Strategic Management
❑ **MSYS 200** Management Information Systems	❑ **INTB 311** Diversity and Intercultural Communication
❑ **ORGA 310** Advanced Leadership Topics	❑ **ORGA 410** Business Consulting
❑ **ORGA 314** Managing Conflict	❑ **ORGA 422** Issues in Management— Senior Seminar
❑ **ORGA 316** Contemporary Organizational Behaviour and Theory	❑ **ORGA 433** Managing Change
❑ **ORGA 330** Managerial Skill Development	
❑ **PROW 210** Advanced Business Writing	Two Business Electives
	_____
One Non-Business Elective	_____
_____	
	Three Open Electives
Two Open Electives	_____
_____	_____
_____	_____
January 2007	

Exhibit 5 Management Major at MacEwan
Bachelor of Commerce Program Plan

experiences. Multilingual education was considered a foundation for intercultural communications and international competence. (See Exhibit 6 for details on the International Business major's program requirements.)

The School of Business also offered a 2-year program with an international orientation in mind: the Asia-Pacific Management Diploma program, which required advanced oral and reading proficiency in Japanese or Chinese. Graduates from this program were eligible to transfer to B. Commerce, providing all prerequisites were met.

To augment the globalization of the College as a whole, the School of Business's international initiatives included the following goals:

1. Inviting international professors for visiting appointments;

2. Developing study tours in India, China and Japan;

3. Hiring additional international academics;

4. Identifying international partners;

5. Internationalizing the curriculum; and

6. International teaching and learning opportunities for faculty members.

The faculty of MacEwan College and the School of Business was increasingly diverse and global. Of the 16 full-time faculty members in B. Commerce, many came from outside Canada, including China, India, Iran, Brazil, the countries of the European Union and the United States. Both Francophone and Anglophone speakers were represented on the faculty.

In addition to its various internationalization initiatives, in 2008 the School of Business planned to develop new majors in the B. Commerce degree in Accounting, Marketing and Human Resources, a number of certificate programs, and study tours to China and Japan, and India.

The School of Business continued to provide higher-education opportunities for career retraining, traditional university training, transfer education credits, applied business degrees and workforce training programs. The new focus on globalization would not undermine current efforts.

How to Globalize the School of Business

MacEwan had gone through the dual transition of (1) becoming a comprehensive college of higher education offering baccalaureate degrees and (2) offering more global education to its students. The School of Business, in parallel with the College, had also gone through this dual transition. Through the hiring of new, Ph.D.-trained international faculty, the development of new international programs, and the establishment of new international relations, it had begun to address the next phase of internationalization.

But what should be the next specific steps? The strategy was in place, but how should the School of Business proceed tactically on its internationalization initiatives? Elford pondered: Would the School of Business be able to distinguish itself through the internationally focused Bachelor of Commerce and Asia-Pacific Management diploma programs?

Globalization for a school of business was multi-dimensional and she needed some insights into prioritizing her goals. Elford found an informative article containing a globalization model written by Alon and McAllaster in *BizEd,* the official publication of the AACSB.[12] (See Exhibit 7.) Could this model help in benchmarking internationalization at MacEwan's School of Business? If so, how could it be used?

---

12. I. Alon and C. McAllaster, "The Global Footprint," *BizEd (AACSB International Journal),* May/June 2006, pp. 32–35.

Year 1	Year 2
❏ **ECON 101** Introduction to Microeconomics	❏ **ACCT 311** Introductory Accounting
❏ **ECON 102** Introduction to Macroeconomics	❏ **ACCT 322** Managerial Information and Control Systems
❏ **ENGL 101** Critical Reading and Writing	❏ **BUSN 201** Introduction to Canadian Business
❏ **LEGL 210** Business Law I	❏ **FNCE 301** Introductory Finance
❏ **MATH 112** Calculus with Business Applications **OR MATH 113/114** Elementary Calculus I **OR MATH 120** Basic Linear Algebra I	❏ **HIST 281** Asia Since 1500 AD
❏ **MGTS 103** Probability and Statistics I	❏ **MARK 301** Fundamentals of Marketing
Two Non-Business Electives	❏ **MGTS 312** Probability and Statistics II
_____	❏ **ORGA 201** Introduction to Management
_____	Two Open Electives
(**CMPT 157** recommended)	_____
One Open Elective	_____
_____	

Year 3	Year 4
❏ **INTB 300** Introduction to International Business	❏ **BUSN 450** Strategic Management
❏ **INTB 311** Diversity and Intercultural Communication	❏ **FNCE 404** International Finance
❏ **INTB 312** Conducting Business in Asia	❏ **INTB 412** Managing in an International Environment
❏ **MGTS 352** Operations Management	❏ **MARK 403** International Marketing
❏ **MSYS 200** Management Information Systems	Intermediate (2xx or above) Full-Year Language
❏ **ORGA 316** Contemporary Organizational Behavior and Theory	_____
❏ **PROW 210** Advanced Business Writing	_____
❏ **POLS 261** Asia Pacific Political Systems	Two Business Electives
Junior (1xx) Full-Year Language	_____
_____	_____
_____	One International Business Option Course
January 2007	_____
	One Open Elective
	_____

Exhibit 6 International Business Major at MACEwan
Bachelor of Commerce Program Plan Suggested Sequencing of Courses

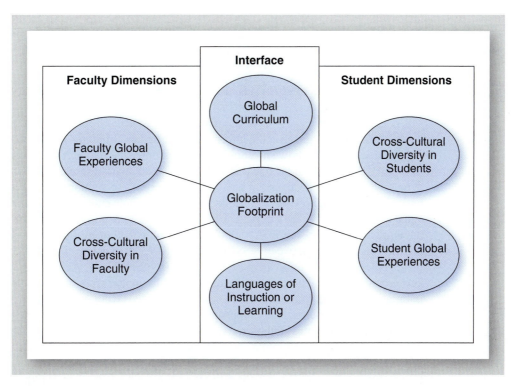

Exhibit 7 A Model for a College's Internationalization

Source: I. Alon and C. McAllaster, "The Global Footprint," *BizEd (AACSB International Journal),* May/June 2006, pp. 32–35.

IVEY

Richard Ivey School of Business
The University of Western Ontario

CASE P1-3

Estimating Demand in Emerging Markets for Kodak Express

Anna Johnson gazed at the information she had accumulated on various countries and wondered how she could use it to estimate the demand for Kodak Express (KE) outlets. She had learned from the Kodak market research department that demand for KE outlets depended on household income. To support one Kodak Express outlet, one of the following was needed: one million households with annual incomes equal to or exceeding the equivalent of US$15,000, two million households earning the equivalent of between US$10,000 and US$14,999, four million households earning the equivalent of between US$5,000 and US$9,999 or 10 million households with incomes less than the equivalent of US$5,000 (see Exhibit 1). According to the market research department, these averages seemed to apply throughout the world, when international dollars (purchasing power parity adjusted) were used as a benchmark.

Unfortunately, the statistics Johnson was able to find did not tell her the household income in United States dollar-equivalents in various countries or how many households in each country fell into a specific income bracket. She would need to complete a series of intermediate calculations to transform the original macroeconomic data to information that was useful for estimating the demand for Kodak Express outlets. Then, on the basis of market demand, Kodak would be able to use this information to decide how to allocate its investments across the various emerging markets.

The purpose of Johnson's calculations was to identify the markets with the most potential. The commitment to open KE outlets in a particular country was a significant investment that needed to have a promising return. Further, determining the markets with the most potential was in line with Kodak's philosophy of "investing where you sell the most."

Income	# of Households
≥ $15,000	1 million
$10,000–$14,999	2 million
$5,000–$9,999	4 million
$0–$4,999	10 million

Exhibit 1 Number of Housholds and Income Levels Needed to Support One Kodak Express Outlet

Source: Company estimates/assumptions.

David M. Currie and Ilan Alon wrote this case solely to provide material for class discussion. The authors do not intend to illustrate either effective or ineffective handling of a managerial situation. The authors may have disguised certain names and other identifying information to protect confidentiality.

Johnson sat in front of her computer, attempting to develop a model that would help her to estimate the market demand for KE outlets. She picked up a pencil and paper and began to sketch the process she would follow to use the data at her disposal to determine demand for KE outlets. Once she determined the process, she would prepare a spreadsheet model, plug in the data for a country and see whether the result was reasonable.

Kodak's Global Strategy

The manufacture and distribution of photography items had been the major focus of Eastman Kodak Corporation since George Eastman commercialized personal cameras using roll film in 1888.[1] The next year, the company became international when it extended distribution of products outside the United States. In 1900, Kodak introduced the first Brownie camera, the company's effort to make photography available to a mass market. By 2002, the company's products were available in more than 150 countries. However, the company was faced with increased competition from two fronts: Japan's Fuji Photo Film Co. produced and marketed many of the same photography products as Kodak, and Kodak had been slow to respond to the emergence of digital photography.[2]

Worldwide revenues for Kodak's products exceeded US$5.5 billion in 2010, a decrease of US$800 million compared with 2009 and a decrease of US$1.6 billion compared with 2008. The decline was partially due to the global economic slowdown, particularly in Europe, Middle East and Africa: revenues from these regions had decreased by more than US$1 billion in the previous two years.[3]

To offset the decline in sales volume in Europe, Middle East and Africa, Kodak's strategy was to expand sales into emerging markets such as India and China. Because of China's enormous population and its citizens' cultural affinity for taking pictures, China was one of the cornerstones of Kodak's emerging market strategy. Even expanding the market to just half of China's population would add the equivalent of another United States or Japan to the world photographic market.[4]

Kodak Express Outlets

Despite Kodak Express outlets being independently owned, they were contractually obliged to buy and display exclusively Kodak products, and they utilized Kodak's store specifications and the company's brand elements. The outlets provided three benefits to Kodak:

1. A front-line retailing presence
2. Wide distribution of Kodak products, services and brand name
3. A strategic asset for Kodak for market development

The company was making an effort to have a more extensive distribution of its Kodak Express outlets throughout the world. Through these outlets, Kodak planned to launch "grass-root marketing development programs."[5]

1. Kodak, "Building the Foundation," http://kodak.com/US/en/corp/kodakHistory/buildingTheFoundation.shtml, accessed January 26, 2004.

2. Daniel Gross, "Photo Finished: Why Eastman Kodak Deserves to Lose Its Dow Jones Industrial Average Membership," *Slate,* January 6, 2004, http://slate.msn.com/id/2093512/, accessed January 26, 2004.

3. Kodak 2010 Annual Report; www.envisionreports.com/EK/2011/22103MA11E/38495aae46f94783a4829c3e66124a12/Kodak_AR_10k_Secured_3-28-11.pdf, accessed June 16, 2011.

4. David Swift, "Remarks of David Swift, Chairman & President, Greater China Region, Eastman Kodak Company," *Goldman Sachs 21st Century China Conference,* September 1999, pp. 1–8.

5. Ilan Alon, "Interview: International Franchising with Kodak in China," *Thunderbird International Business Review,* November/December 2001, pp. 737–754.

Country	Population (in millions)
United States	310
Bangladesh	164
Brazil	193
Cambodia	14
China	1,341
India	1,216
Indonesia	234
Laos	6
Malaysia	28
Nigeria	156
Pakistan	167
Russia	140
South Africa	50
Thailand	64
Vietnam	88

Exhibit 2 Population of Selected Countries, 2010

Source: International Monetary Fund, 2010.

Data Availability

Johnson focused on four sets of data that were readily available from reliable sources for a variety of countries: population, purchasing power, income distribution and average household size. The first data set, population, seemed straightforward. Any analysis of a country's purchasing habits would begin with consumers, whether on an individual (per capita) basis or a household basis. Population estimates for 2010 are shown in Exhibit 2. More recent statistics were difficult to locate because most countries conducted a census only once every 10 years. Between censuses, all population statistics were estimates.

Determining the dollar-equivalent level of income from one country to another was a more challenging task. Many statistics comparing one country with another merely converted data into United States dollars using an average exchange rate for the year. Although this method was useful for some purposes, it was potentially misleading when used for consumption patterns because it ignored the cost of living from one country to another. For example, a family earning RMB65,000 in China earned the equivalent of approximately US$10,000 using an exchange rate conversion of RMB6.5 RMB per United States dollar.[6] But RMB65,000 in China purchased much more than US$10,000 purchased in the United States; thus, the family in China would be considered much better off by Chinese standards, and their consumption patterns might be closer to a family in the United States earning US$48,000.

To account for this difference, economists frequently standardized data for differences in purchasing power, called purchasing power parity (PPP). Johnson was able to find gross domestic product (GDP) per capita in United States dollars using PPP for the countries in which she was interested (see Exhibit 3).

A related problem was that GDP was not the same as national income, and Johnson needed to know a household's income. After some research, she discovered that because the difference usually was not significant, economists frequently used GDP as a proxy for national income. Therefore, the GDP per capita for these countries could serve as a substitute for income per capita. That meant that the average person in India earned the equivalent of US$3,339 annually on a PPP basis in 2010.

6. Exchange rate on April 18, 2011, http://finance.yahoo.com/currency-converter/, accessed June 16, 2011.

Country	Gross Domestic Product Purchasing Power Parity per Capita (in US$)
United States	47,284
Bangladesh	1,572
Brazil	11,239
Cambodia	2,112
China	7,519
India	3,339
Indonesia	4,394
Laos	2,436
Malaysia	14,670
Nigeria	2,422
Pakistan	2,791
Russia	15,837
South Africa	10,498
Thailand	9,187
Vietnam	3,134

Exhibit 3 Gross Domestic Product Purchasing Power Parity per Capita for Selected Countries, 2010

Source: International Monetary Fund, 2010.

Income distribution was another important issue because if more people earned low incomes in a country, they wouldn't be able to support as many KE outlets. Johnson needed to determine how many households corresponded to different income levels for any country. Data on income distribution are shown in Exhibit 4. For any country, population was divided into equal portions called quintiles (fifths), and each quintile showed the share of national income accruing to that quintile. For example, in India the bottom 20 per cent of the population accounted for 8.1 per cent of national income, and the top 20 per cent of the population accounted for 45.3 per cent of national income. Because each quintile represented 20 per cent of the population, about 243 million people (20 per cent of 1,216 million people) earned only 8.1 per cent of the country's total income. At the other extreme, 243.2 million people earned 45.3 per cent of the country's total income. If incomes were distributed evenly in a country, each quintile would account for 20 per cent of the national income (see Exhibit 4).

The average size of a household would help to determine the number of households in a country and, thus, the number of households in each of the quintiles. Data for the average size of household shown as the number of persons per household are shown in Exhibit 5. Dividing the population of a quintile by the number of people per household would yield an estimate for the number of households in the country. Of course, the assumption was that the number of people per household did not change with income. Johnson realized, however, that average household size depended on both cultural and economic factors. In some countries, the custom was for an extended family (parents, children and grandparents) to live in the same household. In most countries, household size varied according to the level of income in the household because families earning higher incomes tended to have fewer children. Household size also varied between urban and rural areas: urban households tended to be smaller. For this analysis, Johnson would need to assume that the average household size applied throughout the country, simply because no reliable statistics were available on the differences between sizes of households for all the countries she wished to examine.

Quintile	United States	Bangladesh	Brazil	Cambodia	China	India	Indonesia	Laos	Malaysia	Nigeria	Pakistan	Russia	South Africa	Thailand	Vietnam
Upper	45.8	40.8	58.7	52	47.8	45.3	45.5	41.4	44.4	48.6	40.5	50.2	62.7	49.4	45.4
Upper Middle	22.4	21.1	19.6	18.9	22	20.4	21.3	21.6	22.8	21.9	21.3	20.7	18.8	21.3	21.6
Middle	15.7	16.1	11.8	12.9	14.7	14.9	14.9	16.2	15.8	14.7	16.3	13.9	9.9	14.1	15.2
Lower Middle	10.7	12.6	6.9	9.7	9.8	11.3	11	12.3	10.8	9.7	12.8	9.6	5.6	9.4	10.8
Lower	5.4	9.4	3	6.5	5.7	8.1	7.4	8.5	6.4	5.1	9.1	5.6	3.1	5.9	7.1

Exhibit 4 Distribution of Income for Selected Countries—Various Dates (as a percentage of income)

Source: World Bank, World Development Indicators, various dates.

Country	Average Household Size (in persons)
United States	2.6
Bangladesh	6.0
Brazil	3.6
Cambodia	3.2
China	3.4
India	5.3
Indonesia	3.4
Laos	5.2
Malaysia	4.4
Nigeria	4.9
Pakistan	7.2
Russia	2.7
South Africa	3.7
Thailand	3.5
Vietnam	4.4

Exhibit 5 Average Household Size for Selected Countries, Various Dates

Source: Euromonitor International, 2010.

Calculating Potential Demand

As Johnson thought more about her task, she realized that she faced a two-step problem. First, she would need to calculate the household income in United States dollars for each quintile of the population. Only by doing this step would she then be able to separate households into each of the income brackets. This difference was important because each category was able to support a different number of KE outlets, as Johnson had learned from Kodak's market research department. The second step would be to calculate the potential demand for KE outlets once she knew the number of households in each spending category.

To attain this number, Johnson knew that she would need to complete several interim steps. Using her available data, she could make some initial calculations: she could determine the PPP GDP for the entire population, the population per quintile and the number of households per quintile. Using the population's GDP and each country's income distribution, she could then calculate the income per quintile.

Dividing the income per quintile by the population per quintile, she knew she would derive the individual income per quintile, from which she could easily conclude the household income per quintile. Then, using at the household income per quintile, she would be able to determine how many households fell into each of the categories in Exhibit 1. Knowing how many households fell in each category, she could then determine the potential demand for KE outlets in a specific market. Her goal was to build a model that would enable her to evaluate each of the countries in Exhibit 2. She would test the model using the data for one country. If it worked, the computer would then do most or all of the subsequent calculations. Once the model was complete, Johnson would use it both to predict demand for Kodak Express outlets in selected emerging markets and to make recommendations to Kodak management regarding market entry and resource allocations in these countries.

Finally, Johnson knew that such a significant investment should take not only today's demand into account. To determine the most attractive markets, she would also need to determine whether those markets would still be attractive in the future. Therefore, she decided to also calculate, in addition to the 2010 calculations, each

Country	Population (in millions)
United States	328
Bangladesh	178
Brazil	199
Cambodia	15
China	1,382
India	1,316
Indonesia	253
Laos	7
Malaysia	31
Nigeria	183
Pakistan	183
Russia	137
South Africa	53
Thailand	66
Vietnam	95

Exhibit 6 Forecasted Population for Selected Countries for 2016

Source: International Monetary Fund, 2011.

Country	Gross Domestic Product Purchasing Power Parity per Capita (in US$)
United States	57,320
Bangladesh	2,340
Brazil	15,193
Cambodia	3,183
China	13,729
India	5,398
Indonesia	6,556
Laos	3,675
Malaysia	19,541
Nigeria	3,242
Pakistan	3,678
Russia	22,717
South Africa	13,607
Thailand	12,681
Vietnam	4,803

Exhibit 7 Forecasted Gross Domestic Product Purchasing Power Parity per Capita for Selected Countries for 2016

Source: International Monetary Fund, 2011.

country's demand for the year 2016. She was able to gather projected data on both PPP GDP per capita and populations for 2016 (see Exhibits 6 and 7); however, she was unable to find reliable forecasts for income distribution and average household sizes. She therefore made the naive assumption that these last two variables, income distribution and average household size, would not change significantly.

What is the potential demand for KE outlets in the various emerging markets in 2010? What would be the demand by 2016? Given the assumptions, which markets will be the top candidates for investment?

We wish to thank Christopher Gassner for the collection of data and the development of new spreadsheets.

CASE P2-1

Ruth's Chris: The High Stakes of International Expansion

Richard Ivey School of Business
The University of Western Ontario

"Well, I was so lucky that I fell into something that I really, really love. And I think that if you ever go into business, you better find something you really love, because you spend so many hours with it . . . it almost becomes your life."

RUTH FERTEL, 1927–2002
FOUNDER OF RUTH'S CHRIS STEAK HOUSE

In 2006, Ruth's Chris Steak House (Ruth's Chris) was fresh off a sizzling initial public offering (IPO). Dan Hannah, vice president for business development since June 2004, was responsible for the development of a new business strategy focused on continued growth of franchise and company-operated restaurants. He also oversaw franchisee relations. Now a public company, Ruth's Chris had to meet Wall Street's expectations for revenue growth. Current stores were seeing consistent incremental revenue growth, but new restaurants were critical and Hannah knew that the international opportunities offered a tremendous upside.

With restaurants in just five countries including the United States, the challenge for Hannah was to decide where to go to next. Ruth's Chris regularly received inquiries from would-be franchisees all over the world, but strict criteria—liquid net worth of at least US$1 million, verifiable experience within the hospitality industry, and an ability and desire to develop multiple locations—eliminated many of the prospects. And the cost of a franchise—a US$100,000 per restaurant franchise fee, a five per cent of gross sales royalty fee, and a two per cent of gross sales fee as a contribution to the national advertising campaign—eliminated some qualified prospects. All this was coupled with a debate within Ruth's Chris senior management team about the need and desire to grow its international business. So where was Hannah to look for new international franchisees and what countries would be best suited for the fine dining that made Ruth's Chris famous?

The House That Ruth Built

Ruth Fertel, the founder of Ruth's Chris, was born in New Orleans in 1927. She skipped several grades in grammar school, and later entered Louisiana State University in Baton Rouge at the age of 15 to pursue degrees in chemistry and physics. After graduation, Fertel landed a job teaching at McNeese State University. The majority of

Allen H. Kupetz and Professor Ilan Alon wrote this case solely to provide material for class discussion. The authors do not intend to illustrate either effective or ineffective handling of a managerial situation. The authors may have disguised certain names and other identifying information to protect confidentiality.

her students were football players who not only towered over her, but were actually older than she was. Fertel taught for two semesters. In 1948, the former Ruth Ann Adstad married Rodney Fertel who lived in Baton Rouge and shared her love of horses. They had two sons, Jerry and Randy. They opened a racing stable in Baton Rouge. Ruth Fertel earned a thoroughbred trainer's license, making her the first female horse trainer in Louisiana. Ruth and Rodney Fertel divorced in 1958.

In 1965, Ruth Fertel spotted an ad in the *New Orleans Times-Picayune* selling a steak house. She mortgaged her home for US$22,000 to purchase Chris Steak House, a 60-seat restaurant on the corner of Broad and Ursuline in New Orleans, near the fairgrounds racetrack. In September of 1965, the city of New Orleans was ravaged by Hurricane Betsy just a few months after Fertel purchased Chris Steak House. The restaurant was left without power, so she cooked everything she had and brought it to her brother in devastated Plaquemines Parish to aid in the relief effort.

In 1976, the thriving restaurant was destroyed in a kitchen fire. Fertel bought a new property a few blocks away on Broad Street and soon opened under a new name, "Ruth's Chris Steak House," since her original contract with former owner, Chris Matulich, precluded her from using the name Chris Steak House in a different location. After years of failed attempts, Tom Moran, a regular customer and business owner from Baton Rouge, convinced a hesitant Fertel to let him open the first Ruth's Chris franchise in 1976. It opened on Airline Highway in Baton Rouge. Fertel reluctantly began awarding more and more franchises. In the 1980s, the little corner steak house grew into a global phenomenon with restaurants opening every year in cities around the nation and the world. Fertel became something of an icon herself and was dubbed by her peers *The First Lady of American Restaurants*.

Ruth's Chris grew to become the largest fine dining steak house in the United States (see Exhibit 1) with its focus on an unwavering commitment to customer satisfaction and its broad selection of USDA Prime grade steaks (USDA Prime is a meat grade label that refers to evenly distributed marbling that enhances the flavor of the steak). The menu also included premium quality lamb chops, veal chops, fish, chicken and lobster. Steak and seafood combinations and a vegetable platter were also available at selected restaurants. Dinner entrees were generally priced between US$18 to US$38. Three company-owned restaurants were open for lunch and offered entrees generally ranging in price from US$11 to US$24. The Ruth's Chris core menu was similar at all of its restaurants. The company occasionally introduced new items as specials that allowed the restaurant to offer its guests additional choices, such as items inspired by Ruth's Chris New Orleans heritage.[1]

Company Name	Number of Restaurants
Ruth's Chris	92
Morton's	66
Fleming's	32
Palm	28
Capital Grille	22
Shula's	16
Sullivan's	15
Smith & Wollensky	11
Del Frisco	6

Exhibit 1 Fine Dining Steak Houses by Brand in the United States (2005)

Source: Ruth's Chris Steak House files.

1. Ruth's Chris Steak House 2005 Annual Report, p. 7.

In 2005, Ruth's Chris enjoyed a significant milestone, completing a successful IPO that raised more than US$154 million in new equity capital. In their 2005 Annual Report, the company said it had plans "to embark on an accelerated development plan and expand our footprint through both company-owned and franchised locations." 2005 restaurant sales grew to a record US$415.8 million from 82 locations in the United States and 10 international locations including Canada (1995, 2003), Hong Kong (1997, 2001), Mexico (1993, 1996, 2001) and Taiwan (1993, 1996, 2001). As of December 2005, 41 of the 92 Ruth's Chris restaurants were company-owned and 51 were franchisee-owned, including all 10 of the international restaurants (see Exhibit 2).

Ruth's Chris's 51 franchisee-owned restaurants were owned by just 17 franchisees, with five new franchisees having the rights to develop a new restaurant, and the three largest franchisees owning eight, six and five restaurants respectively. Prior to 2004, each franchisee entered into a 10-year franchise agreement with three 10-year renewal options for each restaurant. Each agreement granted the franchisee territorial protection, with the option to develop a certain number of restaurants in their territory.

Decade	New Restaurants (total)	New Restaurants (company-owned)	New Restaurants (franchises)
1965–1969	1	1	0
1970–1979	4	2	2
1980–1989	19	8	11
1990–1999	44	19	25
2000–2005	25	12	13
	93[2]	42	51

Figure 1 Ruth's Chris Restaurant Growth by Decade

Source: Ruth's Chris Steak House files.

2. Due to damage caused by Hurricane Katrina, Ruth's Chris was forced to temporarily close its restaurant in New Orleans, Louisiana.

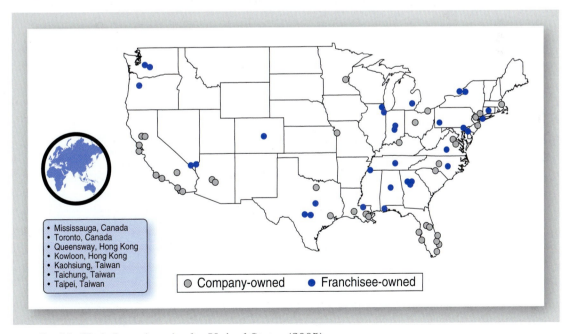

- Mississauga, Canada
- Toronto, Canada
- Queensway, Hong Kong
- Kowloon, Hong Kong
- Kaohsiung, Taiwan
- Taichung, Taiwan
- Taipei, Taiwan

○ Company-owned   ● Franchisee-owned

Exhibit 2 Ruth's Chris Locations in the United States (2005)

Source: Ruth's Chris Steak House files.

Ruth's Chris's franchisee agreements generally included termination clauses in the event of nonperformance by the franchisee.[2]

A World of Opportunities

As part of the international market selection process, Hannah considered four standard models (see Figure 2):

1. Product development—new kinds of restaurants in existing markets
2. Diversification—new kinds of restaurants in new markets
3. Penetration—more of the same restaurants in the same market
4. Market development—more of the same restaurants in new markets

The product development model (new kinds of restaurants in existing markets) was never seriously considered by Ruth's Chris. It had built a brand based on fine dining steak houses and, with only 92 stores, the company saw little need and no value in diversifying with new kinds of restaurants.

The diversification model (new kinds of restaurants in new markets) was also never considered by Ruth's Chris. In only four international markets, Hannah knew that the current fine dining steak house model would work in new markets without the risk of brand dilution or brand confusion.

The penetration model (more of the same restaurants in the same market) was already underway in a small way with new restaurants opening up in Canada. The limiting factor was simply that fine dining establishments would never be as ubiquitous as quick service restaurants (i.e., fast food) like McDonald's. Even the largest cities in the world would be unlikely to host more than five to six Ruth's Chris steak houses.

The market development model (more of the same restaurants in new markets) appeared the most obvious path to increased revenue. Franchisees in the four

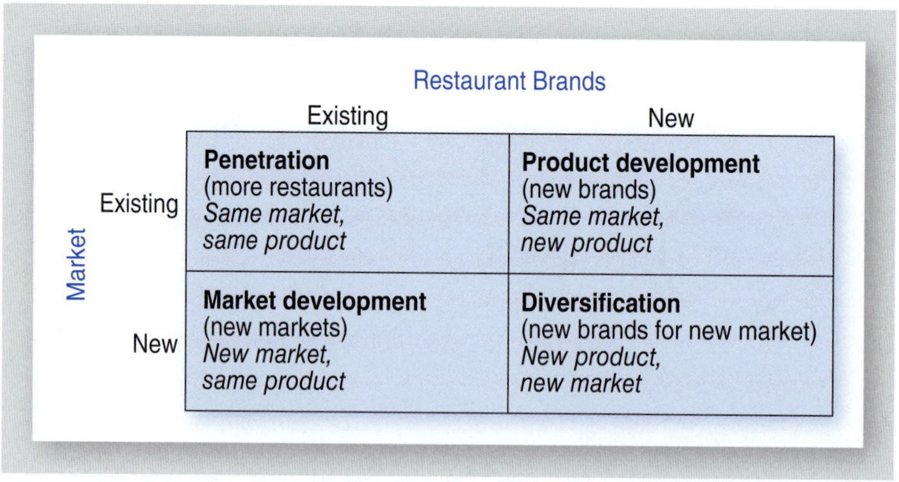

	Restaurant Brands	
	Existing	**New**
Existing	**Penetration** (more restaurants) *Same market, same product*	**Product development** (new brands) *Same market, new product*
New	**Market development** (new markets) *New market, same product*	**Diversification** (new brands for new market) *New product, new market*

(left axis label: **Market**)

Figure 2 Restaurant Growth Paths[3]

2. Ruth's Chris Steak House 2005 Annual Report, p. 10.

3. This diagram is based on Ansoff's Product/Market Matrix, first published in "Strategies for Diversification," Harvard Business Review, 1957.

international markets—Canada, Hong Kong, Mexico and Taiwan—were profitable and could offer testimony to would-be franchisees of the value of a Ruth's Chris franchise.

With the management team agreed on a model, the challenge shifted to market selection criteria. The key success factors were well-defined:

- Beef-eaters: Ruth's Chris was a steak house (though there were several fish items on the menu) and, thus, its primary customers were people who enjoy beef. According to the World Resources Institute, in 2002 there were 17 countries above the mean per capita of annual beef consumption for high-income countries (93.5 kilograms—see Exhibit 3).[4]

- Legal to import United States beef: The current Ruth's Chris model used only USDA Prime beef, thus it had to be exportable to the target country. In some cases, Australian beef was able to meet the same high United States standard.

- Population/high urbanization rates: With the target customer being a well-to-do beef-eater, restaurants needed to be in densely populated areas to have a large enough pool. Most large centers probably met this requirement.

- High disposable income: Ruth's Chris is a fine dining experience and the average cost of a meal for a customer ordering an entrée was over US$70 at a Ruth's Chris in the United States. While this might seem to eliminate many countries quickly, there are countries (e.g., China) that have such large populations that even a very small percentage of high disposable income people could create an appropriate pool of potential customers.

- Do people go out to eat? This was a critical factor. If well-to-do beef-eaters did not go out to eat, these countries had to be removed from the target list.

- Affinity for United States brands: The name "Ruth's Chris" was uniquely American as was the Ruth Fertel story. Countries that were overtly anti-United States would be eliminated from—or at least pushed down—the target list. One measure of affinity could be the presence of existing United States restaurants and successful franchises.

Region/Classification	Growth Rate					
	2002	2001	2000	1999	1998	1998–2002
World	39.7	38.8	38.6	38.0	37.7	5.31%
Asia (excluding Middle East)	27.8	26.9	26.6	25.7	25.4	9.45%
Central America/Caribbean	46.9	45.7	44.8	42.9	41.3	13.56%
Europe	74.3	72.5	70.5	70.6	73.1	1.64%
Middle East/North Africa	25.7	25.7	26.0	25.1	24.7	4.05%
North America	123.2	119.1	120.5	122.2	118.3	4.14%
South America	69.7	68.4	69.1	67.6	64.2	8.57%
Sub-Saharan Africa	13.0	12.9	13.1	12.8	12.6	3.17%
Developed Countries	80.0	78.0	77.2	77.3	77.6	3.09%
Developing Countries	28.9	28.1	28.0	27.1	26.6	8.65%
High-Income Countries	93.5	91.9	92.0	92.2	90.9	2.86%
Low-Income Countries	8.8	8.6	8.4	8.3	8.2	7.32%
Middle-Income Countries	46.1	44.6	43.9	42.7	42.3	8.98%

Exhibit 3 Meat Consumption per Capita (in kilograms)

4. World Resources Institute, "Meat Consumption: Per Capita (1984–2002)," retrieved on June 7, 2006 from http://earthtrends .wri.org/text/agriculture-food/variable-193.html.

Country	Per Capita Beef Consumption (kg)	Population (1,000s)	Urbanization Rate (%)	Per Capita GDP (PPP in US$)
Argentina	97.6	39,921	90%	$13,100
Bahamas	123.6	303	89%	$20,200
Belgium	86.1	10,379	97%	$31,400
Brazil	82.4	188,078	83%	$8,400
Chile	66.4	16,134	87%	$11,300
China	52.4	1,313,973	39%	$6,800
Costa Rica	40.4	4,075	61%	$11,100
Czech Rep	77.3	10,235	74%	$19,500
France	101.1	60,876	76%	$29,900
Germany	82.1	82,422	88%	$30,400
Greece	78.7	10,688	61%	$22,200
Hungary	100.7	9,981	65%	$16,300
Ireland	106.3	4,062	60%	$41,000
Israel	97.1	6,352	92%	$24,600
Italy	90.4	58,133	67%	$29,200
Japan	43.9	127,463	65%	$31,500
Kuwait	60.2	2,418	96%	$19,200
Malaysia	50.9	24,385	64%	$12,100
Netherlands	89.3	16,491	66%	$30,500
Panama	54.5	3,191	57%	$7,200
Poland	78.1	38,536	62%	$13,300
Portugal	91.1	10,605	55%	$19,300
Russia	51	142,893	73%	$11,100
Singapore	71.1	4,492	100%	$28,100
South Africa	39	44,187	57%	$12,000
South Korea	48	48,846	80%	$20,400
Spain	118.6	40,397	77%	$25,500
Switzerland	72.9	7,523	68%	$32,300
Turkey	19.3	70,413	66%	$8,200
UAE/Dubai	74.4	2,602	85%	$43,400
UK	79.6	60,609	89%	$30,300
United States	124.8	298,444	80%	$41,800
Vietnam	28.6	84,402	26%	$2,800

Exhibit 4 Data Table

Sources: World Resources Institute, "Meat Consumption: Per Capita (1984-2002)," retrieved on June 7, 2006 from http://earth-trends.wri.org/text/agriculture-food/variable-193.html and World Bank Key Development Data & Statistics, http://web.world-bank.org/WBSITE/EXTERNAL/DATASTATISTICS/0,,contentMDK:20535285~menuPK:232599~pagePK:64133150~piPK:64133175~theSitePK:239419,00.html, retrieved on June 7, 2006.

What Should Ruth's Chris Do Next?

Hannah had many years of experience in the restaurant franchising business, and thus had both personal preferences and good instincts about where Ruth's Chris should be looking for new markets. "Which markets should we enter first?" he thought to himself. Market entry was critical, but there were other issues too. Should franchising continue to be Ruth's Chris exclusive international mode of entry? Were there opportunities for joint ventures or company-owned stores in certain markets? How could he identify and evaluate new potential franchisees? Was there an opportunity to find a global partner/brand with which to partner?

Hannah gathered information from several reliable United States government and related websites and created the table in Exhibit 4. He noted that many of his top prospects currently did not allow the importation of United States beef, but he felt that this was a political (rather than a cultural) variable and thus could change quickly under the right circumstances and with what he felt was the trend toward ever more free trade. He could not find any data on how often people went out to eat or a measure of their affinity toward United States brands. Maybe the success of United States casual dining restaurants in a country might be a good indicator of how its citizens felt toward United States restaurants. With his spreadsheet open, he went to work on the numbers and began contemplating the future global expansion of the company.

"If you've ever had a filet this good, welcome back."

RUTH FERTEL, 1927–2002
FOUNDER OF RUTH'S CHRIS STEAK HOUSE

CASE P2-2
A Speed Race: Benelli and QJ Compete in the International Motorbike Arena

Marta Zhang, the young Chinese managing director of Italian motorcycle manufacturer Benelli, was sitting in her office in Pesaro, Italy, contemplating the purchase of the company by Qianjiang Group (QJ) in 2005. After the Chinese won a bid to acquire the company, QJ was off to a very good start: the local authorities had helped to create a welcoming environment, the two production lines were operational, new motorbikes were being projected by skilled engineers and the new scooters were very attractive.

While this new relationship began well, many differences were emerging between China and Italy: cultural attitude, work methods, civil and fiscal rules and access to credit were some areas of dispute. Despite industrial investments in order to gain efficiency and reduce prices, penetration of Western markets was difficult due to a high level of competition, especially from Japanese brands.

The European and United States press had welcomed the new motorbike models very enthusiastically, but sales results were not coherent with such technical success and with QJ's plans; moreover, the technical departments in Pesaro and in China had not agreed on the industrial plan to produce a new motorbike, which was projected two years before, and already presented—with great success—to a specialist public.

Mario Tonis, the press office director, interrupted Zhang's thoughts with some good news: the motorbike tests last month had produced brilliant results with the press. *Ultimate Motorcycling* reported the following:

> Retaining the original Benelli staff and leaving all design and manufacturing still in Pesaro, the combination of Asian work ethic and Italian design flair has proven a potent combination, indeed. The result has produced several new Benelli models, and the Tornado, although identical in appearance to previous iterations, has evolved into a superbike that retains the design brilliance of the original but without its quirky nature.[1]

The products were available and potentially successful, but how could Zhang integrate the new company, create a common corporate culture, help transfer the know-how, expand the business and win out over the strong Japanese competition?

Francesca Spigarelli, Ilan Alon and William Wei wrote this case solely to provide material for class discussion. The authors do not intend to illustrate either effective or ineffective handling of a managerial situation. The authors may have disguised certain names and other identifying information to protect confidentiality.

1. Arthur Coldwells, "Stormbringer: Benelli Tornado Tre 1130, A Brilliant Return," *Ultimate Motorcycling,* April/May 2009, p. 27.

The Acquired Company

Benelli was established as a family firm in Pesaro, Italy (in the Marche Region on the Adriatic coast), in 1911. Initially specializing in automobile and motorcycle repairs as well as the manufacturing of spare parts, over the years the firm also began manufacturing motorcycles that were successful in various sports competitions, winning numerous national and international titles.

To offer a stable work for her six sons, Teresa Benelli, a young widow, opened the "Benelli Garage" to repair cars and motorcycles. The business was successful and the sons begun first to produce spare parts and then engines too. In 1920, the first engine was ready: a single-cylinder two-stroke 75 cc model. In the following year, the first Benelli motorcycle was built with a complete in-house engine of 98 cc.

In 1923, a special model of motorcycle was projected and produced to enter race competitions. One of Teresa's sons, Antonio—nicknamed "Tonino the Terrible"— had a natural talent as a rider. Running a Benelli 175, he started a brilliant career winning four Italian championship titles in 1927, 1928 and 1930 with the single overhead camshaft model, and in 1931 with the double overhead camshaft model. The success in races contributed to affirm the brand and capacity of the company in projecting and producing competitive bikes at an international level. In 1932, during a race, Tonino had a terrible accident and had to stop his career. He died in 1937 in a road accident.

In 1949, one of Teresa's sons, Giuseppe, founded his own motorbike company— Motobi—due to disagreements with his brothers. Some years later, as problems with the family were solved, he attached to the parent company.

In 1962, Benelli and Motobi were able to produce about 300 motorcycles per day, with a workforce of 550 employees.[2] Toward the end of the 1960s, growing competition with the Japanese led to the sale of Benelli to De Tomaso Industries Inc. Despite various attempts to differentiate itself from its Japanese competitors, as well as a merger with Moto Guzzi in 1988, the company's manufacturing operations eventually ceased.[3]

In 1989, an entrepreneur also from the Pesaro area attempted to relaunch the company, but his efforts were unsuccessful. Operations only resumed in 1995 when the Indesit Group[4] purchased the brand and again relaunched the company. Although the group focused immediately on the scooter sector (trying to gain profits from the high volume of production despite low margins), in 2001, the group decided to enter the motorcycle sector in a niche market; however, the need for sizable investments, coupled with enormous financial difficulties, eventually brought a halt to production in 2005 and sent the company into liquidation (see Exhibit 1). Following an intense period of negotiations for the acquisition of Benelli by the John Galt Investment Ltd. company owned by Russian Nikolai Smolenski, son of Alexander Smolenski,[5] the company was eventually purchased by QJ.[6]

---

2. www.benelli.com/eng/storia.asp.

3. Francesca Spigarelli and Paola Bellabona, "The transnational dimension of the Chinese Economy," in M. Abbiati, *Economic and cultural characteristics of the Chinese Market*, Ca' Foscarina, Venice, 2006, p. 157.

4. The Indesit Group, the largest company in the Marche Region, Italy (€3,438 million in turnover in 2007 and 17,418 employees), was producing electric home appliances. The company belonged to the Merloni family. See www.indesitcompany.com.

5. Giorgio Leonardi, "A 24 year old Russian billionaire running Benelli's bikes," *La Repubblica*, July 30, 2005, p. 41, http://ricerca.repubblica.it/repubblica/archivio/repubblica/2005/07/30/un-miliardario-russo-di-24-anni-monta.html; accessed July 1, 2009; Federico De Rosa, "Benelli. A rush between Russians and Chinese. Qianjiang Motor Group is arriving," Corriere della Sera, September 6, 2005, http://archiviostorico.corriere.it/2005/settembre/06/Benelli_testa_testa_russo_cinese_co_9_050906051.shtml, accessed July 1, 2009.

6. Jeff Israey, "China in Italy: Kick Start," *Time*, August 9, 2007, www.time.com/time/magazine/article/0,9171,1651236,00.html, accessed June 30, 2009.

2001
■ Launch of a new strategic plan. The main decisions concerned the following: focusing on high displacement motorcycles, partnerships with other producers in the scooter sector and reducing costs to be more competitive in terms of sales prices.
■ Cooperative agreement with Renault Sport in the scooter sector. The commercial purpose was to sell Benelli's products in both France and Italy through the Renault network.
■ Participation in the Superbike championship with the new Tornado 900 cc. Good results helped the company win a consensus in the market (relaunching the company image).
2002
■ Cooperation with Renault Sport did not bring the expected results because of negative market conditions and trends.
■ Management focused on motorbike production. A new motorbike was launched: the Tornado 900 Tre, with 101 units sold within several months (85 per cent abroad).
■ In the scooter sector, the company looked for more flexibility by reducing stocks and outsourcing production. The most knowledge-intensive activities remained inside. The new Velvet 400 cc was projected.
2003
■ Benelli stopped production of scooters to focus exclusively on motorbike production.
■ The new Tornado RS model was launched, with production of 1,600 units. A new motorbike in the naked sector, the Tornado Naked Tre (TNT), was projected, which was due to be launched in 2004. Many orders from both Italy and abroad were placed by customers due to the success in the press.
2004
■ The new TNT was launched in the naked sector. Within seven months 930 units were sold. Good results in race competition supported sales activities. New versions of the TNT were projected and due to be launched in 2005 (many orders were already placed).
■ A new line of accessories and spare parts was projected to enter the market: high margins on those products should have brought higher profits to the company.

Exhibit 1 Company Activities before the Acquisition

Source: Benelli financial statements and balance sheet.

An acquisition by the Russian group would have probably resulted in the company being dismantled, with its machinery transferred to the United Kingdom and the loss not only of the brand but also of local jobs. Instead, QJ intended to relaunch the company by adopting an interesting industrial plan.

The Acquirer Company[7]

QJ was situated in Wenling, China, 480 kilometres from Shanghai. QJ was a large-scale state-owned group, and one of the 520 key state enterprises certified by the Chinese State Council. QJ was the largest Chinese company producing and selling motorcycles, with an annual output of more than one million units. It was chosen by the Motor Cycle Industry Association as one of the 10 best enterprises with strong competitive power in China. At the beginning of 2002, the "Qianjiang" trademark was given the award of "Famous Chinese Trademark."

QJ had formerly been the Wenling Chemical Engineering Machinery Factory, established in 1971. The factory changed its line of production to motorcycles in May

7. The information about the acquirer company and strengths of the company is from Qianjiang Motor Company Profile (Gong si jie jie), www.qjmotor.com/qjmotor/JieShao/aboutus.jsp, accessed December 11, 2009; Qianjiang Motor Financial Report (Cai wu bao gao), First Quarter 2009 accessed December 11, 2009; www.qjmotor.com/qjmotor/newsAction.do?method=view&id=4028882f20f0be69012108d4445e0019, accessed December 11, 2009; Qianjiang Motor Interim Report (Zhong qi bao gao), 2006, http://disclosure.szse.cn/m/finalpage/2006-08-17/18034278.PDF, accessed December 11, 2009.

1985, and then moved to Wenling. In January 1993, its name was changed to the Zhejiang Motorcycle Factory. After restructuring in 1996, the enterprise became Zhejiang Qianjiang Motorcycle Group. With government support, QJ successively merged with and acquired the Wenling Saccharification Factory, the Wenling Locomotive Factory, the Wenling Vehicle Repair Factory and the Wenling Electric Tools Factory, among others. These mergers allowed the group to achieve low-cost expansion and to double its economic indicators within a short time. The Zhejiang Qianjiang Motorcycle Company, Ltd. was established in 1999 with the approval of the People's Government of Zhejiang Province. The group was the primary founder of the subsidiary Zhejiang Wenling Motorcycle Company, and owned 75 per cent equity of Zhejiang Meikeda Motorcycle Company, Ltd., which was co-founded with Bright Steel Pte. Ltd.[8] Zhejiang Qianjiang Motorcycle Company, Ltd. had been a public company listed on the Shenzhen Stock Exchange since May 14, 1999.

Strengths of the Company

The primary business of QJ was research and development (R&D), as well as the manufacturing and marketing of motorcycles and engine parts. The company's motorcycle products constituted approximately seven per cent of market share in China.

The QJ Group designed, developed and produced Qianjiang machinery and electrical products. It produced motorcycles ranging from 50 cc to 250 cc, and also manufactured motorcycle-related products such as engines and parts, as well as race cars, miniature motorcycles, all-terrain vehicles (ATVs), gas scooters, generators, high pressure water cleaners, garden tools, power pumps, vacuum pumps and lawn mowers, among other products. Forty per cent of the group's products were exported to Europe, America, the Middle East, Northeast Asia and Africa—to a total of more than 110 countries throughout the world.

Eight years after the company went public, it had produced and sold more than seven million motorcycles (among which 0.93 million were exported). Total sales reached RMB21.196 billion, and RMB4.537 billion was paid in taxes. Among the total sales, 9,377,000 finished motorcycles were sold on the domestic market and 2,654,000 were exported, earning US$140.38 million in foreign exchange. The assets of QJ totaled RMB3.6 billion, with a total investment of RMB260 million.

The company covered an area of more than seven million square feet in the Wenling Economic Development Zone and was the largest motorcycle production base in Asia and the most advanced in China, with an annual production capacity of 1.5 million finished motorcycles. It had one joint-stock company and five joint-venture companies: these included many sub-departments such as a graduate school, an R&D centre, a testing centre, a machine-processing factory and an assembly factory. The company possessed both high and new technology and first-class equipment, and utilized advanced three-dimensional Pro/ENGINEER and CAD Design Software manufacturing technology. At the same time, it also imported advanced equipment (e.g., a processing-centre machine as well as a line-cutting machine, etc.) from the United States, Germany, Switzerland and Japan to develop its products and to process mouldings and machines.

The enterprise had a complete quality management system, and was issued an International Organization for Standardization certificate (ISO9001) in 1997 by the authorized international attestation organization, TUV Product Service, Ltd. The company's series of products passed CE, GS, CSA and UL standards and received quality

---

8. Zhejiang Meikeda Motorcycle Co., Ltd. was a joint venture of the Qianjiang Group and Singapore Kedeng Investment Co., Ltd., with registered capital of US$2.8 million; 75 per cent of equity was held by the Qianjiang Group and 25 per cent held by Singapore Kedeng Investment Co., Ltd.

licences from the National Import and Export Commodity Inspection Bureau. QJ also received "Well-Known Brand of China," "Chinese Famous Trademark," "Inspection-free Product," "State-level Technical Centre" and "State-level Laboratory" awards.

International Expansion

To upgrade its products, Qianjiang Motor cooperated with AVL—one of the two most important European automobile and motorcycle research institutes—and with a French engine design corporation that was a cooperative partner of Renault to develop motorcycle engines. Working with design company Bluesky Design (www.blueskydsn.com), Qianjiang Motor developed fashionable vehicles such as dune buggies, scooters, beam sport-utility vehicles and off-road vehicles for overseas markets.[9]

In 1999, Jiang Zuyun joined forces with QJ to sell motorcycles in the Indonesian market. Within two years, QJ held almost half of the Indonesian motorcycle market share. On August 20, 2001, the largest joint venture between China and Indonesia, Sanex Qianjiang Motor International (Sanex Qianjiang), inaugurated a US$12 million motorcycle assembly plant in Indonesia. Established as a joint venture in March 2000, Sanex Qianjiang was owned by Qianjiang Motor International, Malaysia's Lion Group and Taiwan's CPI, who together held 35 per cent of the shares, and Indonesia's PT Sanex. Beginning in April 2000, Sanex Qianjiang imported fully-assembled motorcycles from its Chinese headquarter and sold them in Indonesia; however, about two months before the inauguration of the plant, the company gradually began to reduce its imports when the local plant started producing 400 to 500 units per day. The plant eventually had a total production capacity of 30,000 units per month. Sanex Qianjiang thus created many employment opportunities for Indonesians. The company had 43 main dealerships and 273 sub-dealerships across Indonesia, and it also planned to establish a subsidiary called PT Sanex Agung Motor Indonesia to produce spare parts for the company.

To target the European market, QJ established a joint venture with an Austrian company to create the Generic brand that would produce European-style motorcycle products; in the meantime, QJ also acquired Hungarian company Keeway Motor, establishing Qianjiang-Keeway Europe. In 2005, QJ acquired Benelli. With these three leading brands—Benelli, Generic and Keeway—QJ was planning to build and expand its markets in Europe and North America, to accelerate technical innovations and to establish itself in a more competitive position in the international market.

In terms of its strategic development, QJ also targeted the Taiwanese market. Taiwan had the highest density of motorcycles in the world, with more than 300 motorcycles per square kilometre. Approximately 50 per cent of the population owned a motorcycle, and due to the high labour costs for repairs and maintenance, Taiwanese people preferred to buy new motorcycles rather than repairing them.[10] Due to the new leadership in Taiwan, the relationship with mainland China had become closer and therefore opened up shipping, postal communications and trading connections with the mainland. At the same time, the production costs of local Taiwanese companies were increasing and the investment environment had deteriorated, thus providing a great opportunity for the development of the mainland motorcycle industry. Qianjiang Motor, located in Wenling, China, was situated to the northeast of the Taiwan Strait. In addition to its geographical advantages, several senior QJ executives who were dispatched by the foreign shareholders were Taiwanese, giving them the advantage of familiarity with

9. X. Xia, "Qianjiang Motor: Exporting to European and American Markets," April 30, 2007, www.atvchina.com.cn/viewnews-7354.html, accessed December 11, 2009.

10. Q. Li, "Qianjiang Motor: Penetrating Market in Taiwan," April 4, 2008, http://www.tzgb.com/Motorcycle/Qiyezhichuang/200804/3766.html, accessed December 11, 2009.

the Taiwanese motorcycle market. QJ opened up the Taiwan market by relying on its geographical location, advanced techniques and competitive pricing. Its gross profits almost doubled due to the rise in exports to Taiwan.

Industry Analysis

The Industry

Benelli was part of the motorcycle industry, which included companies involved in manufacturing motorcycles and related equipment, parts and accessories. Motorcycles were classified by their engine size and vehicle use. Engines were measured according to their displacement by cubic centimetre (cc): scooters were less than 50 cc, standard were from 50 cc to 650 cc and heavy were more than 650 cc. Motorcycles were usually classified for commercial purposes into one of the following three categories: street, off-road or dual-purpose, depending on the surface on which they were intended to be used.

Street motorcycles were designed for riding on paved roads. Their engines were generally in the 125 cc and greater range. They included the following categories: cruiser, sport bike, touring, sport touring, naked, feet-forward motorcycles, scooters and mopeds. Off-road motorcycles, also known as dirt bikes, included motocross, rally raids, trials and track racing. Dual-purpose motorcycles were street legal motorbikes that were also designed for off-road situations. This class included adventure-touring, enduro and supermotard.

Benelli had products in both the scooter sector and in the heavy segment of the motorcycle industry: in the naked, sport and touring segments. With a wide range of scooters and standard products in a variety of models, QJ focused on the low-price segment of the market. Its slogan was, "Dedicated to a combination of European design, Japanese quality, and Chinese cost." It also had several typical Chinese-style low-power motorcycles.

Global Trends

Several key competitors in the motorcycle industry shared the majority of worldwide sales. The industry could be described as global and highly competitive. Price, design and engine performance were the key elements in customer choice. Japanese manufacturers such as Yamaha, Suzuki, Kawasaki and Honda had large market shares in many countries by combining innovative designs with low prices; however, in certain geographic markets, a single producer may have had a dominant position due to its specific core competencies or due to customer loyalty. For example, this was the case for Harley Davidson in North America, where the company held almost one-third of the market (Exhibit 2),[11] or of Ducati, in the sports or race segments, where the company offered high technical performance, which was supported by good sports/race results.[12]

In the period 2003–2007, the motorcycle market in the United States, Canada, Germany, France, United Kingdom, Italy, Russia and Japan grew by 4.7 per cent. The total value of the so-called G8 market was, at the end of 2007, of US$24.3 billion (41 per cent related to the United States), with a projection of a further grow of 5.1 per cent by 2012.

11. Don J. Brown, "What's Next for the Motor Co.?," *Dealernews,* February 1, 2009, www.dealernews.com/dealernews/Research/Whats-Next-for-the-Motor-Co/ArticleStandard/Article/detail/579349 accessed June 30, 2009. As for Ducati, see "Ducati Grows United States Market Share," Motorcycleusa.com, 2009, www.motorcycle-usa.com/577/3542/Motorcycle-Article/Ducati-Grows-United-States-Market-Share.aspx, accessed December 10, 2009.

12. As for Ducati competitive position, see "Ducati Grows United States Market Share," Motorcycleusa.com, 2009, www.motorcycle-usa.com/577/3542/Motorcycle-Article/Ducati-Grows-United-States-Market-Share.aspx, accessed December 10, 2009.

Producer	Market Share (%)
Harley Davidson	27.3
Honda	20.9
Yamaha	17,0
Kawasaki	13.8
Suzuki	12.5
KTM	2.0
BMW	1.4
Triumph	1.3
Victory	1.3
Ducati	1.0

Exhibit 2 Market share of Top 10 Motorbike Producers in the United States (Sales Estimates for 2008)

Source: Don J. Brown (2009), "What's Next for the Motor Co.?" *Dealernews*, February 1, 2009, www.dealernews.com/dealernews/Research/Whats-Next-for-the-Motor-Co/ArticleStandard/Article/detail/579349, accessed June 30, 2009.

An interesting trend in the global arena was due to the appearance of small companies, from emerging markets, Brazil, Russia, India and China in particular (BRIC area). Those markets were becoming more and more interesting both for supply and demand of motorcycles. In the period 2003–2007, the BRIC motorcycle market grew by 14.5 per cent and its total value was of US$27.2 billion at the end of 2007.[13] Brazil was the fastest growing area with a compound annual growth rate of 28.3 per cent. Following the projections available, by 2012 the BRIC market should reach a value of US$67.4 billion, with an increase of 19.9 per cent from 2007.[14]

Local Trends: Italy

In Italy, the motorcycle industry was very competitive: Japanese manufacturers had the biggest market share, especially in the motorcycle sector. In 2008, Honda and Yamaha held more than 30 per cent of new vehicle registrations and gained a dominant position despite negative market trends (see Exhibit 3). In the same year, Kawasaki sold the most of a single motorcycle model (see Exhibit 4). In the scooter segment, the Italian Piaggio Group had a good market share.[15]

Benelli had a small market share in the Italian industry, operating in a niche segment. The company tried to compete with Aprilia, Ducati and Honda, but its real direct competitors both on the Italian market and abroad were three Italian producers: Moto Morini (Morini), MV Augusta (MV) and Triumph Motorcycles (Triumph). Morini was its direct competitor in terms of both proposed models and annual sales. Although it was in the same market segment, MV produced more exclusive/luxury motorcycles, with higher prices and better performance. Benelli was Triumph's competitor because these two companies were the only manufacturers of three-cylinder Italian motorcycles; however, in comparison to Benelli, Triumph's market share was much larger (Exhibit 5).

13. "Motorcycles—Global Group of Eight (G8) Industry Guide," Research and Markets, www.researchandmarkets.com/reportinfo.asp?report_id=706788, accessed June 30, 2009.

14. "Motorcycles—BRIC (Brazil, Russia, India, China) Industry Guide," Research and Markets, www.researchandmarkets.com/reportinfo.asp?report_id=706787, accessed June 30, 2009.

15. www.ancma.it/common/file/articolo_220sezione_7.pdf and www.ancma.it/common/file/articolo_224sezione_8.pdf, accessed December 10, 2009.

Producer	Market Share (%)
Honda	19.4
Piaggio	16.3
Yamaha	14.9
Kymco	7.8
Suzuki	6.8
Altre	6.7
Aprilia	5.5
Kawasaki	4.2
BMW	3.6
Ducati	2.6

Exhibit 3 Market Share of Top 10 Motorbike Producers in Italy (% on Number of Registrations, February 28, 2009)

Source: Authors calculation on data from www.ancma.it/it/publishing.asp, acquired through Benelli QJ srl.

	Producer	Product	Class	Number
1	Kawasaki	Z 750	Naked	6,745
2	Honda Italia	Hornet 600	Naked	5,207
3	BMW	R 1200 GS	Enduro	5,087
4	Honda	XL 700 V Transalp	Enduro	4,198
5	Yamaha	FZ6 Fazer	Naked	4,025
6	Suzuki	GSR 600	Naked	3,172
7	Ducati	M 696	Naked	3,113
8	Suzuki	DL650 U V-Strom	Enduro	2,655
9	Kawasaki	ER-6n	Naked	2,560
10	BMW	R 1200 R	Naked	2,258

Exhibit 4 Top 10 Motorbikes Sold in Italy in 2008 (Number of Registrations)

Source: Authors calculation on data from www.ancma.it/it/publishing.asp, acquired through Benelli QJ srl.

Producers	2006	2007	2008
Benelli	262	401	484
Moto Morini	340	356	351
MV Augusta	1,987	1,891	1,274
Triumph Motorcycles	3,781	5,233	5,978

Exhibit 5 Motorbike and Scooter (more than 50 cc) Registrations per Year

Source: Authors calculation on data from www.ancma.it/it/publishing.asp, acquired through Benelli QJ srl.

Local Trends: China

The Chinese motorcycle market was the largest in the world and accounted for 59.1 per cent of market volume in the Asia-Pacific region (see Exhibit 6). In 2006, the domestic market grew by 7.9 per cent to reach a value of US$5.8 billion and a volume of 14.9 million units. It was projected to have a value of US$9.9 billion in 2011, an increase of 69.4 per cent since 2006; the forecast volume would reach 24.6 million units, an increase of 65.7 per cent since 2006.

EXHIBIT 6 COUNTRY BACKGROUNDS

China

China was the world's second largest economy in terms of gross domestic product (GDP) at purchasing power parity (PPP), and the world's most populous nation. Huge trade surpluses (China was the third largest world trader) and a large capacity to attract foreign direct investment (FDI)—China was the world's number 1 recipient of FDI—provided China with a huge amount of foreign reserves to be invested.[16] Real GDP grew at 11 per cent from 2003 to 2007 (Table A) and even after the economic crisis the economy was projected to expand at very high rates (Table B). Government stimulus packages, formally launched at the end of 2008 with an initial investment of about US$600 billion (equivalent to 13 per cent of GDP), provided a great boost to the country's economic growth. China would have remained the fastest-growing major economy in the world in the period 2009-10.[17]

While China's outlook appeared promising, extraordinary economic growth was unbalanced and, according to some, even unsustainable. Problems included the growing pollution in urban and industrial areas, the unbalanced growth of the cities compared to the countryside, social pressures, human rights violations and lack of democracy.[18] In the business sector, many Chinese companies that had entered international markets were not profitable, and they faced huge problems in terms of being competitive and adopting international management standards. Chinese companies had difficulties getting their products accepted in Western countries; moreover, some foreign companies were redirecting their investments to other emerging nations or to developing countries where they could find lower labor costs.

TABLE A—Outlook for China

Annual Data	2007	Historical Averages from 2003–2007	%
Population (millions)	1,321.3	Population growth	0.6
GDP (billions of US$; market exchange rate)	3,46	Real GDP growth	11.0
GDP (billions of US$; PPP)	7,316	Real domestic demand growth	9.9
GDP per head (US$; market exchange rate)	2,620	Inflation	2.6
GDP per head (US$; PPP)	5,540	Current account balance (% of GDP)	5.6
Average exchange rate RMB:US$	7.61	FDI inflows (% of GDP)	3.0

Source: Factsheet, May 6, 2009, Economist Intelligence Unit (Country ViewsWire).

16. For a deep analysis on aspects related to Chinese outward and inward foreign direct investments see "OECD Investment Policy Reviews China: Encouraging Responsible Business Conduct," OECD Publishing, 2008.

17. Economist Intelligence Unit, "China Economy: Stimulus Report Card," http://viewswire.eiu.com/index.asp?layout=VWArticleVW3&article_id=715063456&country_id=1800000180&page_title=Latest+analysis, accessed December 10, 2009.

18. Economist Intelligence Unit, Country Profile 2009—*China,* The Economist Intelligence Unit Limited, London, 2009, www.eiu.com.

TABLE B—China's Main Macroeconomic Data: Projections						
Key Indicators	**2008**	**2009**	**2010**	**2011**	**2012**	**2013**
Real GDP growth (%)	9.0	6.0	7.0	8.4	8.7	8.9
Consumer price inflation (%)	5.9	−0.2	2.5	3.5	4.1	4.1
Budget balance (% of GDP)	−0.1	−3.6	−2.1	−1.6	−1.1	−1.0
Current account balance (% of GDP)	10.2	6.1	4.5	3.6	2.9	2.0
Commercial bank prime rate (%)	5.6	5.4	6.6	7.0	7.1	7.4

Source: Factsheet, May 6, 2009, Economist Intelligence Unit (Country ViewsWire).

Italy

Italy was part of the Group of Seven (G7) industrialized nations. Its economic strength was in the processing and manufacturing of goods. Exports of luxury goods, consumer durables and investment goods led its competitiveness abroad. The industrial system was based mainly on small and medium-sized family-owned firms.

Economic growth in Italy ranged from one per cent in 1996 to a 3.7 per cent peak in 2000 and gradually slowed down thereafter in the two periods of recession in 2003 and 2008. Recent growth rates were among the lowest of the industrialized countries, due mainly to several years of low productivity growth and loss of competitiveness. Like many Western countries, Italy was facing the consequences of the global financial turmoil, with a strong decrease in output and a rise in public spending after a period of substantial reductions in the budget deficit (Table C and Table D). The economy weakened during 2008: exports fell sharply due to the export structure. Investment demand also fell sharply, as did consumer expenditures, especially for cars and durables.

The government faced challenges related to long-term budget consolidation. The key issues included the extension of the pension reform process and reforms to improve the efficiency of public administration. At the same time, measures to relaunch firm competitiveness were needed to sustain an industrial system that was based mainly on small and medium enterprises (SMEs).

TABLE C—Outlook for Italy			
Annual Data	**2008**	**Historical Averages from 2004–2008**	**%**
Population (millions)	58.1	Population growth	0.1
GDP (billions of US$; market exchange rate)	2,311	Real GDP growth	0.9
GDP (billions of US$; PPP)	1,797	Real domestic demand growth	0.9
GDP per head (US$; market exchange rate)	39,744	Inflation	2.3
GDP per head (US$; PPP)	30,910	Current account balance (% of GDP)	−2.2
Average exchange rate €:US$	0.680	FDI inflows (% of GDP)	1.3

Source: Factsheet, May 6, 2009, *Economist Intelligence Unit* (Country ViewsWire).

TABLE D—Italy's Main Macroeconomic Data: Projections						
Key Indicators	2008	2009	2010	2011	2012	2013
Real GDP growth (%)	−1.0	−4.5	−0.5	0.6	0.9	0.9
Consumer price inflation (av; %)	3.4	0.5	0.8	1.7	1.9	1.6
Consumer price inflation (av; %: EU harmonized measure)	3.5	0.6	0.9	1.8	2.0	1.7
Budget balance (% of GDP)	−2.7	−5.3	−5.2	−3.6	−3.7	−3.6
Current account balance (% of GDP)	−3.2	−2.2	−2.0	−3.0	−2.8	−2.7
Short-term interest rate (av; %)	4.6	1.7	1.8	2.6	3.5	4.1

Source: Factsheet, May 6, 2009, *Economist Intelligence Unit* (Country ViewsWire).

Based on volume, Jiangmen Grand River Group Company, Ltd. was the leading player in the Chinese motorcycle market, accounting for 16.2 per cent of market share in 2006. In the same year, Chongqing Loncin Industry (Group) Company, Ltd. and China Jialing Industrial Company, Ltd. held 8.3 per cent and 7.4 per cent of market share respectively. Due to the lack of a dominant leading player in the market, there was an increasing number of manufacturers, including Qianjiang Motors and other emerging firms that competed for the remaining 68 per cent of market share.

To understand actual trends in the Chinese market and QJ's position, some background information on the Chinese legal and regulatory environment is required. Focusing on the exhaustion of traditional natural resources, the deterioration of the environment and the excessive carbon dioxide emissions, the Chinese Ministry of Finance, Ministry of Science and Technology, Ministry of Industry and Technology Information and the National Development and Reform Commission issued a financial compensation plan for pure electric and fuel cell-powered vehicles. Energy-saving and environment-protecting vehicles were leading the R&D trend. QJ put the development of new-energy motorcycles onto its agenda: the company took the lead in releasing motorcycles with an engine management system, catering to national policies. Strengthening its technical input, QJ also introduced an electronic control injection system, reducing noise and gas emissions; at the same time, QJ was devoted to developing electric and liquid gas-powered motorcycles, as well as to participating in the formulation of national electric motorcycle standards.

According to a Chinese State Council resolution, motorcycles would officially be included in the "to the countryside" plan. From March 1, 2009 to December 31, 2009, the state was to allocate RMB5 billion for farmers in the countryside to trade old motorcycles and automobiles for new ones. This would mean considerable growth in the domestic motorcycle market. In the countryside, motorcycles were indispensible vehicles for feed, poultry and product transport, as well as for commuting. Compared to computers and other home appliances, farmers relied the most on motorcycles. The plan would be implemented over the course of four years, until 2013. As the leading company in the domestic motorcycle industry, QJ would greatly benefit from this compensation policy.[19]

19. L. Qu, "Great Prospects for Motorcycle Industry in China," March 2009,
http://money.zjol.com.cn/05money/system/2009/03/31/015391068.shtml, accessed December 11, 2009.

The Acquisition

Benelli and QJ made contact for the first time in June 2005: they were looking for an agreement that matched their relative strengths. Benelli had a recognizable brand name, knowledge of Western markets and projection skills, while QJ had high-efficiency plants and low production costs. In September 2005, a deal was reached concerning the founding of Benelli QJ. Industrial activities began in October 2005.

The main reasons for QJ to purchase Benelli was to utilize a well-known and recognized brand in terms of quality and sporting tradition, as well as to capitalize on Benelli's professionalism and knowledge in order to offer a high-quality product in segments that had not yet been penetrated by the QJ Group; therefore, the strategic objective of the initiative was to relaunch the Benelli brand by leveraging its history and tradition in order to achieve high-quality production. Benelli's products and spare parts were also to be used in China in order to increase the quality of domestically-manufactured products and to further diversify production to new categories of clients. Increased efficiency and a wide range of quality products were expected to help QJ to compete with the leading Japanese companies in the motorbike market.

At the time of the acquisition, there were no particular expectations with respect to Benelli's geographic location in central Italy, but QJ actually found some competitive benefits in the Marche Region. There was a lot of support from local public organizations, which facilitated negotiations and helped QJ win in the "competition" with the Russian entrepreneur to purchase the company. The directors of QJ—which was in part a publicly-controlled company—welcomed the involvement of the local organizations, as well as the relationships forged between the Chinese local government and that of town, provincial and regional organizations in Italy.

There was much unexpected common ground in terms of culture and society between Pesaro, the Marche Region and the location in China. In addition to being located in a coastal town, QJ appreciated that the people in Pesaro had a strong work ethic and an approach to work that was similar to that in China.

The Post-Acquisition Phase

Main Organizational and Operating Changes Introduced After the Acquisition

Operations relating to administration, production and R&D were maintained in Pesaro. The main changes related to production operations, which were restructured to increase capacity at the Pesaro site: innovations included an expansion of in-house operations, such as the three-cylinder engine assembly that had previously been outsourced. As a result, the original workforce of 45 at the time of purchase was increased to 100 employees.

As for human resources, the sales director, parts quality manager and managing director were Chinese. The sales director was working on restructuring the sales network and expanding it to the West. The quality manager was handling the production relationship with the parent company especially to coordinate the production of Benelli parts that were made in China and then imported for assembly. All of the engineers, workers and technicians were Italian. The previous technical director became vice managing director. Generally, Chinese employees from the QJ Group came to Pesaro and vice versa for short periods of time, on a rotating basis, to learn from mutual experience (especially for designing and testing of motors).

For Benelli, the greatest positive changes after the acquisition included the following:

- Efficiency-building efforts to reduce some avoidable costs that had been increasing with the previous owners and leading to significant losses;

- A new way of managing human resources: QJ gave increased decision-making power and responsibility to the staff, including young employees and women. QJ was attempting to let all of the staff become involved in the future of the company, by spreading a teamwork approach through periodical meetings and encouraging suggestions and ideas from the bottom to the top.

Industrial Activities: Present and Future

In 2009, two production lines were operating at the original industrial plant: one for engine production and assembly and one for motorcycle production and assembly. Before the acquisition, engines were produced and tested through outsourcing, so only one line of production was in use. The decision to outsource the engines had been a mistake: it resulted in high production costs and problems in quality and performance control. The Chinese thus decided to bring production in-house, following the suggestions of the Italian technical director. In order to realize the new plan, the agreements with local professional and technical schools were reinforced, to create apprenticeships and subsequent placements for students. No changes were made in the relationships with the local suppliers.

The QJ Group devised a challenging industrial plan for the development of the company, with a resulting increase in the workforce: the industrial plan involved manufacturing new products within four years. Motorcycle production increased from only three models prior to the company's acquisition to nine in 2007 and 10 in 2008 (Exhibit 7 shows two 2009 Benelli products). Each motorcycle model was different, and three new engines were used; they were designed in the technical department in Pesaro. Designs and prototypes were then transferred to the QJ technical department, where both the Chinese and Italian technical departments worked cooperatively to oversee the industrial development of the project. Once the industrial plan for the product was completed, production began in Italy.

Exhibit 7 Two 2009 Benelli products

Source: Courtesy of Benelli QJ srl.

Prior to the acquisition, Benelli produced only one model of scooter. Since 2008, two new models were added to their product range. As of August 2009, there were four models: they were all designed and projected in Italy, completely produced in China by QJ, and then imported with Benelli's brand for distribution in Italy.

A key factor in the relaunching of Benelli's activities was to reduce production costs and sales prices. It was estimated that it would take 10 years to achieve a truly competitive price in relation to the Japanese manufacturers. More parts would be produced in China to reach this strategic goal, while all high-value—knowledge-based—activities were maintained in Italy. While trying to win competitiveness in terms of price and build on QJ's strengths, Benelli was working on QJ products to improve their technical performance as well as their style and design.

Benelli's products were expected to enter the Chinese market in 2009–2010. In 2009, import restrictions on motorbikes with a displacement of more than 250 cc were abolished, so sales activities could now be organized; several dealers were ready to sell Benelli's motorbikes in China. Scooters would not be distributed in China because they were not competitive in terms of price. After the industrial plan was completed, the relaunching of Benelli would also focus on racing activity: QJ was planning to have new competitive bikes ready for the MotoGP (in the next five years) and for the World Superbike races.[20]

Sales Activities Abroad and the Commercial Network

Another key element for improving Benelli's competitive position and strengthening QJ's competitiveness on international markets was the commercial network. Benelli's business relationships abroad were being restructured, starting with the development of new branches in Europe and the United States. A great part of Benelli's sales came from the European Union, particularly in Italy. Germany was the most important foreign market. The second most important foreign market for Benelli should have been the United States; however, there was a big differential between *sell in* and *sell out* (i.e., the number of imported motorbikes and the number of motorbikes sold). The key problems related to sales in the United States were customer-assistance services and distribution channels. The United Kingdom was another important market.

The Italian commercial network was based on 179 official sellers: 30 per cent located in the north, 33 per cent in the centre and 37 per cent in the south. Benelli also set up 21 "authorized workshops," eight in the north, three in the centre and 48 in the south.

The distribution network abroad consisted primarily of joint subsidiaries with Benelli and KW brand products. KW was a new brand intended to sell scooters: it was launched by the group after the acquisition of the Hungarian company Keeway (later Qianjiang-Keeway Europe). These brands were differentiated by their price and quality, but they were sold through the same network. Aside from the KW subsidiaries, the commercial network was based on official importers—usually one for each country—that sold to different dealers. The dealers did not usually operate as monobrand sellers. Benelli had importers in 37 countries across Europe, Asia and America.

QJ's commercial strategy was differentiated on the basis of the geographic area: while there was a strong sales network in Indonesia through dealers and subdealers, Qianjiang Motor kept its sales away from the Southeast Asian market where national brands grouped together to compete and force down prices. Companies in countries such as Vietnam mainly relied on low prices to compete, and Qianjiang's prices were entirely uncompetitive.

20. Aaron Frank, "Benelli, BMW, and MV Agusta—Onward and Upward," *Motorcyclist,* www.motorcyclistonline.com/newsandupdates/122_0804_benelli_bmw_mv_agusta/index.html, accessed December 10, 2009.

QJ was now turning to the North American and European markets. Europe had a very strict technical standard to pass as a threshold, so it was difficult to enter the market. In Europe, motorcycle repairs had a high cost per hour that could erode the margins made through sales. Therefore, first-rate products with good quality were needed to enter the European market.

What Is Next?

After the acquisition, some problems arose due to the cultural differences between the Chinese and the Italians in terms of behaviour, specifically concerning business approach. Human relationships were difficult due to different mentalities, habits and background. Problems stemmed not only from differing organizational cultures, but also from the differing working environments in China and Italy.

There were many examples of such communication problems in the technical area. The Chinese and the Italian technical departments should have worked together in harmony to combine and optimize their complementary skills; however, working together was difficult due to language and cultural differences. These problems were delaying the development of important projects.

Another critical field was that relating to rules and laws. In some cases, administrative actions were perceived as nonsense by both Italians and Chinese. Behaviours relating to specific Italian fiscal or civil rules were sometimes judged as "wrong" by the Chinese; likewise, Chinese rules seemed "strange" or unacceptable to Italian employees. In this sense, the problem facing Benelli and its new Chinese owners concerned how to improve cross-cultural understanding. Problems in communications and cultural differences created a rift between management and employees, impeding the implementation of strategy and harming the company's potential.

Other difficulties in managing the "new" Benelli were due to the great focus on efficiency, which also had negative consequences. Domestic consumers in China were price-oriented: in general, this resulted in Chinese companies paying more attention to reducing costs and cutting investments that had long-term or intangible returns. QJ's international expansion required it to give up this traditional way of doing business and to reconsider the low-cost approach. This focus on cost-savings led the company to give less importance to sales promotion.

A key problem for Benelli and its new Chinese owners was to improve the worldwide strength of the brand as well as the effectiveness of the sales network to increase market share. Benelli's products, especially its motorcycles, had a huge potential to compete with the most important players in the market, but their market share in both Europe and in the United States was low. QJ had expected fewer problems in penetrating the western market through the Benelli brand; however, delays were caused as a result of having to rebuild and relaunch the brand image internationally, as well as having to re-establish international supplier relationships. Marketing investments, especially for sales promotion, post-sales assistance and customer care were needed.

The authors would like to thank Gianluca Galasso, Susanna Carloni, Pierluigi Marconi and Yan Haimei for all the information and support they gave us during the writing of the case.

CASE P2-3

Riviera Radio (RR): Developing a Market in a Highly Diverse Community

Paul Kavanagh, managing director of Riviera Radio, was going through some serious thought about the challenges that the radio broadcasting industry has faced recently. Looking out of his office window, he could admire the beauty of Monte Carlo's port, the yachts, and the beautiful sunshine as it danced across the Mediterranean sea.[1]

Having its headquarters in Monaco is a unique setting for any business, not only geographically, but also in terms of the challenges and opportunities of acquiring and retaining clients for the business—a pool of diversity, nationalities, and lifestyles.

Rivera Radio ("RR") transmits its signal "from San Remo to Saint Tropez," as the slogan says, from the Italian Riviera across Monaco into the French Riviera: an area in which French, Italian, and expatriates from over 120 different nationalities work, live, and play amongst the international companies, high tech research centers, banks and numerous film stars, celebrities and tourists.

Paul's immediate concern is now how to continue to grow Riviera Radio's audience and advertising base. After 20 years of more or less steady growth, where would they find new clients and advertisers? Would the diversity of nationalities, ages, and income allow for business development amongst the local or international populations? Or possibly both? Would the main shareholder, Morris Communications of Augusta, Georgia (USA), be satisfied with the positioning of the radio station as strongly Anglo-focused in a Franco-Italian environment? And, last but not least, would the business development activities need adjustment to account for technological advances such as Internet radio broadcasts?

Riviera Radio—History of a Business Plan Inspired by Grace Kelly

Riviera Radio was founded based on an idea encouraged by Princess Grace, formerly known as actress Grace Kelly. When she moved to Monaco in the late 1950s she had promoted the idea with friends and her husband, Prince Rainier, of setting up an English language radio station for the non-French speaking community.

Working through the bureaucracy and acquiring a license from Monaco to operate a station that broadcast primarily in France and Italy took some time, and although Princess Grace passed away in 1982 as a result of a tragic car accident, the idea went ahead, and Riviera Radio was born. With a broadcasting tower located in France and a Monegasque license and studio location, Riviera Radio began to transmit music, news, and advertisements to the Anglophone community in the Riviera—including the estimated 40,000 permanent residents, as well as the hundreds of thousands of Anglophone tourists who vacation in the region each year. Also, it appeared that other non-French listeners increasingly turned to this station for its music content.

Case prepared by Dr. G. Suder, SKEMA Business School, Jean Monnet Chair, France, USA and China; and Dr. W. S. Lightfoot, Brenau University, Georgia (USA). Reprinted with permission.

1. The authors would like to thank Riviera Radio, in particular Paul Kavanagh, for the access to the relevant information material and sources.

In addition to broadening the programming to include access to the British Broadcasting Corporation (the "BBC") news network, an "Anglo" station would not be under the same programming restrictions normally found in French radio. French radio stations are required by law to play between 40 and 50 percent of their songs in French.

Riviera Radio started to serve an important niche in the region. But the challenges of serving a niche market are similar for any business: Are there enough customers willing to "pay" for the products or services? Riviera Radio is no different. The radio stations "home base" in Monaco includes just 32,000 residents of whom less than 20 percent can be considered Anglophone (typically described as native or near native speakers of English—and including citizens of the United Kingdom, United States, Australia, New Zealand, and South Africa, as well as the Nordic region). And while there are an estimated 40,000 or so permanent Anglophones from "San Remo to Saint Tropez," this does not give the station enough of a base to be profitable. Right now, Paul Kavanagh estimates that a market needs about 100,000 people in it before a radio station can become profitable. In fact, if he was to start a new radio station, he says, he would start it in Nice. "Nice has 480,000 people—Monaco only has 32,000. Your local market is where you get most of your loyal listeners from."

Client Profiles

Radio, like other media, has essentially two sets of clients:

1. Listeners (or the "Audience")
2. Advertisers

Riviera Radio's verifiable (according to Media Metrix) listener base is an interesting mix of French and non-French, with the French making up about 40 percent of the total audience of approximately 150,000 listeners. The non-French audience is made up of British, Scandinavians, Germans, South Africans, Australians, Americans, Irish, Russians, and a wide range of other people from over 100 different countries. As Media Metrix only surveys households in the Alpes Maritimes Departments, these numbers do not include listeners from the Var (where Saint Tropez is) or Italy (where San Remo is).

Given the diversity of listeners, it would seem reasonable for the leading non-French station to attempt to "capture" as many of them as possible—offering a wide range of programming that would appeal to their specific interests. According to Paul Kavanagh, this strategy is misguided: "It is a natural assumption to make—try to do everything for everyone—five minutes at a time. The reality is that in the end, you end up not satisfying anyone. We decided it is better to focus on becoming 'best friends' with the people we target. This 'super serving' a specific core leads to building a larger market share—because they give you a bigger portion of their time."

And while the total number of listeners tuning in is important, it is the actual reach that really counts. "Reach" means how many people actually listen to the radio for more than 15 minutes at a time. According to Paul Kavanagh, RR's core audience is currently made up of 60 percent males, generally between the ages of 25 and 59 years old. 80 percent of the core listeners tune in from between 7:00 and 9:00 a.m. in the morning; 45–50 percent listen during the 5:00 to 7:00 p.m. commute time, and 20 percent tune in after 7:00 p.m. As a general rule of thumb, radio dominates daytime media, while television dominates the nighttime.

One interesting note is that there was a shift in the gender of active listeners between 2005 and 2006: The male to female ratio shifted from 53 percent female/47 percent male in 2005, to 40 percent female/60 percent male in 2006. Paul Kavanagh believes this may have had to do with RR's frequent World Cup related broadcasts—often from bars and pubs on the Riviera. He also suggests that they may offer a little too much programming related to sports which might turn off some of their female listeners.

Why all this emphasis on listeners? Without enough listeners, and without a clear understanding of who they are, as well as their habits and tendencies, it is difficult to attract advertisers. Advertising represents the vast majority of the revenue for the radio.

When Paul Kavanagh was brought in during the fall of 2003, his job was to turn around a station that had not been profitable for most of its history. In announcing the appointment of Paul Kavanagh as the General Manager of the station in October of 2003, Michael D. Osterhout, chief operating officer of the Morris broadcast division noted: "Paul's record of achievement in radio proves he has everything it takes to best develop that potential. He gets results."

Results in radio mean advertising money, and profits. The best way to do this was for RR to further define its niche—which, according to Paul Kavanagh, is not just as a non-French, or "Anglo" station, but rather, as a British-focused station. "It is who we are. And it's what people have come to look for—whether to improve their English skills, stay in touch with what's happening in the rest of the world, or simply because they like our programs and music."

In addition to the BBC news every hour on the hour, the four hosts include three English natives and one Australian. The morning show features Rob Harrison and Peter Nugent, who discuss a wide range of topics, from local Monaco and Riviera news to the Ashes Cup (for Cricket Fans), rugby, and football for sports aficionados. Paul Kavanagh is aware that they have lost some female listeners, and to help attract them back, in the spring of 2007, the noontime host Elizabeth Lewis added her sharp wit to the rapport of Peter and Rob, providing both a female voice to the primetime slot, as well as offering other topics beyond sports to the listening public. Advances in technology over the past several decades give radio stations a big advantage, as Paul Kavanagh notes that "a lot of programming can be done automatically—and there are times during the day when people want to sit back and listen to some good music."

This is all meant to further strengthen the relationship RR has with its core listeners (referred to as "P1" listeners). The core age group of listeners is 35 to 45 years—it is the group that determines what music is played, and these days, influences the decisions on what the hosts emphasize. This core also influences the design of the website (www.rivieraradio.mc); over the past decade, this has become a critical dimension for all media companies. Advertisers are looking for people who will spend money with them. They are interested in media that works—and RR has worked hard to cultivate a relationship using all the resources possible. Their objective is to become a real community service platform for the core demographic, offering a range of information from local sources and internationally from BBC. The website adds in additional dimensions such as content and programming that audience can listen to from the internet site, as well as community events, classified ads, blogs, and even the live car or estate sale.

Local and Regional Diversity Management

France and Monaco are interesting places for an Anglo business to operate. "We try to adapt to the style of the client. If the client is French, we try to look and act French. If they are English, we try to look and act English." Noting that 40 percent of the customers are French, and that his core clients tend to be better educated and wealthier than the typical resident of the Riviera, he suggests that advertisers from both the French and non-French speaking communities can be well served by Riviera Radio.

One significant challenge is the way business is done in France. "The French operate their businesses a little differently than we do in England, or in the States. It seems as if the businesses are run to suit the life style and needs of the owners and employees, rather than the clients. In other business sectors, well, I know of several cafés that are closed during lunch—which seems a bit odd."

As a client-focused business, RR tries to bridge the gap between a focus on the British and extended Anglophone community, and the advertisers who seek their money. The key is in the people he hires. For the listeners, RR employs the three "Brits" and one "Aussie" and has an American-based voiceover actor for advertisements and other on-air announcements. Paul Kavanagh, with his slight Irish lilt, can also be heard occasionally.

Calling on advertisers is another matter. His sales team includes non-French and French sales representatives. They align their sales efforts so that culturally, the right person is calling on the potential advertising client. And while the message may be the same—that advertising with RR works—the delivery method is different. Whereas Paul Kavanagh feels that the French tend to make decisions based more on emotions, and spur of the moment opportunity, Anglo businesses want to see results and proof that what they spend with RR will pay off in terms of new revenues and profits.

An interesting trend that Paul Kavanagh notes is the increase in the number of Russian listeners. He found out that Russians account for 18 percent of Societe Bain de Mer's ("SBM") turnover each year and that they tend to be the tourists who spend the most money on a per capita basis. SBM is the tourism and hospitality management company that operates a lot of the hotels and restaurants in Monaco. "They stay in the €6000 per night suites, and buy the most expensive watches." This has gotten Paul Kavanagh thinking again, of possibly adding in programming that increases their listenership. And while they are not in the Anglo core, they are part of the larger audience that includes many of the wealthiest people in the region. "The bottom line is they spend money—loads of it. And that is what our advertising clients want."

Gaining Market Share

With a sizable population of high net worth individuals, it would seem logical that there would be a great deal of competition in the Riviera. Paul Kavanagh indicated that competitors are mainly local or Internet–based radios, with the latter catching those listeners who like to listen in to the same station worldwide. Locally, MC 1 from Monaco is a niche business that aims to serve Monaco residents only, specifically targeting very wealthy listeners. Radio International is the only other English language radio station in the region—it broadcasts from nearby Bordeghera, Italy. The Radio Monte Carlo network is headquartered in Paris and includes Radio Monte Carlo 2 ("RMC2") which broadcasts in Italian, and RMC Info, which broadcasts in French. This network has gone through troubled times and several ownership changes over the past few years.

On the Riviera, the main stations include RMC Info, KISS FM, Nostalgie, Cherie FM, RIRE et CHANSONS, and NRJ—all of which broadcast in French, to a French audience, and under French music regulations. Satellite and Internet radio are potentially very serious challengers—although to what magnitude remains to be seen, as the market regulators are currently imposing rules that prevent broadcasts outside of the home country. This may well translate into an opportunity for Riviera Radio's Internet-based broadcasting that Paul Kavanagh thinks may lead to future increases within Monaco once British and other overseas radio broadcasts are less accessible.

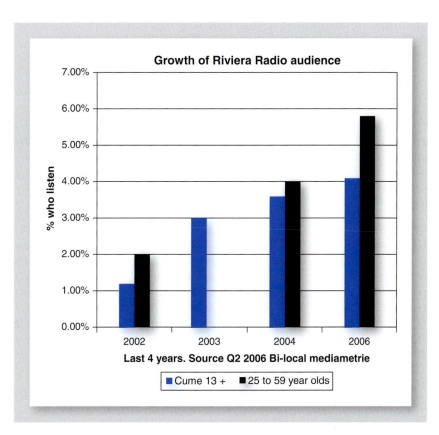

Growth of Riviera Radio audience

% who listen

Last 4 years. Source Q2 2006 Bi-local mediametrie

■ Cume 13 +   ■ 25 to 59 year olds

Despite the challenges, RR's market share has increased significantly over the past several years, with most of it taken from French radio stations in the region. Media Metrix latest data shows that the overall awareness of Riviera Radio has increased from 29 percent in 2002 to 42 percent in 2006, while the actual number of listeners has increased from 2 percent in 2002, to 5.8 percent in 2006—a nearly 300 percent increase in share in just four years!

Paul Kavanagh believes the increase in market share is directly related to the renewed focus on a core audience. He reiterated that while it is tempting to try to serve everyone, in the end, no one is happy. Thus the formula of sounding British. BBC News at the top of each hour, the triumvirate of British/Colonial morning show hosts offering the "full English breakfast"; discussion on cricket and the Premiership league football scores—the programming has a British empire feel that people come to expect and enjoy.

Media Metrix in Paris measures market share by phoning over 120,000 people about media consumption, with household, profession in France. Limitations include the fact they only call on a landline, and they only speak with French-speaking consumers. As a result, RR believes a number of its key consumer groups are under-represented as there are quite a few high net worth, non-French residents who live in the region, using only mobile telephones when here for 6 months a year, or playing on their yachts. Paul Kavanagh also noted that more and more young people prefer mobile lines—so if anything, the Media Metrix numbers are conservatively low. To improve the overall value of the numbers, since 2002 RR has paid for bilingual interviewers in the region "its home region." This extra service helps RR improve the overall quality of its statistics, helping their sales people do a better job of tailoring their sales pitches to prospective advertising clients.

The advertisers, in turn, are interested in targeting Riviera Radio's core listeners—the non-French, mainly Anglophone audience that listen most of the day, instead of French listeners who typically prefer to listen in during "music only" time frames. A good station has 25–30 percent P1 listeners who are passionate and dedicated about the station. This is different than regular listeners who may switch on for shorter periods of time.

Although this core listener group is generally comprised of people between the ages of 35 and 45—as Paul Kavanagh notes, people who come to the Riviera feel as if they are 10 years younger—they socialize more, listen to "younger" music . . . so in reality, the age group of the core audience may be more like 35 to 55.

Concluding Thoughts

The opportunity to work and live in a highly multicultural environment is fascinating. The opportunity to meet and work with people from a wide range of interesting backgrounds can make it a very rewarding experience in many different ways. For the small or medium-sized business, it can be a double-edged sword: the temptation to try to cater to the different niche populations is compelling, while the size of any one niche population may not be sufficient to generate significant profits!

The image of Monaco and of the Riviera, with Cannes and Saint Tropez feeding into the glitz and glamour, suggest it should be a great market for high-end providers of luxury goods and services. And for the non-French community, this seems to ring true. Monaco in particular is seen as an attractive place for vacations with lots of things to see and do. The French, on the other hand, see Monaco as a place full of strange and out-of-touch-with-reality people—a population not to be taken too seriously.

This duality of being the lone significant Anglophone station in a French speaking country presents challenges not easy to overcome. But Riviera Radio, under Paul Kavanagh's able leadership, seems to have turned it around by running toward its Anglophone audience rather than away from it. In the process, he and his team have positioned RR as a centre of a cluster or community. The station entertains, while also acting as a utility—providing a range of services that people depend on in their daily lives.

RR wishes to continue to build its brand—one that fits with what it means to be in Monaco, and on the Riviera, and one that supports its focus on it primary audience of high net worth Anglophone listeners. He envisions a day when people will talk about the radio station as something posh, valuable to their lives, and convenient for their routines. Whether it is shopping, finding a service, recruiting staff and yacht services, renting out flats for the Formula One race period or that of the Monte Carlo Master Series, Riviera Radio would be the luxury service that people will count on for entertainment, news, and utility. And the advertisers will follow suit.

As Paul Kavanagh sat back to further reflect on Riviera Radio's future, he wondered if that was the way to go. . . . and how to continue getting there.

CASE P3-1

Master International Franchising in China: The Athlete's Foot, Inc. (A)

Richard Ivey School of Business
The University of Western Ontario

O ne day in late 2001, Rick Wang, the managing director of RetailCo Inc., the master franchisee for The Athlete's Foot in China, was reviewing the most recent sales report of his company. He found that the sales volume for the past six months had declined precipitously, down almost one-third from what it had been only one year ago. Inevitably, Wang was concerned.

RetailCo Inc. had enjoyed a banner year in 2000; however, the company had experienced a cascade of problems beginning in 2001. At the start of that year, the company was forced to deal with pressure due to a supply shortage of major products, which could deal a deathblow to any small retailer. In quick succession, financial crises and sales problems related to the lack of product created a systemic disaster. Unless Wang acted quickly and decisively, RetailCo might not survive this confluence of major problems.

Rick Wang and RetailCo Inc.

Rick Wang was a typical American-born Chinese, able to speak both American English and Chinese. His parents had immigrated to Taiwan and then America when they were fairly young; regardless of their geographic location, however, the family maintained strong cultural ties to its homeland. Wang was raised in a traditional Chinese family in the United States. After graduating from the University of Southern California with a degree in communications, he began his career as an account director at Lintas, a well-regarded international advertising agency. He then transferred to Foremost Dairies Ltd., a leading manufacturer of milk and ice cream in Taiwan, as its marketing director, and thus gained experience in short–shelf-life consumer goods.

In 1992, he moved to his parents' hometown, Shanghai, and worked for Shanghai Fuller Foods Ltd. as vice president of marketing. He assisted in the building of the company's factory in Jinqiao district and developed new brands of Fuller milk and ice cream. Under Wang's leadership, the brands "Qian Shi Nai" (milk) and "San Marlo" (ice cream) quickly achieved market leadership in the area, known by almost all the residents in Shanghai. In late 1997, Shanghai Fuller Foods Ltd. was sold to Nestlé; Wang decided to strike out on his own.

Amber Xu prepared this case under the supervision of Professor Ilan Alon solely to provide material for class discussion. The author does not intend to illustrate either effective or ineffective handling of a managerial situation. The author may have disguised certain names and other identifying information to protect confidentiality.

As a result of a chance encounter, Rick Wang became acquainted with the athletic footwear industry and became a retailer. Wang retains a vivid memory of the day he was introduced to the possibilities of this retailing niche:

> One day, when I was playing softball with a bunch of my American friends who then worked at Nike, one of them said to me, "Rick, since your ice-cream business has been sold, what do you want to do now?" I said, "I don't know yet. Maybe I'll go back to San Francisco, or back to Taiwan." He said, "Why don't you consider overseeing our Nike stores in Shanghai?" I asked, "Nike stores? Can I make money?" And he replied immediately, "Sure, they can make a lot of money!" I asked for the financial statement, which he showed me the next day. After looking carefully I said, "Ok. Let's do it."

Rick Wang, at that time, had no experience in either the sports footwear industry or any direct knowledge of in-store retailing, but he was very excited about his new business venture. RetailCo Inc. was established with the intention of managing the retail realities of athletic footwear sales.

His optimism notwithstanding, Wang's hasty involvement and lack of experience in the footwear retailing industry led to the poor performance of his stores. In the six months after the company was established, no profit was made. As the situation worsened, Wang anxiously sought expert advice. He began by educating himself on the Internet, searching terms such as "athletic footwear retail," "sport retail" and "sports shoes retail." Surprisingly, he found that almost every page of his searches revealed one American company: The Athlete's Foot, Inc. Like many entrepreneurs, Wang recognized the value inherent in modeling his own activities on those of an industry leader.

The Athlete's Foot, Inc.

The Athlete's Foot, Inc., based in Kennesaw, Georgia, in the United States, was the world's foremost franchisor of athletic-footwear operations. It grew from a small, family-run store to an international retailer in three decades. The Athlete's Foot owned about 800 corporate and franchise stores in more than 40 countries (see Exhibit 1).

The history of the growth of The Athlete's Foot was a model of aggressive business behavior. In 1971, Robert and David Lando opened the world's first athletic-footwear specialty store, named The Athlete's Foot, on Wood Street in Pittsburgh, Pennsylvania. The very next year, The Athlete's Foot, Inc., began franchising its business model domestically. The first franchise agreement was signed by Killian Spanbauer, who opened a store at the Sawyer Street Shopping Center in Oshkosh, Wisconsin. After that, The Athlete's Foot began a period of focused expansion: by 1976 there were more than 100 stores; only two years later (1978), there were more than 200 Athlete's Foot outlets in America.

Antigua	China	Greece	Kuwait	Poland
Argentina	Costa Rica	Guadeloupe	Malaysia	Portugal
Aruba	Curacao	Guatemala	Malta	Republic of Palau
Australia	Cyprus	Hungary	Martinique	Reunion Island
Bahamas	Denmark	Indonesia	Mexico	St. Kitts/ St. Nevis
Barbados	Dominican Republic	Italy	New Zealand	St. Maarten
Canada	Ecuador	Jamaica	Panama	South Korea
Cayman Islands	France	Japan	Peru	United States
Chile	French Guyana	Jersey Island	Philippines	Venezuela

Exhibit 1 Countries Where The Athlete's Foot Stores Are Located

Source: www.theathletesfoot.com.

That same year, the company began to internationalize its franchising efforts; in 1978, the first of what was to become many international franchises opened, at 16 Stevens Place, in Adelaide, Australia. This milestone event encouraged The Athlete's Foot to franchise an additional 150 stores in international markets by 1979.

After a decade of successful market penetration, The Athlete's Foot, in its second decade, began a period of adjustment. In the early 1980s, Group Rallye purchased The Athlete's Foot from the Lando family. This buyout provided crucial financial support to the company at a time when it needed to pay more attention to product design and customer service, rather than focusing exclusively on expansion. For example, the company inaugurated a systemwide commitment to customer service. In order to help customers to find the "right" footwear, or at least to help to determine the proper fit, sales associates underwent training at "Fit University," introduced by The Athlete's Foot Wear Test Center to provide education on the physiology and anatomy of the feet and to enable sales associates to properly fit athletic footwear. This focus on educating its sales force—who, in turn, educated customers about the value of relying on The Athlete's Foot as a consumer-oriented facility—paid almost immediate dividends.

In the 1990s, The Athlete's Foot consolidated its market standing even as it continued its enviable international growth. The Athlete's Foot changed its name to The Athlete's Foot, Inc. and moved its headquarters to Kennesaw, Georgia, after Euris purchased Group Rallye in 1991. The company's structure was reorganized into two divisions as a result of this change in ownership: a marketing team serviced the franchises, and a "store team" operated the company-owned stores. The marketing team did an impressive job in the years following the reorganization. The Athlete's Foot, Inc. grew to more than 650 stores worldwide in 1997 and was named the number-one franchise opportunity by *Success* magazine that same year. After a dynamic new chief executive officer (CEO), Robert J. Corliss, joined the company in 1999, the company experienced a record growth year—opening 37 corporate stores in six countries and 87 franchise stores, the most franchises in company history. The other division, the operations' team that managed company stores, also achieved significant success during this period. The company launched a new store design featuring an innovative, customer-oriented technology called the FitPrint System.[1] This innovation was to lead to a competitive advantage for The Athlete's Foot, Inc. As a result of franchise oversight and marketing innovations, the company was awarded the "Trendsetter of the Year" award by the sporting goods community for 1999 and 2000.

The growth story of The Athlete's Foot became a model for franchising even as it successfully continued its almost 30-year tradition of domestic and international expansion. Many would-be entrepreneurs were drawn to the company, for reasons linked to the company's focus points: customer service, aggressive marketing and control of the pipeline from production to point-of-sale. Comments from franchisees illustrate the company's magnetic effect on franchisee development. Jaclyn Hill from Auburn said that her "decision to join The Athlete's Foot was based primarily upon them having an established, customer-service focused program to sell athletic shoes." Powell's Kyle H. Johnson commented:

> The Athlete's Foot was my choice when I decided to enter the retail industry for several reasons. Some are obvious such as access to vendors, reasonable franchise fees, and fair royalty rates. Beyond that, they offer a tremendous amount of support.[2]

---

1. According to Athlete's Foot, Inc., the FitPrint System is a proprietary state-of-the-art computerized technology that measures pressure points at different phases of a customer's gait.

2. www.theathletesfoot.com, accessed July 2005.

An Athlete's Foot Master Franchisee in China

Rick Wang was one of many entrepreneurs interested in pursuing business opportunities in the footwear retailing sector; Wang, however, had not followed the less risky entrepreneurial path of franchising, but had struck out on his own, with problematic results. His research on the successes of The Athlete's Foot's management model led him to contact that company. At that time, Wang had little knowledge of how franchising worked, or what potential benefits he might realize. In fact, his ostensible reason for contacting the company was his belief that he might pick up some pointers from this more experienced retailer:

> I was not a believer in franchising. I did not believe in franchising because I did not believe in paying so much money to buy somebody's brand and then putting more money in to build it. I can do by myself. But I decided to contact The Athlete's Foot because I really knew that I needed help.

Rick Wang decided to fly to Atlanta, to view the company's headquarters and evaluate the company and its team. This trip was fruitful. As a potential Chinese partner, Wang received a warm welcome from the CEO and the entire management team during his visit. Among his stops, he was especially impressed by the inventory control system in the merchandize department. Wang recalled:

> I wasn't very excited until I walked into the merchandise department and I saw their buying team, how they bought products. I saw how intensively they controlled the inventory system, using a very high-tech system. And then I started to learn the science behind the retailing. And I started to realize perhaps I need to pay the tuition to learn this. It's always the case: if you want to dance, you have to pay the band.

After Wang returned to China, he immediately started his franchise and retail plan. He first persuaded the board of RetailCo to agree to his idea of becoming the master franchisee of an Athlete's Foot structure in China. Second, he efficiently worked out a negotiation plan with the United States franchisor on the subjects of sales territory and royalty fees. He suggested separating the huge Chinese market into three regions: East China Area, North China Area and South China Area. The region of East China, stretching to the cities of Chengdu and Chongqin, was the biggest and potentially the most important market in China; it was in this area that Wang planned to focus his efforts. The region of North China, including Beijing, although a potentially lucrative market, was to be a secondary consideration. Last, development of the South China Area was to be delayed until after the first two regions were penetrated; the proximity to Hong Kong, with its history of appropriating brand names and flooding the market with cheaper copies, made immediate consideration of this region a risky and ambiguous proposition.

In terms of royalty fees, Wang fortunately negotiated a fairly good deal with The Athlete's Foot, Inc. The monthly royalty was to be 2.5 per cent of net sales. Other initial-area development fees—including franchising fees, fees for additional stores, purchasing a management information system (MIS), an employment-control system, etc.—totaled a few thousand dollars per store. In addition, Wang requested discounts related to any future fees for local marketing. All the funds for initiating business were to be self-financed.

When the deal was made, Wang, together with his six colleagues, went to Atlanta for "New Owner Training" at The Athlete's Foot's, Inc. Within six weeks, they had completed their "On Site Training" and had practiced operating the business: they worked in a store, sold shoes, helped people with their fittings and even worked in the warehouse, experiencing first-hand the realities of inventory control. They also learned how to work internal-control systems and marketing procedures. Overall, their training covered issues related to marketing, merchandizing, operations' management and employee sales training. Wang commented: "It was just fascinating, like going back to school. It was very enjoyable."

Their efforts paid off. In September 1998, the first store of the nascent master franchisee's China operation was opened in the Parkson Department Store on the Huaihai Road in Shanghai, in the East China Area. Parkson was the most popular department store with an ideal demographic: the youngest customers between the age of 20 to 35—those considered most devoted to brand names and most style conscious—shopped on fashion-oriented Huaihai Road. Therefore, the first store was actually in the fashion center amid a favorite venue of young consumers. The store was opened on the ground floor of Parkson's with the same store design and equipment as those in the United States. Beautiful store design and abundant/diverse name-brand products made the store attractive to customers.

Wang achieved success in starting his retail franchising at a time when the franchise concept in the Chinese market was new and innovative, and the sports footwear market was underdeveloped. His business instincts, his knowledge of the Shanghai market and his training at The Athlete's Foot, Inc.'s headquarters combined to initiate a signal success in what was then a relatively new entrepreneurial concept.

Business Context

Franchising in the Chinese Market

The franchise concept first entered the Chinese market in the early years of the 1990s with the emergence of reputable international franchising companies, such as KFC and McDonald's. They originally entered China in the early 1990s, building corporate stores first. After having achieved steady sales volumes and sufficient economies of scale, they cautiously but aggressively expanded. These pioneer global franchisors included dominant players in the fast-food industry and various master franchisors in other industries, such as 7-Eleven convenience stores, 21st Century Real Estate, EF education, Avis auto rental, Kodak film developing and Fornet laundry service. These firms contributed to China's franchising market development and created an awareness among an increasingly entrepreneurial class that franchising held substantial positive outcomes for those able to enter into such relationships.

Overseas franchisors tended to adopt one of two approaches when operating in the Chinese market: the franchise of a product or trade name (product name franchising) or the franchise of a particular business model in exchange for fees or royalties (business format franchising). Corporations that had a strong capital background, such as McDonald's and KFC, would choose an offshore franchise retail model (see Exhibit 2) to ensure effective control over product quality and company operations. Small- and medium-sized franchisors would often choose direct franchising by seeking a local franchisee. Franchisors, licensing to local partners, could take advantage of local knowledge, saving the costs resulting from distance—both in terms of logistics and culture.

Since the end of the 1990s, franchising had become a mature, steady growth opportunity in China. By the end of 1997, there were just more than 90 franchisors in China and about 30 franchise stores. One year later, however, the number had grown to more than 120 franchisors with sales volume of more than 50 million RMB (US$6.05 million), of which 40 per cent were franchise stores.[3] By 2000, the number of franchisors

3. Ye-Sho Chen, "Franchise China: She is Ready, Are You?," http://isds.bus.lsu.edu/chen/Franchise.htm, accessed July 2005.

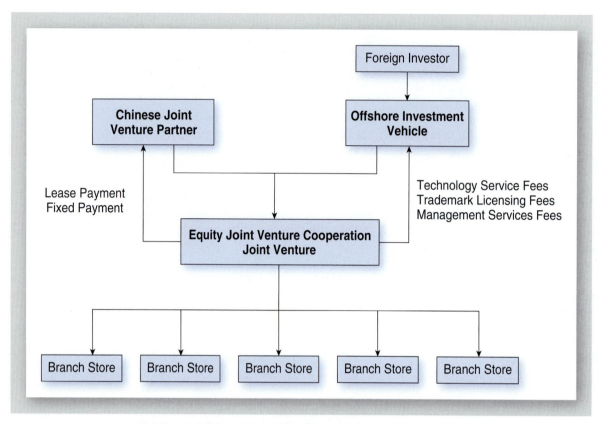

Exhibit 2 Offshore Franchise Retail Model

Source: Fraser Medel, "Legal Issues Related to Franchising in China," *Franchising in China,* November 2003.

approached 600. The sales volume also increased dramatically, jumping about 80 per cent from 1999 to 2000.[4] This remarkable growth (at the time of this article, franchising was growing at a high double-digit growth rate) continued in the years that followed.

Franchised businesses in China varied along a wide spectrum of business sectors. Companies in more than 30 industries had chosen franchising as a business model to sell their products and expand in this market. Retail and food/restaurant operations had always been the dominant franchising industries, accounting for 35 per cent and 30 per cent of total franchisors,[5] respectively. Other segments experiencing significant growth included education, business services, auto services, interior decoration, beauty and health, and laundry. The service sector had also grown in importance in recent years.

Market Environment

In the late 1990s, as many in the global market were aware, China was becoming the land of opportunity. China's strong and steady growth, proven by 10 years of continual gross domestic product (GDP) increases, seemed unstoppable. Economic growth led to an increase in personal incomes, especially in larger cities. The emergence of a large middle class, often consisting of well-educated professionals, added to the consumer demand for globally recognized, quality products.

4. *Franchise: The International Management of a Franchise,* Xinhua Press, Beijing, 2003, p. 181.
5. Ibid.

	1997	**1998**	**1999**	**2000**	**2001**	**2002**	**2003**	**2004**
Per Capita Annual Disposable Income of Urban Households								
Income	5160.3	5425.1	5854.0	6280.0	6859.6	7702.8	8472.2	9421.6
Per Capita Annual Living Expenditures for Consumption in sector of Education, Culture and Recreation Service								
Consumption	448.38	499.39	567.05	669.58	736.63	902.28	934.38	1032.80

Exhibit 3 Consumption of Recreation Goods in Entertainment and Sports Sector, 1997–2003

Source: China Statistics Yearbooks (various years).

Domestically, the Chinese government made great efforts to regulate the market and standardize the business environment. To facilitate access to the World Trade Organization (WTO), China committed itself to removing more market-entry barriers, which created a more open market for international investors. The laws and regulations governing franchise businesses were, thus, improved. On November 14, 1997, the Ministry of Internal Trade published and released the very first Chinese franchise law, *The Regulation on Commercial Franchise Business (for Trial Implementation)*. Afterwards, the Regulation was revised and improved several times: in 2005, *The Law on Commercial Franchise Business Administration* was eventually released as a basic rule for franchise operations in China.

Market competition in China was less rigorous than that in the United States. In the athletic footwear retailing industry in China, for example, there were few capable players in the early to mid-1990s. Meanwhile, the demand for high-quality athletic footwear increased as consumers' incomes increased (see Exhibit 3). Market research for 1998 indicated that people in Shanghai owned only one pair of athletic footwear. By 2005, they had, on average, three pairs. In terms of style, people's preferences changed from choosing footwear for functional purposes to opting for fashion. Athletic footwear retailers selling name-brand shoes had what seemed to be a promising future.

The Glorious Age

The success of his first store encouraged Wang to open more stores, more quickly than he had initially planned. In the months following his franchise premiere in Shanghai in 1998, Wang adopted an aggressive expansion strategy, opening a new store every 22 days. After spreading the business to the North China region, the company opened 40 corporate stores in seven other Chinese cities. The company realized a profit in its second year of operations, reaching a sales volume of US$14 million in 2000.

Every one of RetailCo's stores acted in accord with the standard of global Athlete's Foot, Inc. The stores, equipped with indoor music, sports videos and fashionable designs, established a pleasant atmosphere for shopping. All stores provided the best possible service for their customers. The service staff in every store were trained before they began their work—also in accordance with the model that Wang and his team had seen in Atlanta. In addition, every store was equipped with computers for billing and inventory control. In fact, the inventory-control system was an advantage that distinguished Wang's stores from other retailers. By adhering to strict, computerized tracking of product, store managers were able to react promptly to shortages or excesses of inventory. The company used the franchisor's proprietary pricing model by utilizing aggressive price reductions to manage inventory excesses. More important than the store brands that the store marketed were the famous internationally branded sports goods, such as Nike, Adidas and Reebok, which were available at the stores.

A pioneering store atmosphere, an excellent inventory-management model and the availability of famous brands quickly made The Athlete's Foot a premier competitor in the Chinese sports retailing industry.

Domestic promotion of The Athlete's Foot brand name was also managed aggressively. Besides media advertising, the company put more emphasis on direct and in-store marketing. It organized three-on-three street basketball games and tournaments to grab the attention of young sports lovers. The company also sponsored high-school basketball teams to further inculcate brand-name recognition of both the stores and their products among teenagers. In-store marketing activities included cooperation with the fast-food giant, McDonald's; monthly newsletters advertising The Athlete's Foot were distributed in McDonald's stores. Nevertheless, the brand-building process was not as successful as it had been in the United States. People responded to the brands of products more than to the retail brand itself: consumers visited stores because they could find internationally known products, not necessarily because they were drawn to The Athlete's Foot as a brand. This customer motivation would lead to substantial problems for Wang in future years.

In 2000, Wang started, cautiously, to seek appropriate franchisees in an attempt to expand the business. Wang selected one sporting goods franchising exhibition in Beijing as the venue for promotion of his franchise opportunities. Almost 500 applicants applied for franchises in one day, far exceeding Wang's expectations. Some applicants even came with large amounts of cash as testament to their financial abilities

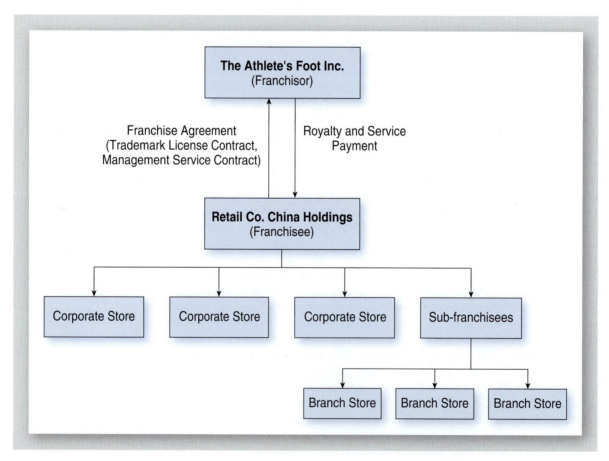

Exhibit 4 Franchise Structures of The Athlete's Foot in China

(and solvency). Wang was concerned, however, about the values of the applicants; he wanted to ensure that the selected candidates were service-oriented and fully understood the partnership requirements related to franchising. Carefully vetting all of the applicants, Wang short-listed 20 candidates. These finalists had strong financial capabilities as well as fine educational backgrounds; they could understand the vital realities involved in franchising partnerships. RetailCo invited these 20 candidates to come to the Shanghai Office for face-to-face meetings with the board. Finally, one— out of 500—was signed with RetailCo to be the first sub-franchisee of The Athlete's Foot, Inc. Later, using the same careful scrutiny, 12 additional sub-franchisee stores were developed in second- and third-tier cities, such as Nanjing, Wuxi and Ningbo.

Signs of Problems

In 2001, in spite of—or possibly due to—its rapid growth, the company gradually felt pressures related to cash flow, marketing and supply. The first "pressure" came from the need to commit large amounts of capital to obtaining retail venues. Since the location of retail stores was related to sales' performance, gaining a quality location was crucial. Wang's good fortune in being able to open his first store at a high-traffic, upscale shopping area in Shanghai was often difficult to replicate at equally moderate rental rates. Obtaining a quality retail space in China usually requires at least a 24-month leasing commitment; in some department stores, a 36-month rental agreement was the norm. To lock in quality locations in this competitive a retail real-estate market, the company signed long-term contracts, looking to best competitors by securing desirable locations. This laudable approach to ensuring franchisee success, however, required an immense commitment of up-front capital. RetailCo took over prime spaces in department stores, but the cost of doing so was great. Unfortunately, when market conditions changed and sales decreased, the pressure caused by an insufficiency of ready reserves of cash inevitably increased.

A second pressure was related to a problem many "breakthrough" franchisors experience in new markets: since 2001, The Athlete's Foot had started to lose its "first-mover" advantage. China began in 2000 to finalize preparations for entry into the WTO. The global financial community was increasingly convinced by then that the immense potential of the Chinese market was soon to become a reality. As a result, the athletic footwear market—along with every other foreign franchise business—underwent major changes, and foreign direct investment (FDI) increased.

In department stores, the space for sporting goods enlarged dramatically from 300 square meters to 700 square meters, then 1,000, 1,500 and finally to an average of 3,000 square meters. This growth spurt meant that franchising space allotted to The Athlete's Foot was, as a percentage of total space, gradually diminished. More footwear retailing players joined the industry; for example, Quest Sports started to open stores in China in 2001. Competition also came from local players, who were able to insinuate themselves in this market due to competitive pricing, enhanced customer service and increased product quality. In other words, these local competitors learned from Wang's Athlete's Foot franchises what Wang had learned from the franchisor. A final concern occurred when individual brands opened more of their own stores.

As a result of its success in the market—partly related to the improved business climate in China as a whole—RetailCo/The Athlete's Foot was, paradoxically, losing its competitive advantage. In 1998, the size of an Athlete's Foot store was almost 100 square meters, often occupying one-third of the total size of the sporting goods section of a large department store. The typical store was supplied by several world-famous brands, such as Nike, Adidas and Reebok. The rest of the sporting goods space was devoted to selling locally branded products and sports equipment: footballs, basketballs, tennis rackets, etc. Although the goods sold in an Athlete's Foot store were exclusive and superior to others, the above-mentioned changes led to a tenfold increase in the amount of store space devoted to sporting goods. Athlete's Foot did not and could not grow as fast, now (post-2001) occupying merely one-fifteenth of the total space devoted to sporting goods in a large department store. Size and visibility matter: the "idea" of Athlete's Foot became increasingly insignificant in customers' minds.

Worse, for Wang, was the fact that his suppliers—the producers of the often-popular styles and models his growing customer base demanded—began to increase their own penetration of what had previously been a fairly wide-open market. The Athlete's Foot multi-brand approach was forced to compete directly with brand-name suppliers who opened their own outlets in direct competition. Inevitably, Wang found it difficult to get the most desirable brand-name products for his stores; the home office—although committed to Wang's status as the master franchisor—was unable to put enough pressure on producers to stem the tide. Wang's stores were unable to keep current inventory of the most recent styles and most in-demand products.

With declines of comparative store size and product varieties, and increases in competition from local and brand-specific market entrants, The Athlete's Foot found itself squeezed out of high-value department store venues. Department stores welcomed the single-brand retailers because they were content with the smaller ratios of retail space; besides, grouping single-brand retailers together made a department store one, huge multi-brand store. The Athlete's Foot had to move to street-front locations that commanded higher rents and were less popular with the purchasing public. Thus, costs increased but revenue decreased.

What Should Wang Do?

Rick Wang realized the company was in risk of bankruptcy if he did not immediately address the radically changed demands of the marketplace.

CASE P3-2

San Francisco Coffee House: An American Style Franchise in Croatia

Richard Ivey School of Business
The University of Western Ontario

On the return to their homeland of Croatia following a six-year visit to the United States, Denis Tensek and Jasmina Pacek decided to open an American-style coffee house reminiscent of San Francisco's atmosphere. While Croatia had many coffee houses, few had the combination of service, quality, products and atmosphere that they remembered from their time living in the United States.

Tensek and Pacek started with a single coffee house. From the beginning, they felt that it had the potential to grow into a franchise. Instead of purchasing a franchise from someone else, they considered creating one that had all the elements of the modern franchise chains that were available on the international market plus the adjustments needed to the local market. They decided to use all of their United States lifestyle and professional experiences as well as understanding of habits and behaviors of the local market to create this new local concept in Croatia.

The initial coffee house became a success. The business steadily grew and operating profits had reached a satisfactory level. Motivated with the success of the first coffee shop in one of Croatia's poorest regions, the couple realized that the potential for this concept was national, if not regional. But, how would they grow? Should they develop their own outlets or open more company-owned outlets?

Organic grow by opening self-owned stores was costly, slow and hard to control. They had neither the means nor the staff. They knew they did not want to put more capital at risk, and did not have the time to travel to various locations around the country. Furthermore, their concept had started to garner local publicity and inquiries from would-be franchisees began to arise. But, how could they franchise in Croatia?

Croatia had a small economy, changing legal system and little experience in franchising. Growing through franchising was appealing, but they only had one store, the business was young, and franchising was unfamiliar to the emerging market of Croatia. The conditions for franchising were not ideal.

Aside from whether to franchise or not, how could they protect their intellectual property and business format know-how? How could they fight off imitators? What would happen if Starbucks or other major coffee chains entered the market? What should be the next steps? How could they become the biggest and most successful coffee house nationally or regionally?

Ilan Alon, Mirela Alpeza and Aleksandar Erceg wrote this case solely to provide material for class discussion. The authors do not intend to illustrate either effective or ineffective handling of a managerial situation. The authors may have disguised certain names and other identifying information to protect confidentiality.

The Entrepreneurs: Tensek and Pacek

Tensek had an MBA from California State University and extensive experience working in large United States corporations. Pacek, on the other hand, had a master's degree in fine arts and design from the University of California, and had worked as an art director in several United States companies. The couple's successful careers and profitable real estate investments in the United States gave them the comfort, confidence and capital to return to Croatia to invest in a new venture while helping their country's development at the same time. They wanted to create a business in Croatia that was world-class, towering above local offerings in service, quality and satisfying customer expectations.

Tensek and Pacek recalled their days in the United States, and the economic success stories of all the major coffee franchise chains such as Starbucks. They even considered taking a master franchise licence for Croatia, but the process was long, complicated and extremely expensive in comparison to the expected return. The fact was that Starbucks had very low local brand recognition in Croatia. The other problem with imported brands was that they often did not allow the adjustments needed to succeed in local markets, the major one being to the pricing of their product when it was simply too high for the local purchasing power of a developing country such as Croatia. They therefore decided to open The San Francisco Coffee House (SFCH) in 2003, a coffee shop with a recognizable visual identity—an interior in which visitors could feel the San Francisco-style coffee shop atmosphere (see Exhibit 1).

The Opening of "San Francisco Coffee House"

Osijek was a town with many coffee shops and bars, and visiting them was part of the lifestyle of the local population. But there was one competitive problem from which they all suffered: they all offered roughly the same limited product line without any differentiating concept. Tensek and Pacek noticed that what was missing in the market was an American-style coffee bar, in which most of the offerings would consist of different types of coffee, and that would include the novel (in Croatia) possibility of getting "coffee to go." They decided to adapt this ubiquitous American concept to the local Croatian market. They were under the impression that the "Made in USA" brand would be positively received in their "new" market, so they named the coffee bar "The San Francisco Coffee House." During the development of the business plan, Tensek traveled several times to the United States researching ideas, studying the technology of coffee making, and personally bringing back with him some of the supplies and crucial ingredients.

Tensek had chosen the location for The San Francisco Coffee House carefully: he was looking for a location with a minimum of 80 square metres near an area with heavy foot traffic, since his and Pacek's main target market was to be businesspeople. He found an excellent location in the town's center—across from the green market, near three university departments, and several lawyers' and public notaries' offices—for which he signed a five-year lease with provisions for extending the lease and a right to pre-emptive purchase in case the owner wanted to sell the premise. After the first few months, they found that their major client markets were students and business professionals of all ages.

Since SFCH was the first American coffee house in Croatia, this unique place where one could enjoy the authentic ambience of the American city received excellent reviews and unusually large media attention in the first six months of existence. *Elle Décor* ranked it among six best-decorated service industry interiors in the country,

Exhibit 1 Pictures of the San Francisco Coffee House (SFCH) Interior and Exterior

complimenting the brave mixture of styles and materials Pacek used to create the urban, bright and sophisticated environment. This was particularly commendable given the entrepreneurs' limited start-up capital of €40,000.

The San Francisco Coffee House assortment was also unique for this market. It offered its customers coffee in 17 different latte (with milk) and mocha variants and American-style muffins in several varieties. Coffee could be taken in the relaxing but urban atmosphere of the bar or it could be taken out in "to-go" packaging. However, SFCH did not have its own coffee brand; instead, in the SFCH in Osijek, coffee cups were marked with a coffee supplier's logo. Coffee suppliers in Croatia also customarily provided the coffee-making machines and their service free of charge (or the cost was included in the price of every kilogram of coffee). In order for Tensek and Pacek to adapt to their target market, guests were provided Croatian and international newspapers and magazines and free wireless access to the Internet (which was extremely rare in Croatia). The ambience was also enhanced by smooth jazz and billboard music from the 1970s, 1980s and 1990s.

SFCH had eight employees and was managed by Tanja Ivelj. The employees were all young people, some of them without any previous working experience and most of whom had worked in SFCH from its inception. When searching for employees, Tensek looked for trustworthy, loyal and honest people. For each workstation, employees had a detailed job description and detailed checklists for each shift and for weekly and monthly routine duties.

All employees underwent training for working in a coffee shop/bar. Their salaries were almost 20 per cent higher than those of comparable employees at other local coffee shops. Every six months all employees had scheduled performance reviews. If a review was satisfactory, there was a further five per cent salary increase. Human resource management was one of the areas where Tensek had brought his American corporate experience into Croatia. In Croatia, employee rights, salaries and general terms of employment were, in most cases, ambiguous. Also contrary to the common practice in Croatia, SFCH provided full paid vacation and benefits for its employees. As a result, in an industry where the turnover rate was extremely high, The San Francisco Coffee House was able to achieve less than 20 per cent turnover over the first three years of operation. As Tensek mentioned, "Satisfied and motivated employees offer a high standard of service to the end customers."

SFCH made an extra effort to maintain excellent relationships with its suppliers, making timely payments in a market that was known for its irregularities. Wise and responsible financial management was the company's priority. The summary of the financial performance of the company's operations is shown in Exhibit 2.

The Environment for Franchising in Croatia

The environment for franchising in Croatia was not ideal because of insufficient regulation, little market know-how about franchising, and low economic development. On the other hand, the emerging market and the new openness to European integration had created opportunities to start bringing in new businesses from the outside.

The Economic Environment

In 1991, after the Republic of Croatia gained its independence, the Croatian market increasingly opened to a great variety of international products and services. Due to the economic growth, which began in the late 1990s, salaries had grown appreciably,

Income Data	2006 (euros)	2007 (euros)
Net Revenues	133,332	166,666
Direct Costs	50,666	54,000
Gross Profit	82,666	112,666
Operating Expenses	36,000	39,333
EBITDA	46,666	73,333
Taxes	9,680	14,520
Depreciation	2,666	7,333

Exhibit 2 SFCH Financial Performance

Annual data	2007	Historical averages (per cent)	2003–07
Population (m)	4.0	Population growth	0.0
GDP (US$ bn; market exchange rate)	51,452	Real GDP growth	4.9
GDP (US$ bn; purchasing power parity)	69,211	Real domestic demand growth	5.0
GDP per head (US$; market exchange rate)	12,863	Inflation	2.6
GDP per head (US$; purchasing power parity)	17,303	Current-account balance (per cent of GDP)	−7.1
Exchange rate (av) HRK:US$	5.35(b)	FDI inflows (per cent of GDP)	6.4

Exhibit 3   Basic Socio-Economic Data on Croatia

Source: The Economist, 2008, http://www.economist.com/countries/Croatia/profile.cfm?folder=Profile-FactSheet, accessed June 11, 2008.

especially in the larger cities and in certain other parts of Croatia.[1] Basic statistics on the economy are shown in Exhibit 3.

Salary growth resulted in increased consumer demand for higher-quality world brand names, which were not widely available in Croatia at the time. After independence, the Croatian market became flooded with imported goods of variable quality. The habits of younger Croatian consumers had changed as a result of this increased supply: international brands became the acquisition target of younger consumers, while older people tended to continue to seek out domestic brands. Inevitably, perhaps, purchasing habits also varied geographically.

Financial institutions in Croatia were mostly owned by foreign banks—around 90 per cent according to one source[2]—and many of these acquisitions had occurred in recent years. Although there was a predictable variety of capitalization options for would-be entrepreneurs, a main characteristic of the Croatian domestic market was the bankruptcy of small entrepreneurs as they struggled to collect their own debts. Although bartering was a common fixture of the domestic market (i.e., between local companies), the international ownership of local banks made such traditional arrangements problematic.

Political Environment

Creating a vibrant business environment in accordance with the standards of the European Union (EU) and with countries embedded in the local market economy was one of the major goals of the Croatian government's policies. The government's dedication to the reform of the national economy could be seen in its desire to attract foreign investment for the development of Croatia's domestic and international markets.

Foreign investments in Croatia were regulated by the Company Act and other legal norms. A foreign investor in Croatia had a number of organizational options available according to this act: a foreign investor would invest alone or as a joint-venture partner with a Croatian company or private citizen; there were no constraints as to the percentage of foreign ownership that was possible. In addition, in keeping with the government's desire for foreign investment, investors gained access to a number of newly opened markets; entrants could take advantage of a number of incentives, tax benefits and customs privileges that were only available to foreign investors.

The Institutions of Franchising

In recent years, the Republic of Croatia had approved a number of laws, which resulted in Croatia's acceptance into the World Trade Organization and CEFTA (Central European Free Trade Agreement); these legal changes also allowed Croatia to

1. Croatian Bureau of Statistics, "Statistical information 2006," 2006, http://www.dzs.hr/Hrv_Eng/StatInfo/pdf/StatInfo2006.pdf, accessed on October 26, 2006.

2. Hrvatska narodna banka, "Standardni prezentacijski format," 2006, http://www.hnb.hr/publikac/prezent/hbanking-sector.pdf, accessed on October 20, 2006.

begin negotiations for acceptance into the EU. Nevertheless, there was no specific legal basis for franchising in Croatia. Franchising was mentioned in Croatian trade law (Narodne Novine, 2003), where the generalities of potential franchising agreements were stated, but mention was made in only one article and that mention was very condensed. Therefore, there was no legal standard for the development of franchising and no legal parameters (yet) for franchising agreements: business practices on the ground determined the appropriateness of such agreements.

Since the concept of franchising was relatively new to Croatia and to its inhabitants, little knowledge existed about franchising. There were two Centers for Franchising, one in Osijek and one in Zagreb, Croatia's most vibrant city. Each of these centers had worked with the Croatian Franchising Association to stimulate franchising development in several ways:

- Educating about franchising—The Franchise Center in Osijek, for example, had organized seminars, "Franchise A to Z," in order to educate entrepreneurs about franchising and its benefits;

- Franchising promotion—both centers and the association were trying to promote franchising as a way of doing business through local media—interviews, articles in the newspapers and magazines, etc.;

- Creating websites with information about franchising on the Internet—information on the portal with current news about franchising in Croatia, information about new franchisors, newly opened franchised locations; connecting franchisors with potential franchisees—one section of the franchise portal contained offers from franchisors interested in the Croatian market; there were several inquiries each week from potential franchisees;

- Helping domestic companies to become franchisors—The Franchise Center in Osijek, with the help of Poduzetna Hrvatska, organized training for potential franchise consultants who could help domestic companies if they decided to use franchising as a growth strategy; and

- Establishing franchise fairs and roundtables.

Foreign franchises tended to choose one of two potential pathways into the Croatian market: distribution-product franchising and/or business-format franchising. Larger, better-known franchisors like McDonald's opened their offices in Croatia and offered franchises to interested entrepreneurs in order to ensure quality control, while smaller and less well-known franchisors sold master franchises to local entrepreneurs in order to ensure the benefits of local knowledge and cost savings.

Barriers to Franchising Development

During September 2006, The Franchise Center of the Center for Entrepreneurship in Osijek conducted a survey of 50 people, asking what examinees (representatives of banks, entrepreneurs and lawyers) thought about the barriers facing franchising in Croatia. Their responses included:

- Laws—there was no legal regulation of franchising in Croatia. The word "franchising" was only mentioned in trade law; the absence of clear legal precedent made it difficult for Croatian lawyers to help their clients, especially during the contracting phase—whether franchisor or franchisee, whether foreign or domestic investor;

- Franchise professionals—there was a dearth of professionals related to franchising; there were too few educational efforts, and too few franchise consultants who could help potential franchisors in developing their own networks or advise franchisees about selecting one;

■ Problems with banks (not familiar with franchising)—banks did not recognize franchising as a relatively safe way of entering into a new business and did not have any specialized loans for the franchising industry; according to a survey conducted by The Franchise Center (2006), some banks' representatives said that they would ask a guarantee for a loan from the franchisor also; banks were not willing to educate their employees in order to learn about this way of doing business; banks seemed unable to distinguish between start-up entrepreneurs creating footholds in new franchise sectors and franchisees who were entering preexisting, proven franchise systems;

■ Small market—because there were only about four million inhabitants in Croatia, examinees were doubtful that the largest franchisors would come to Croatia due to logistical problems: the perception was that it was much easier to open a location in London than in Croatia; large and famous franchisors were looking for bigger areas to capture the population, and they often resisted adapting to local standards and prices; smaller franchisors that would have liked to enter Croatia were not as well known to Croatian entrepreneurs and were, therefore, seldom selected; and

■ Franchising was not a well-known way of doing business—people seldom recognized franchising; many thought it was connected with insurance; this was the biggest barrier according to the survey because people were not willing to enter into something with which they were unfamiliar; further seminars and roundtables needed to be organized in order to educate entrepreneurs about franchising and its costs/benefits.

According to the above-mentioned survey, there were some identifiable reasons for the relatively slow development of franchising in the Republic of Croatia: entrepreneurial thinking, lack of franchising education, and a weak national franchising association. First, many entrepreneurs would rather own their own companies and have complete "business freedom" than submit to the restrictions they saw as related to becoming part of a system—from production and distribution to sales and to the "forced" cleaning of the premises. Second, Croatian entrepreneurs were not completely familiar with the benefits that would be gained by being a member of a successful franchising system.

Despite such a pessimistic tone, industry experts also reported that there was an excellent chance for franchising in Croatia, that there was the possibility of high growth in this sector (up to 30 per cent), and that Croatia's membership in the EU would provide the necessary boost to franchising development. The survey showed that although franchising was not a familiar way of doing business, experts saw a bright future for franchising in Croatia.

Competition

Franchises had become more well-known in Croatia starting in the early 1990s, after the first McDonald's was opened in Zagreb. "McDonald's expansion into the Croatian market has tended to use two franchising methods: direct franchising and business-facility lease arrangements . . . Such lease arrangements allow for franchisees to become entry-level franchisees using less capital at the outset."[3]

Other franchisors followed McDonald's lead. For example, one of the relatively new restaurant franchising concepts in the Croatian market was the Hungarian company Fornetti, which managed to spread quickly its mini-bakeries business throughout Croatia by using franchising. They were founded in 1997, and by 2007 had more than

3. L. Viducic and G. Brcic in I. Alon and D. Welsh, *International Franchising in Emerging Markets: China, India and Other Asian Countries,* CCH Inc., Chicago, 2001, p. 217.

Franchisor	Industry	Number of Outlets
McDonald's	Fast food	16 restaurants
Subway	Fast food	6 restaurants
Fornetti	Bakeries	Over 150 locations
Dama Service	Refilling toner cartridges	3 locations
Berlitz	Foreign language school	1 location
Firurella	Weight loss center for women	2 locations
Berghoff	Kitchen equipment	3 locations
Benetton	Fashion textile industry	Around 20 shops
Remax	Realestate	2 location

Exhibit 4 Foreign Franchisors in Croatia

Source: "Round table—Franchising in Croatia," address given at EFF/IFA International Symposium, Brussels, October 24–25, 2006.

Franchisor	Industry	Number of Outlets
Elektromaterijal	Household appliance distribution	Over 50 stores
X-nation	Fashion clothes	40 stores/corners
Rubelj Grill	Grill	17 restaurants
Skandal	Fashion clothes	15 stores
Body Creator	Weight loss center for women	4 centers
Bio & Bio	Health food	3 shops
Bike Express	Courier service	1 location
The San Francisco Coffee House	Coffee bar	1 location

Exhibit 5 Domestic Franchisors in Croatia

Source: "Round table—Franchising in Croatia," address given at EFF/IFA International Symposium, Brussels, October 24–25, 2006.

3,000 locations in Central and Eastern Europe.[4] Other international franchises represented in Croatia included Benetton, Subway, Dama Service and Remax.

According to the Croatian Franchise Association, there were approximately 125 (25 of them domestic) franchise systems present in the Croatian market. These systems operated approximately 900 locations and employed almost 16,000 people.[5] Companies in more than 20 industries had chosen franchising as a growth option, with the sales industry and fast-food sectors accounting for more than 20 per cent of the market. Other segments with important shares included the tourist industry, rent-a-car companies, courier services and the fashion industry.

Exhibits 4 and 5 show the most well-known foreign and domestic franchisors in Croatia by industry and number of outlets as of 2007.

While a few restaurant franchisors had already entered the Croatian market, no well-known international coffee houses had done so. Competition for coffee houses was mostly local, dating back to Croatia's early days. Local competitors offered a roughly homogeneous product—coffee—and, most did not bother to create a visual identity, a brand or a new concept. Price, location and ambiance distinguished one coffee bar from another. Competitive rivalry from abroad, however, was imminent. The question was not if international coffee houses would come, but when?

Coffee consumption in Croatia was quite high; many Croatians spent time between meals, in the morning, or at night at coffee bars, which often also served beer and

4. K. Mandel, "Franchise in Hungary," address given at The Franchise Center Osijek seminar "Franšiza od A do Ž," Osijek, November 2004.

5. L. Kukec, "Roundtable—Franchising in Croatia," address given at EFF/IFA International Symposium, Brussels, October 24–25, 2006.

other alcoholic products. While regular bars and other restaurants competed with coffee shops for customers, coffee shops were relatively cheaper, providing a comfortable environment for socializing. Suppliers of coffee were many and included both international and local brands. Coffee, itself, was basically a commodity.

What Should Be Done Next?

Tensek and Pacek looked at the facts: franchising was one of several possible models for business growth and was widely used in economically developed countries throughout the world. Some of the reasons why companies preferred to develop franchise networks rather than organic grow included lower financial investment, lower risk, faster growth, local market knowledge by franchisee, and the franchisee's motivation to succeed. They wanted these benefits too.

The barriers which the San Francisco Coffee House faced in franchising in the local market were challenging:

- There was just not enough information about franchising; as a result, entrepreneurial and institutional awareness of franchising was quite low;

- There were no well-established support organizations for the development of franchise networks in Croatia; there were only two Entrepreneurship Centers in Croatia which offered services regarding franchise network development; and

- There was no significant support from financial institutions; banks failed to recognize the relatively lower risk of investment in start-up entrepreneurs/franchisees than in independent start-up entrepreneurs.

Moreover, the company was still young and unproven in other locations. The couple could simply enjoy their local success. They could open additional stores by themselves. Or they could try to sell franchises of their concept. See Exhibit 6 for the entrepreneurs' estimates of store-level expenses and revenues.

Could the couple develop franchising in a market where local conditions were less than conducive? Could they gain national prominence? The couple had never run a franchising business and did not have the necessary experience and knowledge. How could they overcome the weaknesses they possessed and the environmental threats? How could they seize the opportunities in the marketplace using their unique experiences, capabilities and strengths?

	Expenses (based on one year)	Euros (€)
1.	Salaries with Benefits	€ 10,000
	Manager	€ 6,000
	Waiter 1	€ 5,333
	Waiter 2	€ 5,333
	Waiter 3	€ 5,333
	Rent with utilities	€ 32,000
2.	Marketing, Royalties	€ 2,666
3.	Cost of Direct Material (based on €666.66 per day)	€ 72,000
4.	Total Expenses per year	€138,666
	Total Income (based on average of €666.66 per day)	€240,000
	Net Income in the first year	€101,333

Exhibit 6 Expected Revenues and Expenses

This case was supported by The Franchise Center, part of the Center for Entrepreneurship Osijek, and Poduzetna Hrvatska, a USAID project in Croatia.

CASE P3-3

Euro Disney

Euro Disney A

Michael Eisner, CEO and Chairman of Walt Disney, was used to celebrations. He and his team had been recognized numerous times since taking over the company leadership in 1984. Most notably, Eisner and his team were responsible for Disney's growth from a $2 billion to $22 billion dollar enterprise. But now with disappointing 1992 year-end and 1993 peak season financials for the new Euro Disney Theme park, celebrating would have to wait. Euro Disney revenue and profit during this timeframe was well below expectations (see Exhibit 1). This substandard performance was a first for Eisner and the only time one of his ventures was unsuccessful. A lot was at stake due to Disney's 49 percent equity position in Euro Disney SCA, the operating company that offered the remaining shares to the public. Several banks also invested in the park by extending construction loans totaling $3.5 billion.

Attendance at the park fell significantly below expectations and never met the 11 million tourists estimate developed in the original business plan (see Exhibit 2). Eisner was preparing for an upcoming meeting with a prominent independent consulting firm specifically hired to analyze the issues surrounding the Euro Disney launch. Eisner prides himself on attention to detail and his leadership skills, which guided the Euro Disney opening in April of 1991 and the very successful theme park introductions in Florida, California, and Tokyo. Having previously gained the confidence of the Disney board and shareholders, Eisner was determined to identify and correct the Euro Disney issues. Troubling to Eisner, though, was the fact that he and his team followed the same formula used in the previously successful theme park launches. This fact sustained his belief that external forces beyond his control were the major cause of the problems.

Six Months Ending Sept 30		
	1992	1993
Revenue (French Francs)	3.1 billion	1.8 billion
Profit/(Loss)	(1.1 billion)	0.7 billion

Exhibit 1 Euro Disney P&L, 1992–1993

Year Ending April (Initial Opening in April 1991)		
	1992	1993
Attendance	10.5 million	9.5 million

Exhibit 2 Annual Attendance Figures

Case prepared by Kathryn Woodbury Zeno, Doctoral Candidate, Lubin School of Business, Pace University, December 2010. Reprinted with permission.

Eisner and his management team were thought to be unstoppable. The saying around the office was that everything they worked on "turned to gold." Tokyo Disney, for example, one of the newest of the theme parks, records more attendance per year than Disneyland in California and Disney World in Florida combined. Tokyo Disney consumers, as well as the newer Hong Kong Disneyland consumers, enjoy the United States-based themes and attractions and seem to inject themselves right into the fun, fantasy, and magic. With continued global expansion as a key strategic imperative for the theme parks, Eisner was determined to make Euro Disney an even more expansive and successful operation than the previously opened theme parks. Eisner was directly involved with every detail and decision made regarding the development and execution of the Euro Disney launch. Driven to maintain Disney's successful and quality image, Eisner needed to stay intimately involved in sorting through the issues.

Original Business Plan Expectations

Bound like a classic novel, Eisner flipped through the 30-page Euro Disney business plan reviewing the research, financial assumptions, and estimates. He was pleased with the amount and level of detail provided in the plan. The location assessment was a perfect example of the plan's thoroughness. As with all real estate investments, the location selection was an important decision, and over 200 European locations were assessed prior to making the final decision to locate the park east of Paris. Consistent with previous theme park location strategies to build near a major city, Euro Disney was expected to draw from a wide geography and benefit from the proximity to Paris, the number one European tourist destination (see Exhibit 3). The business plan also outlined European vacation trends, which on average reflected two to three weeks more vacation time than Americans. As a result, the plan assumed European tourists would spend more days at Euro Disney than the other theme parks.

Coordination with the French government was also cited as a major initiative. Even with the close proximity to Paris, it was necessary to build transportation infrastructure to facilitate convenient park access. The French government invested hundreds of millions of dollars to develop rail connections from other major European cities, for example. The opening of the Channel Tunnel in 1993 was also built into the attendance figures and was expected to increase UK tourist attendance.

Attendance is a major variable that can make or break theme park projections. Tokyo Disney provided additional learning to Eisner's team on how to operate a theme park in a cooler and rainier environment than California or Florida. Like Tokyo Disney, Euro Disney incorporated covered waiting areas and walkways to minimize tourist exposure to the elements and to maximize length of stay. Other learning incorporated from a separate Tokyo Disney assessment included the appeal and acceptance of American themes and references embedded in the Disney attractions by non-Americans. Main

Theme Park	City Location	Closest Major City	Distance between Major City and Theme Park (Miles)
Disneyland California	Anaheim	Los Angeles	26.2*
Disneyworld Florida	Lake Buena Vista	Orlando	18.4*
Tokyo Disney Japan	Urayasu	Tokyo	10.0**
Euro Disney France	Marne-La-Vallée	Paris	19.0***

Exhibit 3 Disney Theme Parks: Proximity to Major Cities

Data retrieved from http://maps.ask.com/maps.

Street U.S.A., Frontierland, and Michael Jackson's Captain EO 3-D movie were featured attractions transferred to Euro Disney. Euro Disney Chairman Robert Fitzpatrick, a United States citizen, indicated that "it would have been silly to take Mickey Mouse and try to do surgery to create a transmogrified hybrid, half French and half American." Communication did take a hybrid approach, as French and English were the languages used on park signage and by the staff. In Tokyo, English was the predominant language. Eisner decided to look more into the Tokyo Disney file to uncover additional learning and perhaps understand why Euro Disney was less successful.

Tokyo Disney

The Oriental Land Company (OLC), in partnership with Disney, opened Tokyo Disney in 1983. A success since the gates opened, Tokyo Disney attracts 90 percent of its tourists from Japan. Foreigners traveling to Japan also visit the attraction, as buses go straight to the theme park from the Narita airport. Competitor theme parks struggle to keep pace with Tokyo Disney and have been introducing new rides and entertainment to stave off the abrupt and continual declines in attendance. For the most part, Tokyo Disney is described as a copycat of the Disney parks in California and Florida. Some localization has been included, such as traditional Japanese food on some of the restaurant menus and the inclusion of Japanese on some signs and lines spoken by some of the attraction actors. Hamburgers and fried chicken are common fare within the park and seem to be accepted, even though it is common for Japanese traveling for an extended trip to bring box lunches called *obento*. Disney does not allow *obento* into the theme park and conceded by allowing families to eat *obento* on benches set up outside of the park. Totally engrossed in this American fantasy experience, Japan has more than accepted Mickey and his friends as evidenced not only by the strong park attendance, but in spite of the cold and rainy weather and by the magnitude of licensed goods seen on lunch boxes, book bags, and T-shirts. Coordination with labor officials has been positive, and Tokyo Japan, which is managed and owned by OLC, works well with the Disney management team in securing investment funds.

Having reviewed the recent results and the original business plan for Euro Disney, Eisner was prepared to direct the consulting firm and charge them with identifying the causes of the problems and more important, provide solutions to address those issues. He gave them three weeks to report on their findings.

Euro Disney Problems Revealed

With the short timeframe given, the cross-functional consulting team identified four central themes that characterized the Euro Disney problems. The four central themes identified were:

1. Management
2. The environment
3. Marketing and consumer issues
4. Financial debt and interest charges

Sitting on the other side of Eisner at the conference room table, the consulting team indicated that, given the depth and severity of the issues, they needed more time and money to develop more specific and actionable recommendations.

Management

Management issues were extensive and found to be interrelated with several of the other issues. The consultants outlined the management's approach, decisions, and practices as the major issues. The main issue was the inconsistency of the overall Euro Disney vision and how that vision integrated into the overall Disney vision. The top management team for Euro Disney believed the competitive frame of reference for Euro Disney was European Cathedrals and monuments. Other direct and indirect competitors and venues were not seriously considered as a part of the broader competitive frame. Other European theme parks, for example, had a better perceived price value. Instead of a carbon copy transplant of American Disney, the European entry needed a distinct positioning and relied too heavily on the success of the parent Disney brand (ranked number seven overall in a list of the best global brands) and the other Disney theme parks.

In-depth interviews with French government officials, members of the financial community, labor, and transportation representatives revealed significant tension and disdain with the Euro Disney team. This tension spanned across the entire project from development to actual implementation. The Euro Disney team, consisting primarily of United States-based executives, skewed the operations and internal decision making to standardized offerings versus considering recommendations made by local officials and industry partners, which would have allowed maximized local appeal and capitalized on local market opportunities. Local advisers, for example, did not recommend the location northeast of Paris and proposed other ways to structure the financial deals so as not to incur such a high debt profile. While Fitzpatrick cautioned against reinventing Mickey, more of a hybrid approach in the Euro Disney introduction may have increased attendance and length of stay. The unwillingness of the top management team to incorporate ideas from local talent and constituencies reflected poorly on Disney's management style and this lack of cooperation was detrimental to the park's success.

Environment

The impact of weather patterns on attendance was another highlighted issue. Euro Disney average temperatures are approximately nine degrees lower than Tokyo Disney, where the average high temperature between Tokyo Disney and Euro Disney have a difference as much as 20 degrees lower than Disneyworld in Lake Buena Vista, Florida (see Exhibit 4). Minimal and slow development of other entertainment entities around Euro Disney was another market issue affecting length of stay. Euro Disney needed complementary attractions and destinations to entice vacationers with several weeks of vacation to travel and stay in a city outside of Paris.

Labor issues, such as the train strike that occurred on opening day, often occur in France and were not factored into the business plan. Labor groups objected to the nonnegotiable dress code, where no facial hair or eye shadow was allowed but the wearing of underwear was required. The lack of negotiation with labor exacerbated the situation and helped to maintain the tension with Euro Disney management. Coordination with

Theme Park	Location	Average Temperature (degrees F)	Average Temperature Range (degrees F)	Temperature Range (degrees F)
Disneyland	Anaheim, California	69.7°	60.0°–79.5°	55.0°–94.0°
Disneyworld	Lake Buena Vista, Florida	72.4°	62.0°–82.6°	48.6°–91.5°
Tokyo Disney	Urayasu Tokyo, Japan	60.0°	54.0°–66.0°	35.0°–86.0°
Euro Disney	Marne-La-Vallée, France	52.0°	45.0°–59.0°	34.0°–75.0°

Exhibit 4 Location Climate for Disney Theme Parks

Data from: Metro Orlando Economic Development Commission; NOAA, National Weather Service; www.paris.world-guides.com/weather; www.weather.gov-National Weather Service-climate.

labor unions was especially important during this recessionary period in France and most of Europe. Operating in a recessionary period also called into question the price-value relationship, which was at risk and led into the consumer and marketing issues.

Consumer Marketing Issues

Analysis reflected that a majority of consumers who visited Euro Disney came primarily from France (45 percent). England, Belgium, Germany, Luxembourg, and the Netherlands cumulatively account for another 50 percent, at roughly 10 percent each. Spain made up the balance. While this broad attraction was consistent with the business plan expectations, the depth of appeal was sub-optimized, with only French and English communication and language-oriented staff. The lack of consumer segmentation beyond Europeans transcended into a lack of understanding of consumer needs, habits, and expectations. The lack of accommodations for lunch and inadequate parking for the heavily used tour buses are just a few of the consumer issues that proved troublesome for Euro Disney. Most offensive was the decision to prohibit alcoholic beverages in the park. In a culture that drinks wine with meals, French travel editor Pierre Amalou said, "That's unreasonable." In response to the long lines for rides, and especially for food, Amalou indicated that "For the French, lining up is like being back in the war." The consultants hypothesized that the French/European ethnocentric orientation did not allow for full enjoyment of the United States-centric attractions (i.e., Frontierland) even though other popular American imports such as Coca-Cola and Hollywood movies were experiencing success.

Financials

The complexity and depth of the financial issues required that the consulting firm bring in an investment banking firm to help truncate the major issues and to make recommendations given the short turnaround time required by Eisner. Major restructuring was going to be necessary in light of the findings:

- Key assumptions upon which financial projections were based were overly optimistic and did not assume a balanced risk profile. Financial projections relied too heavily on contributions from the hotels and office parks surrounding Euro Disney.

- The deal structure was based primarily on new debt offerings reflecting liberal policies and high leveraging that was typical of practices in Europe. Although Euro Disney had been working to restructure, unrealistic deadlines had been set that did not allow for complete and adequate analysis to fully address the financial concerns.

- External factors that were present when the deals were developed were not factored into the business proposition. Europe was in a multi-year recession, the French real estate market was in a slump, and major fluctuations existed between the various European currencies, particularly the French franc.

- Related to not understanding the market, pricing structures within the park and as compared to competition and other Disney properties were overpriced. Hotel rooms near Euro Disney cost US$340, as much as a four-star hotel in the center of Paris. Pricing was highlighted as an issue that would continue to be problematic given the continued strength of the European currencies versus the French franc and the United States dollar. Europeans were lured to the United States as they were able to buy more, enjoy the year-round warmer Florida weather, and the many attractions contained within the Orlando area.

Where to Begin?

Eisner knew there would be much to do. He had already organized teams to work on solutions to the identified problems. An investment banking team had been retained to develop an immediate debt restructuring which was need by March 31. Rumors began to circulate that Euro Disney might declare bankruptcy. While restructuring was one of the short-term and immediate needs, Eisner also wanted to work on other short-term issues and take aggressive steps on the longer-term issues, such as marketing and the environment. The press was relentless, especially the English media, which Eisner admitted he "was not prepared for." Action plans needed to be put quickly in place—no later than the end of March—so he could directly address the media, build local relationships, and save Euro Disney.

Discussion Questions

1. What did Disney do wrong in its planning for Euro Disney?
2. What recommendations would you make to Disney to deal with the problems of Euro Disney?
3. What lessons can we learn from Disney's problems with Euro Disney?
4. What social/cultural models might assist Disney with better understanding the France/European environment?
5. What might be the cultural universals that Disney should continue to leverage as they expand their theme parks? What might be the associated risks?

Euro Disney B

Taking responsibility for management issues, Eisner made several changes within the Euro Disney management team. He placed several Europeans in top positions, with Philippe Bourguignon as the new Euro Disney Chairman. Bourguignon reviewed first year fiscal numbers which reported losses of US $920 million, due to the following three factors:

- Lower than projected per capita spending by visitor
- The park's overleveraged financial position, in which it paid 1.7 billion francs to service 20.3 billion francs debt and
- The absence of real estate revenue

These "sound bites" were repeatedly provided to the press by Euro Disney spokesman Jacques-Henri Eyraud. Michael Eisner, chairman of Walt Disney Co., which owns a 49 percent stake in Euro Disney, gave a "D" grade to the European theme park for its poor performance. This poor grade also seemed to signal to some that Eisner was beginning to distance himself from the issues Euro Disney continued to face. In an annual report, Eisner stated the following to shareholders:

> We certainly are interested in aiding Euro Disney SCA, the public company that bears our name and reputation. We will deal in good faith. . . . But in doing so, I promise all shareholders of the Walt Disney Company that we will take no action to endanger the health of Disney itself.

Disney typically projects 20 percent growth in annual earnings and return on equity over a five-year period. Disney was able to make its earnings target, driven by successful film features and licensing extensions for these properties, but missed the return on equity promise driven by the $350 million charge taken for Euro Disney. An overhaul in the financial structure was expected by spring of 1994. Euro Disney could not afford the interest charges for fiscal 1993, which were approximately US $1 million per day. Banks involved in the restructuring would not comment, but an analyst of a major investor indicated "there's evidently a bit of pressuring going on."

Pressure was definitely being felt by other Euro Disney executives, stakeholders, and parent company Disney. Bourguignon responded quickly by reducing operating costs, driving efficiency, and by beginning to tackle some of the marketing challenges. Merchandise offering and inventory was lowered from 30,000 to 17,000, magnetic cards replaced meal vouchers in Euro Disney Hotels, and food offerings were consolidated from 5,400 to 2,000. Supply chain operations were decentralized, with decision making authority given to lower-level managers. Additionally, staff cuts were identified for the end of 1993 and into 1994.

Environmental market concerns seemed to be improving as the European economy was rebounding, the Channel Tunnel opened, and a TGV high-speed train was planned to go directly to Euro Disney from major European hubs without having to change trains in Paris. In addition, the fiftieth anniversary of the Normandy invasion raised hopes for higher attendance in 1994. Improved economic conditions coupled with the debt restructuring were expected to build Euro Disney profitability. Major negotiations were still necessary, as the Euro Disney team needed to convince parent Disney of the need to reduce management fees (35 percent of gross revenue), incentive management fees of 30–50 percent of pretax cash flow, and royalties of 5 percent on food and 10 percent on admission. Given these initial plan agreements, the parent company had been profiting since the park opened, even when Euro Disney was operating at a loss. The restructuring sought to reduce these fees to facilitate Euro Disney changes and fortify the park's financial condition and build overall profitability.

Restructuring Plan Agreement

Parent company Disney agreed to eliminate management fees and royalties on ticket fees for five years. Disney also purchased underutilized assets and leased them back to Disney at favorable rates. Negotiators with the banks forgave 18 months of interest payments and postponed principal payments for three years. Another component of the restructuring was to secure agreement from Disney shareholders for the rights to raise money to eliminate debt. The right was approved on June 8, 1994.

The financial bailout provided by the banks and parent company Disney helped to give Euro Disney some breathing room. With the financial and environmental issues moving ahead, Bourguignon and his team also enacted significant changes to the marketing plan strategies. Most significant was the renaming of the theme park to Disneyland Paris. This repositioning grounded the theme park to the French capital and reinforced its proximity to this major city. In the midst of questionable press, a positive press event occurred when Michael Jackson and Lisa Marie Presley visited Disneyland Paris on their honeymoon. Also, at the end of 1994, admission process were reduced by 22 percent for the 1995 peak season. This was important, as attendance dropped in FY ending 1994, to 8.8 million (see Exhibit 5).

(FY Ending 30 September)	
1993	9.8 million
1994	8.8 million
1995	10.7 million

Exhibit 5 Annual Attendance Figures

FY Ending 30 September in French Francs		
	Revenue	**Profit (Loss)**
1993	4.9 billion	(5.3 billion)
1994	4.1 billion	(1.8 billion)
1995	4.8 billion	114 million

Exhibit 6 Euro Disney Profit and Loss

Results from the restructuring and operational changes improved Disneyland Paris's performance and generated a profit for FY ending 1995 (see Exhibit 6).

Discussion Questions

1. Do you agree with the restructuring plan? What else should have been considered?

2. What else does Euro Disney/Disneyland Paris need to do to sustain profitability and remain in the black?

3. Should the name of the park be changed? What are the related benefits and risks?

4. What can be done to make better use of underutilized resources (such as hotels) while increasing the profitability of well-patronized facilities?

5. Did Disney understand the regulatory and labor environments in France and in the EU?

6. What management structure and skill sets would you recommend to Eisner to implement and sustain a Euro Disney turnaround?

7. Should Disney enter into another market with a theme park? Why or why not? Which market would you recommend and why?

Disneyland Paris C

The initial restructuring and bailout plan proved beneficial over the next few years but was difficult to sustain in light of new direct competition from European theme parks and aggressive measures by existing attractions such as Six Flags Europe. The mid-1990s represented a continued recessionary period for Europe, which continued to affect real estate values, particularly in France. In order to remain competitive, Disneyland Paris continues to find itself caught between the need to expand with new properties and attractions and the need to live within a reasonable debt structure and investment profile. The importance of a "second gate" strategy was demonstrated with the expansion of Disney attractions and entertainment destinations in the United States and Japan. Length of stay and attendance increased when the destinations offered multiple attractions and hotels. In an attempt to raise cash, Euro Disney spokesman Jacques-Henri Eyraud stated the desire "to sell one or more hotels in order to ease debt burdens." Difficulty selling hotels caused Euro Disney to reduce hotel room prices to stimulate higher occupancy rates. This strategy eventually seemed to pay off, as hotel occupancy rates climbed to 72 percent, higher than other hotels in France, which were experiencing occupancy rates between 59 and 63 percent. In 1996, Euro Disney reported a net profit of $40 million for its FY, which ended September 30. While Disney would not confirm, the profit gains seem to be driven by the hotel sector. Newly promoted Philippe Bourguignon, now Euro Disney's chief, attributed the strong results to efficient cost controls. By the late 1900s, Disneyland Paris was excited by the benefits expected from the formalization of the European Economic Union. As a unified region consisting of 11 countries, easier border crossing and currency standardization were expected to bolster Disneyland Paris attendance.

The beginning of the new decade was troublesome for Disney. Eisner and Disney President Robert Iger did not receive bonuses in 2001, as the company posted a net loss of $158 million. This loss was the result of a failed dot-com venture, the closing of several Disney retail stores, and theme park declines. Travel across the theme parks was down after the September 11 terrorist attacks in New York City and subsequent terrorist acts in parts of Europe. Airline travel declined significantly during this time period, and the multiplier effect was felt throughout the interrelated industries. While the industries were expected to rebound, these occurrences suppressed the robust growth desired and needed by Disneyland Paris. With the opening of Walt Disney Studios Park and convention centers outside of Paris, Euro Disney was hoping to increase performance by leveraging the successful Disney film equities and business sector. Industry analysts suggested Disney needed to develop new rides to better compete. Other speculations are that the two French-based Disney theme parks would cannibalize each other without unique offerings and entertainment experiences. Long-term strategic plans reflected even more Disney France expansion, given the large amount of acreage owned by Euro Disney SCA. The land mass was larger than any other Disney property. Unofficial reports indicate potential investments of three new major attractions to be unveiled between 2006 and 2008. To expand, though, Euro Disney would need another infusion of cash, investment, and strong partnerships. Parent company Disney's stake in Euro Disney was now down to 39 percent from the initial 49 percent.

While top management at the Disney Company has made strides in improving its arrogant and culturally insensitive image, there was a lot of unrest within the internal management ranks. Eisner was losing many of his soldiers to other top positions in lucrative entertainment venues. Preferring to remain anonymous, some of the former executives indicated there was not enough "room at the top" for them and Eisner, regardless of how much they contributed to the company's growth.

Even with the management turmoil and coverage in the press regarding the need for more objective governance among the Disney board, Eisner maintained his plans and dreams to continue theme park global expansion. The opening of Hong Kong Disney in 2005 was just one of these dreams come true. Forecasts for the venture in China were mixed, although Disney management was confident about the opportunity. The sheer size of the population, relaxed visa restrictions on mainland Chinese visiting Hong Kong, and the strong presales of Disney paraphernalia and tickets were offered as positive indicators for success. Pessimists cautioned that Hong Kong Disneyland may face similar cultural issues to Disneyland Paris. For example, popular American artists such as Britney Spears were not popular in Hong Kong. Other American icons such as KFC (Kentucky Fried Chicken) have expanded into Hong Kong, but have a menu which is 85 percent Chinese food. The ease with which Disney enters and thrives in this new environment, culture, and population, may not be as simple as Disney management believes.

Disney Nods to Chinese Culture

The Hong Kong government has a 57 percent stake in the park. Based on the size of the property, Hong Kong Disneyland is posed to be the largest theme park of all of the Disney parks, overtaking Disneyland Paris in expansion potential. While a majority of the attractions are based on the American themes and designs, Disney hired a Feng Shui expert to help in designing the park. The Hong Kong Disneyland Hotel does not have a fourth floor, as the number four sounds like the word for death in Chinese and is therefore considered unlucky. The hotel ballroom was designed to be 888 square meters, because the number eight is a lucky number. Main Street, a popular component of all Disney parks, has a Chinese restaurant. Interestingly, many of the designs to incorporate the Chinese culture are not always immediately visible but are subtly incorporated into the park's architecture.

Discussion Questions

1. How should the Disney parks differentiate themselves from the competitive threat posed by the growing number of European amusement parks?
2. What target marketing strategy should be pursued in the face of the changing competitive environment?
3. What branding strategy decisions are relevant?
4. How would you contrast the Euro Disney launch to the Hong Kong Disneyland launch?
5. Will Hong Kong Disneyland be successful? Why or why not?
6. What should be the decision criteria for expanding into additional theme parks and attractions versus fortifying existing theme parks and attractions?

References

Disney doesn't rule out closure of Euro Disney. (3 January 1994). *The Wall Street Journal* (Eastern edition), A4.

Geoffrey A. Fowler and, Merissa Marr. (16 June 2005). Disney's china play; its new hong kong park is a big cultural experiment; will 'main street' translate? *Wall Street Journal,* pp. B.1–B.1. Retrieved from http://search.proquest.com/docview/399001620?accountid=13044.

Haberman, C. (5 October 1986). Disneyland carves out a magic kingdom in hearts of Japanese (Final edition, C). *Chicago Tribune* [New York Times News Service, pre-1997 full text], 16.

Harney, A. (18 August 2005). Magic for the middle kingdom. *Financial Times* (London 1st edition), 19.

Jefferson, D. J. (13 April 1992). Euro Disney opens with much hoopla and a train strike—attendance appeared low, but the crowds seemed pleased by attractions. *The Wall Street Journal* (Eastern edition), C1.

Koranteng, J. (17 December 2001). Euro Disney preparing to unwrap $600 mil Walt Disney Studios Park. *Amusement Business, 113*(50); ABI/INFORM Global, 12.

Koranteng, J. (2005, January). Euro threesome gear up for '05. *Amusement Business, 117*(1), 10.

Larsen, P. T. (13 February 2004). Star pupil takes aim at old school management training. *Financial Times* (London 1st edition), 26.

Mahar, M. (20 June 1994). Not-so-magic kingdom. *Barron's, 74*(25), 29–34.

Meyer, M., & McGuire, S. (5 September 1994). Of mice and men. *Newsweek, 124*(10), 40.

Michaud, P. (6 December 1996). Euro Disney's hotel sector drives company's profits. *Hotel and Motel Management, 211*(21), 4.

Moore, M. T. (6 October 1993). Euro Disney's culture shock. *USA Today* (Money, Final edition), 2B.

Orwall, B. (29 April 2002). Disney moves to improve governance—unhappy about criticism, Eisner revamps practices, hires prominent consultant. *The Wall Street Journal* (Eastern edition), A3.

Selwitz, R. (1 February 1994). Euro Disney hobbles into new year. *Hotel and Motel Management, 209*(2), 4–5.

Tokyo Disney resort operator ups FY '06 earnings forecasts. (9 February 2007). *Jiji Press English News Service*, 1.

Turner, R. (30 December 1993). Disney's Eisner gives 'D' grade to Euro Disney. *The Wall Street Journal* (Eastern edition), A2.

Wrighton, J. (29 September 2004). Euro Disney in debt-restructure deal. *The Wall Street Journal*, A3. Retrieved from http://online.wsj.com/article_print/0,SB109636350494229909,00.html.

Additional References

Best global brands. (2006). *Interbrand*, p. 11.

Inkpen, A., & Ramaswamy, K. (2006). Strategic choices in a global marketplace. In *Global Strategy Creating and Sustaining Advantage Across Borders* (pp. 32–53). New York: Oxford University Press.

CASE P4-1

Mobile Language Learning: Praxis Makes Perfect in China

Richard Ivey School of Business
The University of Western Ontario

I think we just approached it differently. We first started by looking for ways that technology could solve problems of the average language student here in Shanghai. From our research we found that students often spent more time traveling to/from class and waiting for class than they actually spent in class. This seemed like a big inefficiency to us and we speculated how things would change if students were able to listen to their instructional materials on the way to class and then use their actual class time more efficiently to practice.[1]

HANK HORKOFF (2006)

Sitting in his office on the third floor in Shanghai near the ZhongShan Park and LouShanGuan Road subway stations, Hank Horkoff was contemplating the next moves for his company, Praxis Language. With the growth of its ChinesePod .com brand, Praxis led the field of mobile learning through the uniqueness of its business model, mobile learning solutions, and tailored content.

Coupled with the explosive growth of smart phones in China, in 2006 the company experienced remarkable growth. What's more, the company had received considerable attention from international media that contributed to its fame and fortune. Chinese language education was coming of age and the advent of technology and globalization made this company a prominent innovator in the mobile language learning category. But Horkoff, a Richard Ivey School of Business alumnus, now faced the challenges of continuing Praxis's growth, capitalizing on its existing assets, fighting off imitators and maintaining its momentum. New competitors were coming online daily. Technology was creating new possibilities for teaching/learning Chinese. And the demand for both Chinese and English language education was on the rise.

Entrepreneurial Opportunities Overseas

After graduating from the University of British Columbia (UBC) in political science in 1996, Horkoff decided to explore opportunities overseas. While studying for his bachelor's degree, he also learned how to program and create web sites. The late 1990s had many opportunities for those who were computer savvy and Horkoff was

1. Huw Collingbourne, "Podcasting Secrets—ChinesePod," *Bitwise Magazine,* August 18, 2006, www.bitwisemag.com/2/ Podcasting-Secrets-ChinesePod.

keen on capitalizing on them. He learned how to program and was able to land a few small projects. This experience proved useful later on.

Leaving Canada, Horkoff decided to venture to Moscow. Russia in the 1990s was exciting. The market had just opened and opportunities for freelance work were available. While getting travel and work experience was fun, Horkoff felt that he wanted more. He wanted to learn more about business and be able to apply this knowledge in the international environment. The Richard Ivey School of Business, which had one of the leading MBA programs in the world, would allow him to obtain exactly these skills. He matriculated in the full-time MBA program and successfully graduated by 2001. After graduation, more international opportunities for business presented themselves.

Horkoff decided to go to Singapore next. There he associated with a bio-technology firm building business plans for various entrepreneurial companies. His knowledge of technology, coupled with his business education, made him especially apt for the position. The job, however, did not provide him with the kind of stimulation he was looking for. Shortly after starting the position, he met a friend who invited him to work as a business planning consultant for Samsung in Beijing. After working there for nine months, he quickly realized that the Beijing job was also not a good fit for him. He felt that working for somebody else, building someone else's business plans, was not what he was destined to do. He quit.

Next, Horkoff went to Shanghai, China's business center and the "land of opportunities." Drawing on his previous skills, he started doing some freelance work and started his own consulting firm doing web consulting and development, customer relations management systems (CRM), backend enterprise development, e-commerce and promotion, etc. Working in Shanghai doing consulting proved to be a life-changing activity.

Through a referral, he started doing some work for the Kaien Language school, which needed a new CRM system. *Kai En English Training Center* was a language school (named after its founders, Ken and Brian) under Western management that provided high-quality language teaching to English learners in Shanghai since 1996.[2] The school offered students the opportunity to improve their business English communication skills in a dynamic environment using modern communicative language teaching methods. The language trainers were qualified and experienced, with a strong interest in developing themselves professionally.

Crawling Out of the Pod

Praxis wanted to find a way to leverage technology to enhance language training. Horkoff realized that much of the time spent learning a language in crowded Shanghai was used traveling to and from the brick-and-mortar training center. And even outside Shanghai, there would be too much time spent listening to lectures and reviewing mundane information that could be replaced easily by podcasting. In early 2005, podcasting—digital audio and/or video media files that are made available for download via web syndication—was becoming increasingly popular as Internet use in China was surging exponentially.

The English language learning market in China was strong. International trade was growing rapidly along with foreign direct investment. Chinese employees who wanted an edge in the job market quickly realized that they needed to be competent in English to take advantage of the growth in international business. Praxis estimated the demand for English language instruction in China to be about 60 million adult learners, but the

2. http://career.kaien.net.cn/index.php?page=about.kaien.

market was highly fragmented. The biggest competitor in the field, New Oriental, had only about five per cent of the market. New Oriental had 30 to 40 students per class-room and little personalization. In addition, in China there were about 50,000 private language schools, international academic institutions and freelance teachers.

Kai En English Language Training Center was well positioned in the marketplace. First, it was an early entrant, having started in Shanghai in 1996. Second, it was owned by two highly competent entrepreneurs with international experience in English as a Second Language (ESL) teaching. Brian McCloskey and Ken Carroll, the founders, were involved in managing language schools in Taiwan before relocating to Shanghai to establish Kai En. By 2007, there were five centers in Shanghai and more than 7,000 annual graduates. The teaching staff included a team of 60-70 full-time native speaking professional English-as-a-First-Language teachers and more than 20 additional Chinese ESL instructors. In short, Kai En was a powerful local brand with a strong reputation.

At first, the founders and Horkoff were keen on leveraging technology to teach English to grow their business. They realized that much of the time of learning a new language was not productive. The real learning happened during the communicative, interactive, and experiential portion of the class when the teacher and students were engaging one another in active speaking, listening, and responding. How can they use technology, they wondered, to maximize the active learning in the classroom?

One way was to shift the passive learning to an online platform. They took the cue from the Wall Street Institute School of English, which early on used computers to aug-ment student learning in the classroom.[3] Wall Street in the 1990s augmented the physi-cal classroom with computer programs to teach English and bundled it with traditional instruction to charge more for its services. The typical foreign language learning envi-ronment consisted of three hours a week. Online added another hour a week to engage—and charge—students. The business model was based on Chris Anderson's *freemium* model in which Praxis gave away audio podcast lessons, while charging for the five types of subscriptions (see Exhibit 1). At the end of 2009, Praxis had more than 10,000

	Price (US$)	Price (RMB)	Discount	Virtual School	Price (US$)	Price (RMB)	Discount
Basic							
1 Month	$ 9	¥ 60		3 Months	$ 249	¥ 1.668	
6 Months	$ 49	¥ 328	9.3%				
12 Months	$ 79	¥ 529	26.9%				
24 Months	$129	¥ 864	40.3%				
Premium				**Executive Plan**			
1 Month	$ 29	¥ 194		1 Month	$ 199	¥ 1,333	
6 Months	$149	¥ 998	14.4%	6 Months	$ 899	¥ 6,023	24.7%
12 Months	$249	¥1,668	28.4%	12 Months	$1,599	¥10,713	33.0%
24 Months	$399	¥2,673	42.7%	24 Months	$2,999	¥20,093	37.2%
Guided				**Praxis Pass**			
1 Month	$ 49	¥ 328		1 Month	$ 39	¥ 261	
6 Months	$249	¥1,668	15.3%	6 Months	$ 169	¥ 1,132	27.8%
12 Months	$429	¥2,874	27.0%	12 Months	$ 299	¥ 2,003	36.1%
24 Months	$699	¥4,683	40.6%	24 Months	$ 549	¥ 3,678	41.3%

Exhibit 1 Product Pricing

Source: Company records.

3. www.wallstreetinstitute.com/students/overview.aspx, retrieved March 6, 2010.

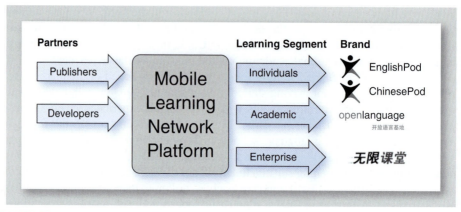

Exhibit 2 Proposed Market Segmentation

Source: Company records.

	Academic	**Enterprise**	**Individual**
Market size (est.)	US$125 million (2013)	US$1 billion (2013)	Billions
Competition	Dyned, Moodle, Blackboard	Wall Street, English First, Global English	Wall Street, Rosetta Stone, New Oriental
Revenue Model	School acts as reseller	Direct	*Freemium*
Marketing	Online, conferences, partnerships	Target HR and training departments	Online, business development

Exhibit 3 Marketing Segmentation Strategy

Source: Company records.

customers paying between US$9–199 per month, resulting in annual income in excess of US$1 million with 50 per cent gross margins. Instructors were paid US$1,000 per month for roughly 160 hours of work. At the end of 2009, Praxis had 50 full-time and 10 part-time employees. It rented a 400 square meter space for US$8,000 per month.

Praxis identified three distinct segments in the English language learning segment in China: academic, enterprise and individual (see Exhibit 2). Praxis believed that each segment required a unique marketing strategy (see Exhibit 3).

Praxis built three different web sites to target each of these markets:

Academic: http://openlanguage.com

Enterprise: http://wxclass.com

Individual: http://chinesepod.com (see Exhibit 4)

Eventually the Praxis management team decided that using technology as a differentiator was not enough to survive and grow given the intense competition for English language education. The partners decided to target an entirely new market: a Chinese language learning center for foreigners. Just as Chinese students saw English as a tool to increase accelerate their career advancement, so too would foreigners need to develop some level of Chinese to survive in their own organizations in the future against locals seeking employment with foreign firms. They could start a new category of business and be the ultimate innovators in this category by infusing technology in the learning/teaching of the language. The Chinese language education market was expanding rapidly, but sophisticated competitors were still largely non-existent.

The birth of ChinesePod.com in 2005 came from the convergence of the growing globalization of the Chinese language, which accompanied China's economic growth,

ChinesePod	
Week Commencing: 10/09/2009	
Week 1	
1.	Intermediate - Ordering Office Supplies
2.	Intermediate - Traditional Chinese Medicine
3.	Intermediate - Tai Chi
4.	Intermediate - Opinions on Poetry
5.	Intermediate - Calligraphy
Week 2	
1.	Intermediate - Wang Tries to Excel at the Office
2.	Intermediate - Up-and-Comer in the Office
3.	Intermediate - A Firing Afoot?
4.	Intermediate - Trimming the Fat at Wang's Office
5.	Intermediate - Lao Wang Plans Revenge
Week 3	
1.	Intermediate - Lao Wang Plans to Sue
2.	Intermediate - Lao Wang in the Doghouse
3.	Intermediate - Delivery Problems
4.	Intermediate - A Dodgy Opportunity for Lao Wang
5.	Intermediate - Requesting a Raise
Week 4	
1.	Intermediate - Job Interview
2.	Intermediate - Studying Chinese
3.	Intermediate - Using a Dictionary
4.	Intermediate - Dorm Life: Late for Class
5.	Intermediate - Signing up for Art Class

Exhibit 4 Sample Lesson Plan and Daily Lesson

Source: http://chinesepod.com.

and the growing use of technology, particularly podcasting and interactive technologies, such as Skype. Furthermore, ChinesePod.com took the computer out of the classroom and put the programs online. This increased the possible engagement with the language learner from 4–5 hours per week to 8–10. Mobile interaction (lab and classroom) provided the potential for 24/7 interaction with the consumer.

The ChinesePod.com business model was fairly simple: offer free Chinese language podcasting for beginner Chinese language learners to draw them into the web site. The podcasts were practical, useful, and short daily conversations about typical subjects such as eating out, making a cell phone call, using the metro, celebrating a birthday, etc. The lessons were divided into several levels: newbie, elementary, intermediate, upper intermediate, advanced, and media. Paid subscribers also had access to dialogue, vocabulary, and exercises. The idea was to break away from the traditional classroom experience and to give potential students a learning experience that was available when they wanted. The company motto was "Learning on Your Terms."

Praxis Language's *Mobile Learning Network* blended podcast lessons, social collaboration tools, classroom integration, mobile distribution and administration features. Different brands targeted the unique market segments of the market in China (see Exhibit 5).

Different levels of paid subscriptions existed. The highest level also included a daily Chinese language teacher who would speak to the student for about 10 minutes

Exhibit 5 Sample Mobile Language Learning Lessons

Source: http://chinesepod.com/.

relating to the podcasted lesson assigned for the day. Because the company used Skype Internet telephone technology, a service that provided free computer-to-computer telephone communications for those who downloaded the program, the learner could be located anywhere in the world and still benefit from a native speaker residing in China. The time difference between China and the host country was a bit of a challenge, but that burden was placed on the teacher in China rather than the students.

Technology: The Lingua Franca

The iPhone is emblematic of a category of mobile devices called smart phones, which actually have more in common with computers than phones in that their primary use is to send and receive data, rather than to talk to other users. Although smart phones were originally sold with hard drives ever-increasing in size, the latest trend pointed to devices that used the "Internet cloud"—large servers like those used by Google to store information. Mobile devices were projected to become little more than access devices, retrieving information and running applications that existed in the cloud. Synonyms for cloud-based computing included cloud computing, software as a service (SAAS), infrastructure as a service, and rent versus own computing.

China was not at the forefront of this cloud computing revolution, but was the world leader in mobile phone subscriptions with more than 700 million cell phone subscribers as of December 2009. According to BDA Limited, an analyst firm that tracked Asian markets, subscribers would grow to around 784 million by 2011, with almost 250 million Chinese accessing the Internet with their cell phone by 2011.[4] Smart phones were used by just a small percentage of Chinese subscribers due to the high cost of the device and the data service. But three of the biggest brands in smart phones, Research in Motion's BlackBerry, Taiwan's HTC (running Google's Android software platform on a Linux operating system), and Apple's iPhone, were launched in China in 2006, May 2009 and October 2009, respectively. According to the Chinese Ministry of Industry and Information Technology, there were almost 10

---

4. "How many new cell phone accounts are opened in China a day?" http://news.cnet.com/8301-10784_3-9724502-7.html.

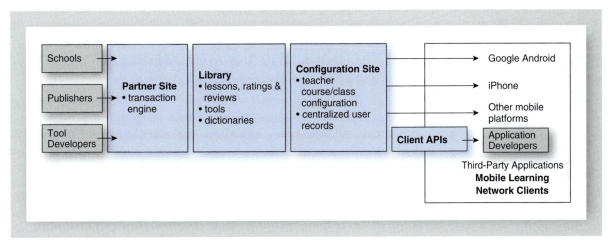

Exhibit 6 Praxis Language's Technology Model

Source: Company records.

million Chinese using third-generation (3G) services in October 2009.[5] 3G networks gave subscribers access to much faster data rates, meaning that more cloud computing and other commercial services that formerly could only be accessed by fixed/wired networks could now migrate to wireless devices (see Exhibit 6).

Praxis identified three technology keys to success in the mobile language learning space:

- using mobile interfaces to simplify access for students;
- using multiple online and offline tools to connect with students to maximize engagement;
- open (non-proprietary) platforms to collaborate with schools, publishers and developers.

Horkoff realized he could not use the technology immediately to address what remained the largest addressable market: English for native Chinese speakers. Most Chinese, while quick to adopt mobile phones, were still completely unfamiliar with podcasting. So Praxis decided to first use this technology to launch ChinesePod.com—Mandarin Chinese for native English speakers. ChinesePod.com offered a viable alternative to potential language learners who would not or could not take evening classes to learn Chinese or couldn't afford a set of books and CDs.

The Opportunity and Challenges Ahead

While ChinesePod.com was doing well, a need existed to examine opportunities for growth. Competitors were coming online daily and the concept had few barriers to entry, technical or otherwise. Should the company move to other language groups? And if so, which ones? Should it simply concentrate on Chinese language education and try to get more customers? Should the company return to its roots and further develop English language training in China? What other services could it add to the platform it had already built?

Two new technologies were coming online in China: the Google Android phone and Apple's iPhone. How could Praxis leverage these new systems? What risks did these and emerging technologies pose to the Praxis business model?

---

5. China's Information Technology and Internet, www.chinatoday.com/it/it.htm.

IVEY

Richard Ivey School of Business
The University of Western Ontario

CASE P4-2

Birzeit Pharmaceutical Company: Marketing from Palestine

Talal Nasereldin sat in his office in the West Bank of Palestine on January 2010, reflecting on the progress of his company. Despite locational disadvantages and a harsh business environment, Birzeit Pharmaceutical Company (BPC) had grown not only locally but also internationally; however, the company was now at a crossroads. It needed to decide on which markets to enter and how to grow further. BPC's growth expanded to new markets and to a diversity of product lines, as explained below.

> Birzeit Pharmaceutical Company (BPC) is Palestine's leading manufacturer of generic medicines. With more than 300 products distributed among 10 production lines and covering different therapeutic ranges, BPC targets all types of customers in the local Palestinian market including the Ministry of Health, local health care organizations, international health care organizations and programs, end users (through pharmacies and physicians). BPC market is not limited to the Palestinian Territory; the company has a well established presence in different export markets—mainly Algeria and Eastern Europe.[1]

BPC had successfully completed several development phases to become not only Palestine's first pharmaceutical company but also the leading manufacturing company in the Palestinian territories and an example of what business entrepreneurs could achieve despite obstacles related to the political and security situation in the West Bank and Gaza. The company had recently completed its most recent development phase in late 2009 by investing in new machinery and expanding its manufacturing facility in Ramallah. In 2008, the company had obtained a Current Good Manufacturing Practices (cGMP) certificate, the result of two decades' hard work and commitment, in addition to generous investments by the company's owners.[2]

BPC realized that the significance of the Palestinian pharmaceutical industry extended far beyond the size of the revenues. Its vision was to be the backbone of the health care security system in Palestine and the region and to offer superior-quality products.[3] Export and import restrictions in Palestine limited the growth of the company. To develop external markets for its products and escape the highly volatile environment of Palestine, the company needed to investigate new markets. In 2006, BPC

Yara Asa'd and Ilan Alon wrote this case solely to provide material for class discussion. The authors do not intend to illustrate either effective or ineffective handling of a managerial situation. The authors may have disguised certain names and other identifying information to protect confidentiality.

1. Birzeit Pharmaceutical Company, "About BPC," www.bpc.ps/index.php?page=about_bpc, accessed March 5, 2010.

2. *Birzeit Pharmaceutical Company Business Plan 2009,* compiled by Dimensions Consulting Company, Ramallah, Palestine, accessed March 2010.

3. Ibid.

invested in an Algerian company with the aim of expanding its export markets and potentially using the site as an external headquarters to serve new markets.

Birzeit Pharmaceutical Company (BPC)

In 1973, Talal Nasereldin graduated from the American University of Beirut with an master's degree in chemistry. Upon his return to Palestine, his family invested in a partnership with Subhi Khoury, who, in 1974, with a total investment of $150,000, had established BPC, a private shareholding company. The small size of the company allowed multi-functional roles for all its employees. Nasereldin, though a chemist, worked in various areas of the company, including packing, management and marketing. He also acted as a representative to promote products to doctors and pharmacists, visiting every community, socializing with the stakeholders and focusing on personalizing all his relationships.

In 1984, Nasereldin became the general manager, which enabled him to work toward growing the company, which he believed held much potential. Under Nasereldin's guidance, BPC witnessed the growth he had envisioned. Growing the product lines was Nasereldin's first goal, which he accomplished first by merging BPC in 1992 with the third-largest pharmaceutical company in Palestine, Palestine Medical Company, and then by acquiring Eastern Chemical Company in 2002. By acquiring these two former competitors, BPC's market share grew substantially.

Nasereldin's second goal was to diversify the business, which was achieved in 1996, when BPC established the Medix Company for Beauty and Care, through which BPC offered international cosmetics and body care products.

In 2005, the company was listed on the Palestine Security Exchange, and, in 2006, BPC partnered with an Algerian pharmaceutical packaging company, Petrapharm, with the goal of expanding its international markets and introducing new technologies to the pharmaceutical manufacturing business.

BPC was in a position of aggressive competition, characterized by its many internal strengths and external opportunities. Such a competitive position allowed the company to gradually follow different business strategies as per below:

- Concentrate growth: Manufacture more of the current products for distribution in the current markets.
- Market development: Offer current products in new markets or through new channels.
- Product development: Modify existing products or offer new related products to current customers.
- Innovation: Introduce new products on an ongoing basis.

The company invested in growing its standards and procedures to prepare for its market growth and expansion. The company's business plan stated,

> BPC combines many factors in order to maintain its success. These factors include: obtaining the latest quality standards certificates such as cGMP (Current Good Manufacturing Practices) and ISO quality systems, strong financial position of the company, highly educated and well trained staff members distributed among the different departments, management team with long experience and high credibility, many strategic investments and alliances (local and international), ongoing product development and market development initiatives, state of the art facilities with a total area of 15,000 square meters, modern production lines operating according to the latest technology in this industry, and best suppliers of raw and packaging materials.[4]

4. *Birzeit Pharmaceutical Company Business Plan 2009*, compiled by Dimensions Consulting Company, Ramallah, Palestine, April 2009, pp. 5–65.

In 2006, BPC initiated an expansion plan to: (1) respond to the continuous increase in demand for its pharmaceutical products in the local market; (2) respond to the increased sales in export markets and especially Algeria; and (3) comply with the cGMP and other quality and regulatory requirements. The company invested more than JD 2 million[5] in new machinery bought from 2006 to 2008. BPC's expansion plan was expected to achieve many positive indicators by the end of the projection period (2015). By 2011, Palestine was still the dominant market for BPC, representing approximately 80 per cent of total sales.[6]

BPC's Competitive Advantage

Given the different levels of competition that BPC faced, it needed to analyse its competitive advantage from different angles. From the perspective of competition with Palestinian manufacturers in the local market, BPC's competitive position stemmed from the following:

- A modern and state-of-the-art production facility equipped with high-tech machinery and production lines
- A well-trained and committed team
- A well-established presence in all selling locations (mainly pharmacies) in the West Bank and Gaza
- A strong financial position that enabled the company to provide the highest credit terms to its customers, provided the company with high flexibility in managing its inventory levels in responding to the changes in Israeli policies and procedures on borders, and demonstrated the credibility that was being provided to the company's stakeholders
- The introduction of new products in demand that were not manufactured by any other Palestinian manufacturer
- Strategic relationships with local health care institutions and donors in addition to investments and business relationships with many key business institutions in Palestine[7]

From another angle, BPC competed with Israeli and foreign products in the local market on a product level. BPC was competing with agents, traders, distributors and drug stores but not necessarily with manufacturers directly. Accordingly, also on the product level, were its three competitive advantages:

1. *The affordable prices of the products.* The affordability of BPC's products reflected the company's cost advantage, which had improved between 2002 and 2007. The company continued to work to improve its cost advantage through the acquisition of modern machinery and equipment and through continuous training and investments in building the skills and capacity of its staff.

2. *The high drug efficacy.* BPC imported its raw materials from the top sources in the world that abided by international standards and best practices. To comply with the requirements of cGMP certification, the machinery and equipment were the most modern in terms of technology and accuracy.

3. *The availability in every retail location in the West Bank and Gaza.* BPC used a detailed distribution map and conducted regular sales analyses by area and

5. JD stands for Jordanian dinar; JD0.71 equals US$1.

6. *Birzeit Pharmaceutical Company Business Plan 2009,* compiled by Dimensions Consulting Company, Ramallah, Palestine, April 2009, pp. 5–65.

7. Ibid.

by selling location. As a result, BPC could quickly respond to customers' needs in any geographical location in the Palestinian territories. BPC could also respond quickly to emergency needs by providing medicines to geographically dispersed communities and maintained good relations with the Ministry of Health and with local communities through its frequent donations of medicines in response to need and urgency.

BPC also benefited from competitive advantages in terms of competition in export markets:

- Quality, which was supported by the company's ISO and cGMP certifications and by its continuous audits, in addition to other specifications and standards that enabled the company to respond to the requirements of entering any export market
- A strong financial position, which enabled the company to provide any working capital and infrastructure investments required to establish a presence in the export markets
- Strong strategic alliances and relationships with key players in the targeted export markets

Market Positioning

BPC positioned itself as the leader of the manufacturing and marketing of generic drugs in the Palestinian territories. The company was seen in the local market as a pioneer in the pharmaceutical industry in terms of its production facilities, machinery and equipment, technology, know-how, financial position, social development role and product development.

BPC's products were positioned in the local market as high-quality products sold at affordable prices. In the export market, BPC's products were seen as high-quality products that were sold at reasonable prices and were available in select selling locations.

BPC Marketing Mix[8]

BPC set its plans and managed them according to the market situation where the company operated. The main features of BPC's plans in managing its marketing mix are summarized below.

Product

- BPC manufactured and marketed generic drugs.
- BPC manufactured 273 products, which covered different therapeutic ranges and were available in approximately 70 different packaging and dosage formats to meet the needs of various customers with respect to distinct export markets, languages and laws.
- BPC focused on achieving a competitive advantage in its products through the raw materials it sourced from around the world. As an example, BPC had a special contract with a Korean company that provided BPC with competitive prices and consistent quality for potassium clavulanate as a raw material.
- The company's products were cGMP- and ISO-certified.

8. Firas Nasiruddin, marketing manager at BPC, personal communication, March 14, 2010.

- BPC invested in human resources, cutting-edge facilities, modern machinery and equipment, and the latest technology.
- BPC planned to introduce new products not manufactured by other local Palestinian pharmaceutical companies, which would provide the company exclusivity in the local market. The company planned to address the demand for unique products, which would raise the company's profits and reduce its competition or limit competition for foreign products. An example of such products would be the third generation cefalosporins in vial form (sterile powder). This line of production had been monopolized by Israeli and international companies in the past.

Pricing

- BPC's domestic products were priced lower than Israeli and foreign drugs, yet were in the same price range as other local manufacturers.
- BPC's products in export markets were moderately priced compared its competitors.
- BPC followed a penetration strategy when pricing in some export markets. For example, BPC sold a product that was used to treat rashes and other dermal infections at 65 per cent off the innovator price. By planning and managing its pricing strategies, BPC benefited from its achieved cost advantage.

Promotion

- BPC used mostly direct selling as a key promotional tool.
- BPC focused its promotional activities on all parties participating in or affected by buying decisions, including pharmacists, physicians and end users, through implementing continuous surveys to study customer's satisfaction, SWOT analysis and product positioning in the market.
- BPC had made substantial investments, both in building the capacity of its sales and promotion team and in obtaining a crew of well-trained sales and promotion personnel covering all targets in the West Bank and Gaza. Policies were implemented throughout the teams and best practices in customer relationship management strategy development were enhanced.
- BPC benefited from strong relationships with the Ministry of Health, health care donor projects and international donors in promoting bulk sales. As a strategy, BPC studied the nationally recognized WHO essential drug list and chose products that were demanded yet not produced locally.
- BPC relied on the long experience and extended networks of its management team in export markets (mainly Algeria) for promoting export sales.
- Public relations and corporate social responsibility (CSR) were valued by BPC's senior management team and board of directors, as reflected through their continuous participation in community activities and events on the national level. BPC sponsored many community activities and events throughout the West Bank and Gaza.

Distribution

- BPC distributed to a wide geographic area, including almost every pharmacy in the West Bank and Gaza.
- BPC kept in contact with all active physicians and pharmacists in the West

Bank and Gaza through continuous field visits, getting direct feedback on its products and its market positioning.

■ BPC's well-experienced team managed its distribution activities in the export markets.

■ BPC outsourced its distribution activities as needed, which reduced costs and contributed to the achievement of its cost advantage.

Business Environment

Political Overview

The Palestinian Minister of Economy described Palestine, "The geographical location of Palestine was excellent, forming an economic and cultural platform and point of contact between three continents: Europe, Asia and Africa. The combined area of the West Bank and Gaza was 6,020 square kilometres."[9]

In 2009, the total population of the Palestinian territories was approximately 3.9 million: 2.4 million in the West Bank and 1.5 million in Gaza. Most of the Palestinian population was young, with approximately 57 per cent younger than age of 20.

The Palestinian National Authority was declared after the Gaza-Jericho Agreement, which was signed in Cairo on May 4, 1994. This agreement created a Palestinian nation governed under the Palestinian National Authority, which was in control of the nation, albeit with restrictions on borders and resources. As a result, the Palestinian National Authority was affected by the Israeli restrictions on borders, which controlled the movement of people and goods in and out of the country, in addition to controlling the resources, imports, exports and even the marketing of the products manufactured in the Palestinian territories, which were not allowed to be marketed in the Israeli neighboring market.

Economic Background

The Palestinian economy had witnessed many ups and downs, mainly due to the general political situation. Gross domestic product (GDP) growth had averaged more than 10 per cent per year between 1994 and 1999, but had slumped following the outbreak of violence in 2000, and the Palestinian economy experienced one of its worst recessions in modern history. However, the GDP rebounded, increasing to 8.5 per cent in 2003 and six per cent in 2005, the same level as in 1999.[10]

As a result of the political situation in Palestine, local companies faced severe export restrictions, not only from international markets (which considered Palestinian products to be below standards), and not only from the Israeli restrictions on borders (aimed at weakening the overall Palestinian economy by enforcing harsh restrictions and regulations on the export of Palestinian goods) but also from the Arab countries that included Palestinian products in the list of Israeli products they boycotted.

Furthermore, the unemployment rate in the West Bank had increased from 15.9 per cent in the second quarter of 2009 to 17.8 per cent in the third quarter of 2009; in Gaza the increase was from 36 per cent in the second quarter of 2009 to 42.3 per cent in the third quarter of 2009.

9. Muhammad Hassouneh and Hasan Abu Libdeh, Palestine Investment Conference, p. 21, www.scribd.com/doc/25577574/Palestine-Investment-Conference-Bethlehem-28, accessed March 26, 2010.

10. Muhammad Hassouneh and Hasan Abu Libdeh, Palestine Investment Conference, www.scribd.com/doc/25577574/Palestine-Investment-Conference-Bethlehem-28, accessed March 26, 2010.

Social Background

Because of continuous political instability, the Palestinian market was dependent on foreign products. Consumers had a negative perception of the quality of locally manufactured products and lacked awareness of the various investments that had been made into upgrading the quality of local products and the local industry, leading to a continued weak positioning of local products within the Palestinian market.

As a result of this negative perception of local products, and due to the maturity of the Palestinian Ministry of National Economy, there was a call to improve the quality and standards of local production by monitoring the compliance of manufacturing processes to international standards. The Palestinian Authority developed its legal system to adapt to the need to trace the safety of the products that its local manufacturers supplied to Palestinian consumers.

Additionally, local companies began their own initiatives. They started to address their local image by participating in sponsorships and corporate social responsibility (CSR) projects aimed at spreading awareness about their companies and by positioning themselves within the local market. The company signed agreements with local manufacturers not to compete locally, building confidence and trust that agreements would be respected. This confidence allowed the companies to build strategies based on long-term visions and agreements, especially in the manufacturing of chronic disease products for diabetes and cardiac diseases. BPC was one of the leading companies in initiating unique and innovative CSR projects that focused on specified segments within the community, such as education, sports, health, environment and communal sustainable development, including investment in infrastructure. The projects were directed through well-studied plans focused on spreading awareness about companies, their status, products, investments, growth and quality. In fewer than five years, the company succeeded in building a solid image within the local market, which heightened Palestinian awareness and increased the number of people requesting to visit the facilities to acknowledge the quality of the facilities and the manufacturing process, and to gain assurance on the quality of the products provided. Increased demand for BPC's products specifically was noted by pharmacists and doctors across the country.

Furthermore, in a call to support local products, the Palestinian Ministry of National Economy initiated, in January 2010, a campaign that had both a sociopolitical dimension and an economic dimension. The campaign called for supporting Palestinian products by promoting them locally, in addition to the boycotting of all Israeli products that were manufactured in settlements established in the Palestinian territories. This campaign had been adopted by all government departments and by the public and was expected to boost the local economy. The launch of this campaign came in response to the Israeli restrictions imposed on Palestinians in general and slow economic development specifically. Statistics announced by the Palestinian Ministry of National Economy noted that Israeli settlements annually pumped more than half a billion U.S. dollars of goods and products into the Palestinian markets.

Local Pharmaceutical Market and Industry

The Palestinian pharmaceutical industry was unique in terms of development. The industry boomed after the events in 1967, which resulted in the closing of its borders with the Arab world. Prior to this time, pharmaceutical products had been imported from foreign companies via importers in Jordan. After 1967, however, imports from Jordan were stopped. The only products available were Israeli products and products imported through Israeli agents.[11]

11. Awad Abu Alia, general director at the Union of Palestinian Pharmaceutical Manufacturers, personal communication, March 14, 2010.

The difficulty in obtaining medicine encouraged nine pharmacists in the West Bank to establish small laboratories to manufacture simple syrups and anti-diarrheal products in 1969. Political and economic instability soon threatened the viability of capital investment in the pharmaceutical industry, and indeed in all industries. In 1970, these nine laboratories merged into three larger companies—Jordan Chemicals in Beit Jala, Palestine Medical Company in Ramallah and Jerusalem Pharmaceutical in Al Bireh.[12]

A period of growth followed, new entrants came to the market, Balsam Company in 1972, followed by Birzeit Pharmaceuticals Company in 1974. In 1979, Eastern Medical Company and Gama entered the market. In 1985, Pharmacare entered the West Bank market, while MASCO entered the Gaza market, to be lastly followed by Al Jaleel Pharmaceutical that entered the West Bank market in 2010.[13]

Later, the big pharmaceutical companies started merging with the smaller ones. In 1993, Birzeit Pharmaceutical Company merged with Palestine Medical Company and, in early 1995, Jerusalem Pharmaceutical Company merged with Balsam Pharmaceuticals Company. Also, in 2003, Birzeit Pharmaceutical Company took over Eastern Chemical Company. As noted by the Birzeit chief executive officer (CEO), "The aim of these mergers was to eliminate weak companies from the market and to raise the standards of the pharmaceutical industry by separating the production of antibiotics from the production of other therapeutics."[14]

By 2010, the Palestinian pharmaceutical industry consisted of six companies, four in Ramallah, one in Beit Jala and one in the Gaza Strip. The six companies covered more than half of local market demand, which positioned the pharmaceutical industry as one of the top Palestinian economic drivers.

The Palestinian pharmaceutical industry employed more than 1,000 employees, 70 per cent of whom held specialized university degrees. Since 2000, the industry had invested more than $US50 million in modernizing the production processes and in improving the industry's premises, leading the Palestinian pharmaceutical industry to increase its market share in the Palestinian market from 20 per cent to 55 per cent.[15] New machineries were acquired, and the manufacturing facilities were reconstructed to meet international manufacturing standards.

By 2009, Palestinian pharmaceutical companies had registered 856 generic products. These companies provided local customers with generic drugs at prices that were competitive with imported products. As a result, Palestinian pharmaceuticals constituted 55 per cent of the pharmaceutical market share.

The industry also invested in creating a presence in the regional and international markets. Jerusalem Pharmaceutical Company owned a pharmaceutical plant in Algeria and a pharmaceutical company in Jordan; BPC owned 50 per cent of Petraharm, a pharmaceutical plant in Algeria; Beit Jala Pharmaceutical Company had strategic relationships with pharmaceutical companies in Saudi Arabia and Jordan; and Pharmacare had a licensing contract with Grunenthal, a pharmaceutical company in Germany.

In March 2008, following decades of efforts and significant investments aimed at the development of resources and production lines, as well as the institution of ISO procedures and international and national compliance audits, four Palestinian pharmaceutical companies were granted the World Health Organization certificate

12. *Birzeit Pharmaceutical Company Business Plan 2009,* compiled by Dimensions Consulting Company, Ramallah, Palestine, April 2009, pp. 5–65.

13. Ibid.

14. T. Nasereldin, personal communication, March 16, 2010.

15. Awad Abu Alia., "Toni Blair Meets with the Union of Palestinian Pharmaceutical Manufacturers," *Al Quds* (newspaper), March 10, 2010, http://web.alquds.com/docs/pdf-docs/2010/3/10/page24.pdf, p. 20.

of Current Good Manufacturing Practices: Birzeit Pharmaceutical Company, Pharmacare, Jerusalem Pharmaceutical Company and Beit Jala Pharmaceutical Company. The award of this certification was a considerable achievement given the difficult working conditions faced by Palestinian companies as a result of the Israeli occupation and restrictions, including the blocking of borders and restrained interaction with the international community. The certification reflected the attainment of international standards in manufacturing practices in a critical industry, which assisted the pharmaceutical industry by strengthening its position in the local market and increasing its ability to penetrate foreign markets.

The Palestinian Ministry of Health played an active role in this achievement by enacting rules and regulations to assist the health sector in general, and the pharmaceuticals sector in particular. The Ministry of Health invested in the capacity of its personnel, who were able to participate in various national audits that confirmed the compliance of the four companies with international standards. Furthermore, with assistance from the World Health Organization, the ministry instituted three guidelines for human, veterinary and cosmetic pharmaceuticals.

Palestinian pharmaceutical products were exported to more than 17 countries, mainly Eastern European countries (Russia and Ukraine), Central Asian countries (Uzbekistan, Georgia and Kazakhstan) and Middle Eastern and African countries (Algeria, Sudan, Yemen, Jordan and the United Arab Emirates).

Competition

BPC faced different levels of competition, including (1) competition with Palestinian manufacturers in the local market; (2) competition with Israeli and foreign products; (3) competition with Palestinian pharmaceutical companies in export markets; and (4) competition with regional and international manufacturers.[16]

BPC's major competition came from five Palestinian manufacturers for the following reasons:

- The majority of BPC's current sales were in the local Palestinian market, which was the case for each of its local competitors.

- Some of the Palestinian manufacturers were competing with BPC in the same export market, which made those local companies not only local competitors but also international competitors in the export market. This was the case with three main companies, BPC, Jerusalem Pharmaceuticals and Pharmacare.

- In many cases, the six Palestinian manufacturers worked as one body (through the Union of Palestinian Pharmaceutical Manufacturers, or UPPM) to jointly face competition from foreign products. Working as one body contributed to the rest of the companies through the strategies adopted by the local companies not to compete with themselves but with the foreign companies, and to try to cover as much as possible of the local market needs by diversifying the product lines.

- The competition from Israeli and foreign products was represented by numerous competitors, including manufacturers, agents, distributors and drugstores, which made analysis of this competition more difficult. Since 1967, the military authorities in the occupied territories relied on Israeli suppliers to fill the needs of the locals, a strategy that was followed until 1980. Local doctors built a positive perception about those products and accordingly affected the growth and positioning of the Palestinian pharmaceutical companies.

16. T. Nasereldin, personal communication, March 13, 2010.

The five Palestinian pharmaceutical manufacturers in the West Bank and Gaza that competed directly with BPC were Pharmacare Ltd., Jerusalem Pharmaceutical Company (JePharm), Jordan Chemical Laboratory (JCL), Middle East Pharmaceutical and Cosmetics Laboratories Co. Ltd. (MEGAPHARM) and Gama Chemical Co. (GAMA).

Market Segments in Palestine[17]

The Palestinian market was divided into three major segments:

1. *Geographic and Demographic Segment:* This key segmentation factor was related to the geographical and demographical distribution of the West Bank and Gaza markets. Those segments divided by the geographic dimensions affected the pharmaceutical industry through the political restrictions and difficulty of movement around cities which increased the cost on the industry to reach some markets.

2. *Health Care Segment:* Health care indicators directed the manufacturing strategy. The pharmaceutical industry used the available indicators to set its strategy on the production plan and the introduction of products as per those needs and indicators. As of the end of 2007, 86 non-governmental health organizations were located in the West Bank.

3. *Pharmacies and Physicians Segment:* Physicians significantly affected the consumption patterns of end users and were considered the pharmaceutical industry's channels for reaching the end users. Pharmacies affected the industry through more lenient terms offered by the pharmaceutical industry, with payment terms being better than those offered by the foreign companies.

Business in Algeria

BPC started exporting to Algeria in early 2004. Exports were limited to bulk solid-dosage formats, which included tablets and capsules. The final step of blister packaging was done by the Algerian company Petrapharm, which operated in two areas, packaging and management. Petrapharm had approximately 25 employees and its main sales were in Algeria.

After the 2006 investment in Petrapharm, Nasereldin initiated a strategy that consisted of two phases. The first phase called for marketing BPC's existing products in the new market. The Algerian partner chose 20 products from BPC's list that were noted to be of high demand in the Algerian market. In Palestine, registering new pharmaceutical products took three years, and a further two years was required to register the product in Algeria, for a total of five years. BPC management chose to wait two years for its already existing products to be registered in Algeria while it worked on registering new products, first in Palestine and later in Algeria. The latter process was the second phase that BPC realized would further grow its profit. In other words, BPC chose to follow a strategy of promoting existing products for new markets, and, as a second step, introducing new products to the new Algerian market and to the new export markets.

In early October 2008, the Algerian Ministry of Health asked all manufacturing companies to meet the local pharmaceutical demand and, hence, disallowed any importation of foreign products that were available locally, including goods manufactured and/or packed in Algeria. This decision would tremendously increase BPC's sales to Petrapharm during the coming years. BPC's pending orders to Petrapharm in

17. *Birzeit Pharmaceutical Company Business Plan 2009,* compiled by Dimensions Consulting Company, Ramallah, Palestine, April 2009, pp. 5–65.

2009 totaled US$1.9 million, resulting in a doubling of Petrapharm's sales, nearing a target of US$5 million.[18] In 2010, BPC's exports to Algeria accounted for 15 per cent of its products, whereas its exports to Eastern Europe accounted for five per cent.

Algerian Pharmaceutical Market

The key characteristics of the Algerian pharmaceutical market were its relatively large size, its potential for growth and its high dependence on imported drugs.

> Algeria remained a key market in Africa, despite dropping to 12th place alongside Nigeria. It was the second-largest African country by territory, and was modernizing its health care system through oil and gas revenues, which had risen considerably in recent years. Despite this increase in revenues, the standard of health care provision across the country was uneven.[19]

The main attractions of the Algerian market were its relatively large and young population (a total population of more than 34 million out of which 24 percent were less than 15 years of age),[20] its high dependence on imported medicines and its steady forecasted growth.[21] However, primitive Algerian investment funds and policies were the major reasons for the slow growth of this market.

BPC hired an external business development consulting firm to forecast the value of the investment in Algeria. The results of the study forecasted the following:

> The value of the Algerian market would rise to US$5 billion within five years. Generics would continue to represent the bulk of consumption in terms of volume. This was especially likely since the Ministry of Health and Population had implemented measures that meant that as a condition of receiving an import license, medicine importers had to pledge that 45 per cent of their imports would be generics. However, with aims for World Trade Organization (WTO) accession, it was likely that conditions for multinationals would improve and gradually result in the further erosion of generics' market share by patented drugs.[22]

Pharmaceutical market growth between 2005 and 2010 would be stimulated by the continuation of the US$2 billion health care modernization program, which envisaged the building of numerous hospitals and clinics. Authorities were aiming to improve health care access.

Pursuing New Markets

Since 2002, BPC had realized that, to grow its business and to overcome the challenges facing its growth in Palestine, it needed to invest in an international facility. Thus, BPC followed a strategy of first pursuing the right market to which it would provide the stipulated products and, next, using the pursued market to diversify its products, as appropriate for the newly acquired export markets.

---

18. T. Nasereldin, personal communication, March 13, 2010.

19. Algerian population, www.piribo.com/publications/country/africa/algeria_pharmaceuticals_healthcare_report_q4_2008.html, accessed March 2010.

20. World Bank, "Algeria," Algerian demographics, http://data.worldbank.org/country/algeria, accessed December 16, 2010. http://world.bymap.org/YoungPopulation.html, accessed February 4, 2011.

21. Bharat Book Bureau, "Middle East and Africa Pharma Sector Forecast to 2010," www.articlesnatch.com/Article/Middle-East-And-Africa-Pharma-Sector-Forecast-To-2012/1790203, accessed December 16, 2010.

22. *Birzeit Pharmaceutical Company Business Plan 2009,* compiled by Dimensions Consulting Company, Ramallah, Palestine, April 2009, pp. 5–65.

The African markets were the company's major interest. The Ivory Coast was the first market BPC investigated, but due to the lack of strong relations, an element that is essential in the Middle Eastern business mindset where personal relations support or push business deals forward, BPC sought markets elsewhere. Next, it considered Tunisia, where, despite massive efforts into making the project work, the lack of an entrepreneurial interest by the Tunisians led BPC to seek a new market. Yemen, Ukraine and Romania were additional markets that BPC approached, but BPC believed that, for this investment to succeed, the company needed to have a strong infrastructure and the right contacts. "Invest in people and relations," said Nasereldin. In 2006, he found the right contact, an Algerian partner that was looking into packaging and marketing pharmaceutical products, and in whom BPC saw a potential partner that could, once the infrastructure and people were in place, turn the business from a packaging and marketing one into a manufacturing one. BPC's vision was to grow its market by finding new markets for its products.

Having decided that the Algerian market presented the best opportunity, the company decided to take this new investment slowly and to execute it in phases. The first phase was to export finished products manufactured in Palestine and to package and market them in Algeria. This phase represented BPC's biggest investment, and the company wanted to execute it with minimal risk. As a result, BPC decided to test the market by first exporting some existing products. The second phase involved transforming the packaging company in Algeria into a manufacturing company that produced the pharmaceutical products that were in highest demand in the Algerian market. As a later phase, the manufacturing company in Algeria would ideally grow to function as an export hub to the rest of the world.

The reasons for BPC's strategy dated back to 2006. At that time, BPC realized it needed a new strategy to deal with the small market size in Palestine and the political instability, restrictions and the duplication of products. The situation was not changing, despite the company's efforts and agreements with local manufacturers on decreasing the level of duplication in an effort to limit the local competition. The company thus sought to expand its export market, believing that the local market was already saturated and that the company's growth would be achieved from the export market by introducing new niche products and/or joint ventures or licensing contracts through which the company could introduce competitive products to both local and export markets.

BPC was required to introduce substantial documentation to prove the competitive quality of the products it offered, as a result of the political situation in Palestine, including the exporting restrictions imposed by Israeli policies and Palestine's negative perception by the export market because it was not yet registered under the WTO Trade-Related Aspects of Intellectual Property Rights (TRIPS) agreement. The situation was worsened by the lack of intellectual property rights in Palestine, which made the Palestinian market, companies and products less attractive and less competitive, thereby limiting the company's opportunities in penetrating new markets.

As he sat in his office envisioning the future of BPC, Nasereldin knew he needed to set BPC's priorities in terms of its strategy in Algeria and the local market by marketing in Algeria products that already existed or that were manufactured in Palestine, or by introducing new products to Algeria other than those already manufactured in Palestine and marketing these products to both countries. But when would it be time to shift to the second phase of the strategy, where the company moved from promoting existing products to introducing new products to the new market, and then diversifying its markets? Additionally, internally in its local market, should BPC continue to sell products produced by competitors or should it focus on new products for the existing market?

Consolidated Statement of Financial Position as of December 31 (in Jordan Dinars)		
	2009	2008
Assets		
Current assets:		
Cash and deposits with banks	3,120,602	2,115,925
Accounts receivable, net	9,978,002	9,648,884
Inventory	4,528,376	4,530,475
Trading securities	1,157,471	1,107,881
Other assets	77,584	77,697
Total current assets	**18,862,035**	**17,480,862**
Non-current assets:		
Deferred tax asset	159,005	135,025
Available for sale securities	796,161	1,708,977
Investment in subsidiaries and associated companies	2,863,520	2,169,918
Properties investments	1,219,350	1,219,350
Property, plant and equipment, net	10,829,435	10,397,547
Total non-current assets	**15,867,471**	**15,630,817**
Total assets	**34,729,506**	**33,111,679**
Liabilities and shareholders' equity		
Current liabilities:		
Accounts payable and accruals	3,296,649	2,927,966
Income tax payable	303,392	1,549,139
Total current liabilities	**3,600,041**	**4,477,105**
Reserve for severance pay	2,301,533	1,907,192
Total liabilities	**5,901,574**	**6,384,297**
Shareholders' equity:		
Capital-authorized ten million shares; fully issued and paid, at JD 1 par value	12,100,000	12,100,000
Compulsory reserve	2,459,481	2,106,271
Optional reserve	1,592,781	1,592,781
General reserve	9,768,731	7,064,352
Retained earnings	2,958,530	3,694,024
Translation difference, subsidiaries	(47,728)	240,311
Minority interest	200,260	137,064
Cumulative change in the fair market value of investments	(204,123)	(207,421)
Total shareholders' equity	**28,827,932**	**26,727,382**
Total liabilities and shareholders' equity	**34,729,506**	**33,111,679**

Exhibit 1 Balance Sheet and Income Statement, 2008–2009

Consolidated Statement of Income, 2008–2009 as of December 31 (in Jordan Dinars)

	2009	2008
Sales	**15,754,980**	**14,471,736**
Cost of goods sold	**(8,628,230)**	**(7,748,917)**
Gross profit on sales	**7,126,750**	**6,722,819**
Selling expenses	(865,222)	(783,073)
Advertising and position expenses	(787,409)	(780,141)
General and administrative expenses	(1,040,919)	(1,035,171)
Net income before other revenues and income tax	**4,433,200**	**4,124,434**
Profit (loss) from investments in securities and affiliates	498,118	(1,995,738)
Financing (expenses) revenues	(370,130)	195,520
Unrealized profits from revaluations properties investments	-	1,126,650
Other revenues	27,859	36,470
Net income before income tax	**4,589,047**	**3,487,336**
Minority interest	(63,196)	(48,457)
Income tax for previous years	(541,050)	-
Income tax for the current year	(365,686)	(350,000)
Deferred tax benefit	23,980	28,745
Net income for the year after income tax	**3,643,095**	**3,117,624**
Board of directors remuneration	(111,000)	(91,000)
Net income	**3,532,095**	**3,026,624**
Earnings per share	**0.292**	**0.250**
Comprehensive income		
Net income	3,532,095	3,026,624
Cumulative change in the fair value of investments	3,298	(6,145)
Net comprehensive income	**3,535,393**	**3,020,479**

Consolidated Statement of Changes in Shareholders' Equity, 2008–2009 as of December 31 (in Jordan Dinars)

	Capital	Compulsory Legal Reserve	Optional Reserve	General Reserve	Retained Earnings	Reserve for investment Revaluation
Balances as of January 1, 2008	**11,000,000**	**1,765,983**	**1,592,781**	**7,064,352**	**3,373,043**	**(201,276)**
Prior years adjustments					(165,355)	
Total comprehensive income	-	-	-	-	**3,026,624**	**(6,145)**
Net income for the year	-	-	-	-	3,026,624	-
Revaluation of securities available for sale	-	-	-	-	-	(6,145)
Dividends	1,100,000	-	-	-	(2,200,000)	-
Appropriation of profits to reserves	-	340,288	-	-	(340,288)	-
Balances as of December 31, 2008	**12,100,000**	**2,106,271**	**1,592,781**	**7,064,352**	**3,694,024**	**(207,421)**
Total comprehensive income	-	-	-	-	**3,532,095**	**3,298**
Profit for the year	-	-	-	-	3,532,095	-
Revaluation of securities available for sale	-	-	-	-	-	3,298
Dividends	-	-	-	-	(1,210,000)	
Appropriation of profits to reserves	-	353,210	-	2,704,379	(3,057,589)	
Balances as of December 31, 2009	**12,100,000**	**2,459,481**	**1,592,781**	**9,768,731**	**2,958,530**	**(204,123)**

Consolidated Statement of Cash Flows, 2008–2009 as of December 31, 2009 (in Jordan Dinars)	2009	2008
Cash flows from operating activities:		
Profit for the year before tax	4,478,047	3,396,336
Non-cash transactions:		
Depreciation	973,035	897,922
Loss (profit) from trading securities	191,777	2,317,969
Provision for severance pay	460,641	413,670
Unrealized profit from revaluation of properties investment	-	(1,126,650)
Net decrease (increase) in other current assets	(326,906)	(1,237,628)
Net increase in other current liabilities	368,683	332,554
Income tax payments	(2,218,217)	(218,730)
Severance benefits paid	(66,300)	(53,920)
Net cash flows from operating activities	**3,860,760**	**4,721,523**
Cash flows from investing activities:		
Increase in investments portfolio	(241,160)	(571,286)
Procurement of fixed assets and projects in progress	(1,404,923)	(1,928,306)
	(1,646,083)	**(2,499,592)**
Cash flows from financing activities:		
Loan payable	-	(1,095,856)
Dividends paid	(1,210,000)	(1,100,000)
	(1,210,000)	**(2,195,856)**
Increase in cash and banks for the year	**1,004,677**	**26,075**
Cash and banks at beginning of year	2,115,925	2,089,850
Cash and banks at end of year	**3,120,602**	**2,115,925**

CASE P4-3

Social Entrepreneurship and Sustainable Farming in Indonesia

IVEY

Richard Ivey School of Business
The University of Western Ontario

Sitting contemplatively in his restaurant and gazing over the rice fields of Sok-Wayah in Ubud, Bali, Oded Carmi mulled over his options to replicate the success of his farm, Sari Organik—specifically, to re-introduce organic rice farming in other parts of Bali and eventually throughout Indonesia. The idea of Sari Organik was initially conceived in 1997 when Carmi sought to build a model farm that would grow organically with market demand and benefit the community while serving as an educational center for small-scale farmers keen to build a "green Bali."

Thirteen years later, the message of the organic farm had not been well embraced by the farmers and landholders and, as a result, diversified food production had not taken place as anticipated. Determined to rejuvenate the community's flagging enthusiasm and carry his mission to fruition, Carmi realized that he needed to analyze his options for replication and sustenance, and act fast. His initial thoughts included some options:

To utilize the established village system and its leadership (religious and civil) to re-introduce the traditional rice-farming culture in Ubud, Bali and eventually Indonesia.

1. To introduce a new model such as microfranchising through which he (the microfranchiser) would recruit a number of local farmers (microfranchisees) and provide them with the resources to grow rice organically.

2. To go into a joint venture with the few existing organic rice farmers in the region.

3. To expand his business as a sole proprietor, i.e. buy more land and increase organic rice production—this was his least favorite option since it would go against his mission of involving the community.

Carmi wasn't sure which of these three options would be best and also wondered if there were other viable options that would help him achieve his mission for the Sari Organik farm.

Oded Carmi's Social Entrepreneurship Background

A budding social entrepreneur,[1] Carmi was born in 1950 in Kibbutz Matsuba, Israel, just south of the Lebanese border, barely two years after the State of Israel's declaration

Ilan Alon and Eve Misati wrote this case solely to provide material for class discussion. The authors do not intend to illustrate either effective or ineffective handling of a managerial situation. The authors may have disguised certain names and other identifying information to protect confidentiality.

1. Ashoka.org defines social entrepreneurs as people who have innovative solutions to social problems and the potential to change patterns across society by demonstrating unrivaled commitment to bold new ideas. Social entrepreneurs prove that compassion, creativity and collaboration are tremendous forces for change. See www.ashoka.org/social_entrepreneur, accessed July 1, 2010.

of independence from the British Mandate of Palestine. The Kibbutz, as it was still identified today, was a large, collective production unit or cooperative settlement whose members jointly owned the means of production and shared social, cultural and economic activities—however, the trend of the Kibbutz was now shifting from farming toward environmental business.[2] During Mr. Carmi's youth, Kibbutz Matsuba owned an agribusiness and provided what it considered relevant agricultural education for its children through a farm (meshek yeladim) where the children worked once a week instead of receiving formal schooling.

At 18 years of age, Carmi joined the Israel Defense Forces (IDF), where he worked for three years as an air traffic controller before relocating to the United States. He first settled in Washington, D.C., where he worked in sheetrock construction for 18 months before moving to Boulder, Colorado, where he continued to work in construction, and also learnt to fly airplanes. After four years in Boulder, he decided to move to Los Angeles, California, but things did not turn out well there; after a nine-month stint at a horse range, he decided to move to New York, where he started a moving company with a friend—Carmi's first entrepreneurial venture. The moving company did not last long so he returned to construction and also got involved in the performing arts, and later moved to San Francisco, where he lived for two years before returning to New York in 1978.

In New York, Carmi continued to work in construction, maintained his involvement in the performing arts, and later, in partnership with four friends, opened a restaurant (gallery bistro) in the East Village, which lasted four years. Carmi continued to live in New York but had a growing desire to settle elsewhere. In search for a place to call home, Carmi first visited Bali in 1992 and later visited Costa Rica and the Dominican Republic, finally getting an opportunity in 1997 when a Balinese acquaintance he had met in New York invited him to Ubud, Bali, and offered him a piece of land for free with permission to build a house.

Once he moved to Ubud, Carmi immersed himself in the Balinese way of life and embarked on subsistence farming close to the nearby river. He first experimented with a variety of organic fruits and vegetables and later organic rice and farm animals. It was at this time that his mission began to hatch—to get farmers to grow complete diets, rather than just rice, as a way to nourish the community and also alleviate poverty. For two years, he travelled back and forth between Bali and New York until his wife, who was still living in New York at the time, suddenly died in 1999, leaving behind an 18-month-old son. Carmi decided to sell the two apartments and a co-op he owned in New York and relocated permanently to Bali with his infant son.

For eight years following the death of his wife, Carmi chose to work solely for the social enhancement of others, living off his savings. He started two non-governmental organizations (NGOs), Senang Hati (Happy Hearts), established in 2000 to assist people living with disabilities, and *Rainbow Mandala*, established in 2003 with a group of Israeli women to provide hope to the community through activities such as hosting special events for orphanages, donating food and presents to the needy, and hosting Christmas day activities. The latter did not last long, but the former had strong organization and had since received foreign support, and was currently operating as *the Senang Hati Foundation*.[3]

As a social entrepreneur, Carmi was passionate about the welfare of the communities in Ubud and was keen to re-introduce sustainable traditional organic rice farming

---

2. "Israel's Kibbutzim shift from red to green," www.businessweek.com/smallbiz/content/jun2010/sb20100623_004082.htm, accessed July 1, 2010.

3. See Senang Hati Foundation, www.senanghati.org, accessed July 1, 2010.

with a commitment to mobilize the community to help replicate this initiative in other parts of Bali, and eventually throughout Indonesia. His dream was to see farmers in the community grow organic rice and, during rotation, use the fallow land to grow vegetables and fruits, and perhaps rear farm animals, thus providing a wholesome diet and a sustainable source of income. Rather than leave this issue to the government and business sector, Carmi realized that it was necessary to engage the local community through its religious and civil leadership to take the initiative of improving its own social and economic welfare.

Sari Organik

The name Sari Organik was obtained in 2005 when Carmi realized that after about eight years of experimenting with organic vegetables he was producing more than he could sell to friends. Two years later, the wife of the landowner who had given him land for free issued an ultimatum to start paying for the land or move out. Carmi chose to stay and decided to invest what was left of his savings (approximately $50,000) to start a small business—an organic farm and restaurant—and thus Sari Organik farm and the restaurant, Bodag Maliah (overflowing basket), were established in December 2007. Exhibit 1 shows pictures of the farm, the restaurant and a sample of the product offerings.

To supplement their existing land, Carmi and his Balinese wife, Nila, who was also their restaurant's head chef, acquired more land from another friend and later befriended their mentors, the owners of "The Big Tree Farms."[4] The latter were the largest organic American expatriate farmers in Bali and the couple sought advice from them on how to turn their experimental farm into a socially responsible yet profitable venture that would enhance the community's well being and augment the couple's dwindling savings.

Through Sari Organik, Carmi hoped to re-establish the severed connection between consumers and farmers, which in his opinion was endangered by the rise of multi-national corporations (MNCs), leading to a disconnect between food processing and farming and posing a major threat to small-scale organic farmers. The objective of Sari Organik was to process food in a transparent manner, close to the consumer; thus Sari Organik processed and sold food directly to the consumer without middlemen, i.e. wholesalers and retailers. The farm's survival was dependent upon consumers' willingness to buy the local organic produce at a slightly higher price than imported food sold by MNCs, which was a real challenge in a world where consumers were used to the MNCs' discount pricing.

Sari Organik employed 35 people as of 2010—five organic rice farmers who were involved in the growing, processing, transportation and delivery of the farm's produce, and 30 restaurant workers involved in food processing, watering, cooking and various restaurant functions. Besides varieties of organic rice, Sari Organik had produced the following products thus far: fruit jams, natural syrups, fruit wines, tofu, soy feta and soy ricotta cheeses, natural sauces, different kinds of bread, pickled products, seeds, fermented teas and roasted nuts. The restaurant served healthy organic meals made from the farm's produce.

Carmi's goal was to keep the organic rice prices as low as possible and pay the organic rice farmers a much higher percentage of the sales price than what they would earn on their own. Sari Organik paid more than double the normal salary in Bali, but the work was harder because it was organic and the yield was lower because no chemicals were used—and because the land needed reconditioning after years of using

---

4. See Big Tree Farms, www.bigtreefarms.com/story, accessed July 1, 2010.

The Restaurant—Warung Bodag Maliah (Overflowing Basket)

Exhibit 1 Sari Organik Farm and Sample of Product Offerings

harmful fertilizers. The restaurant depended on the level of tourism; during high season, it generated about 200 million rupiahs a month in revenue (before accounting for tax and expenses), with a profit of about 80 million rupiahs a month. During low season, the restaurant sometimes did not break even and Carmi had to pump in his savings. Exhibit 2 shows Sari Organik's consolidated income statement for the month ending April 30, 2010.

Carmi had embraced his responsibility to manage his farm responsibly and sustainably in order to contribute to and not just exploit Sari Organik's stakeholders. He realized that it was vital to establish the confidence of the community at large and the village leaders (religious and civil), and even of individual farmers and consumers, to assure them that Sari Organik was worthy of their trust. Carmi knew that any business with a desire to survive into the future would be well advised to adopt the best practice of "sustainable development," defined by the United Nations (UN) as a process of change in which the exploitation of resources, the direction of investments, the orientation of technological development and institutional change are all in harmony and enhance both current and future potential to meet human needs and aspirations.[5] Like MNCs and other large-scale businesses, small entrepreneurs are equally charged with the responsibility of running sustainable, responsible businesses.

As a small business owner, Carmi fulfilled his corporate social responsibility (CSR)[6] not only through the generation of employment opportunities for the community, but also through (1) the provision of an educational and nurturing work environment for his employees (Sari Organik was a model farm for the community); (2) the sustainable use of land and agricultural resources (he did not use fertilizers, but instead used animal manure and organic composts to fertilize the soil, and also strived to maintain the ecological balance of his land through biodiversity, leaving animals such as snakes, eels, frogs, fish, dragonflies, freshwater crabs and a variety of insects in their natural habitats in the rice fields so that they could contribute to the health of the soil and water systems); (3) allowing his land to lie fallow from time to time to prevent exhaustion, and rotating the crops to replace depleted nitrogen in the soil; and (4) the sales of healthy, nutritious organic food from his farm to the community at reasonable prices.

The Environment: Indonesia

Home to the world's largest Muslim population, Indonesia gained its independence from the Netherlands in 1949, but only held its first free parliamentary general elections in 1999, ending a repressive rule. Indonesia was also the third-largest democracy after India and the United States, respectively, the fourth most populous country in the world (approximately 242 million)[7] after China, India and United States, respectively, and the world's largest archipelagic state (about three times the size of Texas). According to Worldwide Governance Indicators (WGI) for 2008,[8] Indonesia ranked in the 10th to 25th percentile on political stability, and ranked in the 25th to 50th percentile on voice and accountability, government effectiveness, regulatory quality, rule of law and control of corruption. The Indonesian government was involved in legal

---

5. "Toward sustainable development," www.un-documents.net/ocf-02.htm#I, accessed July 1, 2010.

6. Corporate social responsibility may be defined as any activity that promotes the welfare of a business corporation's stakeholders; this includes philanthropic programs targeting employees and the community, commitment to promote suppliers' welfare, and other activities designed to promote environmental stewardship (sustainability).
See Ludescher and Mashud, "CSR exposed," *The Independent Review*, 15:1, 2010, p. 123.

7. CIA World Factbook, 2009. https://www.cia.gov/library/publications/the-world-factbook//index.html

8. http://info.worldbank.org/governance/wgi/sc_chart.asp, accessed July 1, 2010.

Revenue		
Warung Bodag Maliah (Sari Organik Restaurant)		
Sales		153,302,500
Sari Organic Café (Little Tree)		
Processed products	4,801,200	
Fresh produce	262,250	5,063,450
Farmers market		
Processed products	760,000	
Fresh produce	206,000	966,000
Sari Organik Farm		
Garden vegetables and salads	13,054,800	
Rice plantation	570,000	
Other produce	12,897,500	26,522,300
Total revenue		**185,854,250**
Expenditure		
Warung Bodag Maliah (Sari Organik Restaurant)		
Cost of goods sold		
Makro	6,819,641	
Garden vegetables and salads	13,054,800	
Rice	570,000	
Ginger juice	5,154,000	
Lemon	1,140,000	
Lemon marquisa	1,210,000	
Storm beer	3,420,000	
Other menu items	44,200,000	75,568,441
Equipment purchase		
Jars	924,000	
Food processor	450,000	
Juicer	2,500,000	
Blender	670,000	
Glasses and soup bowls	1,180,000	5,724,000
Other expenses		
Printing notes and memos	420,000	
Menu covers	300,000	
Central bill (promotions)	7,312,300	
Employee salaries	21,585,250	
Maintenance	632,000	
Air conditioning	825,000	
Electricity	1,100,000	32,174,550
Sari Organik Farm		
Farm workers' salaries		
Kintamani farm	925,000	
Others	6,982,500	7,907,500
Purchases		
Brown rice	960,000	
Sabu vegetables (Jan. to Mar.)	5,191,750	
Other farm inputs	13,381,500	
Nets and maintenance	454,000	19,987,250
Miscelleneous		
Gas, salary, phone, security, full moon offerings, advertising		19,905,000
Total expenditure		**161,266,741**
Income before tax		**24,587,509**
Less tax 10%		2,458,751
Income after tax		**22,128,758**
		=US$2,445

Exhibit 2 Consolidated Income Statement for the Month Ending April 30, 2010 (in IDR)

Source: Company records.

Note: The exchange rate on July 3, 2010, was 9050.0194 Indonesian rupiahs (IDR) = 1 United States dollar.

and economic reforms and had shown a remarkable turnaround under President Susilo Bambang Yudhoyono's watch.

A highly collectivist society, Indonesia ranked as follows on Hofstede's cultural dimensions[9]: 78 on power distance (United States, 40), 48 on uncertainty avoidance (United States, 46), 14 on individualism (United States, 91) and 46 on masculinity (United States, 62). Doing business in this society required patience and an understanding of the influences affecting business culture and the legal and regulatory environments. The country was facing challenges with issues such as poverty, unemployment, inadequate infrastructure, underdeveloped education, corruption and a complex regulatory environment, among others. The economy was emerging: 52 per cent of its population lived in urban areas, with an annual urban growth rate of 3.3 per cent. Agriculture contributed 42 per cent to Indonesia's labor workforce, while industry contributed 18 per cent and services contributed 39 per cent. Indonesia was industrializing, but remained an agrarian society in transition. Indonesian economic growth relied mainly on domestic consumption, and its GDP had been increasing (ranked 16th in the world with PPP at $969 billion, 33rd with a real growth rate at 4.5 per cent, and 155th with per capita PPP at $4,000[10]), with agriculture contributing 15 per cent, industry contributing 47 per cent, and services contributing 37 per cent, as of 2009.[11]

A developing country, Indonesia was also facing a number of environmental challenges including deforestation, water pollution from industrial waste, sewage, air pollution in urban areas, smoke and haze from forest fires, etc. The country boasted a sophisticated irrigation system covering 45,000 square kilometers of land, with only 11 per cent arable land. There was a dire need for sustainable development (going green) in order to manage the natural resources that would reduce poverty and support human development.

Rice Farming in Bali

Research into the history of rice farming in Bali indicates that Bali had been producing rice for more than 1,100 years.[12] The region originally grew a variety of rice grains, each with a distinct flavor, texture, aroma and even color: pink, white, brown, red and black. All farming was originally done with no harmful chemicals, using only natural compost and animal manure. The "Green Revolution"[13] was launched in Indonesia in the late 1960s over concerns of food security in the country. The Indonesian government, with the help of the World Bank, developed a grain rice hybrid that was supposed to give a higher yield and, therefore, increase the productivity of farmers. Government mandates to use the new rice variety as well as related pesticides and chemicals led to increased production and Indonesia became agriculturally independent, making enough rice to feed itself. Short run gains, however, were difficult to maintain in the long run as the ill effects of the policy were not fully foreseen.[14]

---

9. www.geert-hofstede.com/hofstede_indonesia.shtml, accessed July 1, 2010.

10. CIA World Fact Book, 2009. https://www.cia.gov/library/publications/the-world-factbook//index.html

11. Ibid.

12. C. Wheeler, "A bowl of honest rice," *Tales from Rural Bali,* 2nd edition, Tokay Press, Indonesia, 2009, pp. 199–206.

13. Green Revolution refers to the renovation of agricultural practices that began in Mexico in the 1940s. Due to its success in producing more agricultural products there, Green Revolution technologies spread worldwide in the 1950s and 1960s, significantly increasing the amount of calories produced per acre of agriculture. See http://geography.about.com/od/globalproblemsandissues/a/greenrevolution.htm, accessed July 10, 2010.

14. Economists call these ill effects *negative externalities*.

To continue this trend, the use of chemicals and pesticides was intensified while the use of animal manures and organic composts slowly stopped. This led to depravation of the soil of rich natural ingredients over the years, and eventually rice yields and quality began to decline even with the intensified use of chemicals; farmers thought they could turn things around by using even more chemicals and fertilizers and this increased the costs of producing rice, while the yields continued to decline and the supply could not meet demand anymore—leading to the need for the country to import rice through MNCs in 1985.

The use of chemicals upset the ecological balance and destroyed biodiversity as animals and insects died from the harmful chemicals. Although not substantiated in the case, it is likely that those chemicals and fertilizers may also have affected the health of the people since local farmers applied the chemicals without the use of gloves and masks for protection. The communities also depended on a single water source flowing through the rice fields, and therefore any chemicals introduced into the water system would inherently contaminate all the fields downstream. During the shift in rice farming, some farmers, especially in the remote areas, held onto a little organically grown traditional rice for their own consumption since they found the hybrid white rice odorless and tasteless. Organic rice farming became a boutique item in Bali, but a few more farmers expressed interest in shifting to this practice. The initial yields were disheartening as the soil was contaminated over the years and would need reconditioning before it could produce yields to match its original level.

Growing rice without chemical inputs could save the farmers money, but they had to be willing to recondition their farms, a process that could take about 18 months according to one American expat farmer who had tried it successfully. Once the land was reconditioned, the yields were great, but the crops had to be rotated and the land made fallow between harvests in order to sustain rice farming. There were indications that the government was supportive of such initiatives by farmers in the local communities as demonstrated by the "go organic campaign" launched in 2001 to develop a certification system, give incentives to farmers developing organic farming techniques, promote the concept of organic farming through training and workshops, and provide financial assistance to farmers to enable them to build organic fertilizer processing equipment.[15] Exhibit 3 provides additional key facts on general and organic farming in Bali.

The Village System in Bali

Bali was made up of basic territorial units or villages known as *Desa* (the equivalent of a city in the United States). *Desa* covered both the wetland where rice is grown and the dry land that consisted of compounds, gardens, temples and roads. Each wetland had a corresponding irrigation unit known as *Subak*. Bali's equivalence of the city's suburbs were called *Banjar*. Each *Banjar* had its temples and organizations. A *Banjar*'s basic social unit was the couple (*pekurenan*); only married couples were full members of the *Banjar*, and were subject to *Banjar* rights and obligations. Decisions were taken by the male members of the social unit and passed after reaching unanimity. The *Banjar* made up an association called the *Banjar suka duka* (the association for the sharing of joy and pain), whose bonds were arguably the most important of all in the network of village associations. Each *Banjar* was made up of anything between fifty and two hundred individual compounds, and in every *Banjar* there were two main leaders, one

---

15. "Indonesia—the Organic Boom," www.meattradenewsdaily.co.uk/news/070610/indonesia___the_organic_boom_.aspx, accessed July 10, 2010.

Farming in General	Organic Farming
■ Bali has the ideal conditions for agriculture: climate—dry and wet season, fertile soil, and availability of abundant water for irrigation. ■ In 2009, Bali only had 228,153 hectares of fertile rice fields left. Various housing and hotel construction projects have been eating up at least 700 hectares of fertile rice fields every year.[16] ■ About 80% of Bali's economy depends on tourism—which some consider a threat to farming in the region. ■ Agriculture, however, is still Bali's biggest employer; specifically, rice cultivation. ■ Other agricultural outputs include fruits, vegetables, Arabica coffee, fish, tuna, seaweed, vanilla, cattle/dairy, goats, sheep, and poultry. ■ Farming is dependent on the traditional farming system, *Subak Abian*, based on the Hindu philosophy of *Tri Hita Karana* (God, other people, and the environment), and about 93.8% of Bali's population adheres to Balinese Hinduism. ■ Bali's administration is developing 40 integrated farming sites to promote both new farming technology and traditional farming systems.[17]	■ Promotes healthy, wholesome eating for the community. ■ Promotes the local economy and community awareness of social entrepreneurship and sustainable development. ■ About 40 years ago, most farming was organic, then the government/World Bank started to promote the use of chemicals to increase output. ■ More labor-intensive, lower output, and relatively expensive. ■ Bali Organic Association (BOA)[18] exists but isn't well developed yet. ■ Organic farms include The Organic Farm—Bali, Big Tree Farms (Island Organics), *Sari Organik*, and Pegasus Farm. ■ Organic Farmers Markets held in Ubud and Sanur provide an opportunity for growers and businesses to sell their organic wares. ■ A sustainable agriculture project—System of Rice Intensification (SRI)[19] has been funded by The Funding Network (TFN) through the Rotary club to train farmers on how to grow rice organically and the social and economic benefits of doing so.

Exhibit 3 Farming in Bali—Key Facts

religious (*Kelian Adat*) and one civilian (*Kelian Dinas*, who sometimes doubled as the village headman, *Bendesa Adat*).[20]

Civilian leaders were either elected or appointed by the villagers, while the religious leader was chosen by village elders. Since 1979, the *Banjar* had been recognized as the lowest administrative structure of the national Indonesian administration, directly under the authority of the *perbekel* or *lurah* (village head) and beyond the traditional village headman (*Bendesa Adat*). In many villages, elders were used to settle disputes, and in many communities in Bali, where Hinduism permeated lifestyles, religious leaders had great power and influence over civilian leaders, whose main responsibilities were to issue ID cards, marriage certificates, death certificates, land rights use and approvals for construction. The Balinese had a respect for authority, and were used to following their leaders' orders.

About 93.8 per cent of Bali's population adhered to Balinese Hinduism—a combination of the existing local beliefs and Hindu influences from South Asia and Southeast Asia. As a result, Balinese Hinduism had a strong influence on the Balinese way of life; most notable was the deeply entrenched concept of *Tri Hita Karana* (*Tri* means "three," *Hita* means "well being," and *Karana* means "cause"). This concept promoted a harmonious relationship among the spiritual, social and natural environments based on the belief that such harmony generated a maximum benefit to human spiritual, mental and physical well being.[21] Organic farming promoted a relationship similar to that of the *Tri Hita Karana* philosophy, and if the community leaders chose

16. www.indonesiaorganic.com/detail.php?id=199&cat=12, accessed July 10, 2010.

17. www.thejakartapost.com/news/2010/02/10/bali-administration-develops-40-integrated-farming-sites.html, accessed July 10, 2010.

18. www.indonesiaorganic.com/detail.php?id=37&cat=21, accessed July 10, 2010.

19. www.rotaryubud.org/projects/susAg-project.htm, accessed July 10, 2010.

20. http://balimagic.com/BaliAdat.html, accessed May 28, 2011.

21. Bali Tri Hita Karana, www.balitrihitakarana.com/abouttrihitakarana.htm, accessed July 1, 2010.

to use this philosophy to increase awareness of the benefits of organic farming, the community would undoubtedly follow.

Bali experienced a tropical climate all year, with two main seasons: dry (April to September) and wet (October to March). To sustain their rice paddies during the dry season, the Balinese had used community rice-growing associations (*Subaks*), which utilized a water irrigation system, for hundreds of years. *Subaks* aimed to ensure that the water was fairly distributed to all farmers during the dry season and *Subaks* had been considered a foundation of society in Bali, headed by a respected elected leader, *Kelian Subak*.

Subak members had equal rights, regardless of caste or title or the size of their land holding, and worked together to bring water from sometimes distant sources, e.g. springs, rivers or lakes, through sophisticated hydraulic engineering systems that consisted of continuously maintained, hand-built aqueducts, small dams, canals and underground tunnels dug through solid rock. The *Subak* met monthly under the leadership of the *Kelian Subak*, and together they decided all issues concerning rice cultivation, e.g. planting, harvesting, offerings, ceremonies, repairing dams and fertilizing; the *Kelian Subak* had the authority to grant or withhold permission for new rice terrace construction and was responsible for ensuring compliance with government regulations.[22]

Modern life had infiltrated the community, and nobody desired to be a farmer because of the low status and minimal income associated with this profession; farmers were not respected.[23] Despite the "modernization" of agriculture in Indonesia, certain traditions held; from Carmi's balcony, farmers could be seen using their ancestors' farming techniques, for example, the use of hand tools to till the land.

Ubud, Bali, Indonesia

A beautiful town located amongst rice paddies and steep ravines in the middle of the island of Bali, Ubud was one of the island's major fine arts and cultural centers and was supported largely by tourism—from back packers to art connoisseurs, the town drew people who were actively involved in art, nature, anthropology, music, dance, architecture, environmentalism and "alternative modalities," among others, and boasted scenic rice fields, small villages, arts and crafts communities, ancient temples, palaces, rivers and cooler temperatures than the main tourist area in southern Bali. Ubud provided accommodation and dining ranging from small boutique hotels to more elegant hotels. The town derived its name from the Balinese word *ubad* (medicine), as the region was originally an important source of medicinal herbs and plants.[24] Exhibit 4 presents the maps of Indonesia and Bali, with an arrow showing the location of Ubud.

About 80 per cent of Bali's economy came from tourism, although agriculture (mostly rice cultivation) was still Bali's biggest employer. The government saw these two industries as a way to raise money through taxes.[25] Sari Organik*'s* model was not well embraced and Carmi speculated that one of the reasons could be that rice farming did not generate much income for the farmers anymore due to land overuse and destruction of top soil from the use of harmful chemicals. Hence, about 90 per cent of farmers had second jobs, and only dedicated a bare minimum of effort to farming just to get their share of the rice. For every eight sacks of rice, one went to the picker

---

22. "Subak—Bali Irrigation System," www.balitravelportal.com/bali/indonesia/travel/culture/subak-bali-irrigation-system, accessed July 1, 2010.

23. C. Wheeler, "Respect," *Tales from Rural Bali*, 2nd edition, Tokay Press, Indonesia, 2009, pp. 271–273.

24. Scores of holistic medicine practitioners lived around Ubud, and many spas and meditation centers had opened up. One could easily find all types of Eastern and Western massage centers, reiki healers, herbal medicine shops, and even acupuncture practitioners in this town. See "Things To Do in Ubud, Bali," http://goseasia.about.com/od/bali/tp/8_things_to_do_in_ubud_bali .htm, accessed July 1, 2010.

25. www.balidiscovery.com/messages/message.asp?Id=6824, accessed May 10, 2011.

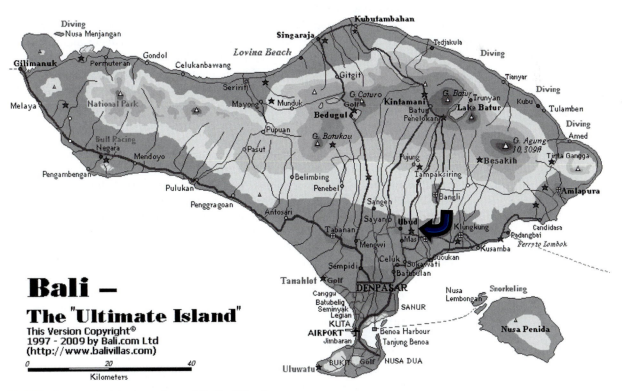

Exhibit 4 MAPS of Indonesia and Bali—Ubud

or harvester, 3.5 went to the landowner, and 3.5 went to the farmer—this was only enough to feed a landowner/farmer's family, without much left to sell. The other reason that Sari Organik's model was not well embraced could have been that farming was not considered a respectable profession due to the "dirty" nature of the work, and because many people preferred an office job over working in the fields.

Sari Organik Striving for a Green Bali

Even though Sari Organik was established as a model to demonstrate this sustainable technique for local farmers to emulate, the effect had been very minimal and quite disappointing. As Carmi strove to realize his dreams of alleviating poverty and encouraging healthy, wholesome eating in Bali and eventually Indonesia at large through Sari Organik's socially responsible business model, he realized that he had a lot to consider. It was clear that certain changes had to be implemented, but it was not clear which changes.

After being visited by an American University expert on franchising, Carmi wondered if microfranchising could be used to reproduce the success of his farm in other parts of Indonesia.[26] Microfranchising models proliferated in the emerging markets and with social causes geared toward development.[27] Microfranchising had its roots in the modern concept of franchising, where the knowledge and concept were transferred to a local entrepreneur, who was typically from a low income bracket, to implement a business practice that would sustain the individual and the local community.

One researcher, Hoyt Edge,[28] indicated that there was a growing movement of people who would like to re-adopt traditional rice-farming practices. Bali was a place in the world where a cultural argument for change could work because the community's culture was so deep rooted in religion and tradition that the people considered it second nature; every person willingly followed strict civil and religious rules known as *Adat*[29] (the rules required one to live and act rightly, fulfill one's secular and religious duties, live with grace and honor, and follow the customs of the family, village, and land).

According to Carmi, the *Subak* system was no longer functioning effectively and the atmosphere was competitive rather than cooperative; everyone was on their own, leading farmers to fight over water or guard water flowing into their farms late into the night. However, Carmi was confident that with the help of the village system's civil and religious leadership in re-establishing the *Tri Hita Karana* philosophy, things could be turned around.

Carmi's objective was to replicate this organic rice-farming model in as many parts of Bali as possible and eventually diversify throughout Indonesia, and he realized that he had to weigh the available options fast. His initial thoughts included (1) utilizing the village system and its religious and civil leadership to increase awareness of the benefits of organic rice farming and re-invigorate community interest in Sari Organik's model—Carmi wondered whether this initiative would be as successful as a similar undertaking that had mobilized a nearby village for the purpose of healing by cultural activity[30] through a month-long event featuring health seminars

26. Micro-franchising is an economic development tool aimed to provide sound business opportunities and services to the poor by introducing scaled-down business concepts found in successful franchise organizations with the overall objective of promoting economic development by developing sound business models that can be replicated by micro-entrepreneurs at the base of the pyramid. See http://marriottschool.byu.edu/selfreliance/microfranchise/about, accessed July 1, 2010.

27. www.acumenfund.org/uploads/assets/documents/Microfranchising_Working%20Paper_XoYB6sZ5.pdf, accessed April 10, 2011.

28. An interview with Dr. Edge, Rollins College; see profile at http://web.rollins.edu/~hedge, accessed July 8, 2010.

29. "Bali Adat," www.balimagic.com/BaliAdat.html, accessed July 10, 2010.

30. http://news.ubud.com/2006/07/first-ubud-festival.html, accessed July 10, 2010.

and activities related to the environment, e.g. competitions by *Banjars* to clean up their streets and maintain their public garden areas; (2) adopting a model such as microfranchising that would pull in microentrepreneurs; (3) going into a joint venture with the few organic rice farmers in the region; and/or (4) finding ways to expand his own business as a sole proprietor, although this was his least favorite option. Carmi also wondered whether there could be other viable options that might help him fulfill his mission for Sari Organik and, more generally, organic farming in Indonesia.

NAME INDEX

SUBJECT INDEX